Beginning

T-SQL with Microsoft® SQL Server® 2005 and 2008

Beginning
T-SQL with Microsoft® SQL Server® 2005 and 2008

Paul Turley and Dan Wood

WILEY

Wiley Publishing, Inc.

Beginning T-SQL with Microsoft® SQL Server® 2005 and 2008

Published by
Wiley Publishing, Inc.
10475 Crosspoint Boulevard
Indianapolis, IN 46256
www.wiley.com

ISBN: 978-0-470-25703-6

Manufactured in the United States of America

10 9 8 7 6 5 4 3 2 1

Library of Congress Cataloging-in-Publication Data is available from the publisher.

For general information on our other products and services please contact our Customer Care Department within the United States at (877) 762-2974, outside the United States at (317) 572-3993 or fax (317) 572-4002.

About the Authors

Paul Turley (Vancouver, WA) is a Manager of Specialized Services for Hitachi Consulting Education Services. Paul manages the Business Intelligence training team and teaches classes for companies throughout the world on Microsoft SQL Server technologies. He works with companies to architect and build BI and reporting solutions. He has been developing business database solutions since 1991 for companies like Microsoft, Disney, Nike, and Hewlett-Packard. He has been a Microsoft Certified Trainer since 1996 and holds several industry certifications, including MCTS and MCITP for BI, MCSD, MCDBA, MSF Practitioner, and IT Project+.

Paul has authored and co-authored several books and courses on database, business intelligence, and application development technologies. He is the lead courseware developer for the Hitachi Consulting courses: SQL Server 2008 Business Intelligence Solutions and SQL Server 2008 Reporting Services Solutions. Books include the prior edition of this book, the 2008, 2005 and 2000 editions of *Professional SQL Server Reporting Services, Beginning SQL Server 2005 Administration, Beginning Access 2002 VBA, Data Warehousing with SQL Server 2000 Analysis Services*, and *Professional Access 2000 Programming*—all from Wrox. He is also a contributing author for *SQL Server 2005 Integration Services Step by Step* from Microsoft Press.

Dan Wood (Silverdale, WA) is the senior database administrator for Avalara, a sales tax compliance company, where he both administers and develops database solutions for several enterprise applications that handle global address validation, tax rate calculation, and sales tax remittance for e-commerce and ERP clients. He has been working with SQL Server as a DBA, consultant, and trainer since 1999. Dan was a contributing author on *Beginning Transact-SQL with SQL Server 2000 and 2005* and the lead author of *Beginning SQL Server Administration*, both from Wrox.

Credits

Executive Editor
Robert Elliott

Development Editor
John Sleeva

Technical Editor
David Norton

Production Editor
Daniel Scribner

Copy Editor
Nancy Rapoport

Editorial Manager
Mary Beth Wakefield

Production Manager
Tim Tate

Vice President and Executive Group Publisher
Richard Swadley

Vice President and Executive Publisher
Joseph B. Wikert

Project Coordinator, Cover
Lynsey Stanford

Proofreader
Publication Services, Inc.

Indexer
Robert Swanson

Acknowledgments

This book wouldn't exist without the hard work and dedication of my coauthor, Dan Wood. Dan's a good friend, a true professional, a great father and husband - and I hear he's an okay football coach. Thanks to Bob Elliot and John Sleeva at Wrox who have been incredibly patient and professional with two completely over-committed authors for the past year. DJ Norton did a great job with the technical review. Thanks, DJ, for breaking my code and making more work for me. Thanks to Lance Baldwin and Drew Naukam on Hitachi Consulting's Microsoft Strategic Alliance team for giving me the space to complete this and the Reporting Services book this year. To all of the amazing people I work with at Hitachi Consulting, thanks for making this such a terrific organization for our clients and a great place to call home.

—Paul Turley

I'd like to thank Paul Turley, who is not only a great friend, but an amazing person, and I appreciate the opportunity to work with him again. Many thanks to our Wrox development editor, John Sleeva, who did an outstanding editing job — not to mention the job he did working with us, which was probably very much like herding cats. Special thanks go to the awesome development team at Avalara for a rewarding and stimulating work environment and for giving me inspiration for many of the examples in this book. Most important, I would like to thank my wonderful wife, Sarah, for all her patience and support as I disappeared for hours at a time and spent many a late night trying to finish the latest chapter. I would also like to thank my kids, Lukas, Tessa, and Caleb, who think it's cool that Dad is writing a book but would much prefer that I spend time with them.

—Dan Wood

Contents

Contents

Contents

Contents

Contents

Contents

Contents

Introduction

Welcome to the world of Transact-Structured Query Language programming with SQL Server 2005 and 2008. Transact-SQL, or T-SQL, is Microsoft Corporation's powerful implementation of the ANSI standard SQL database query language, which was designed to retrieve, manipulate, and add data to relational database management systems (RDBMS).

You may already have a basic idea of what SQL is used for, but you may not have a good understanding of the concepts behind relational databases and the purpose of SQL. This book will help you build a solid foundation of understanding, beginning with core relational database concepts and continuing to reinforce those concepts with real-world T-SQL query applications.

If you are familiar with relational database concepts but are new to Microsoft SQL Server or the T-SQL language, this book will teach you the basics from the ground up. If you're familiar with earlier versions of SQL Server, it will get you up to speed on the newest features. And if you know SQL Server 2005, you'll learn about some exciting new capabilities in SQL Server 2008.

A popular online encyclopedia lists about 800 distinct programming languages in use today. These languages are used to develop different types of applications for different types of computer systems and specialized devices. Needless to say, we have a lot of software in our information-rich society. Programming languages rapidly evolve and come and go, but one of few constants in the industry is that most business applications read, store, and manipulate data — data stored in relational databases. If you use Microsoft SQL Server in any capacity, the need to learn and use T-SQL is inescapable. Amazing things are possible with just a few keystrokes of powerful SQL script.

Indeed, SQL is one of the few standard languages in the industry that doesn't come and go and has remained constant over the decades. The capabilities of T-SQL expand as features are added to each version of the SQL Server product. The concepts and exercises in this book will help you to understand and use the core language and its latest features.

Who This Book Is For

Information Technology professionals in many different roles use T-SQL. Our goal is to provide a guide and a reference for IT pros across the spectrum of operational database solution design, database application development, and reporting and business intelligence solutions.

Database solution designers will find this book to be a thorough introduction and comprehensive reference for all aspects of database modeling, design, object management, query design, and advanced query concepts.

Application developers who write code to manage and consume SQL Server data will benefit from our thorough coverage of basic data management and simple and advanced query design. Several examples of ready-to-use code are provided to get you started and to continue to support applications with embedded T-SQL queries.

Report designers will find this book to be a go-to reference for report query design. You will build on a thorough introduction to basic query concepts and learn to write efficient queries to support business reports and advanced analytics.

Finally, database administrators who are new to SQL Server will find this book to be an all-inclusive introduction and reference of mainstream topics. This can assist you as you support the efforts of other team members. Beyond the basics of database object management and security concepts, we recommend *Beginning SQL Server 2005 Administration* and *Beginning SQL Server 2008 Administration* from Wrox, co-authored in part by the same authors.

What This Book Covers

This book introduces the T-SQL language and its many uses, and serves as a comprehensive guide at a beginner through intermediate level. Our goal in writing this book was to cover all the basics thoroughly and to cover the most common applications of T-SQL at a deeper level. Depending on your role and skill level, this book will serve as a companion to the other Wrox books in the Microsoft SQL Server *Beginning* and *Professional* series. Check the back cover of this book for a road map of other complementary books in the Wrox series.

This book will help you to learn:

- ❑ How T-SQL provides you with the means to create tools for managing databases of different size, scope, and purpose
- ❑ Various programming techniques that use views, user-defined functions, and stored procedures
- ❑ Ways to optimize query performance
- ❑ How to create databases that will be an essential foundation to applications you develop later

How This Book Is Structured

Each section of this book organizes topics into logical groups so the book can be read cover-to-cover or used as a reference guide for specific topics.

We start with an introduction to the T-SQL language and data management systems, and then continue with the SQL Server product fundamentals. This first section teaches the essentials of the SQL Server product architecture and relational database design principles. This section (Chapters 1–3) concludes with an introduction to the SQL Server administrator and developer tools.

The next section, encompassing Chapters 4 through 9, introduces the T-SQL language and teaches the core components of data retrieval, SQL functions, aggregation and grouping, and multi-table queries. We start with the basics and build on the core structure of the SQL SELECT statement, progressing to advanced forms of SELECT queries.

Chapter 10 introduces transactions and data manipulation. You will learn how the INSERT, UPDATE, and DELETE statements interact with the relational database engine and transaction log to lock and modify data rows with guaranteed consistency. You will not only learn to use correct SQL syntax but will understand how this process works in simple terms.

More advanced topics in the concluding section will teach you to create and manage T-SQL programming objects, including views, functions, and stored procedures. You learn to optimize query performance and use T-SQL in application design, applying the query design basics to real-world business solutions. Chapter 15 contains a complete tutorial on using SQL Server 2008 Reporting Services to visualize data from the T-SQL queries you create.

The book concludes with a comprehensive set of reference appendixes for command syntax, system stored procedures, information schema views, file system commands, and system management commands.

What You Need to Use This Book

The material in this book applies to all editions of Microsoft SQL Server 2005 and 2008. To use all the features discussed, we recommend that you install the Developer Edition, although you can also use the Enterprise, Standard, or Workgroup editions.

SQL Server 2005 Developer Edition or SQL Server 2008 Developer Edition can be installed on a desktop computer running Windows 2000, Windows XP, or Windows Vista. You can also use Windows 2000 Server, Windows Server 2003, or Windows Server 2008 with the Enterprise or Standard edition. The SQL Server client tools must be installed on your desktop computer and the SQL Server relational database server must be installed on either your desktop computer or on a remote server with network connectivity and permission to access.

Consult www.microsoft.com/sql for information about the latest service packs, specific compatibilities, and minimum recommend system requirements.

The examples throughout this book use the following sample databases, which are available to download from Microsoft: the sample database for SQL Server 2005 is called *AdventureWorks*, and the sample database for SQL Server 2008 is called *AdventureWorks2008*. Because the structure of these databases differs significantly, separate code samples are provided throughout the book for these two version-specific databases.

An example using the AdventureWorks2008DW database for SQL Server 2008 is also used in Chapter 15.

To download and install these sample databases, browse www.codeplex.com.

Conventions

To help you get the most from the text and keep track of what's happening, we've used a number of conventions throughout the book.

Try It Out

The *Try It Out* is an exercise you should work through, following the text in the book.

1.   They usually consist of a set of steps.

2.   Each step has a number.

3.   Follow the steps through with your copy of the database.

> Boxes like this one hold important, not-to-be forgotten information that is directly relevant to the surrounding text.

Notes, tips, hints, tricks, and asides to the current discussion are offset and placed in italics like this.

As for styles in the text:

❑   We *highlight* new terms and important words when we introduce them.

❑   We show keyboard strokes like this: Ctrl+A.

❑   We show filenames, URLs, and code within the text like so: `persistence.properties`.

❑   We present code in two different ways:

```
We use a monofont type with no highlighting for most code examples.
We use gray highlighting to emphasize code that's particularly important in
the present context.
```

Source Code

As you work through the examples in this book, you may choose either to type in all the code manually or to use the source code files that accompany the book. All the source code used in this book is available for download at `www.wrox.com`. Once at the site, simply locate the book's title (either by using the Search box or by using one of the title lists) and click the Download Code link on the book's detail page to obtain all the source code for the book.

Because many books have similar titles, you may find it easiest to search by ISBN; this book's ISBN is 978-0-470-25703-6.

Once you download the code, just decompress it with your favorite compression tool. Alternatively, you can go to the main Wrox code download page at www.wrox.com/dynamic/books/download.aspx to see the code available for this book and all other Wrox books.

Errata

We make every effort to ensure that there are no errors in the text or in the code. However, no one is perfect, and mistakes do occur. If you find an error in one of our books, like a spelling mistake or faulty piece of code, we would be very grateful for your feedback. By sending in errata you may save another reader from hours of frustration and at the same time you will be helping us provide even higher quality information.

To find the errata page for this book, go to www.wrox.com and locate the title using the Search box or one of the title lists. Then, on the book details page, click the Book Errata link. On this page you can view all errata that has been submitted for this book and posted by Wrox editors. A complete book list including links to each book's errata is also available at www.wrox.com/misc-pages/booklist.shtml.

If you don't spot "your" error on the Book Errata page, go to www.wrox.com/contact/techsupport .shtml and complete the form there to send us the error you have found. We'll check the information and, if appropriate, post a message to the book's errata page and fix the problem in subsequent editions of the book.

p2p.wrox.com

For author and peer discussion, join the P2P forums at p2p.wrox.com. The forums are a Web-based system for you to post messages relating to Wrox books and related technologies and interact with other readers and technology users. The forums offer a subscription feature to e-mail you topics of interest of your choosing when new posts are made to the forums. Wrox authors, editors, other industry experts, and your fellow readers are present on these forums.

At http://p2p.wrox.com you will find a number of different forums that will help you not only as you read this book, but also as you develop your own applications. To join the forums, just follow these steps:

1. Go to p2p.wrox.com and click the Register link.
2. Read the terms of use and click Agree.
3. Complete the required information to join as well as any optional information you wish to provide, and click Submit.
4. You will receive an e-mail with information describing how to verify your account and complete the joining process.

   You can read messages in the forums without joining P2P but in order to post your own messages, you must join.

Once you join, you can post new messages and respond to messages other users post. You can read messages at any time on the Web. If you would like to have new messages from a particular forum e-mailed to you, click the Subscribe to this Forum icon by the forum name in the forum listing.

For more information about how to use the Wrox P2P, be sure to read the P2P FAQs for answers to questions about how the forum software works as well as many common questions specific to P2P and Wrox books. To read the FAQs, click the FAQ link on any P2P page.

Introducing T-SQL and Data Management Systems

This first chapter introduces you to some of the fundamentals of the design and architecture of relational databases and presents a brief description of SQL as a language. If you are new to SQL and database technologies, this chapter will provide a foundation to help ensure the rest of the book is as useful as possible. If you are already comfortable with the concepts of relational databases and Microsoft's implementation, you might want to skip ahead to Chapter 2, "SQL Server Fundamentals," or Chapter 3, "SQL Server Tools." Both of these chapters introduce the features and tools in SQL Server 2005 and 2008 and discuss how they are used to write T-SQL.

T-SQL Language

I have mentioned to my colleagues and anyone else who might have been listening that one day I was going to write a version of Parker Brother's Trivial Pursuit entitled "Trivial Pursuit: Geek Edition." This section gives you some background on the T-SQL language and provides the information you need to get the orange history wedge on the topic of "Database History" in Trivial Pursuit: Geek Edition.

T-SQL is Microsoft's implementation of a standard established by the American National Standards Institute (ANSI) for the Structured Query Language (SQL). SQL was first developed by researchers at IBM. They called their first pre-release version of SQL "SEQUEL," which is a pseudo-acronym for **S**tructured **E**nglish **QUE**ry Language. The first release version was renamed to SQL, dropping the English part but retaining the pronunciation to identify it with its predecessor. As of the release of SQL Server 2008, several implementations of SQL by different stakeholders are in the database marketplace. As you sojourn through the sometimes mystifying lands of database technology you will undoubtedly encounter these different varieties of SQL. What makes them all similar is the ANSI standard to which IBM, more than any other vendor, adheres to with tenacious rigidity. However, what makes the many implementations of SQL different are the customized programming objects and extensions to the language that make it unique to that particular platform.

Microsoft SQL Server 2008 implements the 2003 ANSI standard. The term "implements" is of significance. T-SQL is not fully compliant with ANSI standards in any of its implementations; neither is Oracle's P/L SQL, Sybase's SQLAnywhere, or the open-source MySQL. Each implementation has custom extensions and variations that deviate from the established standard. ANSI has three levels of compliance: Entry, Intermediate, and Full. T-SQL is certified at the entry level of ANSI compliance. If you strictly adhere to the features that are ANSI-compliant, the same code you write for Microsoft SQL Server should work on any ANSI-compliant platform; that's the theory, anyway. If you find that you are writing cross-platform queries, you will most certainly need to take extra care to ensure that the syntax is perfectly suited for all the platforms it affects. The simple reality of this issue is that very few people will need to write queries to work on multiple database platforms. The standards serve as a guideline to help keep query languages focused on working with data, rather than other forms of programming. This may slow the evolution of relational databases just enough to keep us sane.

Programming Language or Query Language?

T-SQL was not really developed to be a full-fledged programming language. Over the years, the ANSI standard has been expanded to incorporate more and more procedural language elements, but it still lacks the power and flexibility of a true programming language. Antoine, a talented programmer and friend of mine, refers to SQL as "Visual Basic on Quaaludes." I share this bit of information not because I agree with it, but because I think it is funny. I also think it is indicative of many application developers' view of this versatile language.

T-SQL was designed with the exclusive purpose of data retrieval and data manipulation. Although T-SQL, like its ANSI sibling, can be used for many programming-like operations, its effectiveness at these tasks varies from excellent to abysmal. That being said, I am still more than happy to call T-SQL a programming language if only to avoid someone calling me a SQL "queryers." However, the undeniable fact still remains: as a programming language, T-SQL falls short. The good news is that as a data retrieval and set manipulation language it is exceptional. When T-SQL programmers try to use T-SQL like a programming language, they invariably run afoul of the best practices that ensure the efficient processing and execution of the code. Because T-SQL is at its best when manipulating sets of data, try to keep that fact foremost in your thoughts during the process of developing T-SQL code.

With the release of SQL Server 2005, Microsoft muddied the waters a bit with the ability to write calls to the database in a programming language like C# or VB.NET, rather than in pure SQL. SQL Server 2008 also supports this very flexible capability, but use caution! Although this is a very exciting innovation in data access, the truth of the matter is that almost all calls to the database engine must still be manipulated so that they appear to be T-SQL based.

Performing multiple recursive row operations or complex mathematical computations is quite possible with T-SQL, but so is writing a .NET application with Notepad. When I was growing up my father used to make a point of telling me that "Just because you can do something doesn't mean you should." The point here is that oftentimes SQL programmers will resort to creating custom objects in their code that are inefficient as far as memory and CPU consumption are concerned. They do this because it is the easiest and quickest way to finish the code. I agree that there are times when a quick solution is the best, but future performance must always be taken into account.

One of the systems I am currently working on is a perfect example of this problem. The database started out very small, with a small development team and a small number of customers using the database. It worked great. However, the database didn't stay small, and as more and more customers started using the system, the number of transactions and code executions increased exponentially. It wasn't long before inefficient code began to consume all the available CPU resources. This is the trap of writing expedient code instead of efficient code. Another of my father's favorite sayings is "Why is there never enough time to do the job right, but plenty of time to do it twice?" This book tries to show you the best way to write T-SQL so that you can avoid writing code that will bring your server to its knees, begging for mercy. Don't give in to the temptation to write sloppy code just because it is a "one time deal." I have seen far too many times when that one-off ad-hoc query became a central piece of an application's business logic.

What's New in SQL Server 2008

When SQL Server 2005 was released, it had been five years since the previous release and the changes to the product since the release of SQL Server 2000 were myriad and significant. Several books and hundreds of websites were published that were devoted to the topic of "What's New in SQL Server 2005." With the release of SQL Server 2008, however, there is much less buzz and not such a dramatic change to the platform. However, the changes in the 2008 release are still very exciting and introduce many changes that T-SQL and application developers have been clamoring for. Since these changes are sprinkled throughout the capabilities of SQL Server, I won't spend a great deal of time describing all the changes here. Instead, throughout the book I will identify those changes that are applicable to the subject being described. In this introductory chapter I want to quickly mention two of the significant changes to SQL that will invariably have an impact on the SQL programmer: the incorporation of the .NET Framework with SQL Server and the introduction of Microsoft Language Integrated Query (LINQ).

Kiss T-SQL Goodbye?

I have been hearing for years that T-SQL and its ANSI counterpart, SQL, were antiquated languages and would soon be phased out. However, every database vendor, both small and large, has devoted millions of dollars to improving their version of this versatile language. Why would they do that if it were a dead language? The simple fact of the matter is that databases are built and optimized for the set-based operations that the SQL language offers. Is there a better way to access and manipulate data? Probably so, but with every major industry storing their data in relational databases, the reign of SQL is far from over.

I worked for a great guy at a Microsoft partner company who was contracted by Microsoft to develop and deliver a number of SQL Server and Visual Studio evangelism presentations. Having a background in radio sales and marketing, he came up with a cool tagline about SQL Server and the .NET Framework that said "SQL Server and .NET — Kiss T-SQL Goodbye." He was quickly dissuaded by his team when presented with the facts. However, Todd wasn't completely wrong. What his catchy tagline could have said and been accurate was "SQL Server and .NET — Kiss Inefficient, CPU-Hogging T-SQL Code Goodbye."

Two significant improvements in data access over the last two releases of SQL Server have offered fuel for the "SQL is dead" fire. As I mentioned briefly before, these are the incorporation of the .NET Framework and the development of LINQ. LINQ is Microsoft's latest application data-access technology. It enables Visual Basic and C# applications to use set-oriented queries that are developed in C# or VB, rather than requiring that the queries be written in T-SQL. Building in the .NET Framework to the SQL Server engine enables developers to create SQL Server programming objects such as stored procedures, functions, and aggregates using any .NET language and compiling them into Common Language Runtime (CLR) assemblies that can be referenced directly by the database engine.

So with the introduction of LINQ in SQL Server 2008 and CLR integration in SQL Server 2005, is T-SQL on its death bed? No, not really. Reports of T-SQL's demise are premature and highly exaggerated. The ability to create database programming objects in managed code instead of SQL does not mean that T-SQL is in danger of becoming extinct. Likewise, the ability to create set-oriented queries in C# and VB does not sound the death knell for T-SQL. SQL Server's native language is still T-SQL. LINQ will help in the rapid development of database applications, but it remains to be seen if this technology will match the performance of native T-SQL code run from the server. This is because LINQ data access still must be translated from the application layer to the database layer, but T-SQL does not. It's a fantastic and flexible access layer for smaller database applications, but for large, enterprise-class applications, LINQ, like embedded SQL code in applications before it, falls short of pure T-SQL in terms of performance.

What was true then is true now. T-SQL will continue to be the core language for applications that need to add, extract, and manipulate data stored on SQL Server. Until the data engine is completely re-engineered (and that day will inevitably come), T-SQL will be at the heart of SQL Server.

Database Management Systems

A database management system (DBMS) is a set of programs designed to store and maintain data. The role of the DBMS is to manage the data so that the consistency and integrity of the data is maintained above all else. Quite a few types and implementations of database management systems exist:

- ❑ **Hierarchical database management systems (HDBMS)** — Hierarchical databases have been around for a long time and are perhaps the oldest of all databases. They were (and in some cases still are) used to manage hierarchical data. They have several limitations, such as being able to manage only single trees of hierarchical data and the inability to efficiently prevent erroneous or duplicate data. HDBMS implementations are getting increasingly rare and are constrained to specialized, and typically non-commercial, applications.

- ❑ **Network database management system (NDBMS)** — The NDBMS has been largely abandoned. In the past, large organizational database systems were implemented as network or hierarchical systems. The network systems did not suffer from the data inconsistencies of the hierarchical model, but they did suffer from a very complex and rigid structure that made changes to the database or its hosted applications very difficult.

- ❑ **Relational database management system (RDBMS)** — An RDBMS is a software application used to store data in multiple related tables using SQL as the tool for creating, managing, and modifying both the data and the data structures. An RDBMS maintains data by storing it in tables that represent single entities, such as "Customer" and "Sale" and storing information about the relationship of these tables to each other in yet more tables managed by the system which define the relationship between the Sale table and the Customer table. The concept of a relational database was first described by E. F. Codd, an IBM scientist who defined the relational model in 1970. Relational databases are optimized for recording transactions and the resultant transactional data. Most commercial software applications use an RDBMS as their data store. Because SQL was designed specifically for use with an RDBMS, I will spend a little extra time covering the basic structures of an RDBMS later in this chapter.

- ❑ **Object-oriented database management system (ODBMS)** — The ODBMS emerged a few years ago as a system where data was stored as objects in a database. ODBMS supports multiple classes of objects and inheritance of classes along with other aspects of object orientation. Currently, no international standard exists that specifies exactly what an ODBMS is and what it isn't.

Because ODBMS applications store objects instead of related entities, they make the system very efficient when dealing with complex data objects and object-oriented programming (OOP) languages such as the .NET languages from Microsoft as well as C and Java. When ODBMS solutions were first released, they were quickly touted as the ultimate database system and predicted to make all other database systems obsolete. However, they never achieved the wide acceptance that was predicted. They do have a very valid position in the database market, but it is a niche market held mostly within the Computer-Aided Design (CAD) and telecommunications industries.

❑ **Object-relational database management system (ORDBMS)** — The ORDBMS emerged from existing RDBMS solutions when the vendors who produced the relational systems realized that the ability to store objects was becoming more important. They incorporated mechanisms to be able to store classes and objects in the relational model. ORDBMS implementations have, for the most part, usurped the market that the ODBMS vendors were targeting for a variety of reasons that I won't expound on here. However, Microsoft's SQL Server, with its xml data type, the incorporation of the .NET Framework, and the new filestream data type introduced with SQL Server 2008, could arguably be labeled an ORDBMS. The filestream data type is discussed in more detail later in this chapter and in Appendix E.

SQL Server as a Relational Database Management System

This section introduces you to the concepts behind relational databases and how they are implemented from a Microsoft viewpoint. This will, by necessity, skirt the edges of database object creation, which is covered in great detail in Chapter 13, so for the purpose of this discussion I will avoid the exact mechanics and focus on the final results.

As I mentioned earlier, a relational database stores all its data inside tables. Ideally, each table will represent a single entity or object. You would not want to create one table that contained data about both dogs and cars. That isn't to say you couldn't do this, but it wouldn't be very efficient or easy to maintain if you did.

Tables

Tables are divided up into rows and columns. Each row must be able to stand on its own, without a dependency to other rows in the table. The row must represent a single, complete instance of the entity the table was created to represent. Each column in the row contains specific attributes that help define the instance. This may sound a bit complex, but it is actually very simple. To help illustrate, consider a real-world entity, such as an employee. If you want to store data about an employee, you would need to create a table that has the properties you need to record data about your employee. For simplicity's sake, call your table Employee.

When you create your employee table, you also need to decide which attributes of the employee you want to store. For the purposes of this example, suppose that you have decided to store the employee's last name, first name, Social Security number, department, extension, and hire date. The resulting table would look something like that shown in Figure 1-1.

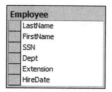

Figure 1-1

The data in the table would look something like that shown in Figure 1-2.

LastName	FirstName	SSN	Dept	Extension	HireDate
Flintstone	Fred	123456789	Operations	9876	11/12/2000
Slate	George	987654321	Management	3456	4/14/1999

Figure 1-2

Primary Keys

To manage the data in your table efficiently, you need to be able to uniquely identify each individual row in the table. It is much more difficult to retrieve, update, or delete a single row if there is not a single attribute that identifies each row individually. In many cases, this identifier is not a descriptive attribute of the entity. For example, the logical choice to uniquely identify your employee is the Social Security number attribute. However, there are a couple of reasons why you would not want to use the Social Security number as the primary mechanism for identifying each instance of an employee, both boiling down to two different areas: security and efficiency.

When it comes to security, what you want to avoid is the necessity of securing the employee's Social Security number in multiple tables. Because you will most likely be using the key column in multiple tables to form your relationships (more on that in a moment), it makes sense to substitute a non-descriptive key. In this way you avoid the issue of duplicating private or sensitive data in multiple locations to provide the mechanism to form relationships between tables.

As far as efficiency is concerned, you can often substitute a non-data key that has a more efficient or smaller data type associated with it. For example, in your design you might have created the Social Security number with either a character data type or an integer. If you have fewer than 32,767 employees, you can use a double-byte integer instead of a 4-byte integer or 10-byte character type; besides, integers process faster than characters.

So, instead of using the Social Security number, you will assign a non-descriptive key to each row. The key value used to uniquely identify individual rows in a table is called a *primary key*. (You will still want to ensure that every Social Security number in your table is unique and not null, but you will use a different method to guarantee this behavior without making it a primary key.)

A non-descriptive key doesn't represent anything else with the exception of being a value that uniquely identifies each row or individual instance of the entity in a table. This will simplify the joining of this table to other tables and provide the basis for a "relation." In this example you will simply alter the table by adding an EmployeeKey column that will uniquely identify every row in the table, as shown in Figure 1-3.

Figure 1-3

With the EmployeeKey column, you have an efficient, easy-to-manage primary key.

Each table can have only one primary key, which means that this key column is the primary method for uniquely identifying individual rows. It doesn't have to be the only mechanism for uniquely identifying individual rows; it is just the "primary" mechanism for doing so. Primary keys can never be null, and they must be unique. Primary keys can also be combinations of columns (though I'll explain later why I am a firm believer that primary keys should typically be single-column keys). If you have a table where two columns in combination are unique, while either single column is not, you can combine the two columns as a single primary key, as illustrated in Figure 1-4.

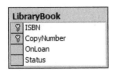

Figure 1-4

In this example, the LibraryBook table is used to maintain a record of every book in the library. Because multiple copies of each book can exist, the ISBN column is not useful for uniquely identifying each book. To enable the identification of each individual book, the table designer decided to combine the ISBN column with the copy number of each book. Personally, I avoid the practice of using multiple column keys. I prefer to create a separate column that can uniquely identify the row. This makes it much easier to write join queries (covered in detail in Chapter 8). The resulting code is cleaner and the queries are generally more efficient. For the library book example, a more efficient mechanism might be to assign each book its own number. The resulting table would look like that shown in Figure 1-5.

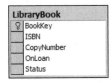

Figure 1-5

Table Columns

As previously described, a table is a set of rows and columns used to represent an entity. Each row represents an instance of the entity. Each column in the row will contain at most one value that represents an attribute, or property, of the entity. For example, consider the employee table; each row represents a single instance of the employee entity. Each employee can have one and only one first name, last name, SSN, extension, or hire date, according to your design specifications. In addition to deciding which attributes you want to maintain, you must also decide how to store those attributes. When you define columns for your tables, you must, at a minimum, define three things:

- ❑ The name of the column
- ❑ The data type of the column
- ❑ Whether the column can support null

Column Names

Keep the names simple and intuitive (such as LastName or EmployeeID) instead of more cumbersome names (such as EmployeeLastName and EmployeeIdentificationNumber). For more information, see Chapter 8.

Data Types

The general rule on data types is to use the smallest one you can. This conserves memory usage and disk space. Also keep in mind that SQL Server processes numbers much more efficiently than characters, so use numbers whenever practical. I have heard the argument that numbers should be used only if you plan on performing mathematical operations on the columns that contain them, but that just doesn't wash. Numbers are preferred over string data for sorting and comparison as well as mathematical computations. The exception to this rule is if the string of numbers you want to use starts with a zero. Take the Social Security number, for example. Other than the unfortunate fact that some Social Security numbers begin with a zero, the Social Security number would be a perfect candidate for using an integer instead of a character string. However, if you tried to store the integer 012345678, you would end up with 12345678. These two values may be numeric equivalents, but the government doesn't see it that way. They are strings of numerical characters and therefore must be stored as characters rather than as numbers.

When designing tables and choosing a data type for each column, try to be conservative and use the smallest, most efficient type possible. But at the same time, carefully consider the exception, however rare, and make sure that the chosen type will always meet these requirements.

The data types available for columns in SQL Server 2005 and 2008 are specified in the following table. Those that are unique to SQL Server 2008 are prefixed with an asterisk (*).

Data Type	Storage	Description
Integers		Note: Signed integers can be both positive and negative, whereas unsigned integers have no inherent signed value
bigint	8 bytes	An 8-byte signed integer. Valid values are −9223372036854775808 through +9223372036854775807.
int	4 bytes	A 4-byte signed integer. Valid values are −2,147,483,648 through +2,147,483,647.
smallint	2 bytes	A double-byte signed integer. Valid values are −32,768 through +32,767.
tinyint	1 byte	A single-byte unsigned integer. Valid values are from 0 through 255.
bit	1 bit	Integer data with either a 1 or 0 value.
Exact Numerics		
decimal	5–17 bytes	A predefined, fixed, signed decimal number ranging from −100000000000000000000000000000000000001 ($-10^{38}+1$) to 99999999999999999999999999999999999999 ($-10^{38}-1$). A decimal is declared with a precision and scale value that determines how many decimal places to the left and right are supported. This is expressed as decimal[(precision, [scale])]. The precision setting determines how many total digits to the left and right of the decimal point are supported. The scale setting determines how many digits to the right of the decimal point are supported. For example, to support the number 3.141592653589793, the decimal data type would have to be specified as decimal(16,15). If the data type were specified as decimal(3,2), only 3.14 would be stored. The scale defaults to zero and must be between 0 and the precision. The precision defaults to 18 and can be a maximum of 38.
numeric	5–17 bytes	The numeric data type is identical to the decimal data type, so use decimal instead, for consistency. The numeric data type is much less descriptive because most people think of integers as being numeric.
money	8 bytes	The money data type can be used to store values from −922,337,203,685,477.5808 to +922,337,203,685,477.5807 of a monetary unit, such as a dollar, euro, pound, and so on. The advantage of the money data type over a decimal data type is that developers can take advantage of automatic currency formatting for specific locales. Notice that the money data type supports figures to the fourth decimal place. Accountants like that. A few million of those ten thousandths of a penny add up after a while!

(continued)

Data Type	Storage	Description
smallmoney	4 bytes	Bill Gates needs the money data type to track his portfolio, but most of us can get by with the smallmoney data type. It consumes 4 bytes of storage and can be used to store values of −214,748.3648 to +214,748.3647 of a monetary unit.
Approximate Numerics		
float	4 or 8 bytes	The float data type is an approximate value (SQL Server performs rounding) that supports real numbers in the range of $-1.79E + 308$ to $-2.23E - 308$, 0 and $2.23E - 308$ to $1.79E + 308$. float can be used as a 4-byte or 8-byte data type, depending on an optional mantissa value (the number of bits used to store the mantissa of the float). float(24) or any value between 1 and 24 will cause the float to be defined as a 4-byte value that can store real numbers in the range of $-3.40E + 38$ to $-1.18E - 38$, 0 and $1.18E - 38$ to $3.40E + 38$. Any number between 25 and 53 will cause the float to be defined as an 8-bit float (aka, a double precision) in the default manner of float(53).
real	4 bytes	The real data type is a synonym for a 4-byte float.
Date and Time Data Types		
datetime	8 bytes	The datetime data type is used to store date and time from January 1, 1753 through December 31, 9999. The accuracy of the datetime data type is 3.33 milliseconds.
*datetime2	8 bytes	The datetime2 data type is used to store date and time from January 1, 0001 through December 31, 9999. The accuracy of the datetime2 data type is variable but defaults to 100 nanoseconds.
smalldatetime	4 bytes	The smalldatetime data type stores date and time from January 1, 1900 through June 6, 2079, with an accuracy of 1 minute.
*date	3 bytes	The date data type stores dates only from January 1, 0001 through December 31, 9999, with an accuracy of 1 day.
*time	5 bytes	The time data type stores time-only data, with a variable precision of up to 100 nanoseconds

Data Type	Storage	Description
*datetimeoffset	10 bytes	The datetimeoffset data type is used to store date and time from January 1, 0001 through December 31, 9999. The accuracy of the datetimeoffset data type varies based on the type of server hardware SQL Server is installed on, but defaults to 100 nanoseconds if supported. When defined, the datetimeoffset data type expects a date and time string to be specified along with a time zone offset. Possible time zone offsets are between −14.00 and +14.00 hours. For example, to define a variable that is time-zone aware for Pacific Standard Time, the following code would be used: `DECLARE @PacificTime AS datetimeoffset(8)`
Character Data Types		
char	1 byte per character. Maximum 8000 characters.	The char data type is a fixed-length data type used to store character data. The number of possible characters is between 1 and 8000. The possible combinations of characters in a char data type are 256. The characters that are represented depend on what language, or collation, is defined. English, for example, is actually defined with a Latin collation. The Latin collation provides support for all English and western European characters.
varchar	1 byte per character. Up to 2GB characters.	The varchar data type is identical to the char data type, but with a variable length. If a column is defined as char(8), it will consume 8 bytes of storage even if only three characters are placed in it. A varchar column consumes only the space it needs. Typically, char data types are more efficient when it comes to processing and varchar data types are more efficient for storage. The rule of thumb is to use char if the data will always be close to the defined length, but use varchar if it will vary widely. For example, a city name would be stored with varchar(167) if you wanted to allow for the longest city name in the world, which is Krung thep mahanakhon bovorn ratanakosin mahintharayutthaya mahadilok pop noparatratchathani burirom udomratchanivetmahasathan amornpiman avatarnsathit sakkathattiyavisnukarmprasit (the poetic name of Bangkok, Thailand). Use char for data that is always the same. For example, you could use char(12) to store a domestic phone number in the United States: (123)456-7890. The 8000-byte limitation can be exceeded by specifying the (MAX) option (varchar(MAX)), which allows for the storage of 2,147,483,647 characters at the cost of up to 2GB storage space.

(continued)

Data Type	Storage	Description
text	1 byte per character. Maximum 2,147,483,648 characters (2GB).	The text data type is similar to the varchar data type in that it is a variable-length character data type. The significant difference is the maximum length of about 2 billion characters (including spaces) and where the data is physically stored. With a varchar data type on a table column, the data is stored physically in the row with the rest of the data. With a text data type, the data is stored separately from the actual row and a pointer is stored in the row so that SQL Server can find the text. The text data type is functionally equivalent to the varchar(MAX) data type.
nchar	2 bytes per character. Maximum 4000 characters (8000 bytes).	The nchar data type is a fixed-length type identical to the char data type, with the exception of the number of characters supported. char data is represented by a single byte and thus only 256 different characters can be supported. nchar is a double-byte data type and can support 65,536 different characters. The cost of the extra character support is the double-byte length, so the maximum nchar length is 4000 characters or 8000 bytes.
nvarchar	2 bytes per character. Up to 2GB.	The nvarchar data type is a variable-length type identical to the varchar data type, with the exception of the amount of characters supported. varchar data is represented by a single byte and only 256 different characters can be supported. nvarchar is a double-byte data type and can support 65,536 different characters. The cost of the extra character support is the double-byte length, so the maximum nvarchar length is 4000 characters or 8000 bytes. This limit can be exceeded by using the (MAX) option, which allows for the storage of 1,073,741,823 characters in 2GB.
ntext	2 bytes per character. Maximum 1,073,741,823 characters.	The ntext data type is identical to the text data type, with the exception of the number of characters supported. text data is represented by a single byte and only 256 different characters can be supported. ntext is a double-byte data type and can support 65,536 different characters. The cost of the extra character support is the double-byte length, so the maximum ntext length is 1,073,741,823 characters or 2GB. The ntext data type is functionally equivalent to the nvarchar(MAX) data type.
Binary Data Types		
binary	1–8000 bytes	Fixed-length binary data. Length is fixed when created between 1 and 8000 bytes. For example, binary(5000) specifies the reserving of 5000 bytes of storage to accommodate up to 5000 bytes of binary data.

Data Type	Storage	Description
varbinary	Up to 2,147,483,647 bytes	Variable-length binary data type identical to the binary data type, with the exception of consuming only the amount of storage that is necessary to hold the data. Using the (MAX) option allows for the storage of up to 2GB of binary data. However, only 1 through 8000 or MAX can be specified as storage options.
image	Up to 2,147,483,647 bytes	The image data type is similar to the varbinary data type in that it is a variable-length binary data type. The significant difference is the maximum length of about 2GB and where the data is physically stored. With a varbinary data type on a table column, the data is stored physically in the row with the rest of the data. With an image data type, however, the data is stored separately from the actual row and a pointer is stored in the row so that SQL Server can find the data. Typically, image data types are used to store actual images, binary documents, or binary objects. The image data type is functionally identical to varbinary(MAX).
Other Data Types		
timestamp	8 bytes	The timestamp data type has nothing to do with time. It is more accurately described as a data type that maintains row version data. In light of this fact, a system alias of rowversion is available for this data type and is generally preferred to avoid confusion. What timestamp actually provides is a database unique identifier to identify a version of a row. Every time a row that contains a timestamp data type is modified, the value of the timestamp changes.
uniqueidentifier	32 bytes	A data type used to store a globally unique identifier (GUID).
*hierarchyid	Up to 892 bytes	The hierarchyid data type is a variable length data type that is used to represent position in a hierarchy.
sql_variant	Up to 8016 bytes	sql_variant is used when the exact data type is unknown. It can be used to hold any data type with the exception of text, ntext, image, and timestamp.
xml	Up to 2GB	The xml data type is used to store well-formed XML. The XML stored can be specified to be well-formed fragments or complete documents and can be enforced with an XML schema bound to the variable, parameter, or column containing the XML data.

SQL Server supports additional data types, listed in the following table, that can be used in queries and programming objects, but they are not used to define columns.

Data Type	Description
cursor	The cursor data type is used to point to an instance of a cursor.
table	The table data type is used to store an in-memory rowset for processing. It was developed primarily for use with the table-valued functions that were introduced in SQL Server 2000.

Nullability

All rows from the same table have the same set of columns. However, not all columns will necessarily have values in them. For example, a new employee is hired, but he has not been assigned an extension yet. In this case, the extension column may not have any data in it. Instead, it may contain null, which means the value for that column was not initialized. Note that a null value for a string column is different from an empty string. An empty string is defined; a null is not. You should always consider a null as an unknown value. When you design your tables, you need to decide whether to allow a null condition to exist in your columns. Nulls can be allowed or disallowed on a column-by-column basis, so your employee table design could look like that shown in Figure 1-6.

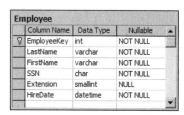

Figure 1-6

Relationships

Relational databases are all about relations. To manage these relations, you use common keys. For example, your employees sell products to customers. This process involves multiple entities:

- ❑ The employee
- ❑ The product
- ❑ The customer
- ❑ The sale

To identify which employee sold which product to which customer, you need some way to link together all the entities. Typically, these links are managed through the use of keys — primary keys in the parent table and foreign keys in the child table.

As a practical example, you can revisit the employee example. When your employee sells a product, his or her identifying information is added to the Sale table to record who the responsible employee was, as illustrated in Figure 1-7. In this case, the Employee table is the parent table and the Sale table is the child table.

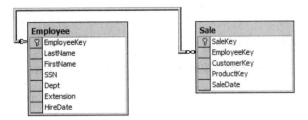

Figure 1-7

Because the same employee could sell products to many customers, the relationship between the Employee table and the Sale table is called a *one-to-many relationship*. The fact that the employee is the unique participant in the relationship makes it the *parent table*. Relationships are very often *parent-child relationships*, which means that the record in the parent table must exist before the child record can be added. In the example, because every employee is not required to make a sale, the relationship is more accurately described as a *one-to-zero-or-more relationship*. In Figure 1-7 this relationship is represented by a key and infinity symbol, which doesn't adequately model the true relationship because you don't know if the EmployeeKey field is nullable. In Figure 1-8, the more traditional and informative "crows feet" symbol is used. The relationship symbol in this figure represents an exactly one (the double vertical lines) to zero (the ring) or more (the crows feet) relationship. Figure 1-9 shows the two tables with an exactly one to one or more relationship symbol. The PK abbreviation stands for primary key, while the FK stands for foreign key. Because a table can have multiple foreign keys, they are numbered sequentially starting at 1.

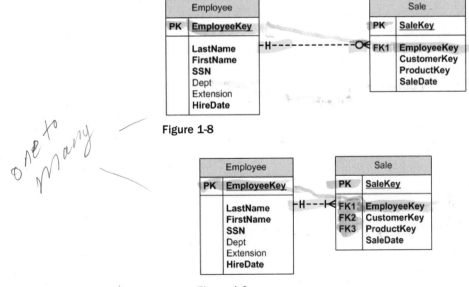

Figure 1-8

Figure 1-9

Relationships can be defined as follows:

- ❏ One-to-zero or more
- ❏ One-to-one or more
- ❏ One-to-exactly-one
- ❏ Many-to-many

The many-to-many relationship requires three tables because a many-to-many constraint would be unenforceable. An example of a many-to-many relationship is illustrated in Figure 1-10. The necessity for this relationship is created by the relationships between your entities: In a single sale many products can be sold, but one product can be in many sales. This creates the many-to-many relationship between the Sale table and the Product table. To uniquely identify every product and sale combination, you need to create what is called a ***linking table***. A linking table is simply another table that contains the combination of primary keys from the two tables, as illustrated in Figure 1-10. The Order table manages your many-to-many relationship by uniquely tracking every combination of sale and product.

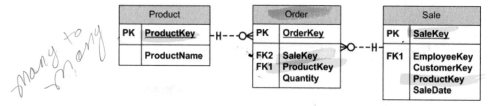

Figure 1-10

As an example of a one-to-one relationship, suppose that you want to record more detailed data about a sale, but you do not want to alter the current table. In this case, you could build a table called SaleDetail to store the data. To ensure that the sale can be linked to the detailed data, you create a relationship between the two tables. Because each sale should appear in both the Sale table and the SaleDetail table, you would create a one-to-one relationship instead of a one-to-many, as illustrated in Figures 1-11 and 1-12.

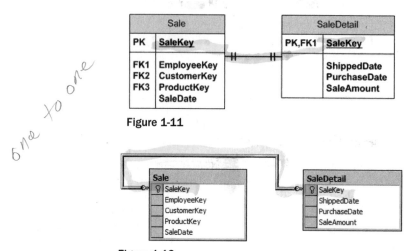

Figure 1-11

Figure 1-12

RDBMS and Data Integrity

An RDBMS is designed to maintain data integrity in a transactional environment. This is accomplished through several mechanisms implemented through database objects. The most prominent of these objects are as follows:

- ❑ Locks
- ❑ Constraints
- ❑ Keys
- ❑ Indexes

Before I describe these objects in more detail, it's important to understand two other important pieces of the SQL architecture: connections and transactions.

Connections

A connection is created anytime a process attaches to SQL Server. The connection is established with defined security and connection properties. These security and connection properties determine which data you have access to and to a certain degree, how SQL Server will behave during the duration of the query in the context of the query. For example, a connection can specify which database to connect to on the server and how to manage memory-resident objects.

Transactions

Transactions are explored in detail in Chapter 10, so for the purposes of this introduction I will keep the explanation brief. In a nutshell, a SQL Server transaction is a collection of dependent data modifications that is controlled so that it completes entirely or not at all. For example, you go to the bank and transfer $100.00 from your savings account to your checking account. This transaction involves two modifications — one to the checking account and the other to the savings account. Each update is dependent on the other. It is very important to you and the bank that the funds are transferred correctly, so the modifications are placed together in a transaction. If the update to the checking account fails but the update to the savings account succeeds, you most definitely want the entire transaction to fail. The bank feels the same way if the opposite occurs.

With a basic idea about these two objects, let's proceed to the four mechanisms that ensure integrity and consistency in your data.

Locks

SQL Server uses locks to ensure that multiple users can access data at the same time with the assurance that the data will not be altered while they are reading it. At the same time, the locks are used to ensure that modifications to data can be accomplished without affecting other modifications or reads in progress. SQL Server manages locks on a connection basis, which simply means that locks cannot be held mutually by multiple connections. SQL Server also manages locks on a transaction basis. In the same way that multiple connections cannot share the same lock, neither can transactions. For example, if an application opens a connection to SQL Server and is granted a shared lock on a table, that same application cannot open an additional connection and modify that data. The same is true for transactions. If an application begins a transaction that modifies specific data, that data cannot be modified in any other transaction until the first has completed its work. This is true even if the multiple transactions share the same connection.

SQL Server utilizes six lock types, or more accurately, six resource lock modes:

- ❏ Shared
- ❏ Update
- ❏ Exclusive
- ❏ Intent
- ❏ Schema
- ❏ Bulk Update

Shared, update, exclusive, and intent locks can be applied to rows of tables or indexes, pages (8-kilobyte storage page of an index or table), extents (64-kilobyte collection of eight contiguous index or table pages), tables, or databases. Schema and bulk update locks apply to tables.

Shared Locks

Shared locks allow multiple connections and transactions to read the resources they are assigned to. No other connection or transaction is allowed to modify the data as long as the shared lock is granted. Once an application successfully reads the data, the shared locks are typically released, but this behavior can be modified for special circumstances. For instance, a shared lock might be held for an entire transaction to ensure maximum protection of data consistency by guaranteeing that the data that a transaction is based on will not change until the transaction is completed. This extended locking is useful for situations where transactional consistency must be 100% assured, but the cost of holding the locks is that concurrent access to data is reduced. For example, you want to withdraw $100.00 from your savings account. A shared lock is issued on the table that contains your savings account balance. That data is used to confirm that there are enough funds to support the withdrawal. It would be advantageous to prevent any other connection from altering the balance until after the withdrawal is complete. Shared locks are compatible with other shared locks so that many transactions and connections can read the same data without conflict.

Update Locks

Update locks are used by SQL Server to help prevent an event known as a *deadlock*. Deadlocks are bad. They are mostly caused by poor programming techniques. A deadlock occurs when two processes get into a standoff over shared resources. Let's return to the banking example: In this hypothetical banking transaction both my wife and I go online to transfer funds from our savings account to our checking account. We somehow manage to execute the transfer operation simultaneously and two separate processes are launched to execute the transfer. When my process accesses the two accounts, it is issued shared locks on the resources. When my wife's process accesses the accounts, it is also granted a shared lock to the resources. So far, so good, but when our processes try to modify the resources, pandemonium ensues. First my wife's process attempts to escalate its lock to exclusive to make the modifications. At about the same time my process attempts the same escalation. However, our mutual shared locks prevent either of our processes from escalating to an exclusive lock. Because neither process is willing to release its shared lock, a deadlock occurs.

SQL Server doesn't particularly care for deadlocks. If one occurs, SQL Server will automatically select one of the processes as a victim and kill it. SQL Server selects the process with the least cost associated with it, kills it, rolls back the associated transaction, and notifies the responsible application of the termination by returning error number 1205. If properly captured, this error informs the user that

"Transaction ## was deadlocked on x resources with another process and has been chosen as the deadlock victim. Rerun the transaction." To avoid the deadlock from ever occurring, SQL Server will typically use update locks in place of shared locks. Only one process can obtain an update lock, preventing the opposing process from escalating its lock. The bottom line is that if a read is executed for the sole purpose of an update, SQL Server may issue an update lock instead of a shared lock to avoid a potential deadlock. This can all be avoided through careful planning and implementation of SQL logic that prevents the deadlock from ever occurring.

Exclusive Locks

SQL Server typically issues exclusive locks when a modification is executed. To change the value of a field in a row, SQL Server grants exclusive access of that row to the calling process. This exclusive access prevents a process from any concurrent transaction or connection from reading, updating, or deleting the data being modified. Exclusive locks are not compatible with any other lock types.

Intent Locks

SQL Server issues intent locks to prevent a process from any concurrent transaction or connection from placing a more exclusive lock on a resource that contains a locked resource from a separate process. For example, if you execute a transaction that updates a single row in a table, SQL Server grants the transaction an exclusive lock on the row, but also grants an intent lock on the table containing the row. This prevents another process from placing an exclusive lock on the table.

Here is an analogy I often use to explain the intent lock behavior in SQL programming classes: You check in to Room 404 at the SQL Hotel. You now have exclusive use of the fourth room on the fourth floor (404). No other hotel patron will be allowed access to this room. In addition, no other patron will be allowed to buy out every room in the hotel because you have already been given exclusive control to one of the rooms. You have what amounts to an intent exclusive lock on the hotel and an exclusive lock on Room 404. Intent locks are compatible with any less-exclusive lock, as illustrated in the following table on lock compatibility.

Requested Lock Type	Existing Granted Lock				
	IS	S	U	IX	X
Intent shared (IS)	Yes	Yes	Yes	Yes	No
Shared (S)	Yes	Yes	Yes	No	No
Update(U)	Yes	Yes	No	No	No
Intent exclusive (IX)	Yes	No	No	Yes	No
Exclusive (X)	No	No	No	No	No

Schema Locks

There are two types of schema locks SQL Server will issue on a table: schema modification locks (Sch-M) and schema stability locks (Sch-S). Schema modification locks prevent concurrent access to a table while the table is undergoing modification — for example, a name change or a column addition. A schema stability lock prevents the table from being modified while it is being accessed for data retrieval.

Bulk Update Locks

A bulk update lock on a table allows multiple bulk load threads to load data into a table while preventing other types of data access. Bulk update locks are issued when table locking is enabled at the table or the chosen as an option with the bulk operation.

Key Range Locks

Key-range locks protect a range of rows implicitly included in a record set being read by a Transact-SQL statement while using the serializable transaction isolation level. The serializable isolation level requires that any query executed during a transaction must obtain the same set of rows every time it is executed during the transaction. A key range lock protects this requirement by preventing other transactions from inserting new rows whose keys would fall in the range of keys read by the serializable transaction.

SQL Server and Other Products

Microsoft has plenty of competition in the client/server database world and SQL Server is a relatively young product by comparison. However, it has enjoyed wide acceptance in the industry due to its ease of use and attractive pricing. If our friends at Microsoft know how to do anything exceptionally well, it's taking a product to market so it becomes very mainstream and widely accepted.

Microsoft SQL Server

Here is a short history lesson on Microsoft's SQL Server. Originally, SQL Server was a Sybase product created for IBM's OS/2 platform. Microsoft engineers worked with Sybase and IBM but eventually withdrew from the project. Then, Microsoft licensed the Sybase SQL Server code and ported the product to work with Windows NT. It took a couple of years before SQL Server really became a viable product. The SQL Server team went to work to create a brand new database engine using the Sybase code as a model. They eventually rewrote the product from scratch.

When SQL Server 7.0 was released in late 1998, it was a major departure from the previous version, SQL Server 6.5. SQL Server 7.0 contained very little Sybase code with the exception of the core database engine technology, which was still under license from Sybase. SQL Server 2000 was released in 2000 with many useful new features, but was essentially just an incremental upgrade of the 7.0 product. SQL Server 2005, however, is a major upgrade and some say it's the very first completely Microsoft product. Any vestiges of Sybase are long gone. The storage and retrieval engine has been completely rewritten, the .NET Framework has been incorporated, and the product has significantly risen in both power and scalability. SQL Server 2008 is to SQL Server 2005 what SQL Server 2000 was to SQL Server 7.0. There are some very interesting and powerful improvements to the server, which we will address in the coming chapters, but the changes are not as dramatic as the changes that SQL Server 2005 brought.

Oracle

Oracle is probably the most recognizable enterprise-class database product in the industry. After IBM's E. F. Codd published his original papers on the fundamental principles of relational data storage and design in 1970, Larry Ellison, founder of Oracle, went to work to build a product to apply those principles. Founded in 1977, Oracle has had a dominant place in the database market for quite some time with a comprehensive suite of database tools and related solutions. Versions of Oracle run on UNIX, Linux, and Windows server operating systems.

The query language of Oracle is known as Procedure Language/Structured Query Language (PL/SQL). Indeed, many aspects of PL/SQL resemble a C-like procedural programming language. This is evidenced by syntax such as command-line termination using semicolons. Unlike T-SQL, statements are not actually executed until an explicit run command is issued (preceded with a single line containing a period.) PL/SQL is particular about using data types and includes expressions for assigning values to compatible column types.

IBM DB2

This is really where it all began. Relational databases and the SQL language were first conceptualized and then implemented in IBM's research department. Although IBM's database products have been around for a very long time, Oracle (then Relational Software) actually beat them to market. DB2 database professionals perceive the form of SQL used in this product to be purely ANSI SQL and other dialects such as Microsoft's T-SQL and Oracle's PL-SQL to be more proprietary. Although DB2 has a long history of running on System 390 mainframes and the AS/400, it is not just a legacy product. IBM has effectively continued to breathe life into DB2 and it remains a viable database for modern business solutions. DB2 runs on a variety of operating systems today, including Windows, UNIX, and Linux.

Informix

This product had been a relatively strong force in the client/server database community, but its popularity waned in the late 1990s. Originally designed for the UNIX platform, Informix is a serious enterprise database. Popularity slipped over the past few years, as many applications built on Informix had to be upgraded to contend with year 2000 compatibility issues. Some organizations moving to other platforms (such as Linux and Windows) have also switched products. The 2001 acquisition of Informix nudged IBM to the top spot over Oracle as they brought existing Informix customers with them. Today, Informix runs on Linux and integrates with other IBM products.

Sybase SQLAnywhere

Sybase has deep roots in the client/server database industry and has a strong product offering. At the enterprise level, Sybase products are deployed on UNIX and Linux platforms and have strong support in Java programming circles. At the mid-scale level, SQLAnywhere runs on several platforms, including UNIX, Linux, Mac OS, NetWare, and Windows. Sybase has carved a niche for itself in the industry for mobile device applications and related databases.

Microsoft Access (Jet)

To be perfectly precise, Access is not really a database platform. Access is a Microsoft Office application that is built to use the Microsoft Jet database platform. Access and Jet were partially created from the ground up but also leverage some of the technology gleaned from Microsoft's acquisition of FoxPro. As a part of Microsoft's Office Suite, Access is a very convenient tool for creating simple business applications. Although Access SQL is ANSI 92 SQL–compliant, it is quite a bit different from T-SQL. For this reason, I have made it a point to identify some of the differences between Access and T-SQL throughout the book.

Access has become the non-programmer's application development tool. Many people get started in database design using Access and then move on to SQL Server as their needs become more sophisticated. Access is a powerful tool for the right kinds of applications, and some commercial products have actually been developed using Access. Unfortunately, because Access is designed (and documented) to be an end user's tool rather than a software developer's tool, many Access databases are often poorly designed and power users learn through painful trial and error about how not to create database applications.

The Jet Database Engine was designed in 1992. Jet is a simple and efficient storage system for small to moderate volumes of data and for relatively few concurrent users, but it falls short of the stability and fault-tolerance of SQL Server. For this reason, a desktop version of the SQL Server engine (now called SQL Server Express, but formally known as Microsoft SQL Desktop Engine [MSDE]) has shipped with Access since Office 2000. SQL Server Express is an alternative to using Jet and really should be used in place of Jet for any serious database. Starting smaller-scale projects with SQL Server Express provides an easier path for migrating them to full-blown SQL Server editions later on.

MySQL

MySQL is a developer's tool embraced by the open source community. Like Linux and Java, it can be obtained free of charge and includes source code. Compilers and components of the database engine can be modified and compiled to run on most any computer platform. Although MySQL supports ANSI SQL, it promotes the use of an application programming interface (API) that wraps SQL statements. As a database product, MySQL is a widely accepted and capable product. However, it appeals more to the open source developer than to the business user.

Many other database products on the market may share some characteristics of the products discussed here. The preceding list represents the most popular database products that use ANSI SQL.

Summary

Microsoft SQL Server 2005 has earned a very good reputation in the marketplace and remains a very capable and powerful database management server. SQL Server 2005 took T-SQL and database management a huge step forward. Now SQL Server 2008 promises to continue the maturation of the product with new and very powerful T-SQL commands and functions.

The upcoming chapters explore most of the longstanding features and capabilities of T-SQL and preview the awesome new capabilities that SQL Server 2005 and SQL Server 2008 have brought to the field of T-SQL programming. So sit back and hold on; it's going to be an exciting ride.

If the whole idea of writing T-SQL code and working with databases doesn't thrill you like it does me, I apologize for my overt enthusiasm. My wife has reminded me on many occasions that no matter how I may look, I really am a geek. I freely confess it. I also eagerly confess that I love working with databases. Working with databases puts you in the middle of everything in information technology. There is absolutely no better place to be. Can you name an enterprise application that doesn't somehow interface with a database? You see? Databases are the sun of the IT solar system!

In the coming months and years you will most likely find more and more applications storing their data in a SQL Server database, especially if that application is carrying a Microsoft logo. Microsoft Exchange Server doesn't presently store its data in SQL, but it will. Active Directory will also reportedly move its data store to SQL Server. Microsoft has been exploring for years the possibility and feasibility of moving the Windows file system itself to a SQL-type store. For the T-SQL programmer and Microsoft SQL Server professional, the future is indeed bright.

SQL Server Fundamentals

Where does SQL Server fit in the grand scheme of business applications? At one time, this was a simple question with a simple answer. Today, SQL Server is at the core of many different types of applications and business solutions large and small. The new generation of servers and operating systems blend file storage and document and data management in a seamless, uniform approach — and at the core of all this technology is SQL Server. Under the hood, this is not the same SQL Server as it was in years past. SQL Server 2005 and SQL Server 2008 are complex, multipurpose data storage engines, capable of doing some very sophisticated things. This new-and-improved SQL Server can manage complex binary streams, hierarchies, cubes, files, and folders in addition to text, numbers, and other simple data types.

For the purposes of this book, we're concerned only with using SQL Server to store and manage *relational* data. This is what it was designed for years ago — and what it does even better today. However, SQL Server can also be used to store and manage application objects in the form of XML. The addition of native XML storage to SQL Server has opened up many doors and possibilities.

Who Uses SQL Server?

Not very long ago, enterprise databases were hidden away on large servers that were never visible to the casual business computer user. Any interaction with these systems was performed only by members of the elite order of database administrators and data developers. These highly revered professionals worked in large, noisy, sealed server rooms on special consoles and workstations. Even after many companies migrated their database systems from mainframe and mid-range computer platforms to PC-based servers, the databases were still hands-off and carefully protected from all but a select few.

A generation of smaller-scale database products evolved to fill the void left for the casual application developer and power user. Products such as the following became the norm for department-level applications because they were accessible and inexpensive:

- ❏ dBase
- ❏ FoxPro
- ❏ Paradox

- ❑ Clipper
- ❑ Clarion
- ❑ FileMaker
- ❑ Access

The big databases were in another class and were simply not available outside of formal IT circles. They were complicated and expensive. Database administrators and designers used cumbersome command-line scripts to create and manage databases. It was a full-time job; DBAs wrote the script to manage the databases and application developers wrote the code for the applications that ran against them. Life was good. Everyone was happy. However, there is only one real constant in the IT world and that is change. In the past ten years, there have been significant changes in the world of application development, database design, and management.

At the launch event for SQL Server 7.0, Steve Ballmer, the President of Microsoft Corporation, was on the road to introduce this significant product release. After demonstrating several simple, wizard-based features, he asked for all the career database administrators to stand up. There were probably 1500 people in the audience and 100 or so DBAs came to their feet. He said, "I'd like to do you all a favor and give you some career advice." He paused with a big smile before he continued, "Learn Visual Basic." Needless to say, there were several uneasy DBAs leaving the launch event that day. Steve's advice was evidence of the harsh reality of changing times. Today, SQL Server and other related Microsoft products represent a toolkit in the hands of a different kind of business IT professional — not a full-time DBA, specialized Business Analyst, or single-minded Application Developer, but a Solution Architect who creates a variety of software solutions consisting of all these pieces. From the initial requirement gathering and solution concept to the database design, component architecture, and user-interface construction, the Database Solution Developer often covers all these bases. Just a quick note to help clarify Mr. Ballmer's point: What do SQL Server and Visual Basic have to do with one another? Chapter 15 answers this question more completely by showing you some examples of complete application solutions. In short, solving business problems requires the use of multiple tools, SQL and programming languages working together.

Although we have certainly seen a lot of change recently in the database world, I won't be so naïve to say that traditional database servers are going away. On the contrary, most large companies have centralized most of their data on large-scale servers and the largest corporate databases are now in the ballpark of 10–20 terabytes in size. In just the past few years, these volumes have been doubling about every three years. There are really two separate trends: Corporate, mission-critical data is growing more than ever, stored on large-scale (albeit physically much smaller) servers, managed by full-time database administrators. The other trend is that small-scale, regional data marts (relatively small reporting databases) and data silos (specialized, departmental databases) have emerged. Unlike the ad-hoc, desktop databases of the past decade, these are stored on department-level database servers. They are managed and used primarily by business unit power users, rather than career IT folks.

A new class of SQL Server user has recently emerged. Computer power users now have access to SQL Server using a variety of tools. Bill Gates refers to these individuals as the "knowledge worker" of the twenty-first century. Desktop applications such as Microsoft Excel and Access can easily be used as front-ends for SQL Server. Microsoft Access gives users the ability to create and manage database objects, much like an administrator would using Management Studio. This means that more casual users have the ability to create and utilize these powerful databases that were available only to highly trained professionals a few years ago. Microsoft Excel enables information workers to connect to and analyze data stored on a SQL Server like never before. Of course, this also means that untrained users can use these powerful tools to make a big mess. Yes, this means that more users now have the tools to create poorly designed databases, more efficiently than ever before.

Let's hope your organization has standards and policies in place to manage production database servers and to control access to sensitive data. With a little guidance and the appropriate level of security access, SQL Server can be a very useful tool in the hands of new users who possess some fundamental skills.

SQL Server Editions and Features

SQL Server comes in five different flavors, each having its specific place in the data management infrastructure. At the top is the Enterprise Edition, which supports absolutely everything that SQL Server 2005 has to offer. On the other end of the spectrum is the Express Edition, which offers very limited but still exciting features.

SQL Server Compact Edition

SQL Server Compact is the replacement for SQL Server CE first offered in SQL Server 2000. The Compact Edition enables the installation of a small SQL Server database on a mobile device to support a Windows mobile application. SQL Server Compact also enables the support of a database that is replicated from a database hosted on a Windows Server. This ability creates a world of opportunity for collecting data in a remote scenario and synchronizing that data with a land-based database. For example, consider an overnight delivery service that must maintain a record of a delivery truck's inventory, including packages delivered and picked up. The truck inventory could be uploaded via replication to a mobile device where a mobile application kept track of the deliveries and new packages picked up at delivery locations. Once the truck arrived back to the delivery center, the mobile device could be synchronized with the central database via replication or data upload.

SQL Server Express Edition

SQL Server Express is at the lowest end of functionality and scalability as far as a non-mobile application goes. However, I am very excited about this particular edition. SQL Server Express has a great price for a lot of functionality — it's free! For its very low price (you can't beat free), it still contains a great deal of functionality.

The reason this edition excites me is that it is perfect for many of my customers who are starting or running small businesses. They have a genuine need for a centralized managed database but aren't ready to pay for a more scalable and robust solution. At the risk of offending my friends in the open source community, most of my customers are not very technically savvy, so very flexible and viable solutions such as MySQL running on Linux or Windows is just not appropriate when a database engine with an intuitive and free graphical management tool exists.

One of the most exciting improvements to Microsoft's free version of their database system is that it comes with a graphical management environment. It also supports databases up to 4 gigabytes in size and contains much of the same functionality as the other editions.

SQL Server Express is a big step up from MSDE (Microsoft SQL Server Desktop Engine), its predecessor, and is a very viable solution for stand-alone applications that require a managed data-store or even distributed applications with a minimal number of connections.

SQL Server Express can be installed on any Microsoft desktop or server operating system from Windows 2000 and beyond, so a very small company can still leverage the database technology without making a large investment. (Did I mention that it's free?) Once the company starts to grow, it inevitably will need to make the move to one of the more robust editions, but the upgrade process from SQL Server Express to its bigger siblings is a piece of cake because the data structures are near identical.

SQL Server Workgroup Edition

The Workgroup Edition contains all the functionality of SQL Server Express Edition and then some. This edition is targeted to those small companies that have either outgrown the Express Edition or need a more flexible solution to begin with and yet do not need all the features of the Standard or Enterprise Edition.

The Workgroup Edition is very flexible and contains many of the features of the more expensive editions. What the Workgroup Edition doesn't provide is support for more advanced business intelligence applications because SQL Server Integration Services and Analysis Services are not included in this edition. The Workgroup Edition also has a reduced feature set in regards to reporting services, although the reporting services features supported should satisfy most small organizations.

Like the Express Edition, the Workgroup Edition can be installed on both desktop and server operating systems, with the exception of Windows XP Home, which is not supported.

SQL Server Standard Edition

Most of the capabilities of SQL Server are supported in the Standard Edition, making it the ideal data platform for many organizations. What the Standard Edition does not provide are many of the features designed for the support of large enterprise databases. These features include many of the high availability and scalability enhancements, such as partitioned tables and parallel online index operations. It also lacks some of the more advanced business intelligence features of Integration Services, Reporting Services, and Analysis Services.

SQL Server Enterprise Edition

The Enterprise Edition is the full-meal deal. Nothing is held back. Parallel operations, physical table partitioning, complete business intelligence, and data-mining support — you name it, the Enterprise Edition has it.

If you require an easy to implement and maintain platform that can support millions of transactions a second, terabytes of RAM, and 64 64-bit processors, then this release is for you. It is also an appropriate solution if you just require advanced business analytics and not necessarily the millions of transactions a second that this edition offers. Another important aspect of the Enterprise Edition is performance. Although the feature set between the Enterprise Edition and the Standard Edition is not huge, the differences in performance between the two editions can be. The Enterprise Edition fully optimizes read-ahead execution and table scans, resulting in marked improvement in read and scan performance.

Relational Database Engine

Big differences exist between a true relational database management system (RDBMS) and a file-based database product. Although a true RDBMS product, such as SQL Server, does store its data in files managed by the file system, the data in these files cannot be accessed directly. The concepts of relational integrity have been applied to file-based databases for several years. Programmers wrote these rules into their program code. The difference is that the RDBMS system contains this code to enforce business rules and doesn't allow a user or developer to work around them once a database has been designed with certain rules applied.

The language used to access nearly all relational database products is SQL. The dialect of SQL used in Microsoft SQL Server is called Transact-SQL. Using SQL is the front door to the data in a database and the administrative objects of the database server. Specialized programmatic interfaces also exist that developers can use to access a database with the appropriate security clearance. Unlike file-based databases, RDBMS systems are designed so there is no "back door" to a database.

Semantics

The words used to describe data concepts are often different, depending a great deal upon the context of the discussion. Data lives in tables. Usually, a table represents some kind of business entity, such as a *Product* or *Customer*, for example. Each item in a table is called a **row** or **record**. For our purposes, these mean the same thing. I may use these words interchangeably throughout the book. Envision several rows in an Excel worksheet representing different products. Each product has a manufacturer, supplier, packaging quantity, and price. In Excel, these values would be contained in different cells. In a table, separate values are referred to as a **column** or **field**. As far as we're concerned, these words have the same meaning as well. How do you decide how data should be organized into tables and columns? That is the fine art of database design and is often no easy task. To arrive at an optimal database design, you must first have a thorough understanding of the business process and the how data will be used.

So, what is data, really? We often hear the words "information" and "data" used to mean the same thing. In reality, they are very different concepts. As humans, we generally concern ourselves with meaningful information we can use day-to-day. Information has a context — it makes sense to us. If my wife asks me to stop by the store on the way home from work and pick up eggs and milk, I should have enough information to accomplish this simple task. I have a few informational items to contend with in this scenario: the store, eggs, and milk. If we were to ask some people in the database business about these simple things, we might get some interesting (or not so interesting) answers. For example, my friend Greg, a city geographic information systems (GIS) expert employed by the city government, might point out that in his database, the *store* is a building with an address, property plot number, city zoning record, water, sewer, and electrical service locations. It has latitude and longitude coordinates, a business license, and a tax record. If we were to talk to someone in the grocery business, they might tell us that *eggs* and *milk* exist in a *products* table in their point of sale and inventory management database systems. Each is assigned a product record ID and UPC codes. The product supplier, vendors, shipping companies, and the dairies likely have their own systems and deal with these items in different ways. However, as a consumer, I'm not concerned with such things. I just need to stop by the store and pick up the eggs and milk.

Here's the bottom line: data is just numbers and letters in a database or computer application somewhere. At some point, all that cryptic data was probably useful information until it was entered into the database. For the database designer or programmer, these values may be meaningful. For the rest of us, it isn't useful at all until it gets translated back into something we understand — information. Part of the job description of SQL programmers is to retrieve data from one or more databases and turn that data into information. By combining data from multiple entities, or simplistically, tables, the SQL programmer puts context to the data, turning it into information.

Changing Terminology

One of the greatest challenges in our relatively new world of technology is how we use common language to communicate both technical and non-technical concepts. Even when dealing with the same system, terminology often changes as you progress through the different stages of the solution design and construction. These stages are generally as follows:

❏ Conceptual or architectural design

❏ Logical design

❏ Physical design

Conceptual Design

As you approach the subject of automating business processes through the use of databases and software, one of the first and most important tasks is to gather business requirements from users and other business stakeholders. Beginning with non-technical, business, and user-centric language, you must find terms to describe each unit of pertinent information to be stored and processed. A complete unit of information is known as an **entity**. Business entities generally represent a whole unit that can stand on its own. For example, a *customer* and a *product* are examples of entities.

Another conceptual unit of information is an **attribute**. This unit of information describes a characteristic of an entity. An attribute may be something as simple as the color or price of a product. It could also be something more complex, such as the dimensions of a package. The important thing during conceptual design is to deal with the simple and conceptual aspects and not all of the implementation details. This way you leave your options open to consider creative ways to model and manage the data according to your business requirements.

In most processes, different terms may be used to describe the same or similar concepts. For example, in an order processing environment, the terms *customer, shopper,* and *purchaser* could mean the same thing. Under closer evaluation, perhaps a *shopper* is a person who looks for products and a *customer* is a person who actually purchases a product. In this case, a *shopper* may become a *customer* at some point in the process. In some cases, a *customer* may not actually be a person. A *customer* could also be an *organization*. It's important to understand the distinction between each entity and find agreeable terms to be used by anyone dealing with the process, especially non-technical users and business stakeholders. Conceptual design is very free-form and often takes a few iterations to reveal all of the hidden requirements.

Along with the entity and attribute concepts, another important notion is that of an *instance*. You may have 100,000 customers on record, but as far as your database system is concerned, these customers don't really exist until you need to deal with their information. Sure, these people do exist out in customer land, but your unfeeling database system couldn't care less about customers who are not currently engaged in buying products, spending money, or updating their billing information. Your system was designed to process orders and purchase products — that's it. If a customer isn't involved in ordering, purchasing, or paying, the system pays no attention. When a customer places an order, you start caring about this information and your order processing system needs to do something with the customer information. At this point, your system reaches into the repository of would-be customers and activates an instance of a specific customer. The customer becomes alive just long enough for the system to do something useful with it and then put it back into cold storage, moving on to the next task. Therefore, in our database system a single customer record is an instance of the Customer entity. All instances of an entity have prescribed attributes, but they don't necessarily share all attributes. For example, it could be possible that not all customers have phone numbers, or middle names. During the conceptual design phase it's best to identify what attributes must be shared by all instances of an entity and what ones are optional.

Logical Design

This stage of design is the transition between the abstract, non-specific world of conceptual design and the very specific, technical world of physical design. After gaining a thorough understanding of business requirements in the language of users, this is an opportunity to model the data and the information flow through the system processes. With respect to data, you should be able to use the terms *entity*, *attribute*, and *instance* to describe every unit of data. Contrasted with conceptual design, logical design is more formalized and makes use of diagramming models to confirm assumptions made in conceptual design.

Prototyping is also part of the logical design effort. A quick mock-up database can be used to demonstrate design ideas and test business cases. It's important, though, that prototypes aren't allowed to evolve into the production design. Fredrick P. Brooks said in his book, *The Mythical Man Month*, "When designing a new kind of system, a team should factor in the fact that they will have to throw away the first system that is built since this first system will teach them how to build the system. The system will then be completely redesigned using the newly acquired insights during building of the first system." When you finally happen upon a working model, throw it out and start fresh. This gives you the opportunity to design a functional solution without the baggage of evolutionary design. In logical design, you decide what you're going to build and for what purpose.

In particular, logical database design involves the definition of all the data entities and their attributes. For example, you know that a customer entity should have a name, a shipping location, and a line of credit. Although you realize that the customer's name may consist of a first name, middle initial, and last name, this is unimportant in this stage of design. Likewise, the customer's location may consist of a street address, city, state, and zip code; you also leave these details for the physical design stage. The point during this stage is to understand the need and recognize how this entity will behave with other data entities and their attributes.

Physical Design

One of the greatest reasons to have a formal design process is to find all of the system requirements before attempting to build the solution. It has been said, "Requirements are like water. They're easier to build on when they're frozen." So any attempt to define requirements as you go along instead of before you start will inevitably lead to disastrous results. Ask any seasoned software professional and I guarantee their response will be preceded with either a tear or a smile.

Physical design is like drawing the blueprints for a building. It's not a sketch or a rough model. It is the specification for the real project in explicit detail. As your design efforts turn to the physical database implementation, entities may turn into tables and attributes into columns. However, there is not always a one-to-one correspondence between conceptual entities and physical tables. That is the simplification I mentioned earlier. The value of appropriate design is to find similarities and reduce redundant effort. You will likely discover the need for more detail than originally envisioned. For instance, a company may have customers that are individuals, but other customers might be a collection of individuals or a corporation.

I worked on a project for a training center where much more detail was needed than first believed. After careful requirements gathering, we found that students attending a class may have paid for the training themselves or had their entire class paid for by their employer. In addition students might have had to pay part of the cost themselves with their employer covering the rest. Then there were the cases that part of the cost was paid by the employer, part by the student, and another part by state agencies. Who was the customer in this last case? As it turned out, according to the company's business rules, the individual student, the employer, and the state agency were all customers. As a result, in the physical design, entities of customer, transaction, and invoice were designed to encompass situations where more than one customer paid for an individual instance of a course.

Relationships

Although entity relationships were discussed briefly in Chapter 1, I want to devote a little more time expounding on the concepts to add clarity to the current topic of design. The purpose of nearly all database systems is to model elements in our physical world. To do this effectively, you need to consider the associations that exist between the various entities you want to keep track of. This concept of an item or multiple items being related to a different item or multiple items is known as *cardinality* or *multiplicity.* To illustrate this concept, just look around you. Nearly everything fits into some kind of collection or set of like objects. The leaves on a tree, the passengers in a car, and the change in your pocket are all examples of this simple principle. These are sets of similar objects in a collection and associated with some kind of container or attached to some type of parent entity. In the previous section, I described the somewhat complex scenario of many customers and a single transaction. In that case, a relationship was defined between an instance of a class, an instance of a student, an instance of multiple invoices, and instances of multiple customers. Relationships can be described and discovered using common language. As you describe associations, listen for words such as *is, have,* and *has.* For example, a customer *has* orders. Now turn it around: an order *has* a customer. By looking at the equation from both sides, you've discovered a *one-to-many relationship* between customers and orders.

Relationships generally can be grouped into three different types of cardinality:

❑ One-to-one

❑ One-to-many

❑ Many-to-many

The one-to-one and one-to-many relationships are fairly easy to define using a combination of foreign keys and unique constraints, but many-to-many relationships cannot actually be defined using two tables. To reduce redundancy, minimize data storage requirements, and facilitate these relationships, you apply standard rules of normalization (the rules of normal form), which are described briefly in this section.

Primary Keys

According to the rule of first normal form (1NF), which says that each column must contain a single type of information or a single value with no repeating groups of data, it is imperative that each row (or record) be stamped with a unique key value. This key could be either a meaningful value that is useful for other reasons, or a surrogate key, a value generated only for the sake of uniqueness. The uniqueness of a record depends entirely on the primary key. Be very cautious and think twice (or three times) before choosing to use non-surrogate key values. I've designed more than a few database systems where it seemed to make sense to use an intelligent value for the primary key (for example, social security number, address, phone number, product code, and so on) and later wished I had just generated a unique value for the key. Most experienced database folks have horror stories to share about such experiences.

So, what's a surrogate key? Two common forms of surrogate key values exist, although there certainly could be more. The first and probably most common form is the IDENTITY property. A SQL Server IDENTITY property is simply an integer value that is automatically incremented by the database system. In the world of Microsoft Access, the identity function is known as an Auto-Number field. SQL Server's IDENTITY property is more flexible, however, since the integer can be seeded at any supported value and incremented by an integer value. This can serve as a unique value as long as all data is entered into a single instance of the database and uniqueness on the identity value is enforced. In distributed systems consisting of multiple, disconnected databases, it can be a bit challenging and next to impossible to keep these values unique. In these cases another type of automatically generated key can be used. This special data type is called a *unique identifier* or globally unique identifier (GUID). This SQL data type is equipped to store a large binary value that is automatically generated by the system. A complex algorithm is used to produce a value that is partially random and partially predictable. The result is what I call a *big ugly number*. It is *statistically guaranteed* to be unique — any time and anywhere. The emphasis on "statistically guaranteed" is intentional. The reason is that chances of this value being duplicated are astronomically improbable, but *not* impossible.

To see surrogate keys in action, you need to build a table that will auto-populate field values. We will cover building objects with T-SQL in Chapter 13, but to clarify the principle of surrogate keys it is useful to take a sneak peek.

The following code creates a table that uses a uniqueidentifier data type with the NEWID() function along with an integer with an IDENTITY() function to auto-populate field values when new rows are added to the table:

```
CREATE TABLE dbo.SurrogateTable
(IdentityColumn int IDENTITY (1,1) NOT NULL
,GUIDColumn uniqueidentifier NOT NULL DEFAULT NEWID()
,DataColumn nvarchar(50) NOT NULL )
GO
```

The IDENTITY() function can accept two values to specify which number to start with and which number to increment by. If the values are not specified, the function defaults to starting at one and incrementing by one, which is also what we specified specifically. It's important to note that neither the

IdentityColumn nor the GUIDcolumn in the preceding example will enforce uniqueness by default, so it is very important to add some type of unique value enforcement to the table to avoid a duplicate from being manually added. This enforcement takes the form of primary key constraints, unique constraints, and unique indexes. Constraints are covered in more detail in Chapter 13.

Now that we have a table that auto-populates fields, let's give it a try. For both SQL Server 2005 and SQL Server 2008 the following code will add two rows of data to the new table:

```
INSERT dbo.SurrogateTable
(DataColumn)
VALUES
('Fred')
INSERT dbo.SurrogateTable
(DataColumn)
VALUES
('Barney')
```

In SQL Server 2008, the code can be simplified to the following:

```
INSERT dbo.SurrogateTable
(DataColumn)
VALUES
('Fred'),('Barney')
```

Now that we have added the rows, let's check out the results by querying our table:

```
SELECT * FROM dbo.SurrogateTable
```

Here are the results:

```
IdentityColumn  GUIDColumn                            DataColumn
--------------  ------------------------------------  ----------------------
1               594FB9AB-C92C-4B4A-A438-1AEF5EC65F67  Fred
2               3D020CA5-6F64-4EF7-90A9-7DEBFFC11E0B  Barney
```

Remember, because the GUID value was automatically generated, the odds that your results are the same as those listed above are astronomical!

Foreign Keys

One purpose for keys is to enforce the relationship between the records in one table to those in another table. A column in the table containing related records is designated as a *foreign key.* This usually means that it contains the same values found in the primary key column(s) of the primary table. However, with SQL Server it could also mean that it contains the same values as those defined by an object known as a *unique constraint.* The only difference between a primary key and a unique constraint is that all primary key values must be defined, whereas a SQL Server unique constraint allows for a single undefined, or null, value. Unlike a primary key or unique constraint, a foreign key doesn't have to be unique. Using the Customer/Order example, one customer can have multiple orders but one order has only one customer. This describes a one-to-many relationship. The primary key column of the Customer table is related to the foreign key column of the Order table through a relationship known as a *foreign key constraint.* Later, in Chapter 13, you see how this relationship is defined in T-SQL.

Normalization Rules

Because this is not a book about database design, I will not engage in a lengthy discussion on the background behind these rules. Volumes have been written on these subjects. On the surface, a short discussion on database design is an important prerequisite to using the T-SQL language. The problem with this is that it's nearly impossible to engage in a short discussion on a topic that is so conceptual and subject to individual style and technique. Like so many "simple" concepts in this industry, this one can be debated almost endlessly. Having written and rewritten this section a few times now, I have decided not to walk through an example and align this with the true rules of normal form, as so many books on this subject do. Rather, I'll briefly present the definitions of each rule and then walk you through an example of distilling an unnormalized database into a practical, normalized form without the weighty discussion of the rules.

Unless you have a taste for mathematical theory, you may not even be interested in the gory details of normalized database design. Throughout this book, I discuss query techniques for normalized and de-normalized data. It would be convenient to say that when a person designs any database, he or she should do so according to certain rules and patterns. In fact, a number of people do prescribe one single approach regardless of the system they intend to design. Everyone wants to be normal, right? Well, maybe not. Perhaps it will suffice to say that most folks want their data to be normal. But, what does this mean in terms of database design? Are different values stored in one table or should they be stored in multiple tables with some kind of association between them? If the latter approach is taken, how are relationships between these tables devised? This is the subject of a number of books on relational database design. If you are new to this subject and find yourself in the position of a database designer, I recommend that you pick up a book or research this topic to meet your needs. This subject is discussed in greater detail in Rob Vieira's books on SQL Server programming, also published by Wrox. I'll discuss some of the fundamentals here, but this is a complex topic that goes beyond the scope of the T-SQL language.

> *The AdventureWorks and AdventureWorks2008 databases supplied with SQL Server 2005 and SQL Server 2008 are very normalized. In order to adequately describe the normalization process, we will be using a hypothetical case in which we are building tables to contain information about a company's employees. We will normalize the tables as the discussion progresses. The queries given as examples will not work on any specific database, unless of course you were to build a database and populate it with tables like those in the example.*

In the early 1970s, a small group of mathematicians at IBM proposed a set of standards for designing relational data systems. In 1970, Dr. Edgar (E. F.) Codd wrote a paper entitled "A Relational Model of Data for Large Shared Data Banks" for the Association of Computing Machinery. He later published a set of 12 principles for relational database design in 1974. These principles described the low-level mechanics of relational database systems as well as the higher-level rules of entity-relation design for a specific database. Dr. Codd teamed with others who also wrote papers on these subjects, including Chris (CJ) Date and Raymond F. Boyce. Boyce and Codd are now credited as the authors of relational database design. Codd's original 12 principles of design involved using set calculus and algebraic expressions to access and describe data. One of the goals of this effort was to reduce data redundancy and minimize storage space requirements. Something to consider is that, at the time, data was stored on magnetic tape, paper punch cards, and, eventually disks ranging from 5 to 20 megabytes in capacity. As the low-level requirements were satisfied by file system and database products, these 12 rules were distilled into the five rules of normal form taught in college classes today.

In short, the rules of normal form, or principles of relational database design, are aimed at the following objectives:

❑   Present data to the relational engine that is set accessible

❑   Label and identify unique records and columns within a table

❑   Promote the smallest necessary result set for data retrieval

❑   Minimize storage space requirements by reducing redundant values in the same table and in multiple tables

❑   Describe standards for relating records in one table to those in another table

❑   Create stability and efficiency in the use of the data system while creating flexibility in its structure

To apply these principles, tables are created with the fewest number of columns (or fields) to define a single entity. For example, if your objective is to keep track of customers who have ordered products, you will store only the customer information in a single table. The order and product information would be stored their own respective tables.

The idea behind even this lowest form of normalizations is to allow straightforward management of the business rules and the queries that implement these rules against data structures that are flexible to accommodate these changes.

The real purpose of first normal form is to standardize the shape of the entity (relation) — to form a two-dimensional grid that is easily accessed and managed using set-based functions in the data engine.

It's really quite difficult to take a table and apply just one rule. One of the tenets of all the rules of normal form is that each rule in succession must conform to its predecessor. In other words, a design that conforms to second normal form must also conform to first normal form. Also, to effectively apply one, you may also be applying a subsequent rule. Although each of these rules describes a distinct principle, they are interrelated. This means that generally speaking, normalization, up to a certain level, is kind of a package deal.

In the next sections I'll briefly describe the different forms of normalization and then take you through the exercise of normalizing employee data to clarify the rules.

First Normal Form

First normal form (1NF) states that:

❑   A table is two-dimensional. It has rows and columns and each row must have the same number of columns.

❑   Each column in a table contains a single attribute and all attributes in the column must be the same type.

❑   Each row must be uniquely identifiable.

To convert flat data to first normal form, additional tables are created by the database designer. Duplicate columns are eliminated and the corresponding values are placed into unique rows of a second table. This rule is applied to reduce redundancy along the horizontal axis (columns).

Second Normal Form

The second normal form (2NF) rule states that non-key fields cannot depend on only a portion of the primary key. These fields are placed into a separate table from those that depend on the key value alone. For instance, if you had a table that had a primary key made up of two columns, all other columns in the row must depend on both of the two columns, not just one.

To meet second normal form, you must satisfy first normal form and then identify any columns that have partial dependencies to the table's primary key. Columns that have a partial dependency are placed in separate tables.

By avoiding multi-column primary keys or by removing partially dependent columns, you arrive at second normal form. Then move to third normal form.

Third Normal Form

The first rule states that rows are assigned a key value for identification. Third normal form (3NF) takes this principle one step further by stating that the uniqueness of any row depends entirely upon the primary key. My friend Rick, who teaches and writes books on this topic, uses a phrase to help remember this rule: "The uniqueness of a row depends on the key, the whole key, and nothing but the key; so help me Dr. Codd."

In some cases it makes sense for the primary key to be a combination of columns. For example, a linking table that is created to manage a many-to many-relationship, as discussed in Chapter 1, can be configured so that the combination of the primary keys from the linked tables is the primary key for the linking table. Redundant values along multiple rows should be eliminated by placing these values into a separate table as well. Compared with first normal form, this rule attempts to reduce duplication along the vertical axis (rows).

Boyce-Codd Normal Form, Fourth and Fifth Normal Form

Boyce and Codd built their standard — Boyce-Codd normal form (BCNF) — on earlier ideals that recognized only those discussed thus far. You must satisfy first and second and third normal forms before moving on to satisfy subsequent forms. In fact, it is the process of the first, second, and third normal forms that drives the need for BCNF. Through the decomposition of attribute functional dependencies, many-to-many relationships develop between some entities. This is sometimes inaccurately left in a state where each entity involved has duplicate candidate keys in one or more of the entities.

Attributes upon which non-key attributes depend are candidate keys. BCNF deals with the dependencies within candidate keys. The short version of what could be a lengthy and complex discussion of mathematical theory is that fourth and fifth normal forms are used to resolve many-to-many relationships. On the surface this seems to be a simple matter — and for our purposes, we'll keep it that way. Customers can buy many different products, and products can be purchased by multiple customers. Concerning ourselves with only customers and products, these two entities have a many-to-many relationship. The fact is that you cannot perform many-to-many joins with just two tables. This requires another table, sometimes called a *bridge* or *intermediary table,* to make the association. The bridge table typically doesn't need its own specific key value, because the combination of primary key values from the two outer tables will always be unique. (Keep in mind that this is not a requirement of this type of association but is typically the case.) Therefore, the bridge table conforms to third normal form by defining its primary key as the composite of the two foreign keys, each corresponding to the primary keys of the two outer, related tables. Fifth normal form is a unique variation of this rule, which factors in additional business logic, disallowing certain key combinations. For our purposes, this should suffice.

Other Normal Forms

A number of disciplines and conceptual approaches to data modeling and database design exist. Among others, these include Unified Modeling Language (UML) and Object Role Modeling (ORM). These include additional forms that help to manage special anomalies that might arise to describe constraints within and between groups or populations of information. The forms that qualify these descriptions usually move into user-defined procedures added to the database and not the declarative structures that have been addressed so far.

Transforming Information into Data

In the real world, the concepts and information you deal with exist in relationships and hierarchies. Just look around you and observe the way things are grouped and associated. As I write this, I'm sitting on a ferry boat. The ferry contains several cars, and cars have passengers. If I needed to store this information in a relational database, I would likely define separate tables to represent each of the entities I just mentioned. These are simple concepts, but when applied at all possible levels, some of the associations may take a little more thought and cautious analysis. At times the business rules of data are not quite so straightforward. Often, the best way to discover these rules (and the limits of these rules) is to ask a series of "what if" questions. Given the ferry/car/passenger scenario, what if a passenger came onto the ferry in one car and left in another? What if she walked on and then drove off? Is this important? Do we care? These questions are not arbitrarily answered by a database designer but through the consensus of designers and system stakeholders.

At some point you will need to decide upon the boundaries of your business rules. This is where you decide that a particular exception or condition is beyond the scope of your database system. Don't treat this matter lightly. It is imperative to define specific criteria while also moving quickly past trivial decision points so that you can move forward and stay on schedule. This is the great balancing act of project management.

When you attempt to take this information and store it in a flat, two-dimensional table as rows and columns, you can't help but create redundant or repeating values. Take a look at a simple example using data from a fictitious small company with only nine employees. The table in Figure 2-1 shows employee records. Each employee has a name and may have two addresses and two phone numbers. Most employees also have a supervisor. This is the way this data might appear in a simple spreadsheet.

EmployeeName	Title	Address1	CityLine1	Address2	CityLine2	HomePhone	WorkPhone	SupervisorName
Nancy Davolio	Sales Representative	507 - 20th Ave. E.	Seattle, WA 98122	<NULL>	<NULL>	(206) 555-9857	(425) 555-1101	Andrew Fuller
Andrew Fuller	Vice President, Sales	908 W. Capital Way	Tacoma, WA 98401	9317 Clear Creek Ln	Vashon Is, WA 98070	(206) 555-9482	(425) 555-1100	<NULL>
Janet Leverling	Sales Representative	722 Moss Bay Blvd.	Kirkland, WA 98033	<NULL>	<NULL>	(206) 555-3412	(425) 555-1119	Andrew Fuller
Margaret Peacock	Sales Representative	4110 Old Redmond Rd.	Redmond, WA 98052	<NULL>	<NULL>	(206) 555-8122	(425) 555-1108	Andrew Fuller
Steven Buchanan	Sales Manager	14 Garrett Hill	London, SW1 8JR	9035 Pike Place	Olalla, WA 98367	(71) 555-4848	(425) 555-1123	Andrew Fuller
Michael Suyama	Sales Representative	Coventry House	London, EC2 7JR	<NULL>	<NULL>	(71) 555-7773	(425) 555-1103	Steven Buchanan
Robert King	Sales Representative	Edgeham Hollow	London, RG1 9SP	<NULL>	<NULL>	(71) 555-5598	(425) 555-1132	Steven Buchanan
Laura Callahan	Inside Sales Coordinator	9317 Clear Creek Ln	Vashon Is, WA 98070	<NULL>	<NULL>	(206) 555-1189	(425) 555-1114	Andrew Fuller
Anne Dodsworth	Sales Representative	7 Houndstooth Rd.	London, WG2 7LT	<NULL>	<NULL>	(71) 555-4444	(425) 555-1124	Steven Buchanan

Figure 2-1

The <NULL> text is SQL Server's way of telling you that there is nothing in that field. Each employee has a name, title, one or two residence locations, a home and work phone number, and a supervisor. This data is easy to read in this form but it may be difficult to use in a proper database system.

Applying Normalization Rules

Using the Employees table shown in Figure 2-1, look for violations of first normal form. Does more than one column contain information about the same type of attributes? Beginning with the numbered Address and CityLine fields, each "location" consists of a column for the address and another column for the city, state, and zip code. Because there are two pairs of these columns, this may be a problem. Each phone number is a single column, designated as either the home or work phone. How would I make a single list of all phone numbers? What happens if I need to record a mobile phone for an employee? I could add a third column to the table. How about a fourth? How about the Title column? The SupervisorName column may be viewed as a special case, but the fact is that the EmployeeName and SupervisorName columns store the same type of values. They both represent employees.

I can move all these columns into separate tables, but how do I keep them associated with the employee? This is accomplished through the use of keys. A key is just a simple value used to associate a record in one table to a record in another table (among other things). To satisfy first normal form, I'll move these columns to different tables and create key values to wire up the associations. In the following example, I have removed the address and city information and have placed it into a separate table.

I have devised a method to identify each employee with a six-character character key, using part of their last and first names. I chose this method because this was once a very popular method for assigning key values. This allows me to maintain the associations between employees and their addresses. In this first iteration (see Figure 2-2), I use this method to make a point. This is a relatively small database for a small company and I don't have any employees with similar first and last names, so this method ought to work just fine, right? Hold that thought for now.

EmployeeKey	EmployeeName	Title	SupervisorName
DAV_NA	Nancy Davolio	Sales Representative	Andrew Fuller
FUL_AN	Andrew Fuller	Vice President, Sales	<NULL>
LAV_JA	Janet Leverling	Sales Representative	Andrew Fuller
PEA_MA	Margaret Peacock	Sales Representative	Andrew Fuller
BUC_ST	Steven Buchanan	Sales Manager	Andrew Fuller
SUY_MI	Michael Suyama	Sales Representative	Steven Buchanan
KIN_RO	Robert King	Sales Representative	Steven Buchanan
CAL_LA	Laura Callahan	Inside Sales Coordinator	Andrew Fuller
DOD_AN	Anne Dodsworth	Sales Representative	Steven Buchanan

Figure 2-2

I do the same thing with the new Addresses table (see Figure 2-3). Each address record is assigned an EmployeeKey value to link it back to the Employees table.

EmployeeKey	AddressLine	CityLine
DAV_NA	507 - 20th Ave. E.	Seattle, WA 98122
FUL_AN	908 W. Capital Way	Tacoma, WA 98401
LEV_JA	722 Moss Bay Blvd.	Kirkland, WA 98033
PEA_MA	4110 Old Redmond Rd.	Redmond, WA 98052
BUC_ST	14 Garrett Hill	London, SW1 8JR
SUY_MI	Coventry House	London, EC2 7JR
KIN_RO	Edgeham Hollow	London, RG1 9SP
DOD_AN	7 Houndstooth Rd.	London, WG2 7LT
CAL_LA	9317 Clear Creek Ln	Vashon Is, WA 98353
FUL_AN	9317 Clear Creek Ln	Vashon Is, WA 98353
BUC_ST	9035 Pike Place	Olalla, WA 98367

Figure 2-3

I have lost a significant piece of information in doing this. I've flattened the address information so that I no longer have one address designated as either primary or secondary for an employee. I'll get to this later. For now, I'm only concerned with adhering to first normal form. Besides, does the information in the old Address1 and CityLine1 columns imply that this is the employee's primary residence? Did I have a complete understanding of the business rules when I began working with this data? Unfortunately, in most ad-hoc projects, it is more often a case of making things up as we go along.

For the phone numbers I'll do the same thing as before — move the phone number values into their own table and then add the corresponding key value to associate them with the employee record. I'm also going to add a column to designate the type of phone number this represents (see Figure 2-4). I could use this as an argument to do the same thing with the addresses, but I'll hold off for now.

EmployeeKey	PhoneNumber	PhoneType
DAV_NA	(206) 555-9857	Home
FUL_AN	(206) 555-9482	Home
LAV_JA	(206) 555-3412	Home
PEA_MA	(206) 555-8122	Home
BUC_ST	(71) 555-4848	Home
SUY_MI	(71) 555-7773	Home
KIN_RO	(71) 555-5598	Home
CAL_LA	(206) 555-1189	Home
DOD_AN	(71) 555-4444	Home
DAV_NA	(425) 555-1101	Work
FUL_AN	(425) 555-1100	Work
LAV_JA	(425) 555-1119	Work
PEA_MA	(425) 555-1108	Work
BUC_ST	(425) 555-1123	Work
SUY_MI	(425) 555-1103	Work
KIN_RO	(425) 555-1132	Work
CAL_LA	(425) 555-1114	Work
DOD_AN	(425) 555-1124	Work

Figure 2-4

Now that I have three tables with common column values, do I have a relational database? Although it may be true that this is related data, it's not a fully relational database. The key values only give me the ability to locate the related records in other tables, but this does nothing to ensure that my data stays intact. Take a look at what I have done so far (see Figure 2-5). The presence of the same key value in all three of these tables is an implied relationship. There is currently no mechanism in place for the database to prevent users from making silly mistakes (such as deleting an employee record without also removing the corresponding address and phone information). This would create a condition, common in early database systems, called *orphaned records.*

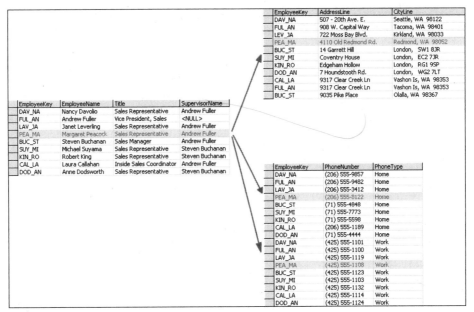

Figure 2-5

Before continuing, I must correct a horrible indiscretion. I told you that this business of using parts of different field values (such as the first and last name) to form a meaningful unique key was once a common practice. This is because database system designers in the past often had to create a system where users had to provide a special number to look up a record. To make this easier, they would come up with some kind of intelligent, unique value. It might include characters from a customer or patient's name, or perhaps a series of numbers with digits in specific positions representing an account type or region. For example, when was the last time you called the bank or the telephone company and were asked for your account number? This happens to me all the time. It amazes me that the companies in possession of the most sophisticated, state-of-the-art technology on the planet require me to memorize my account number. How about looking up my account using my name, address, phone number, mother's maiden name, or any of the other information they required when I set up my account?

Using this simple name-based key may have seemed like the right thing to do at the time, but the fact is that it will likely get me into a whole lot of trouble down the road. I worked for a company that used this approach in a small, commercial application. The program even appended numbers to the end of the keys so there could be nearly a hundred unique key values for a given last name/first name combination. What they didn't anticipate was that their product would eventually become the most popular medical billing software in the country and would be used in business environments they couldn't possibly have imagined. Eventually this got them into trouble, and they had to completely re-architect the application to get around this limitation. One customer, a medical office in the Chicago area, had so many patients with the same or similar names, that they actual ran out of key values.

Thinking Ahead

I'll resolve the EmployeeKey issue by changing it to an auto-sequencing integer called an *identity* (see Figure 2-6). This is known as a ***surrogate key***, which simply means that key values are absolutely meaningless as far as the user is concerned. The database assigns numbers that will always be unique within this column. The purpose of the key is to uniquely identify each row, not to give employees or users something to memorize.

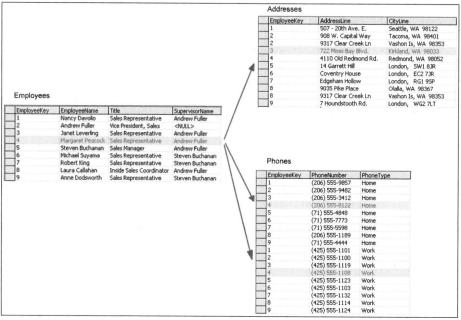

Addresses

EmployeeKey	AddressLine	CityLine
1	507 - 20th Ave. E.	Seattle, WA 98122
2	908 W. Capital Way	Tacoma, WA 98401
2	9317 Clear Creek Ln	Vashon Is, WA 98353
3	722 Moss Bay Blvd.	Kirkland, WA 98033
4	4110 Old Redmond Rd.	Redmond, WA 98052
5	14 Garrett Hill	London, SW1 8JR
6	Coventry House	London, EC2 7JR
7	Edgeham Hollow	London, RG1 9SP
8	9035 Pike Place	Olalla, WA 98367
8	9317 Clear Creek Ln	Vashon Is, WA 98353
9	7 Houndstooth Rd.	London, WG2 7LT

Employees

EmployeeKey	EmployeeName	Title	SupervisorName
1	Nancy Davolio	Sales Representative	Andrew Fuller
2	Andrew Fuller	Vice President, Sales	<NULL>
3	Janet Leverling	Sales Representative	Andrew Fuller
4	Margaret Peacock	Sales Representative	Andrew Fuller
5	Steven Buchanan	Sales Manager	Andrew Fuller
6	Michael Suyama	Sales Representative	Steven Buchanan
7	Robert King	Sales Representative	Steven Buchanan
8	Laura Callahan	Inside Sales Coordinator	Andrew Fuller
9	Anne Dodsworth	Sales Representative	Steven Buchanan

Phones

EmployeeKey	PhoneNumber	PhoneType
1	(206) 555-9857	Home
2	(206) 555-9482	Home
3	(206) 555-3412	Home
4	(206) 555-8122	Home
5	(71) 555-4848	Home
6	(71) 555-7773	Home
7	(71) 555-5598	Home
8	(206) 555-1189	Home
9	(71) 555-4444	Home
1	(425) 555-1101	Work
2	(425) 555-1100	Work
3	(425) 555-1119	Work
4	(425) 555-1108	Work
5	(425) 555-1123	Work
6	(425) 555-1103	Work
7	(425) 555-1132	Work
8	(425) 555-1114	Work
9	(425) 555-1124	Work

Figure 2-6

The next step is to designate the EmployeeKey in the Employees table as a primary key and the related keys as foreign keys. The foreign key constraints cause the database engine to validate any action that could cause these relationships to be violated. For example, the database would not allow an employee record to be deleted if there were existing, related address or phone records. Related tables are often documented using an entity-relationship diagram (ERD). The diagram in Figure 2-7 shows the columns and relationships between these tables.

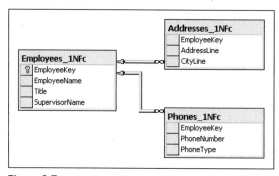

Figure 2-7

There is still work to do. The SupervisorName is also a violation of first normal form because it duplicates some employee names. This is a special case, however, because these names already exist in the Employees table. This can be resolved using a self-join, or relationship, on the same table (see Figure 2-8).

EmployeeKey	EmployeeName	Title	SupervisorEmployeeID
1	Nancy Davolio	Sales Representative	2
2	Andrew Fuller	Vice President, Sales	<NULL>
3	Janet Leverling	Sales Representative	2
4	Margaret Peacock	Sales Representative	2
5	Steven Buchanan	Sales Manager	2
6	Michael Suyama	Sales Representative	5
7	Robert King	Sales Representative	5
8	Laura Callahan	Inside Sales Coordinator	2
9	Anne Dodsworth	Sales Representative	5

Figure 2-8

The supervisor designation within the Employees table is now just an integer value referring to another employee record.

The Title column is also in violation of first normal form and could be moved into its own table, as well. A title isn't uniquely owned by an employee, but each employee only has one title. To discern this relationship, you must look at it from both directions:

❑ One employee has one title.

❑ One title can have multiple employees.

This is a one-to-many relationship from the title to the employee. Resolving this is a simple matter of placing one instance of each title value in a separate table, identified by a unique primary key. A similar column is added to the Employees table as a non-unique foreign key (see Figure 2-9).

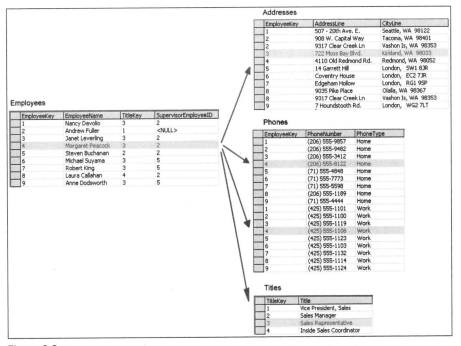

Figure 2-9

You should see a pattern developing. This is an iterative process that will typically send you in one of two directions in each cycle. You will either continue to move these values into related tables with related keys, or you will find discrepancies between your business rules and the data, and then head back to the drawing board to correct the data and table structure.

Multiple Associations

I know that a title can be associated with more than one employee, but what happens if an address is shared by more than one individual? This is a problem in the current database model. I can't use one primary key value and have multiple associations going in both directions. The only way I can do this is to create a primary key that includes two separate values: one for the employee key and one for the address key. However, I can't do this using either of these two tables. If I add the EmployeeKey to the Addresses table, I'm back to the original problem, where I would have duplicate address rows. Because a record in the Addresses table will no longer be directly tied to a record in the Employees table, I must remove the EmployeeKey and create a new primary key for this table and remove the duplicate values. Now the Addresses table conforms to first normal form and third normal form.

Many-to-many relationships are solved using a separate table, often called a *join or bridge table*. Often, this table contains no user-readable values, only keys to bridge one table to another. However, you may recall that we have a missing bit of information. Remember when I moved the address information from the Address1/CityLine1 columns and Address2/CityLine2 columns into the Address table? I said that we had no way to trace these back to their roots and recall which location was the employee's primary residence? I can now resolve this within the bridge table by adding an additional column (see Figure 2-10).

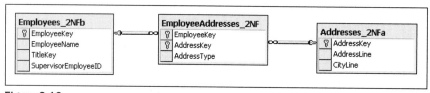

Figure 2-10

The new AddressType column is used to indicate the type of residence. This allows employees to share addresses while eliminating redundant address records. Does the AddressType column violate first normal form? Technically, yes. This could be an opportunity to optimize the database even more by creating yet another table for these values. It looks like there would only be three address type records related to the nine employees (see Figure 2-11).

EmployeeKey	AddressKey	AddressType
1	1	Primary Home
2	2	Primary Home
2	10	Weekend Home
3	3	Primary Home
4	4	Primary Home
5	5	Primary Home
5	11	Vacation Home
6	6	Primary Home
7	7	Primary Home
8	10	Primary Home
9	9	Primary Home

Figure 2-11

A simple query is used to obtain detail information about employees at a common address:

```
SELECT    EmployeeName, AddressLine, CityLine, AddressType
FROM      Employees
   INNER JOIN EmployeeAddresses
          ON Employees.EmployeeKey = EmployeeAddresses.EmployeeKey
   INNER JOIN Addresses
          ON EmployeeAddresses.AddressKey = Addresses.AddressKey
WHERE     Addresses.AddressKey = 10
```

It looks like the Vice President of Sales and the Inside Sales Coordinator share a residence only on weekends (see Figure 2-12).

	EmployeeName	AddressLine	CityLine	AddressType
1	Andrew Fuller	9317 Clear Creek Ln	Vashon Is, WA 98353	Weekend Home
2	Laura Callahan	9317 Clear Creek Ln	Vashon Is, WA 98353	Primary Home

Figure 2-12

Multi-Valued Columns

The last issue to contend with is that of having multiple values stored in a single column. There are quite a few examples in these tables. For example, the EmployeeName column in the Employees table contains both the first and last name, the AddressLine column in the Addresses table includes all parts of a street address, and the CityLine contains the city name, U.S. state, and zip code/postal code. Before I just willy-nilly start parsing all the values into separate columns, it's important for me to consider how this data will be used and the advantages and disadvantages of breaking it into pieces. Here are some sample questions that can help to define these business requirements:

❑   Will the employee first name and last name ever be used separately?

❑   Will I ever need to sort on one single value (such as last name)?

❑   Does every employee have a first name and last name? Do they only have a first name and last name (middle names/initials, hyphenated names, and so on)?

❑   Is there any value or need in separating parts of the address line (will I need a list of streets, and so on)?

❑   If I separate parts of the AddressLine or CityLine into separate columns, do I need to accommodate international addresses?

Apparently I do need to consider addresses in at least two locales because I have locations in the UK and the United States, so I will need to think beyond only one style of address. So, suppose that I have consulted my sponsoring customer and have learned that it would be useful to store separate first names and last names and we don't care about middle names or initials. We also don't plan to accommodate anyone without a first and last name. We have no need to break up the address line. This practice is highly uncommon outside of specialized systems and would be very cumbersome to maintain. We would benefit from storing the city, postal code or zip code, and state or province. It would also be useful to store the country, which is currently not included. Storing geographic information can be tricky because of the lack of consistency across international regions. This may require that you devise your own synonyms for different regional divisions (such as city, township, municipality, county, state, province, and country). In distributing these values into separate columns, you may find even more redundancies. Should these be further normalized and placed into separate tables? Does this ever end? I'll cite one example where the city, state, and zip code is normalized. I maintain a system that stores U.S. addresses and stores only the zip code on the individual's record. A separate table contains related city and state information obtained from the U.S. Postal Service.

I won't bore you will the mechanics of separating all these fields. The process is quite straightforward and very similar to what's already been done. Figure 2-13 shows the completed data model, based on the original flat table.

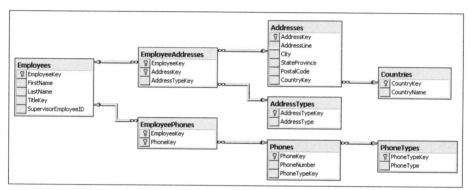

Figure 2-13

To Normalize or To De-normalize?

Depending on how a database is to be used (generally, it will be used for data input or for reporting), it may or may not be appropriate to apply all the rules just presented. The fact of the matter is that fully normalized databases require some gnarly, complex queries to support reporting and business analysis requirements. Complying fully with all the rules of normal form often adds more overhead to the application. Without going into detail, here's something to think about: If you are designing a new database system to support a typical business process, you will usually want to follow these rules completely and normalize all your data structures. After a time, when you have a large volume of data to extract and analyze through reports and business intelligence tools, you may find it appropriate to create a second database system for this purpose. In this database, you will strategically break the rules of normal form, creating redundant values in fewer, larger tables. Here's the catch: Only after you fully understand the rules of normal form will you likely know when and where you should break them.

Question Authority

You should ask yourself an important question as you encounter each opportunity to normalize: "Why?" Know why you should apply the rules and what the benefits and cost are. One of the challenges of applying normalization rules is to know just how far to go and to what degree it makes sense to apply them. At times it just makes sense to break some of the rules. There are good arguments to support both sides of this issue and without a complete understanding of business requirements I would be hard pressed to make a general statement about how data elements (such as phone numbers, titles, or addresses) should always be managed. In short, you need to understand the business requirements for your application and then apply the appropriate level of database normalization to reach that goal. If ever in doubt, it's usually best to err on the side of keeping the rules.

That being said, don't let yourself be bullied into adhering strictly to normalization rules if they don't make sense. A case in point: I worked for a very smart guy who had virtually no database experience. Very often he would read an article or a chapter of a book and suddenly became an expert on that particular technology. When he noticed that duplicate state codes were showing up repeatedly in our database, he decided that we needed a State table so that the states were not duplicated and that only valid states were added to a record. Because the addition of state code data was completely controlled by the application and not by ad-hoc changes to the database tables, his reasoning was not very valid. The data team finally got him to relent after pretending to enthusiastically endorse his opinion and add to it by claiming we also needed a street number table to avoid erroneous addresses as well as an area code table and a phone prefix table. He got the message almost immediately and decided that separating the state codes out didn't make as much sense as he originally thought.

Normalization is very important to database integrity, but remember that the more tables involved in a query to extract data, the worse the performance of the query.

We have discussed some abstract normalization concepts, which can be a bit confusing to someone new to databases. It is important to understand the basics if you are ever going to be called on to build data entities and not just to query them. Another important aspect of T-SQL programming is to understand how queries are processed by SQL Server. This will give you insight on how you should formulate your queries. The next section gives a brief description of the query processing process.

The Mechanics of Query Processing

To drive a car, it's not essential to understand how the engine works. However, if you want to be able to drive a car well (and perhaps maintain and tune it for optimal performance), it's helpful to have a fundamental understanding of the engine mechanics and to know what's going on inside. Likewise, it's possible to use SQL Server without fully understanding its mechanics, but if you want to create queries that work efficiently, it will help to understand what goes on within the relational database engine and the query processor.

When a SQL statement is presented to the database engine, the engine begins to analyze the request and break it down into steps. Based on characteristics of the data stored in tables, decisions are made resulting in the selection of appropriate operations. Many factors are considered including the table structures, existence of indexes, and the relative uniqueness of relevant data values.

It would be inefficient for the query-processing engine to analyze all the data prior to each query, so SQL Server gathers statistical information it uses to make these decisions. By default, SQL Server will gather statistical data about data stored in columns, such as the amount of rows, the ratio of rows to unique values and the distribution of the data in the rows. SQL Server uses this statistical data to build an efficient data retrieval plan and will adapt over time as the data changes.

Complex queries are broken down into individual steps — smaller queries — that process granular operations. This list of steps and operations is known as an *execution plan.* Chapter 14 gives a more detailed description of execution plans and how to analyze them. The query's syntax may actually be rewritten by the query optimizer into a standard form of SQL. SQL Server doesn't actually execute SQL; that's just how we talk to it. Before SQL Server can send instructions to the computer's processor, these commands must be compiled into low-level computer instructions, or object code. The optimized, compiled query is placed into an in-memory cache. Depending on how the query is created (for example, it may be saved as a view or stored procedure), the execution plan is saved with that object in a memory location called the *procedure cache*. Even ad-hoc queries can benefit from this process. The cached compiled query and execution plan is held into memory and reused until the plan is aged out. This way, if the same query is executed multiple times, it should run faster and more efficiently after the first time.

Additionally, the data that is read from disk during the query is placed in a memory location called the *buffer cache*. When the same query (or similar queries) is executed, the data can be retrieved from memory instead of making repeated trips to the disk.

In SQL Server, the same mechanism is used to manage both buffer cache and procedure cache. Here's a closer look at this process, also illustrated in Figure 2-14:

1. First, the query is parsed for syntactic accuracy. The text is flat-lined and translated into a standardized form of SQL.

2. Objects and then permissions are resolved, replacing object names with data-specific numeric identifiers and security context. These identifiers streamline conversations between the relation and storage engine.

3. The query processor then analyzes the query to find the lowest cost method of executing it. This includes looking for appropriate indexes, determining the order in which to search and retrieve data from referenced objects, and determining whether to use multiple or single CPU's to process the query.

4. The query is translated, or compiled, from SQL to Tabular Data Stream (TDS), the native language of the SQL Server network libraries. In this translation, operations are simplified and further optimized.

5. A compiled version of the plan and call are placed into cache for reuse.

6. The relational engine spawns threads for calling logical and physical I/O and operational execution. Database object locks are placed and managed by the transactional engine.

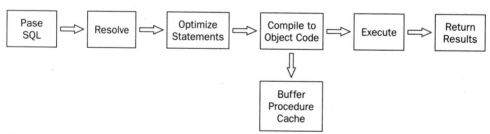

Figure 2-14

After the initial processing of a query, subsequent processing gets to take a shortcut. Because the query has already been parsed, resolved, optimized, and compiled, the compiled plan can be retrieved from cache and executed as shown in Figure 2-15.

Figure 2-15

The AdventureWorks Databases

Through the remainder of the book, you'll be working with a database used by the fictitious company Adventure Works Cycles, which sells bicycles and related products. This database, called *AdventureWorks* with SQL Server 2005 and *AdventureWorks2008* with SQL Server 2008, is a sample database included with SQL Server. There have actually been several different versions of this database as it evolved from the first edition in 2004 and then through the SQL Server 2008 CTP test period. The version that installs with SQL Server 2005 is slightly different from the version installed with SQL Server 2008. To accommodate for these differences, we have done one of three things. For the most part, we have attempted to use tables in our examples that are the same in structure in both SQL versions. When that was not possible, we either wrote two sets of examples, one for SQL Server 2005 and the other for SQL Server 2008, or we built views to emulate the table structure of SQL Server 2005 in SQL Server 2008. With this caveat in mind, all the query examples shown in the book will work with both versions, unless specified otherwise, but queries run with the 2005 version may return different results from those shown in this book. For the sake of simplicity and consistency, all references to the sample database will be to AdventureWorks2008 only. However, AdventureWorks2008 implies either AdventureWorks2008 or AdventureWorks.

You can download and install either the AdventureWorks or AdventureWorks2008 sample database from the support site for this book at www.wrox.com. Keep in mind that while the 2005 version of the database will work with either SQL Server 2005 or 2008, the 2008 version will work with SQL Server 2008 only. To install the sample database, follow these steps:

1.   Click the Download button for the database you want, click Open in the File Download dialog, and then follow the directions in the InstallShield Wizard.

2.   Double-check that the AdventureWorks or AdventureWorks2008 database has been added to the list of available databases on your server. If it hasn't, right-click the Databases node in SQL Server Management Studio's Object Explorer and choose Refresh.

3.   If the new database is not displayed on the database tree, the database file may need to be attached manually. Simply right-click the database server node in the SQL Server Management Studio object browser and select Attach Database. Then click the Add button in the middle of the window, browse to the location of the database file, and click OK.

Summary

SQL Server is widely used by many different people in many different ways. At its core is the relational database engine, and sitting on this foundation is a wealth of features and capabilities. The way that SQL Server databases are designed and administered has changed as the client applications have improved and been integrated into Microsoft's suite of solution development tools. SQL Server is now accessible to business users in addition to technical professionals.

In this chapter, you read about the conceptual, logical, and physical phases of solution design and how they apply to designing a database. A relational database stores data in separate tables, associated through primary key/foreign key relationships that implement the rules of normal form. You saw how flat, spreadsheet-like data is transformed into a normalized structure by applying these rules. Normalizing data structures is not an absolute necessity for all databases and it sometimes is prudent to ignore the rules to simplify the design. Both normalizing and de-normalizing a database design come at a cost that must be carefully considered and kept in balance with the business rules for the solution. These business rules and the user's requirements ultimately drive the capabilities and long-term needs of a project.

You also learned about the client/server database execution model and how SQL Server uses both client-side and server-side components to process requests and to execute queries. The execution and procedure caches allow SQL Server to optimize performance by compiling execution plans for ad-hoc queries and prepared stored procedures.

In the next chapter, you learn how to use the different tools available to the SQL programmer to create and manage database scripts and projects.

SQL Server Tools

It's said that a craftsman's work is only as good as his tools. To some degree, this principle applies to SQL Server. However, many database professionals from the old school choose not to use sophisticated tools, just as many craftsmen use old manual tools (chisels, carving knives, and so on) to do the work that is often simplified through automation. Many would even argue that the results are different, perhaps even better, when you remove automation from the equation. Regardless of the ideals to which you subscribe, a number of tools and applications are available that you can use to create and debug queries. Which tools do you need? This depends a great deal on what you need to do.

Common SQL Server Tasks

Here's a breakdown of some of the common tasks you may need to perform with SQL Server:

- ❏ **Administrative tasks**
    - ❏ Creating databases
    - ❏ Creating and managing server logins and database roles and users
    - ❏ Granting and managing security permissions
    - ❏ Scheduling backups
    - ❏ Auditing and error checking
    - ❏ Diagnosing failures and application errors
    - ❏ Performance tuning
    - ❏ Configuring data replication
    - ❏ Managing disk space and data files

- ❑ **Database management tasks**

  - ❑ Adding and managing tables, views, stored procedures, and functions

  - ❑ Creating indexes

  - ❑ Creating views, stored procedures, and functions

  - ❑ Importing, exporting, or transforming data

- ❑ **Data operations**

  - ❑ Inserting, updating, and deleting records

  - ❑ Supporting application features

  - ❑ Defining business rules

  - ❑ Selecting records from a table or multi-table join

Whether you are using SQL Server 2005 or SQL Server 2008, this chapter walks you through exercises that will work for either version of the product. Where there are differences (and they are very few), I will identify them. I'm assuming that you have SQL Server installed on your local computer with all the server and client tools. If your database server is on another computer, you may need to install the client tools on your local computer to follow these directions. I am also assuming that you are using Integrated Windows authentication and that your Windows account has sufficient permissions to create objects and run queries against the database server. If you have installed SQL Server on your local computer with default options, this should be the case — unless, of course, you are using Windows Vista as your operating system. If you have installed SQL Server on a Vista machine and your normal logon is not the administrator account (which it probably shouldn't be), you will need to add an account for your normal logon to avoid having to run the client tools as Administrator.

You can perform the following steps to create a logon to a local server running on a Vista machine:

1. Click the Windows logo in the bottom-left corner to bring up the program menu.

2. Click All Programs and then on Microsoft SQL Server 2008 (or 2005).

3. Right-click the SQL Server Management Studio link on the menu and click Run as Administrator. When prompted, enter the administrator password. (You do know what the administrator password is, right?)

4. After Management Studio opens you will be prompted to connect to a server. In the ServerName box you can type either the name of your local computer or **(local)**, or just a period (.) to connect to the local default instance of SQL Server.

5. After the connection has been made to your local SQL Server, click the New Query button to open a new query window (see Figure 3-1).

Figure 3-1

6. In the new query window, type the following code to create a privileged user account mapped to your normal login account that has permissions to perform all the exercises in this book. I don't want to insult your intelligence, but keep in mind that you will have to replace the name of the server and the login name with those on your computer. My computer name is WoodVista and my login name is DanW.

```
CREATE LOGIN [WOODVISTA\DanW] FROM WINDOWS
WITH DEFAULT_DATABASE=[master]
EXEC sp_addsrvrolemember @loginame = N'WOODVISTA\DanW'
                        ,@rolename = N'sysadmin'
```

Now that you have a SQL account with database administrator access, you can launch and use Management Studio without having to use the Windows Vista elevated permission feature.

If you are working with a remote database server, you should talk to your system administrator and make sure you have the client tools correctly installed and that you have the appropriate permissions to run queries. As you work through these exercises, the only difference will be that you will be connecting to a remote server rather than to the local server.

SQL Server Management Studio

SQL Server Management Studio completely replaces Enterprise Manager and Query Analyzer. It also replaces some of the functionality formerly found in Analysis Manager. It does an excellent job of both replacing the old tools and exceeding them in almost every possible way.

The SQL Server Management Studio interface looks a lot like the Visual Studio IDE and is in actuality a Visual Studio shell. The Visual Studio shell brings many very useful tools and features to the creation and organization of database objects, as well as the full feature set of the old tools.

If you have SQL Server 2000 or SQL Server 7 experience, you will notice that when SQL Server Management Studio is first launched, the default view is a great deal like the old Enterprise Manager, with a slight Query Analyzer influence (see Figure 3-2).

Figure 3-2

Many different windows can be viewed in Management Studio, so the management of screen real estate becomes critical. Most of the windows have the ability to either be pinned open or configured to fly out when the mouse pointer is placed over the menu bar or auto hide when the mouse cursor is placed elsewhere. If you are familiar with the Visual Studio IDE, this will be very familiar; if not, it may take a little while to get used to.

For those of you who are unfamiliar with the Visual Studio interface, the following bit of instruction is offered: Any window that supports the pinned and unpinned option will have a pin at the top right of the window. When the window is pinned, the pin will appear vertically oriented. When the window is unpinned, it will be horizontal (see Figure 3-3) and the toolbar will auto hide or fly out, depending on the mouse cursor location.

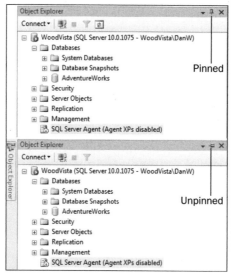

Figure 3-3

Most of the toolbars and windows also support the ability to be repositioned or configured to float. To reposition a tool window, you can just grab it by the title bar using the mouse pointer, and then drag to undock and move it around the design surface (see Figure 3-4). Something interesting happens when you do this.

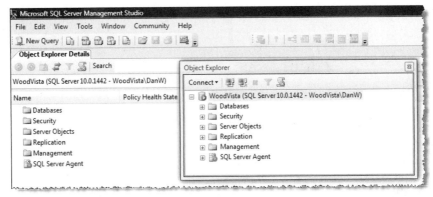

Figure 3-4

When a window is undocked and you drag it around the main window, guide diamonds are displayed, like points of a compass, to assist with the docking window placement (see Figure 3-5).

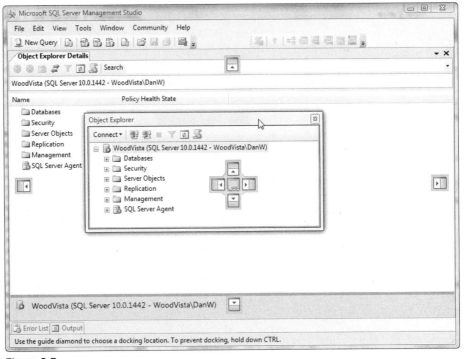

Figure 3-5

When you hover over one of the guide diamonds, the docking target area of the window is designated with a translucent shaded rectangle. As you see in Figure 3-6, you can also use the guide diamonds in the center cluster of the window. If a window is already docked in that area, using the center guide will dock your window adjacent to the existing window.

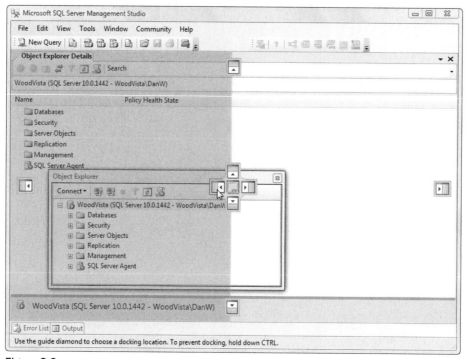

Figure 3-6

If you hover over an existing docked window, a separate set of guides will appear, allowing you to dock within this space or to create tabbed documents where the windows share screen real estate with other windows in the same space (see Figure 3-7).

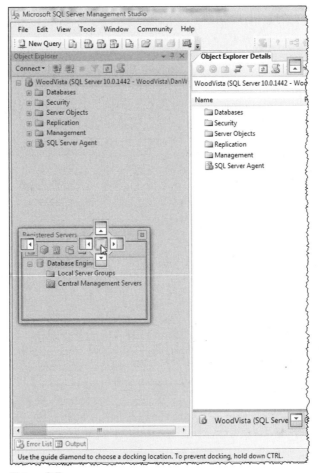

Figure 3-7

If you get into trouble and can't place a window where you want it, click to set focus to the window and then use the Window menu on the standard menu bar to toggle the window back to either Floating or Dockable. This should allow you to reposition the window as you like.

If you don't have any experience with Microsoft's development environment, the Visual Studio interface may take a little getting used to, but once you do, it is hard to imagine any interface that works as well. It offers the advantage of being able to hide windows when you don't need them but make them visible when you do, without having to reconfigure the interface. This conserves a great deal of screen real estate without having to click on several menus to expose the features you want.

Tool Windows

SQL Server Management Studio offers many different tool windows that facilitate the development and modification of database objects as well as the effective management of SQL Server. The various views are accessible from the View menu as well as the Standard toolbar. Each window can be configured as dockable, which is the default, but it can also be configured as a tabbed document or a floating window.

Object Explorer

Object Explorer is more than just a way to explore the database objects on a server; it is also a tool that can be used to create basic template scripts for selecting, inserting, updating, and deleting data. As shown in Figure 3-8, Object Explorer is arranged in a standard tree view with different groups of objects nested in folders.

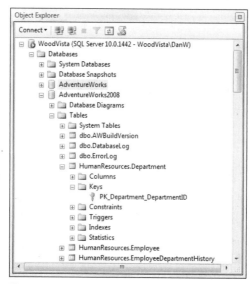

Figure 3-8

Object Explorer's functionality is exposed through the context menu. Right-clicking on any object or folder within Object Explorer exposes the list of available options. For example, right-clicking on a table exposes the context menu shown in Figure 3-9. Putting the mouse over the Script Table As option exposes additional options for creating basic scripts for that table, as also shown in Figure 3-9.

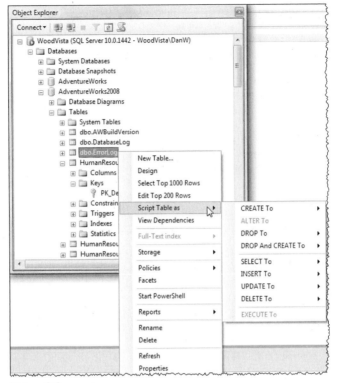

Figure 3-9

The context menu also presents the ability to create scripts that manipulate the object. For example, right-clicking on a table exposes a context menu that allows the user to either view or modify the table structure through the graphical interface. This functionality exists for virtually every object that is visible in Object Explorer.

Another great feature of SQL Server Management Studio that is exposed through Object Explorer and other areas of the studio interface is the ability to create scripts based on actions performed in the graphical designers. For instance, right-clicking on the table folder and choosing to create a new table launches a graphical interface where the table structure can be defined. Once the table design is complete, you can either save the table, which creates it, or you can click the Generate Change Script button on the Table Designer toolbar (see Figure 3-10), which will write the appropriate T-SQL to complete the task.

Figure 3-10

Likewise when working with other objects in Management Studio, a Script button will appear at the top of the respective designer, which will cause the actions performed in the designer to be scripted to a new editor window. This feature is especially useful when several different objects of the same type are to be created. The first one can be designed in the designer, the script generated for it, and that script modified to create the remaining objects. It is also very useful to learn the syntax for creating and modifying objects.

In this example you will use Object Explorer to create a script to select data from the HumanResources. Department table.

1. In Object Explorer, click the + symbol to the left of Databases to expand the database folder. Then expand the AdventureWorks database folder and then the Tables folder.

2. Right-click the HumanResources.Department table.

3. On the context menu, click the Select Top 1000 rows item. Management Studio will generate a new query window with the script and execute it.

    The new query window and the query results are displayed to the right of the Object Explorer (see Figure 3-11). Notice that the script generator places brackets around all the object names. This isn't really required for the objects in this query, but the script generator defaults to this behavior in case an object has an embedded space or reserved word in it. We'll discuss the particulars of object delimiting in Chapter 4.

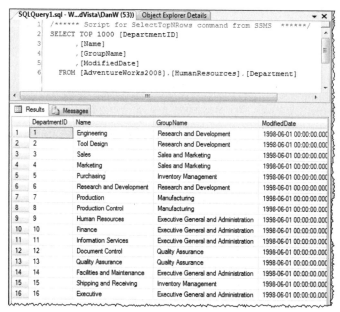

Figure 3-11

Code Editor

SQL Server Management Studio's Code Editor provides the ability to open, edit, or create new queries. When you click New Query, the query window that opens is also known as the Code Editor. The Code Editor supports the following types of queries:

❑ **Database engine queries** — Database engine queries are written in T-SQL.

❑ **Data mining queries** — Data mining queries are created by using extensions to the SQL language called DMX, or Data Mining Extensions. DMX queries are written to return information from data mining models created in SQL Server Analysis Services.

❑ **Multidimensional queries** — Multidimensional queries are written using Multidimensional Expressions (MDX). MDX queries are used to retrieve information from multidimensional cubes created in SQL Server Analysis Services.

❑ **XML for analysis queries** — XMLA queries are built to create, manage, and manipulate Analysis Server objects.

❑ **SQL Server Compact Edition queries** — Compact edition queries are used in mobile applications hosted by the Windows Mobile operating system and SQL Server Compact Edition.

The Code Editor is essentially a word processor. It provides color coding of syntax, multiple query windows, and partial code execution by highlighting the desired code and clicking the execute button or pressing F5. SQL Server documentation refers to the Code Editor as the Query Editor, the Text Editor, or simply the Editor, depending on what aspect of SQL Server you are reading about.

In SQL Server 2008, the basic functionality that the Code Editor brings is the same for all the possible types of queries it supports. For example, the Code Editor provides support for basic IntelliSense functions and code completion such as those found in Visual Studio. In SQL Server 2005 the code-completion and IntelliSense features are not available with T-SQL queries. IntelliSense and code-completion are discussed later in this chapter. The Code Editor window also provides direct access to a graphical query builder. Right-clicking on the Code Editor window, when that window is associated with a database engine query, results in a context menu that includes the Design Query in Editor option (see Figure 3-12). The Query Designer is very useful when writing queries against databases that you are not familiar with. At the end of this chapter is an exercise to show you how to use this useful tool to quickly create T-SQL queries.

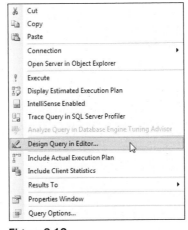

Figure 3-12

Solution Explorer

Before SQL Server 2005, organizing queries and object definitions was completely left to the DBA or database developer. The ability to organize and group scripts together or to check them in to a source control system was completely manual. SQL Server Management Studio takes full advantage of Visual Studio's solution system by providing the means of grouping one or more projects that contain various connection objects and scripts into a single solution called a SQL Server Management Studio *solution*. Each solution can have one or more projects associated with it. For example, if you are developing several objects for a new application that includes both database engine and analysis engine objects, you can create a new solution that links them all together by creating a SQL Server Management Studio solution and creating both a SQL Server Scripts and Analysis Server Scripts project in that solution. You do this, oddly enough, not by creating a new solution, which there is no option for, but instead by creating a new project by clicking the File menu and choosing New Project, which launches the New Project dialog (see Figure 3-13).

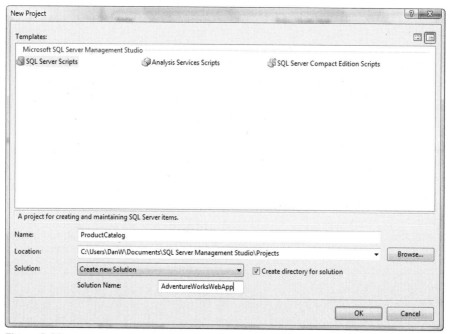

Figure 3-13

If no solution is currently open, Management Studio will create a new solution. If a solution is presently open, you will be given the choice of adding the project to the existing solution or closing the present solution and creating a new one. As you can see in Figure 3-13, there are three types of projects from which to choose:

- ❑ SQL Server Scripts projects contain T-SQL database engine queries.

- ❑ Analysis Services Scripts projects contain MDX, DMX, and XMLA analysis queries.

- ❑ SQL Server Compact Edition Scripts projects contain queries for the Compact Edition of SQL Server that is used in Windows Mobile devices.

The solution is managed through a solution file with an .ssmssln extension. The example shown in Figure 3-13 created a new solution folder called AdventureWorksWebApp that contains a project folder called ProductCatalog. By default the solution folder and the first project folder will have the same name, so it is generally a good idea to change the name of the solution. The Create directory for solution option can also be cleared and a base solution folder specified. In this way only a project folder will be created in the specified directory. If a solution is already opened, creating a new project can add the project to the solution or be configured to create a whole new solution and close the open one.

In the solution folder are two files. One file is the solution file, which in this case is called AdventureWorksWebApp.ssmssln and contains a list of all the projects in the solution and their location. The second file is the solution options file, called AdventureWorksWebApp.sqlsuo. The solution options file contains information about the options that customize the development environment.

The solution folder will contain a project folder for every project added to the solution. The project folder contains all the project files including the project definition file. The project definition file is a XML file with the .ssmssqlproj extension. In the previous example this file is called ProductCatalog.ssmssqlproj. The project definition file contains the connection information as well as metadata about the remaining files in the project.

A rather annoying aspect of the Solution Explorer is that new queries are not automatically added to the solution if they are not added from the Solution Explorer itself. For example, suppose that you have created a new project and then click on the New Query button at the top left of Management Studio. A new query window will open, but the query will not be part of your open project. To ensure that new queries are added to the project, you need to right-click on the Queries folder and select New Query.

Properties Window

As shown in Figure 3-14, the Properties window is linked to the Solution Explorer and simply displays the properties for the currently selected item in the Solution Explorer window. Editable properties will be bolded. If the Properties window is not visible, you can open it from the View menu or by pressing F4.

Figure 3-14

Registered Servers

Multiple servers can be registered and connected to with Management Studio. This allows the DBA to manage multiple servers in a single environment. The Registered Servers window is not visible by default. To display it, click the View menu and choose Registered Servers, or press Ctrl+Alt+G. Right-clicking anywhere in the Registered Servers window will expose a context menu that allows for the addition of new server registrations. It also allows for the creation of server groups. If you have multiple servers in your organization, server groups can be very useful. For instance, server registrations can be segregated so that all the test and development servers are in one group and the production servers are in another, or servers could be grouped based on function or department. Instances of the database engine, analysis services, reporting services, integration services, and SQL Server Compact Edition can be registered in the Registered Servers window. Once registered, the Registered Servers window provides the ability to manage the associated services or quickly connect Object Explorer to that server instance, as shown in Figure 3-15.

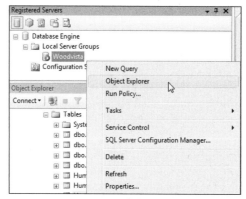

Figure 3-15

Bookmark Window

When working with very large scripts in the Code Editor, it is very useful to be able mark a location in the script. Bookmarks enable this functionality. The Bookmark window is made visible with the View menu and is enabled when working with any SQL Server script type. Any number of bookmarks can be created and then renamed with an intuitive name that identifies the bookmark. If the script is part of a solution, the bookmarks are saved with the solution in the solution options file. Bookmarks can be organized in to multiple folders for each project. Figure 3-16 shows the bookmark window open and a bookmark called Catch Block.

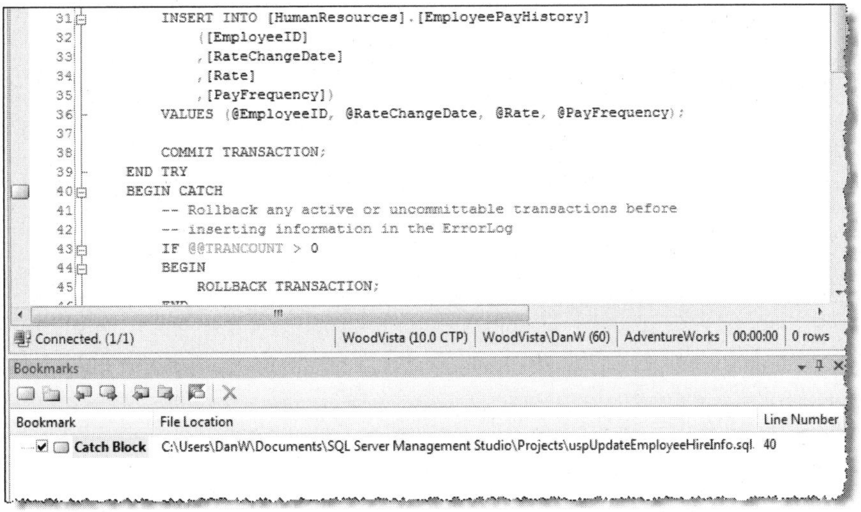

```
31    INSERT INTO [HumanResources].[EmployeePayHistory]
32       ([EmployeeID]
33       , [RateChangeDate]
34       , [Rate]
35       , [PayFrequency])
36    VALUES (@EmployeeID, @RateChangeDate, @Rate, @PayFrequency);
37
38    COMMIT TRANSACTION;
39    END TRY
40    BEGIN CATCH
41       -- Rollback any active or uncommittable transactions before
42       -- inserting information in the ErrorLog
43       IF @@TRANCOUNT > 0
44       BEGIN
45          ROLLBACK TRANSACTION;
```

Connected. (1/1)   WoodVista (10.0 CTP) | WoodVista\DanW (60) | AdventureWorks | 00:00:00 | 0 rows

Bookmarks

Bookmark	File Location	Line Number
☑ ☐ **Catch Block**	C:\Users\DanW\Documents\SQL Server Management Studio\Projects\uspUpdateEmployeeHireInfo.sql	40

Figure 3-16

Toolbox

The toolbox contains maintenance plan tasks that can be dragged to the Maintenance Plan designer used by database administrators to create maintenance plans for routine scheduled maintenance, such as database backups and index maintenance operations.

Object Explorer Details

The Object Explorer Details pane is displayed by default and is a great deal like the list or detail view in Windows Explorer.

Web Browser

Your default web browser can be launched from within SQL Server Management Studio to minimize the number of open applications and to allow direct access to Internet content from within the Management Studio application. This is done from the View menu by choosing Web Browser.

Template Explorer

The Template Explorer contains hundreds of SQL Server, Analysis Server, and SQL Mobile scripts. Each script is grouped into folders based on their function. The template scripts can be opened by being dragged on to an open query window. If no query window is open, the templates can be opened through a double mouse click, the Edit menu, or right-click context menu, all of which cause a new query window to open. Once a template is open in the Query Editor, the parameters of the template can be replaced with actual values by launching the Specify Values For Template Parameters dialog. This dialog can be launched from the SQL Editor toolbar or through the Query menu.

Error List

The Error List window is available only with SQL Server 2008 and contains a list of all errors detected in the open query window (see Figure 3-17).

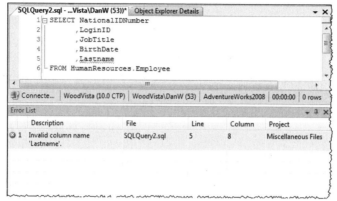

Figure 3-17

Toolbars

SQL Server Management Studio provides several different toolbars that expose features from various menus. Each toolbar can be displayed or hidden in the typical Windows toolbar method of selecting View ⇨ Toolbars and choosing which toolbars to display. In addition, you can customize the toolbars to display only the buttons most often used by right-clicking the toolbar and choosing Customize.

Database Diagram Toolbar

The Database Diagram toolbar exposes a great deal of functionality for use on database diagrams. The toolbar is not used just for diagramming the database, but also for modifying or creating database objects from within the diagram interface. The toolbar is not displayed by default when working with database diagrams. It must be selected through the View ⇨ Toolbars menu. In addition, a menu item labeled Database Diagram will appear on the menu bar when a database diagram is open. The menu has the same options as the toolbar. The Database Diagram toolbar features are described in the following table.

Feature	Purpose
New Table	Enables the creation of new tables from within the database diagram.
Add Table	Adds an existing table from the database to the diagram.
Add Related Tables	If you select a table in the database diagram and click on the Add Related Tables button, all the tables that are related by a declarative Foreign Key constraint will be added to the diagram.
Delete Tables From Database	Not only removes the table from the diagram, but deletes the table and its contents as well.
Remove From Diagram	Removes the selected table from the diagram.

Feature	Purpose
Generate Change Script	Any changes made to database objects in the diagram, such as creating, deleting, or modifying of attributes, can be sent to a script. If changes are made to underlying objects and the diagram is saved, a prompt is shown asking to confirm changes to the underlying objects.
Set Primary Key	Sets or changes the primary key assignment to the selected column.
New Text Annotation	Adds a textbox for annotation to the database diagram.
Table View	Enables the changing of table presentation in the diagram, including a customized view to configure exactly what aspects of the table are displayed.
Show Relationship Labels	Displays or hides the name of the foreign key constraints.
View Page Breaks	Displays or hides page break lines to enable the organization of diagrams for printing.
Recalculate Page Breaks	Re-centers table objects onto as few pages as possible after being manually arranged on the diagram.
Autosize Selected Tables	Resizes tables to fit the diagram in the smallest size that still shows all fields.
Arrange Selection	Arranges selected tables so that they do not overlap and are viewable in the diagram.
Arrange Tables	Arranges all tables so that they do not overlap and are viewable in the diagram.
Zoom	Increases or decreases the zoom factor on the displayed diagram.
Relationships	Launches a dialog that displays existing foreign keys defined on a selected table and enables the defining of additional foreign keys.
Manage Indexes and Keys	Launches a dialog that displays existing primary and unique keys defined on a selected table and enables the defining of additional keys.
Manage Full-Text Index	Launches a dialog that displays existing full-text indexes on a selected table and enables the defining of additional full-text indexes on full-text index enabled databases.
Manage XML Indexes	Launches a dialog that displays existing XML Indexes on a selected table and enables the defining of additional XML indexes.
Manage Check Constraints	Launches a dialog that displays existing check constraints on a selected table and enables the defining of additional check constraints.
Manage Spatial Indexes	Launches a dialog that displays existing spatial indexes on a selected table and enables the defining and creation of new spatial indexes that are associated with the new `geometry` data type included with SQL Server 2008.

Help Toolbar

The Help toolbar provides a very easy and convenient mechanism for consulting online help articles while using Management Studio.

Query Designer Toolbar

The Query Designer toolbar is enabled when a table is opened with SQL Server 2005's Object Explorer or when the top 200 rows are opened for edit in SQL Server 2008.

To open a table in SQL Server 2005:

1. Right-click the table you want to open in Object Explorer.
2. Click Open Table.

To open the top 200 rows for edit in SQL Server 2008:

1. Right-click the table you want to open in Object Explorer.
2. Click Edit Top 200 Rows.

If the Query Designer toolbar was not visible, it will be when the table is opened. If it was visible, it will now be enabled. Although opening a table in a test and development environment is probably acceptable, opening a table in this manner in a production environment is not recommended. Opening a table with Object Explorer dumps the data from the table into a memory object called an *updateable scrollable cursor*. What this means is that while the table data is exposed in the results window, any change to the displayed data is made to the underlying data in the table. This can be very dangerous. Displaying the entire contents of the table also can consume a great deal of server resources if the table is large. As a general rule, if the entire contents of a table need to be exposed the best way is to write a query with no filters, such as:

```
SELECT * FROM Person.Address
```

This exposes the same information as opening the table but does not populate an updateable cursor, so the results are read-only. If the data in that table needs to be updated, an update command (which is covered in Chapter 10) is more appropriate than modifying the data in an open table results window. Because the ability to open a large table is generally not a good idea, SQL Server 2008 replaced that ability with the new Edit Top 200 Rows feature.

The following table describes the Query Designer toolbar features.

Feature	Purpose
Show Diagram Pane	Displays or hides the diagram pane that can be used to add or remove tables from the query, add derived tables, and configure table join criteria.
Show Criteria Pane	Displays or hides the criteria pane which can be used to alias column names, establish sort orders, and configure filter criteria.
Show SQL Pane	Displays or hides the SQL pane which displays the resultant SQL syntax from the diagram pane. The SQL syntax can also be manipulated in the SQL pane resulting in changes to the criteria and diagram panes.
Show Results Pane	Displays or hides the results of the query if it has been executed.
Change Type	Allows changing the type of query from SELECT to INSERT, DELETE or UPDATE.
Execute SQL	Executes the query against the database.
Verify SQL Syntax	Validates the syntax of the query, but does not execute it.
Add Group By	Adds a GROUP BY expression and formats the query so that non-aggregated columns in the SELECT list are present in the GROUP BY list.
Add Table	Adds an existing table to the diagram pane and SQL pane.
Add New Derived Table	Adds an empty table to the diagram pane and the shell syntax for creating a derived table subquery to the SQL pane.

Source Control Toolbar

The Source Control toolbar is enabled when working with scripts and a Source Control plug-in has been configured, such as Visual Source Safe or Visual Studio Team System. The following table describes the toolbar options.

Feature	Purpose
Change Source Control	Displays a dialog that enables the linking of new and existing items in the Solution Explorer to a source control database folder.
Get Latest Version	Opens the latest version of the item or items selected in the Solution Explorer.
Get	Returns a list of all versions of the selected item and allows the selection of a particular version.
Check Out for Edit	Opens the selected items for editing and marks its status in the source control database as Open for Edit, preventing other users from editing it at the same time.
Check In	Saves changes and marks the selected items in the source control database as Checked In, and allows editing by other users.
Undo Checkout	Discards any changes and marks the selected item in the source control database as Checked In, and allows editing by other users.
View History	Displays the history of a project, which includes a list of everything done to the project from creation to deletion.
Refresh Status	Queries the source control database for the most recent status of all project items.
Share	Allows for a single item to be shared in multiple projects. Changes made to shared items are reflected in all the projects that use the item.
Compare	Compares an item to a previous version to expose the changes made.
Properties	Displays detailed status information on the selected item.
Source Control Manager	Launches the associated source control application as identified in the Managements Studio options settings.

SQL Editor Toolbar

The SQL Editor toolbar becomes visible, or is enabled if already visible, when a new SQL query window is opened. The toolbar provides the most common features used by SQL programmers and DBAs. The supported features are described in the following table.

Feature	Purpose
Connect	Queries can be written without being connected to a database. So, when it comes time to execute the query or validate its syntax against a database, the Connect button displays a server connection dialog that enables the selection of the applicable server and database.
Change Connection	Enables you to change the connected server. A script can be created and tested on a test and development server and then the connection changed to the production server for execution.

Feature	Purpose
Available Databases	Displays a drop-down list box for selecting the database context for the query.
Execute	Executes the SQL in the current window against the selected database.
Debug	The debug feature is only included with SQL Server 2008. It enables the SQL programmer to systematically step through large scripts to debug and track logic flow. Debugging is covered in more detail later in the chapter.
Parse	Checks the SQL in the current window for valid structure and syntax. It does *not* check to ensure that referenced objects actually exist.
Cancel Executing Query	Terminates the present query.
Display Estimated Execution Plan	Displays a graphical execution plan for the current window. It does not actually execute the query, but simply checks the metadata of the referenced object and builds a query plan based on current information.
Design Query in Editor	Launches the Graphical Query Editor.
Specify Values for Template Parameters	Displays a dialog that enables the replacement of template parameters with defined values.
Include Actual Execution Plan	Returns a graphical query plan used during execution, along with the results of the query.
Include Client Statistics	Returns client statistics, including statistics about the query, network packets, and the elapsed time of the query, along with the query results.
SQLCMD Mode	SQLCMD replaces OSQL as the command-line SQL tool. SQLCMD Mode allows the editing and testing of command-line scripts in the editor.
Results to Text	Formats the results of any query executed in the Query Editor as text.
Results to Grid	Returns query results in a grid. By default, grid results cannot exceed 65,535 characters.
Results to File	When a query is executed, a Save Results window will appear, prompting for a file name and location.
Comment Out Selected Lines	Adds in-line comment marks to comment out the selected lines.
Uncomment Selected Lines	Removes in-line comment marks.
Decrease Indent	Decreases the indent of selected text.
Increase Indent	Increases the indent of selected text.

SQL Compact Edition Toolbar

The SQL Compact Edition toolbar becomes visible, or is enabled if already visible, when a new SQL Compact Edition query window is opened. The tools on the toolbar are a subset of the SQL Editor tools showing only those that are applicable for SQL Compact Edition queries.

SQL Server Analysis Services Editor Toolbar

The Analysis Services toolbar also becomes visible, or is enabled if already visible, when a new analysis query is opened or created. The tools on this toolbar are also a subset of the SQL Editor tools, but contain only those tools applicable to Analysis Services queries (DMX, MDX, XMLA).

Standard Toolbar

The Standard toolbar provides buttons to execute the most common actions, such as opening and saving files. It also provides buttons that will launch new queries and expose different tool windows.

Table Designer Toolbar

The Table Designer toolbar becomes visible, or is enabled if already visible, when either a new table is created using Table Designer or an existing table is modified using the Table Designer. The Table Designer is launched by right-clicking on the table node in the Object Explorer and choosing New Table from the context menu, or by right-clicking on an existing table in the table node of Object Explorer and choosing Design. The Table Designer toolbar has buttons that enable the creation or deletion of primary keys on a table, as well as launching dialogs for creating and managing indexes, constraints, and table relationships.

Text Editor Toolbar

As previously described, Management Studio supports a few different languages, with each language having its own specific toolbar. The Text Editor toolbar offers additional shortcuts to those provided in the other language-specific editors. The features are described in the following table.

Feature	Purpose
Display an Object Member List	When you are editing DMX, MDX, or XMLA scripts, this feature invokes an IntelliSense window that displays a list of possible script members. IntelliSense features are not available when working with SQL scripts.
Display Parameter Info	Displays the parameter list for system stored procedures and functions used with Analysis Services.
Display Quick Info	Displays declaration information for XML objects created or referenced in an XMLA script.
Display Word Completion	Displays possible words to complete a variable, command, or function call. If only one possible option exists, it is implemented.
Decrease Indent	Decreases the indent of selected text.

Feature	Purpose
Increase Indent	Increases the indent of selected text.
Comment Out Selected Lines	Adds in-line comment marks to comment out the selected lines.
Uncomment Selected Lines	Removes in-line comment marks.
Toggle a Bookmark on the Current Line	Adds or removes a bookmark to the current script at the position of the cursor.
Move the caret to the previous bookmark	Moves the cursor to the previous set bookmark in the current script project.
Move the caret to the next bookmark	Moves the cursor to the next set bookmark in the current script project.
Move the caret to the previous bookmark in the current folder	Moves the cursor to the previous set bookmark in the currently selected bookmark folder of the bookmark window.
Move the caret to the next bookmark in the current folder	Moves the cursor to the next set bookmark in the currently selected bookmark folder of the bookmark window.
Move the caret to the previous bookmark in the current document	Moves the cursor to the previous set bookmark in the current script window.
Move the caret to the next bookmark in the current document	Moves the cursor to the next set bookmark in the current script window.
Clear all bookmarks in all files	Removes all configured bookmarks from the current project.

View Designer Toolbar

The View Designer toolbar is almost exactly like the Query Designer toolbar, with the exception of being limited to writing SELECT queries. In addition, queries written with the View Designer are saved as views and not just as query scripts.

SQL Server Management Studio Configuration

Management Studio's look and feel can be customized through the Tools ⇨ Options menu. The Options dialog, shown in Figure 3-18, enables you to customize the Management Studio IDE. The configuration options are divided into the following seven areas.

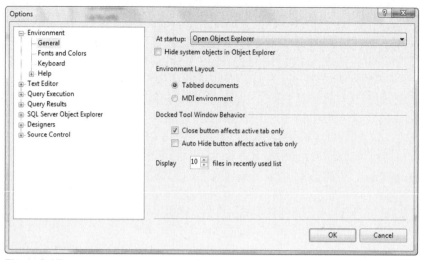

Figure 3-18

Environment

The Environment section is broken down into the following four sub-areas:

❑   **General** — The General section provides startup options and environment layout, such as tabbed windows versus MDI (Multiple Document Interface) windows and how the windows behave.

❑   **Fonts and Colors** — The fonts and colors used in the text editor are extraordinarily customizable in this area. The color and font used for reserved words, stored procedures, comments, and background colors are just a sampling of what can be changed.

❑   **Keyboard** — For those database administrators who are used to Query Analyzer's keyboard shortcuts, this configuration area enables the setting of the keyboard shortcuts to the same ones used in Query Analyzer. The keyboard configuration area also allows for the addition of custom keyboard shortcuts.

❑   **Help** — The Help area enables the integration of Help into a Management Studio window or the ability to launch Help externally. It also enables you to customize local and online help resources.

Text Editor

The Text Editor section, which enables you to customize various text editors, is divided into the following four sub-areas:

❑   **File Extension** — File extensions for all the possible script and configuration files can be configured in the File Extension area. Known file extensions such as .sql, .mdx, .dmx, and .xml are not listed but are automatically associated with their respective editors. They can be reassigned with a "with encoding" option so that Management Studio will prompt for specific language encoding every time an associated file type is opened. Custom file extensions can also be added.

❑ **All Languages** — The All Languages area is divided into two parts — General and Tabs — and provides configuration settings for IntelliSense features, word-wrap, line numbers, and indentation for all script languages. Keep in mind that IntelliSense options have no impact on SQL scripts in SQL Server 2005. IntelliSense for T-SQL scripts is new to SQL Server 2008.

❑ **Plain Text** — The Plain Text configuration settings are for plain text documents not associated with a particular scripting language.

❑ **XML** — This area provides configuration settings for XML documents. These settings consist of the same settings from the All Languages area as well as XML-specific settings such as automatic formatting and schema download settings.

Query Execution

The Query Execution section provides configuration options for how queries are executed as well as connection properties and timeout settings. The Query Execution section is divided into two sub-areas:

❑ **SQL Server** — The SQL Server area has configuration options that control the maximum row count and the maximum amount of text or Unicode text that is returned to the Management Studio results window. This area also has options to specify a batch delimiter other than GO and to specify query execution time-out settings. Batch delimiters are discussed in Chapter 4. There is also an advanced and ANSI area that provides for the configuration of specific connection-level options.

❑ **Analysis Services** — This area provides configuration setting to control the execution timeout setting for Analysis Services queries.

Query Results

The Query Results section provides configuration options for how query results are formatted and is also divided into the same two sub-areas as the Query Execution settings.

❑ **SQL Server** — The SQL Server section has configuration options to specify the default location for query results — to a grid, as text, or to a file — as well as the default location for results sent to a file.

❑ **Analysis Services** — Configuration settings for Analysis Services query results include showing grids in separate tabs and playing the default windows beep when the query completes. Both settings are disabled by default.

SQL Server Object Explorer

SQL Server 2008 provides an additional section that enables you to configure the amount of records displayed by default when querying the audit log, as well as the amount of records returned in SQL Server 2008's new context menu choices of Edit Top <n> Rows and Select Top <n> Rows (see Figure 3-19). The new choices are shown when right-clicking a table in Object Explorer, as shown in Figure 3-20. This section also provides the ability to configure scripting defaults. The scripting menu is also available in SQL Server 2005.

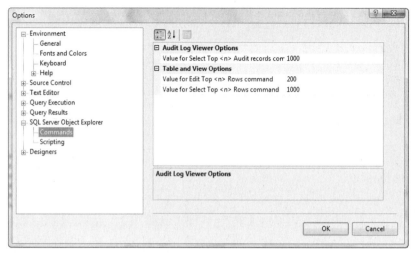

Figure 3-19

Figure 3-20

Designers

The Designers section provides configuration options for the graphical designers used in Management Studio. The Designers section is divided into three sub-areas:

- **Table and Database Designers** — The Table and Database Designers area allows for the configuration of specific designer behavior.

- **Maintenance Plans** — The Maintenance Plans options determine the way new shapes are added to the maintenance plan design area.

- **Analysis Services Designers** — The Analysis Services Designers page provides options to set the connection timeout for the Analysis designers and the colors for the Data Mining Model viewer.

Source Control

The Source Control configuration section allows for the integration of a source control plug-in, such as Visual Source Safe or Visual Studio Team System.

SQL Server Business Intelligence Development Studio

The SQL Server Business Intelligence Development Studio, or BI Studio, is actually Visual Studio. Regardless of whether Visual Studio is launched from the SQL Server menu as BI Studio or from the Visual Studio menu as Visual Studio, it launches the exact same application. If the full Visual Studio suite has not been installed, the only available project templates will be Business Intelligence projects. However, if the full suite is installed, all the installed features and templates will be available.

A complete discussion of the Visual Studio IDE is beyond the scope of this book, but a brief description is definitely in order.

Microsoft has divided business intelligence into three distinct pieces: integration, analysis, and reporting. These three parts of the business intelligence package are implemented through SQL Server Integration Services, SQL Server Analysis Services, and SQL Server Reporting Services, respectively. Correspondingly, the BI Studio provides business intelligence project templates that focus on these three areas. The following table briefly describes the available templates.

Template	Description
Integration Services Project	Integration Services projects are used to create robust Extract-Transform-Load (ETL) solutions to enable the moving and transforming of data.
Analysis Services Project	Analysis Services projects are used to create SQL Server Analysis Services databases that expose the objects and features of analysis cubes used for complex data analysis.
Import Analysis Services 9.0 Database	The import project enables the creation of an Analysis Services project from an existing SQL Server Analysis Services database. It essentially reverse-engineers the project from an existing database and creates a project from an existing Analysis Services database.
Report Server Project	Report Server projects are used to create and deploy enterprise reports for both traditional (paper) and interactive reports.
Report Server Project Wizard	The Report Server Project Wizard offers the same functionality as the Report Server Project option, but starts the development of the project in a step-by-step process that guides the user through the various tasks required to create a report. As with many wizards, this one leaves the project in a skeleton phase that will require more detailed finalization.
Report Model Project	Report Model projects are used to create and deploy SQL Server Reporting Services report models, which can in turn be used by end users to create reports using the Report Builder tool.

SQL Server Profiler

The SQL Server Profiler is an absolutely essential tool for both database administrators and database developers alike. The Profiler provides the ability to monitor and record virtually every facet of SQL Server activity. It is actually a graphical interface for SQL Trace, which is a collection of stored procedures and functions that are used to monitor and record server activity. A complete discussion of Profiler is beyond the scope of this book. For more information on the Profiler, check out *Beginning SQL Server 2005 Administration* (Wrox).

Database Tuning Advisor

The Database Tuning Advisor (DTA) can analyze SQL Server scripts or SQL Server Profiler traces to evaluate the effective use of indexes. It can also be used to get recommendations for building new indexes, indexed views, or for creating physical table partitions. The DTA is a useful tool for database administrators and is described in detail in the book *Beginning SQL Server 2005 Administration* (Wrox).

SQL Server Configuration Manager

The SQL Server Configuration Manager is a Microsoft Management Console (MMC) snap-in used to manage all the services and protocols used by an instance of SQL Server. Each instance of SQL Server is divided into three nodes: SQL Server Services, SQL Server Network Configuration, and SQL Native Client Configuration. This tool is almost exclusively used by database administrators and is explained in detail in *Beginning SQL Server 2005 Administration* (Wrox).

Command-Line Tools

SQL Server comes with plenty of great graphical tools to accomplish almost everything you could ever need to do, but there also comes a time when a simple command-line tool is the best tool for the job. The two tools used most frequently are SQLCMD and BCP, but there are many more. This section will describe just the SQLCMD utility because it is the one that will be used with T-SQL. For more information about all the command-line tools supported by SQL Server, check out SQL Server Books Online under the topic "Command Prompt Utilities."

SQLCMD

The SQLCMD utility replaced OSQL starting with SQL Server 2005 as the utility used to execute T-SQL statements, stored procedures, and SQL script files from the command prompt. SQLCMD utilizes OLE DB (Object Linking and Embedding, Data Base) as the interface to connect to SQL Server and execute T-SQL. OLE DB is a very efficient mechanism for connecting to databases and provides many more error handling and connection options than the classic ODBC (Open Data Base Connectivity) connection objects used with OSQL.

The SQLCMD utility enables you to use variables, connect to servers dynamically, query server information, and pass error information back to the calling environment.

SQLCMD supports several arguments that change the way it behaves and how it connects to an instance of SQL Server. An abbreviated list is included in the following table. For a complete list of the argument options, consult SQL Server Books Online under the topic "SQLCMD Utility." Note that SQLCMD command-line arguments are case sensitive.

Argument	Description
-S	Specifies the SQL Server instance name for SQLCMD to connect to
-E	Configures SQLCMD to use a trusted connection
-U	Specifies the user name to use when connecting with a SQL Server login
-P	Specifies the password to use when connecting with a SQL Server login
-i	Specifies the T-SQL script input file to run
-o	Specifies the output text file to return the results of a SQLCMD execution
-v	Specifies the parameter(s) to pass to a SQLCMD script execution
-A	Designates the SQLCMD connection as a Dedicated Administrator Connection (DAC)

The SQLCMD utility typically is used to execute saved T-SQL scripts in batch processes. This functionality is further enhanced by the ability of SQLCMD to accept scripting parameters. SQL Server Management Studio makes the creation of SQLCMD scripts even easier with its SQLCMD Mode. You can write and test the scripts with Management Studio by selecting SQLCMD Mode on the SQL Editor toolbar.

Multiple variables can be declared and their values set with the SETVAR command as well as passed in to a SQLCMD script with the -v argument. The following example shows how to use multiple SETVAR commands by creating two variables, ColumnName and TableName. The SETVAR command not only creates the variables, it also specifies the value of the variables.

```
USE AdventureWorks2008
GO
:SETVAR ColumnName "Name"
:SETVAR TableName "Production.Product"
SELECT $(ColumnName)
FROM $(TableName)
```

When testing this example, make sure to select the SQLCMD mode on the Query menu so that the query is run through the SQLCMD command. (see Figure 3-21).

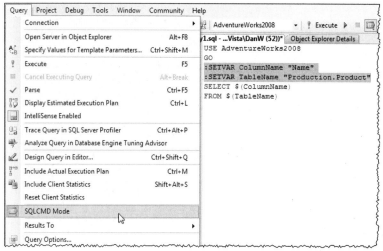

Figure 3-21

Now let's use the SQLCMD utility from the command prompt. First, modify the preceding example and remove the SETVAR commands. Then save the script to a file as GetProducts.SQL. I am saving it to the root of my C: drive. The script should look like the following example:

```
USE AdventureWorks2008
GO
SELECT $(ColumnName)
FROM $(TableName)
```

You could execute this script with the SQLCMD utility by using the following command line:

```
SQLCMD /E /S WoodVista /i C:\GetProducts.SQL /v ColumnName="Name" TableName =
"Production.Product"
```

Because SQLCMD isn't a particularly interactive environment, actions must be performed using a single-line command. When you launch SQLCMD, you must provide login information — either a username and password for SQL Server authentication, or a switch to indicate that you want to use integrated Windows security. The following example uses integrated security by using the /E switch. (This stands for Enterprise security.) Note that the documentation for the /E switch shows that this means *trusted connection.* I am using it with the /S switch that specifies the server to connect to. If the server is not specified, the SQLCMD utility will attempt to connect to the local default instance of SQL Server. When you press Enter, a new prompt is displayed that shows the first line of a T-SQL batch along with a caret symbol:

```
SQLCMD /E /S WoodVista
1>
```

This indicates that you are now working in the SQLCMD environment rather than at the command prompt. It also lets you know that this is the first line in a batch process. SQLCMD runs all commands in batch mode and doesn't actually execute any commands until you explicitly tell it to, using the GO command. You can write as many lines of code as you want, but they will not be executed until the GO command is specified. You can think of the GO command very much the same as the Execute button on the SQL Editor toolbar. SQL batches are explained in detail in Chapter 4. For now, I'll continue to enter SQL commands and then type **GO** when I'm ready to execute the entire batch. Notice that the batch line number resets after every GO statement (Figure 3-22).

```
SQLCMD -E -S WoodVista
1>USE AdventureWorks2008
2>GO
Changed database context to 'AdventureWorks2008'
1>SELECT Name, ListPrice FROM Production.Product WHERE ProductID = 879
2>GO
Name                                                ListPrice
--------------------------------------------------- ---------
All-Purpose Bike Stand                              159.0000

<1 Rows affected>
1>
```

Although the SELECT command asked only to return two columns, the results used up most of my screen real estate. Each character type column will use the maximum number of allocated characters. This means that if you have a column defined as varchar(255), even if the actual data doesn't take up this much space, this column will require 255 characters of screen space, not allowing much room for anything else. Another drawback to using this interface for returning data is that little of the result set is held in memory after the query runs. You can scroll the command window up to view some text, but this is very limited.

The EXIT command is used to leave SQLCMD and return to a command prompt. Type **EXIT** again to close the command prompt window.

Writing Queries

Now that we have taken a look at the tools available, let's spend a little time using Management Studio to create queries.

Creating a query in SQL Server Management Studio involves defining a connection to a data source and opening an editor window. A query can be saved to a script file or simply used as a temporary workspace. To create a new SQL query, use the New Query button on the Standard toolbar, as shown in Figure 3-22.

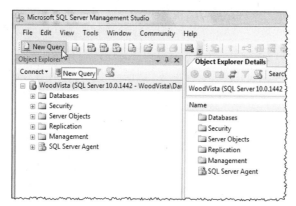

Figure 3-22

If you are presently connected to a server with the Object Explorer, a new Query window will open connected to that server. If you are connected to multiple servers with Object Explorer, the query window will open connected to whichever server was last selected. When working with multiple servers, be careful that the query window is associated with the correct server. Running ad-hoc code accidently on a production system can quickly get you into deep trouble with the DBA. If you are not connected to a server with Object Explorer, a connection dialog for the query window will open.

With the new query window open, you will probably need to specify the database you would like to use. If the database of interest was selected in Object Explorer when you opened the new query window, the window's database context will be set to it. If not, you will have to specify the database manually. You can do this in one of two ways. With a query window open, the SQL Editor toolbar is displayed with a drop-down list of available databases from the current data source (server), as shown in Figure 3-23. In the drop-down list, select the database you want to use. All the examples in this book use the AdventureWorks2008 database, but they will also work with SQL Server 2005 version of the database, regardless if it is running on SQL Server 2005 or 2008. Simply omit the 2008 from the names if you are not using the SQL Server 2008 version. Using the database drop-down list has the same effect as the second way of setting context — typing the SQL command **USE (*database_name*)**, as shown in following example.

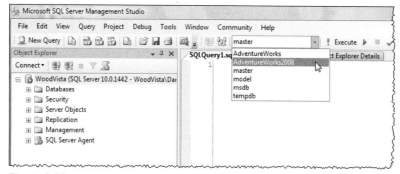

Figure 3-23

Now for a simple query: To set the database context and then list all the columns and rows in the Production.Product table, type the following SQL expression:

```
USE AdventureWorks2008
GO
SELECT * FROM Production.Product
```

After typing this text into the query window, run the query by either clicking the Execute button on the SQL Editor toolbar (that's the button with the red exclamation mark) or by pressing F5. When you do this, your computer will go to work and look up about 500 product records. While the query is running, a small, animated icon of a spinning green circle is displayed in the status bar at the bottom of the window. When it's done, summary information will be displayed with the running time and the number of records returned. The rows are displayed in a new window pane at the bottom of the Management Studio window. Although this is a very simple example, anything else that you would do to retrieve data, regardless of how complex, will be an extension of this simple exercise.

Scripting Options

SQL statements can be very verbose and often require a lot of typing. Much of this work can be minimized by letting the Management Studio do the work for you. Most common actions can be scripted automatically using a few simple menu selections. There are too many methods for scripting a query and too many actions to perform to demonstrate here. And the menu selections are, for the most part, self-explanatory. But the following Try It Out section should get you started.

Try It Out

1. Using the Object Explorer, expand the AdventureWorks2008 database and then the Tables folder. Under this folder, you will see a list of all the tables in the database. You want to generate a script to return all the columns in the Sales.SalesOrderDetail table.

2. Scroll down until you see Sales.SalesOrderDetail . Right-click this item and navigate through the menus, as shown in Figure 3-24. You want to generate a SELECT statement to read and return rows from the table. You also want to display the script in a new query window, so choose New Query Editor Window.

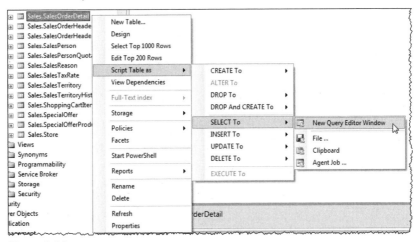

Figure 3-24

The SELECT statement is generated and displayed in a new window (see Figure 3-25). You should know that many options can affect the way a query looks on the screen but the way the code looks doesn't matter significantly to SQL Server. The automated script is formatted based on the creators of the scripting engine and is designed to make the script runnable in almost every environment. You should note a couple things about the format of this SQL script. The first thing to notice is the use of square brackets. Square brackets are used by the scripting engine to define object names. This is the defined behavior in case the object contains a reserved word, such as Transaction, or contains an embedded space, such as My Column. The use of square brackets is discussed in more detail in Chapter 4, but know that their use is optional. The only time that it is required to define an object name is when that object name contains an embedded space or reserved word. There are no names in this query that meet those criteria, so it really doesn't matter. Also, take a look at the line starting with the word "FROM." The script includes the database name, schema name, and then the table name separated by periods. The database name is optional when you have elected to set this as a current database. Auto-generated script is generally very descriptive. Another interesting feature of the editor window is that a colored line will appear to the left of the code indicating the status of the code. By default, new code will be indicated by a yellow vertical line. After the script is saved, however, the line turns green.

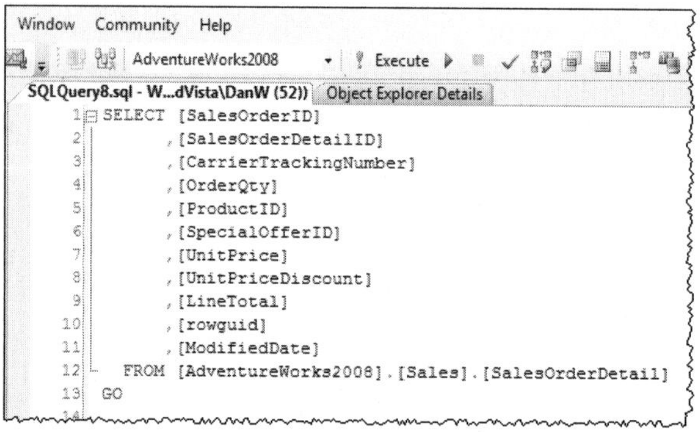

Figure 3-25

3. Finally, execute this query using the Execute button on the SQL Editor toolbar. After a few seconds the results will be displayed in a grid at the bottom of the window. Look at the status bar shown in Figure 3-26. More than 121,000 rows were returned in about 4 seconds. The time it takes to run a query will depend on several factors, of course, so your results might differ from my results.

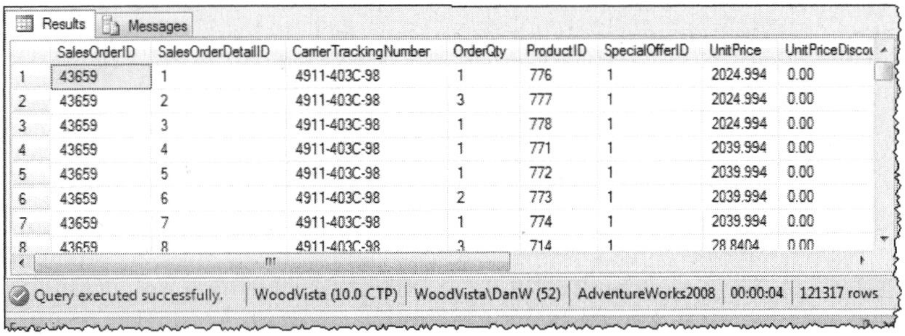

Figure 3-26

Using the Graphical Query Designer

The single-table queries written so far are fairly simple. Now you can start building a more complex query. To use the graphical query designer, right-click an empty query window and choose Design Query in Editor from the menu. If you need to edit existing query text, you can highlight the SQL and use this same technique to make changes using the query builder. The following Try It Out section demonstrates building a query using the AdventureWorks sample database.

Try It Out

1. Open a new query window by clicking the New Query button on the standard toolbar, which is located on the upper-left of Management Studio by default.

2. Set the database context to the AdventureWorks2008 database by choosing AdventureWorks2008 from the Available Databases drop-down on the SQL Editor toolbar (see Figure 3-27).

Figure 3-27

3. Right-click anywhere in the new query window and select the Design Query in Editor option (see Figure 3-28).

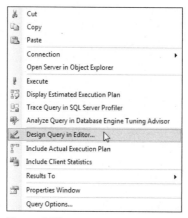

Figure 3-28

The Query Designer opens with the Add Table dialog to prompt you for the tables to be used in this query (see Figure 3-29). The tables listed are from the database context of the query window. If you forget to set the context, you may not see any tables or not see the tables you expected because the wrong database context is selected. Note that the schema names are displayed in parentheses following the table names. You can either double-click each table one at a time or hold down the Ctrl key and click to select multiple tables. For this exercise, choose the Product, ProductCategory, and ProductSubCategory tables to be added to this query. Click the Add button to add these tables to the query and then click Close when you're done.

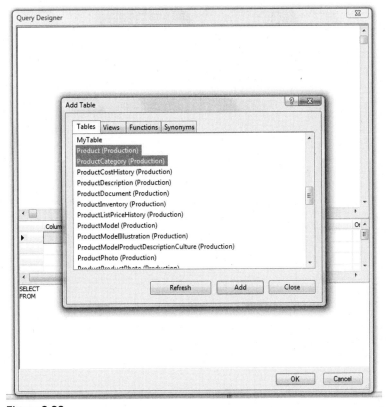

Figure 3-29

There are three panes in the designer window, each representing the query in a different way:

❑ Diagram pane

❑ Columns pane

❑ SQL pane

The three panes are synchronized, and changes made to the query in any one of these panes will be reflected in the others. A window graphically representing each table is placed into the top-most diagram pane of the designer. The graphical query designer draws lines from column names in each of these tables, with a diamond on each. This represents an inner join derived from the existence of corresponding relationships that exist in the database design. For example, in the definition for the ProductCategory table, a relationship, or foreign key constraint, is defined between the ProductCategoryID column and the ProductCategoryID column in the ProductSubCategory table. The Query Designer is smart enough to translate this relationship into a join statement between these tables. The diamond tells you that this is an inner join and that records will only be returned if corresponding values exist in the joined columns for both of these tables. Joins will be discussed in great detail in Chapter 8.

One thing that can be a little confusing when discussing your interaction with the columns pane is the use of the word "columns." Each column that is to be returned from the query is displayed as a row in the columns pane grid. It would be convenient if they could be referred to as "fields" rather than "columns"; however, the tool makes reference to "Columns" in the first column of the grid. This means that in our conversations regarding this interface, we are left to distinguish the columns (or fields) of the query from the columns in the grid, which represent attributes or characteristics to the query columns.

To choose columns to be returned, check the boxes in the table windows in the order that they appear in Figure 3-30. As you do this, these column names will be added to the columns pane and to the SELECT clause in the SQL pane. Note that there are three different Name columns between the three tables. Because the column names in a query must be unique, the designer creates aliased names for the ProductSubCategory and Product Name columns as Expr1 and Expr2. This satisfies this rule, but the aliases' names aren't exactly optimal.

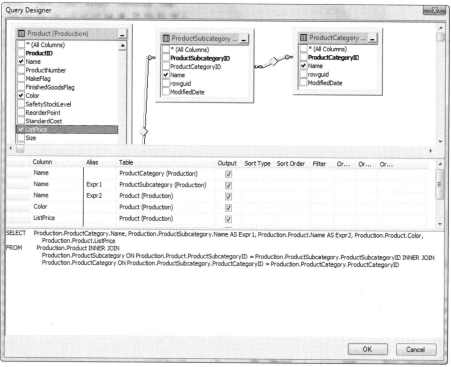

Figure 3-30

I'd prefer to use more intuitive names for the three Name columns. In the columns pane (second section of the designer), add or replace the text with the alias names from Figure 3-31. Call the ProductSubCategory.Name field "SubCategory," and the Product.Name field "Product." To be consistent, also change the alias of the ProductCategory.Name field to "Category." Finally, under the Sort Order column, type or select the values 1, 2, and 3 for the first three columns, respectively.

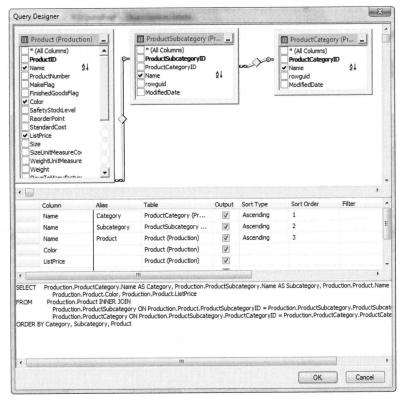

Figure 3-31

The query is now ready to be run. Click the OK button to transfer the script to the open query window. Click the Execute button and you should see rows returned in the results grid below your query window.

You can experiment by adding and removing columns and changing the sort order and alias names. I didn't intend to save this query as a script file, so if you close the query window, just indicate that you don't want to save changes.

The Query Designer is very useful for creating queries on databases that you are not very familiar with and even, at times, with ones you are familiar with. However, it does create what I call "ugly code." It is not particularly easy to read or edit. In Chapter 4, we will discuss formatting code in more detail, but for now take a look at the previous query the way the Query Designer wrote it:

```
SELECT      Production.ProductCategory.Name AS Category,
Production.ProductSubcategory.Name AS Subcategory, Production.Product.Name AS
Product, Production.Product.Color, Production.Product.ListPrice
FROM        Production.Product INNER JOIN
Production.ProductSubcategory ON Production.Product.ProductSubcategoryID =
Production.ProductSubcategory.ProductSubcategoryID INNER JOIN
Production.ProductCategory ON Production.ProductSubcategory.ProductCategoryID =
Production.ProductCategory.ProductCategoryID
ORDER BY Category, Subcategory, Product
```

Now look at the same query with some appropriate formatting:

```
SELECT   Production.ProductCategory.Name AS Category
       , Production.ProductSubcategory.Name AS Subcategory
       , Production.Product.Name AS Product
       , Production.Product.Color
       , Production.Product.ListPrice
FROM     Production.Product
INNER JOIN Production.ProductSubcategory
    ON Production.Product.ProductSubcategoryID =
       Production.ProductSubcategory.ProductSubcategoryID
INNER JOIN Production.ProductCategory
    ON Production.ProductSubcategory.ProductCategoryID =
       Production.ProductCategory.ProductCategoryID
ORDER BY Category
       , Subcategory
       , Product
```

We will fine-tune this formatting in the next chapter, but as you can see, the formatted code is easier to read and modify, which makes life much easier for the SQL programmer.

Using Templates

Unless you have a perfect memory, there will be many times in your journey with SQL Server that you will need some assistance. I'd say that about 98 percent of the SQL I write is from memory because the vast majority of the time, I need to do fairly common things: select, insert, update, delete, and so on. The rest of the time, I either need to jog my memory or learn to use a command I haven't had to use before. I have enough trouble just remembering the names of my kids let alone how to rebuild an index with a specific fill-factor. So, I'll either need to look this up in Books Online and/or go find an example. Most of the time, it's more helpful to see the script than it is to learn about the command and exactly how it affects the mechanics of the database engine. This is where script templates come in.

Script templates simply provide a starting point for queries. A template is really just a piece of script saved to a file that you open in the SQL Query Designer and then modify to suit your needs. The Templates Explorer window is optional. Use the View menu or Templates Explorer button on the toolbar to enable this window if it isn't already visible (see Figure 3-32). As mentioned earlier, templates are organized into categories. Simply expand the folder icons on the tree view to find the template you are looking for.

Figure 3-32

Now, create a query to add columns to an existing table. This is easy to do using a template. Find the folder for table-related templates, expand it, and then find the template labeled Add Column. Right-click this item to display the pop-up menu, and then select Open to use the template in a new query, as shown in Figure 3-33.

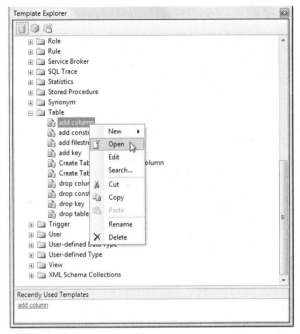

Figure 3-33

This action opens a new Query Editor window with a copy of the template. Note the color-coding used to help distinguish keywords, commands, and comments in the SQL text. With the skeleton of the query written for you, it's a fairly simple matter to replace the generic placeholders with your own text. In fact, there is a tool to help you do just that.

With the template script open, click on the Query menu and choose the Specify Values for Template Parameters item (see Figure 3-34).

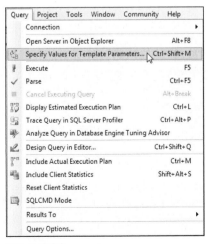

Figure 3-34

This opens a dialog that allows you to quickly replace all the template parameters with your own values (see Figure 3-35). In my example, I simply added some generic values for the table name and column name so that we could see the results of our work.

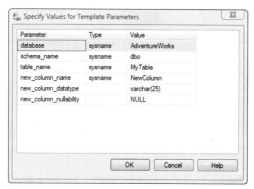

Figure 3-35

After clicking OK to close the Specify Values for Template Parameters dialog, you are ready to run the new script. As you can see in Figure 3-36, the script has been written and has incorporated the values specified earlier.

```
-- ===========================================================================
-- Add column template
--
-- This template creates a table, then it adds a new column to the table.
-- ===========================================================================
USE AdventureWorks
GO

IF OBJECT_ID('dbo.MyTable', 'U') IS NOT NULL
    DROP TABLE dbo.MyTable
GO

CREATE TABLE dbo.MyTable
(
    column1 int       NOT NULL,
    column2 char(10) NULL
)
GO

-- Add a new column to the table
ALTER TABLE dbo.MyTable
    ADD NewColumn varchar(25) NULL
GO
```

Figure 3-36

Using the Debug Feature

SQL Server 2000 had a very useful feature for debugging SQL stored procedures, but it was removed with the release of SQL Server 2005 and the change to the SQL user interfaces. With the release of SQL Server 2008, the debug feature is back and bigger and better than before. Now instead of just being able to debug stored procedures, you can run any SQL code through the debugger.

The debug feature is particularly useful for stepping through large batches of T-SQL code to ensure that the defined logic and data manipulation is handled in a way that is intended. Instead of attempting to step through a large and complicated script, which could become very confusing, I will show you the basics of the debug feature with a simple script that populates two variables. Although the script is simple, it does contain a couple of features that have not been adequately explained — functions and variables. Because both of these concepts will be explained in later chapters, I will not spend a great deal of time here defining them. Suffice it to say at this point that a variable is a named memory location that is assigned a specific data type. That memory location can be populated and modified by the SQL programmer through the use of SET and SELECT commands. A function is a programmatic object that when called always returns a value. It can optionally be passed in values to manipulate. This example uses the PI() function, which, as you would expect, returns the mathematical value of π (3.14159265358979).

The script that will be sent through the debug process is as follows:

```
DECLARE @Terra as float, @Description as varchar(20)
SET @Terra = 24901.55
SET @Description = 'Terra C Mi'
EXEC sp_who2
SELECT @Terra AS 'Distance', @Description AS 'Terra Defined'
SET @Terra = @Terra / PI()
SET @Description = 'Terra D Mi'
SELECT @Terra AS 'Distance', @Description AS 'Terra Defined'
```

Type the script in a new query window. Because we are not accessing a database in this example, it doesn't matter which database the query window's context is set to.

Now on the SQL Editor toolbar, click the green debug triangle (see Figure 3-37) or press Alt+F5 to begin the debugging process.

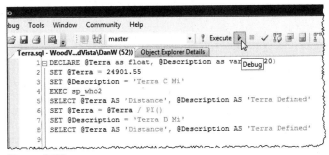

Figure 3-37

The script will be opened in a debug window with a cursor pointing to the first line of executable code (see Figure 3-38). In our case, that is the first SET statement.

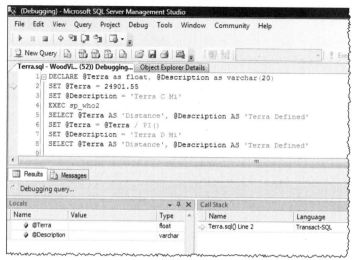

Figure 3-38

Notice in Figure 3-38 that the values for the two variables are empty. The variables have been declared at this point but not populated. Also note that the Debug toolbar has been enabled (see Figure 3-39).

Figure 3-39

The Debug toolbar has eight buttons by default, as described in the following table.

Feature	Purpose
Continue (Alt+F5)	Runs the remainder of the code until the next breakpoint or until the end of the code. (Breakpoints are described later in this section.)
Break All (Ctrl+Alt+Break)	Stops the code processing at its current position. It can be resumed with the Continue button.
Stop (Shift+F5)	Stops code execution and exits the debugger.
Select Next Statement	Moves the cursor to the next statement to be executed.
Step Into (F11)	Executes the next line of code. If the next line is a programming object, such as a stored procedure or user-defined function, the debugger opens the object so that each line of code in the object can be stepped through.
Step Over (F10)	Executes the next line of code. If the next line is a programming object, such as a stored procedure or user-defined function, the debugger executes the object in its entirety and moves to the next line of code in the calling code.
Step Out (Shift F11)	Used to return to the calling code after using the Step Into feature to step into a stored procedure or function. The Step Out feature runs the remaining lines of code in the programming object and returns to the next line of executable code.
BreakPoints	The Breakpoint button launches the Breakpoints window (see Figure 3-40), which enables the programmer to mark a portion of code for the debugger to break on. The purpose of this feature is to enable the programmer to run large portions of code that are known to be bug free and to break right before a problematic section of code in order to step through that code systematically. Breakpoints are added to code with the F9 key or by selecting Toggle Breakpoint on the Debug menu.

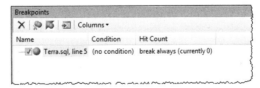

Figure 3-40

Now that you have a basic understanding of the debug features, let's step through our code. In Management Studio, click the Step Into button twice (see Figure 3-41) or press F11 twice to execute the next two lines of code that assign our variable values.

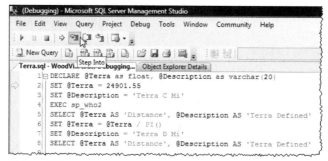

Figure 3-41

Notice that in the Locals window, which shows the value of variables, the variable @Terra has now been assigned a `float` number and the @Description has been assigned a string, or `varchar`, value. The Call Stack window also shows the new line that the cursor is on (see Figure 3-42).

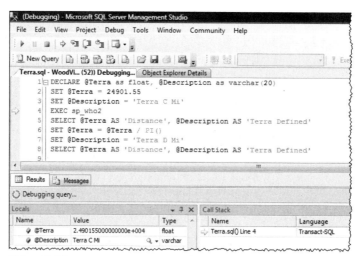

Figure 3-42

The next line of code in our script is one that executes the system stored procedure sp_who2, which returns information about all or one connection presently active on the server. When we step into the EXEC sp_who2 line of code, we will be stepping in to the sp_who2 code. Click the Step Into button once to step into the sp_who2 stored procedure. Notice that the code that makes up the stored procedure has been opened in a new query window (see Figure 3-43) and now it is possible to step through each line of code in the sp_who2 stored procedure. Click the Step Into button several times to step through the different sections of the stored procedure.

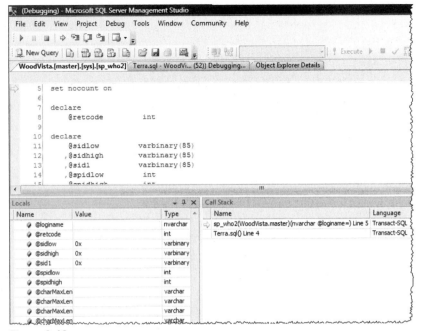

Figure 3-43

Because we can be fairly certain that there are no bugs in the sp_who2 system stored procedure, we can click Step Out or press Shift+F11 to run the rest of the stored procedure and return to the next line of executable code in our calling code.

What happens when you know that large portions of your code are problem free and you want to focus on the sections of code that are problematic? That's where breakpoints come in. Breakpoints can be placed only on lines of executable code, which essentially means that on that line the code has to *do* something. Declaring variables or placing comments in code does not count.

Place a breakpoint in the code by clicking line 7 of the code and pressing F9 (see Figure 3-44). A red ball appears to the left of that line of code. In very large scripts it is advantageous to use breakpoints to quickly run through the majority of code by clicking the Continue button. The code will be executed until the breakpoint is encountered. In our particular example, the cursor is sitting on Line 5. You can now click the Continue button to advance the cursor to the breakpoint (see Figure 3-45).

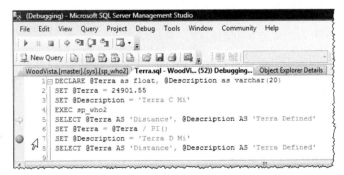

Figure 3-44

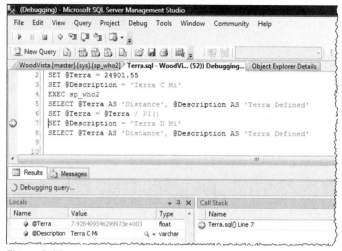

Figure 3-45

As shown in Figure 3-45, also note that the values in the Locals window have been updated. Click the Continue button one more time to execute the remaining lines of code. Notice that the debugger exits and the typical query result window is displayed with the results of the code (see Figure 3-46).

Notice that the results window shows the result of the sp_who2 stored procedure and the SELECT statements in the code.

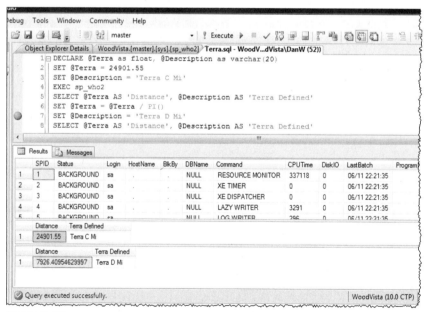

Figure 3-46

Summary

I could have written a complete book about the features of the SQL Server client and management tools. The application is very rich and very powerful. Even after using it for the past few years, since SQL Server 2005 was in early beta, I continue to find new aspects of the application that make my life as a development DBA much easier. However, in this book you get just a taste, albeit a fairly thorough one, of all the aspects and options available with the SQL Server 2005 and 2008 toolset.

In this chapter you learned what you will need to know to write SQL queries and choose the best tool for the job. Depending on your role and objectives, you will use different tools to do different things.

If you are a database administrator, you will invariably spend some time using the SQL Configuration Manager to configure servers and manage the services that comprise SQL Server. You will also spend much of your time using SQL Server Management Studio to secure databases, create, monitor, and tune various database objects, and occasionally use the SQLCMD utility to run SQL scripts on the command line.

If you are an architect or solution designer, you may use the SQL Server Management Studio to diagram and generate database objects and the SQL Query Editor to create stored procedures, functions, and views to optimize database access. You may also use Microsoft Visio and the advanced solution design tools in Visual Studio and the Business Intelligence Studio to design and manage database projects.

If you are an application developer, you will likely spend most of your time developing software and creating integrated stored procedures and views in the Visual Studio integrated database design environment, and using SQL Server Management Studio to create and manage database objects.

It's often difficult to draw a clear distinction between these roles anymore. This is why these tools are tightly integrated and contain overlapping features and capabilities. Fortunately, they have been designed to work together and provide a consistent user experience. Once you have mastered Management Studio, for example, you should be able to open the Business Intelligence Studio and work comfortably with the menus, toolbars, tool windows, and similar features.

As you read on, I will make reference to some of these other tools, but you will spend most of your time using the SQL Server Management Studio. To use the T-SQL language, you don't need to be concerned about the features of a particular design application, but you will find these features useful when you go to design entire database solutions, debug queries, and tune database objects.

Exercises

The exercises for this chapter and Chapter 4 provide numbered, step-by-step instructions. The solutions for these exercises are the final query, commands, or result and are located in Appendix F. The exercises for subsequent chapters provide less-detailed instructions. You should use the material in each chapter to determine the appropriate steps and to find the solutions. The instructions specify the AdventureWorks2008 database, but will also work for the SQL Server 2005 version of the database and the SQL Server 2005 database engine.

Exercise 1

1. Using SQL Server Management Studio, create a new query using the AdventureWorks2008 database.

2. Add the Product table to the designer.

3. Select the ProductID, Name, and ListPrice columns by checking the corresponding boxes in the table window.

4. Sort the results by the Name column in ascending order using the Sort Type option.

5. Check the SQL expression in the third pane of the graphical query designer with the solution.

Exercise 2

1. Using SQL Server Management Studio, create a new query using the AdventureWorks2008 database, as you did in Exercise 1.

2. Add two tables: Product and ProductSubCategory.

3. For the ProductSubCategory table, select the Name column and create an alias for it named SubCategory. For the Product table, select the Name column and create an alias for it named ProductName. Also select the ListPrice column from this table.

4. Sort the query by the ProductSubCategory Name column and then the Product table Name column, both in ascending order.

5. Execute the query and scroll through the results. Check the SQL expression displayed with the solution.

Exercise 3

Write a simple query using the Query Editor window in SQL Server Management Studio using the following steps:

1. Open SQL Server Management Studio.

2. Enter **localhost** for the server name (or enter the name of your server, if connecting remotely).

3. Create a new query and select the AdventureWorks2008 database from the database selection list in the toolbar.

4. Enter the following SQL script in the query window:

```
SELECT * FROM Production.Product WHERE ListPrice > 3000
```

5. To find out how many products have a list price greater than $3000, execute this query, and check the row count in the status bar.

Exercise 4

Execute a simple query using command-line utilities:

1. Use the SQLCMD utility to utilize Windows Integrated (Enterprise) security. Each statement should be followed by a batch delineation (GO) command.

2. Indicate that you want to run statements using the AdventureWorks2008 database.

3. Execute the following SQL statement and view the results:

```
SELECT ProductCategoryID, Name FROM Production.ProductCategory
```

4. Exit the command-line utility and then the command window.

5. Check your statements with the solution.

Introducing the T-SQL Language

In the early days of relational databases, a number of industry-wide efforts were made to unify different, proprietary query languages. IBM had established an early standard called *Structured English Query Language*. This name was condensed to spell the word *SEQUEL*. Another effort resulted in a language called *Select Query Language* (SQL), which included commands allowing data to be read only for reporting and record look-up. This became a popular, product-independent standard to which the "Sequel" acronym was still applied by members of the database community. Eventually, additional commands were added, enabling records to be added, deleted, and modified. This created a quandary: they had worked so hard to create a standard language with a cute name that no longer fit. The word *Select* was finally replaced with the word *Structured*, and the universe was once again brought back to a state of balance. Of course, the purists will insist that SQL is pronounced ESS CUE EL, rather than "SEQUEL." So, how should you pronounce it? Any way you want. Disagree if you like, but I save one syllable and say "SEQUEL." For the SQL language to survive outside of a specific product or company, the standard was published and held by an independent standards organization. The SQL standard was originally registered with the American National Standards Institute and officially called the *ANSI SQL* standard, established in 1986. This standard has been revised a few times, resulting in revisions known as the following:

- ❑ ANSI SQL-86
- ❑ ANSI SQL-89
- ❑ ANSI SQL-92
- ❑ ANSI SQL:1999
- ❑ ANSI SQL:2003
- ❑ ANSI SQL:2006

The concept seems quite simple but there is a little more to this story. The ANSI SQL standard is actually no longer held exclusively by the American National Standards Institute. This is a common tale of American-born standards that are later implemented internationally. In 1987,

SQL became an international standard and was registered with the International Organization for Standardization (ISO) using its previously copyrighted title, ANSI SQL. This means that the 1992 revision of the SQL standard is actually known as *ISO ANSI SQL-92*. Even though the standard was updated in 1999, 2003, and 2006, most SQL-based database products had been established on the ANSI SQL-92 standard, and they have not been revised to fully conform to the ANSI SQL-99, 2003, or 2006 specifications. Like most of its competition, T-SQL does not fully conform to any of the more recent ANSI versions, but it does implement many of the selected features.

Finally, the ANSI SQL standard actually defines three conformance levels: Entry, Intermediate, and Full. Most products, including SQL Server, conform entirely to the entry-level standard and partially to the higher levels.

The Nature of SQL

Many people who work with T-SQL have had some experience with other languages. If you've never done any programming, please don't close the book at this point and give up. This is certainly not a prerequisite for writing SQL, but it is a reference point for many who have worked with computer systems in other capacities.

Comparing T-SQL to a procedural or object-oriented programming language (such as Java, C, C++, C#, or Visual Basic) is like comparing apples to pomegranates. It's not better than or worse than, but quite different than, a true programming language — even though you may see some similarities in the syntax and structure of certain statements. For different types of operations, T-SQL may be far superior or much worse than these languages, simply because of what it is designed to accomplish. One of the challenges in making broad statements about the capabilities of different languages is that as they continue to grow and evolve, version after version, additional capabilities are added. The problem with industry standards is that everyone is out to protect and enhance their own product. Over time, the capabilities of each technology (or language, in this case) begin to overlap, leaving us with a number of different options to perform the same tasks.

Is it possible to perform data access or data manipulation (to insert, modify, or delete values in a database) with a procedural programming language without using SQL? Yes, but it's cumbersome and usually inefficient. Can you perform complex mathematical operations, looping, string parsing, or multidimensional array management in T-SQL? Certainly, but it won't be a very good experience. Chapter 1 mentioned that SQL Server 2005 gives programmers the capability of writing stored procedures and user-defined functions entirely in object-oriented program code, rather than SQL. This doesn't make T-SQL any less capable as SQL Server's native query language. It simply gives programmers another option.

T-SQL is designed primarily to work with relational data. No big surprise here. Secondarily, T-SQL also has a number of useful capabilities for working with scalar (single value) data, logical operations, mathematics, decision structures, text string parsing, and looping mechanisms. However, compared with most programming languages, SQL is not as powerful or as capable as a true programming language. If your needs call for advanced functionality that may be outside the realm of SQL's native capabilities, you may need to carefully consider using a different approach, such as a custom, extended, stored procedure, application programming interface (API), .NET assembly, or other programming solution. This is why SQL Server's Integration Services can utilize both programming code and T-SQL. With that settled, what can you do with T-SQL? Quite a lot. What should you do with T-SQL? That's an even better question. I hope to give you a good idea by the time you finish this chapter.

T-SQL is the language used to talk to SQL Server, and query expressions are essentially used to ask the server to do things. It's important to know what you can ask for — and what SQL Server can do. Query operations are divided into three different categories. I'll briefly describe them and then take some time to look at specific examples. Like everything else in the technical world, these categories are best known by three-letter abbreviations (that's TLA, for short.) Locally, these fall in the order I've listed here:

❑ **Data Definition Language (DDL)** — DDL statements are used to create and manage the objects in a database. They can be used to create, modify, and drop databases, tables, indexes, views, stored procedures, and other objects.

Examples include CREATE, ALTER, and DROP.

❑ **Data Control Language (DCL)** — DCL statements control the security permissions for users and database objects. Some objects have different permission sets. You can grant or deny these permissions to a specific user or users who belong to a database role or Windows user group.

Examples include GRANT, REVOKE, and DENY.

❑ **Data Manipulation Language (DML)** — DML statements are used to work with data. This includes statements to retrieve data, insert rows into a table, modify values, and delete rows.

Examples include SELECT, INSERT, UPDATE, and DELETE.

Where to Begin?

Where should we begin? This is one of those chicken and egg questions. Before you can query data, you have to have it stored somewhere. I think it would be a bit distracting to start from the very beginning and step through the entire process to create a new database. For simplicity's sake, I'd like to start out working with data stored in an existing database so we don't get too far off topic. I'll cover DDL and DCL statements, used primarily for database construction and administration, at the end of this chapter.

You'll be working with the AdventureWorks2008 sample database. The versions of this database that Microsoft includes with SQL Server 2005 and SQL Server 2008 are a bit different in content, but the same in structure. The SQL Server 2008 version was updated to better normalize the data, but in most cases the data returned from either database will be very similar.

Because you've already learned the basics of using the Query Editor in SQL Server Management Studio, I'm not going to be giving you specific instructions regarding the use of the tool. The purpose here is to focus on the language. If you need to, review these instructions in Chapter 3. To begin, open the SQL Server Management Studio Query Editor and connect to your database server.

Data Manipulation Language

The basic statements of Data Manipulation Language (DML) are introduced in this chapter with elaboration to follow in later chapters.

You can do only four things with data. You can *Create* records, *Read* them, *Update* record values, and you can *Delete* records. That spells *CRUD* — we do CRUD with data. Cool, huh? When SQL was devised, they chose to use different words for these four operations: *Insert, Select, Update*, and *Delete*. Somehow,

ISUD isn't quite as easy to remember as CRUD. If you can master these four types of statements, you will be able to do just about anything with data using SQL.

Queries Have Layers

In the movie *Shrek*, Mike Myers' character, Shrek the Ogre, explains to his friend Donkey that "Ogres are like onions — they have layers." To some degree, the SELECT statement is like an Ogre, or rather it's like an onion — it has layers. On the surface, there isn't that much to it. However, when you start peeling back the layers, there's quite a lot to it. You've likely discovered this fact on your own. Here's the important point: it's not complicated. It's really just layers upon simple layers. The fundamentals are quite simple. I call this principle *compounded simplicity.*

Before I can effectively introduce the next topic, I need to jump the gun a little bit and briefly discuss the SELECT statement. This statement is covered thoroughly in Chapter 5. For now, it's important to understand that to return data from tables in SQL Server, you will use the SELECT statement. In relational databases, information gets transformed into data, typically by storing it in multiple tables. It would stand to reason, then, that to turn data back into useful information it must be retrieved from multiple tables. This is accomplished by using a handful of techniques: joins, subqueries, and unions. You learn more about these topics in future chapters. For now, know that these represent the bulk of the work you will do as you create and use queries.

Here's a simple example. When the following query runs, the query processor parses the query and breaks it down into individual steps.

```
SELECT TOP 10 Production.Product.Name
              ,Sales.SalesOrderDetail.LineTotal
FROM Production.Product
INNER JOIN Sales.SalesOrderDetail
   ON Production.Product.Productid = Sales.SalesOrderDetail.ProductID
WHERE Sales.SalesOrderDetail.SpecialOfferID = 1
ORDER BY Sales.SalesOrderDetail.LineTotal DESC
```

The different steps are covered in detail in Chapter 14, but for now it is sufficient to understand that the query processor works the query essentially from the bottom up, excluding the row ordering. The first thing that happens is the query processor looks at the filter, which in this case is SpecialOffer=1. Then it proceeds to figure out how best to return the product name and line total for all products sold with the special offer.

The low-level instructions used to process these steps are compiled into executable instruction code and cached in-memory so that subsequent executions don't require the same degree of preparation and resource overhead. Depending on whether this query is part of an ad-hoc SQL statement or a saved database object, the compiled instructions may also be saved to permanent storage, improving efficiency in the long term.

Set-Based Operations

When SQL Server processes a SELECT command, it builds a structure in memory to return a result set. This structure, essentially a two-dimensional array of rows and columns, is known as a *cursor*. The word "cursor" is an acronym for **CUR**rent **S**et **O**f **R**ecords. As such, it represents the entire set of rows returned from a table or query. SQL Server's query-processing engine is built on a foundation of cursor processing and is optimized to work with data as a set of records, rather than individual rows.

Row-Based Operations

A technique more popular in other database products is to populate a cursor type variable from a SELECT query and then step through each row. You can do this in SQL Server, but it generally works against the query-processing engine. Whenever possible, it is advisable to work with set-based results rather than trying to process individual rows. That being said, row-level cursor operations certainly have their place. That place, however, is rarely transactional code. The cursor object and its place in the grand scheme of things are discussed more thoroughly in Chapter 13.

Query Syntax Basics

The term *query* is a bit misleading. Normally, you would think of a query as a question. People often will associate the term *query* with a SELECT statement in T-SQL. However, whether the T-SQL contains a SELECT, UPDATE, DELETE, or INSERT statement, it is still a query. A query is like a sentence; it must to be a complete statement with at least a subject and a verb. The semantic rules of SQL define a simple structure. You start with a clause that states what you intend to do: Select, Insert, Update, or Delete — these are the verbs. You also must define the columns or values to be returned. Usually, you will indicate the table or other database object you want to work with — this is the subject or noun. Depending on the type of operation, there are connecting words such as From and Into.

You'll learn about each of these statements in greater detail later but, for now, some simple examples follow. If you want to retrieve all of the column values from all rows in the Product table, you would execute the following query:

```
SELECT * From Production.Product
```

If you need to raise the cost of all product records by 10 percent, this statement would work:

```
UPDATE Production.Product SET StandardCost = StandardCost * 1.1
```

The T-SQL language is very forgiving when it comes to formatting statements. The SQL Server query-processing engine doesn't care about whether commands are in upper- or lowercase. It doesn't care about spaces, tabs, and carriage returns as long as they don't interfere with the name of a command or value. This means that you can format your script for readability just about any way you like. For example, the following query returns product sales information for a range of dates, sorted by product category and subcategory. The query could be written like this:

```
SELECT Production.ProductCategory.Name AS Category, Production.
ProductSubCategory.Name AS SubCategory, Production.Product.Name AS
ProductName ,Sales.SalesOrderHeader.OrderDate, Sales.SalesOrderDetail.
OrderQty, Sales.SalesOrderDetail.UnitPrice
FROM   Sales.SalesOrderHeader INNER JOIN Sales.SalesOrderDetail ON
Sales.SalesOrderHeader.SalesOrderID = Sales.SalesOrderDetail.SalesOrderID
INNER JOIN Production.Product ON Sales.SalesOrderDetail.ProductID = Product.
ProductID INNER JOIN Production.ProductSubCategory ON Production.Product.
ProductSubCategoryID = Production.ProductSubCategory.ProductSubCategoryID
INNER JOIN Production.ProductCategory ON Production.ProductSubCategory.
ProductCategoryID = Production.ProductCategory.ProductCategoryID
WHERE Sales.SalesOrderHeader.OrderDate BETWEEN '1/1/2003' AND '12/31/2003'
ORDER BY Production.ProductCategory.Name, Production.ProductSubCategory.Name,
Production.Product.Name
```

Or, it could be written like this:

```
SELECT Production.ProductCategory.Name AS Category
     ,Production.ProductSubCategory.Name AS SubCategory
     ,Production.Product.Name AS ProductName
     ,Sales.SalesOrderHeader.OrderDate
     ,Sales.SalesOrderDetail.OrderQty
     ,Sales.SalesOrderDetail.UnitPrice
FROM   Sales.SalesOrderHeader
     INNER JOIN Sales.SalesOrderDetail
        ON Sales.SalesOrderHeader.SalesOrderID =
           Sales.SalesOrderDetail.SalesOrderID
     INNER JOIN Production.Product
        ON Sales.SalesOrderDetail.ProductID = Product.ProductID
     INNER JOIN Production.ProductSubCategory
        ON Production.Product.ProductSubCategoryID =
           Production.ProductSubCategory.ProductSubCategoryID
     INNER JOIN Production.ProductCategory
        ON Production.ProductSubCategory.ProductCategoryID =
           Production.ProductCategory.ProductCategoryID
WHERE Sales.SalesOrderHeader.OrderDate BETWEEN '1/1/2003' AND '12/31/2003'
ORDER BY Production.ProductCategory.Name
        ,Production.ProductSubCategory.Name
        ,Production.Product.Name
```

Obviously, the second query is easier to read and would be much easier for someone to look at and figure out what's going on. It's entirely up to the T-SQL programmer to make sure the code is formatted for readability. The first example was very messy, but I took the time to format the second example so that it was easy to read. However, we're not done yet. The code is still messier than it needs to be. To clean up the code and remove the redundant schema and table references, we will use table aliases. To do this, you simply create an alias after the table is referenced for the first time in the FROM or JOIN clauses. An alias is sort of like a nickname. You simply give the object a new name by placing the nickname after the object's given name, as shown in the following example:

```
SELECT PC.Name AS Category
     ,PSC.Name AS SubCategory
     ,P.Name AS ProductName
     ,SOH.OrderDate
     ,SOD.OrderQty
     ,SOD.UnitPrice
FROM   Sales.SalesOrderHeader AS SOH
     INNER JOIN Sales.SalesOrderDetail AS SOD
        ON SOH.SalesOrderID = SOD.SalesOrderID
     INNER JOIN Production.Product AS P
        ON SOD.ProductID = P.ProductID
     INNER JOIN Production.ProductSubCategory AS PSC
        ON P.ProductSubCategoryID = PSC.ProductSubCategoryID
     INNER JOIN Production.ProductCategory AS PC
        ON PSC.ProductCategoryID = PC.ProductCategoryID
WHERE SOH.OrderDate BETWEEN '1/1/2003' AND '12/31/2003'
ORDER BY PC.Name
        ,PSC.Name
        ,P.Name
```

Referencing columns from aliased tables can be confusing, depending on who wrote the code. The official rule is that the only columns that require the table alias are those that are ambiguous — or more simply, ones that appear in multiple tables. So, technically we could write our query like this:

```
SELECT PC.Name AS Category
      ,PSC.Name AS SubCategory
      ,P.Name AS ProductName
      ,OrderDate
      ,OrderQty
      ,UnitPrice
FROM   Sales.SalesOrderHeader AS SOH
    INNER JOIN Sales.SalesOrderDetail AS SOD
        ON SOH.SalesOrderID = SOD.SalesOrderID
    INNER JOIN Production.Product AS P
        ON SOD.ProductID = P.ProductID
    INNER JOIN Production.ProductSubCategory AS PSC
        ON P.ProductSubCategoryID = PSC.ProductSubCategoryID
    INNER JOIN Production.ProductCategory AS PC
        ON PSC.ProductCategoryID = PC.ProductCategoryID
WHERE SOH.OrderDate BETWEEN '1/1/2003' AND '12/31/2003'
ORDER BY PC.Name
        ,PSC.Name
        ,P.Name
```

Note that in this example the OrderDate, OrderQty, and UnitPrice columns are not labeled as far as their source table is concerned. Personally, I don't believe this is a good practice. The reason being is that if you are not familiar with the database structure, it is very difficult to figure out where the OrderDate, OrderQty and UnitPrice columns are coming from. Are they in the SalesOrderHeader table or the SalesOrderDetail Table? In my opinion, you should always provide the source table or table alias with the column name whenever your query references more than one table.

As I mentioned in the previous chapter, the AS keyword is almost always optional. Most SQL programmers I have worked with use them for column aliasing but not for table aliasing. Using the AS keyword with columns makes the code much easier to read. Using the keyword with Tables definitely doesn't hurt readability either, but whether it helps is a matter of personal taste. The important thing is to be consistent.

By now you have also probably noticed that whenever a T-SQL keyword is used, it is written in all uppercase. This is by no means a requirement. T-SQL is very indifferent to how you write your code, as long as the words are spelled correctly. However, this flexibility should not be used as an excuse to write poorly formatted code. Properly well-formatted code is easy to read and easy to debug. But because both uppercase and lowercase statements are acceptable, a query could be written as follows:

```
select Name, StandardCost from Production.Product
```

Although the preceding statement would execute just fine, it's not quite as easy to read as the following:

```
SELECT Name, StandardCost FROM Production.Product
```

This is especially true if you happen to be using a tool that does not color code the T-SQL. Also, there will be times when you are dealing with data in a database that has been configured to be case-sensitive. In that case, selecting from the product table will raise an error if the name of the table is Product.

The last things I want to discuss about formatting are indenting and commas. Indenting makes the code easy to read and gives it a professional look. You may not think that is very important, but when you have to look at as much code as I do every day, you soon learn to appreciate those programmers who put the extra effort into making the code as easy to read as possible. As for commas, you will probably have noticed that when a list spans more than one line I have placed the comma at the beginning of the line and not the end. This probably goes against everything you learned in school. Commas, of course, go at the end of a line, not the beginning. In T-SQL there is a very good reason for placing commas at the beginning of a line. It makes it very easy to remove or comment out that line during the course of development. For example, using the previous example, what happens if we decide to comment out or remove the UnitPrice column so that the price value is not returned by the query (code commenting is covered in a later section in this chapter)?

```
SELECT PC.Name AS Category
      ,PSC.Name AS SubCategory
      ,P.Name AS ProductName
      ,SOH.OrderDate
      ,SOD.OrderQty
--      ,SOD.UnitPrice
FROM    Sales.SalesOrderHeader AS SOH
    INNER JOIN Sales.SalesOrderDetail AS SOD
        ON SOH.SalesOrderID = SOD.SalesOrderID
    INNER JOIN Production.Product AS P
        ON SOD.ProductID = P.ProductID
    INNER JOIN Production.ProductSubCategory AS PSC
        ON P.ProductSubCategoryID = PSC.ProductSubCategoryID
    INNER JOIN Production.ProductCategory AS PC
        ON PSC.ProductCategoryID = PC.ProductCategoryID
WHERE SOH.OrderDate BETWEEN '1/1/2003' AND '12/31/2003'
ORDER BY PC.Name
        ,PSC.Name
        ,P.Name
```

By placing the double-dash in front of the UnitPrice field, it is effectively removed from the query. However, if the commas were at the end of the line, I would have broken the query since there would be a trailing comma with no additional columns specified.

```
SELECT PC.Name AS Category,
       PSC.Name AS SubCategory,
       P.Name AS ProductName,
       SOH.OrderDate,
       SOD.OrderQty,
--       SOD.UnitPrice
FROM    Sales.SalesOrderHeader AS SOH
...
Msg 156, Level 15, State 1, Line 7
Incorrect syntax near the keyword 'FROM'
```

Naming Conventions

There seems to be a universal concept that anything that can be very simple and uncomplicated *must* become confusing and overly complicated. When a database is created, objects should be named according to some kind of sensible naming convention. There is no industry-wide standard, and people have different ideas about appropriate naming conventions. Most folks perceive this as a simple matter of common sense, so they don't put much effort into it. The problem with common sense is that it's not very common and everyone seems to have their own idea about what is sensible.

It would be very convenient to have one simple standard to follow, and if things were that simple, I'd tell you exactly what to do. Most of it is quite easy, but object naming is a bit of an art. There are many considerations. For example, it's a good idea to use names that are descriptive and complete, describing the purpose of each object. On the other hand, you should keep names short and simple so users don't have to do a lot of extra typing. These are conflicting directions.

A general rule of thumb when creating objects in SQL Server is that if the Query Editor turns the color of the name from black to any other color, you should probably avoid using it. However, you will quickly learn that Microsoft violates this rule repeatedly with the names it gives to both system objects and sample objects in the AdventureWorks2008 database. Also keep in mind that the Query Editor changes the color of all words it has been configured to recognize. These words include SQL reserved words, functions and system objects, ODBC reserved words, and even future reserved words. So, not all words that change color are really reserved words. For example, the word "Description" turns blue when typed into an open query window. It can still be used without any special handling, but Management Studio recognizes it as a potential reserved word.

Some older database products don't support mixed-case names or names containing spaces. For this reason, many database administrators continue to use all lowercase names with words separated by underscores. Personally, I find mixed-case names a little easier on the eyes.

Trends come and go. With Windows 95, Microsoft promoted the use of long filenames. Microsoft Access, which was developed at about the same time, also promoted the use of long database object names. From a certain perspective, it makes sense to use friendly, sentence-like, descriptive names. The fact is that SQL Server will have no problem with names containing spaces, but other components of a solution may have issues with this. As values are handled at different levels of an application, they may move from the controls in the user interface to variables in the program code, then to the method parameters or properties of a class. Eventually, these values are passed into a stored procedure as parameters or as field names in a SQL statement. The point is that it is much easier on everyone involved if these items all have the same, or very similar, names.

You could argue that there would be no harm in using space-filled field names in the database and similar names, sans spaces, elsewhere — and you'd probably be right. The general belief among database professionals is that spaces don't belong in object names. Frankly, this is probably more of an issue of perception, rather than technical feasibility. However, writing code that references objects with embedded spaces is prone to errors and application exceptions. If you want to stay on friendly terms with the application developers who create programs to access your database, avoid embedded spaces.

I've done a lot of one-man solution development where I create the database, write the software components, design and develop the user interfaces, and write all the program code to glue the pieces together. Even in these applications, it's easy to get lost if related object names aren't the same. I have always insisted that they be consistent throughout the entire solution. I've also worked on some fairly large, complex projects where the database was designed by someone else long ago. If the names aren't clear and concise in the beginning, I'm faced with a quandary: change the names in my program code to something easier to understand (accepting that they don't match the table and field names), or consistently apply the same cryptic and confusing names throughout the entire solution.

It's not uncommon for a database designer to model and create tables, applying his or her own naming standards to table and field names. After this person has moved on to a different job, another database expert comes in and adds stored procedures. He might disagree with the names applied by the original designer, so he names the procedures and input parameters differently than the fields in the table. Along comes an outside consultant developing software components, and he uses abbreviated names for the related class properties that correspond to the fields and parameters. Later, a junior-level software developer is assigned to create a user application for the data. He takes a class or reads a book about appropriate object naming standards and decides to fix the problem by applying his own names in spite of those that already exist. Coincidentally, I just finished modifying some report queries today. I had designed the tables these reports used. In testing, I discovered that performance wasn't ideal and decided to build another table with pre-aggregated data. Another database designer stepped in to help and named some of the columns differently than mine. For example, I have a column named FiscalMonthYearNumber and his was FiscalMonthNum. Is this a big deal? Not really, but it does require that I fix the queries for all of my reports.

There is no easy solution to this common problem. Ideally, the person who designs the database should carefully consider the impact of the names chosen and document them thoroughly. This sets the standard for all those who follow — and all names should remain consistent. I typically use mixed-case names, capitalizing each word and concatenating them. In programming circles, this is often referred to as *Pascal case*, named after the Pascal programming language. The following table shows a few common naming standards with some of the history and pros and cons regarding each.

Naming Standard	Example	Description
Pascal Case	CustomerFirstName	All words are capitalized and concatenated without delimiting characters.
Camel Case	customerFirstName	All characters are lowercase except the first letter of each word after the first word. This standard is common in XML element names but not as common in database object naming.
Hungarian Notation	VcCustomerFirstNamemstr CustomerFirstName	Objects are prefixed with characters used to denote data type and/or scope. This standard is more common in programming code than in database object naming. True Hungarian Notation can be very complicated and verbose.
Lower-Case, Delimited	customer_first_name	Comes from legacy database products that don't support mixed-case names. Still commonly used due to backward compatibility and tradition.
Long Names	Customer First Name	Promoted in Microsoft products such as Access. Has the advantage of being readable but not commonly used in serious software solutions. Incompatible with related programming code.

Object Delimiting

As I have previously discussed, it is probably best to avoid using embedded spaces or reserved words when creating objects. However, you will undoubtedly encounter databases where the designer did not adhere to this best practice. For example, I currently work with a database that has an audit table named "Transaction." Transaction is most definitely a reserved word and should not have been used. To make things worse the table has a column named Timestamp and another one named LineNo. The table was obviously created by a developer using visual tools because creating it any other way would have been problematic. Here is a simplified version of the table creation script:

```
CREATE TABLE Transaction
(TransactionId bigint NOT NULL
,Timestamp datetime NOT NULL
,Service varchar(75) NOT NULL
,LineNo int )
```

If you attempt to run this script, it will fail with the following error:

```
Msg 156, Level 15, State 1, Line 1
Incorrect syntax near the keyword 'Transaction'
```

In order to create the table successfully, the keywords in its definition must be delimited. SQL Server supports two types of delimiting characters: square brackets and double quotes. In the following example you see how to delimit the objects with square brackets:

```
CREATE TABLE [Transaction]
(TransactionId bigint NOT NULL
,[Timestamp] datetime NOT NULL
,Service varchar(75) NOT NULL
,[LineNo] int )
```

In the next example, double quotes are used to delimit the object names:

```
CREATE TABLE "Transaction"
(TransactionId bigint NOT NULL
,"Timestamp" datetime NOT NULL
,Service varchar(75) NOT NULL
,"LineNo" int )
```

By default, Management Studio sets the connection property of new query windows to support double-quote delimiting, but it can be turned off. If it is turned off, double quotes will be considered illegal operators. The code to set double-quote support on and off is as follows:

```
SET QUOTED_IDENTIFIER ON
...
SET QUOTED_IDENTIFIER OFF
```

If you type in the table definition for the Transaction table in the example, you will also notice that the word "Service" is blue as well as the other delimited keywords. "Service" is a keyword in SQL Server; however, it is one of those keywords like "Description" that can be used and not delimited.

The other types of names that must be delimited are those with embedded spaces. I don't believe embedded spaces should ever be used in object names, but I am sure there are very smart people who would disagree. In my experience, they complicate an already complex technology. So, while you could create a table with the following code, why would you?

```
CREATE TABLE [My long named table that holds customer data]
([Customer data key] int NOT NULL
,[Customer Last Name] varchar(75) NOT NULL
,[Customer First Name]varchar(75)
)
```

Writing an interface to access a table with this type of naming structure will be problematic at best. As I mentioned before, SQL Server's flexibility should not be used as an excuse to write bad code or create objects that will create more problems than they are worth.

You will notice as you use Management Studio's scripting tools that SQL Server delimits all objects. This is not because it is necessary or even the best way to write code. It was just easier to wrap all objects in delimiters than to write a scripting engine that had to look for objects that required delimiting.

Commenting Script

When you write SQL script, it will inevitably be easy to read and understand — at the time you write it. Programming is something we do in a certain context. When I work on a project, my head is in that project and most everything makes perfect sense at the time. I once developed a database application for a consulting client. A few different people had been involved in writing queries and program code over a few months. They asked me to come back in to create some new reports. As I opened the project and read through the code, I found it difficult to understand the logic. In my frustration, I said, "I don't understand what is going on in this code. Who wrote this?" My customer replied to my dismay, "That's your code. You wrote it last year." Needless to say, I was embarrassed as well as frustrated.

I learned a valuable lesson: comment everything. No matter how plain the logic seems. No matter how much sense it makes at the time, it probably won't make so much sense to the next person who reads it, especially months or years later. If nothing else reminds you of this simple lesson, just remember this: Every one of us leaves a legacy. Other query designers and programmers will remember you for what you leave behind for them to maintain. They will most likely either remember you for making their job difficult or for making their job easier.

T-SQL comments come in two forms. One is a block comment and the other is an in-line comment. Block comments are very often used in header blocks. A header block is a formal block of text that precedes every scripted object, such as a stored procedure or user-defined function. It should conform to a standard format and should contain information such as the following:

- ❑ The name of the scripted object
- ❑ The name of the designer or programmer
- ❑ Creation date
- ❑ Revision dates and notes
- ❑ Information about what the object does and how it's called
- ❑ Validation testing and approval notes

Block comments begin with a forward slash and at least one asterisk (/*) and end with an asterisk and a forward slash (*/). Everything in between is treated as a comment and ignored by the query parser. A header block doesn't need to be complicated. It should just be consistent. Here's an example of a simple header block preceding the script for a stored procedure used to insert product records:

```
/***************************************************************************
 *    spInsProduct - Inserts product records
 *
 *    Accepts ProductName, StandardPrice, QtyInStock, CategoryID
 *    Returns new ProductID, Int
 *
 *    Created: 6-12-08 (Paul Turley)
 *
 *    Revisions:
 *    7-10-08 - (Dan Wood)      Added MarkupPercent parameter
 *    7-12-08 - (Paul Turley)   Changed MarkupPercent parameter data type from
 *                              int to decimal(10,2)
 ***************************************************************************/
```

In-line comments are placed in the body of the script to document the process and flow along with the actual script. Comments are preceded by two hyphens (--). The query parser ignores the remainder of the line. In-line comments can be placed after the executable script on the same line or can be written on a separate line, as you can see in the following example:

```
CREATE PROCEDURE spGetProductHistory
-- Define date parameters, set NULL defaults to make parameters optional
  @StartDate datetime = NULL
 ,@EndDate datetime = NULL
AS
--Check date values. If NULL set default dates to cover entire product history
  IF @StartDate IS NULL
     SET @StartDate = '1900-01-01'
  IF @EndDate IS NULL
     SET @EndDate = GETDATE()

     -- Return all product history for defined time period
     SELECT PC.Name AS Category
           ,PSC.Name AS SubCategory
           ,P.Name AS ProductName
           ,SOH.OrderDate
           ,SOD.OrderQty
--         ,SOD.UnitPrice
        FROM   Sales.SalesOrderHeader AS SOH
        INNER JOIN Sales.SalesOrderDetail AS SOD
          ON SOH.SalesOrderID = SOD.SalesOrderID
        INNER JOIN Production.Product AS P
          ON SOD.ProductID = P.ProductID
        INNER JOIN Production.ProductSubCategory AS PSC
           ON P.ProductSubCategoryID = PSC.ProductSubCategoryID
        INNER JOIN Production.ProductCategory AS PC
           ON PSC.ProductCategoryID = PC.ProductCategoryID
        WHERE SOH.OrderDate BETWEEN @StartDate AND @EndDate
     ORDER BY PC.Name
           ,PSC.Name
           ,P.Name
```

Note that in this example the comments are used by the programmer to tell anyone coming along afterward what the script is meant to do. If in doubt, add a comment. If not in doubt, add one anyway. Don't worry about overdoing it. Granted, some of your script will make sense without commenting and may be somewhat self-documenting, but don't take a chance. Don't listen to yourself when that little voice says, "Don't worry about commenting your code now. You can do it later." Maybe you're more disciplined than I am, but if I don't write comments when I'm writing code, it won't get done. In fact many books on writing good programming code insist that comments should be written first without writing any actual code. This is sometimes inaccurately referred to as *pseudo code.* After you have several comment blocks and in-line comments, you go back in and fill in the actual code. Using our previous example the code would look like the following example prior to writing the actual code:

```
CREATE PROCEDURE spGetProductHistory
-- Define date parameters, set NULL defaults to make parameters optional
-- Check date values. If NULL set default dates to cover entire product history

    -- Return all product history for defined time period
```

Another important application of in-line comments is as temporary development notes both to myself and to others. Inevitably, on the first pass through my script, I'm most concerned about getting core functionality working. Exceptions to basic logic, problem workarounds, error-handling, and less-common conditions are usually secondary to just getting the code to work once under ideal conditions. As I consider all of these secondary factors, I make notes to myself that may include to-do items and reminders to go back and add clean-up code and polished features.

In addition, there invariably will be times when building large scripts when you want to prevent certain lines of code from executing — either to locate faulty code or to prevent code from running that is unnecessary — but for documentation sake the code is left behind, but commented out. Again, there are two ways of commenting out code: block comments and in-line comments. Generally, in-line comments are the preferred method of commenting out sections of code. SQL Server Management Studio makes this easy by providing both a keyboard and button shortcut to comment out any highlighted code. Simply highlight the section of code that you want to disable or *comment out,* and then click the Comment Selection button on the SQL Editor toolbar (see Figure 4-1). If you would rather use the keyboard shortcut, simply highlight the section of code and then press Ctrl+K and then Ctrl+C. To uncomment the selection, click the Uncomment button or press Ctrl+K and then Ctrl+U.

Figure 4-1

Using Templates

Management Studio provides a very useful, and often underutilized, feature called *templates.* Templates provide a starting place for a variety of database object scripts. Several templates come with SQL Server and adding your own is an easy task. In Chapter 3, you learned how to use the script template features in Management Studio. In reality, a template is just a text file containing SQL commands and placeholders for object names. Using a template can save considerable time and effort, especially when writing script that you may not use very often.

Template scripts provide a basic pattern to get you started. If you'd like to create your own templates, this is very easy to do. Simply write the script in a new query window and then select File ⇨ Save As to save it to a Template SQL file.

Template files saved to the standard template folders will be added to the available templates for SQL Management Studio. In a default SQL Server installation, these folders are found in the following locations:

Version	Templates Folder Path
SQL Server 2005	C:\Program Files\Microsoft SQL Server\90\Tools\Binn\VSShell\Common7\IDE\sqlworkbenchnewitems\Sql
SQL Server 2008	C:\Program Files\Microsoft SQL Server\100\Tools\Binn\VSShell\Common7\IDE\sqlworkbenchnewitems\Sql

Generating Script

The term *script* simply refers to a bunch of SQL statements typically used together to perform some useful purpose. This could vary from a simple SQL query to a group of several queries and commands used to create an entire database. The SQL Server client and administrative tools (Management Studio and Visual Studio) have the ability to generate script for just about any object or combination of objects. You can even generate the script to re-create an entire database. Scripts are usually saved to a file with a .sql extension and are simply plain text. You could easily create or edit a script file with Notepad or any other text editor.

Managing Script

I suggest that you have a designated folder for your script files. I usually create a folder for each database project or application I'm working on. I will also make it a point to back up and archive the script files in these folders. Just like program source code, my scripts are treated like gold. Especially for the programming objects in your database (views, functions, and stored procedures), these objects should be scripted and saved on a CD or protected network folder. This practice will be invaluable in case (make that *when*) something goes wrong.

Version Control

One of the greatest challenges in managing scripts is how to keep track of multiple versions of the same file. The natural order of application development involves prototyping a feature, working through iterations of design, testing, and debugging until the feature is stable. At this point, it is important to keep a copy of the working SQL script and program source code before any changes are made. Adding features and capabilities to a query or programming object nearly always has adverse effects, at least in the short term. The secret to success is to script and save your queries and objects to script files after you get them working.

On many occasions, I have been asked to make some minor change or enhancement to a project. It may involve adding a column to a table or just adding a calculation to a query. If the changes are not scripted and rigorously tested, they will inevitably have some unforeseen impact. Perhaps my customer calls in a panic to inform me that she's getting an error, it's the end of the month, and they can't print invoices. These are not the kind of calls you want to take.

Making minor changes often seems like a good idea at the time. If objects were originally scripted before making any changes, it's usually a simple task to either review the original script or make corrections, or to run the original script, returning the query to its previous, working state. Script version management is not complicated, but without having a system in place and making a deliberate effort to follow it, it's easy to lose track of your changes.

A few simple approaches to version control exist. Version control software, such as Microsoft Visual SourceSafe, automates this task by storing files in a central database. As files are checked out and checked in, a separate copy is time-stamped and stored in the SourceSafe database. Any version of the file can then be retrieved at any time. Source control is the best bet if a group of people will be sharing script files and working on different, networked development computers. SQL Server Management Studio integrates with Visual SourceSafe or Visual Studio team System as well as a number of third-party source control applications. Much like Visual Studio, files can be checked out, checked in, and managed from within the Management Studio design environment.

A less-sophisticated approach is to simply append filenames with the date they are created and the initials of the person creating them. Keep these files in project-related folders and back them up regularly. The following are examples of the script files for a stored procedure called `spGetCustomerAccountDetail`:

- ❏ Create spGetCustomerAccountDetail – 7-02-07 PT.sql
- ❏ Create spGetCustomerAccountDetail – 7-09-07 DW.sql
- ❏ Create spGetCustomerAccountDetail – 7-11-07 PT.sql
- ❏ Create spGetCustomerAccountDetail – 7-15-07 PT.sql
- ❏ Create spGetCustomerAccountDetail – 8-03-07 DW.sql

Data Definition Language

If you have used Management Studio, Visual Studio, Access, or any other tools to create and design SQL Server databases, you have used Data Definition Language (DDL) — perhaps not directly but by using these user interface tools to manage database objects. Nearly all database maintenance operations are scripted and then that script is executed. This is one reason why there are so many scripting options in the SQL Server management tools. The scripting engine has been there for years in one form or another.

This is a simple topic because you can do only three things with any database object: create it, modify it, or delete it. The table that follows lists the corresponding DDL statements.

Statement	Description
CREATE	Used to create a new object. This applies to many common database objects, including databases, tables, views, procedures, triggers, and functions.
ALTER	Used to modify the structure of an existing object. The syntax for each object will vary, depending on its purpose.
DROP	Used to delete an existing object. Some objects cannot be dropped because they are schema-bound. This means that you will not be able to drop a table if it contains data participating in a relationship or if another object depends on the object you intend to drop.

The syntax of DDL statements is quite simple. A quick tour through each of the common database objects and an example for each follows. Because this isn't a database programming book, we won't be exploring the nuances and uses for these objects, but the syntax used to manage them.

Creating a Table

In its simplest form, to add a new table to the current database, you specify the table name and then list the table's new columns in parentheses, followed by their data type. Here's an example:

```
CREATE TABLE Appointment
 (  AppointmentID    int
    ,Description      varchar(50)
    ,StartDateTime    datetime
    ,EndDateTime      datetime
    ,Resource         varchar(50) NULL
 )
```

You can specify several options for each column definition. Briefly, this might include options such as auto-sequencing identity, default values, constraints, and whether the column value may be set to Null. For a complete list of options, check the SQL Server Books Online documentation.

Creating a View

A view is similar to a table in that users can select from a view like a table, and, in some cases, update or delete values as well. Views are stored in the database, but they don't really store data. A view is really just a SELECT query that gets optimized to make it execute more efficiently than if you were to make up the query every time you wanted to select data. However, views can do some very interesting things that we're not going to get into (like actually storing data.). They can be indexed and they can be used with other programming objects to make SQL Server do some very powerful things. Enough for now. The finer points of views are discussed in Chapter 13.

When you create a view, you're really just naming a SELECT statement. The syntax looks like this:

```
CREATE VIEW vwProductByCategory
AS
SELECT PC.Name AS Category
      ,PSC.Name AS SubCategory
      ,P.Name AS Product
FROM    Production.ProductCategory PC
INNER JOIN Production.ProductSubcategory PSC
   ON PC.ProductCategoryID = PSC.ProductCategoryID
INNER JOIN Production.Product P
   ON P.ProductSubcategoryID = PSC.ProductSubcategoryID;
```

Creating a Stored Procedure

Stored procedures can perform a wide range of actions and business functionality. For example, a stored procedure can insert, update, or delete records in a table. By passing parameter values, it can make decisions and either select data or perform other operations accordingly. Because stored procedures can be used in so many unique ways, it's hard to exemplify a "typical" stored procedure. The syntax for creating a stored procedure is similar to that of a view. Note the input parameters defined just before the word AS:

```
/**********************************************************
 *   Checks for existing Product record
 *   If exists, updates the record.  If not,
 *   inserts new record
 **********************************************************/
CREATE PROCEDURE spInsertOrUpdateProduct
   -- Input parameters --
   @ProductName nvarchar(50)
  ,@ProductNumber nvarchar(25)
  ,@StdCost money
AS
   IF EXISTS(SELECT *
               FROM Production.Product
               WHERE ProductNumber = @ProductNumber)
      UPDATE Production.Product
        SET NAME = @ProductName, StandardCost = @StdCost
      WHERE ProductNumber = @ProductNumber
   ELSE
      INSERT INTO Production.Product
      (Name, ProductNumber, StandardCost)
      SELECT @ProductName
            ,@ProductNumber
            ,@StdCost
```

Creating a Trigger

Creating a trigger is similar to creating a stored procedure. Actually, a trigger is a special type of stored procedure that gets executed when specific operations are performed on the records in a table (such as an Insert, Update, or Delete). Business logic similar to that of a standard stored procedure may be performed within a trigger, but it is typically used to apply specialized business rules to ensure data integrity. Some of the unique characteristics of triggers include their assignment to a DML operation (Insert, Update, and/or Delete), implicit transaction control, and virtual table references that are used to represent the record or records involved in the transaction that caused the trigger to fire.

In the following example, note the reference to a virtual table called Deleted. This "table" is actually a virtual set of rows that are in the process of being deleted as the trigger is automatically executed. There is no script to explicitly begin processing a transaction because the trigger execution is the result of a transaction in progress. The ROLLBACK TRANSACTION command affects this inherent transaction and prevents the delete operation from being completed.

```
/*******************************************************
   Checks for existing sales orders using
   the product being deleted.
   Prevents deletion if orders exist.
*******************************************************/
CREATE TRIGGER tr_DelProduct
ON Production.Product
FOR DELETE
AS
  IF (SELECT Count(*)
      FROM Sales.SalesOrderDetail
      INNER JOIN Deleted
        ON SalesOrderDetail.ProductID = Deleted.ProductID) > 0
  BEGIN
    RAISERROR ('Cannot delete a product with sales orders',14,1)
    ROLLBACK TRANSACTION
    RETURN
  END
```

Creating a User-Defined Function

User-defined functions are used to apply custom business logic such as performing calculations, parsing values, and making value comparisons. Functions are often called within views and stored procedures to reduce code redundancy and to encapsulate functionality. The script used to create a new user-defined function is similar to that of a stored procedure. The function is defined on the first executable line of the script (preceded in this example by a comment block). Immediately following the CREATE command, the function name references one or more parameters followed by a data type, in parentheses. The text following the Returns keyword indicates the data type that the function will return. This is a simple scalar (single value) function that returns a datetime type value. In Chapter 10, you also learn how user-defined functions can return complex, multi-value results and table-type result sets, similar to a view or stored procedure. This function utilizes local variables and system functions to perform its internal logic.

```
/*******************************************************
 Returns a date representing the last date
 of any given month.
*******************************************************/
CREATE Function dbo.fn_LastOfMonth(@TheDate datetime)
Returns datetime
AS
BEGIN
```

(continued)

(continued)

```
DECLARE @FirstOfMonth  datetime
DECLARE @DaysInMonth int
DECLARE @RetDate datetime
SET @FirstOfMonth = DATEADD(mm, DATEDIFF(mm,0,@TheDate), 0)
SET @DaysInMonth = DATEDIFF(d, @FirstOfMonth, DATEADD(m, 1, @FirstOfMonth))
RETURN  DATEADD(d, @DaysInMonth - 1, @FirstOfMonth)
END
```

Scripting Practices

When scripting objects, a common practice is to check for the existence of the object before creating it. Although this isn't necessary when you know the object isn't already in the database, if you generate script using SQL Server Management Studio, logic is typically included to remove the object if it exists and then re-create it. Keep in mind that dropping and re-creating an object will remove any security privileges that have been granted to users. If you simply need to modify an object to add capabilities, it may be advisable to use the ALTER command rather than DROP followed by the CREATE command. A number of different scripting options can be used to customize auto-generated script, and many of the non-default options may be unnecessary.

Every SQL Server database contains a number of standard system views that provide information about the different objects in a database. This information is known as *metadata*. Ask any database professional to define metadata and you will undoubtedly get the same response: "Metadata is data about data." Although this definition is technically correct, it is also pretty much useless in defining what metadata really is. The problem with defining metadata is that metadata is contextual. Depending on how you are looking at the information changes its context. It can be metadata or just data. For example, is the name of the columns on the Production.Product table data or metadata? In the context of the table, it is metadata, but if you were to query the sys.columns system view, the names become data, as the query in Figure 4-2 shows.

SQLQuery4.sql - ...Vista\DanW (53))* | Object Explorer Details

```
1 SELECT *
2 FROM sys.columns
3 WHERE [object_id] = OBJECT_ID('Production.Product');
4
```

Results | Messages

	object_id	name	column_id	system_type_id	user_type_id	max_length	precision	scale	collation_name
1	1717581157	ProductID	1	56	56	4	10	0	NULL
2	1717581157	Name	2	231	260	100	0	0	SQL_Latin1_General_CP1_CI_AS
3	1717581157	ProductNumber	3	231	231	50	0	0	SQL_Latin1_General_CP1_CI_AS
4	1717581157	MakeFlag	4	104	258	1	1	0	NULL
5	1717581157	FinishedGoodsFlag	5	104	258	1	1	0	NULL
6	1717581157	Color	6	231	231	30	0	0	SQL_Latin1_General_CP1_CI_AS
7	1717581157	SafetyStockLevel	7	52	52	2	5	0	NULL
8	1717581157	ReorderPoint	8	52	52	2	5	0	NULL
9	1717581157	StandardCost	9	60	60	8	19	4	NULL
10	1717581157	ListPrice	10	60	60	8	19	4	NULL
11	1717581157	Size	11	231	231	10	0	0	SQL_Latin1_General_CP1_CI_AS
12	1717581157	SizeUnitMeasureCode	12	239	239	6	0	0	SQL_Latin1_General_CP1_CI_AS
13	1717581157	WeightUnitMeasureCode	13	239	239	6	0	0	SQL_Latin1_General_CP1_CI_AS
14	1717581157	Weight	14	106	106	5	8	2	NULL
15	1717581157	DaysToManufacture	15	56	56	4	10	0	NULL

Figure 4-2

So, yes, metadata is data about data. But more important, it is data that describes other data and gives it context.

You can get a lot of useful information about your database from these views. The following script searches the sys.objects system view to find out if the Person.Address table exists in the current database. If it does exist, the DROP statement is conditionally executed to delete the table.

```
IF  EXISTS (SELECT * FROM sys.objects
              WHERE object_id = OBJECT_ID('Person.Address')
                AND type in (N'U'))
DROP TABLE Person.Address
GO
```

A line of script may fail for a variety of reasons. Because of referential constraints and other dependencies, tables must be dropped in the right order. In case the table isn't successfully dropped, it may be a good idea to check again for the existence of the table before attempting to create it. This is performed in the following script:

```
IF NOT EXISTS (SELECT * FROM sys.objects
                 WHERE object_id = OBJECT_ID('Person.Address')
                   AND type in (N'U'))
BEGIN
  CREATE TABLE Person.Address(
   AddressID int IDENTITY(1,1) NOT NULL
  ,AddressLine1 nvarchar(60) NOT NULL
  ,AddressLine2 nvarchar(60) NULL
  ,City nvarchar(30) NOT NULL
  ,StateProvinceID int NOT NULL
  ,PostalCode nvarchar(15) NOT NULL
  ,Rowguid uniqueidentifier ROWGUIDCOL  NOT NULL
  ,ModifiedDate datetime NOT NULL)
END
```

As useful as they are, system views didn't appear to be designed for ease of use or readability, so they can be somewhat cryptic. Another problem if you use system views is that there are no guarantees that they won't change in later versions of SQL Server, possibly breaking your code if you were to upgrade and migrate your database. In lieu of directly querying system views, a set of views is provided with SQL Server to simplify the structure and data in the system views. These *information schema views* are available in each database. Essentially, these views are just saved queries that extract information from the underlying system views, but the data is formatted and cleansed so that it's easy to read and query. Each view is prefixed with the name INFORMATION_SCHEMA, followed by a period and a general object type. In place of the script in the previous example, which selects from the sys.objects table, a similar script may be used with the INFORMATION_SCHEMA.TABLES view, such as in the following:

```
IF  EXISTS (SELECT *
              FROM INFORMATION_SCHEMA.Tables
              WHERE TABLE_NAME = 'Address'
                AND TABLE_SCHEMA = 'Person')
    DROP TABLE Person.Address
  GO
```

As Figure 4-3 shows, the output and query of the information schema view is much simpler and straightforward. Appendix D contains a reference for the information schema views included with SQL Server.

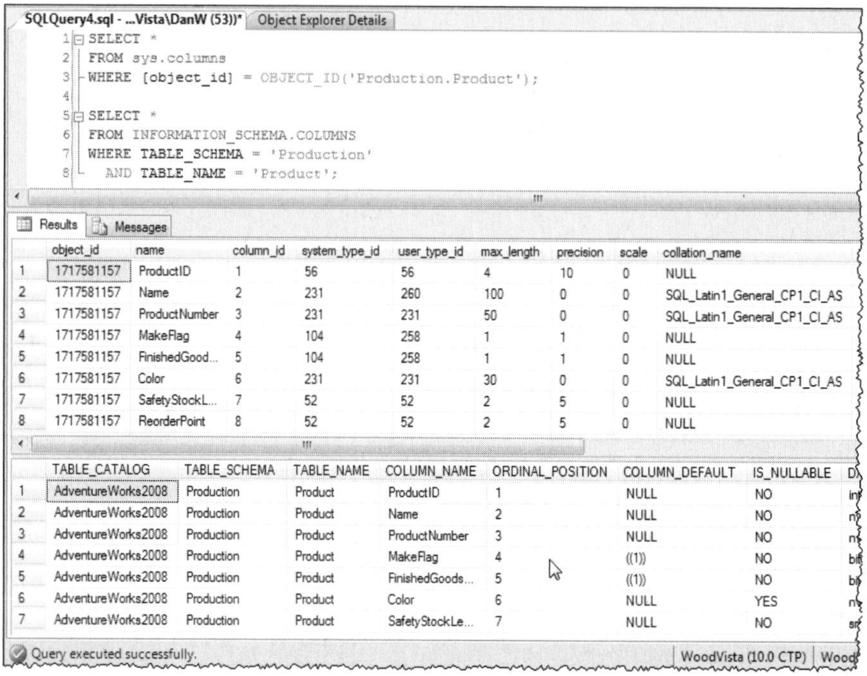

Figure 4-3

Altering Objects

The script used to modify some existing objects is very similar to the syntax used to create objects, using the ALTER command in place of CREATE. This is the case for objects that contain SQL expressions such as views, stored procedures, and user-defined functions. The following script is very similar to the example used to demonstrate how to create a stored procedure. An additional input parameter and error handling have been added.

```
/************************************************************
 *    Checks for existing Product record
 *    If exists, updates the record.  If not,
 *    inserts new record
 *    Revised: 2-12-08 Dan Wood
 ************************************************************/
ALTER PROCEDURE spInsertOrUpdateProduct
  -- Input parameters --
   @ProductName nvarchar(50)
  ,@ProductNumber nvarchar(25)
  ,@StdCost money
  ,@ListPrice money
AS
```

```
BEGIN TRY
    BEGIN TRANSACTION
        IF EXISTS(SELECT *
                    FROM Production.Product
                    WHERE ProductNumber = @ProductNumber)
            UPDATE Production.Product
              SET NAME = @ProductName, StandardCost = @StdCost
            WHERE ProductNumber = @ProductNumber
        ELSE
            INSERT INTO Production.Product
            (Name, ProductNumber, StandardCost, ListPrice)
            SELECT @ProductName
                  ,@ProductNumber
                  ,@StdCost
                  ,@ListPrice
    COMMIT TRANSACTION
END TRY
BEGIN CATCH
    DECLARE @ErrMsg varchar(1000)
    SET @ErrMsg = ERROR_MESSAGE()
    ROLLBACK TRANSACTION
    RAISERROR(@ErrMsg, 14,1)
    RETURN
END CATCH
```

After the ALTER statement has been executed, the object retains all of its previous properties and security access privileges or restrictions, but its definition is updated with any of the script changes. This includes the comment block before the ALTER statement line.

Some objects require different syntax used to alter their definition than the language used to create them. For example, when creating a table, columns are defined within parentheses after the table name. To alter the design of a table and change the columns, you would use the ADD or DROP keyword before each column definition. Any existing columns that are not addressed in the ALTER TABLE script remain in the table's definition.

```
ALTER TABLE Appointment
ADD  LeadTime smallint NULL
```

Each column or constraint change must be performed in a separate ALTER TABLE statement. For example, if my goal was to add the LeadTime column and to drop the Resource column, this can be performed using the previous and next statements but can't be done in a single statement.

```
ALTER TABLE Appointment
DROP COLUMN Resource
```

Dropping Objects

Why is it that the most dangerous commands are the easiest to perform? Dropping an object removes it from the database catalog, completely deleting it from the database. Tables containing data and their related indexes are de-allocated, freeing the storage space for other data. To quote a well-known former president of the United States, "Let me make one thing perfectly clear" — there is no Undo command in SQL Server. If you have dropped an object or deleted data, it's gone.

The syntax for dropping all objects is the same: `DROP objecttype objectname`. Here are a few examples of script used to drop the objects I previously created:

```
DROP TABLE Appointment
DROP VIEW vwProductOrderDetails
DROP PROCEDURE spInsertOrUpdateProduct
DROP TRIGGER TR_Del_Product
DROP FUNCTION dbo.fn_LastOfMonth
```

Some objects cannot be dropped if there are dependent objects that would be affected if they no longer existed. Examples are tables with foreign key constraints, user-defined types, and rules. This safety feature is called *schema binding*. Some objects don't enforce schema binding by default but it can be created to explicitly enforce this rule. Views, stored procedures, and user-defined functions can optionally be created with schema binding and prevent orphaned dependencies. This feature is discussed in greater detail in Chapter 12.

Data Control Language

Data Control Language (DCL) is by far the simplest subset of the SQL language. The goal of DCL is to manage users' access to database objects. After the database has been designed and objects are created using DDL, a security plan should be implemented to provide users and applications with an appropriate level of access to data and database functionality, while protecting the system from intrusion. Access privileges can be controlled at the server or database level, and groups of privileges can be assigned to individual users and to groups of users who are assigned role membership. Although database security involves simple concepts, it is not a task to be approached in a haphazard manner. It's important to devise a comprehensive plan and to consider all of the business requirements and the organization's security standards when devising a database security plan.

SQL Server recognizes two separate security models. These include SQL Server Security, where roles and users are managed entirely within the database server, and Integrated Windows Security, which maps privileges to groups and users managed in a Windows-based network system. This topic is discussed in greater detail in Chapter 16, but some of the basic principles are explained in this section.

The easiest way to think about permissions is in layers. Because users can have memberships to multiple roles, they may have a mixed set of privileges for different database objects. Like placing multiple locks on a door, a user can only gain access to an object if all restrictive permissions are removed and they have been granted access through at least one role membership. Using the lock analogy, if you had a key to one of three locks, you would not be able to open the door. Likewise, if a user is a member of three roles, two of which are denied access to an object, access won't be allowed even if it is explicitly granted. The user must be either removed from the restrictive roles or these permissions must be revoked.

In short, DCL consists of three commands that are used to manage security privileges for users or roles on specific database objects:

❑ The GRANT command gives permission set to a user or role.

❑ The DENY command explicitly restricts a permission set.

❑ The REVOKE command is used to remove a permission set on an object.

Revoking permissions removes an explicit permission (GRANT or DENY) on an object so that permissions that may have been applied at a less-specific level are used. Before permissions can be applied to objects, users and roles are defined. SQL Server provides a set of standard roles for both the database server and for each database. You learn how to manage permissions for roles and users in Chapter 13.

Following are some examples. This statement grants SELECT permission to the user Paul on the Production.Product table:

```
GRANT SELECT ON Production.Product TO Paul
```

Tables and views have permissions to allow or restrict the use of the four DML statements: SELECT, INSERT, UPDATE, and DELETE. Stored procedures and functions recognize the EXECUTE permission. On tables, views, and functions, permissions can also be given or restricted on a user's ability to implement referential integrity, using the REFERENCE permission. The REFERENCE permission means that if a user is given access to a table that has a foreign key defined on it that references another table, the user will need access to the other table. At a minimum the permission is REFERENCE.

This example grants EXECUTE permission to members of the db_datawriter built-in role but denies this permission to a user named Martha:

```
GRANT EXECUTE ON spAddProduct TO db_datawriter
DENY EXECUTE ON spAddProduct TO Martha
```

Multiple permissions can be applied on an object by placing permissions in a comma-delimited list, as in the following:

```
GRANT SELECT, INSERT, UPDATE ON Production.Product TO Paul
```

An important aspect to remember about SQL Server security is that SQL Server does not enforce logical combinations of permissions. For example, assume that user Paul is a member of a security role called Authors and the following DCL scripts are executed:

```
GRANT UPDATE ON dbo.PublishedBooks TO Authors
DENY SELECT ON dbo.PublishedBooks TO Paul
```

Because Paul is a member of the Authors role, he inherits the UPDATE permission granted to that role. He was also specifically denied the SELECT permission on the table PublishedBooks. The logical assumption would be that Paul could not update the PublishedBooks table, but this assumption would be wrong. Paul cannot update any specific rows due to this permission combination so the following command would fail:

```
UPDATE PublishedBooks
  SET Author = 'Paul Turley'
WHERE BookID = 222
```

However this command would succeed:

```
UPDATE PublishedBooks
  SET Author = 'Paul Turley'
```

125

Because the WHERE expression is, in essence, a SELECT command that is processed prior to the update, Paul is prevented from making the change. Unfortunately, Paul is a savvy SQL user, and he knows that by updating all the rows in the table he circumvents the denied SELECT permission and changes all the published book records to show that he is the author. The moral to this story is to use care and planning when applying permissions.

This short discourse should have provided a cursory introduction to the concepts and practices of DCL. As previously mentioned, like database design, security is a matter that should be carefully planned and implemented in a uniform and standard approach. It's usually best to have a small number of database administrators charged with the task of security to keep tight reins over how privileges are applied for users of a database.

Summary

By now, you should have a good understanding about what the T-SQL language is used for and how it is implemented with Microsoft SQL Server. You learned that T-SQL is a dialect of the Structured Query Language, based on the industry-wide ANSI SQL standard.

Three categories of statements within SQL are used to define and manage a database and the objects contained therein, to control access to data and database functionality, and to manage the data in a database. Data Definition Language (DDL) encompasses the CREATE and ALTER statements, used to define database objects. Data Control Language (DCL) is used to manage security access and user privileges to data and database objects. Finally, Data Manipulation Language (DML) is the subset of SQL you will typically use most often. DML contains the SELECT, INSERT, UPDATE, and DELETE statements and several variations of these statements that you will use to populate tables with records, modify, remove, and read data values. The SELECT statement has several modifiers and additional commands and clauses you will use to do useful things with, and make sense of, the data stored in a database.

The SQL Server database engine uses intelligent logic to process queries as efficiently as possible. The query parser and optimizer translate a SQL query into distinct operations, which are then compiled into low-level machine instructions. This compiled execution plan is cached in memory and can be stored permanently within the database with database programming objects to run more efficiently.

You also learned about the proper way to write SQL script, using comments and naming standards. Script can be saved in script files for safekeeping and templates can be used to save time and effort when writing new queries.

This chapter, along with the first three chapters, is the foundation on which more specific topics are based. As you move forward, you will be using the scripting techniques discussed here and the tools you learned to use in Chapter 2. The rest of the book focuses on specific types of queries and objects.

Exercises

Exercise 1

Use SQL Server Management Studio to create and execute a new query, and view the results:

1. Open a connection to your local or remote test server.

2. Indicate that you want to run queries against the AdventureWorks2008 database.

3. Execute the following SQL statement:

```
SELECT * FROM Production.Product
```

4. Check the status bar for the numbers of rows returned by the query.

5. Check the results with the solution.

Exercise 2

Insert a row using generated SQL script:

1. Using SQL Server Management Studio, expand the AdventureWorks2008 database in the object browser. Right-click the Production.ProductCategory table and select Script Table As ⇨ Insert to ⇨ New Query Editor Window.

2. With the new query opened, click on the Query menu and select the Specify Values for Template Parameters option. Specify "Widgets" as the value for Name (with single quotes), and the keyword DEFAULT for both the RowGuid and ModifiedDate values.

3. Execute the query.

4. Enter the following query to view the contents of the ProductCategory table:

```
SELECT * FROM Production.ProductCategory
```

5. Highlight this statement and execute this query.

6. Verify that a new row was added to the results. Check the modified SQL expression that you generated with the solution.

Data Retrieval

In Chapter 4, you learned that as the SQL language has evolved, it has expanded to add more capabilities. In this chapter you learn the fundamentals of the Data Manipulation Language (DML) aspects of T-SQL as they relate to retrieving data. Topics include filtering results with the WHERE clause, limiting results to specific table attributes, and ordering results to conform to business requirements. Subsequent chapters build on these concepts as you learn about more advanced implementations of these DML components.

Storage and Retrieval

I'm not a particularly organized person by nature. When I am done using an item, my first impulse is to toss it on my dresser or a table. The workbench in my garage hasn't seen the light of day for several months. I tell you this so you can understand my deep appreciation for the orderliness of a relational database. Perhaps this is the element in my life that helps me compensate for the lack of order in other areas. I also love containers of all kinds. The cool thing about having containers is that when you need to put something away, there's always a place for it, but when it comes time to find it, that's often another story.

Retrieving data through queries is really about finding stuff. SQL queries are used to reach into the database and pull out useful information; sometimes you need to get all of the details and sometimes you need only a subset of data based on common characteristics. At times, the value or values you'll want to return are an aggregation of data that tell you something about the data, rather than just returning all of the data in raw form.

As you will see later on, queries can be nested within queries and can be saved as programming objects such as functions, stored procedures, and views. Queries can then get their data from these objects. Queries can be joined, nested, and compounded in many different ways. Just remember that it all boils down to the same basic components.

The SELECT Statement

The SELECT statement consists of four clauses or components, as explained in the following table.

Clause	Explanation
SELECT	Followed by a list of columns or an asterisk, indicating that you want to return all columns
FROM	Followed by a table or view name, or multiple tables with join expressions
WHERE	Followed by filtering criteria
ORDER BY	Followed by a list of columns for sorting

The SELECT statement and FROM clause are required. The others are optional. Think of a table as a grid, like an Excel worksheet, consisting of cells arranged in rows and columns. Often, when you want to view the data in a table, you're only interested in seeing some of the information. To control what data gets returned, you can either display a subset of the columns, a subset of the rows, or a combination of the two. In any case, the *result set* is a list of rows, each consisting of the same number of columns.

The first few examples in this chapter show you two different views of the same data. I have pasted the contents of the Product table into an Excel workbook. For each query, you will see the first 66 rows and all 10 columns. As I filter the rows and columns, I'll highlight the selected rows and columns. This will provide a different perspective alongside the filtered result set. Keep in mind that Excel presents values a little differently than the results grid. For example, Null values are displayed as empty cells, whereas the results grid displays the text Null by default (this can be configured to display anything you like). Figure 5-1 shows a sampling of data from the Product table in an Excel worksheet.

ProductID	Name	ProductNumber	MakeFlag	FinishedGoodsFlag	Color	StandardCost	ListPrice	Size	Weight
749	Road-150 Red, 62	BK-R93R-62	TRUE	TRUE	Red	2171.2942	3578.27	62	15
750	Road-150 Red, 44	BK-R93R-44	TRUE	TRUE	Red	2171.2942	3578.27	44	13.77
751	Road-150 Red, 48	BK-R93R-48	TRUE	TRUE	Red	2171.2942	3578.27	48	14.13
752	Road-150 Red, 52	BK-R93R-52	TRUE	TRUE	Red	2171.2942	3578.27	52	14.42
753	Road-150 Red, 56	BK-R93R-56	TRUE	TRUE	Red	2171.2942	3578.27	56	14.68
771	Mountain-100 Silver, 38	BK-M82S-38	TRUE	TRUE	Silver	1912.1544	3399.99	38	20.35
772	Mountain-100 Silver, 42	BK-M82S-42	TRUE	TRUE	Silver	1912.1544	3399.99	42	20.77
773	Mountain-100 Silver, 44	BK-M82S-44	TRUE	TRUE	Silver	1912.1544	3399.99	44	21.13
774	Mountain-100 Silver, 48	BK-M82S-48	TRUE	TRUE	Silver	1912.1544	3399.99	48	21.42
775	Mountain-100 Black, 38	BK-M82B-38	TRUE	TRUE	Black	1898.0944	3374.99	38	20.35
776	Mountain-100 Black, 42	BK-M82B-42	TRUE	TRUE	Black	1898.0944	3374.99	42	20.77
777	Mountain-100 Black, 44	BK-M82B-44	TRUE	TRUE	Black	1898.0944	3374.99	44	21.13
778	Mountain-100 Black, 48	BK-M82B-48	TRUE	TRUE	Black	1898.0944	3374.99	48	21.42
789	Road-250 Red, 44	BK-R89R-44	TRUE	TRUE	Red	1518.7864	2443.35	44	14.77
790	Road-250 Red, 48	BK-R89R-48	TRUE	TRUE	Red	1518.7864	2443.35	48	15.13
791	Road-250 Red, 52	BK-R89R-52	TRUE	TRUE	Red	1518.7864	2443.35	52	15.42
792	Road-250 Red, 58	BK-R89R-58	TRUE	TRUE	Red	1554.9479	2443.35	58	15.79
793	Road-250 Black, 44	BK-R89B-44	TRUE	TRUE	Black	1554.9479	2443.35	44	14.77
794	Road-250 Black, 48	BK-R89B-48	TRUE	TRUE	Black	1554.9479	2443.35	48	15.13
795	Road-250 Black, 52	BK-R89B-52	TRUE	TRUE	Black	1554.9479	2443.35	52	15.42
796	Road-250 Black, 58	BK-R89B-58	TRUE	TRUE	Black	1554.9479	2443.35	58	15.68
954	Touring-1000 Yellow, 46	BK-T79Y-46	TRUE	TRUE	Yellow	1481.9379	2384.07	46	25.13
955	Touring-1000 Yellow, 50	BK-T79Y-50	TRUE	TRUE	Yellow	1481.9379	2384.07	50	25.42
956	Touring-1000 Yellow, 54	BK-T79Y-54	TRUE	TRUE	Yellow	1481.9379	2384.07	54	25.68
957	Touring-1000 Yellow, 60	BK-T79Y-60	TRUE	TRUE	Yellow	1481.9379	2384.07	60	25.9
966	Touring-1000 Blue, 46	BK-T79U-46	TRUE	TRUE	Blue	1481.9379	2384.07	46	25.13
967	Touring-1000 Blue, 50	BK-T79U-50	TRUE	TRUE	Blue	1481.9379	2384.07	50	25.42
968	Touring-1000 Blue, 54	BK-T79U-54	TRUE	TRUE	Blue	1481.9379	2384.07	54	25.68
969	Touring-1000 Blue, 60	BK-T79U-60	TRUE	TRUE	Blue	1481.9379	2384.07	60	25.9
779	Mountain-200 Silver, 38	BK-M68S-38	TRUE	TRUE	Silver	1265.6195	2319.99	38	23.35
780	Mountain-200 Silver, 42	BK-M68S-42	TRUE	TRUE	Silver	1265.6195	2319.99	42	23.77
781	Mountain-200 Silver, 46	BK-M68S-46	TRUE	TRUE	Silver	1265.6195	2319.99	46	24.13
782	Mountain-200 Black, 38	BK-M68B-38	TRUE	TRUE	Black	1251.9813	2294.99	38	23.35
783	Mountain-200 Black, 42	BK-M68B-42	TRUE	TRUE	Black	1251.9813	2294.99	42	23.77
784	Mountain-200 Black, 46	BK-M68B-46	TRUE	TRUE	Black	1251.9813	2294.99	46	24.13

Figure 5-1

Choosing Columns

Specify the columns you want your query to return immediately after the SELECT statement. The following statement returns three columns and all records in the Product table:

```
SELECT Name, StandardCost, Color
FROM Production.Product
```

Even though there may be dozens of columns of data in this table, you're just returning data values for the Name, StandardCost, and Color columns. You're still going to get all of the rows that exist in the table. Figure 5-2 shows the Excel worksheet with only the selected columns highlighted.

ProductID	Name	ProductNumber	MakeFlag	FinishedGoodsFlag	Color	StandardCost	ListPrice	Size	Weight
749	Road-150 Red, 62	BK-R93R-62	TRUE	TRUE	Red	2171.2942	3578.27	62	15
750	Road-150 Red, 44	BK-R93R-44	TRUE	TRUE	Red	2171.2942	3578.27	44	13.77
751	Road-150 Red, 48	BK-R93R-48	TRUE	TRUE	Red	2171.2942	3578.27	48	14.13
752	Road-150 Red, 52	BK-R93R-52	TRUE	TRUE	Red	2171.2942	3578.27	52	14.42
753	Road-150 Red, 56	BK-R93R-56	TRUE	TRUE	Red	2171.2942	3578.27	56	14.68
771	Mountain-100 Silver, 38	BK-M82S-38	TRUE	TRUE	Silver	1912.1544	3399.99	38	20.35
772	Mountain-100 Silver, 42	BK-M82S-42	TRUE	TRUE	Silver	1912.1544	3399.99	42	20.77
773	Mountain-100 Silver, 44	BK-M82S-44	TRUE	TRUE	Silver	1912.1544	3399.99	44	21.13
774	Mountain-100 Silver, 48	BK-M82S-48	TRUE	TRUE	Silver	1912.1544	3399.99	48	21.42
775	Mountain-100 Black, 38	BK-M82B-38	TRUE	TRUE	Black	1898.0944	3374.99	38	20.35
776	Mountain-100 Black, 42	BK-M82B-42	TRUE	TRUE	Black	1898.0944	3374.99	42	20.77
777	Mountain-100 Black, 44	BK-M82B-44	TRUE	TRUE	Black	1898.0944	3374.99	44	21.13
778	Mountain-100 Black, 48	BK-M82B-48	TRUE	TRUE	Black	1898.0944	3374.99	48	21.42
789	Road-250 Red, 44	BK-R89R-44	TRUE	TRUE	Red	1518.7864	2443.35	44	14.77
790	Road-250 Red, 48	BK-R89R-48	TRUE	TRUE	Red	1518.7864	2443.35	48	15.13
791	Road-250 Red, 52	BK-R89R-52	TRUE	TRUE	Red	1518.7864	2443.35	52	15.42
792	Road-250 Red, 58	BK-R89R-58	TRUE	TRUE	Red	1554.9479	2443.35	58	15.79
793	Road-250 Black, 44	BK-R89B-44	TRUE	TRUE	Black	1554.9479	2443.35	44	14.77
794	Road-250 Black, 48	BK-R89B-48	TRUE	TRUE	Black	1554.9479	2443.35	48	15.13
795	Road-250 Black, 52	BK-R89B-52	TRUE	TRUE	Black	1554.9479	2443.35	52	15.42
796	Road-250 Black, 58	BK-R89B-58	TRUE	TRUE	Black	1554.9479	2443.35	58	15.68
954	Touring-1000 Yellow, 46	BK-T79Y-46	TRUE	TRUE	Yellow	1481.9379	2384.07	46	25.13
955	Touring-1000 Yellow, 50	BK-T79Y-50	TRUE	TRUE	Yellow	1481.9379	2384.07	50	25.42
956	Touring-1000 Yellow, 54	BK-T79Y-54	TRUE	TRUE	Yellow	1481.9379	2384.07	54	25.68
957	Touring-1000 Yellow, 60	BK-T79Y-60	TRUE	TRUE	Yellow	1481.9379	2384.07	60	25.9
966	Touring-1000 Blue, 46	BK-T79U-46	TRUE	TRUE	Blue	1481.9379	2384.07	46	25.13
967	Touring-1000 Blue, 50	BK-T79U-50	TRUE	TRUE	Blue	1481.9379	2384.07	50	25.42
968	Touring-1000 Blue, 54	BK-T79U-54	TRUE	TRUE	Blue	1481.9379	2384.07	54	25.68
969	Touring-1000 Blue, 60	BK-T79U-60	TRUE	TRUE	Blue	1481.9379	2384.07	60	25.9
779	Mountain-200 Silver, 38	BK-M68S-38	TRUE	TRUE	Silver	1265.6195	2319.99	38	23.35
780	Mountain-200 Silver, 42	BK-M68S-42	TRUE	TRUE	Silver	1265.6195	2319.99	42	23.77
781	Mountain-200 Silver, 46	BK-M68S-46	TRUE	TRUE	Silver	1265.6195	2319.99	46	24.13
782	Mountain-200 Black, 38	BK-M68B-38	TRUE	TRUE	Black	1251.9813	2294.99	38	23.35
783	Mountain-200 Black, 42	BK-M68B-42	TRUE	TRUE	Black	1251.9813	2294.99	42	23.77
784	Mountain-200 Black, 46	BK-M68B-46	TRUE	TRUE	Black	1251.9813	2294.99	46	24.13

Figure 5-2

If you want to return values for all available columns, you can either specify every column by name or use the asterisk (*) to indicate "all columns." This query returns all of the columns in the table, as if you had listed every available column in the SELECT statement:

```
SELECT * FROM Production.Product
```

Occasionally, I hear the asterisk in this context referred to as a *splat*. So if you hear an old-timer DBA say "Select Splat From Products," you'll know what he's talking about.

Using the SELECT * technique of returning rows is acceptable only in an ad hoc query environment. Using this technique in an application environment will cause nothing but aggravation down the road. Data consumers such as ADO.NET or any other interface generally require column name mapping. As long as the number of columns and the names of the columns in your database will *never* change, you can most likely get away with using SELECT *. However, if there is any one constant in the universe, it's change. Column names will invariably change and so will the number of columns in a table. As a best practice avoid this technique for returning all rows. There are a number of reasons to explicitly list the columns in your query, including the following:

❑ Including columns you don't need may produce unnecessary disk I/O and network traffic.

❑ Sensitive information may be available to unauthorized users.

❑ In complex, multi-table queries, including all columns produces redundant column values, confusing users and complicating application development.

❑ Results are more predictable and easier to manage.

Later on, you'll learn about writing queries for multiple tables. However, in the following Try It Out, you take a quick look at such a query so that you can see how to address columns from more than one table with identical names.

Try It Out   Multi-Table Query

Open SQL Server Management Studio and connect to your database server. Select the AdventureWorks2008 database from the selection list on the toolbar. Type the following query into the query editor and execute the query:

```
SELECT ProductID
      ,Name
      ,Color
      ,StandardCost
      ,ListPrice
FROM Production.Product
```

In the results pane, you should see five columns of values representing Product records — all 504 of them. The record count is displayed in the lower status bar, near the right side. Your results should look something like those shown in Figure 5-3.

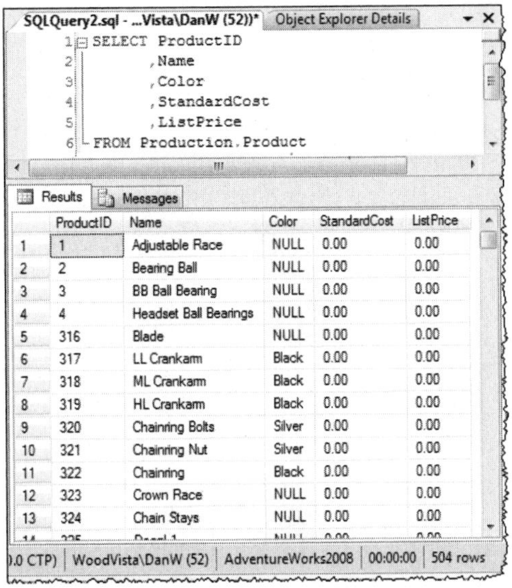

Figure 5-3

Expand the query to get model information from a related table. Amend the query as in the following example.

```
SELECT ProductID
       ,Name
       ,Color
       ,StandardCost
       ,ListPrice
       ,ProductModelId
       ,Name
FROM Production.Product
INNER JOIN Production.ProductModel
ON Production.Product.ProductModelID = Production.ProductModel.ProductModelID
```

Now when you execute this query, what happens? You get an error that looks like that shown in Figure 5-4.

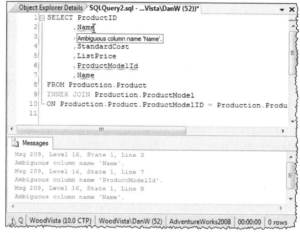

Figure 5-4

The query parser is unhappy because you have referred to two different tables that contain columns with identical names. If you are using SQL Server 2008, the query window will tell you your query isn't going to work before you ever execute it. It underlines the ambiguous column names and if you hover the mouse over the underlines text, it will tell you what the error is (refer to Figure 5-4). This feature is new to SQL Server 2008. Both the Product and ProductModel tables contain columns named Name and ProductModelID. This problem is easily remedied by prefixing the column names with the table name. The corrected query would look like this:

```
SELECT ProductID
       ,Production.Product.Name
       ,Color
       ,StandardCost
       ,ListPrice
       ,Production.ProductModel.ProductModelId
       ,Production.ProductModel.Name
FROM Production.Product
INNER JOIN Production.ProductModel
ON Production.Product.ProductModelID = Production.ProductModel.ProductModelID
```

However, as I mentioned in the previous chapter, this is still not the best way to format the query. It's very advantageous to look at a query and know exactly which data is coming from which table, as the following example shows:

```
SELECT Production.Product.ProductID
      ,Production.Product.Name
      ,Production.Product.Color
      ,Production.Product.StandardCost
      ,Production.Product.ListPrice
      ,Production.ProductModel.ProductModelId
      ,Production.ProductModel.Name
FROM Production.Product
INNER JOIN Production.ProductModel
ON Production.Product.ProductModelID = Production.ProductModel.ProductModelID
```

Now there is an additional issue with our query. It will work, but it will return two columns called Name. A database application attempting to consume this data is going to get very confused. When there are duplicate named columns it is very important to give one or both alias names. Column aliases are covered in detail later in this section, but for now take a look at the following example and how it alleviates the duplicate name problem:

```
SELECT Production.Product.ProductID
      ,Production.Product.Name AS Product
      ,Production.Product.Color
      ,Production.Product.StandardCost
      ,Production.Product.ListPrice
      ,Production.ProductModel.ProductModelId
      ,Production.ProductModel.Name AS Model
FROM Production.Product
INNER JOIN Production.ProductModel
ON Production.Product.ProductModelID = Production.ProductModel.ProductModelID
```

You will also notice that when referencing the table, the schema name is also required. In database terminology, a schema is a namespace. It is a way you can group common objects together in a common namespace. A schema is also a securable object, so the DBA can grant explicit permissions to a schema. For example, a DBA can grant a user the SELECT permission to a schema. In that way the user will be allowed to select rows from any table or view that is in that schema.

Every object in a SQL Server database is identified with a four-part name. The name takes the form of Server.Database.Schema.Object. In the case of the table columns, they are not really objects, but attributes of an object. In the SELECT clause, the server is not specified, only the database, schema, object, and attribute. The FROM clause is where the server may be specified. So, to select the ProductID attribute of the Product object from the Production schema in the AdventureWorks2008 database on the WoodVista server, I would write the query as follows:

```
SELECT AdventureWorks2008.Production.Product.ProductID
FROM WoodVista.AdventureWorks2008.Production.Product
```

As you have seen previously, some parts of the four-part name are optional. If the server name is omitted, SQL Server assumes the query is being run on the server connection where the query is being run. The same is true for the database. SQL Server will assume that whatever database context is currently set is the database where the objects of interest reside.

Things get more complicated when you get to the schema. In SQL Server, every user is assigned a default schema, or namespace.

If you have never used SQL Server before, or if you have used versions prior to SQL Server 2005, the schema object may need just a bit more explanation.

A *schema* is a named collection of database objects that forms a namespace. The namespace is owned by a single user. Within the namespace, objects cannot have duplicate names. However, objects can have the same name if they exist in different namespaces, or more specifically, different schemas. For instance, if a table called MyTable is created in the schema Sales on my server called AughtEight, its name becomes `AughtEight.Sales.MyTable`. An additional table called MyTable can still be created in the Marketing schema and its name would be `AughtEight.Marketing.MyTable`. Schemas also form a security scope, which can be used by the database administrator to control access to all objects within the schema namespace.

Schemas and Name Resolution

Because schemas are, in fact, namespaces, it is important to set the context of object references when calling on database objects in SQL Server. As I mentioned earlier, every user is assigned a default schema. When a user logs in to a SQL Server and calls on database objects, this default schema will play a distinct role in how the objects must be referenced.

Because SQL Server, as with many other database products, organizes objects in schemas, it is important to understand how to properly access these objects.

Here's how it works: The database designer defines schemas, which are really just category names. These schema names can have associated ownership and permissions, which provides the same capabilities available in earlier SQL Server versions.

If you are using the AdventureWorks2008 database that installs with SQL Server and the login you are using has been assigned the default schema of DBO, you must use the following syntax to access the Product table:

```
SELECT * FROM Production.Product
```

In earlier versions of SQL Server, objects were typically owned by a user called *DBO*, and if you didn't prefix an object reference with a username, the DBO user was just assumed. The same is true with schemas in SQL Server 2005 and 2008. Objects can belong to the DBO schema, and if you don't use a schema name in an object reference, the DBO schema is assumed as long as it is your default schema. However, if your default schema has been changed to something other than DBO, then this is no longer true. If an object is part of any other schema, the schema name must be used in the expression. Here is an example to illustrate this feature.

User Fred connects to the AdventureWorks2008 database on a SQL Server instance called Bedrock1. Fred's default schema has not been explicitly assigned, and so it is set to DBO by default. Fred then executes the following query:

```
SELECT * FROM Product
```

The query processor attempts to resolve the Product table name to *Bedrock1.AdventureWorks2008.dbo. Product*, but the query fails because the Product table exists in the Production schema and not the DBO schema. Now I change Fred's default schema like this:

```
ALTER USER Fred WITH DEFAULT_SCHEMA = Production
```

When Fred executes the product query again, the Query Processor resolves the product table to *Bedrock1. AdventureWorks2008.Production.Product,* and the query succeeds.

Now take a look at an opposite example. User Barney, who is the assistant DBA, connects to the same instance that user Fred did, but he wants to retrieve the contents of the DBAudit table that exists in the DBO schema, but Barney's default schema has also been set to Production. Barney runs the following query:

```
SELECT * FROM DBAudit
```

The Query Processor first attempts to resolve the DBAudit table to Barney's default schema, *Bedrock1. AdventureWorks2008.Production.DBAudit*, but the resolution fails. However, because the Query Processor started in a schema other than DBO, it then falls back to the DBO schema and attempts to resolve the table to *Bedrock1.AdventureWorks.dbo.DBAudit*. This resolution succeeds, and the contents of the table are returned.

This fallback resolution works in two cases: if the object does not exist in the user's default schema, but does in the DBO schema, or if the object does not exist in the user's default schema, but does in the SYS schema. The SYS schema is reserved for system objects and contains system views that are very useful in the management of SQL Server databases.

One final point that is very important to understand is that a table can have the same name as another table in a different schema. So it is very possible to have a table called User in the Sales schema, the Production schema and the HumanResources schema. If this is true, it becomes even more important that the tables are referenced with their two-part name to ensure the correct data is returned. "Why would anyone do something like creating three tables all with the same name?" Good question. The answer is that a SQL Server schema is not only a namespace, it is also a security context. The DBA could grant permissions to the sales manager to add and delete users in the Sales.User table, but prevent her from having access to the Production.User table. It is just another way of managing security and application access.

Column Aliasing

You may want to change column names in a query for a variety of reasons. These may include changing a column name to make it easier to understand or to provide a more descriptive name. Changing a column name can also provide backward compatibility for application objects if column names were renamed after design.

In a previous example you saw that the Query Processor needs to know what table to retrieve a column from if the column exists in more than one referenced table. The same can also be true for the person reading the results. They might need to know exactly what table the values were extracted from. The following example clarifies the source of an ambiguous column by using an alias:

```
SELECT SalesOrderHeader.CustomerID AS SalesCustomerID
      ,SalesOrderHeader.SalesPersonID
      ,PurchaseOrderNumber
FROM   Sales.Customer
INNER JOIN Sales.SalesOrderHeader
    ON Customer.CustomerID = SalesOrderHeader.CustomerID
```

In the result set shown in Figure 5-5, you can see that the first column now shows up as SalesCustomerID and not CustomerID.

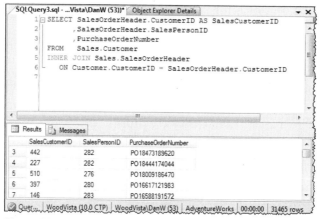

Figure 5-5

Months later, this could save someone a lot of grief and aggravation. Imagine getting a call from the accounting department when they discover that they have been billing the wrong customer.

You can alias a column in three different ways. The technique used in the preceding example is probably the most descriptive. A popular technique leaves out the AS keyword so the actual column name simply precedes the alias. The following table shows each of these techniques. The last one isn't common, but it can come in handy in limited situations.

Syntax	Description
Column AS Alias	Most readable technique, but not popular with SQL purists
Column Alias	Common technique, but not very readable
Alias = Column	Not common in T-SQL

Here are examples of these three techniques:

```
SELECT ListPrice - StandardCost AS Margin
FROM Production.Product
SELECT ListPrice - StandardCost Margin
FROM Production.Product
SELECT Margin = ListPrice - StandardCost
FROM Production.Product
```

As you can see, the first example, using the AS keyword is probably the most descriptive and easiest to read.

Calculated and Derived Columns

One of the most common types of column aliases is when a new column is created from an expression or calculation, such as in the previous example using the Product table. As you can see in Figure 5-6, this produces a single column called Margin, which contains the difference between the products cost and price.

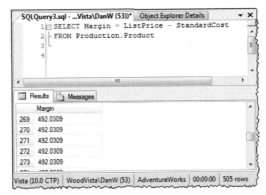

Figure 5-6

Following are a few examples using various functions and column data types. This first simple example uses the UnitPrice and OrderQty columns from the Sales.SalesOrderDetail to calculate the purchase amount for a line item by multiplying these two values. The resulting alias column is called PurchasePrice:

```
SELECT SalesOrderID
    ,ProductID
    ,UnitPrice * OrderQty As PurchasePrice
FROM Sales.SalesOrderDetail
```

In the result set shown in Figure 5-7, the PurchasePrice column shows the calculated figure.

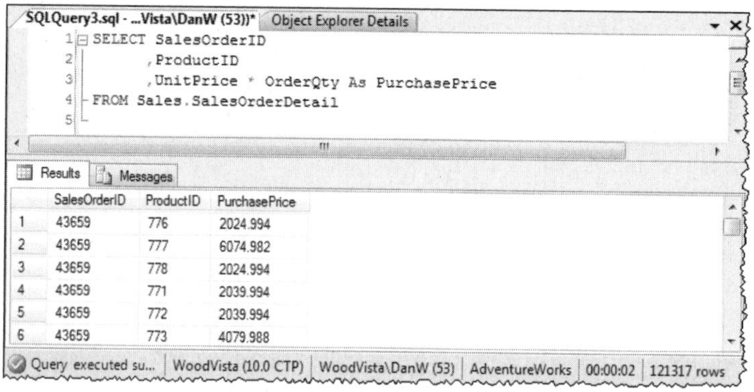

Figure 5-7

In the following scenario, you need to calculate each employee's age based on their birth date and the current date. Using the DATEDIFF function, you ask SQL Server to calculate the number of years between the two dates to get the approximate result. The query would look like this:

```
SELECT NationalIDNumber
     ,BirthDate
     ,DATEDIFF(YY, BirthDate, GETDATE()) As Age
FROM HumanResources.Employee
```

The result set should resemble that shown in Figure 5-8.

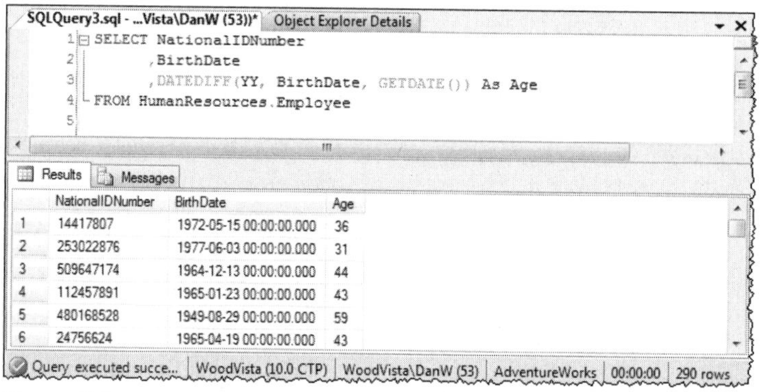

Figure 5-8

In the next example, the Product's table SubCategoryID, is related to a column in the ProductSubCategory table. Without using a join between these tables, I would like to see the subcategory name in the output from my query. Because I know that SubCategoryID 1 represents mountain bikes,

I can add this description using an alias column. In the WHERE clause, I filter product rows based on the subcategory and then add an alias column called SubCategoryName:

```
SELECT Name, ListPrice, 'Mountain Bike' AS SubCategoryName
FROM Production.Product WHERE ProductSubCategoryID = 1
```

Figure 5-9 shows the results from this query. Note the SubCategoryName column.

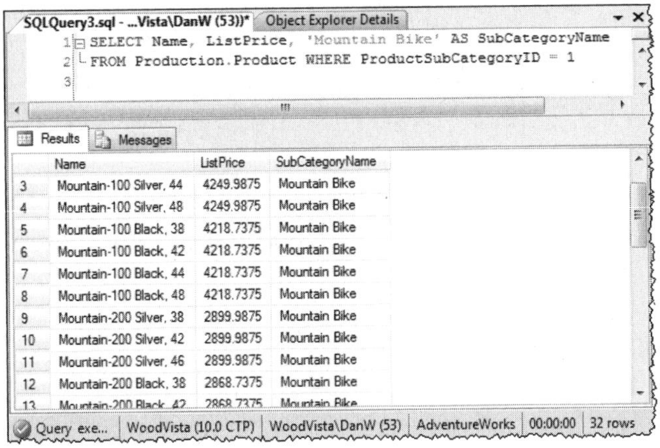

Figure 5-9

I'll come back to this example and expand on it in Chapter 8 when you learn about multi-table queries.

Filtering Rows

It's safe to say that most of the time you won't want to return every record, especially from your largest tables. Many production databases in business are used to collect and store records for many years of business activity. For small to medium-sized businesses, this is a common practice. In larger-scale systems, data is usually archived yearly or monthly and useful, historical information may be moved into a data warehouse for reporting. Regardless, it often doesn't make sense to return all rows in a table. Two basic techniques exist for returning some of the rows from a query: The WHERE clause is used to qualify each row based on filter criteria, and the TOP clause is used to limit the list to a defined number of rows.

The WHERE Clause

Filtering is largely the job of the WHERE clause, which is followed by some sort of filtering expression. The syntax of this statement is very natural and should be easy to translate to or from a verbal statement. I'll continue to use the Excel worksheet example that I began using earlier in this chapter. In this example, all columns for products that are black are returned:

```
SELECT * FROM Production.Product
WHERE Color = 'Black'
```

I'm essentially asking SQL Server to filter the rows for the table only vertically, returning slices that meet only the specified color criteria, as reflected in Figure 5-10.

ProductID	Name	ProductNumber	MakeFlag	FinishedGoodsFlag	Color	StandardCost	ListPrice	Size	Weight
749	Road-150 Red, 62	BK-R93R-62	TRUE	TRUE	Red	2171.2942	3578.27	62	15
750	Road-150 Red, 44	BK-R93R-44	TRUE	TRUE	Red	2171.2942	3578.27	44	13.77
751	Road-150 Red, 48	BK-R93R-48	TRUE	TRUE	Red	2171.2942	3578.27	48	14.13
752	Road-150 Red, 52	BK-R93R-52	TRUE	TRUE	Red	2171.2942	3578.27	52	14.42
753	Road-150 Red, 56	BK-R93R-56	TRUE	TRUE	Red	2171.2942	3578.27	56	14.68
771	Mountain-100 Silver, 38	BK-M82S-38	TRUE	TRUE	Silver	1912.1544	3399.99	38	20.35
772	Mountain-100 Silver, 42	BK-M82S-42	TRUE	TRUE	Silver	1912.1544	3399.99	42	20.77
773	Mountain-100 Silver, 44	BK-M82S-44	TRUE	TRUE	Silver	1912.1544	3399.99	44	21.13
774	Mountain-100 Silver, 48	BK-M82S-48	TRUE	TRUE	Silver	1912.1544	3399.99	48	21.42
775	Mountain-100 Black, 38	BK-M82B-38	TRUE	TRUE	Black	1898.0944	3374.99	38	20.35
776	Mountain-100 Black, 42	BK-M82B-42	TRUE	TRUE	Black	1898.0944	3374.99	42	20.77
777	Mountain-100 Black, 44	BK-M82B-44	TRUE	TRUE	Black	1898.0944	3374.99	44	21.13
778	Mountain-100 Black, 48	BK-M82B-48	TRUE	TRUE	Black	1898.0944	3374.99	48	21.42
789	Road-250 Red, 44	BK-R89R-44	TRUE	TRUE	Red	1518.7864	2443.35	44	14.77
790	Road-250 Red, 48	BK-R89R-48	TRUE	TRUE	Red	1518.7864	2443.35	48	15.13
791	Road-250 Red, 52	BK-R89R-52	TRUE	TRUE	Red	1518.7864	2443.35	52	15.42
792	Road-250 Red, 58	BK-R89R-58	TRUE	TRUE	Red	1554.9479	2443.35	58	15.79
793	Road-250 Black, 44	BK-R89B-44	TRUE	TRUE	Black	1554.9479	2443.35	44	14.77
794	Road-250 Black, 48	BK-R89B-48	TRUE	TRUE	Black	1554.9479	2443.35	48	15.13
795	Road-250 Black, 52	BK-R89B-52	TRUE	TRUE	Black	1554.9479	2443.35	52	15.42
796	Road-250 Black, 58	BK-R89B-58	TRUE	TRUE	Black	1554.9479	2443.35	58	15.68
954	Touring-1000 Yellow, 46	BK-T79Y-46	TRUE	TRUE	Yellow	1481.9379	2384.07	46	25.13
955	Touring-1000 Yellow, 50	BK-T79Y-50	TRUE	TRUE	Yellow	1481.9379	2384.07	50	25.42
956	Touring-1000 Yellow, 54	BK-T79Y-54	TRUE	TRUE	Yellow	1481.9379	2384.07	54	25.68
957	Touring-1000 Yellow, 60	BK-T79Y-60	TRUE	TRUE	Yellow	1481.9379	2384.07	60	25.9
966	Touring-1000 Blue, 46	BK-T79U-46	TRUE	TRUE	Blue	1481.9379	2384.07	46	25.13
967	Touring-1000 Blue, 50	BK-T79U-50	TRUE	TRUE	Blue	1481.9379	2384.07	50	25.42
968	Touring-1000 Blue, 54	BK-T79U-54	TRUE	TRUE	Blue	1481.9379	2384.07	54	25.68
969	Touring-1000 Blue, 60	BK-T79U-60	TRUE	TRUE	Blue	1481.9379	2384.07	60	25.9
779	Mountain-200 Silver, 38	BK-M68S-38	TRUE	TRUE	Silver	1265.6195	2319.99	38	23.35
780	Mountain-200 Silver, 42	BK-M68S-42	TRUE	TRUE	Silver	1265.6195	2319.99	42	23.77
781	Mountain-200 Silver, 46	BK-M68S-46	TRUE	TRUE	Silver	1265.6195	2319.99	46	24.13
782	Mountain-200 Black, 38	BK-M68B-38	TRUE	TRUE	Black	1251.9813	2294.99	38	23.35
783	Mountain-200 Black, 42	BK-M68B-42	TRUE	TRUE	Black	1251.9813	2294.99	42	23.77
784	Mountain-200 Black, 46	BK-M68B-46	TRUE	TRUE	Black	1251.9813	2294.99	46	24.13

Figure 5-10

The result set shows only the matching rows (as much as you can see in the results grid), as shown in Figure 5-11.

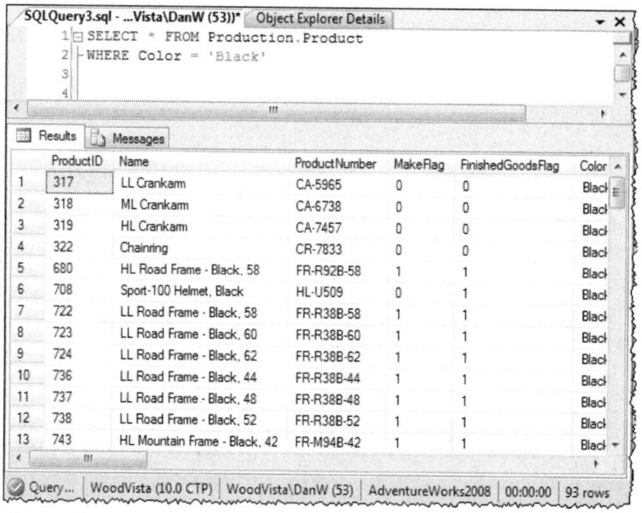

Figure 5-11

It's important to note that the WHERE clause is evaluated by SQL Server *before* the data is retrieved. SQL Server will find just the rows that match the filter criteria and return them. This conserves memory and I/O resources. In Chapter 14, we look a little more closely at this aspect of queries and how to best write queries for optimal performance.

Recall that I used this workbook to demonstrate selecting specific columns to be returned from the query. So far, I've selected specific columns and specific rows. Now, I'll combine the two to return a subset of both columns and rows using the following SELECT expressions:

```
SELECT Name, StandardCost, Color
FROM Production.Product
WHERE Color = 'Black'
```

Before you examine the results, refer to Figure 5-12 for another look at that workbook data with highlighted columns and rows.

The result set contains only the values in the intersection of the columns and rows. As you can see in Figure 5-13, only the Name, StandardCost, and Color columns are included, and the only rows are those where the Color value is Black.

ProductID	Name	ProductNumber	MakeFlag	FinishedGoodsFlag	Color	StandardCost	ListPrice	Size	Weight
749	Road-150 Red, 62	BK-R93R-62	TRUE	TRUE	Red	2171.2942	3578.27	62	15
750	Road-150 Red, 44	BK-R93R-44	TRUE	TRUE	Red	2171.2942	3578.27	44	13.77
751	Road-150 Red, 48	BK-R93R-48	TRUE	TRUE	Red	2171.2942	3578.27	48	14.13
752	Road-150 Red, 52	BK-R93R-52	TRUE	TRUE	Red	2171.2942	3578.27	52	14.42
753	Road-150 Red, 56	BK-R93R-56	TRUE	TRUE	Red	2171.2942	3578.27	56	14.68
771	Mountain-100 Silver, 38	BK-M82S-38	TRUE	TRUE	Silver	1912.1544	3399.99	38	20.35
772	Mountain-100 Silver, 42	BK-M82S-42	TRUE	TRUE	Silver	1912.1544	3399.99	42	20.77
773	Mountain-100 Silver, 44	BK-M82S-44	TRUE	TRUE	Silver	1912.1544	3399.99	44	21.13
774	Mountain-100 Silver, 48	BK-M82S-48	TRUE	TRUE	Silver	1912.1544	3399.99	48	21.42
775	Mountain-100 Black, 38	BK-M82B-38	TRUE	TRUE	Black	1898.0944	3374.99	38	20.35
776	Mountain-100 Black, 42	BK-M82B-42	TRUE	TRUE	Black	1898.0944	3374.99	42	20.77
777	Mountain-100 Black, 44	BK-M82B-44	TRUE	TRUE	Black	1898.0944	3374.99	44	21.13
778	Mountain-100 Black, 48	BK-M82B-48	TRUE	TRUE	Black	1898.0944	3374.99	48	21.42
789	Road-250 Red, 44	BK-R89R-44	TRUE	TRUE	Red	1518.7864	2443.35	44	14.77
790	Road-250 Red, 48	BK-R89R-48	TRUE	TRUE	Red	1518.7864	2443.35	48	15.13
791	Road-250 Red, 52	BK-R89R-52	TRUE	TRUE	Red	1518.7864	2443.35	52	15.42
792	Road-250 Red, 58	BK-R89R-58	TRUE	TRUE	Red	1554.9479	2443.35	58	15.79
793	Road-250 Black, 44	BK-R89B-44	TRUE	TRUE	Black	1554.9479	2443.35	44	14.77
794	Road-250 Black, 48	BK-R89B-48	TRUE	TRUE	Black	1554.9479	2443.35	48	15.13
795	Road-250 Black, 52	BK-R89B-52	TRUE	TRUE	Black	1554.9479	2443.35	52	15.42
796	Road-250 Black, 58	BK-R89B-58	TRUE	TRUE	Black	1554.9479	2443.35	58	15.68
954	Touring-1000 Yellow, 46	BK-T79Y-46	TRUE	TRUE	Yellow	1481.9379	2384.07	46	25.13
955	Touring-1000 Yellow, 50	BK-T79Y-50	TRUE	TRUE	Yellow	1481.9379	2384.07	50	25.42
956	Touring-1000 Yellow, 54	BK-T79Y-54	TRUE	TRUE	Yellow	1481.9379	2384.07	54	25.68
957	Touring-1000 Yellow, 60	BK-T79Y-60	TRUE	TRUE	Yellow	1481.9379	2384.07	60	25.9
966	Touring-1000 Blue, 46	BK-T79U-46	TRUE	TRUE	Blue	1481.9379	2384.07	46	25.13
967	Touring-1000 Blue, 50	BK-T79U-50	TRUE	TRUE	Blue	1481.9379	2384.07	50	25.42
968	Touring-1000 Blue, 54	BK-T79U-54	TRUE	TRUE	Blue	1481.9379	2384.07	54	25.68
969	Touring-1000 Blue, 60	BK-T79U-60	TRUE	TRUE	Blue	1481.9379	2384.07	60	25.9
779	Mountain-200 Silver, 38	BK-M68S-38	TRUE	TRUE	Silver	1265.6195	2319.99	38	23.35
780	Mountain-200 Silver, 42	BK-M68S-42	TRUE	TRUE	Silver	1265.6195	2319.99	42	23.77
781	Mountain-200 Silver, 46	BK-M68S-46	TRUE	TRUE	Silver	1265.6195	2319.99	46	24.13
782	Mountain-200 Black, 38	BK-M68B-38	TRUE	TRUE	Black	1251.9813	2294.99	38	23.35
783	Mountain-200 Black, 42	BK-M68B-42	TRUE	TRUE	Black	1251.9813	2294.99	42	23.77
784	Mountain-200 Black, 46	BK-M68B-46	TRUE	TRUE	Black	1251.9813	2294.99	46	24.13

Figure 5-12

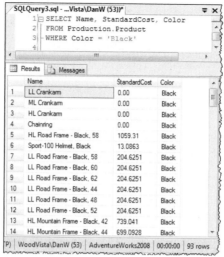

Figure 5-13

For example, consider the following verbal request: "I would like to see a list of products, including the product name and price that have a price less than $5.00." The SQL version of this request would look like this:

```
SELECT Name, ListPrice
FROM Production.Product
WHERE ListPrice < 5.00
```

Easy, right? Filtering statements should be very natural and easy to read. You just need to get used to the flow.

Comparison Operators

Qualifying values to match a set of criteria is a relatively straightforward proposition, especially when working with numeric and date/time types. Testing a numeric value to see if it is greater than 10 makes sense and there is little room for confusion. However, testing to see if the value Fred is greater than the value Bob may not seem to make much sense, but in reality you will likely find yourself using this technique while searching through character strings.

Comparing and qualifying values generally boils down to this: A value is either equal to, less than, or greater than another value. When matching character values, you can be a little more creative, looking for partial strings of characters to match a value that is "like" another value. Starting with the simplest comparisons, value-matching operators are described in the following table.

Operator	Description
=	Equal to. Matches a value that is exactly equal to another value. Can be used with nearly all data types.
<> or !=	Not equal to.
<	Less than. Typically used with numeric and date/time data types.
>	Greater than.
!<	Not less than.
!>	Not greater than.
<=	Less than or equal to.
>=	Greater than or equal to.
Like	Used to perform wildcard matches with character values.

As you can see, most of the comparison operators are very straightforward. Here are just a couple of examples of their use:

To return the name and list price of all products that cost $75.00 or more, the query would look like this:

```
SELECT Name, ListPrice
FROM Production.Product
WHERE ListPrice >= 75.00
```

In a previous example we looked for all products with a list price less than $5.00 using the less than (<) operator. We could also have written the query like this:

```
SELECT Name, ListPrice
FROM Production.Product
WHERE ListPrice !> 5.00
```

The LIKE operator is a bit more complicated than the rest of the comparison operators. The first thing to know is that "like" does not mean "similar" when it comes to SQL Server. It means "exactly like." The power that the LIKE operator brings is the ability to use wildcards for character string comparisons. For example, what if you know that a store's name that sells AdventureWorks products begins with "Top," but you can't remember the rest of the name. The LIKE operator enables you to search through the list of store names that begin with "Top," as the following example demonstrates:

```
SELECT Name FROM Sales.Store
WHERE Name LIKE 'Top%'
```

The percent (%) character tells SQL Server that you want to return all rows where the first three letters are "Top" and zero or more characters follow.

The following table lists the wildcards that may be used and their description:

Wildcard	Description
%	Any string of zero or more characters
_	Any single character
[ ]	Any single character within the specified range or set
[^]	Any single character not within the specified range or set

Following are some examples of how to use the LIKE expression to search character strings in a column, but first let's create a simple table to practice on.

Begin by running the following SQL code to create and populate a table called SlateGravel. The first block will run in either SQL Server 2005 or 2008. The second block, however, is optimized using new SQL Server 2008 (only) syntax.

```
--SQL Server 2005/2008 syntax:
USE AdventureWorks2008
GO
CREATE TABLE dbo.SlateGravel
(LastName varchar(25) NULL
,FirstName varchar(25) NULL
,Position varchar(25) NULL);
INSERT SlateGravel
VALUES
('Flintstone', 'Fred', 'Bronto Driver')
INSERT SlateGravel
VALUES
('Rubble', 'Barney', 'Accountant')
INSERT SlateGravel
VALUES
('Turley', 'Paul', 'Developer')
INSERT SlateGravel
VALUES
('Wood', 'Dan', 'DBA')
INSERT SlateGravel
VALUES
('Rockhead', 'Don', 'System Administrator')
INSERT SlateGravel
VALUES
('Rockstone', 'Pauline', 'Manager')
--SQL Server 2008 syntax:
USE AdventureWorks2008
GO
CREATE TABLE dbo.SlateGravel
(LastName varchar(25) NULL
,FirstName varchar(25) NULL
```

```
,Position varchar(25) NULL);
INSERT SlateGravel
VALUES
  ('Flintstone', 'Fred', 'Bronto Driver')
,('Rubble', 'Barney', 'Accountant')
,('Turley', 'Paul', 'Developer')
,('Wood', 'Dan', 'DBA')
,('Rockhead', 'Don', 'System Administrator')
,('Rockstone', 'Pauline', 'Manager')
```

As you have seen before, to return every string starting with a string of characters you use the following syntax:

```
SELECT * FROM SlateGravel
WHERE LastName LIKE 'Flint%'
```

Be aware that if the data is stored in a case-sensitive collation searching for "flint%" will not return strings beginning with "Flint."

To find strings ending with certain values simply place the wildcard at the beginning of the string.

```
SELECT * FROM SlateGravel
WHERE LastName LIKE '%stone'
```

To find a value that that contains a certain string you can use both leading and trailing wildcards.

```
SELECT * FROM SlateGravel
WHERE LastName LIKE '%sto%'
```

To find a value when only a single character is unknown, the underscore can be used.

```
SELECT * FROM SlateGravel
WHERE LastName LIKE '_urley'
```

To find a value when a single character is within a specified range or set, square brackets are used. This example looks for first names of either Dan or Don.

```
SELECT * FROM SlateGravel
WHERE FirstName LIKE 'D[ao]n'
```

To search within a range, a dash is added between the letters.

```
SELECT * FROM SlateGravel
WHERE FirstName LIKE 'D[a-o]n'
```

Finally, to search for a value that does not contain specific characters, the caret symbol is used.

```
SELECT * FROM SlateGravel
WHERE FirstName LIKE 'D[^o]n'
```

Another variation of the LIKE operator is to use the NOT keyword. So, instead of looking for all first names like "Dan," you can search for all first names *not* like "Dan."

```
SELECT * FROM SlateGravel
WHERE FirstName NOT LIKE 'Dan'
```

Logical Comparisons

Using logical comparisons is how we make sense of things and it's how we simplify matters. It's how we dispel the gray area between "yes" and "no" or "true" and "false."

It would be convenient if all decisions were based on only one question, but this is rarely the case. Most important decisions are the product of many individual choices. It would also be convenient if each unique combination of decisions led to a unique outcome, but this isn't true either. The fact is that, often, multiple combinations of individual decisions can lead to the same conclusion. This may seem to be very complicated. Fortunately for us, in the 1830s mathematician George Bool boiled all of this down to a few very simple methods for combining outcomes called *logical gates*. There are only three of them: AND, OR, and NOT.

It's important to realize that every SQL comparison and logical expression yields only one type of result: True or False. When combining two expressions, there are only three possible outcomes: they are both True, they are both False, or one is True and the other False. With the groundwork laid, let's apply Bool's rules of logic to the SQL WHERE clause and combine multiple expressions.

The AND Operator

The AND operator simply states that for the entire expression to yield a True result, all individual statements must be true. For example, suppose you're looking for product records where the SubCategoryID is 1 (mountain bikes) and the price is less than $1,000. You're not interested in road bikes under $1,000, nor mountain bikes costing $1,000 or more. Both criteria must be met.

```
SELECT ProductID, Name, ListPrice
FROM Production.Product
WHERE ProductSubCategoryID = 1 AND ListPrice < 1000
```

Assuming that there are records matching either criterion, the AND operator will always reduce the rows in the result set. For example, the Product table contains 32 mountain bikes and 418 rows of products with a list price under $1,000. However, as you can see in Figure 5-14, only 14 rows match both of these filters.

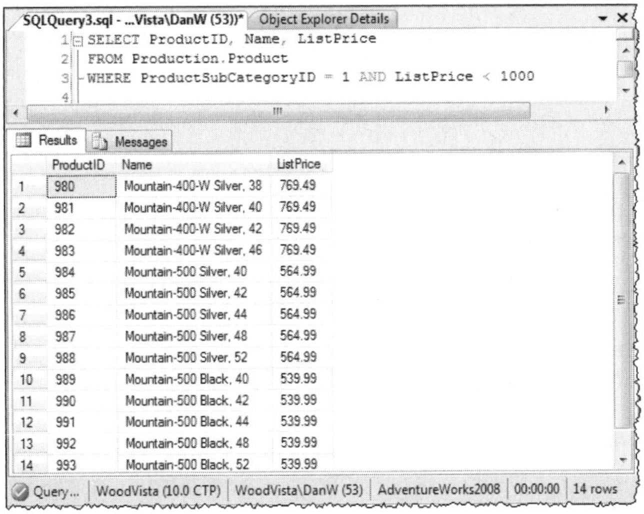

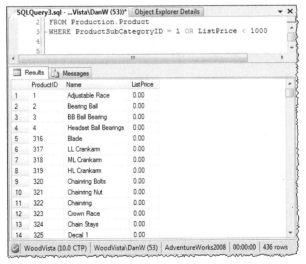

Figure 5-14

The OR Operator

When statements are combined using the OR operator, rows are returned if they match any of the criteria. Using the previous statement, changing the AND to an OR produces a different result:

```
SELECT ProductID, Name, ListPrice
FROM Production.Product
WHERE ProductSubCategoryID = 1 OR ListPrice < 1000
```

Rather than seeing only mountain bikes under $1,000, you see all mountain bikes, regardless of their price, and all products having a price under $1,000. This query returns 436 rows (14 of which are shown in Figure 5-15).

Figure 5-15

The NOT Operator

The NOT operator doesn't stand alone. It's simply a modifier that can precede any logical expression. The job of this operator is to reverse the result. So, if an expression yields True, you get a False. If it's False, you see True. Sometimes it's easier to test for the opposite of what you are looking for. However, the NOT operator is often less efficient because SQL Server actually processes the base expression first (perhaps returning all qualifying rows), and then fetches the rows that were not included in the original result. Depending on the complexity of the statement and the number of rows in the table, using NOT may still be more efficient than having to build an expression that selects everything but the records you want to ignore.

If you wanted to return all product records except for road bikes, you could use this expression:

```
SELECT ProductID, Name, ListPrice
FROM production.Product
WHERE NOT ProductSubCategoryID = 2
```

In the result set, shown in Figure 5-16, all rows are returned except for those having a ProductSubCategoryID value of 2.

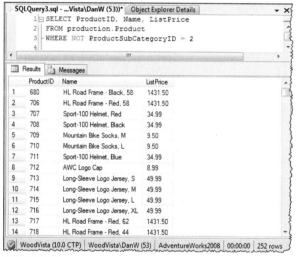

Figure 5-16

I'm not particularly fond of this syntax because it makes much more sense to write the expression as follows:

```
SELECT ProductID, Name, ListPrice
FROM Production.Product
WHERE ProductSubCategoryID != 2
```

or this way:

```
SELECT ProductID, Name, ListPrice
FROM Production.Product
WHERE ProductSubCategoryID <> 2
```

However, all three queries will return duplicate results and consume the same resources.

The Mighty Null

In the earlier days of databases, designers often found it difficult to consistently express the concept of "no value." For example, if a product invoice line is stored but you don't have the price of the product at the time, do you store a zero? How would you differentiate this row from another where you intended not to charge for the product?

Character data can be particularly strange at times. Within program code, string variables initialize to an empty string. In older file-based databases, what would now be considered to be a field would consist of a designated number of characters in a specific position within the file. If a field wasn't assigned a value, the file stored spaces in place of the data. Programs returned all of the characters including the spaces, which had to be trimmed off. If there wasn't anything left after removing the spaces, the program code concluded that there was no value in the field. So, what if you had intended to store spaces? How would you differentiate between a space and no value at all? Numeric types initialize to zero. The Bit or Boolean data type in some programming languages initializes to zero or False. If you store this value, does this mean that the value is intentionally set to False, or is this just its default state? What about dates that haven't been set to a value? As you can see, there is plenty of room for confusion regarding this topic. For this and other reasons, the ANSI SQL standard for representing the concept of "no value" is to use a special value called *Null*. Internally, Null is actually a real character (on the ANSI character chart, it's character zero — not to be confused with the number zero). It means "nothing," that this field doesn't have a value. Every significant data type supports the use of the Null value.

The Null value has an interesting behavior — it never equals anything, not even itself. To make it stand out, a special operator distinguishes Null from all other values. To test for Null, use the IS operator. So, Null does not equal Null … Null *IS* Null.

Some of the products in the product table have a color value, and some don't. To intentionally state that the product does not have a color (or, perhaps, that the color isn't known), this column is set to Null. Now you'd like to return a list of products with no color attribute, so use the following query:

```
SELECT ProductID, Name, Color
FROM Production.Product
WHERE Color IS NULL
```

As shown in Figure 5-17, the results contain a list of products with no color attribute.

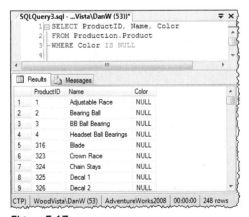

Figure 5-17

151

To reverse the logic and return a list of products with known color attributes, you simply add the NOT operator, as follows:

```
SELECT ProductID, Name, Color
FROM Production.Product
WHERE Color IS NOT NULL
```

The result contains all of the rows from the table that were not listed in the previous result, some of which are shown in Figure 5-18.

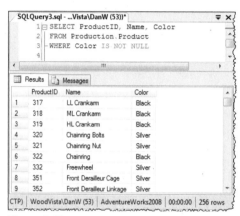

Figure 5-18

Extended Filtering Techniques

As you've seen, expressions using simple comparison operators can be combined to narrow down results and explicitly return the records you are looking for. Sometimes, even simple filtering expressions can get a little complicated. To simplify common expressions, operators were added to the SQL language. If nothing more, it makes expressions more natural and easier to read. One common example is a query for records in a date range. If you needed to return all employee records for employees born between 1962 and 1985, you would need to specify that the birth date should be greater than or equal to the first day of the first year in the range, January 1, 1962, and that the same column should also be less than or equal to the last day of the last year, December 31, 1985. This query would look like this:

```
SELECT NationalIDNumber, LoginID
FROM HumanResources.Employee
WHERE BirthDate >= '1962-1-1'
  AND BirthDate <= '1985-12-31'
```

The results contain only Employee records where the birth date falls within the specified range.

The BETWEEN Operator

Rather than managing the date range, the BETWEEN statement simplifies the range expression, helping state your intentions more explicitly:

```
SELECT NationalIDNumber, LoginID
FROM HumanResources.Employee
WHERE BirthDate BETWEEN '1962-1-1' AND '1985-12-31'
```

Granted, the first statement wasn't really that complicated, but if you combine this expression with others in the same query, every attempt to simplify a query helps. Keep in mind that the definition of BETWEEN is actually between and including both extremes of the value range.

When the query is executed, SQL Server's query processor parses the expression and reformats the query in more explicit, standardized form. If you wrote and executed the second query using the BETWEEN statement, the query that actually runs against the query engine would be exactly the same as the first. BETWEEN is really just a programming shortcut.

The IN() Function

Another shortcut command is the IN function. This function is designed to match a field to any number of values in a list. This shortcut function saves effort and keeps your queries shorter and easier to read. For example, suppose that you're interested in a list of just the bikes produced by AdventureWorks Cycles. The database identifies products by category and subcategory. To find a list of all the bikes from the Products table, you could use the following query:

```
SELECT ProductID
       ,Name AS Product
FROM   Production.Product
WHERE ProductSubCategoryID IN (1,2,3)
```

As before with the BETWEEN operator, the IN function is a shortcut. The query could have been written as follows with the same results:

```
SELECT ProductID
       ,Name AS Product
FROM   Production.Product
WHERE ProductSubCategoryID = 1
   OR ProductSubCategoryID = 2
   OR ProductSubCategoryID = 3
```

As the preceding example illustrates, when using a shortcut function, the query processor interprets the IN function as multiple OR statements. Functionally, there is no difference between the two queries, but the IN function makes it easier to write and easier to read.

check (Season IN ('Fall', 'winter', 'summer', 'fall'))

The `IN` function can also be used with subqueries, which you will learn more about in Chapter 8. As an example, suppose you wanted to know all the bike-related products, not just bikes? You could use the following query:

```
SELECT ProductID
      ,Name AS Product
FROM Production.Product
WHERE ProductSubCategoryID IN (SELECT ProductSubCategoryID
                               FROM Production.ProductSubCategory
                               WHERE ProductCategoryID IN (1,2))
```

Operator Precedence

It's important to consider the order in which multiple operations are carried out. If not, you may not get the results you'd expect. The precedence (order of operations) is determined by a few different factors. The first and most important is whether the precedence is explicitly stated. This is covered shortly. Operations involving different data types may be processed in a different order. Lastly, the operators are considered: `NOT` is processed first, then `AND`, then `OR` operations. Before you look up this topic in Books Online and attempt to memorize the operator precedence for every data type, please read on.

Here's an example. A user says that she would like a list consisting of mountain bikes and road bikes priced over $500 and under $1,000. You know that the product subcategories for mountain bikes and road bikes are 1 and 2, respectively. This query follows the logic of the stated requirement:

```
SELECT  Name
       ,ProductNumber
       ,ListPrice
       ,ProductSubCategoryID
FROM Production.Product
WHERE ProductSubCategoryID = 1
   OR ProductSubCategoryID = 2
   AND ListPrice > 500
   AND ListPrice < 1000
```

If you run this query, you see that it returns 48 records that appear to meet the requirements (see Figure 5-19).

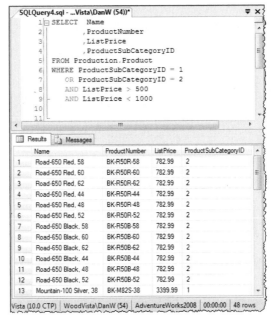

Figure 5-19

However, upon closer examination, you can see that you have mountain bikes on the list that cost over $1000.00. Why is that? Go back and take a look at the query. When the query parser has to contend with more than one logical operator, it has to decide how to process them. The order of precedence for logical operators is NOT, AND, then OR. So it will always process an AND expression before an OR expression. The mechanics of query processing are really up to the query optimizer, but the results for a given statement will always be the same. Later on you'll learn how to find out what the query optimizer does when it breaks down and processes a query. Most likely, in this case, it took the first AND expression,

```
ProductSubCategoryID = 2 AND ListPrice > 500
```

processed and buffered the results, and then the next AND expression,

```
AND  ListPrice < 1000
```

and used this to filter the first set of results. So far, so good, but it's the next step that gets you into trouble. Because the query parser processes an OR expression after all of the AND logic, it went back to the beginning of the WHERE clause and processed this statement:

```
ProductSubCategoryID = 1
```

Because this statement preceded the OR operator, it found all of the mountain bike records in the table and appended these to the first set of results. So, the query processor did what you told it to do but not necessarily what you wanted it to do.

Frankly, rearranging these statements will not give you the results you're looking for. Unless you find a way to tell the query-processing engine the order in which you want it to process these operations, you're not going to get a list of affordable bikes.

Using Parentheses

Filter expressions are often combined to return a very specific range and combination of records. When combining the individual expressions, it's often necessary (or at least a good idea) to use parentheses to separate expressions and to specify the operation precedence and order. Making a point to use parentheses when multiple operations are processed makes it unnecessary to be concerned with the complexities of normal operator precedence.

For example, I would like a list consisting of mountain bikes priced over $1,000 and road bikes priced over $500. I know that the product subcategories for mountain bikes and road bikes are 1 and 2, respectively. My query looks like this:

```
SELECT Name
     , ProductNumber
     , ListPrice
     , ProductSubCategoryID
FROM Production.Product
WHERE (ProductSubCategoryID = 1 AND ListPrice > 1000)
   OR (ProductSubCategoryID = 2 AND ListPrice > 500)
```

The parentheses in this example serve only to clarify the order of operations. Because the AND operator is processed before the OR operator, the parentheses are not actually necessary in this expression.

When combining OR operators with AND operators, a different combination of parenthetical and non-parenthetical comparisons would yield different results. The following queries exemplify this point. The previous example (with or without parentheses) returns 61 rows.

The following query is similar, but uses the OR operator. With the parentheses removed, it returns 136 rows (a sampling of which is shown in Figure 5-20).

```
SELECT    Name
     , ProductNumber
     , ListPrice
     , ProductSubCategoryID
FROM Production.Product
WHERE ProductSubCategoryID = 1 OR ListPrice > 1000
   AND ProductSubCategoryID = 2 OR ListPrice > 500
```

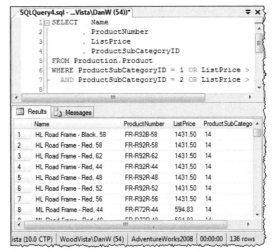

Figure 5-20

With parentheses grouping the two OR operators and separating the AND operators, the same query returns only 100 rows:

```
SELECT    Name
        , ProductNumber
        , ListPrice
        , ProductSubCategoryID
FROM Production.Product
WHERE (ProductSubCategoryID = 1 OR ListPrice > 1000)
  AND (ProductSubCategoryID = 2 OR ListPrice > 500)
```

The results are shown in Figure 5-21.

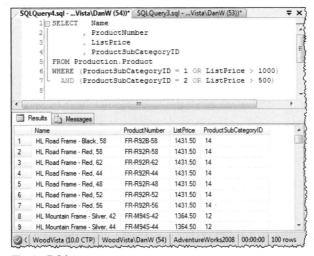

Figure 5-21

The bottom line is, whether or not parentheses are required, use them to state your intentions and to make your queries easier to read. When multiple operations are combined, it becomes increasingly important to group and separate operations using parentheses. Just as in mathematical expressions, parentheses can be nested any number of levels deep.

Sorting Results

Typically, you will want records to be returned in some sensible order. Rows can be sorted in order of practically any combination of columns. For example, you may want to see employee records listed in order of last name and then by first name. This means that for employees who have the same last name, records would be sorted by first name within that group. When writing and testing queries, you may see that some tables return rows in a specific order even if you don't make it a point to sort them. This may be due to existing indexes on the table, or it may be that records were entered in that order. Regardless, as a rule, if you want rows to be returned in a specific order, you should use the ORDER BY clause to enforce your sorting requirements and guarantee that records are sorted correctly if things change in the table.

The ORDER BY clause is always stated after the WHERE clause (if used) and can contain one or more columns in a comma-delimited list. If not stated otherwise, values will be sorted in ascending order. You can optionally specify ascending order using the ASC keyword. This means that the following two statements effectively do the same thing:

```
SELECT Name AS Product
       ,ListPrice
FROM Production.Product
WHERE ListPrice > 0
ORDER BY ListPrice
```

Or

```
SELECT Name AS Product
       ,ListPrice
       ,StandardCost
FROM Production.Product
WHERE ListPrice > 0
ORDER BY ListPrice ASC
```

As you see, records are sorted by the ListPrice column in ascending order. In the result set shown in Figure 5-22, I've scrolled down the list to view the products with a list price between 20 and 25.

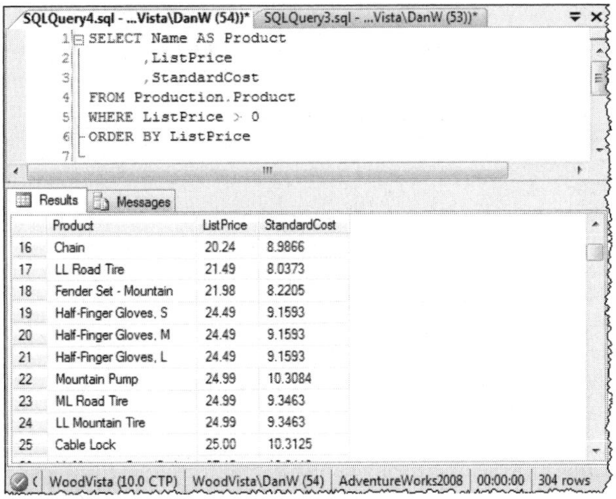

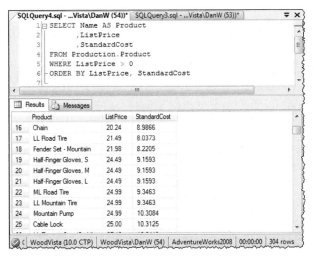

Figure 5-22

Note that the standard cost values are not sorted. As far as we're concerned, this order is completely arbitrary. You can change this by adding the StandardCost column to the ORDER BY list, as follows:

```
SELECT Name AS Product
      ,ListPrice
      ,StandardCost
FROM Production.Product
WHERE ListPrice > 0
ORDER BY ListPrice, StandardCost
```

Now the results show the products sorted in order of ListPrice and then subsorted by StandardCost. The standard cost values for products with a list price of $24.99 are now also in ascending order, as shown in Figure 5-23.

Figure 5-23

One more example shows how rows can be sorted in descending order. Suppose that you want the list of company products listed from most expensive to least expensive. This is a simple task. Using the ORDER BY clause, indicate that the ListPrice column should be sorted in descending order:

```
SELECT Name, ListPrice
FROM Production.Product
ORDER BY ListPrice DESC
```

Top Values

So far, you've seen that if you want to return a subset of the rows in a table, it's necessary to filter the results based on some sort of criteria. In some cases, you will want to simply return a specific number of records regardless of the number of qualifying rows. You have two options for returning top values: including a fixed number of rows or a percentage of total rows.

This example also involves the products sold by the AdventureWorks Cycles Company. As with the previous example, the following query returns a list of all products sorted by their list price from most expensive to least expensive. However, the list is limited to the 10 most expensive products.

```
SELECT TOP 10 Name, ListPrice
FROM Production.Product
ORDER BY ListPrice DESC
```

SQL Server doesn't try to make much sense out of this data. It doesn't even consider the sorted values when chopping off the list. It simply truncates the results after the tenth row has been returned, regardless of any values.

For the products that are bicycles, a unique product record represents a different color and frame size, so there are actually several rows for the same model. The most expensive bike, the road bike model 150, costs $3,578.27. Given all of the color and frame size combinations, there are five products at this price followed by five more Mountain Model 100 bikes in the TOP query. However in the example without the TOP statement you will notice that there were actually eight model 100 mountain bikes, but only five of them are returned with our TOP 10 query. The list is arbitrarily truncated after ten records.

Keep this in mind when asking for a "top" list.

WITH TIES

There is an easy way to solve the dilemma caused by tied values in the last position of your top list arbitrarily capping the results. First of all, you need to go back and clarify the business rule. Often, this means going back to your users or project sponsor to seek a restatement of requirements. That conversation might go something like this:

"You said that you wanted a report showing the top 25 most expensive products. What if the price of the 25th product were the same as one or more products down the list? Do you want to include other products that are tied for the same price as the item in the 25th position?"

If the answer is "Yes," the solution is quite simple. The WITH TIES statement simply continues to populate the list as long as subsequent rows' sorted values are the same as the last item in the Top list.

For example, the following requests a list of the top ten most expensive products using the same statement as before, except using TOP 10 WITH TIES:

```
SELECT TOP 10 WITH TIES Name, ListPrice
FROM Production.Product
ORDER BY ListPrice DESC
```

Figure 5-24 shows the complete results for this query.

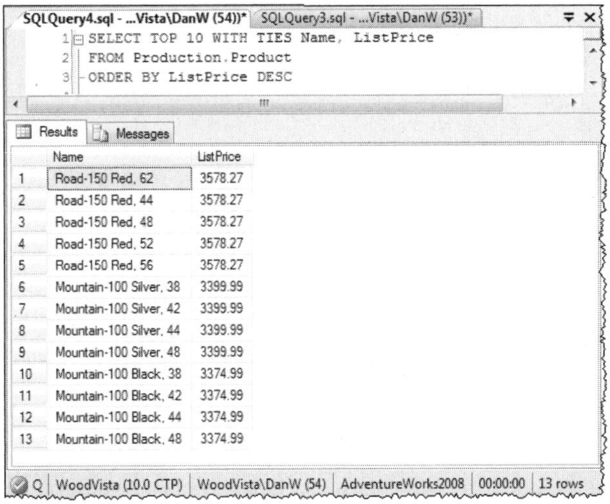

Figure 5-24

As you can see, 13 rows are returned because rows 11 through 13 have the same ListPrice value as row 10.

Percent

Rather than specifying a number of records to be returned with the TOP statement, you can also specify a percentage of the entire result set. SQL Server will do the math for you and then round to the nearest whole number. It essentially performs this calculation and then issues a Top X clause in place of the Top X Percent. Do this using the list price example. If you were to select all products without using the TOP statement, 504 rows would be returned. If you ask for the top 10 percent, a subset of rows is returned. Try it out:

```
SELECT TOP 10 PERCENT Name, ListPrice
FROM Production.Product
ORDER BY ListPrice DESC
```

As you can see in Figure 5-25, 51 rows are returned because SQL Server rounds up to the nearest whole record.

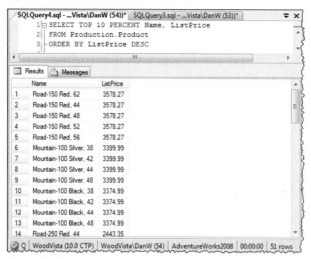

```
SELECT TOP 10 PERCENT Name, ListPrice
FROM Production.Product
ORDER BY ListPrice DESC
```

	Name	ListPrice
1	Road-150 Red, 62	3578.27
2	Road-150 Red, 44	3578.27
3	Road-150 Red, 48	3578.27
4	Road-150 Red, 52	3578.27
5	Road-150 Red, 56	3578.27
6	Mountain-100 Silver, 38	3399.99
7	Mountain-100 Silver, 42	3399.99
8	Mountain-100 Silver, 44	3399.99
9	Mountain-100 Silver, 48	3399.99
10	Mountain-100 Black, 38	3374.99
11	Mountain-100 Black, 42	3374.99
12	Mountain-100 Black, 44	3374.99
13	Mountain-100 Black, 48	3374.99
14	Road-250 Red, 44	2443.35

Figure 5-25

The same rules apply as if you had just used the Top X version of this statement. You can use WITH TIES and sort the result in either ascending or descending order.

Summary

Although you haven't seen a lot of complexity in this introduction to the SELECT statement and its fundamental nuances, it's a very powerful tool. As you continue to build more complex statements, the SELECT statement will be center stage. This chapter started by explaining selecting all rows using the asterisk (*) to return values for all available columns in a table and then moved on to specify selected columns. It is more efficient to return only the columns needed. This is especially the case when standard queries will be called routinely by software code, a report, or an application component. You learned how columns can be aliased to either rename a column or return a new column from a literal value, calculation, or expression based on multiple column values.

Filtering rows is the function of the WHERE clause, using logical comparisons. Values may be equal to, less than, greater than, or the opposite of any of the above by using the NOT operator. Character data types can also be compared using the LIKE operator to perform partial matching, wildcard, and pattern matching. Using Null is the accepted method to indicate that a column value has not been set — and testing for Null gives you an exact method to test for this condition. When combining comparison operators, it's often necessary to indicate the order of operations using parentheses. Not only does this ensure that operations are performed in the appropriate order, but it also makes queries much easier to read and maintain.

Rows can be sorted on any number of columns and can be placed in ascending or descending order. Finally, this chapter discussed the use of the TOP keyword, used to truncate a result set either by a specific number of rows or by a percentage of the entire result set.

Exercises

Exercise 1

Using SQL Server Management Studio, write a query to return employee records from the AdventureWorks2008 database. Include the NationalIDNumber, LoginID, JobTitle, BirthDate, MaritalStatus, and HireDate columns in the result set. Execute this query and view the results.

Exercise 2

Modify the query from Exercise 1 so that a new column, called AgeAtHire, can be added to the results that is a result of an expression using the HireDate column and the Birthdate column. (Hint: Use the DATEDIFF() function.)

Exercise 3

Return all Product records from the Production.Product table in the AdventureWorks2008 database that take 3 days or longer to manufacture. Include the Name and ListPrice columns.

Exercise 4

Return a list of the 10 most expensive products from the Production.Product table in the AdventureWorks database that have a product number beginning with "BK." Include only the ProductId, Name, ProductNumber, Color, and ListPrice columns. When complete, check to see if there are any products the same price as the number 10 product.

SQL Functions

Now that you understand how to formulate SQL queries and return result sets, you need to do something useful with this data. Once you have successfully retrieved values from tables, it's very common to further manipulate values to provide useful and meaningful results. This may involve performing calculations and mathematical operations, converting data, parsing values, combining values, and aggregating a range of values.

The purpose of this chapter is to help you learn the mechanics of using functions of all kinds. It introduces you to some of the more common value manipulation functions and some less-common functions to give a sample of these powerful capabilities.

At the end of the book, you'll find a reference for most of the system-supplied functions and the syntax needed to use them. Additionally, subsequent chapters contain more detailed information about specific groups of functions. For example, Chapter 7 discusses specific uses for aggregate functions in more advanced SQL queries, and Chapter 11 shows you how to use functions to support full-text index searches.

T-SQL functions are grouped into the categories described in the following table.

Function Category	Purpose
Aggregation	Return a scalar value representing an aggregation over a range of values, applying a specific aggregate selection or summary.
Configuration variables	Return information about the SQL Server execution environment that may be useful in programming objects.
Conversion	Convert values of one data type to another. Also used to apply formatting characteristics to dates, times, and numeric values.
Cursor	Loop through the rows in a result set in a procedural manner when iterating through a cursor.

(continued)

Function Category	Purpose
Date and time	Parse the date and time portions of a date value, as well as compare and manipulate date/time values.
Mathematical	Perform a variety of common and specialized mathematical operations. Useful in performing algebraic, trigonometric, statistical, approximating, and financial operations.
Metadata	Utility functions that return information about the SQL Server configuration details and details about the server and database settings.
Ranking	Enumerate sorted and top-valued result sets.
Security	Return role membership and privilege information for SQL Server users. Also include a set of functions to manage events and traces.
String manipulation	Used to parse, replace, and manipulate character values.
System	Utility functions used to perform a variety of tasks. These include value comparisons and value type testing. This category is also a catch-all for other functionality.
System statistical	Administrative utilities used to discover database system usage and environment information.

The Anatomy of a Function

The purpose of a function is to return a value. Most of the functions you will use return a *scalar value,* meaning a single unit of data, or a simple value. However, functions can return practically any data type, and this includes types such as Table and Cursor, which could be used to return entire, multi-row result sets. I won't take the discussion to that level in this chapter. Chapter 12 explains how to create and utilize user-defined functions to return more complex data.

Functions have been around for a long time, even long before SQL. The pattern used to call functions is the same in nearly all programming languages:

```
Result = Function()
```

In T-SQL, values are typically returned using the SELECT statement. If you just want to return a value in a query, you treat SELECT as the output operator without using an equals sign:

```
SELECT Function()
```

I'd Like to Have an Argument

When it comes to SQL functions, the term *argument* is used to mean an input variable or placeholder for a value. Functions can have any number of arguments and some arguments are required, whereas others are optional. Optional arguments are typically at the end of the comma-delimited argument list, making them easier to exclude if they are not to be provided in the function call.

When you read about functions in SQL Server Books Online or on-line help, you'll see optional arguments denoted in square brackets. In this example for the CONVERT() function, both the length argument for the data type and the style argument for the CONVERT() function are optional:

```
CONVERT ( data_type [ ( length ) ] , expression [ , style ] )
```

I'll simplify this because we're really not discussing how to use data types at the moment:

```
CONVERT ( data_type, expression [ , style ] )
```

According to this, the CONVERT() function will accept either two or three arguments. So, either of these examples would be acceptable:

```
SELECT CONVERT(varchar(20), GETDATE())
SELECT CONVERT(varchar(20), GETDATE(), 101)
```

The first argument for this function is the data type, varchar(20), and the second argument is another function, GETDATE(). The GETDATE() function returns the current system date and time in the datetime data type. The third argument in the second statement determines the style for the date information returned. The 101 in this case returns the date in the *mm/dd/yyyy* format. The GETDATE() function is described in more detail later in the chapter. Even if a function doesn't take an argument, or doesn't require an argument, it is called with a set of empty parentheses, like the GETDATE() function. Note that when a function is referred to by name throughout the book, the parentheses are included because this is considered standard form.

Deterministic Functions

Because of the inner-workings of the database engine, SQL Server has to separate functions into two different groups based on what's called *determinism*. This is not a new-age religion. It's simply a statement about whether the outcome of a function can be predicted based on its input parameters or by executing it one time. If a function's output is not dependent on any external factors, other than the value of input parameters, it is considered to be a deterministic function. If the output can vary based on any conditions in the environment or algorithms that produce random or dependent results, the function is *nondeterministic*. For instance, the GETDATE() function is nondeterministic because it will never return the same value twice in a single batch. Why make a big deal about something that seems so simple? Well, nondeterministic functions and global variables can't be used in some database programming objects, such as user-defined functions. This is due partially to the way SQL Server caches and precompiles executable objects. For simple, ad-hoc queries, knock yourself out and use any type of function you like; however, if you plan on building more advanced, reusable programming objects, it's important to understand this distinction.

As a brief example, the following functions are deterministic:

❑   AVG() (all aggregate functions are deterministic)

❑   CAST()

❑   CONVERT()

❑   DATEADD()

❑ DATEDIFF()

❑ ASCII()

❑ CHAR()

❑ SUBSTRING()

These functions and variables are nondeterministic:

❑ GETDATE()

❑ @@ERROR

❑ @@SERVICENAME

❑ CURSORSTATUS()

❑ RAND()

Using User Variables with Functions

Variables can be used for both input and output. In T-SQL, a user variable is prefixed with the @ symbol, declared as a specific data type, and can then be assigned a value using either the SET or SELECT statements. The following example shows the use of an integer (int) data type variable called @MyNumber, passed to the SQRT() function:

```
DECLARE @MyNumber int
SET @MyNumber = 144
SELECT SQRT(@MyNumber)
```

The result of this call is 12, the square root of 144.

Using SET to Assign Variables

The following example uses another int type variable, @MyResult, to capture the return value for the same function. This technique is most like the pattern used in procedural programming languages in which the SET statement is combined with an expression to assign a value to a parameter.

```
DECLARE @MyNumber int, @MyResult int
SET @MyNumber = 144
-- Assign the function result to the variable:
SET @MyResult = SQRT(@MyNumber)
-- Return the variable value
SELECT @MyResult
```

Using SELECT to Assign Variables

You can achieve the same result of assigning values to a variable by using a variation of the SELECT statement. A variable is declared prior to assigning a value. The chief advantage of using the SELECT statement instead of the SET command is that multiple variables can be assigned values in a single operation. The value is assigned using the SELECT statement and then can be used for any purpose after the SELECT statement has been executed:

```
DECLARE @MyNumber1 int, @MyNumber2 int, @MyResult1 int, @MyResult2 int
SELECT @MyNumber1 = 144, @MyNumber2 = 121
-- Assign the function result to the variable:
SELECT @MyResult1 = SQRT(@MyNumber1), @MyResult2 = SQRT(@MyNumber2)
-- Return the variable value
SELECT @MyResult1, @MyResult2
```

In the preceding example, the four variables are first declared, and then their values are assigned with two SELECT statements, instead of four separate SET statements. Functionally, these techniques are identical. However, populating multiple variables with a SELECT statement is generally more efficient in regards to server resources than multiple SET commands. The limitation of selecting multiple or even single values into parameters is that the population of variables cannot be combined with data retrieval operations. This is why the preceding example used a SELECT statement to populate the variables followed by a second SELECT statement to retrieve the data in the variables. For example, the following script will not work:

```
DECLARE @RestockName varchar(50)
SELECT ProductId
       ,@RestockName = Name + ':' + ProductNumber
FROM Production.Product
```

This script will generate the following error:

```
Msg 141, Level 15, State 1, Line 2
A SELECT statement that assigns a value to a variable must not be combined
with data-retrieval operations.
```

Using Functions in Queries

Functions are often combined with query expressions to modify column values. This is easily done by passing column names to function arguments. The function reference is inserted into the column list of a SELECT query, as follows:

```
SELECT JobTitle, NationalIdNumber, YEAR(BirthDate) AS BirthYear
FROM HumanResources.Employee
```

In this example, the BirthDate column value is passed into the YEAR() function as an argument. The function's result becomes the aliased column BirthYear.

Nested Functions

Often, you will find that the functionality you need doesn't exist in a single function. By design, functions are intended to be simple and focused on providing a specific feature. If functions did a lot of different things, they would be complicated and difficult to use (and some are, but fortunately, not many). For this and other reasons, each function simply does one thing. To get all of the functionality I need, I may pass the value returned from one function into another function. This is known as a *nested function call.*

Here's a simple example: The purpose of the GETDATE() function is to return the current date and time. It doesn't return elegantly formatted output; that's the job of the CONVERT() function. To get the benefit of both functions, I pass the output from the GETDATE() function into the value argument of the CONVERT() function, like this:

```
SELECT CONVERT(varchar(20), GETDATE(), 101)
```

You'll see a few examples of this pattern throughout this chapter.

Aggregate Functions

The essence of reporting is typically to distill a population of data into a value or values representing a trend or summary. This is what aggregation is all about. Aggregate functions answer the questions asked by the consumers of data:

❏   "What were the total sales of chicken gizzard by-products for last month?"

❏   "What is the average price paid for food condiments by male Brazilians between the ages of 19 and 24?"

❏   "What was the longest order-to-shipping time of all orders last quarter?"

❏   "Who is the oldest employee still working in the mail room?"

Aggregate functions return a scalar value (a single value) applying a specific aggregate operation. The return data type is comparable to that of the column or value passed to the function. Aggregates are often used along with grouping, rollup, and pivoting operations to produce results for data analysis. This is covered in greater detail in Chapter 7. The focus here is on some of the more common functions in simple SELECT queries.

Aggregate functions can be used with scalar input values, rather than in a SELECT query, but what's the point? I can pass the value 15 to each of these aggregate functions and each will return the same result:

```
SELECT AVG(15)
SELECT SUM(15)
SELECT MIN(15)
SELECT MAX(15)
```

They all return 15. After all, the average, sum, smallest, and largest value in a range of one value is that value. What happens if I count one value?

```
SELECT COUNT(15)
```

I get 1. I counted one value.

Now let's do something useful. Aggregate functions really are valuable only when used with a range of values in a result set. Each function performs its magic on all non-null values of a column. Unless you are applying grouping (which you will see in Chapter 7) you cannot return both aggregated values and regular column values in the same SELECT statement.

The AVG() Function

The AVG() function returns the average for a range of numeric values, for all non-null values. For example, a table contains the following gymnastics meet scores:

Gymnast	Event	Score
Sara	Vault	9.25
Cassie	Vault	8.75
Delaney	Vault	9.25
Sammi	Vault	8.05
Erika	Vault	8.60
Sara	Beam	9.70
Cassie	Beam	9.00
Delaney	Beam	9.25
Sammi	Beam	8.95
Erika	Beam	8.85

The following query is executed with these values:

```
SELECT AVG(Score)
```

The result would be 8.965.

If three girls didn't compete in some events and the table had some missing scores, these might be represented as NULLs:

Gymnast	Event	Score
Sara	Vault	9.25
Cassie	Vault	8.75
Delaney	Vault	NULL
Sammi	Vault	8.05
Erika	Vault	8.60
Sara	Beam	9.70
Cassie	Beam	NULL
Delaney	Beam	9.25
Sammi	Beam	NULL
Erika	Beam	8.85

In this case, the NULL values are not considered, and the average is calculated based on the existing numerical values. The result would be 8.921429.

However, if the missing scores were counted against the team, and the column contained zero values instead, this would seriously affect the overall score (6.245) and their chances of moving on to state competition.

The COUNT() Function

The COUNT() function returns an integer value for the number of non-null values in the column range. For instance, if the gymnastics data in the previous example were in a table called GymEvent and I wanted to know the number of events that Sammi received a score on, I could execute the following query:

```
SELECT COUNT(Score) FROM GymEvent WHERE Gymnast = 'Sammi'
```

The result would be 1 because Sammi participated only in the vault event, which is indicated by the score for Sammi's beam event being NULL.

If you need a count of all rows in a table, regardless of NULL values, use the following syntax:

```
SELECT COUNT(*) FROM table
```

Using the previous example with Sammi, a COUNT(*) query would look like this:

```
SELECT COUNT(*) FROM GymEvent WHERE Gymnast = 'Sammi'
```

Because the COUNT(*) function ignores NULL values, the result of this query would be 2.

The MIN() and MAX() Functions

The MIN() function returns the smallest (minimum) non-null value for a column range. The MAX() function returns the largest (maximum) value. These functions can be used with most data types and work according to the sorting rules of the type. To make this point, suppose that a table contains the following values stored in two different columns, one as an integer type and the other as a character type:

Column1 (int type)	Column2 (varchar type)
2	2
4	4
12	12
19	19

What will the MIN() and MAX() functions return? You may be surprised.

	Column1 (int type)	Column2 (varchar type)
MIN()	2	12
MAX()	19	4

Because values in Column2 are stored as characters rather than numbers, it is sorted according to the ASCII value of each character, from left to right. This is why 12 is less than any other value and 4 is greater than any other value.

The SUM() Function

The SUM() function is one of the most commonly used aggregates and is fairly self-explanatory. As with the AVG() function, it works with numeric data types and returns the additive sum of all non-null values in a column range.

You'll learn to use all of the aggregate functions in Chapter 7, including statistical functions. You'll also see how to create user-defined aggregates.

Configuration Variables

These aren't really functions, but they can be used in much the same way as system functions. Each global variable returns scalar information about the SQL Server execution environment. Following are some common examples.

The @@ERROR Variable

This variable contains the last error number for the current connection. The value for @@ERROR is 0 when a statement is executed with no errors. Errors are raised by the database engine when standard error conditions occur. All the standard error numbers and messages are viewable from the sys.messages system view and can be queried using the following script:

```
SELECT * FROM sys.messages
```

Custom errors can be raised manually using the RAISERROR statement and can be added to the sysmessages table using the sp_addmessage system stored procedure.

Following is a simple example of the @@ERROR variable. First I try to divide a number by 0. This causes the database engine to raise the standard error number 8134. Make sure to look at the Results tab to see the results of the query. By default, when an error occurs the Messages tab of Management studio is shown on top of the Results tab.

```
SELECT 5 / 0
SELECT @@ERROR
```

Successfully retrieving the value of @@ERROR causes the value of @@ERROR to return to 0 because @@ERROR holds only the error number for the previously executed statement. If I want to retrieve additional error information, I could get it from the sys.messages view using the following script:

```
SELECT 5 / 0
SELECT * FROM master.dbo.sysmessages WHERE error = @@ERROR
```

Later in this section I'll show you how to use error functions for a more efficient way of returning error data.

SQL Server is installed by default with languages in addition to U.S. English. Each language-specific error message has a language identifier (msglangid) that corresponds to a language in the syslanguages table, as shown in Figure 6-1.

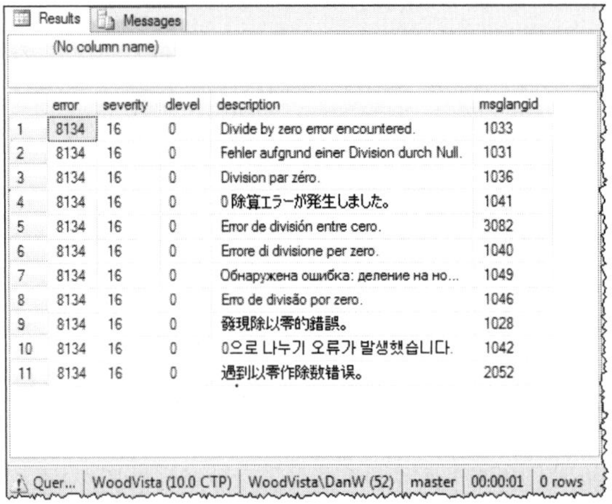

Figure 6-1

In case you were wondering, the attribute name msglangid has been unofficially defined as "Microsoft Global Language Identifier." Microsoft uses this identifier to identify a language or a combination of a language and a country, which Microsoft defines as a *locale*. For instance, the English language installed with SQL Server is United States English with a msglangid of 1033, as opposed to United Kingdom English with a msglangid of 2057. The following table describes the language identifiers installed by default with SQL Server 2008. The only difference in SQL Server 2005 is the absence of msglangid 1046 (Portuguese).

Language	Msglangid
Chinese (Traditional/Taiwan)	1028
German (Germany)	1031
English (United States)	1033
French (France)	1036

Language	Msglangid
Italian (Italy)	1040
Japanese	1041
Korean	1042
Portuguese (Brazil)	1046
Russian	1049
Chinese (Simplified/PRC)	2052
Spanish (International Sort)	3082

To retrieve a list of all installed and supported languages, execute the following query:

```
SELECT alias, name, msglangid
FROM sys.syslanguages
```

The @@SERVICENAME Variable

This is the name of the Windows service used to execute and maintain the current instance of SQL Server. This will typically return the value MSSQLSERVER for the default instance of SQL Server. However, named instances of SQL Server have uniquely named service names. For example, on my computer named WoodVista, I have two instances of SQL Server: a default instance and a named instance called AughtEight. Retrieving the contents of the @@SERVICENAME global variable on the default instance returns MSSQLSERVER, but on the named instance it returns AUGHTEIGHT

The @@TOTAL_ERRORS Variable

This is the total number of errors that have occurred since the current connection was opened. As with the @@ERROR variable, this is unique for each user session and is reset when each connection closes.

The @@TOTAL_READ Variable

This is a count of the total disk read operations that have occurred since the current connection was opened. This variable is interesting to the DBA to see disk read activity over time.

The @@VERSION Variable

This variable contains the complete version information for the current instance of SQL Server.

```
SELECT @@VERSION
```

For example, for an instance of SQL Server 2005 Developer Edition running on Windows XP, this script returns the following:

```
Microsoft SQL Server 2005 - 9.00.3050.00 (Intel X86)   Mar  2 2007 20:01:28
Copyright (c) 1988-2005 Microsoft Corporation  Developer Edition on Windows
NT 5.1 (Build 2600: Service Pack 2)
```

For an instance of SQL Server 2008 (RTM) Developer Edition running on Windows Vista, the script returns the following:

```
Microsoft SQL Server 2008 (RTM) - 10.0.1600.22 (Intel X86)   Jul  9 2008
14:43:34   Copyright (c) 1988-2008 Microsoft Corporation  Developer Edition on
Windows NT 6.0 <X86> (Build 6000: )
```

The actual version number, used internally at Microsoft, is a simple integer value, although released products may have other branded names. In this case, SQL Server 2005 is really version 9, and SQL Server 2008 is version 10. Windows XP Professional shows up as Windows NT version 5.1 and Vista shows up as 6.0. The build number is used for internal control and reflects changes made in beta and preview product releases, and post-release service packs.

Error Functions

Previously, you learned how to use the @@ERROR global variable to retrieve error information. However, a better way of returning all the available error data is by using error functions. The information returned by these functions can be returned and stored in an error tracking table for error auditing. The error functions are nested inside an error-handling routine. We'll discuss error handling in more detail Chapter 11, but it is implemented by using a block of code nested inside a TRY and END TRY statement, followed by a block of code inside a CATCH and END CATCH statement.

```
--Try to do something
BEGIN TRY
   SELECT 5 / 0
END TRY
--If it causes an error, do this
BEGIN CATCH
   PRINT ERROR_MESSAGE()
END CATCH
```

Be advised that when we speak of error catching, that is exactly what is meant. Running the previous example causes no discernable error because the error was caught and "handled" within the catch block. It is imperative that when writing error handling code that the SQL programmer includes in the catch block code that will raise a system error, if that is appropriate. Error handling is covered in detail in Chapter 12.

There are several error functions that return specific information about the error:

❑ ERROR_MESSAGE() — Returns the description of the error.

❑ ERROR_NUMBER() — Returns the number of the error.

❑ ERROR_SEVERITY() — Returns the error severity. Error severity is an integer value ranging from 0 to 25. The following table briefly describes the severity levels:

Severity Level	Description
0 through 10	Informational messages. Will not cause any system error flag to be raised.
11 through 16	User-correctable errors, such as a foreign key or primary key violation.
17	Non-fatal insufficient resource error
18	Non-fatal internal error
19	Fatal insufficient resource error
20	Fatal error in current process
21	Fatal database error in all processes
22	Fatal table integrity error
23	Fatal database integrity error
24	Fatal hardware error
25	Fatal system error

❑ ERROR_STATE() — Returns the error state number. The error state is an integer value that can be used to uniquely identify the cause of a system error.

❑ ERROR_LINE() — Returns the line number inside the routine that caused the error.

❑ ERROR_PROCEDURE() — Returns the name of the stored procedure or trigger where the error occurred.

The following script uses T-SQL's built-in error handling to capture and print the error data returned when a divide by 0 is encountered. The results of the PRINT command are shown in the Messages tab of Management Studio.

```
BEGIN TRY
    SELECT 5/0
END TRY
BEGIN CATCH
    PRINT 'Error Message='
    PRINT ERROR_MESSAGE()
    PRINT 'Error Number='
    PRINT ERROR_NUMBER()
```

(continued)

(continued)

```
      PRINT 'Error Severity='
      PRINT ERROR_SEVERITY()
      PRINT 'Error State='
      PRINT ERROR_STATE()
      PRINT 'Error Line='
      PRINT ERROR_LINE()
      PRINT 'Error Procedure='
      PRINT ERROR_PROCEDURE()
   END CATCH
```

As you can see, executing this script returns more detailed error information in the Messages tab than just the error number.

```
(0 row(s) affected)
Error Message=
Divide by zero error encountered.
Error Number=
8134
Error Severity=
16
Error State=
1
Error Line=
2
Error Procedure=
```

The ERROR_PROCEDURE() function did not return the procedure name because the error was generated in an ad-hoc query.

Conversion Functions

Data type conversion can be performed using the CAST() and CONVERT() functions. For most purposes, these two functions are redundant and reflect the evolutionary history of the SQL language. The functionality may be similar, but the syntax is different. Not all values can be converted to other data types. Generally speaking, any value that can be converted can be done so with a simple function call.

The CAST() Function

The CAST() function accepts one argument, an expression, which includes both the source value and a target data type separated by the word AS. Here is an example, using the literal string '123' converted to an integer:

```
SELECT CAST('123' AS int)
```

The return value will be the integer value 123. However, what happens if you try to convert a string representing a fractional value to an integer?

```
SELECT CAST('123.4' AS int)
```

Neither the CAST() nor the CONVERT() functions will do any guessing, rounding, or truncation for you. Because the value 123.4 can't be represented using the int data type, the function call produces an error:

```
Server: Msg 245, Level 16, State 1, Line 1
Syntax error converting the varchar value '123.4' to a column of data type int.
```

If you need to return a valid numeric equivalent value, you must use a data type equipped to handle the value. There are a few that would work in this case. If you use the CAST() function with your value to a target type of decimal, you can specifically define the precision and scale for the decimal value. In this example, the precision and scale are 9 and 2, respectively. Precision is the total number of digits that can be stored to both the left and right of the decimal point. Scale is the number of digits that will be stored to the right of the decimal point. This means that the maximum whole number value would be 9,999,999 and the smallest fractional number would be .01.

```
SELECT CAST('123.4' AS decimal(9,2))
```

The decimal data type displays the significant decimal positions in the results grid:

```
123.40
```

The default values for precision and scale are 18 and 0 respectively. Without providing values for precision and scale of the decimal type, SQL Server effectively truncates the fractional part of the number without causing an error.

```
SELECT CAST('123.4' AS decimal)
```

The result looks like an integer value:

```
123
```

Applying data type conversions to table data is very easy to do. The next example uses the Product table, and starts with the following query:

```
SELECT ProductNumber, ProductLine, ProductModelID
FROM Production.Product
WHERE ProductSubCategoryID < 4
```

The production manager has been tasked with creating a system to uniquely identify each bike that is produced so that it is trackable as to model, type, and category. She has decided to combine the product number, product line identifier, and product model identifier, along with a sequential number, to create this unique serial number for every bike produced. In the first step of the process, she has asked that you provide a list of all the possible product root identities that include all the attributes except for the sequential number.

If you use the following expression, you don't get the result you're looking for. In fact, as you can see in Figure 6-2, you don't get any result at all.

```
SELECT ProductNumber
        + '-'
        + ProductLine
        + '-'
        + ProductModelID AS BikeSerialNum
FROM Production.Product
WHERE ProductSubCategoryID < 4
```

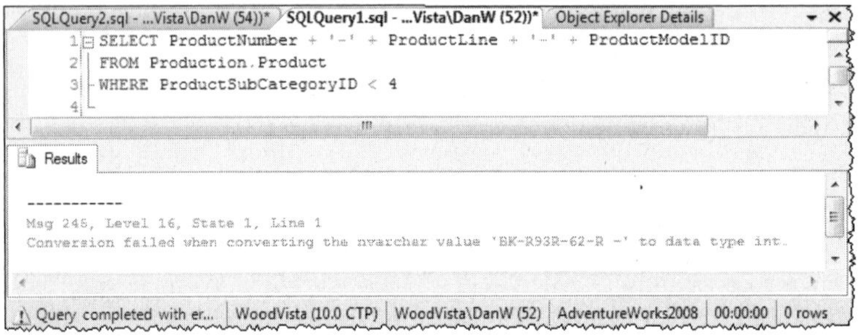

Figure 6-2

Instead of retrieving the results you anticipated, you get the somewhat cryptic error message about converting an `nvarchar` value to an `int`. Because you didn't actually ask for any conversion, this error can be confusing. The problem with this query is that you're trying to concatenate the character value (`ProductNumber`) with the first hyphen, and then another character value (`ProductLine`) with another character value (the second hyphen), and finally adding in the `ProductModelID`, which is an `int`.

The query engine perceives the hyphen to be a mathematical operator, rather than a character. Regardless of the outcome, you need to fix the expression and make sure you are working with the appropriate data types. This expression makes the necessary type conversions and returns a result, as shown in Figure 6-3.

```
SELECT ProductNumber
        + '-'
        + ProductLine
        + '-'
        + CAST(ProductModelID AS char(4)) AS BikeSerialNum
FROM Production.Product
WHERE ProductSubCategoryID < 4
```

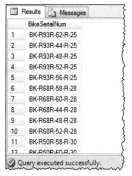

Figure 6-3

Converting the integer values to character data types makes these character values without adding any extra spaces. These values are combined with the hyphen using the plus sign to concatenate string values rather than adding and subtracting the previous numeric values.

The CONVERT() Function

For simple type conversion, the CONVERT() function does the same thing as the CAST() function, only with different syntax. The CAST() function is generally easier to use and is simple in its function. The chief advantage of the CONVERT() function is its capability to format dates as well as numeric data. It requires two arguments: the first for the target data type and the second for the source value. Here are a couple of quick examples similar to those used in the preceding section:

```
SELECT CONVERT(int, '123')
SELECT CONVERT(decimal(9,2), '123.4')
```

The CONVERT() function's enhanced features make it useful for returning formatted string values. Date values can be formatted in a variety of ways. There are 28 predefined date formats to accommodate international and special-purpose date and time output. The following table shows how these break down.

Format Number	Year Digits	Hour Format	Description	Example
0	2	12	Default	Apr 25 2005 1:05PM
1	2		US	04/25/05
2	2		ANSI	05.04.25
3	2		UK/French	25/04/05
4	2		German	25.04.05
5	2		Italian	25-04-05

(continued)

Format Number	Year Digits	Hour Format	Description	Example
6	2		Custom - Date Only	25 Apr 05
7	2		Custom - Date Only	Apr 25, 05
8		24	Custom - Time Only	13:05:35
9	4	12	Default, milliseconds	Apr 25 2005 1:05:35:123PM
10	2		US	04-25-05
11	2		Japan	05/04/25
12	2		ISO	050425
13	4	24	Europe	25 Apr 2005 13:05:35:123
14		24	Custom Time, milliseconds	13:05:35:123
100	4	12	Default	Apr 25 2005 1:05PM
101	4		US	04/25/2005
102	4		ANSI	2005.04.25
103	4		UK/French	25/04/2005
104	4		German	25.04.2005
105	4		Italian	25-04-2005
106	4		Custom - Date Only	25 Apr 2005
107	4		Custom - Date Only	Apr 25, 2005
108		24	Custom - Time Only	13:05:35
109	4	12	Default, milliseconds	Apr 25 2005 1:05:35:123PM
110	4		US	04-25-2005
111	4		Japan	2005/04/25
112	4		ISO	20050425
113	4	24	Europe	25 Apr 2005 13:05:35:123
114		24	Custom Time, milliseconds	13:05:35:123

The third argument to this function is optional and accepts the format number integer value. The examples provided in the grid apply to the datetime data type. When converting from the smalldatetime data type, the formatting remains the same but some elements will display 0 because it does not support milliseconds. Here are a few examples of some related script along with formatted date output:

```
SELECT 'Default Date: '  + CONVERT(varchar(50), GETDATE(), 100)
Default Date: Apr 25 2005 1:05PM
SELECT 'US Date: ' + CONVERT(varchar(50), GETDATE(), 101)
US Date: 04/25/2005
SELECT 'ANSI Date: '  + CONVERT(varchar(50), GETDATE(), 102)
ANSI Date: 2005.04.25
SELECT 'UK/French Date: ' + CONVERT(varchar(50), GETDATE(), 103)
UK/French Date: 25/04/2005
SELECT 'German Date: ' + CONVERT(varchar(50), GETDATE(), 104)
German Date: 25.04.2005
```

Format numbers 0, 1, and 2 also apply to numeric types and affect the format of decimal and thousand separators. The effect is different for different data types. In general, using the format number 0 (or no value for this argument) returns a formatted value in the data type's most native form. Using 1 or 2 generally displays a more detailed or precise value. The following example uses 0:

```
DECLARE @Num Money
SET @Num = 1234.56
SELECT CONVERT(varchar(50), @Num, 0)
```

It returns the following:

```
1234.56
```

Using 1 returns the following:

```
1,234.56
```

And using 2 returns the following:

```
1234.5600
```

This example does the same thing with a float type:

```
DECLARE @Num float
SET @Num = 1234.56
SELECT CONVERT(varchar(50), @Num, 2)
```

Using the value 0 doesn't change the format from what you've provided but using 1 or 2 returns the number expressed in scientific notation, the latter using 15 decimal positions:

```
1.234560000000000e+003
```

The STR() Function

This is a quick-and-easy conversion function that converts a numeric value to a string. The function accepts three arguments: the numeric value, the overall length, and the number of decimal positions. If the integer part of the number and decimal positions is shorter than the overall length, the result is left-padded with spaces. In this first example, the value (including the decimal) is five characters long. I've made it a point to show the results in the grid so you can see any left padding. This call asks for an overall length of eight characters with four decimal positions:

```
SELECT STR(123.4, 8, 4)
```

The result has the decimal value right-filled with 0s: 123.4000.

Here I'm passing in a ten-character value and asking for an eight-character result, with four decimal positions:

```
SELECT STR(123.456789, 8, 4)
```

The result must be truncated to meet my requirements. The STR() function rounds the last digit: 123.4568.

Now I'll pass in the number 1 for the value and ask for a six-character result with four decimal positions. In this case, the STR() function right-fills the decimal value with zeros.

```
SELECT STR(1, 6, 4)
    1.0000
```

However, if I specify an overall length greater than the length of the value, decimal point, and the decimal value, the result will be left-padded with spaces.

```
SELECT STR(1, 12, 4)
```

1.0000

```
SELECT STR(1, 6, 4)
1.0000
SELECT STR(1, 12, 4)
_____   1.0000
```

Cursor Functions and Variables

Chapter 9, "Advanced Queries and Scripting," discusses the use of cursors along with some of the pros and cons of using this technique. The short version of this topic is that cursors can provide the ability to process multiple rows of data, one row at a time, in a procedural loop. This ability comes at a cost when compared with more efficient, set-based operations. One function and two global variables are provided to help manage cursor operations.

The CURSOR_STATUS() Function

The CURSOR_STATUS() function returns an integer indicating the status of a cursor-type variable passed into the function. A number of different types of cursors can affect the behavior of this function. For simplicity, the return value typically will be one of those listed in the following table.

Return Value	Description
1	Cursor contains one or more rows (dynamic cursor contains 0 or more rows).
0	Cursor contains no rows.
−1	Cursor is closed.
−2	Cursor is not allocated.
−3	Cursor doesn't exist.

The @@CURSOR_ROWS Global Variable

This variable is an integer value representing the number of rows in the cursor that are open in the current connection. Depending on the cursor type, this value may or may not represent the actual number of rows in the result set.

The @@FETCH_STATUS Global Variable

The @@FETCH_STATUS variable is a flag that indicates the state of the current cursor pointer. It is used primarily to determine whether a row still exists and when you have reached the end of the result set after executing a FETCH NEXT statement. When you open a cursor, the @@FETCH_STATUS value is -1. Once the first value is fetched into the cursor, the @@FETCH_STATUS value changes to 0. It stays at 0 until there are no more rows to fetch, at which time it changes back to -1. The use of this function is shown in Chapter 9.

Date Functions

These functions are used for working with datetime and smalldatetime type values. Some are used for parsing the date and time portions of a date value and for comparing and manipulating date/time values. The difference between the datetime and smalldatetime types is shown in the following table:

Data Type	Storage Requirement	Date Range
datetime	8 bytes	1/1/1753 – 12/31/9999
smalldatetime	4 bytes	1/1/1900 – 6/6/2079

The DATEADD() Function

The DATEADD() function adds a specific number of date unit intervals to a date/time value. For example, to determine the date 90 days after April 29, 1988, you could use the following statement:

```
SELECT DATEADD(Day, 90, '4-29-2007')
```

The answer is as follows:

```
2007-07-28 00:00:00.000
```

Any of the values in the following table can be passed in the interval argument.

Interval	Interval Argument Values
Year	Year, yyyy, yy
Quarter	Quarter, qq, q
Month	Month, mm, m
Day of the year	DayOfYear, dy, y
Day	Day, dd, d
Week	Week, wk, ww
Hour	Hour, hh
Minute	Minute, mi, n
Second	Second, ss, s
Millisecond	Millisecond, ms

Using the same date as before, here are some more examples. This time, I'll include the time as well. The results are on the following line:

18 years later:

```
SELECT DATEADD(Year, 18, '4-29-1988 10:30 AM')
2006-04-29 10:30:00.000
```

18 years before:

```
SELECT DATEADD(yy, -18, '4-29-1988 10:30 AM')
1970-04-29 10:30:00.000
```

9,000 seconds after:

```
SELECT DATEADD(Second, 9000, '4-29-1988 10:30 AM')
1988-04-29 13:00:00.000
```

9,000,000 milliseconds before:

```
SELECT DATEADD(ms, -9000000, '4-29-1988 10:30 AM')
1988-04-29 08:00:00.000
```

You can combine the CONVERT() and the DATEADD() functions to format a return date value nine months before September 8, 1989, as follows:

```
SELECT CONVERT(varchar(20), DATEADD(m, -9, '9-8-1989'), 101)
12/08/1988
```

This returns a variable-length character value, which is a little easier to read than the default dates you saw in the previous results. This is a nested function call where the results from the DATEADD() function (a datetime type value) are fed to the value argument of the CONVERT() function.

The DATEDIFF() Function

I think of the DATEADD() and DATEDIFF() functions as cousins — sort of like multiplication and division. There are four elements in this equation: the start date, the interval (date unit), the difference value, and the end date. If you have three, you can always figure out what the fourth one is. I use a start date, an integer value, and interval unit with the DATEADD() function to return the end date value relative to a starting date. The DATEDIFF() function returns the difference integer value if I provide the start and end dates and interval. Do you see the relationship?

To demonstrate, I simply choose any two dates and an interval unit as arguments. The function returns the difference between the two dates in the interval unit provided. I want to know what the difference is between the dates 9-8-1989 and 10-17-1991 in months:

```
SELECT DATEDIFF(month, '9-8-1989', '10-17-1991')
```

The answer is 25 months. How about the difference in days?

```
SELECT DATEDIFF(day, '9-8-1989', '10-17-1991')
```

It's 769 days.

How about the difference in weeks between 7-2-1996 and 8-4-1997?

```
SELECT DATEDIFF(week, '7-2-1996', '8-4-1997')
```

It's 57 weeks.

You can even figure out how old you are in seconds:

```
DECLARE @MyBirthDate datetime
SET @MyBirthDate = '7-16-1962'
SELECT DATEDIFF(ss, @MyBirthDate, GETDATE())
```

Someone is almost 1.5 billion seconds old!

You can apply this function to a query by passing a column name to the value argument. First let's build a simple table with some names and birthdates in it. We'll use the same basic table structure that we used in Chapter 5.

```
--SQL Server 2005/2008 syntax:
USE AdventureWorks2008
GO
CREATE TABLE dbo.SlateGravelEmployee
(LastName varchar(25) NULL
,FirstName varchar(25) NULL
,Position varchar(25) NULL
,BirthDate datetime NULL);
INSERT SlateGravelEmployee
VALUES
('Flintstone', 'Fred', 'Bronto Driver', '12-31-1960')
INSERT SlateGravelEmployee
VALUES
('Rubble', 'Barney', 'Accountant', '02-14-1964')
INSERT SlateGravelEmployee
VALUES
('Turleyrock', 'Paul', 'Developer', '03-24-1967')
INSERT SlateGravelEmployee
VALUES
('Petriwood', 'Dan', 'DBA', '07-16-1962')
INSERT SlateGravelEmployee
VALUES
('Johnstone', 'Randy', 'System Administrator', '03-14-1961')
INSERT SlateGravelEmployee
VALUES
('Witherstone', 'Mark', 'Vice President', '09-27-1967')
```

```
--SQL Server 2008 syntax:
USE AdventureWorks2008
GO
CREATE TABLE dbo.SlateGravelEmployee
(LastName varchar(25) NULL
,FirstName varchar(25) NULL
,Position varchar(25) NULL);
,BirthDate datetime NULL);
INSERT SlateGravelEmployee
VALUES
  ('Flintstone', 'Fred', 'Bronto Driver', '12-31-1960')
,('Rubble', 'Barney', 'Accountant', '02-14-1964')
,('Turleyrock', 'Paul', 'Developer', '03-24-1967')
,('Petriwood', 'Dan', 'DBA', '07-16-1962')
,('Johnstone', 'Randy', 'System Administrator', '03-14-1961')
,('Witherstone', 'Mark', 'Vice President', '09-27-1967')
```

The following query will return the name and birthdates from our table. The DATEDIFF() function is used to extract information from a column containing datetime data. This will tell you the approximate age of each Slate Gravel employee.

```
SELECT LastName
      ,FirstName
      ,BirthDate
      ,DATEDIFF(YEAR, BirthDate, GETDATE()) AS ApproximateAge
FROM SlateGravelEmployee
ORDER BY LastName
```

Figure 6-4 shows the results.

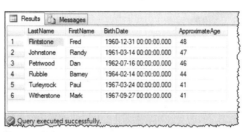

Figure 6-4

This may look right at first glance, but it's not accurate to the day. For example, according to the data, Fred's birth date is on December 31 and he would be celebrating his 48th birthday this year (I'm running the query in July, 2008). If I were to use the previous calculation to determine when his age changes, I would be sending Fred a birthday card sometime in January, about eleven months early.

Unless you find the difference between these dates in a more granular unit and then do the math, the result will only be accurate within a year of the employee's actual birth date. This example factors the number of days in a year (including leap year). Converting to an int type truncates, rather than rounds, the value:

```
SELECT LastName
      ,FirstName
      ,BirthDate
      ,DATEDIFF(YEAR, BirthDate, GETDATE()) AS ApproximateAge
      ,CONVERT(int, DATEDIFF(day, BirthDate, GETDATE())/365.25) AS Age
FROM SlateGravelEmployee
ORDER BY LastName
```

Compare the results shown in Figure 6-5 with those of the previous example.

Now Fred is 47 and the rest of the employees' ages should be accurate within about a day. The BirthDate column in this table stores the employee's birth date as of midnight (00:00:00 AM). This is the first second of a date. The GETDATE() function returns the current date and time. This means that I'm comparing two dates with a difference of about eight hours (it's about 8:00 AM as I write this). If you want this calculation to be even more accurate, you need to convert the result of the GETDATE() function to a datetime value at midnight of the current date.

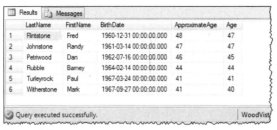

Figure 6-5

The DATEPART() and DATENAME() Functions

These functions return the date part, or unit, for a `datetime` or `smalldatetime` value. The `DATEPART()` function returns an integer value, and the `DATENAME()` function returns a string containing the descriptive name, if applicable. For example, passing the date 4-29-1988 to the `DATEPART()` function and requesting the month returns the number 4:

```
SELECT DATEPART(month, '4-29-1988')
```

Whereas, with the same parameters, the `DATENAME()` function returns April:

```
SELECT DATENAME(month, '4-29-1988')
```

Both of these functions accept values from the same list of date part argument constants as the `DATEADD()` function.

The GETDATE() and GETUTCDATE() Functions

Both of these functions return the current date and time as a DateTime type. The `GETUTCDATE()` function uses the time zone setting on the server to determine the equivalent Universal Time Coordinate time. This is the same as Greenwich Mean Time or what pilots call "Zulu Time." Both functions are accurate to 3.33 milliseconds:

```
SELECT GETDATE()
SELECT GETUTCDATE()
```

Executing these functions returns the unformatted result shown in Figure 6-6.

Figure 6-6

Because I'm in the Pacific time zone and currently in daylight savings time, there is a seven-hour difference between the current time and UTC. When in standard time, there would be an eight-hour difference. I can verify this using the following `DATEDIFF()` function call:

```
SELECT DATEDIFF(hour, GETDATE(), GETUTCDATE())
```

The SYSDATETIME() and SYSUTCDATETIME() Functions

These SQL Server 2008 functions are identical to `GETDATE()` and `GETUTCDATE()` functions, respectively, with the exception that instead of returning the results in the `datetime` data type, they return the results in the new SQL Server 2008 data type `datetime2`, which is accurate up to 100 nanoseconds, depending on the hardware the server is installed on.

```
SELECT SYSDATETIME()
SELECT SYSUTCDATETIME()
```

The DAY(), MONTH(), and YEAR() Functions

These three functions return an integer date part of a `datetime` or `smalldatetime` type value. They serve a variety of useful purposes, including the ability to create your own unique date formats. Suppose that you need to create a custom date value as a character string. By converting the output from each of these functions to character types and then concatenating the results, you can arrange them practically any way you want:

```
SELECT 'Year: ' + CONVERT(varchar(4), YEAR(GETDATE()))
    + ', Month: ' + CONVERT(varchar(2), MONTH(GETDATE()))
    + ', Day: ' + CONVERT(varchar(2), DAY(GETDATE()))
```

As I write this, the script produces the following:

```
Year: 2008, Month: 2, Day: 20
```

The next section discusses string manipulation functions and uses a similar technique to build a compact custom time stamp.

String Manipulation Functions

String functions are used to parse, replace, and manipulate character values. One of the great challenges when working with quantities or raw character data is to reliably extract meaningful information. A number of string parsing functions are available to identify and parse substrings (a portion of a larger character type value). As humans, we do this all the time. When presented with a document, an invoice, or written text, we intuitively identify and isolate the meaningful pieces of information. Automating this process can be a cumbersome task when dealing with even moderately complex text values. These functions contain practically all the tools necessary. The challenge is to find the simplest and most elegant method.

The ASCII(), CHAR(), UNICODE(), and NCHAR() Functions

These four functions are similar because they all deal with converting values between a character and the industry standard numeric representation of a character. The American Standard Code for Information Interchange (ASCII) standard character-set includes 128 alpha, numeric, and punctuation characters. This set of values is the foundation of the IBM PC architecture, and although some of it is now somewhat antiquated, much remains and is still central to modern computing. If you use the English language on your computer, every character on your keyboard is represented in the ASCII character-set. This is great for English-speaking (or at least English-typing) computer users, but what about everyone else on the planet?

In the evolution of the computer, it didn't take long for the ASCII set to become obsolete. It was soon extended from a 128 to a 256 ANSI character-set which uses a single byte to store every character. Still an American standard (held by the American National Standards Institute), this extended list of characters meets the needs of many other users, supporting most western European language characters, but is still founded on the original English-language character-set. To support all printable languages, the Unicode standard was devised to support multiple language-specific character-sets. Each Unicode character requires 2 bytes of storage space, twice the space as ASCII and ANSI characters. However, with 2 bytes, more than 65,000 unique characters can be represented providing support for Eastern European and Asian characters. SQL Server supports both ASCII and Unicode standards.

The two ASCII-based functions are ASCII() and CHAR(). The fundamental principle here is that every character used on the computer is actually represented as a number. To find out which number is used for a character, pass a single-character string to the ASCII() function, as follows:

```
SELECT ASCII('A')
```

This returns 65.

What if you know the number and want to convert it to a character? That's the job of the CHAR() function:

```
SELECT CHAR(65)
```

This returns the letter A.

To get a complete list of ASCII character values, you can populate a temporary table with the values 0 through 127 and then use the CHAR() function to return the corresponding characters. I'll shorten the script but include the entire result set in multi-column format, to save space:

```
-- Create temporary table for numbers:
Create Table #ASCIIVals (ASCIIValue smallint)
-- Insert numbers 0 - 127 into table:
Insert Into #ASCIIVals (ASCIIValue) Select 0
Insert Into #ASCIIVals (ASCIIValue) Select 1
Insert Into #ASCIIVals (ASCIIValue) Select 2
Insert Into #ASCIIVals (ASCIIValue) Select 3
Insert Into #ASCIIVals (ASCIIValue) Select 4
...
Insert Into #ASCIIVals (ASCIIValue) Select 123
Insert Into #ASCIIVals (ASCIIValue) Select 124
Insert Into #ASCIIVals (ASCIIValue) Select 125
Insert Into #ASCIIVals (ASCIIValue) Select 126
Insert Into #ASCIIVals (ASCIIValue) Select 127
-- Return all integer values and corresponding ASCII characters:
SELECT ASCIIValue, CHAR(ASCIIValue) AS Character FROM #ASCIIVals
```

Here are the results reformatted in a multi-column grid. Note that non-printable control characters show as small squares in the results grid. Depending on a number of factors, such as fonts or languages installed, these may be displayed a little differently.

ASCII Value	Character	ASCII Value	Character	ASCII Value	Character	ASCII Value	Character
0		32		64	@	96	'
1		33	!	65	A	97	a
2		34	"	66	B	98	b
3		35	#	67	C	99	c
4		36	$	68	D	100	d
5		37	%	69	E	101	e
6		38	&	70	F	102	f
7		39	'	71	G	103	g
8		40	(	72	H	104	h
9		41	)	73	I	105	i
10		42	*	74	J	106	j
11		43	+	75	K	107	k
12		44	,	76	L	108	l
13		45	-	77	M	109	m
14		46	.	78	N	110	n
15		47	/	79	O	111	o
16		48	0	80	P	112	p
17		49	1	81	Q	113	q
18		50	2	82	R	114	r
19		51	3	83	S	115	s
20		52	4	84	T	116	t
21		53	5	85	U	117	u
22		54	6	86	V	118	v
23		55	7	87	W	119	w
24		56	8	88	X	120	x
25		57	9	89	Y	121	y

(continued)

ASCII Value	Character	ASCII Value	Character	ASCII Value	Character	ASCII Value	Character
26		58	:	90	Z	122	z
27		59	;	91	[	123	{
28		60	<	92	\	124	|
29		61	=	93	]	125	}
30	-	62	>	94	^	126	~
31		63	?	95	_	127	☐

The UNICODE() function is the Unicode equivalent of the ASCII() function, and the NCHAR() function does the same thing as the CHAR() function only with Unicode characters. SQL Server's nchar and nvarchar types will store any Unicode character and will work with this function. For extremely large values, the ntext and nvarchar(MAX) types also support Unicode characters.

To return extended characters, you can execute the NCHAR() function with sample character codes, as follows:

```
SELECT NCHAR(220)
```

This returns the letter Ü.

```
SELECT NCHAR(233)
```

This returns an accented lowercase e, é.

```
SELECT NCHAR(241)
```

This returns a Spanish "enya," or n with a tilde, ñ.

Of course, because the ASCII standard supports all the European characters, using the CHAR() function would work for these extended characters as well. However, things get interesting when you start using the NCHAR() function with values between 256 and 65536. For instance, the following query returns the Greek character Omega.

```
SELECT NCHAR(433)
```

The Cyrillic letter Ya (Я) is returned with the following query:

```
SELECT NCHAR(1071)
```

The CHARINDEX() and PATINDEX() Functions

CHARINDEX() is the original SQL function used to find the first occurrence of a substring within another string. As the name suggests, it simply returns an integer that represents the index of the first character of the substring within the entire string. The following script looks for an occurrence of the string 'sh' within the string 'Washington':

```
SELECT CHARINDEX('sh', 'Washington')
```

This returns 3 to indicate that the "s" is the third character in the string "Washington." Using two characters for the substring wasn't particularly useful in this example but could be if the string contained more than one letter s.

The PATINDEX() function is the CHARINDEX() function on steroids. It will perform the same task in a slightly different way, but has the added benefit of supporting wildcard characters (such as those you would use with the LIKE operator). As its name suggests, it will return the index of a pattern of characters. This function also works with large character types such as ntext, nchar(max), and nvarchar(max). Note that if PATINDEX() is used with these large data types, it returns a bigint type rather than an int type. Here's an example:

```
SELECT PATINDEX('%M_rs%', 'The stars near Mars are far from ours')
```

Note that both percent characters are required if you want to find a string with zero or more characters before and after the string being compared. The underscore indicates that the character in this position is not matched. The string could contain any character at this position.

Compare this to the CHARINDEX() function used with the same set of strings:

```
SELECT CHARINDEX('Mars', ' The stars near Mars are far from ours')
```

Both of these functions return the index value 16. Remember how these functions work. I'll combine this with the SUBSTRING() function in the following section to demonstrate how to parse strings using delimiting characters.

The LEN() Function

The LEN() function returns the length of a string as an integer. This is a simple but useful function that is often used alongside other functions to apply business rules. The following example tests the Month and Day date parts integers, converted to character types, for their length. If just one character is returned, it pads the character with a zero and then assembles an eight-character date string in US format (MMDDYYYY):

```
DECLARE @MonthChar varchar(2), @DayChar varchar(2), @DateOut char(8)
SET @MonthChar = CAST(MONTH(GETDATE()) AS varchar(2))
SET @DayChar = CAST(DAY(GETDATE()) AS varchar(2))
-- Make sure month and day are two char long:
IF LEN(@MonthChar) = 1
  SET @MonthChar = '0' + @MonthChar
```

(continued)

(continued)

```
IF LEN(@DayChar) = 1
   SET @DayChar = '0' + @DayChar
-- Build date string:
SET @DateOut = @MonthChar + @DayChar + CAST(YEAR(GETDATE()) AS char(4))
SELECT @DateOut AS OutputDate
```

The return value from this script will always be an eight-character value representing the current date. At this writing, the output is:

```
07012008
```

The LEFT() and RIGHT() Functions

The LEFT() and RIGHT() functions are similar in that they both return a substring of a specified size. The difference between the two is what part of the character string is returned. The LEFT() function returns characters from the left-most part of the string, counting characters to the right. The RIGHT() function does exactly the opposite. It starts at the right-most character and counts to the left, returning the specified number of characters. Take a look at an example that uses the string "George Washington" to return substrings using these functions.

If you ask to return a five-character substring using the LEFT() function, as follows, the function locates the left-most character, counts five characters to the right, and returns the substring "Georg."

```
DECLARE @FullName varchar(25)
SET @FullName = 'George Washington'
SELECT LEFT(@FullName, 5)
```

If you ask to return a five-character substring using the RIGHT() function, the function locates the right-most character, counts five characters to the left, and returns the substring "ngton."

```
DECLARE @FullName varchar(25)
SET @FullName = 'George Washington'
SELECT RIGHT(@FullName, 5)
```

Neither of these functions is particularly useful for consistently returning a meaningful part of this string. What if you want to return the first name or last name portions of the full name? This takes just a little more work. The LEFT() function may be the correct method to use for extracting the first name if you can determine the position of the space in every name you might encounter. In this case, you can use either the CHARINDEX() function or the PATINDEX() function to locate the space, and then use the LEFT() function to return only these characters. The following example takes a procedural approach, breaking this process into steps:

```
DECLARE @FullName varchar(25), @SpaceIndex tinyint
SET @FullName = 'George Washington'
-- Get index of the delimiting space:
SET @SpaceIndex = CHARINDEX(' ' , @FullName)
-- Return all characters to the left of the space:
SELECT LEFT(@FullName, @SpaceIndex - 1)
```

I don't want to include the space, so it's necessary to subtract one from the @SpaceIndex value to include only the first name.

The SUBSTRING() Function

The SUBSTRING() function starts at a position and counts characters to the right, returning a substring of a specified length. Unlike the LEFT() function, you can tell it at what index position to begin counting. This allows you to extract a substring from anywhere within a character string. This function requires three arguments: the string to parse, the starting index, and the length of the substring to return. If you want to return all text to the end of the input string, you can use a length index larger than necessary. The SUBSTRING() function will return characters up to the last position of the string and will not pad the string with spaces.

The SUBSTRING() function can easily replace the LEFT() function by designating the left-most character of the string (1) as the starting index.

Continuing with the earlier example, you can set the starting position and length, returning a value from the middle of the name string. In this case, you'll start at position 4 and return the 6-character substring "rge Wa."

```
DECLARE @FullName varchar(25)
SET @FullName = 'George Washington'
SELECT SUBSTRING(@FullName, 4, 6)
```

Now, you can put it all together and parse the first name from the full name in a way that will work for any full name string formatted as FirstName + space + LastName. Using the same logic as before, you are going to nest the function calls to reduce the number of lines of script and get rid of the @SpaceIndex variable. Instead of the LEFT() function, use SUBSTRING().

```
DECLARE @FullName varchar(25)
SET @FullName = 'George Washington'
-- Return first name:
SELECT SUBSTRING(@FullName, 1, CHARINDEX(' ', @FullName) - 1)
```

Similar logic is used to extract the last name. You simply have to change the start index argument to the position following the space. The space is at position seven, and the last name begins at position eight. This means that the start index will always be one plus the CHARINDEX() result:

```
DECLARE @FullName varchar(25)
SET @FullName = 'George Washington'
--Return last name:
SELECT SUBSTRING(@FullName, CHARINDEX(' ', @FullName) + 1, LEN(@FullName))
```

Putting it all together, you can run the following query to extract the first and last name from the full name variable:

```
DECLARE @FullName varchar(25)
SET @FullName = 'George Washington'
-- Return first name:
SELECT SUBSTRING(@FullName, 1, CHARINDEX(' ', @FullName) - 1) AS FirstName,
       SUBSTRING(@FullName, CHARINDEX(' ', @FullName) + 1, LEN(@FullName))
       AS LastName
```

The values passed into the SUBSTRING() function are the position of the space plus one as the start index. This will be the first letter of the last name. Because you won't always know the length of the name, you can pass in the LEN() function for the length of the substring. The SUBSTRING() function will reach the end of the string when it reaches this position and simply include all characters after the space to the end of the string.

To set up an example, let's create and populate a temporary table:

```
CREATE TABLE #MyNames (FullName varchar(50))
GO
INSERT INTO #MyNames (FullName) SELECT 'Fred Flintstone'
INSERT INTO #MyNames (FullName) SELECT 'Wilma Flintstone'
INSERT INTO #MyNames (FullName) SELECT 'Barney Rubble'
INSERT INTO #MyNames (FullName) SELECT 'Betty Rubble'
INSERT INTO #MyNames (FullName) SELECT 'George Jetson'
INSERT INTO #MyNames (FullName) SELECT 'Jane Jetson'
```

Now execute a query using the function calls to parse the first name and last name values as one-line expressions. Note that references to the @FullName variable are replaced with the FullName column in the table:

```
SELECT
    SUBSTRING(FullName, 1, CHARINDEX(' ' , FullName) - 1) AS FirstName
  , SUBSTRING(FullName, CHARINDEX(' ' , FullName) + 1, LEN(FullName)) AS LastName
FROM #MyNames
```

The results, shown in Figure 6-7, display two distinct columns as if the first and last names were stored separately.

Figure 6-7

The LOWER() and UPPER() Functions

These functions are pretty easy to figure out. Each simply converts a character string to all lowercase or all uppercase characters. This is most useful when comparing user input or stored strings for comparison. String comparisons are typically case-insensitive, depending on settings chosen during SQL Server setup. Used along with other string manipulation functions, strings can be converted to use proper case for data storage and presentation. This example accounts for mixed-case last names, assuming the name contains a single space before the second capitalized substring. You could argue that some of these names normally wouldn't contain spaces, and I agree. This demonstration could easily be extended to include provisions for other mixed-case names (names beginning with Mc, hyphenated names, and so on).

```
DECLARE @LastName varchar(25), @SpaceIndex tinyint
SET @LastName = 'mc donald'                -- Test value
-- Find space in name:
SET @SpaceIndex = CHARINDEX(' ' , @LastName)
IF @SpaceIndex > 0                         -- Space: Capitalize first &
substring
    SELECT UPPER(LEFT(@LastName, 1))
  + LOWER(SUBSTRING(@LastName, 2, @SpaceIndex - 1))
  + UPPER(SUBSTRING(@LastName, @SpaceIndex + 1, 1))
  + LOWER(SUBSTRING(@LastName, @SpaceIndex + 2, LEN(@LastName)))
ELSE                                       -- No space: Cap only first char.
    SELECT UPPER(LEFT(@LastName, 1))
  + LOWER(SUBSTRING(@LastName, 2, LEN(@LastName)))
```

This script returns Mc Donald. You can also extend the example to deal with last names containing an apostrophe. The business rules in this case expect no space. If an apostrophe is found, the following character is to be capitalized. Note that to test an apostrophe in script, it must be entered twice (' ') to indicate that this is a literal, rather than an encapsulating single quote. Last name values are stored with only an apostrophe.

```
DECLARE @LastName varchar(25), @SpaceIndex tinyint, @AposIndex tinyint
SET @LastName = 'o''malley'                -- Test value
-- Find space in name:
SET @SpaceIndex = CHARINDEX(' ', @LastName)
-- Find literal ' in name:
SET @AposIndex = CHARINDEX('''', @LastName)
IF @SpaceIndex > 0                         -- Space: Capitalize first & substring
    SELECT UPPER(LEFT(@LastName, 1))
  + LOWER(SUBSTRING(@LastName, 2, @SpaceIndex - 1))
  + UPPER(SUBSTRING(@LastName, @SpaceIndex + 1, 1))
  + LOWER(SUBSTRING(@LastName, @SpaceIndex + 2, LEN(@LastName)))
ELSE IF @AposIndex > 0                     -- Apostrophe: Cap first & substring
    SELECT UPPER(LEFT(@LastName, 1))
  + LOWER(SUBSTRING(@LastName, 2, @AposIndex - 1))
  + UPPER(SUBSTRING(@LastName, @AposIndex + 1, 1))
  + LOWER(SUBSTRING(@LastName, @AposIndex + 2, LEN(@LastName)))
ELSE                                       -- No space: Cap only first char.
    SELECT UPPER(LEFT(@LastName, 1))
  + LOWER(SUBSTRING(@LastName, 2, LEN(@LastName)))
```

This script returns O'Malley. For this to be of use, you can wrap it into a user-defined function, as follows:

```
CREATE FUNCTION dbo.fn_FixLastName ( @LastName varchar(25) )
RETURNS varchar(25)
AS
BEGIN
  DECLARE   @SpaceIndex tinyint
          , @AposIndex tinyint
```

(continued)

(continued)

```
        , @ReturnName varchar(25)
-- Find space in name:
SET @SpaceIndex = CHARINDEX(' ', @LastName)
-- Find literal ' in name:
SET @AposIndex = CHARINDEX('''', @LastName)
IF @SpaceIndex > 0                  -- Space: Capitalize first & substring
        SET @ReturnName = UPPER(LEFT(@LastName, 1))
    + LOWER(SUBSTRING(@LastName, 2, @SpaceIndex - 1))
    + UPPER(SUBSTRING(@LastName, @SpaceIndex + 1, 1))
    + LOWER(SUBSTRING(@LastName, @SpaceIndex + 2, LEN(@LastName)))
ELSE IF @AposIndex > 0              -- Apostrophe: Cap first & substring
        SET @ReturnName = UPPER(LEFT(@LastName, 1))
    + LOWER(SUBSTRING(@LastName, 2, @AposIndex - 1))
    + UPPER(SUBSTRING(@LastName, @AposIndex + 1, 1))
    + LOWER(SUBSTRING(@LastName, @AposIndex + 2, LEN(@LastName)))
ELSE                                -- No space: Cap only first char.
        SET @ReturnName = UPPER(LEFT(@LastName, 1))
    + LOWER(SUBSTRING(@LastName, 2, LEN(@LastName)))
RETURN @ReturnName
END
```

To test the function, populate a temporary table with sample values so that you can query the names from this table:

```
CREATE TABLE #MyIrishFriends (FirstName varchar(25), LastName varchar(25) )
INSERT INTO #MyIrishFriends (FirstName, LastName) SELECT 'James', 'O''grady'
INSERT INTO #MyIrishFriends (FirstName, LastName) SELECT 'Nancy', 'o''brian'
INSERT INTO #MyIrishFriends (FirstName, LastName) SELECT 'George', 'MC kee'
INSERT INTO #MyIrishFriends (FirstName, LastName) SELECT 'Jonas', 'mc intosh'
INSERT INTO #MyIrishFriends (FirstName, LastName) SELECT 'Florence', 'MC BRIDE'
```

The results as they are stored are shown in Figure 6-8.

```
SELECT FirstName, LastName
FROM #MyIrishFriends
```

Figure 6-8

Using the custom function returns the results shown in Figure 6-9.

```
SELECT FirstName, dbo.fn_FixLastName(LastName) AS LastName
FROM #MyIrishFriends
```

Figure 6-9

The LTRIM() and RTRIM() Functions

The LTRIM() and RTRIM() functions simply return a string with white space (spaces) trimmed from either the left or right side of significant characters, respectively.

```
DECLARE @Value1 char(10), @Value2 char(10)
SET @Value1 = 'One'
SET @Value2 = 'Two'
SELECT @Value1 + @Value2
SELECT CONVERT(varchar(5), LEN(@Value1 + @Value2)) + ' characters long. '
SELECT RTRIM(@Value1) + RTRIM(@Value2)
SELECT CONVERT(varchar(5), LEN(RTRIM(@Value1) + RTRIM(@Value2)))
        + ' characters long trimmed. '
```

The abbreviated results in text form follow:

```
------------------------------
One        Two
------------------------------
13 characters long.
------------------------------
OneTwo
------------------------------
6 characters long trimmed.
```

The REPLACE() Function

The REPLACE() function can be used to replace all occurrences of one character or substring with another character or substring. This can be used as a global search and replace utility.

```
DECLARE @Phrase varchar(1000)
SET @Phrase = 'I aint gunna use poor grammar when commenting script and
I aint gunna complain about it. '
SELECT REPLACE(@Phrase, 'aint', 'am not')
```

As you can see, this was quite effective (well, kind of):

```
I am not gunna use poor grammar when commenting script and I am not gunna
complain about it.
```

If your result line cuts off with "...", expand the column to the right until you can see the entire line.

The REPLICATE() and SPACE() Functions

REPLICATE() is a very useful function when you need to fill a value with repeating characters. I'll use the same temporary table I created for the list of names in the SUBSTRING() example to pad each name value to 20 characters. I subtract the length of each value to pass the right value to the REPLICATE() function:

```
SELECT FullName + REPLICATE('*', 20 - LEN(FullName))
FROM #MyNames
```

The result is a list of names padded with asterisk characters, each 20 characters in length:

```
Fred Flintstone*****
Wilma Flintstone****
Barney Rubble*******
Betty Rubble********
George Jetson*******
Jane Jetson*********
```

The SPACE() function does the same thing, only with spaces. It simply returns a string of space characters of a defined length.

```
SELECT FullName + SPACE(20 - LEN(FullName))
FROM #MyNames
```

If you get an error that the #MyNames table doesn't exist, just re-run the CREATE TABLE script from the section "The SUBSTRING Function" earlier in this chapter.

The REVERSE() Function

As its name implies, the REVERSE() function reverses the characters in a string. This might be useful if you need to work with single-character values in a concatenated list.

```
SELECT REVERSE('The stars near Mars are far from ours. ')
.sruo morf raf era sraM raen srats ehT
```

I'm sure there's a practical application for this.

The STUFF() Function

The STUFF() function enables you to replace a portion of a string with another string. It essentially will stuff one string into another string at a given position and for a specified length. This can be useful for string replacements where the source and target values aren't the same length. For example, I need to replace the price in this string, changing it from 99.95 to 109.95:

```
Please submit your payment for 99.95 immediately.
```

The price value begins at position 32 and is five characters in length. It really doesn't matter how long the substring is that I want to stuff into this position. I simply need to know how many characters need to be removed.

```
SELECT STUFF('Please submit your payment for 99.95 immediately. ', 32, 5,
'109.95')
```

The resulting string follows:

```
Please submit your payment for 109.95 immediately.
```

The QUOTENAME() Function

This function is used with SQL Server object names so they can be passed into an expression. It simply returns a string with square brackets around the input value. If the value contains reserved delimiting or encapsulating characters (such as quotation marks or brackets), modifications are made to the string so SQL Server perceives these characters as literals, as you can see in the following example. The results of the query are shown in Figure 6-10.

```
SELECT QUOTENAME(COLUMN_NAME) AS ColumnName
FROM INFORMATION_SCHEMA.COLUMNS
```

Figure 6-10

Mathematical Functions

The functions listed in the following table are used to perform a variety of common and specialized mathematical operations and are useful in performing algebraic, trigonometric, statistical, approximating, and financial operations.

Function	Description
ABS()	Returns the absolute value for a numeric value.
ACOS()	Computes the arccosine (an angle) in radians.
ASIN()	Computes the arcsine (an angle) in radians.
ATAN()	Computes the arctangent (an angle) in radians.
ATN2()	Computes the arctangent of two values in radians.
CEILING()	Returns the smallest integer value that is greater than or equal to a number.

(continued)

Function	Description
COS()	Computes the cosine of an angle in radians.
COT()	Computes the cotangent of an angle in radians.
DEGREES()	Converts an angle from radians to degrees.
EXP()	Returns the natural logarithm raised to a specified exponent.
FLOOR()	Returns the largest integer value that is less than or equal to a number.
LOG()	Calculates the natural logarithm of a number using base-2 (binary) numbering.
LOG10()	Calculates the natural logarithm of a number using base-10 numbering.
PI()	Returns the value for PI() as a float type.
POWER()	Raises a value to a specified exponent.
RADIANS()	Converts an angle from degrees to radians.
RAND()	Returns a fractional number based on a randomizing algorithm; accepts an optional seed value.
ROUND()	Rounds a fractional value to a specified precision.
SIGN()	Returns −1 or 1 depending on whether a single argument value is negative or positive.
SIN()	Computes the sine of an angle in radians.
SQRT()	Returns the square root of a value.
SQUARE()	Returns the square (n^2) of a value.
TAN()	Computes the tangent of an angle in radians.

Metadata Functions

These are utility functions that return information about the SQL Server configuration details and details about the server and database settings. This includes a range of general and special-purpose property-related functions that will return the state of various object properties. These functions wrap queries from the system tables in the Master database and a user database. It's recommended that you use these and other system functions rather than creating queries against the system tables yourself, in case schema changes are made in future versions of SQL Server. Some of the information listed in the following table can also be obtained using the INFORMATION_SCHEMA views. These views are described in Appendix D.

Function	Description
COL_LENGTH()	Returns the length of a column from the column name.
COL_NAME()	Returns the name of a column from the object ID.
COLUMNPROPERTY()	Returns a flag to indicate the state of a column property. Properties include AllowsNull, IsComputed, IsCursorType, IsDeterministic, IsFulltextIndexed, IsIdentity, IsIdNotForRepl, IsIndexable, IsOutParam, IsPrecise, IsRowGuidCol, Precision, Scale, and UsesAnsiTrim.
DATABASEPROPERTY()	This function is maintained for backward compatibility with older SQL Server versions. It returns a flag to indicate the state of a database property. Properties include IsAnsiNullDefault, IsAnsiNullsEnabled, IsAnsiWarningsEnabled, IsAutoClose, IsAutoCreateStatistics, IsAutoShrink, IsAutoUpdateStatistics, IsBulkCopy, IsCloseCursorsOnCommitEnabled, IsDboOnly, IsDetached, IsEmergencyMode, IsFulltextEnabled, IsInLoad, IsInRecovery, IsInStandBy, IsLocalCursorsDefault, IsNotRecovered, IsNullConcat, IsOffline, IsQuotedIdentifiersEnabled, IsReadOnly, IsRecursiveTriggersEnabled, IsShutDown, IsSingleUser, IsSuspect, IsTruncLog, and Version.
DATABASEPROPERTYEX()	Returns a flag to indicate the state of a database property. Properties include Collation, IsAnsiNullDefault, IsAnsiNullsEnabled, IsAnsiPaddingEnabled, IsAnsiWarningsEnabled, IsArithmeticAbortEnabled, IsAutoClose, IsAutoCreateStatistics, IsAutoShrink, IsAutoUpdateStatistics, IsCloseCursorsOnCommitEnabled, IsFulltextEnabled, IsInStandBy, IsLocalCursorsDefault, IsMergePublished, IsNullConcat, IsNumericRoundAbortEnabled, IsQuotedIdentifiersEnabled, IsRecursiveTriggersEnabled, IsSubscribed, IsTornPageDetectionEnabled, Recovery, SQLSortOrder, Status, Updateability, UserAccess, and Version.
DB_ID()	Returns the database ID from the database name.
DB_NAME()	Returns the database name from the database ID.
FILE_ID()	Returns the file ID from the file name.
FILE_NAME()	Returns the file name from the file ID.

(continued)

Function	Description
fn_listextendedproperty()	Returns a table object populated with extended property names and their settings.
FULLTEXTCATALOGPROPERTY()	Returns a flag to indicate the state of a full-text catalog property. Properties include PopulateStatus, ItemCount, IndexSize, UniqueKeyCount, LogSize, and PopulateCompletionAge.
FULLTEXTSERVICEPROPERTY()	Returns a flag to indicate the state of a full-text service property. Properties include ResourceUsage, ConnectTimeout, IsFulltextInstalled, and DataTimeout.
INDEX_COL()	Returns the name of a column contained in a specified index, by table, index, and column ID.
INDEXKEY_PROPERTY()	Returns a flag to indicate the state of an index key property. Properties are ColumnId and IsDescending.
INDEXPROPERTY()	Returns a flag indicating the state of an index property. Properties include IndexDepth, IndexFillFactor, IndexID, IsAutoStatistics, IsClustered, IsFulltextKey, IsHypothetical, IsPadIndex, IsPageLockDisallowed, IsRowLockDisallowed, IsStatistics, and IsUnique.
OBJECT_ID()	Returns an object ID from the object name.
OBJECT_NAME()	Returns an object name from the object ID.
OBJECTPROPERTY()	Enables you to get property information from several different types of objects. It is advisable to use a function designed to query specific object types, if possible. Returns a flag indicating the state of an object property. Properties include CnstIsClustKey, CnstIsColumn, CnstIsDeleteCascade, CnstIsDisabled, CnstIsNonclustKey, CnstIsNotRepl, CnstIsNotTrusted, CnstIsUpdateCascade, ExecIsAfterTrigger, ExecIsAnsiNullsOn, ExecIsDeleteTrigger, ExecIsFirstDeleteTrigger, ExecIsFirstInsertTrigger, ExecIsFirstUpdateTrigger, ExecIsInsertTrigger, ExecIsInsteadOfTrigger, ExecIsLastDeleteTrigger, ExecIsLastInsertTrigger, ExecIsLastUpdateTrigger, ExecIsQuotedIdentOn, ExecIsStartup, ExecIsTriggerDisabled, ExecIsUpdateTrigger, HasAfterTrigger, HasInsertTrigger, HasInsteadOfTrigger, HasUpdateTrigger, IsAnsiNullsOn, IsCheckCnst, IsConstraint, IsDefault,

Function	Description
	IsDefaultCnst, IsDeterministic, IsExecuted, IsExtendedProc, IsForeignKey, IsIndexable, IsIndexed, IsInlineFunction, IsMSShipped, IsPrimaryKey, IsProcedure, IsQuotedIdentOn, IsReplProc, IsRule, IsScalarFunction, IsSchemaBound, IsSystemTable, IsTable, IsTableFunction, IsTrigger, IsUniqueCnst, IsUserTable, IsView, OwnerId, TableDeleteTrigger, TableDeleteTriggerCount, TableFullTextBackgroundUpdateIndexOn, TableFulltextCatalogId, TableFullTextChangeTrackingOn, TableFulltextKeyColumn, TableFullTextPopulateStatus, TableHasActiveFulltextIndex, TableHasCheckCnst, TableHasClustIndex, TableHasDefaultCnst, TableHasDeleteTrigger, TableHasForeignKey, TableHasForeignRef, TableHasIdentity, TableHasIndex, TableHasInsertTrigger, TableHasNonclustIndex, TableHasPrimaryKey, TableHasRowGuidCol, TableHasTextImage, TableHasTimestamp, TableHasUniqueCnst, TableHasUpdateTrigger, TableInsertTrigger, TableInsertTriggerCount, TableIsFake, TableIsPinned, TableTextInRowLimit, TableUpdateTrigger, and TableUpdateTriggerCount.

Ranking Functions

Ranking functions are used to enumerate sorted and top-valued result sets using a specified order, independent from the order of the result set.

The ROW_NUMBER() Function

The ROW_NUMBER() function returns an integer with a running incremental value based on an ORDER BY clause passed to this function. If the ROW_NUMBER's ORDER BY matches the order of the result set, the values will be incremental and in ascending order. If the ROW_NUMBER's ORDER BY clause is different than the order of the results, these values will not be listed in order but will represent the order of the ROW_NUMBER function's ORDER BY clause, as shown in the following examples and results.

```
SELECT
    ProductCategoryID
  , Name
  , ROW_NUMBER() OVER (ORDER BY Name) AS RowNum
FROM Production.ProductCategory
ORDER BY Name
```

With the ORDER BY clause on the ROW_NUMBER() call matching the order of the query, these values are listed in order (see Figure 6-11).

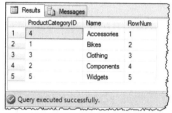

Figure 6-11

However, when using a different ORDER BY clause in the function call, these values are not ordered.

```
SELECT
    ProductCategoryID
  , Name
  , ROW_NUMBER() OVER (ORDER BY Name) AS RowNum
FROM production.ProductCategory
ORDER BY ProductCategoryID
```

This provides an effective means to tell how the result would have been sorted using the other ORDER BY clause, as shown in Figure 6-12.

	ProductCategoryID	Name	RowNum
1	1	Bikes	2
2	2	Components	4
3	3	Clothing	3
4	4	Accessories	1
5	5	Widgets	5

Query executed successfully.

Figure 6-12

The RANK() and DENSE_RANK() Functions

Both of these functions are similar to the ROW_NUMBER() function in that they return a value based on an ORDER BY clause, but these values may not always be unique. Ranking values are repeated for duplicate results from the provided ORDER BY clause, and uniqueness is only based on unique values in the ORDER BY list. Each of these functions takes a different approach to handling these duplicate values. The RANK() function preserves the ordinal position of the row in the list. For each duplicate value, it skips the subsequent value so that the next non-duplicate value remains in its rightful position.

```
SELECT
    ProductID
  , Name
  , ListPrice
  , RANK() OVER (ORDER BY ListPrice DESC) AS Rank
FROM Production.Product
ORDER BY Rank
```

Note in the result set shown in Figure 6-13 that the values are repeated for duplicated price values and the skipped values following each tie. For example, rows for product name "Road-150 Red, 52" and "Road-150 Red, 56" are ranked number 1, and the following row, "Mountain-100 Silver, 38" is ranked number 6.

	ProductID	Name	ListPrice	Rank
1	749	Road-150 Red, 62	4472.8375	1
2	750	Road-150 Red, 44	4472.8375	1
3	751	Road-150 Red, 48	4472.8375	1
4	752	Road-150 Red, 52	4472.8375	1
5	753	Road-150 Red, 56	4472.8375	1
6	771	Mountain-100 Silver, 38	4249.9875	6
7	772	Mountain-100 Silver, 42	4249.9875	6
8	773	Mountain-100 Silver, 44	4249.9875	6
9	774	Mountain-100 Silver, 48	4249.9875	6
10	775	Mountain-100 Black, 38	4218.7375	10
11	776	Mountain-100 Black, 42	4218.7375	10
12	777	Mountain-100 Black, 44	4218.7375	10

Query executed successfully.

Figure 6-13

The DENSE_RANK() function works exactly the same way, but it doesn't skip numbers after each tie. This way, no values are skipped, but the ordinal ranking position is lost whenever there are ties.

```
SELECT
     ProductID
    ,Name
    ,ListPrice
    ,DENSE_RANK() OVER (ORDER BY ListPrice DESC) AS Rank
FROM Production.Product
ORDER BY Rank
```

The result, shown in Figure 6-14, repeats ranked values but doesn't skip any numbers in this column.

	ProductID	Name	ListPrice	Rank
1	749	Road-150 Red, 62	3578.27	1
2	750	Road-150 Red, 44	3578.27	1
3	751	Road-150 Red, 48	3578.27	1
4	752	Road-150 Red, 52	3578.27	1
5	753	Road-150 Red, 56	3578.27	1
6	771	Mountain-100 Silver, 38	3399.99	2
7	772	Mountain-100 Silver, 42	3399.99	2
8	773	Mountain-100 Silver, 44	3399.99	2
9	774	Mountain-100 Silver, 48	3399.99	2
10	775	Mountain-100 Black, 38	3374.99	3
11	776	Mountain-100 Black, 42	3374.99	3
12	777	Mountain-100 Black, 44	3374.99	3

Query executed successfully.

Figure 6-14

The NTILE(n) Function

This function also ranks results, returning an integer ranking value. However, rather than enumerating the results into uniquely ranked order, it divides the result into a finite number of ranked groups. For example, if a table has 10,000 rows and the NTILE() function is called with an argument value of 1000, as NTILE(1000), the result would be divided into 1000 groups of 10, with each group being assigned the same ranking value. The NTILE() function also supports the OVER (ORDER BY...) syntax like the other ranking functions discussed in this section. The following example divides the product table into 20 groups of products based on their price from highest to lowest. The partial results are shown in Figure 6-15.

```
SELECT
    ProductID
    ,Name
    ,ListPrice
    ,NTILE(20) OVER (ORDER BY ListPrice DESC) AS GroupedProducts
FROM Production.Product
ORDER BY GroupedProducts
```

	ProductID	Name	ListPrice	GroupedProducts
1	749	Road-150 Red, 62	3578.27	1
2	750	Road-150 Red, 44	3578.27	1
3	751	Road-150 Red, 48	3578.27	1
4	752	Road-150 Red, 52	3578.27	1
5	753	Road-150 Red, 56	3578.27	1
6	771	Mountain-100 Silver, 38	3399.99	1
7	772	Mountain-100 Silver, 42	3399.99	1
8	773	Mountain-100 Silver, 44	3399.99	1
9	774	Mountain-100 Silver, 48	3399.99	1
10	775	Mountain-100 Black, 38	3374.99	1
11	776	Mountain-100 Black, 42	3374.99	1
12	777	Mountain-100 Black, 44	3374.99	1
13	778	Mountain-100 Black, 48	3374.99	1
14	789	Road-250 Red, 44	2443.35	1
15	790	Road-250 Red, 48	2443.35	1
16	791	Road-250 Red, 52	2443.35	1
17	792	Road-250 Red, 58	2443.35	1
18	793	Road-250 Black, 44	2443.35	2
19	794	Road-250 Black, 48	2443.35	2
20	795	Road-250 Black, 52	2443.35	2
21	796	Road-250 Black, 58	2443.35	2

Figure 6-15

Security Functions

The security-related functions return role membership and privilege information for SQL Server users. This category also includes a set of functions to manage events and traces, as described in the following table.

Function	Description
fn_trace_geteventinfo()	Returns a table type populated with event information for a specified trace ID.
fn_trace_getfilterinfo()	Returns a table type populated with information about filters applied for a specified trace ID.
fn_trace_getinfo()	Returns a table type populated with trace information for a specified trace ID.
fn_trace_gettable()	Returns a table type populated with file information for a specified trace ID.
HAS_DBACCESS()	Returns a flag indicating whether the current user has access to a specified database.
IS_MEMBER()	Returns a flag indicating whether the current user is a member of a Windows group or SQL Server role.
IS_SRVROLEMEMBER()	Returns a flag indicating whether the current user is a member of a database server role.
SUSER_SID()	Returns either the security ID for a specified user's login name or (if the parameter is omitted) returns the security ID of the current user. Returns either the user ID for a specified username or (if the parameter is omitted) returns the user ID of the current user.
SUSER_SNAME()	Returns the login name for a specified security ID. If no security ID is provided it returns the login for the current connection.
USER_ID()	Returns either the user ID for a specified username or (if the parameter is omitted) returns the user ID of the current user.
USER_NAME()	Returns a username for a specified user ID.

System Functions and Variables

This section discusses utility functions used to perform a variety of tasks. These include value comparisons and value type testing. This category is also a catch-all for other functionality.

Function	Description
APP_NAME()	Returns the name of the application associated with the current connection.
COALESCE()	Returns the first non-null value from a comma-delimited list of expressions.

(continued)

Function	Description
COLLATIONPROPERTY()	Returns the value of a specific property for a specified collation. Properties include CodePage, LCID, and ComparisonStyle.
CURRENT_TIMESTAMP()	Returns the current date and time and is synonymous with the GETDATE() function. It exists for ANSI-SQL compliance.
CURRENT_USER()	Returns the name of the current user and is synonymous with the USER_NAME() function.
DATALENGTH()	Returns the numbers of bytes used to store or handle a value. For ANSI string types, this will return the same value as the LEN() function, but for other data types, the value may be different.
fn_helpcollations()	Returns a table type populated with a list of collations supported by the current version of SQL Server.
fn_servershareddrives()	Returns a table type populated with a list of drives shared by the server.
fn_virtualfilestats()	Returns a table type populated with I/O statistics for database files, including log files.
FORMATMESSAGE()	Returns an error message from the sysmessages table for a specified message number and comma-delimited list of parameters.
GETANSINULL()	Returns the nullability setting for the database, according to the ANSI_NULL_DFLT_ON and ANSI_NULL_DFLT_OFF database settings.
HOST_ID()	Returns the workstation ID for the current session.
HOST_NAME()	Returns the workstation name for the current session.
IDENT_CURRENT()	Returns the last identity value generated for a specified table regardless of the session and scope.
IDENT_INCR()	Returns the increment value specified in the creation of the last identity column.
IDENT_SEED()	Returns the seed value specified in the creation of the last identity column.
IDENTITY()	Used in a SELECT... INTO statement to insert an automatically generated identity value into a column.
ISDATE()	Returns a flag to indicate whether a specified value is or is not capable of being converted to a date value.
ISNULL()	Determines whether a specified value is null and then returns a provided replacement value.

Function	Description
ISNUMERIC()	Returns a flag to indicate whether a specified value is or is not capable of being converted to a numeric value.
NEWID()	Returns a newly generated uniqueidentifier type value. This is a 128-bit integer, globally unique value, usually expressed as an alpha-numeric hexadecimal representation (for example, 89DE6247-C2E2-42DB-8CE8-A787E505D7EA). This type is often used for primary key values in replicated and semi-connected systems.
NULLIF()	Returns a NULL value when two specified arguments have equivalent values.
PARSENAME()	Returns a specific part of a four-part object name.
PERMISSIONS()	Returns an integer whose value is a bit-wise map indicating the permission or combination of permissions for the current user on a specified database object.
ROWCOUNT_BIG()	As with the @@ROWCOUNT variable, returns the number of rows either returned or modified by the last statement. Returns a bigint type.
SCOPE_IDENTITY()	As with the @@IDENTITY variable, this function returns the last Identity value generated but is limited to the current session and scope (stored procedure, batch, or module).
SERVERPROPERTY()	Returns a flag indicating the state of a server property. Properties include Collation, Edition, Engine Edition, InstanceName, IsClustered, IsFullTextInstalled, IsIntegratedSecurityOnly, IsSingleUser, IsSyncWithBackup, LicenseType, MachineName, NumLicenses, ProcessID, ProductLevel, ProductVersion, and ServerName.
SESSION_USER	Returns the current username. Note that this function is called without parentheses.
SESSIONPROPERTY()	Returns a flag indicating the state of a session property. Properties include ANSI_NULLS, ANSI_PADDING, ANSI_WARNINGS, ARITHABORT, CONCAT_NULL_YIELDS_NULL, NUMERIC_ROUNDABORT, and QUOTED_IDENTIFIER.
STATS_DATE()	Returns a date that statistics for a specified index were last updated.
SYSTEM_USER	Returns the current username. Note that this function is called without parentheses.
USER_NAME()	Returns the username for a specified user ID. If no ID number is provided, the function returns the current database user.

Some examples related to a few of the functions listed in the preceding table follow.

The COALESCE() Function

The COALESCE() function can be very useful in returning the first non-null value from a list of arguments, saving quite a lot of IF or CASE decision logic. The following example populates a table of products, showing up to three prices each:

```
CREATE TABLE #ProductPrices (ProductName varchar(25), SuperSalePrice Money
NULL, SalePrice Money NULL, ListPrice Money NULL)
GO
INSERT INTO #ProductPrices VALUES('Standard Widget', NULL, NULL, 15.95)
INSERT INTO #ProductPrices VALUES('Economy Widget', NULL, 9.95, 12.95)
INSERT INTO #ProductPrices VALUES('Deluxe Widget', 19.95, 20.95, 22.95)
INSERT INTO #ProductPrices VALUES('Super Deluxe Widget', 29.45, 32.45, 38.95)
INSERT INTO #ProductPrices VALUES('Executive Widget', NULL, 45.95, 54.95)
GO
```

All products have a list price, some have a sale price, and others may have a super sale price. The current price of a product is going to be the lowest existing price, or the first non-null value when reading each of the price columns as they are listed:

```
SELECT ProductName, COALESCE(SuperSalePrice, SalePrice, ListPrice) AS CurrentPrice
FROM #ProductPrices
```

This method is far more elegant than using multiple lines of branching and decision logic, and the result is equally simple, as illustrated in Figure 6-16.

Figure 6-16

The DATALENGTH() Function

The DATALENGTH() function returns the number of bytes used to manage a value. This can be used to reveal some interesting differences between data types. It's probably no surprise that when a varchar type is passed to both the DATALENGTH() and LEN() functions, they return the same value:

```
DECLARE @Value varchar(20)
SET @Value = 'abc'
SELECT DATALENGTH(@Value)
SELECT LEN(@Value)
```

These statements both return 3 because the varchar type uses three single-byte characters to store the three-character value. However, if an nvarchar type is used, it takes twice as many bytes to manage a value of the same length:

```
DECLARE @Value nvarchar(20)
SET @Value = 'abc'
SELECT DATALENGTH(@Value)
SELECT LEN(@Value)
```

The DATALENGTH() function returns 6 because 2 bytes are used to store each character using a Unicode character set. The LEN() function returns 3 because this function returns the number of characters, not the number of bytes. Here's an interesting test. How many bytes does it take to store an integer variable set to the value 2? How about an integer variable set to 2 billion? Let's find out:

```
DECLARE @Value1 int, @Value2 int
SET @Value1 = 2
SET @Value2 = 2000000000
SELECT DATALENGTH(@Value1)
SELECT LEN(@Value1)
SELECT DATALENGTH(@Value2)
SELECT LEN(@Value2)
```

The DATALENGTH() function returns 4 in both cases because the int type always uses 4 bytes, regardless of the value. The LEN() function essentially treats the integer value as if it were converted to a character type, returning the number of digits, in this case, 1 and 10, respectively.

The following global system variables all return an int type. These may be useful in stored procedures and other programming objects to implement custom business logic.

Variable	Description
@@ERROR	Returns the last error number for the current session.
@@IDENTITY	Returns the last identity value generated in the current session.
@@ROWCOUNT	Returns the row count for the last execution in the current session that returned a result set.
@@TRANCOUNT	Returns the number of active transactions in the current session. This would result from multiple, nested BEGIN TRANSACTION statements before executing corresponding COMMIT TRANSACTION or ABORT TRANSACTION statements.

Global System Statistical Variables

The following table describes administrative utilities used to discover database system usage and environment information.

Variable	Description
@@CONNECTIONS	Returns the number of open connections.
@@CPU_BUSY	Returns the number of milliseconds that SQL Server has been working since the service was last started.
@@IDLE	Returns the number of milliseconds that SQL Server has been idle since the service was last started.
@@IO_BUSY	Returns the number of milliseconds that SQL Server has been processing I/O since the service was last started.
@@PACK_RECEIVED	Returns the number of network packets that SQL Server has received since the service was last started.
@@PACK_SENT	Returns the number of network packets that SQL Server has sent since the service was last started.
@@PACKET_ERRORS	Returns the number of network packet errors that SQL Server has received since the service was last started.
@@TIMETICKS	Returns the number of microseconds per tick.
@@TOTAL_ERRORS	Returns the number of disk I/O errors that SQL Server has received since the service was last started.
@@TOTAL_READ	Returns the number of physical disk reads since the SQL Server service was last started.
@@TOTAL_WRITE	Returns the number of physical disk writes since the SQL Server service was last started.

Summary

Functions do the heavy lifting of your business logic and can be used to apply programming functionality to queries. Several useful and powerful functions are standard features of T-SQL. You learned that SQL functions, like functions in procedural and object-oriented programming languages, encapsulate programming features into a simple and reusable package. This takes a lot of the work out of the query designer's hands. You know that T-SQL is a task-oriented language rather than a procedural language. Although functions give you the option to tread the procedural line, building fairly complex logic into queries, the strength of the language is in allowing the designer to state his intentions rather than the exact steps and methods that must be used to perform a task. Used correctly, functions allow you to do just that.

In T-SQL, arguments are used to pass values into a function and most functions return a scalar, or single-value, result. Functions are categorized as either deterministic or nondeterministic. A deterministic function will always return the same value when called with the same argument values. Nondeterministic functions depend on other resources to determine the return value; therefore SQL Server must execute the function explicitly. For this reason, there are some restrictions on the use of nondeterministic functions in custom SQL programming objects.

SQL functions perform a wide variety of important tasks including mathematical operations, comparisons, date parsing and manipulation, and advanced string manipulation. Several categories of specialized functions are introduced along with their related topics in following chapters. A complete function syntax reference is also provided in Appendix B.

Exercises
Exercise 1

Write a query to return the average weight of all touring bikes sold by Adventure Works Cycles that list for more than $2,500. Use the ProductSubCategory table to determine how you should filter these products.

Exercise 2

Designate a variable called @ProCount to hold the number of product records on record. Execute a query to return this value and assign it to the variable. Use the variable in an expression to return the value in the phrase "There are X products on record."

Exercise 3

Calculate the square root of the absolute value of the cosine of PI.

Exercise 4

How many days has it been since the signing of the Treaty of Versailles on June 28, 1919, which ended World War 1? Calculate the answer using T-SQL functions.

Exercise 5

Using the SlateGravelEmployee table defined earlier in the chapter, return the FirstName, LastName, and the two-letter initials of all the employees.

Aggregation and Grouping

When creating reports or analyzing business data, viewing the individual records in a table can be like looking at a map through a microscope. It's just a little too close to get the right perspective. Looking up a single record to find out when a customer bought a specific product may be valuable when that's all you care about, but perhaps you're more interested in how many products the customer bought during a period of time, or how much he or she spent on all purchases. Business leaders most often want to understand the bigger picture still — maybe they need to know how many products various customers in different geographic regions bought over a period of time. As you need to "zoom out" to view data from a larger point of view, you will inevitably need to group individual records together and then sum up, average, or count the details. This is called *aggregation*.

The term "aggregation" refers to something that is a summary of something else. In this context, an aggregate function returns a single value for a group of records. You can use aggregate functions in two different ways. You can "roll up," or summarize, all the rows returned by a query. Or, you also can apply aggregation at a group level, showing summarized values for the rows having the same values in the columns you designate for grouping. Remember that information is meaningful; data is little more than values stored in a table. Often, the information part of the equation comes from analyzing groups of records along with aggregated values, and then comparing how one range of records relates to another.

In this chapter, you learn how to use aggregate functions to summarize data and to perform statistical analysis. You also see how records can be grouped and aggregated into subtotals. Finally, you learn to use specialized grouping features to generate ad hoc grouped reports.

To Group or Not to Group

Before deciding if you should summarize data using aggregate functions, you need to determine if you should group these records by distinct value ranges. The criteria used for grouping may be the values in one column or a combination of multiple columns. More than likely, the results of a query will be handed off to some application code or a reporting tool. If this query client is going to show summarized data but will also need access to the detail records, then it will have to do the grouping and aggregating itself. If, however, it only needs to see grouped and summarized values, it makes sense to do the grouping in the query.

Grouping and aggregating data can provide a meaningful context for analyzing business information. It allows users to perform comparisons and to spot trends or anomalies in the data. Typically, we group data on *attribute* fields, which usually describe characteristics (for example, category, color, or a time period, such as "Month"). The fields used to aggregate are a type of field known as *measures* or *facts*. These fields typically store numeric values that can be summed, averaged, or otherwise aggregated for reporting. One exception to this rule is that keys and attribute fields are often used for counting records, which is a form of aggregation.

If the data is grouped and then aggregated, the result will be a list of distinct grouped values along with an aggregated value for each group. If no grouping is performed, the results will simply be a single row containing the aggregated value(s) for all the records.

Using Aggregate Functions

Aggregate functions fall into two categories: simple aggregates and statistical functions. The simplest technique for using aggregate functions is aggregating all rows in a query. Aggregate functions include the means to summarize a range of values in a variety of ways. For example, you may simply want to count the rows that match certain criteria or get the sum for a range of numeric values. The following table contains all the system-supplied aggregate functions supported by T-SQL used to summarize column values.

Function	Description
COUNT()	Calculates the count of all non-null values for a specific column. Can also be used as COUNT(*) to return the absolute count of rows regardless of null values. Returns int data type.
COUNT_BIG()	Same as the COUNT() function but returns the bigint data type. This would be necessary only when the table contains more than two billion rows.
SUM()	Returns the sum of all non-null values in the range. The return data type is the same as the numeric column data type.
AVG()	Returns the average of all non-null values in the range. The return data type is the same as the numeric column data type.
MIN()	Returns the smallest non-null value in the range. Can be used with any sortable data type.
MAX()	Returns the largest non-null value in the range. Can be used with any sortable data type.
STDEV()	Returns the simple standard deviation for all non-null values in a numeric range. Returns a float data type, regardless of the column type.

Function	Description
STDEVP()	Returns the standard deviation for a population, for all non-null values in a numeric range. Returns a `float` data type, regardless of the column type.
VAR()	Returns the simple variance for all non-null values in a numeric range. Returns a `float` data type, regardless of the column type.
VARP()	Returns the variance for a population, for all non-null values in a numeric range. Returns a `float` data type, regardless of the column type.
CHECKSUM_AGG	Returns a checksum of values in an aggregate range. This is used to compare a range of values against another range to tell if they are the same. The resulting value is generally not useful except as a comparison to another checksum.

An aggregate function is called and applied to a specific column. The aggregate function is applied to the range of values in that column, either for the entire table or a group of rows when used along with a GROUP BY clause. Most aggregates work on numeric values, but some, such as the COUNT, MIN, and MAX functions, can work with other data types. The following sections break down each aggregate function, with examples and instructions for you to try it out for yourself.

The COUNT() Function

When you just need to know how many records there are in a table, or how many records share common attribute values, use the COUNT() function. It simply counts rows or non-null values in a column's value range. Because the data type of the column isn't considered, it will work with columns of practically any type of data.

Consider the following two examples. If you execute this query against the Product table, the total number of rows is returned:

```
SELECT COUNT(*) FROM Production.Product
```

As you can see, the Product table contains 504 rows (unless you've added or removed any rows). Now, count only the values in the Color column using the following expression:

```
SELECT COUNT(Color) FROM Production.Product
```

Because 248 records don't have a Color value (these rows contain the value NULL for this column), only 256 rows get counted. Now add the word DISTINCT before the column reference and execute the query again:

```
SELECT COUNT(DISTINCT Color) FROM Production.Product
```

Because so many of the products have the same prices, only nine records are counted. The DISTINCT modifier can be used with any of the aggregate functions except when using the CUBE or ROLLUP statements, which are discussed later in this chapter.

The SUM() Function

The SUM() function simply returns the sum of a range of numeric column values. Like the others, this function only considers non-null values. A simple example returns the subtotal for a product order. This query adds up the UnitPrice for each detail line in the order whose SalesOrderID is 50189:

```
SELECT SUM(UnitPrice)
FROM Sales.SalesOrderDetail
WHERE SalesOrderID = 50189
```

The result is a single row with a single column just like the previous examples, as shown in Figure 7-1. This is the sum of all UnitPrice values in the SalesOrderDetail table.

Figure 7-1

I have two issues with this result. The first is that the column doesn't have a name. When applying aggregate functions, the resulting column won't be named unless you specifically define an alias for the column name. If you use visual query design tools, such as Access or the T-SQL Designer (in Visual Studio or to create a view in SQL Server Management Studio), these tools will devise column aliases such as SumOfUnitPrice or Expr1. The first order of business is to assign an alias so that this column has a sensible name. The other problem with this simple example is that it assumes that the customer purchased one of each product. The fact is that there are three detail rows for this order with respective quantities 1, 3, and 4. To total the order accurately, you'll have to do a little math. This query resolves both of these issues, calculating extended price and defining an alias for the column:

```
SELECT SUM(UnitPrice * OrderQty) AS OrderTotalPrice
FROM Sales.SalesOrderDetail
WHERE SalesOrderID = 50189
```

The result shown in Figure 7-2 contains the correct amount (the total of all three order detail rows, considering the quantity for the product purchased), and the column has a name.

Figure 7-2

The AVG() Function

The AVG() function returns the calculated average for a range of numeric values. Internally, the query processor calculates the sum of all the values and then divides by the number of rows in the range (containing non-null values). Optionally, the AVG() function can make a distinct selection of values and then perform the same calculation on this abbreviated set of values. Using a distinct selection can greatly affect the results and is not as common.

I'd like to use the product sales data in the AdventureWorks2008 database to demonstrate the practical application of these aggregate functions. In this scenario, the director of marketing has asked for an analysis of road bike sales in 2003. This information exists in three related tables. Pay no attention to the join statements for the time being; they are covered in Chapter 8. The following query uses the SalesOrderHeader table to filter the sales order, the Product table to filter by ProductSubCategoryID (2 is road bikes), and the UnitPrice is retrieved from the SalesOrderDetail table. For simplicity, I'm not considering the quantity of bikes purchased.

I'll start with the lowest price paid for a bike. Using the MIN() function should return only one value:

```
SELECT    MIN(UnitPrice)
FROM      Sales.SalesOrderHeader
          INNER JOIN Sales.SalesOrderDetail ON
          SalesOrderHeader.SalesOrderID = SalesOrderDetail.SalesOrderID
          INNER JOIN Production.Product
            ON SalesOrderDetail.ProductID = Product.ProductID
WHERE     Product.ProductSubCategoryID = 2
          AND SalesOrderHeader.OrderDate BETWEEN '1-1-03' And '12-31-03'
```

You can see that the lowest UnitPrice value in this range is $296.99. (I've rounded the results to the nearest penny.) Just modify the query, substituting the following functions in place of the MIN() function in the example. The following table shows the results.

Question	Function	Result
What was the lowest price paid?	MIN()	296.99
What was the highest price paid?	MAX()	2,443.35
What is the average price paid?	AVG()	1,019.98

Understanding Statistical Functions

The functions you've seen so far perform simple aggregation over a range of values. The following statistical functions apply more complex algorithms to a range of values. Fundamentally, the principle is the same, but the application is a little more specialized.

Statistics wasn't my best subject in school. Although I understood the relevance and importance of statistics, my brain just wasn't wired for it. Fortunately, now that I use these functions regularly in consulting and application development work, I no longer struggle with it, but I often need to jog my memory by looking at an example. This section explains these concepts in simple terms and provides some useful examples for those of us who don't think statistically.

The STDEV() Function

Have you ever taken a class where the teacher graded on a curve? If so, you were the victim of standard deviation (or, perhaps, the benefactor).

The standard deviation is a calculation based on the variance of a numeric range of values. Actually, it's simply the square root of the variance. In a normal distribution, values can be plotted in a bell curve, with the mean value represented by the center of the curve. If you were to slice off the center of the curve, taking about 68% of the most common values, this would represent the standard deviation (or "first standard deviation"). If you were to move outward the same variation of values, you would take off another 27% (a total of 95%), leaving only 5%.

Standard deviation is an effective method for analyzing and making sense of large distributions of data. It is also a common method to calculate risk and probability.

To measure the standard deviation for your sample values table, simply use the following query:

```
SELECT STDEV(MyValue) FROM MyValues
```

The result, 1.5811... , tells you that for the values in your table, those values that are in the range from 2.4198 to 5.5811 (within 1.5811 of the mean) are in the first standard deviation.

Using the AdventureWorks or AdventureWorks2008 sales data, you can apply this analysis to bicycle sales. Suppose that the director of marketing asks "How much did most of our customers pay for road bikes in 2003?" Just modify the query you used before, using the STDEV() function like this:

```
SELECT    STDEV(UnitPrice)
FROM      Sales.SalesOrderHeader
          INNER JOIN Sales.SalesOrderDetail ON
          Sales.SalesOrderHeader.SalesOrderID = Sales.SalesOrderDetail
.SalesOrderID
          INNER JOIN Production.Product ON Sales.SalesOrderDetail
.ProductID = Product.ProductID
WHERE     Production.Product.ProductSubCategoryID = 2
          AND Sales.SalesOrderHeader.OrderDate BETWEEN '1-1-03'
And '12-31-03'
```

The result is 634.11. This means that most of your customers paid between $385.87 and $1,654.09 for their road bikes — at least those purchases in the first standard deviation (the average price: $1019.98 ± $634.11).

The STDEVP() Function

This function calculates standard deviation based on the variance of a population. It's a special-purpose function, generally used only in statistical analysis.

The VAR() Function

The VAR() function returns the statistical variance for a range of values — that is, a value that indicates how "spread out" the values are in the range. The value returned by this function is actually the measure of how far the extreme low range or high range value is from the middle — or mean value of the range, weighted by the greatest concentration of similar values. For example, given the range of values on a number line, 2, 3, 4, 5, and 6, the number 4 is the mean — it's in the middle of the range.

The variance is a calculation based on the standard deviation. In short, the variance is simply the standard deviation squared. This is useful because it defines a range of "normal" values within one standard deviation on both sides of the mean. In this simple example, the variance of this range is 2.5. This is very simple if you have a list of distinct, incremental values but it gets a little more complex as the values are less uniform.

You can do some simple experimenting with values in a single-column table created by running the following query:

```
Create Table MyValues (MyValue Float)
```

Now, insert the values given in the previous example, using this query:

```
Insert Into MyValues (MyValue) SELECT 2
Insert Into MyValues (MyValue) SELECT 3
Insert Into MyValues (MyValue) SELECT 4
Insert Into MyValues (MyValue) SELECT 5
Insert Into MyValues (MyValue) SELECT 6
```

To return the variance of this range, use this query:

```
SELECT VAR(MyValue) FROM MyValues
```

The result is 2.5. If you insert more values close to the center of the range, you will see that this changes the outcome and returns a smaller variance. This is because the result is computed as the average squared deviation (difference) of each number from its mean. This is done so negative numbers behave appropriately and to weight the equation toward the center of the greatest concentration of values. Regardless, it's a standard statistical function and, fortunately, you probably don't need to concern yourself with the specifics of the internal calculation. Calculating variance is the first step in performing other statistical functions, such as standard deviation.

As you can see, using integer values to keep things simple, you've created a bell-curve around the mean value, 4:

```
INSERT INTO MyValues (MyValue) SELECT 3
INSERT INTO MyValues (MyValue) SELECT 4
INSERT INTO MyValues (MyValue) SELECT 4
INSERT INTO MyValues (MyValue) SELECT 4
INSERT INTO MyValues (MyValue) SELECT 5
```

You then return the deviation for the range again:

```
SELECT VAR(MyValue) FROM MyValues
```

The result should now be about 1.33333. This number is smaller because adding values closer to the mean reduces the value of the standard deviation to indicate that values, on average, are less spread out.

The VARP() Function

The variance over a population is simply another indicator of the same variance principle, using a different formula. This formula is sometimes called *biased estimate of variance*. Although this method is used in some complex calculations, the other form of variance is more common. (I'm sure I saw this used once in college, but, frankly, I've never seen it used. Please don't tell anyone I've admitted to this.)

User-Defined Aggregate Functions

SQL Server 2005 and SQL Server 2008 allow application developers to add custom aggregate functions to a database. These functions are written in a .NET programming language, such as C# or Visual Basic .NET, and must be compiled into a .NET assembly using the Microsoft .NET Common Language Runtime. As a SQL query designer, all you need to know is that once aggregate functions are deployed and correctly configured, you can use them in your queries as you would any of the system-supplied aggregate functions.

Grouping Data

So far, your work with aggregate functions has been for a group of records that return a single value. An operation that returns a single value is known as a *scalar* result. Although this may be appropriate for very simple data analysis, aggregate functions can be used in far more sophisticated and useful ways. Groups are used to distill rows with common column values into one row. This gives you the opportunity to perform aggregated calculations on each of the groupings. There are some restrictions and it's important to understand the rules regarding groups. Columns returned by a grouped query must either be referenced in the GROUP BY list or use an aggregate function. Other columns can be used for filtering or sorting but these column values cannot be returned in the result set.

The GROUP BY Clause

Often, you will need to distill all the rows in a table, or the results of a multi-table join, into summary rows with a grand total or subtotals for groups of rows. Grouping is the process of summarizing ranges of rows based on some kind of distinct match or similarity between common rows. Typically, all the rows within the group are aggregated into a single row using one or more of the aggregate functions we just looked at.

Grouping occurs after records are retrieved and then aggregated. The GROUP BY clause is added to the query after the WHERE and ORDER BY clauses. Consider that the query runs first without the aggregate functions and grouping to determine which rows will be considered for grouping. After these results are read into memory, SQL Server makes a pass through these records, applying groupings and aggregate calculations.

Consider the following example using the SUM() function:

```
SELECT SalesOrderID, SUM(OrderQty) FROM Sales.SalesOrderDetail
GROUP BY SalesOrderID
```

The SalesOrderID value can be returned because it appears in the GROUP BY list. The query will return one distinct row for each SalesOrderID value. For each group of related records, all the OrderQty values are added together as the result of the SUM() function. The result should include two columns, the SalesOrderID and the sum of the OrderQty for the related detail rows, as shown in Figure 7-3.

	SalesOrderID	(No column name)
1	43659	26
2	43660	2
3	43661	38
4	43662	54
5	43663	1
6	43664	14
7	43665	20
8	43666	7
9	43667	6
10	43668	93

Figure 7-3

Because detail rows contain multiple quantities, you really can't tell if these rows are aggregated. To get a better view, add another column to the previous query using the COUNT() function. Also, add column aliases to label these values:

```
SELECT  SalesOrderID
      , SUM(OrderQty) AS QtySum
      , COUNT(SalesOrderID) AS DetailCount
FROM Sales.SalesOrderDetail
GROUP BY SalesOrderID
```

Execute this query and check the result.

The result, displayed in Figure 7-4, shows that all but two of the visible rows were grouped and the SUM() function was applied to the OrderQty column value.

	SalesOrderID	QtySum	DetailCount
1	43659	26	12
2	43660	2	2
3	43661	38	15
4	43662	54	22
5	43663	1	1
6	43664	14	8
7	43665	20	10
8	43666	7	6
9	43667	6	4
10	43668	93	29

Figure 7-4

If you were to view the ungrouped records in this table, you could clearly see what's going on. The result shown in Figure 7-5 is just a simple SELECT query on the SalesOrderDetail table showing the first few rows.

	SalesOrderID	OrderQty
1	43659	1
2	43659	3
3	43659	1
4	43659	1
5	43659	1
6	43659	2
7	43659	1
8	43659	3
9	43659	1
10	43659	6
11	43659	2
12	43659	4
13	43660	1
14	43660	1
15	43661	1

Figure 7-5

Sales order 43659 has 12 detail rows, whose OrderQty values add up to 26, and order 43660 has two detail rows with a total quantity of 2.

When grouping on more than one column, every unique combination of grouped values produces a row in the result set. The following query demonstrates this scenario. Because the SalesOrderDetail table isn't preordered by the two columns you want to group on, you're explicitly ordering the results:

```
SELECT ProductID
     , SpecialOfferID
FROM Sales.SalesOrderDetail
GROUP BY ProductID, SpecialOfferID
ORDER BY ProductID, SpecialOfferID
```

The query returns a distinct list of ProductID and SpecialOfferID values, as shown in Figure 7-6.

	ProductID	SpecialOfferID
1	707	1
2	707	2
3	707	3
4	707	8
5	707	11
6	708	1
7	708	2
8	708	3
9	708	8
10	708	11
11	709	1
12	709	2
13	709	3
14	709	4
15	710	1

Figure 7-6

Although this may be interesting, it's not particularly useful information. Let's find out how many rows are actually being used to produce this list of distinct values. I'm going to change up the query a bit because I want to introduce another element. In the following query, I group on the SalesOrderID and the CarrierTrackingNumber, and include a count aggregation for both of these columns. Note the alias columns defined for these two count aggregates.

```
SELECT SalesOrderID, COUNT(SalesOrderID) AS SalesOrderIDCount
    , CarrierTrackingNumber, COUNT(CarrierTrackingNumber) AS
CarrierTrackingNumberCount
FROM Sales.SalesOrderDetail
GROUP BY SalesOrderID, CarrierTrackingNumber
ORDER BY SalesOrderID, CarrierTrackingNumber
```

In the result set shown in Figure 7-7, you can see that the results were similar to the previous query with the added counts.

	SalesOrderID	SalesOrderIDCount	CarrierTrackingNumber	CarrierTrackingNumberCount
1	43659	12	4911-403C-98	12
2	43660	2	6431-4D57-83	2
3	43661	15	4E0A-4F89-AE	15
4	43662	22	2E53-4802-85	22
5	43663	1	1E90-4FBF-B6	1
6	43664	8	2F44-4BA1-BB	8
7	43665	10	19F0-4638-8E	10
8	43666	6	D46A-40CA-8D	6
9	43667	4	4DFB-4B10-A6	4
10	43668	29	365D-4C9A-BE	29
11	43669	1	B65C-4867-86	1
12	43670	4	F101-4649-85	4
13	43671	11	DFD9-41B7-94	11
14	43672	3	F4B5-48D0-BA	3

Figure 7-7

It's probably not a surprise that sales orders and the shipping tracking numbers usually correspond because all the items for an order typically would ship together. Because this is the case for most of the records, the counts are the same. However, if you scroll down in the results, you can see that the counts are not the same when there are Null values. These records might indicate orders that have not yet shipped, were cancelled, or where the customer picked up the items instead of having them shipped. Figure 7-8 shows that omitted CarrierTrackingNumber values are not processed by the aggregate function, resulting in a count of 0.

	SalesOrderID	SalesOrderIDCount	CarrierTrackingNumber	CarrierTrackingNumberCount
32	43690	4	7A3C-492F-A6	4
33	43691	1	272B-4319-9E	1
34	43692	28	BFA9-470E-B4	28
35	43693	10	EC62-4BB3-9B	10
36	43694	11	EC3D-48E0-A6	11
37	43695	8	A89C-4D25-B9	8
38	43696	1	50C1-41FA-BE	1
39	43697	1	NULL	0
40	43698	1	NULL	0
41	43699	1	NULL	0
42	43700	1	NULL	0
43	43701	1	NULL	0

Figure 7-8

For more of a real-world example, because of the complexity of the AdventureWorks or AdventureWorks2008 database, it's necessary to create a fairly complex query with several table joins. Again, don't be concerned with the statements in the FROM clause, but do pay attention to the column list after the SELECT statement. You'll see this query again in the next chapter.

The purpose of the following query is to find out what products your customers have purchased. The Individual table contains personal information about human being–type customers (rather than stores that buy wholesale products). You've already seen that sales orders have order details, and a sales order detail line is related to a product.

This query works with AdvertureWorks2008:

```
SELECT
        Store.Name AS StoreName
    , Product.Name AS ProductName
    , COUNT(SalesOrderDetail.ProductID) AS PurchaseCount
FROM
        Sales.Customer INNER JOIN Sales.SalesOrderHeader
        ON Customer.CustomerID = SalesOrderHeader.CustomerID
        INNER JOIN Sales.SalesOrderDetail
        ON SalesOrderHeader.SalesOrderID = SalesOrderDetail.SalesOrderID
        INNER JOIN Production.Product
        ON SalesOrderDetail.ProductID = Product.ProductID
        INNER JOIN Sales.Store ON Customer.StoreID = Store.BusinessEntityID
GROUP BY Product.Name, Store.Name
ORDER BY Store.Name, Product.Name
```

This query works with AdventureWorks (for SQL Server 2005):

```
SELECT
        Store.Name AS StoreName
    , Product.Name AS ProductName
    , COUNT(SalesOrderDetail.ProductID) AS PurchaseCount
FROM
        Sales.Customer INNER JOIN Sales.SalesOrderHeader
        ON Customer.CustomerID = SalesOrderHeader.CustomerID
        INNER JOIN Sales.SalesOrderDetail
        ON SalesOrderHeader.SalesOrderID = SalesOrderDetail.SalesOrderID
        INNER JOIN Production.Product
        ON SalesOrderDetail.ProductID = Product.ProductID
        INNER JOIN Sales.Store ON Customer.CustomerID = Store.CustomerID
GROUP BY Product.Name, Store.Name
ORDER BY Store.Name, Product.Name
```

Three columns are returned from the query: the StoreName, the ProductName, and the number of product records in each group (PurchaseCount), using the COUNT() function. This returns the number of times a store purchased the same product. You could use the product Name in the COUNT() function, but it's usually more efficient to use primary key columns. Note that even though the StoreName and ProductName columns are aliased in the SELECT list, when used in the GROUP BY and ORDER BY statements, the alias name is not used — only the qualified column names are used.

Figure 7-9 shows the first 35 rows in the result set.

	StoreName	ProductName	PurchaseCount
1	A Bike Store	LL Road Frame - Black, 52	2
2	A Bike Store	LL Road Frame - Black, 58	1
3	A Bike Store	LL Road Frame - Red, 44	2
4	A Bike Store	LL Road Frame - Red, 48	2
5	A Bike Store	LL Road Frame - Red, 60	1
6	A Bike Store	LL Road Frame - Red, 62	2
7	A Bike Store	Long-Sleeve Logo Jersey, M	1
8	A Bike Store	ML Road Frame - Red, 48	2
9	A Bike Store	Road-150 Red, 44	2
10	A Bike Store	Road-150 Red, 48	1
11	A Bike Store	Road-150 Red, 52	1
12	A Bike Store	Road-150 Red, 56	4
13	A Bike Store	Road-150 Red, 62	2
14	A Bike Store	Road-450 Red, 44	3
15	A Bike Store	Road-450 Red, 48	3
16	A Bike Store	Road-450 Red, 52	3
17	A Bike Store	Road-450 Red, 58	3
18	A Bike Store	Road-450 Red, 60	3
19	A Bike Store	Road-650 Black, 44	4
20	A Bike Store	Road-650 Black, 48	2
21	A Bike Store	Road-650 Black, 52	3
22	A Bike Store	Road-650 Black, 58	2
23	A Bike Store	Road-650 Black, 60	2
24	A Bike Store	Road-650 Black, 62	2
25	A Bike Store	Road-650 Red, 44	4
26	A Bike Store	Road-650 Red, 48	3
27	A Bike Store	Road-650 Red, 52	2
28	A Bike Store	Road-650 Red, 58	3
29	A Bike Store	Road-650 Red, 60	2
30	A Bike Store	Road-650 Red, 62	4
31	A Bike Store	Sport-100 Helmet, Black	1
32	A Bike Store	Sport-100 Helmet, Blue	1
33	A Great Bicycle Company	AWC Logo Cap	1
34	A Great Bicycle Company	ML Road Pedal	1
35	A Great Bicycle Company	Road-450 Red, 52	2

Figure 7-9

Suppose that the purpose of this query was to locate stores that have purchased more than four of any product. Rather than scrolling through 20,501 rows, you can modify the query for rows with a count greater than four. This type of post aggregated filtering is performed with the HAVING clause, discussed next.

The HAVING Clause

If you need to filter the results of a grouped query based on the result of an aggregated value, then the aggregation must be performed first. You can't use the WHERE clause because it is processed prior to grouping and aggregation; therefore, you need some way to filter the rows after the grouping has been completed. This is the job of the HAVING clause.

This technique is very similar to using the WHERE clause, but the HAVING clause is limited to those columns and aggregate expressions that have already been specified on the SELECT statement. Typically, you will refer to aggregate values simply by repeating the aggregate function expression in the HAVING clause, just like you did in the SELECT statement. Here is the previous query with this expression added:

AdventureWorks2008:

```
SELECT
        Store.Name AS StoreName
    , Product.Name AS ProductName
    , COUNT(SalesOrderDetail.ProductID) AS PurchaseCount
FROM
        Sales.Customer INNER JOIN Sales.SalesOrderHeader
          ON Customer.CustomerID = SalesOrderHeader.CustomerID
        INNER JOIN Sales.SalesOrderDetail
          ON SalesOrderHeader.SalesOrderID = SalesOrderDetail.SalesOrderID
        INNER JOIN Production.Product
          ON SalesOrderDetail.ProductID = Product.ProductID
        INNER JOIN Sales.Store ON Customer.StoreID = Store.BusinessEntityID
GROUP BY Product.Name, Store.Name
HAVING COUNT(SalesOrderDetail.ProductID) > 4
ORDER BY Store.Name, Product.Name
```

AdventureWorks:

```
SELECT
        Store.Name AS StoreName
    , Product.Name AS ProductName
    , COUNT(SalesOrderDetail.ProductID) AS PurchaseCount
FROM
        Sales.Customer INNER JOIN Sales.SalesOrderHeader
          ON Customer.CustomerID = SalesOrderHeader.CustomerID
        INNER JOIN Sales.SalesOrderDetail
          ON SalesOrderHeader.SalesOrderID = SalesOrderDetail.SalesOrderID
        INNER JOIN Production.Product
          ON SalesOrderDetail.ProductID = Product.ProductID
        INNER JOIN Sales.Store ON Customer.CustomerID = Store.CustomerID
GROUP BY Product.Name, Store.Name
HAVING COUNT(SalesOrderDetail.ProductID) > 4
ORDER BY Store.Name, Product.Name
```

The result set is now reduced to 2,138 rows (about one-tenth of the original results), including only the store/product purchases. Examining the results reveals something very interesting. In the previous results, you saw that there appeared to be a lot of transactions for the store called A Bike Store. However, when you look at the results in this way, you see that this customer purchased only small quantities of each product. As such, they are not included in these results, as shown in Figure 7-10.

	StoreName	ProductName	PurchaseCount
1	Advanced Bike Components	AWC Logo Cap	12
2	Advanced Bike Components	Half-Finger Gloves, M	8
3	Advanced Bike Components	Half-Finger Gloves, S	7
4	Advanced Bike Components	LL Road Frame - Black, 52	9
5	Advanced Bike Components	LL Road Frame - Black, 58	8
6	Advanced Bike Components	LL Road Frame - Red, 44	7
7	Advanced Bike Components	LL Road Frame - Red, 60	7
8	Advanced Bike Components	Long-Sleeve Logo Jersey, L	11
9	Advanced Bike Components	Long-Sleeve Logo Jersey,...	11
10	Advanced Bike Components	Long-Sleeve Logo Jersey,...	11
11	Advanced Bike Components	ML Road Frame-W - Yello...	5
12	Advanced Bike Components	ML Road Frame-W - Yello...	6
13	Advanced Bike Components	Road-250 Black, 44	5
14	Advanced Bike Components	Road-250 Black, 48	6
15	Advanced Bike Components	Road-550-W Yellow, 38	7
16	Advanced Bike Components	Road-550-W Yellow, 40	7
17	Advanced Bike Components	Road-550-W Yellow, 48	7
18	Advanced Bike Components	Road-650 Black, 44	6
19	Advanced Bike Components	Road-650 Black, 52	5
20	Advanced Bike Components	Road-650 Black, 58	7
21	Advanced Bike Components	Road-650 Black, 60	8
22	Advanced Bike Components	Road-650 Red, 44	6

Figure 7-10

This data makes sense because most of the products listed with higher product counts are lower-priced items, which tend to sell quickly.

Like the WHERE clause, you can use the HAVING clause with any combination of comparison expressions and logical operators. Just be mindful that it is processed after the initial record selection (which is filtered by the WHERE clause) and that you are limited to the columns and aggregate expressions in the SELECT statement.

I'll use an example from the AdventureWorks or AdventureWorks2008 database so that you can follow along and work with the data yourself.

Grouping the Employee table on the FirstName and Gender columns will return all the combinations of these values. I'll aggregate the Employee primary key column using the COUNT() function so that you can see how many records there are for each FirstName/Gender combination.

AdventureWorks2008:

```
SELECT
    FirstName
  , Gender
  , COUNT(E.BusinessEntityID)
FROM HumanResources.Employee AS E INNER JOIN Person.Person AS P
 ON E. BusinessEntityID = P.BusinessEntityID
GROUP BY  FirstName, Gender
ORDER BY FirstName, Gender
```

AdventureWorks:

```
SELECT
    FirstName
  , Gender
  , COUNT(E.EmployeeID)
FROM HumanResources.Employee AS E INNER JOIN Person.Contact AS C
  ON E.ContactID = C.ContactID
GROUP BY  FirstName, Gender
ORDER BY FirstName, Gender
```

Figure 7-11 shows the first few employee records grouped by name and gender with the count of names for that gender.

	First Name	Gender	(No column name)
1	A. Scott	M	1
2	Alan	M	1
3	Alejandro	M	1
4	Alex	M	1
5	Alice	F	1
6	Amy	F	1
7	Andreas	M	1
8	Andrew	M	2
9	Andy	M	1
10	Angela	F	1
11	Anibal	F	1
12	Annette	F	1
13	Annik	M	1
14	Arvind	M	1
15	Ashvini	M	1
16	Barbara	F	2
17	Baris	M	1
18	Barry	M	1
19	Belinda	F	1

Figure 7-11

I've shown you a few examples of queries using grouping and filtering that use the HAVING clause. Here's a simplified version to try out on your own. Before you look at the following query, cover it up or bookmark and close the book (after reading these instructions, of course). Your challenge is to return the average list price of mountain bike products, grouped by color only where the average price is greater than $1,200. Mountain bikes have a ProductSubcategoryID = 2.

Try it out on your own and then compare your results with the following query:

```
SELECT Color, AVG(ListPrice)
FROM Production.Product
WHERE ProductSubcategoryID = 2
GROUP BY Color
HAVING AVG(ListPrice) > 1200
```

You'll recall that the WHERE clause filters rows before they get to the GROUP BY clause or aggregate function. The HAVING clause is processed after the grouping and aggregation have already taken place.

In the previous edition of this book, using the AdventureWorks database that had originally been created for SQL Server 2000, I pointed out that some of our friends at Microsoft had some fun when populating this table. Most of the names in the Employee table were actually Microsoft employees or friends and colleagues in the SQL Server community, and many of these names were strategically entered with the wrong gender. Apparently, someone had a sense humor, but all good things must come to an end and this table has since been "cleaned up." Looks like the party's over. As a result of the apparent cleansing of AdventureWorks, we've had to rework many of our demonstrations and sample queries to keep pace with these changes. Keep this in mind if you've read the previous edition of this book or if you are working with sample queries written for SQL Server 2000 or 2005.

Total and Subtotal Group Modifiers

The GROUP BY clause, along with aggregate functions, is useful in many common query scenarios. It offers a convenient way to reduce the number of rows returned by a query while continuing to return a uniform set of columns and rows that are easily consumed by applications and reporting tools.

Before getting into a discussion about the techniques available for totaling grouped aggregates and creating subtotal breaks, a discussion of how you will use this data is needed. SQL Server is typically used as the back-end data store for some type of application or data consumer product. Many data presentation and reporting tools exist that will take care of formatting and totaling values from your queries. The technique you choose will largely depend on the tool or application that will consume this data.

One important consideration is whether you want the data to be grouped, aggregated, and subtotaled by the database server or by the client application after results have been returned from the database. There is little doubt that it is more efficient to let the database server do the work and send less data across the network. However, consider the case where an application allows users to interact with data, choosing different sorting and grouping options. It might make more sense to send raw data to the application one time so it can be manipulated by the client rather than refreshing the result set and resending a different result each time the user chooses a grouping or sorting option. These are decisions that your solution designers might need to make on a larger scale. The purpose here is to discuss the options in SQL Server to do the grouping and subtotaling at the database server.

Old and New Subtotal Techniques

With SQL Server 2008, Microsoft released support for a new set of techniques for performing in-query subtotal breaks. These are new techniques that you will not see in existing queries created with previous product versions. The older techniques are "deprecated." Get used to this term because we're seeing it a lot lately. "Deprecated" means that there's a newer, cooler way of doing something, and the old method, though it might still be supported, may not be sometime in the future. I'll point out the old and new techniques in this section as we continue.

By introducing subgrouping and the related techniques introduced in the following section, you can enhance the functionality of data grouping and aggregation. However, you should carefully consider how you intend to use the results, as many tools may not be able to interpret the outcome. If you're not careful, you could get inaccurate or confusing results. Reporting tools such as Access, Crystal Reports, or SQL Server Reporting Services are perfectly capable of producing breaks and calculating subtotals without any special provisions within the query. However, these features can be useful for creating breaks and totals in an ad hoc query and without the aid of a reporting client.

Note that I use the terms "totaling" and "subtotaling" in a general sense to mean applying whatever aggregate functions you choose at various group levels. For example, if I were using the AVG() function to return the average purchase price per product, and per quarter at the quarter level, I would want to see the average calculation for all the product price averages. I'm using the term "subtotal" loosely, even though I expect to see an average calculation rather than a sum or total.

Subgrouping

With more than one column referenced in the GROUP BY clause, some interesting things happen. For the sake of simplicity, a hypothetical table follows with simplified values.

ID1	ID2	MyValue
A	X	2
A	X	1
A	Y	2
A	Y	1
B	X	3
B	Y	2
B	Y	2

In a query for my hypothetical table, I include the first two columns, ID1 and ID2, in the GROUP BY clause, and then use the SUM() function to total the values in the third column:

```
SELECT ID1, ID2, Sum(MyValue)
FROM MyHypotheticalTable
GROUP BY ID1, ID2
```

Multiple rows are returned, one for each unique combination of values, as shown in the following table.

ID1	ID2	MyValue
A	X	3
A	Y	3
B	X	3
B	Y	4

What I don't have in this result set is the sum for all occurrences where ID1 is equal to A or where ID2 is equal to Y. To get the aggregate result of a grouped query, you can use the ROLLUP and CUBE statements, as described in the following sections. Essentially, these statements will take the results from the grouped query and apply the same aggregation to either the first column's values or all combinations of values for each column that appears in the GROUP BY column list.

The ROLLUP Clause

This is the simplest option for calculating subtotals and totals on the first column in the GROUP BY column list. In the case of my hypothetical example, in addition to calculating the sum of each unique column value, totals would be tallied for the value A and B in the ID1 column only.

There are two different ways to apply ROLLUP in SQL Server 2008. The older method has you add WITH ROLLUP after the GROUP BY statement, like this:

```
SELECT ID1, ID2, SUM(MyValue)
FROM MyHypotheticalTable
GROUP BY ID1, ID2
WITH ROLLUP
```

The newer technique, introduced with SQL Server 2008, uses ROLLUP as a modifier for the GROUP BY clause:

```
SELECT ID1, ID2, SUM(MyValue)
FROM MyHypotheticalTable
GROUP BY ROLLUP(ID1, ID2)
```

The results would look something like those shown in the following table.

ID1	ID2	MyValue
A	X	3
A	Y	3
B	X	3
B	Y	4
A	(null)	6
B	(null)	7

Null values are used to indicate that the corresponding column was ignored when calculating the aggregate value.

The CUBE Clause

The CUBE operator is an expanded version of the ROLLUP operator. Rather than just rolling up the aggregate values for the first column in the GROUP BY list, CUBE performs this rollup for every combination of grouped column values. In the case of the hypothetical tables used in the previous example, three additional rows are added to the result set. Here is the same query using WITH CUBE rather than WITH ROLLUP:

```
SELECT ID1, ID2, SUM(MyValue)
FROM MyHypotheticalTable
GROUP BY ID1, ID2
WITH CUBE
```

And the following is the newer, recommended form that applies CUBE as a modifier to the GROUP BY clause:

```
SELECT ID1, ID2, SUM(MyValue)
FROM MyHypotheticalTable
GROUP BY CUBE(ID1, ID2)
```

The corresponding result set is shown in the following table.

ID1	ID2	MyValue
A	X	3
A	Y	3
B	X	3
B	Y	4
A	(null)	6
B	(null)	7
(null)	X	6
(null)	Y	7
(null)	(null)	13

Null values in the first column indicate that this is a rollup on the values in the second column. In this case, these rows contain subtotal values for all rows where ID2 is equal to X or Y. The last row has null values in both grouped columns. This indicates that it is a grand total, the sum of all rows.

The GROUPING() Function

Let's go back to the AdventureWorks Cycles Product table example used earlier. I made a point not to use this table for the ROLLUP and CUBE examples because it would throw a wrench into the works.

Go back and take another look at Figure 7-8, noting the null values in the CarrierTrackingNumber column. You'll recall that when using the ROLLUP and CUBE modifiers, a null is used to indicate a rollup or subtotal row where that column's value isn't being considered. What if a column in the GROUP BY list actually contains null values? Here's the earlier example again, with the added ROLLUP modifier that is now available in SQL Server 2008:

```
SELECT SalesOrderID, COUNT(SalesOrderID) AS SalesOrderIDCount
    , CarrierTrackingNumber, COUNT(CarrierTrackingNumber) AS
        CarrierTrackingNumberCount
FROM Sales.SalesOrderDetail
GROUP BY ROLLUP(SalesOrderID, CarrierTrackingNumber)
ORDER BY SalesOrderID, CarrierTrackingNumber
```

In the result set shown in Figure 7-12, additional rows are added with subtotals.

	SalesOrderID	SalesOrderIDCount	CarrierTrackingNumber	CarrierTrackingNumberCount
1	NULL	121317	NULL	60919
2	43659	12	NULL	12
3	43659	12	4911-403C-98	12
4	43660	2	NULL	2
5	43660	2	6431-4D57-83	2
6	43661	15	NULL	15
7	43661	15	4E0A-4F89-AE	15
8	43662	22	NULL	22
9	43662	22	2E53-4802-85	22
10	43663	1	NULL	1
11	43663	1	1E90-4FBF-B6	1
12	43664	8	NULL	8
13	43664	8	2F44-4BA1-BB	8
14	43665	10	NULL	10
15	43665	10	19F0-4638-8E	10
16	43666	6	NULL	6
17	43666	6	D46A-40CA-8D	6
18	43667	4	NULL	4
19	43667	4	4DFB-4B10-A6	4
20	43668	29	NULL	29

Figure 7-12

Looking at these results, you should see a pattern. For each set of distinct SalesOrderID values, there is a row with a NULL in the CarrierTrackingNumber column and a row with a legitimate value in this column. The NULL indicates that this row is a subtotal for the group. That's great, but what if the CarrierTrackingNumber actually contains a NULL? This can be confusing and difficult to keep track of. Imagine the added confusion if you were grouping on more than two columns, or using the CUBE operator rather than ROLLUP. Imagine taking the results of this query to your software developer and asking him to create a custom report with subtotals and totals and then try to explain this grouping criterion. This is where the GROUPING() function comes in.

The GROUPING() function returns a bit value (1 or 0) to indicate that a row is a rollup. This makes it easy to separate the aggregation of null values. Any application or tool that consumes grouped data can easily distinguish the rolled-up subtotal rows from simple grouped rows. Here's a better example of a query using the GROUPING() function:

```
SELECT Color, Size
    , AVG(ListPrice) AS AvgPrice
    , GROUPING(Size) AS IsRollup
FROM Production.Product
GROUP BY ROLLUP(Color, Size)
```

In the results shown in Figure 7-13, you can see that each individual rollup row is flagged with a 1. The NULL value for the Size column on line 3 is literal. This row shows the average price for all Black products that have no size specified. Line 18, however, is a rollup for all sizes that have Black for the color. So, what do the NULL values for both Color and Size represent on line 2? The rollup flag is 1, so this is a total – in fact, this row is the grand total for all colors and all sizes.

	Color	Size	AvgPrice	IsTotal
1	NULL	NULL	16.8641	0
2	NULL	NULL	16.8641	1
3	Black	NULL	180.2259	0
4	Black	38	1689.6660	0
5	Black	40	554.6325	0
6	Black	42	1561.8720	0
7	Black	44	1134.3790	0
8	Black	46	1822.2950	0
9	Black	48	1134.3790	0
10	Black	52	903.5471	0
11	Black	58	1107.0100	0
12	Black	60	560.1050	0
13	Black	62	850.5700	0
14	Black	L	53.4900	0
15	Black	M	53.4900	0
16	Black	S	53.4900	0
17	Black	XL	59.9900	0
18	Black	NULL	725.1210	1
19	Blue	NULL	34.9900	0
20	Blue	44	537.8850	0

Figure 7-13

Because this is a ROLLUP query, only the Size values get rolled up into their respective Color combination counterparts. As such, this query doesn't show grouped Size values for every combination of Color. If you substitute CUBE for the ROLLUP function, you will see additional Grouping flags for the Size and you will see all of the unique combinations for each.

Note that if the results of these grouped and aggregated queries will be fed to a custom reporting solution or a similar application, application developers will appreciate the output from the GROUPING() function. This can make life much easier for a custom software developer or report designer.

The COMPUTE and COMPUTE BY Clauses

Regardless of the data you might work with, SQL Server was designed, and is optimized, to return rows and columns — two dimensions. Likewise, software designed to consume SQL data expects to receive two-dimensional data. All of the components, application programming interfaces (APIs), and connection utilities are engineered to work with two-dimensional result sets. For example, a programmer, using the .NET Framework, may populate a `DataTable` object from a T-SQL query, which builds a two-dimensional object in memory to be consumed by additional programming code. Standard user interface components, such as a grid or chart, are designed to consume data in this form.

Why am I making such a big deal out of this two-dimensional result set business? The COMPUTE clause is a very simple means for viewing data with totals and subtotals, but it breaks all the rules when it comes to standard results. It's also important to note that this is a proprietary SQL Server feature and isn't recognized by the ANSI SQL specification. It's an effective technique for viewing summary data, but its usefulness may be somewhat limited in many real software solutions, and its usefulness is really limited to SQL Server Management Studio. If that isn't a good enough reason to convince you not to use this feature in a production application, here's an even better argument: SQL Server 2008 will most likely be the last version of SQL Server to support it. For years, the SQL Server team at Microsoft has been telling us that there may be limited future support, and they have finally decided to deprecate this feature altogether. Whether you plan to use it in the future or not, it's important to realize its limitations. The bottom line is that you should be performing subtotal breaks in your reporting applications, rather than ad hoc T-SQL queries. If you need to output the results of an ad hoc query with subtotals and totals for your users to read in a quick-and-dirty report, you should use the ROLLUP or CUBE modifiers. You can paste the results into Excel and use colors, borders, and shading to indicate the rollups and subtotals to make the data easier to understand.

Because this feature is still supported in the current product version and you may encounter it in existing queries, I've provided a brief example to illustrate the application of the COMPUTE clause:

Suppose that the sales manager calls you on the phone and asks you to tell her what the total sales were for last month. She doesn't need a formal report, and you're not going to develop a custom application for users to do this themselves. She just wants a list of sales orders with the total. Using this technique may be the best choice.

Here's a simple example of the COMPUTE clause:

```
SELECT ProductID, SalesOrderID, OrderQty
FROM Sales.SalesOrderDetail
ORDER BY ProductID, SalesOrderID
COMPUTE SUM(OrderQty)
```

The query editor splits the result into two grids because the result doesn't fit into a standard two-dimensional grid, as shown in Figure 7-14.

I had asked for SQL Server to compute the sum of the OrderQty for the entire result set. This created a grand total for the entire range of data. Because of the formatting restrictions of viewing results in grid view, I'd like to show you the same result in text view.

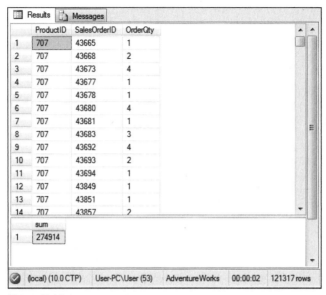

Figure 7-14

This may be useful if you are interested in the grand total following the entire range of values. If you want to see grouped sections of rows with subtotals, it's a simple matter to add the column name or list of columns to the end of the COMPUTE clause. Modify the previous query to group by the ProductID:

```
SELECT ProductID, SalesOrderID, OrderQty
FROM Sales.SalesOrderDetail
WHERE SalesOrderID > 75100
ORDER BY ProductID, SalesOrderID
COMPUTE SUM(OrderQty) BY ProductID
```

The result set shows the same list of SalesOrderDetail records with a subtotal break after each ProductID. (I've shortened the result and returned it in text format to save space.)

```
ProductID    SalesOrderID OrderQty
-----------  ------------ --------
707          75105        1
707          75121        1
sum
-----------
2
ProductID    SalesOrderID OrderQty
-----------  ------------ --------
708          75103        1
708          75107        1
708          75111        1
sum
-----------
3
...
```

```
ProductID    SalesOrderID OrderQty
-----------  ------------ --------
931          75114        1
931          75115        1
sum
-----------
2

(83 row(s) affected)
```

The COMPUTE clause is an easy and convenient technique for producing a detailed list of column values with total and grouped subtotal breaks. It doesn't do grouping and aggregation on every row like the GROUP BY clause. Just keep in mind that the output isn't compatible with most standard data consumer software and programming components. If you just need to view or print a quick, ad hoc report, this may be the easiest way to get there. Otherwise, use the ANSI standard GROUP BY clause with the ROLLUP or CUBE modifiers. Also, remember that the COMPUTE clause will no longer be supported in future versions of SQL Server.

From a database design standpoint, it is imperative that large tables are indexed on columns that will be used for grouping and aggregation. Few other functions and SQL statements will stress the database engine to the same degree. Consider using a clustered index on a column that is usually used in queries to join to another table or specify the usual sort order. You can find more information about indexing strategies in *Professional Microsoft SQL Server 2008 Programming*, also from Wrox.

As previously mentioned, cube operations can be especially intensive. As you have run some of these queries, you've probably noticed that it takes a little while to perform calculations and return the aggregated results. It's best to use the ROLLUP and CUBE modifiers with filtered data. If you do need to perform intensive grouping operations on a large volume of data, try to do this at a time when you won't be competing with other large operations.

Although it usually makes sense to let SQL Server do a majority of the work, sometimes returning a larger volume of data that can be reused in the client application, rather than running numerous query operations, is best. This is especially true with dynamic reporting solutions. Make a point to understand your users' needs and try to strike a balance between the flexibility of an application or reporting solution and the efficiency of the whole system. As a rule, don't return any more data than is necessary. Finally, make a point to order records explicitly using the ORDER BY clause. This will guarantee the sort order of your queries. Even if records in the table already exist in the correct order, using the ORDER BY clause will not cause any processing overhead.

Summary

This chapter introduced nine aggregate functions that can be used in a simple SELECT statement to return summary values for the entire range or with the GROUP BY clause to roll up groups of rows with similar values. The aggregate functions include simple mathematical operations, such as Count and Sum, and statistical functions such as variance and standard deviation.

The GROUP BY clause can be used to reduce the results of a query to distinct combinations of grouped values. When used with aggregate functions, this produces value summaries within the grouping.

The ROLLUP and CUBE statements extend grouping functionality by adding summary rows. Adding WITH ROLLUP to a grouped query will produce summary rows for the first column in the GROUP BY list. Adding WITH CUBE will add summary rows for every possible combination of grouped column values. The GROUPING() function can be used along with these operators to flag summary rows and to avoid confusion.

Use the COMPUTE statement sparingly and only for quick reports in the Query Editor. Although it's simple compared to using some of the other techniques discussed in this chapter, it is not ANSI SQL–compliant and doesn't work with most software and programming tools. It is, however, a convenient method for viewing summary information quickly (but will not be supported in future versions of SQL Server).

Exercises

Exercise 1

For SQL Server 2008, using the AdventureWorks2008 database:

Write a query to return the JobTitle and lowest LoginID value for each group of employees. Include only employees with an OrganizationLevel of 0, 1, or 2.

For SQL Server 2005, using the AdventureWorks database:

Write a query to return the title, gender, and lowest LoginID value for each group of employees. Include only employees with a title of Buyer, Recruiter, or Stocker.

Exercise 2

Return a list of ProductSubCategoryID values from the Product table. Include only subcategories that occur more than 20 times. In addition to the ID value, also return the first product name in alphabetical order and the highest price for products in this subcategory.

Exercise 3

For SQL Server 2008, using the AdventureWorks2008 database:

Produce a list of organization levels from the Employee table. For each level, include the average vacation hours for all employees of each gender. Also produce an additional subtotaling row for each level that includes the average vacation hours for all employees of that level. This should be done using only one SELECT expression.

For SQL Server 2005, using the 2005 version of the AdventureWorks database:

Produce a list of employee titles and genders from the Employee table. For each title, include the average vacation hours for all employees of each gender. Also produce an additional subtotaling row for each title that includes the average vacation hours for all employees of that title. This should be done using only one SELECT expression.

Multi-Table Queries

At the beginning of this book, we briefly discussed some of the concepts of database design. You'll recall that information is often broken down into pieces and stored in several tables to improve accuracy and reduce redundancy. This leaves you with one of the greatest challenges in relational database work — putting the information back together.

In this chapter, you learn about

- ❏ Combining columns from multiple tables using subqueries and joins
- ❏ Using legacy and ANSI standard join syntax applied in the FROM and WHERE clauses
- ❏ The difference between inner, outer, full, and cross joins
- ❏ Applying the UNION operator to combine parallel result sets

A few years ago I rented a diesel front loader to level some property and put in a gravel driveway. I had never operated one before, but I figured that it couldn't be too difficult. It was the kind with four wheels and big rubber tires with deep tread. It had a big lever on each side for each hand that controlled power to the wheels on the left and right sides of the vehicle. The hydraulics were controlled using foot pedals that swiveled in each direction. It really felt like a big video arcade game at first (you know, the big ones that cost a whole dollar per game). Needless to say, it took coordination that I had yet to develop when I started. It handled a little differently than my Ford Mustang. The first thing I did was ease the throttle forward and try to go up a slight incline. The clutches on the traction controls were very sensitive. I pushed the hand levers too quickly, and it lunged forward. I found myself heading nose-up, popping a wheelie on the rear wheels. The thought of rolling over backward in a five-ton, diesel-powered steel box was not very appealing.

My wife was watching (and giggling) from a safe distance and suggested that perhaps she could do a better job. Not about to let my wife show me how to operate a big piece of machinery, I eventually got used to the controls and learned to work with it. By the end of the day, I was tearing up the woods like a five-year-old with a Tonka truck.

The key was to learn how this piece of machinery was engineered to work. Like a racehorse, I had to find that middle ground between what *it* wanted to do and what *I* wanted it to do. After I found that space, we got along just fine. Although it's hard to get SQL Server to pop a wheelie, like any other industrial-strength tool, you have to work *with* it. One of the key factors to achieving this goal is to understand how the tool is designed to work. There are nearly always different ways to approach a problem and different techniques that will ultimately achieve the same end result, but the shortest path will usually be the most efficient.

To fully explain some concepts in this chapter, I'll need to use some simple examples of some things we have yet to cover completely but will in later chapters. This is kind of a chicken and egg thing. For example, we discuss subqueries at length in Chapter 9, but I'll show you the basics of how to join a table to a subquery a little later in this chapter.

When a relational database is designed, tables are typically created with defined relationships between them. When the data is queried, join operations are often employed to utilize these relationships and "reassemble" the original information. Although it usually makes sense to join tables using predefined relationships, there are times when you will not use related columns to join tables. If your database has been designed correctly, this should be the rare exception to the rule.

Here's a simple example. I have used the Database Diagram feature in SQL Server Management Studio to create an entity relation diagram for part of the AdventureWorks database (see Figure 8-1).

The lines interconnecting the tables represent **relationships** (also called **referential constraints**). These lines connect to each table in the diagram, and although they may represent associations between specific fields, relationship lines don't necessarily point to the fields because some relationships may be based on multiple fields. You can see that relationships have been defined between these tables that are based on primary and foreign key columns. As you know, primary keys are used to uniquely identify rows in a table, and foreign keys are used to relate one table's rows to another. For example, the Customer table's designated primary key is the CustomerID column. Every customer record has a unique value assigned in this column. The SalesOrderHeader table also contains a CustomerID column, but values in this column are not necessarily unique because a single customer can have multiple orders. However, every SalesOrderHeader record with a CustomerID value must have a corresponding CustomerID value in the Customer table. This rule is enforced in the foreign key constraint rule defined in the SalesOrderHeader table.

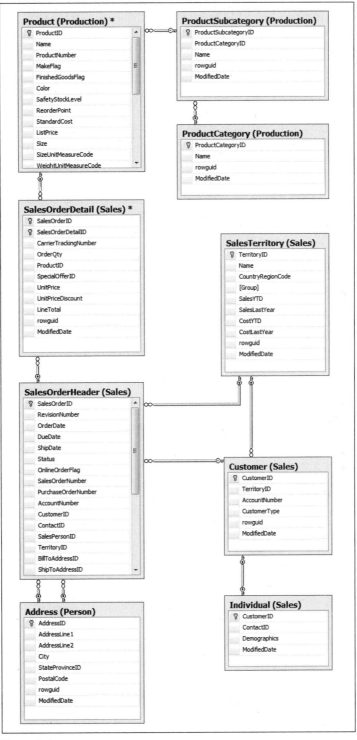

Figure 8-1

Understanding Subqueries and Joins

There's a right way and a wrong way to do everything, but unfortunately, there isn't always just one right or wrong method. The subject of correct join syntax is debatable, and there are recommended methods for different products. In the material that follows, I will show you a few different techniques, all of which are currently supported in SQL Server 2005 and 2008. Read on as I describe the methods recommended and guaranteed to provide future support and optimal performance.

As the SQL language has evolved and as it has been implemented in different products, a few different techniques have been devised for joining tables to match up related records. Although there are a few variations of these techniques, there are essentially three different options to join records from two different tables. The first two are different forms of join operations within a single SELECT statement. You can either join tables in the WHERE clause or in the FROM clause. The third technique involves more than one SELECT statement, where one query encompasses a second SELECT statement. This is often called a *subquery* — a query within a query. The tables in a subquery can be independent of each other or can be related through some kind of matching expression. One technique, used to match rows of the subquery to a row or rows of the main query, is often referred to as a *correlated subquery*. Subqueries are covered in Chapter 9. For now, I will concentrate on the bread and butter of SQL Server queries: the join operation.

Joining Tables in the WHERE Clause

If you work with long-time database professionals who cut their teeth on other products such as Oracle, Informix, or DB2, you are likely to encounter an older style of join syntax that is discouraged in SQL Server. In fact (since 1992 when the most accepted ANSI SQL standard was penned), the traditional form has been mildly discouraged by most of the database product vendors, but old-timers get downright religious about continuing to use the old-school method. Because it's an older technique, it is often referred to as a **legacy join**. Although it is still partially supported by SQL Server, this is not the recommended approach for SQL Server 2008. You may encounter this syntax in existing code. In this example, both the Customer and SalesOrderHeader are referenced in the FROM clause, and the join operation is performed in the WHERE clause:

```
SELECT Customer.AccountNumber, SalesOrderHeader.OrderDate
FROM Sales.Customer, Sales.SalesOrderHeader
WHERE Customer.CustomerID = SalesOrderHeader.CustomerID
```

The query returns 31,465 rows, comprised of a combination of records from the Customer and SalesOrderDetail tables. Figure 8-2 shows the first few of these rows.

This query implements an inner join, discussed shortly. The equal sign between each of the column references means that this query returns only rows where there are matching records in each of the tables. This is known as an *equijoin*, meaning that the values in two tables compared in the join operation must be equal to one another. Microsoft is making good on its threat to deprecate this feature of T-SQL. As of SQL Server 2008, the outer join form is no longer supported. I'll discuss this a little later in this chapter.

	AccountNumber	OrderDate
1	AW00000676	2001-07-01 00:00:00.000
2	AW00000117	2001-07-01 00:00:00.000
3	AW00000442	2001-07-01 00:00:00.000
4	AW00000227	2001-07-01 00:00:00.000
5	AW00000510	2001-07-01 00:00:00.000
6	AW00000397	2001-07-01 00:00:00.000
7	AW00000146	2001-07-01 00:00:00.000
8	AW00000511	2001-07-01 00:00:00.000
9	AW00000646	2001-07-01 00:00:00.000
10	AW00000514	2001-07-01 00:00:00.000
11	AW00000578	2001-07-01 00:00:00.000
12	AW00000504	2001-07-01 00:00:00.000
13	AW00000200	2001-07-01 00:00:00.000
14	AW00000119	2001-07-01 00:00:00.000
15	AW00000618	2001-07-01 00:00:00.000

Figure 8-2

Joining Tables in the FROM Clause

The same operation can also be performed using the ANSI standard method. In the FROM clause, the two tables are referenced with a JOIN statement followed by the ON keyword and the same column references used in the preceding example:

```
SELECT Customer.AccountNumber, SalesOrderHeader.OrderDate
FROM Sales.Customer INNER JOIN Sales.SalesOrderHeader
ON Customer.CustomerID = SalesOrderHeader.CustomerID
```

The result is the same. If you view the execution plan for both of these queries, you'll note that they both cause SQL Server to perform exactly the same operations. There is no difference in time, cost, or efficiency. You can view the execution plan for a query by enabling this option in the Query menu. Run the query, and the Execution Plan tab appears below the results window, as shown in Figure 8-3. Note that we've removed some of the irrelevant elements from the diagram to keep things simple.

Reading from right to left, each icon represents an operation. The records are retrieved from both tables and held in memory. Because each of the columns referenced in the JOIN statement are indexed, the query-processing engine chooses to scan and retrieve records using these indexes. Rows in the Customer table are retrieved using a separate, non-clustered index. Records in the SalesOrderDetail table are physically ordered by the CustomerID column based on a clustered index. The width of the arrows indicates the relative volume of data returned from the respective operation. The rows are combined using a hash join method to produce the final result. If you execute either of these two queries, you will see that the execution plans are the same. Float the mouse pointer over the left-most icon to see statistics for the finished product. The Subtree cost shows the total time in seconds for this and all operations that lead to it.

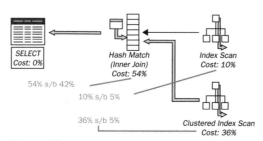

Figure 8-3

So here's the bottom line on this topic: In most cases, legacy joins, performed in the WHERE clause, and ANSI standard joins, performed in the FROM clause, will result in the same execution plan and achieve the same relative performance. However, this doesn't guarantee that you will see the same effect when joins are combined in large, complex queries. Microsoft recommends that you use ANSI standard joins going forward. As of SQL Server 2008, some forms of non-ANSI standard joins are no longer supported. To keep things simple, just use the recommended syntax.

Types of Joins

Two major types of joins exist: inner joins, which return only corresponding records in two tables, and outer joins, which return all the rows in one table and then corresponding rows in a second table.

To demonstrate the behavior of different join types, keep the following facts in mind: The AdventureWorks2008 database contains 19,820 customer records. All but 701 customers have corresponding sales orders. These are corresponding rows in the SalesOrderHeader table, where the CustomerID column value is equal to an existing value in the Customer table's CustomerID. There are 31,465 rows in the SalesOrderHeader table.

The record counts in the SQL Server 2005 AdventureWorks database are different from these, but you should see the same general patterns and behavior when using the same queries.

Inner Joins

This is the most common type of join operation. The purpose of the inner join is to match up rows in one table with corresponding rows in another table where the associated columns contain the same value. If one of these tables' columns has a different value, or no value at all, these rows will not be returned by the query.

Before showing you an example, I'll make this request using common language: I'd like to see all of the customers who have orders — and all of the orders that have corresponding customers. For each customer, show me the customer's account number, and for each order, the order date.

Again, the SQL statement that makes this same request is as follows:

```
SELECT Customer.AccountNumber, SalesOrderHeader.OrderDate
FROM Sales.Customer INNER JOIN Sales.SalesOrderHeader
ON Customer.CustomerID = SalesOrderHeader.CustomerID
```

You just saw the results from this query in Figure 8-2, so I won't show them to you again. Just remember that it returns 31,465 rows that consist of customers with orders as well as orders that have customers.

The INNER JOIN statement can also be abbreviated by simply using JOIN. Although this is not as explicit, it works just as effectively as the earlier statement:

```
SELECT Customer.AccountNumber, SalesOrderHeader.OrderDate
FROM Sales.Customer JOIN Sales.SalesOrderHeader
ON Customer.CustomerID = SalesOrderHeader.CustomerID
```

Outer Joins

The job of an outer join is to return all of the rows from one table and then to match those rows in a corresponding table where the joining column has the same value. The difference between this and an inner join is that the unmatched rows in the first table are still returned by the query.

In common language, an outer join request might look like this: I'd like to see all of the customers, and for the customers who have orders, I'd also like to see related order information. Show me the account number for every customer, and if the customer has orders, show me a row for each combination of customers and orders.

Here's the SQL statement for this request:

```
SELECT Customer.AccountNumber, SalesOrderHeader.OrderDate
FROM Sales.Customer LEFT OUTER JOIN Sales.SalesOrderHeader
ON Customer.CustomerID = SalesOrderHeader.CustomerID
```

Outer joins always favor one table — the table from which you choose all rows. In this case, the table on the left side of the JOIN statement From Customer LEFT OUTER JOIN SalesOrderHeader is the Customer table. This means that all customer rows will be returned from the query and then from the corresponding SalesOrderHeader rows. If you think about it, this makes sense because the SalesOrderDetail table has a foreign key constraint that requires a matching CustomerID value. Given the relationship between these tables, it wouldn't make sense to join them the other way around.

When you execute this query, the results will initially look much the same as before. However, notice the row count: 32,166 rows — 635 more than before. What's going on here? Go back and look at the numbers I gave you just before I introduced inner joins. The Customer table contains 31,465 rows, including 701 without any orders. The outer join returned the customers who don't have orders. When an outer join doesn't have matching rows in the outer table (in a left outer join, the table on the right is the outer table), NULL values are returned. To find customers without orders, look for a NULL in the OrderDate column. But can't you use a query to do this? Rather than making you scroll through over 31,000 rows looking for those missing an order date, just alter the query, adding a WHERE clause:

```
SELECT Customer.AccountNumber, SalesOrderHeader.OrderDate
FROM Sales.Customer LEFT OUTER JOIN Sales.SalesOrderHeader
ON Customer.CustomerID = SalesOrderHeader.CustomerID
WHERE SalesOrderHeader.OrderDate IS NULL
```

This query returns 701 rows, customers who have no orders, as shown in Figure 8-4.

	AccountNumber	OrderDate
1	AW00000507	NULL
2	AW00000132	NULL
3	AW00000192	NULL
4	AW00000375	NULL
5	AW00000209	NULL
6	AW00000547	NULL
7	AW00000189	NULL
8	AW00000298	NULL
9	AW00000261	NULL
10	AW00000367	NULL
11	AW00000324	NULL
12	AW00000341	NULL
13	AW00000619	NULL
14	AW00000447	NULL
15	AW00000347	NULL
16	AW00000450	NULL
17	AW00000035	NULL
18	AW00000158	NULL
19	AW00000032	NULL
20	AW00000413	NULL
21	AW00000356	NULL

Figure 8-4

So, what is the purpose of a right outer join? Using a right in place of left in this expression would have the same effect as reversing the order of the tables and columns. In most cases, you could choose to use one or the other. However, if you have an outer join on both sides of a table, you may be constrained to use either a left or a right outer join. Fortunately, visual query design tools can be used to create complex queries. This is easy to do using the Transact SQL Query Builder.

Try It Out

Applying the following steps, you will use the graphic query editor feature in SQL Server Management Studio to build a simple inner join query. Before you begin, make sure you have Management Studio open with a connection to your database server instance.

1. Open the Query Builder in SQL Server Management Studio.

2. In the Object Browser, drill down into Databases. Right-click the AdventureWorks2008 (or AdventureWorks for SQL Server 2005) database and choose New Query.

3. In the New Query window, right-click over the white space and choose Design Query in Editor. This opens the graphical query designer in a separate window with the Add Tables dialog on top.

4. From the Add Table dialog window, select the "Customer (Sales)" table and click Add.

5. Select the "SalesOrderHeader (Sales)" table (see Figure 8-5) and click Add. Click "Close" to close the Add Table dialog window.

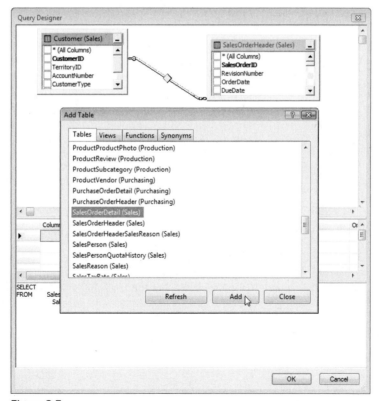

Figure 8-5

The designer always assumes you will want an inner join. The diamond on the join line between these tables represents the join, and the logic is quite simple.

6. Right-click the diamond icon to view a pop-up menu of join operations. From the menu, choose Select All Rows from Customer, as shown in Figure 8-6.

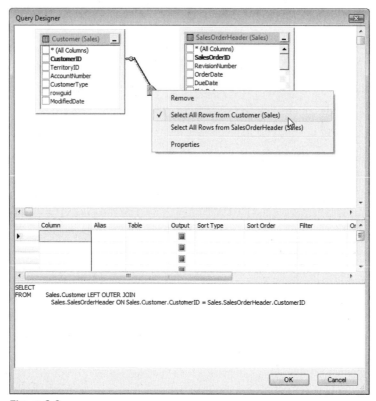

Figure 8-6

The diagram adds a rectangular "cap" to the left side of the join to indicate that all rows will be returned from the table on the corresponding side of the join.

7. Now scroll down or resize the Customer table window and check the box next to the AccountNumber column. Also, for the SalesOrderHeader table, check the OrderDate column (see Figure 8-7).

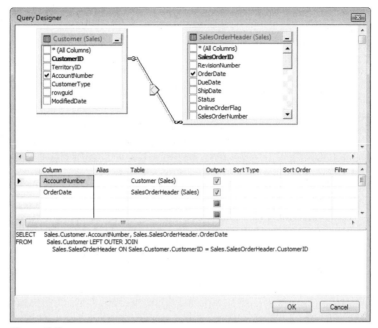

Figure 8-7

Take a look at the SQL statement in the third pane of the designer. It should look like this:

```
SELECT   Sales.Customer.AccountNumber, Sales.SalesOrderHeader.OrderDate
FROM     Sales.Customer LEFT OUTER JOIN
         Sales.SalesOrderHeader ON Sales.Customer.CustomerID =
         Sales.SalesOrderHeader.CustomerID
```

This is a great tool for learning join syntax. When in doubt, build your queries this way and then examine the SQL. Rather than using the designer as a crutch so you don't have to learn to do it the hard way, use it as a learning tool and then challenge yourself by rewriting the same queries in the Query Editor. As we mentioned earlier, there are those purists who refuse to use these design tools to create queries. In our opinion, it all comes down to time, money, and effort. If you can get the job done more effectively using a utility of some kind without sacrificing functionality, then by all means, do it.

There is also shorthand syntax for outer joins. You can abbreviate the join statement by using LEFT JOIN or RIGHT JOIN rather than LEFT OUTER JOIN and RIGHT OUTER JOIN, respectively.

Legacy Outer Joins

A little earlier in this chapter, I told you that support for legacy joins is going away. In the previous edition of this book, written for SQL Server 2000 and 2005, we showed you how to use a technique — common in other database products — that we refer to as *legacy join syntax*. We also recommended that this technique not be used because Microsoft had threatened to stop supporting it. Well, guess what?

They stopped supporting legacy outer joins in SQL Server 2008. You can still get away with implementing an inner join in the WHERE clause, but you can no longer perform outer joins in the WHERE clause unless you set the compatibility of your database to emulate an older version of SQL Server.

In case you encounter this in existing, older queries, I'll show you an example so that you can recognize queries that must be rewritten to work. A legacy outer join is performed in the WHERE clause by placing an asterisk next to the equal sign between the column references. Either precede the equal sign (*=) or proceed the equal sign (=*) to denote a left or right outer join, respectively. The asterisk points to the table that will return all rows regardless of matching rows in the other table. The most significant issue with this is that ambiguous results can be returned by a legacy outer join when an expression is placed on the side of the join where all records are to be returned (the "*" side). Under certain conditions, the query parser just can't figure out how to build the right execution plan and doesn't apply the correct execution logic.

Here is the same query as the previous example using the legacy join syntax in the WHERE clause:

```
SELECT Customer.AccountNumber, SalesOrderHeader.OrderDate
FROM Sales.Customer, Sales.SalesOrderHeader
WHERE Customer.CustomerID *= SalesOrderHeader.CustomerID
```

Unless your database is in 8.0 or previous compatibility mode, this query will not run and will return an error. Because legacy inner joins are supported but outer joins are not, this leaves the door open for poor and inefficient query design. If any of these working old-school inner joins need to be converted to outer joins, I guess you're stuck. Now it's your job to convince the 25 year DB2 veteran, turned SQL Server DBA, to stop using them.

Multicolumn Joins

Some databases are designed with multicolumn keys and may require that you define multicolumn joins in your queries. There is no stated limit to the number of columns that can be used in a join. Typically, you would only need to use more than one joining column to support specific business rules (because joins are usually performed on primary and foreign key columns). The logic of a join expression is very similar to that of a WHERE clause. Multiple comparisons can be combined using the AND and OR operators.

Let's use this technique to find product sales records (in the SalesOrderDetail table) for products sold at dealer cost. This involves matching the ProductID between the two tables and matching the ListPrice from the Product table to the UnitPrice from the SalesOrderDetail table:

```
SELECT    Product.ProductID
        , Product.Name
        , Product.StandardCost
        , Product.ListPrice
        , SalesOrderDetail.UnitPrice
FROM      Production.Product
          INNER JOIN Sales.SalesOrderDetail
          ON  Product.ProductID = SalesOrderDetail.ProductID
          AND Product.ListPrice = SalesOrderDetail.UnitPrice
```

57,949 transactions were recorded where the product was sold for the list price. The first few rows of this result are shown in Figure 8-8. Of course, if you were to change any of the StandardCost or UnitPrice values (as we do in Chapter 10), your results will be a little different.

	ProductID	Name	StandardCost	ListPrice	UnitPrice
1	749	Road-150 Red, 62	2171.2942	3578.2700	3578.2700
2	773	Mountain-100 Silver, 44	1912.1544	3399.9900	3399.9900
3	773	Mountain-100 Silver, 44	1912.1544	3399.9900	3399.9900
4	773	Mountain-100 Silver, 44	1912.1544	3399.9900	3399.9900
5	750	Road-150 Red, 44	2171.2942	3578.2700	3578.2700
6	749	Road-150 Red, 62	2171.2942	3578.2700	3578.2700
7	778	Mountain-100 Black, 48	1898.0944	3374.9900	3374.9900
8	771	Mountain-100 Silver, 38	1912.1544	3399.9900	3399.9900
9	751	Road-150 Red, 48	2171.2942	3578.2700	3578.2700
10	751	Road-150 Red, 48	2171.2942	3578.2700	3578.2700
11	752	Road-150 Red, 52	2171.2942	3578.2700	3578.2700
12	753	Road-150 Red, 56	2171.2942	3578.2700	3578.2700
13	753	Road-150 Red, 56	2171.2942	3578.2700	3578.2700
14	750	Road-150 Red, 44	2171.2942	3578.2700	3578.2700
15	749	Road-150 Red, 62	2171.2942	3578.2700	3578.2700

Figure 8-8

Non-Equijoins

So far, the join operations you've seen (in their various forms) have all used comparisons of equality. In other words, the values compared between two tables must be equal for the query to return matching records. Although far less common, joins can also be performed using any other valid method of comparison. This can include any of those listed in the following table.

Operator	Comparison
<>	Not equal to
<	Less than
>	Greater than
<=	Less than or equal to
>=	Greater than or equal to

I can modify the previous example to find sales orders for products that were sold at a discounted price:

```
SELECT     Product.ProductID
         , Product.Name
         , Product.StandardCost
         , Product.ListPrice
         , SalesOrderDetail.UnitPrice
FROM       Production.Product
           INNER JOIN Sales.SalesOrderDetail
           ON   Product.ProductID = SalesOrderDetail.ProductID
           AND  Product.ListPrice > SalesOrderDetail.UnitPrice
```

This returns 63,368 rows of sales orders that weren't sold at full list price, some of which are shown in Figure 8-9.

	ProductID	Name	StandardCost	ListPrice	UnitPrice
1	776	Mountain-100 Black, 42	1898.0944	3374.9900	2024.9940
2	777	Mountain-100 Black, 44	1898.0944	3374.9900	2024.9940
3	778	Mountain-100 Black, 48	1898.0944	3374.9900	2024.9940
4	771	Mountain-100 Silver, 38	1912.1544	3399.9900	2039.9940
5	772	Mountain-100 Silver, 42	1912.1544	3399.9900	2039.9940
6	773	Mountain-100 Silver, 44	1912.1544	3399.9900	2039.9940
7	774	Mountain-100 Silver, 48	1912.1544	3399.9900	2039.9940
8	714	Long-Sleeve Logo Jersey, M	38.4923	49.9900	28.8404
9	716	Long-Sleeve Logo Jersey, XL	38.4923	49.9900	28.8404
10	709	Mountain Bike Socks, M	3.3963	9.5000	5.7000
11	712	AWC Logo Cap	6.9223	8.9900	5.1865
12	711	Sport-100 Helmet, Blue	13.0863	34.9900	20.1865
13	762	Road-650 Red, 44	486.7066	782.9900	419.4589
14	758	Road-450 Red, 52	884.7083	1457.9900	874.7940
15	745	HL Mountain Frame - Black, 48	699.0928	1349.6000	809.7600
16	743	HL Mountain Frame - Black, 42	739.0410	1349.6000	714.7043

Figure 8-9

Of course, I can easily turn this query around to show inflated sales by changing the comparison expression to read `Product.ListPrice < SalesOrderDetail.UnitPrice`, then find that we haven't jacked up the price above list for even one transaction. Wow! We're running an honest business after all.

Special-Purpose Join Operations

I think it's safe to say that you have seen 99 percent of the join operations you will use day-to-day. Two more types of joins are quite rare: full joins and cross joins. Unless you need to do some very unusual things, you will likely not use them. I can think of just three or four times I've used a full join or cross join in the past few years to solve unique problems.

Full Joins

A *full join* (or *full outer join*) is an outer join that doesn't favor one of the two tables. The result set will return unmatched values on both sides of the join.

Consider the following hypothetical example. A Parent table contains parent names and a Child table contains child names and parent names. One Parent record doesn't have a matching Child record, and one Child record doesn't have a matching Parent.

Parent
ParentName
Fred
Wilma
Barney
Betty
Mr. Slate

Child	
ChildName	**ParentName**
Pebbles	Fred
Pebbles	Wilma
Bam Bam	Barney
Bam Bam	Betty
Dino	NULL

If you were to join these two tables on the ParentName columns from both tables using a full outer join, as follows, all records would be returned, including the mismatched parent and the child.

```
SELECT Child.ChildName, Parent.ParentName
FROM Child FULL OUTER JOIN Parent
  ON Child.ParentName = Parent.ParentName
```

The results would look like the following example. Note that Mr. Slate and Dino are both returned with NULL values in the joining columns.

ParentName	**ChildName**
Fred	Pebbles
Wilma	Pebbles
Barney	Bam Bam
Betty	Bam Bam
Mr. Slate	NULL
NULL	Dino

This hypothetical example demonstrates this point in its simplest form. The AdventureWorks database has a highly normalized design, and there aren't many simple examples of related tables with unmatched records. The following real example requires some extra joins to present the necessary data. Wholesale customers (or stores) exist as records in both the Customer and Store tables. Store records have a corresponding SalesPersonID, which relates to an Employee. A left outer join between the Store and Customer tables is necessary to include mismatched SalesPersonID values (such as mismatched ParentName values in the previous example).

Here's a quick example using the AdventureWorks database in SQL Server 2005. Note that because the SQL Server 2008 sample data was "cleaned up," this query no longer works with the newer sample database. Customer records exist that do not have an assigned sales person employee, and employee records exist that are not assigned to a customer as a sales person. This query will return customers and employees — and the combination of the two when they are related:

```
SELECT Customer.CustomerID
    , EmployeeID
FROM Sales.Customer LEFT OUTER JOIN Sales.Store
    ON Customer.CustomerID = Store.CustomerID
    FULL OUTER JOIN
    HumanResources.Employee ON Store.SalesPersonID = Employee.EmployeeID
ORDER BY CustomerID, EmployeeID
```

In Figure 8-10, you will notice NULL values in the CustomerID column returned from the Customer table. If you scroll-down, you will also see NULL values in the EmployeeID column returned from the Employee table.

	CustomerID	EmployeeID
1	NULL	1
2	NULL	2
3	NULL	3
4	NULL	4
5	NULL	5
6	NULL	6
7	NULL	7
8	NULL	8
277	NULL	288
278	1	280
279	2	283
280	3	277
977	700	279
978	701	282
979	11000	NULL
980	11001	NULL
981	11002	NULL
982	11003	NULL
983	11004	NULL

Figure 8-10

This query returned 19,462 results. This is essentially every possible combination of distinct values for the two columns participating in the join, including NULL values.

The last time I used this type of join was for a medical patient scheduling application. Business requirements called for the user interface to display the available appointment blocks for all doctors in the clinic. Doctors with appointments scheduled were to be displayed in a different color. For example, each of three doctors in the clinic could see patients scheduled for appointments that could begin every 15 minutes. An appointment slot table contained scheduling blocks beginning at 9:00 A.M. and ending at 4:45 P.M. Each row in this table represented a 15-minute block (9:00, 9:15, 9:30, and so on). In the scheduling application, my client wanted to see every possible appointment for each doctor, including those that had no appointments scheduled. A full join between the appointment slot table and the appointment table did the trick.

Cross Joins

This is the granddaddy of all joins. When using a cross join, you don't designate columns for the join to match values. The query will simply return every possible combination of rows for two tables without regard for matching column values. This produces what is known as a *Cartesian product*. Needless to say, this can produce a large volume of rows and could be an effective way to populate a test database table with sample data. Frankly, I have yet to find a practical use for this technique in a production database.

If you were to create a cross join between the Customer and SalesOrderHeader tables, this is what you should expect to see: The Customer table contains 19,185 records, and the SalesOrderHeader table contains 31,465 records. This means that for every Customer row, 31,465 rows will be added to the result set. If you do the math, the result will contain 603,656,025 possible combinations. Please do not run this query on a production server in the middle of the day. If you do, please don't tell your system administrator what book you were reading when you learned to do this. Joking aside, running this query would take several minutes and would consume a fair amount of server resources.

A somewhat more conservative example would be to cross join customers with employees. This query returns about five and a half million records:

```
SELECT CustomerID, LoginID
FROM Sales.Customer CROSS JOIN HumanResources.Employee
ORDER BY CustomerID, LoginID
```

You can also simply omit the CROSS JOIN statement and separate the table references with commas:

```
SELECT CustomerID, LoginID
FROM Sales.Customer, HumanResources.Employee
ORDER BY CustomerID, LoginID
```

In my experience cross joins are more often created by accident than by intent. This is especially true when using the Query Builder. If two tables are added to the diagram that do not have a relationship defined, the Query Builder will generate a cross join query automatically.

Filtering Records in the Join Clause Using a Predicate

This is a lesser-known technique that can be used to filter rows before a join operation is executed. When a traditional multi-table query is executed, the join is processed first and then filtering takes place afterward; at least this is what you're telling SQL Server to do. Fortunately, SQL Server is smart enough to perform filtering ahead of time when it makes sense to do this (as long as indexes and column statistics are up-to-date, which they should be under normal conditions). Regardless, this technique guarantees that records not matching the filtering criteria will not be considered in the join operation.

Here is the example for the AdventureWorks2008 database in SQL Server 2008:

```
SELECT Customer.CustomerID
     , LoginID
FROM   Sales.Customer INNER JOIN Sales.Store
         ON Customer.StoreID = Store.BusinessEntityID
       INNER JOIN HumanResources.Employee
         ON Store.SalesPersonID = Employee.BusinessEntityID
       AND Customer.CustomerID < 10
ORDER BY CustomerID, LoginID
```

And here is the same query for the AdventureWorks database in SQL Server 2005:

```
SELECT  Customer.CustomerID
      , EmployeeID
      , CustomerType
FROM    Sales.Customer INNER JOIN Sales.Store
          ON Customer.CustomerID = Store.CustomerID
        INNER JOIN HumanResources.Employee
          ON Store.SalesPersonID = Employee.EmployeeID
        AND Customer.CustomerID < 10
ORDER BY CustomerID, EmployeeID
```

However unconventional, this method would have the same effect as if the filter criteria (`Customer.CustomerID < 10`) were specified in the WHERE clause. For readability, I believe that using the WHERE clause is the preferred method.

Joining on an Expression

Chapter 9 discusses the idea of using an AS statement as a derived table. For the purpose of the current discussion, it's good to know that joins can be used not only for tables, but also for any SELECT expression. An example follows so that you can see how this works.

The director of marketing wants to reduce the cost of selling small-ticket items but doesn't want to discontinue low-priced items that are selling well. The director would like to see the cumulative sales for the ten least-expensive products. This will require two separate SELECT expressions. The first will return the product rows for the ten least-expensive products, and the second will return the aggregate sales filtered by this product selection.

I'm working from the inside out, so the second expression will actually become the first part of the final query. I'll start with the first step and then add the second expression to the beginning of the query filtering criteria.

The first query simply returns the ten least-expensive products:

```
SELECT TOP 10
         ProductID
       , Name
       , ListPrice
FROM Production.Product
WHERE ListPrice <> 0
ORDER BY ListPrice ASC
```

The ProductID column is essential, but the other two columns shown in Figure 8-11 are included just for reference in the results.

	ProductID	Name	ListPrice
1	873	Patch Kit/8 Patches	2.2900
2	922	Road Tire Tube	3.9900
3	870	Water Bottle - 30 oz.	4.9900
4	921	Mountain Tire Tube	4.9900
5	923	Touring Tire Tube	4.9900
6	877	Bike Wash - Dissolver	7.9500
7	712	AWC Logo Cap	8.9900
8	872	Road Bottle Cage	8.9900
9	874	Racing Socks, M	8.9900
10	875	Racing Socks, L	8.9900

Figure 8-11

This expression must be given an alias so that I can refer to it in another SELECT expression. In the following example, I refer to the results of the first query by the alias CheapProducts. The second step is to create another query for the aggregated sales orders. This becomes the outer query that refers to the first inner query by its alias, as if it were a physical table.

```
SELECT
        SalesOrderDetail.ProductID
      , CheapProducts.Name
      , CheapProducts.ListPrice
      , SUM(LineTotal) AS SalesTotal
FROM Sales.SalesOrderDetail
      INNER JOIN
          (SELECT TOP 10
                  ProductID
                , Name
                , ListPrice
          FROM Production.Product
          WHERE ListPrice <> 0
          ORDER BY ListPrice ASC) AS CheapProducts
      ON SalesOrderDetail.ProductID = CheapProducts.ProductID
GROUP BY
        SalesOrderDetail.ProductID
      , CheapProducts.Name
      , CheapProducts.ListPrice
```

The alias I created for the derived table has a descriptive name. The traditional approach is to use a single letter for table aliases. Personally, I find this to be a bit cryptic. You will likely refer to the alias several times, so it's a good idea to keep the name short — but also make it meaningful. To include columns from the inner products query in the outer result set, reference them by using the alias, as if this were just another table. Finally, because I'm aggregating the LineTotal column for records sharing the same product, all of the columns except for the aggregate must be included in the GROUP BY column list. This works because each of these column values is unique to a specific product. The results are displayed in Figure 8-12.

	ProductID	Name	ListPrice	SalesTotal
1	922	Road Tire Tube	3.9900	9480.240000
2	877	Bike Wash - Dissolver	7.9500	18406.972080
3	923	Touring Tire Tube	4.9900	7425.120000
4	874	Racing Socks, M	8.9900	9387.149432
5	875	Racing Socks, L	8.9900	13784.589952
6	872	Road Bottle Cage	8.9900	15390.880000
7	712	AWC Logo Cap	8.9900	51229.445623
8	921	Mountain Tire Tube	4.9900	15444.050000
9	873	Patch Kit/8 Patches	2.2900	8232.597632
10	870	Water Bottle - 30 oz.	4.9900	28654.163327

Figure 8-12

I'll take some more time to cover derived tables and other subquery techniques in the next chapter. This gives you an idea about using joins in creative ways to address unique business rules. What I've learned (and continue to learn) about using SQL to address unique challenges is that there is almost always a method to solve the problem — and there are often several options. The ideal solution is usually not all that complicated. However, the ideal and most elegant solution is often not the one we use on the first attempt.

Multi-Table Joins

Let's put it all together. I need a list of all stores and, for those store/customers that have purchased products, details of the order and the product information. In this database, a store is a type of a customer, which requires a join between the Store and Customer tables. Because I want all stores regardless of matching orders, this will require an outer join to the SalesOrderHeader table. All other tables are included through inner joins. Figure 8-13 provides an illustration.

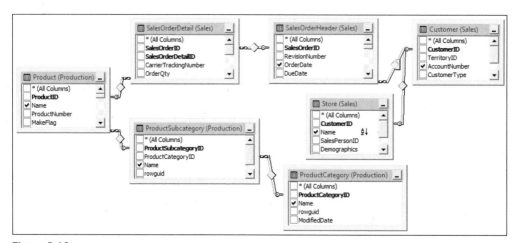

Figure 8-13

This query might be particularly tricky if you were to write it without the help of the designer. Because the SalesOrderHeader table participates in two joins, an inner join with SalesOrderDetail and an outer join with the Customer table, this breaks up the SQL syntax. Note the mispairing of JOIN and related ON statements in the SQL statement for this query.

This query runs against the AdventureWorks2008 database in SQL Server 2008:

```
SELECT      Store.Name AS StoreName
          , Customer.AccountNumber
          , SalesOrderHeader.OrderDate
          , ProductCategory.Name AS Category
          , ProductSubCategory.Name AS SubCategory
          , Product.Name AS ProductName
FROM        Sales.Store INNER JOIN Sales.Customer
                ON Store.BusinessEntityID = Customer.StoreID
            LEFT OUTER JOIN Sales.SalesOrderDetail
            INNER JOIN Sales.SalesOrderHeader
              ON Sales.SalesOrderDetail.SalesOrderID = SalesOrderHeader
.SalesOrderID
            INNER JOIN Production.Product
                ON SalesOrderDetail.ProductID = Product.ProductID
            INNER JOIN Production.ProductSubCategory
              ON Product.ProductSubCategoryID =
                  ProductSubCategory.ProductSubCategoryID
            INNER JOIN Production.ProductCategory
                ON ProductSubCategory.ProductCategoryID =
                    ProductCategory.ProductCategoryID
                ON Customer.CustomerID = SalesOrderHeader.CustomerID
ORDER BY Store.Name
```

This is the same query designed to work with the AdventureWorks database in SQL Server 2005:

```
SELECT      Store.Name AS StoreName
          , Customer.AccountNumber
          , SalesOrderHeader.OrderDate
          , ProductCategory.Name AS Category
          , ProductSubCategory.Name AS SubCategory
          , Product.Name AS ProductName
FROM        Sales.Store INNER JOIN Sales.Customer
                ON Store.CustomerID = Customer.CustomerID
            LEFT OUTER JOIN Sales.SalesOrderDetail
            INNER JOIN Sales.SalesOrderHeader
              ON Sales.SalesOrderDetail.SalesOrderID = SalesOrderHeader
.SalesOrderID
            INNER JOIN Production.Product
                ON SalesOrderDetail.ProductID = Product.ProductID
            INNER JOIN Production.ProductSubCategory
              ON Product.ProductSubCategoryID =
                  ProductSubCategory.ProductSubCategoryID
            INNER JOIN Production.ProductCategory
                ON ProductSubCategory.ProductCategoryID =
                    ProductCategory.ProductCategoryID
                ON Customer.CustomerID = SalesOrderHeader.CustomerID
ORDER BY Store.Name
```

When you need to write a complex query, it may be a good idea to at least start with the graphical query designer. Figure 8-14 shows the result set for this query from the results pane of the SQL Query Designer. Note the NULL values in the first row indicating that the store/customer has no related order records.

	StoreName	AccountNumber	OrderDate	Category	SubCategory	ProductName
1	A Bicycle Association	AW00000324	NULL	NULL	NULL	NULL
2	A Bike Store	AW00000001	NULL	NULL	NULL	NULL
3	A Bike Store	AW00029773	2002-02-01 00:00:00.000	Accessorie	Helmets	Sport-100 Helmet, I
4	A Bike Store	AW00029773	2002-02-01 00:00:00.000	Accessorie	Helmets	Sport-100 Helmet, I
5	A Bike Store	AW00029773	2002-02-01 00:00:00.000	Bikes	Road Bikes	Road-150 Red, 44
6	A Bike Store	AW00029773	2002-05-01 00:00:00.000	Bikes	Road Bikes	Road-150 Red, 44
7	A Bike Store	AW00029773	2002-02-01 00:00:00.000	Bikes	Road Bikes	Road-150 Red, 48
8	A Bike Store	AW00029773	2002-02-01 00:00:00.000	Bikes	Road Bikes	Road-150 Red, 52
9	A Bike Store	AW00029773	2001-08-01 00:00:00.000	Bikes	Road Bikes	Road-150 Red, 56
10	A Bike Store	AW00029773	2001-11-01 00:00:00.000	Bikes	Road Bikes	Road-150 Red, 56
11	A Bike Store	AW00029773	2002-02-01 00:00:00.000	Bikes	Road Bikes	Road-150 Red, 56
12	A Bike Store	AW00029773	2002-05-01 00:00:00.000	Bikes	Road Bikes	Road-150 Red, 56
13	A Bike Store	AW00029773	2002-05-01 00:00:00.000	Bikes	Road Bikes	Road-150 Red, 62
14	A Bike Store	AW00029773	2001-11-01 00:00:00.000	Bikes	Road Bikes	Road-150 Red, 62
15	A Bike Store	AW00029773	2001-08-01 00:00:00.000	Bikes	Road Bikes	Road-450 Red, 44
16	A Bike Store	AW00029773	2001-11-01 00:00:00.000	Bikes	Road Bikes	Road-450 Red, 44

Figure 8-14

Union Queries

Joins expand the result set horizontally. That is, columns are added to the results from multiple tables, essentially widening the result. A UNION query expands the results vertically as records are piled on top of one another. A simple example follows. The Employee table and the Individual table both contain records of people. To shorten the list, I'm just going to select the top five rows from each table:

```
SELECT TOP 5 FirstName FROM Person.Person
SELECT TOP 5 Name FROM Purchasing.Vendor
```

These two queries, even if executed at the same time, return two different result sets, as shown in Figure 8-15.

Figure 8-15

Now, I'll put them together. A union combines multiple results with the same number of columns. Columns must have compatible data types. To keep things simple, I suggest that columns have the same names and the same data types. Actually, the column names don't have to match. If the names are different for a corresponding column, the name from the last set will be used in the results. Because these two queries contain the same column names and types, combining them is simple.

Try It Out

Enter and execute the following query:

In SQL Server 2008:

```
SELECT TOP 5 FirstName FROM Person.Person
UNION
SELECT TOP 5 Name FROM Purchasing.Vendor
```

In SQL Server 2005:

```
SELECT TOP 5 FirstName FROM Person.Contact
UNION
SELECT TOP 5 Name FROM Purchasing.Vendor
```

Note that each SELECT statement could be executed as an independent query. Although not absolutely necessary, all of the columns have the same name. Figure 8-16 shows the results.

Figure 8-16

A potential problem with this result set is that you have no way of knowing what table each of the rows came from. Depending on what you intend to do with this data, this may or may not be important. In case it is, you need to tag each row with a value indicating its source. This is easily accomplished by adding an alias in the individual SELECT statements. I've also cleaned this query up a bit by naming the columns uniformly. You'll recall that the column name returned by a UNION query is determined by the last query in the union. As a matter of standard convention, I would recommend that all columns have the same names and data types just to avoid surprises. This is the modified query for SQL Server 2008:

```
SELECT TOP 5 FirstName AS Name, 'Contact' AS Source
FROM Person.Person
UNION
SELECT TOP 5 Name, 'Vendor' AS Source
FROM Purchasing.Vendor
```

By creating a Source alias, you provide a literal value. In the results shown in Figure 8-17, this indicates whether the person is an individual customer or an employee, as defined by each of the two queries.

Figure 8-17

The UNION operator when used by itself is actually a UNION DISTINCT. This means that the two queries are merged and sorted and have any duplicates removed. Notice the FirstName column in Figure 8-16. The values are in alphabetical order. This is the result of the implied DISTINCT/SORT operation that accompanies the UNION. On the surface this may seem like a good idea, and it may be, but the additional overhead of sorting and removing duplicates can be quite costly when used against large tables. For best performance, use the UNION ALL operator instead. The UNION ALL operator simply concatenates the two results. Just keep in mind that if the same first name–last name combination existed in both the Employee and Individual table, it would appear twice.

Partitioning and Federating Data

In the early days of client/server computing, there were two different approaches to managing data. A database was either managed centrally, in a mainframe- or midrange-hosted environment, or data was stored in small-scale, file-based data stores. There really wasn't a middle ground between these two options. To compensate for the lack of desktop database scalability, programmers found creative ways to replicate and synchronize data, but none of these work-arounds provided true concurrency. In a large-scale, multi-regional business environment, it often makes sense to store the data that will be used by local users on a server relatively close to them. This approach may provide less network overhead and faster query performance. This provides for the needs of users in the region who need access to the region-specific data, but it also means that users who need access to data from another region must retrieve it from a remote server.

Here's a scenario that nearly all of us can relate to: When you make a purchase with a credit card, the store uses a merchant service provider to authorize and transact the purchase. This could be a service offered by their bank, credit card company, or a third-party clearinghouse. Your card number is sent to a data center, a query is executed against a database to retrieve your account information, and then records are added to complete the transaction. Most likely, the bank doesn't have one central data center. A data center is a facility housing a group of computer servers. PC-based servers are often clustered together to form a single, virtual server. Essentially, it's a bunch of PCs lumped together, pretending to be a more powerful computer — almost like a mainframe. The bank probably has a few regional data centers, and merchants connect to one closest to them. For simplicity, assume that my bank has merchant services data centers in Seattle (west coast accounts) and Atlanta (east coast accounts).

I live, and my bank accounts are based, in Washington State. If I were to make a purchase at a local store — or a store anywhere in the western United States — the transaction would be processed in the Seattle data center. If someone whose bank account is managed in another data center were to make a purchase in the Seattle area, a connection from the local data center to the customer's home data center would be used to retrieve their account information. Here's how this might work.

If these accounts were managed in SQL Server, a remote server connection may be used to provide on-demand connectivity to a database in another regional data center. In this example, I use the server names EastCoastServer and WestCoastServer to represent the remote servers and LocalHost to represent the respective local server. At each data center, the local database contains a view (a stored SELECT query) called vw_AllAccounts. In the Seattle regional center, the SQL script for the view looks like this:

```
SELECT AccountNumber, Balance, CreditLimit, CustomerName
FROM LocalHost.dbo.AccountDatabase.WestCoastAccounts
UNION
SELECT AccountNumber, Balance, CreditLimit, CustomerName
FROM EastCoastServer.AccountDatabase.dbo.EastCoastAccounts
```

In Atlanta, a view with the same name looks like this:

```
SELECT AccountNumber, Balance, CreditLimit, CustomerName
FROM LocalHost.dbo.AccountDatabase.EastCoastAccounts
UNION
SELECT AccountNumber, Balance, CreditLimit, CustomerName
FROM WestCoastServer.AccountDatabase.dbo.WestCoastAccounts
```

Of course, these are hypothetical examples that won't run with our sample databases.

In each of the regional databases, the local accounts table (either WestCoastAccounts or EastCoastAccounts) is used to manage accounts in that region. The account lookup is performed using a stored procedure that accepts the account number as an input parameter and then looks up a record by matching this value to the AccountNumber column. Because there will only ever be one matching record, the stored procedure's SELECT statement uses a TOP 1 modifier that causes the database to stop searching for records after it locates one. The stored procedure script looks like this:

```
CREATE PROCEDURE spGetAccount
        @AccountNumber Int
AS
        SELECT TOP 1 * FROM vw_AllAccounts
```

As you can see, this is just a simple SELECT statement with a parameterized value (@AccountNumber) that gets passed in when it is executed. Chapter 13 uses the views and stored procedure to discuss what happens when the credit card transaction is processed.

Performance and Scaling Considerations

Now, let's look at a smaller-scale implementation to improve performance and efficiently manage a large volume of data. In this scenario, sales records are stored in a single table. Perhaps several thousand records are inserted each month. To report on this data over a period of years, it would be necessary to keep perhaps millions of rows in the sales table. Managing such a large volume of data in an active database will inevitably slow performance and raise administrative costs. At first glance this may seem like a perplexing challenge.

Let's view the facts and consider the options to resolve this quandary. To effectively deal with performance issues, you must first identify the bottlenecks. What's typically the slowest part of a computer system? Nearly all system components are solid-state, route electronic signals moving at nearly the speed of light and rely on transistors switching pulses at millions of times per second. Computers process data at incredible speeds but continue to store it on spinning disks, using mechanical armatures to write and read values. The hard disk is almost always the slowest part of a system. When retrieving data, other components wait while the disk controller finds and moves the read/write head to the right track and then waits for the disk to rotate to the sectors containing the data bits, assembling interlaced values as the disk rotates multiple times. The head is relocated again until all data is retrieved. You can't speed up the disk, but you can spread data across multiple disks to speed up the overall process.

In a partitioned storage solution, data is split up onto multiple disks. This affords SQL Server the opportunity to retrieve data in parallel and make more efficient use of multiple disk drives. There are actually a few different approaches to multiple-disk storage. In this scenario, I'll present an unsophisticated but very effective technique using multiple tables and a Union query.

At the end of every year, a routine removes year-old sales records from the current sales table and inserts them into a specific archive table containing only that year's sales. Each of these tables is placed on a separate physical disk drive. Over a few years, there may be several tables. Suppose that this system has been in place for five years, and the disks and tables are set up as shown in Figure 8-18.

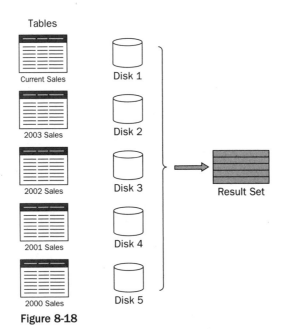

Figure 8-18

For reporting, a view is created that contains a series of UNION statements:

```
SELECT * From CurrentSales
UNION ALL
SELECT * From 2003Sales
UNION ALL
SELECT * From 2002Sales
UNION ALL
SELECT * From 2001Sales
UNION ALL
SELECT * From 2000Sales
```

When this query is executed, all of these disk drives may be accessed at the same time. Assuming there are no other performance barriers, this could theoretically improve performance by a factor of five. Not only is this query going to run faster, but it will also ease the burden on competing operations rather than blocking processes and other users' requests. You'll see some more specific examples of this type of query in the discussion on creating database objects in Chapter 13.

Summary

Dialects of SQL have evolved over the years, and SQL Server understands different expressions and techniques that do the same thing. The ANSI-92 SQL standard helps to distill a variety of join techniques to a manageable number. This not only simplifies the choices, but it also provides some guidance when maintaining code and scripts written by others. Follow the ANSI standard and use the techniques promoted by SQL Server. This will ensure that your queries will continue to work most efficiently going forward.

Joins provide a means to reassemble data back into meaningful information. The inner join matches rows between two tables whereas the outer joins select all rows from one side of the join and only matching rows from the other. Cross joins and full joins, although less common in most applications, provide a means to match up combinations of rows from two tables that may not be related.

Union queries allow records from multiple tables to be combined rather than joined, bringing rows into a single result set. This is an effective technique for partitioning and federating data in archive tables and databases in different geographic locations.

It's important to understand the impact of multi-table joins and unions. Query performance is significantly impacted by the use of indexes and data types. If done correctly, SQL Server can work very efficiently with a large volume of data. If not, complex queries can demand significant server resources and impede overall system performance and availability. Test your queries with real data, and analyze the execution plans to make sure your queries execute as you expect them to.

Exercises

Exercise 1

Create a list of vendors and the subtotal amounts for their purchase orders, sorted by vendor names. This list should include the vendor name and the subtotal amount for all vendors who have purchase orders recorded in the PurchaseOrderHeader table.

Exercise 2

Using either the AdventureWorksDW2008 or AdventureWorksDW sample database, write a query that returns a list of employees with their managers. It should return four aliased columns, including the ManagerTitle, ManagerName, EmployeeTitle, and EmployeeName. Using two aliased instances of the DimEmployee table, join the table to itself using the EmployeeKey and ParentEmployeeKey columns.

Exercise 3

Write a query that returns a list of product subcategories and related products that don't have any sales order detail records. Include two columns, including the subcategory name labeled SubCategoryName and the product name labeled ProductName.

Advanced Queries and Scripting

Writing queries is like driving to work. There are probably 18 different ways to get there, and most likely, some routes are clearly better than others. Under different conditions, different choices may be preferable. This might depend on variable traffic conditions, the time of day, or whether you need to stop by the grocery store to pick up milk and flowers. In my case, the route I choose depends largely on the ferry schedule. If I can't make the ferry, I save time by driving a much greater distance rather than waiting for the next boat. Some opt for consistency, choosing to take the same route regardless of changing conditions, whereas others weave through traffic to find the fastest lane, and shave off a few seconds here and there.

Similarly, many queries can be written more than one way. Traditional SQL statements, written for other database products, often use subqueries, whereas SQL Server leans toward ANSI-standard join expressions. Most SQL Server professionals will tell you that if you have the option to choose between using a subquery and a join, the joins will execute faster. Generally speaking, I think this is true, but it depends on the expression and other conditions. Using joins gives the database engine more leeway to implement the best type of operations for a query, whereas subqueries may not afford SQL Server as many options.

An even more flexible option was introduced in SQL Server 2005 with *common table expressions* (CTEs), a technique used to define a named SELECT statement that may later be referred to as a table. CTEs are a bit of a fence-sitter depending on how they are used. For more complex logic that can't be handled in a join, the CTE may be the way to go. You'll learn more about CTEs later in this chapter.

Depending on the query, the same results can be achieved using any one of these techniques. Graphical design tools, such as the Query Designer, build ANSI join statements. This is considered to be SQL Server's native form for combining column data from more than one table. To implement some business logic, joins simply may not give you the flexibility you need and a subquery or CTE may be the only answer. We introduce CTE toward the end of this chapter because this feature builds on the concept of subqueries. CTEs offer far more flexibility than traditional subqueries, so we strongly recommend that you get through this section before you put your code into production.

A number of architectural improvements were made in SQL Server 2008 that may help with query performance. However, the language syntax covered in this chapter hasn't changed since SQL Server 2005.

Subqueries

A subquery is simply a SELECT query within a SELECT query. Several forms of subqueries exist, ranging from expressions that return a single, or scalar, value to a multi-row result set. We are going to show you several examples of each type, beginning with scalar expressions.

Scalar Expressions

Within the column selection list of a SELECT statement, embedded SELECT statements can be used to return a single-column value, otherwise known as a *scalar valued expression*. One of the most common examples of a scalar expression is to use an aggregate function to return a value based on the scope of multiple rows.

Consider this example. We would like to compare the price paid for a product with the average price of all product sales. This can be done by using a simple SELECT statement that uses the AVG() function to produce a column in the query's result set given the alias AvgPrice:

```
SELECT    ProductID
        , UnitPrice
        , (SELECT AVG(UnitPrice) FROM Sales.SalesOrderDetail)
    AS AvgPrice
FROM Sales.SalesOrderDetail
```

In the results shown in Figure 9-1, you can see that the values in this column are constant. This is because the subquery expression has no correlation or dependency on the outer query. It simply calculates the average price for all product sales again and again, and returns this value in every row of the result.

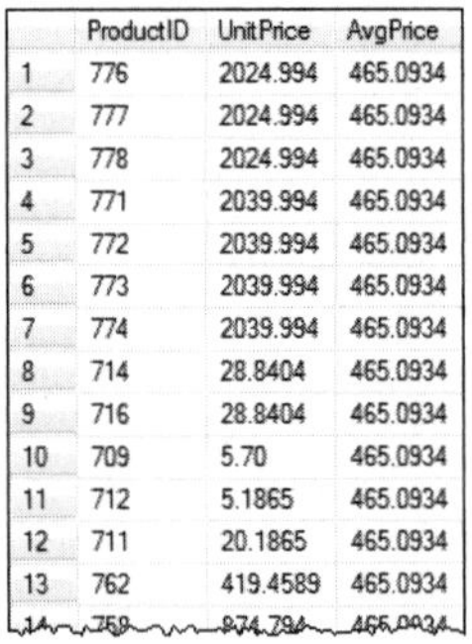

	ProductID	UnitPrice	AvgPrice
1	776	2024.994	465.0934
2	777	2024.994	465.0934
3	778	2024.994	465.0934
4	771	2039.994	465.0934
5	772	2039.994	465.0934
6	773	2039.994	465.0934
7	774	2039.994	465.0934
8	714	28.8404	465.0934
9	716	28.8404	465.0934
10	709	5.70	465.0934
11	712	5.1865	465.0934
12	711	20.1865	465.0934
13	762	419.4589	465.0934
14	759	874.794	465.0934

Figure 9-1

Fortunately, SQL Server is smart enough to perform the calculation once and then simply return a cached value for each request. Can you imagine how wasteful it would be to recalculate the average of 121,317 values, and then repeat the same calculation 121,317 times? It's important to note that the database engine doesn't just do exactly what you ask it to. It has intelligence built in to find shortcuts like this one.

Speaking of intelligence, let's do something a little more intelligent with this data. Rather than showing the average price of all sales on each row, we'll use this value to calculate the difference between this row's sale price and the average for all sales:

```
SELECT    ProductID
        , UnitPrice
        , UnitPrice - (SELECT Avg(UnitPrice) FROM Sales.SalesOrderDetail)
    AS AvgPriceDifference
FROM Sales.SalesOrderDetail
```

Now the result shows the difference between the value returned by the subquery and the sale price in the UnitPrice column (see Figure 9-2).

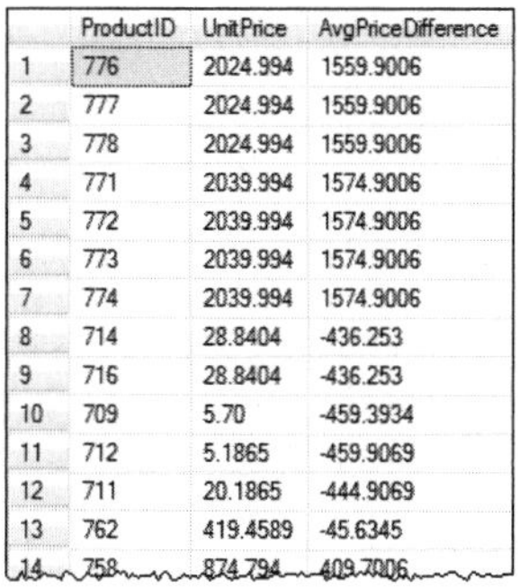

	ProductID	UnitPrice	AvgPriceDifference
1	776	2024.994	1559.9006
2	777	2024.994	1559.9006
3	778	2024.994	1559.9006
4	771	2039.994	1574.9006
5	772	2039.994	1574.9006
6	773	2039.994	1574.9006
7	774	2039.994	1574.9006
8	714	28.8404	-436.253
9	716	28.8404	-436.253
10	709	5.70	-459.3934
11	712	5.1865	-459.9069
12	711	20.1865	-444.9069
13	762	419.4589	-45.6345
14	758	874.794	409.7006

Figure 9-2

As you can see, subqueries can be used to add dimension to data in flat tables. We are going to build on this query to show some variations.

Try It Out

Rather than getting a scalar value from an aggregate on the same table, you can also use another table. Try out the following query. Use the ProductID value to join the SalesOrderDetail and Product tables and get the ListPrice for the corresponding product:

```
SELECT    ProductID
        , UnitPrice AS SalePrice
        , (SELECT ListPrice FROM Production.Product
            WHERE Product.ProductID = SalesOrderDetail.ProductID)
            AS ProductListPrice
FROM Sales.SalesOrderDetail
```

In Figure 9-3, the results show the list price in the third column.

	ProductID	SalePrice	ProductListPrice
1	776	2024.994	3374.99
2	777	2024.994	3374.99
3	778	2024.994	3374.99
4	771	2039.994	3399.99
5	772	2039.994	3399.99
6	773	2039.994	3399.99
7	774	2039.994	3399.99
8	714	28.8404	49.99
9	716	28.8404	49.99
10	709	5.70	9.50
11	712	5.1865	8.99
12	711	20.1865	34.99
13	762	419.4589	782.99
14	758	874.794	1457.99
15	745	809.76	1349.60

Figure 9-3

Now take it one step further. Use this value to calculate the difference between the product's list price and price charged. By adding the expression UnitPrice — before the subquery, you can tell whether the sale price is inflated or discounted from the list price:

```
SELECT    ProductID
        , UnitPrice AS SalePrice
        , UnitPrice - (SELECT ListPrice FROM Production.Product
          WHERE Product.ProductID = SalesOrderDetail.ProductID)
            AS PriceDifference
FROM Sales.SalesOrderDetail
```

The results are shown in Figure 9-4.

	ProductID	SalePrice	PriceDifference
1	776	2024.994	-1349.996
2	777	2024.994	-1349.996
3	778	2024.994	-1349.996
4	771	2039.994	-1359.996
5	772	2039.994	-1359.996
6	773	2039.994	-1359.996
7	774	2039.994	-1359.996
8	714	28.8404	-21.1496
9	716	28.8404	-21.1496
10	709	5.70	-3.80
11	712	5.1865	-3.8035
12	711	20.1865	-14.8035
13	762	419.4589	-363.5311
14	758	874.794	-583.196

Figure 9-4

The negative values in the third column indicate that these products were sold for less than the list price in the product table. Apparently, Adventure Works Cycles makes it a point to sell all of its products below list price (too bad that this is a fictitious business).

Alternate Join Operations

Before we show you the following examples, we want to answer what may seem to be an obvious question: Why learn to use subqueries that do the same thing as join operations when joins are preferable? All by themselves, it probably doesn't make sense to use subqueries in place of joins. So why take this route? As you will see, some business rules are best implemented using a subquery expression. Under the right conditions join-type subqueries used in concert with specialized business logic subqueries may be the right choice. Although the exception rather than the rule, sometimes you may need more flexibility than an ANSI join will offer.

Inner Join Subqueries

An inner join subquery is a simple expression. The main difference between this technique and the ANSI-SQL INNER JOIN statement is that this join is performed in the WHERE clause rather than the FROM clause. Note that two tables are referenced in the FROM clause as a comma-delimited list:

```
SELECT SOH.OrderDate
     , SOD.ProductID
     , SOD.UnitPrice
FROM Sales.SalesOrderHeader AS SOH, Sales.SalesOrderDetail AS SOD
WHERE SOH.SalesOrderID = SOD.SalesOrderID
ORDER BY SOH.OrderDate
```

There are no surprises in the result set shown in Figure 9-5. Just like an inner join, you will only see matching records between the SalesOrderHeader and SalesOrderDetail tables.

	OrderDate	ProductID	UnitPrice
1	2001-07-01 00:00:00.000	776	2024.994
2	2001-07-01 00:00:00.000	777	2024.994
3	2001-07-01 00:00:00.000	778	2024.994
4	2001-07-01 00:00:00.000	771	2039.994
5	2001-07-01 00:00:00.000	772	2039.994
6	2001-07-01 00:00:00.000	773	2039.994
7	2001-07-01 00:00:00.000	774	2039.994
8	2001-07-01 00:00:00.000	714	28.8404
9	2001-07-01 00:00:00.000	716	28.8404
10	2001-07-01 00:00:00.000	709	5.70
11	2001-07-01 00:00:00.000	712	5.1865
12	2001-07-01 00:00:00.000	711	20.1865
13	2001-07-01 00:00:00.000	762	419.4589
14	2001-07-01 00:00:00.000	758	874.794

Figure 9-5

Before adding anything to the script in this example, we would like to compare this query to its ANSI-SQL equivalent:

```
SELECT SOH.OrderDate
     , SOD.ProductID
     , SOD.UnitPrice
FROM Sales.SalesOrderHeader AS SOH INNER JOIN Sales.SalesOrderDetail AS SOD
ON SOH.SalesOrderID = SOD.SalesOrderID
ORDER BY SOH.OrderDate
```

There is no reason to show the result set because it is going to look exactly like that for the previous example.

You can compound join operations for more than two tables very easily. We'll add the Product table so you can see the product name for each sales record:

```
SELECT  SalesOrderHeader.OrderDate
      , SalesOrderDetail.ProductID
      , SalesOrderDetail.UnitPrice
      , Product.Name
FROM    Sales.SalesOrderHeader, Sales.SalesOrderDetail, Production.Product
WHERE   SalesOrderHeader.SalesOrderID = SalesOrderDetail.SalesOrderID
        AND SalesOrderDetail.ProductID = Product.ProductID
ORDER BY SalesOrderHeader.OrderDate
```

Using the AND operator, you can extend the WHERE clause with the join between the SalesOrderDetail and Product tables. The result shows the OrderDate column from the SalesOrderHeader table, the ProductID and UnitPrice from SalesOrderDetail, and the Name column from the table (see Figure 9-6).

	OrderDate	ProductID	UnitPrice	Name
1	2001-07-01 00:00:00.000	776	2024.994	Mountain-100 Black, 42
2	2001-07-01 00:00:00.000	777	2024.994	Mountain-100 Black, 44
3	2001-07-01 00:00:00.000	778	2024.994	Mountain-100 Black, 48
4	2001-07-01 00:00:00.000	771	2039.994	Mountain-100 Silver, 38
5	2001-07-01 00:00:00.000	772	2039.994	Mountain-100 Silver, 42
6	2001-07-01 00:00:00.000	773	2039.994	Mountain-100 Silver, 44
7	2001-07-01 00:00:00.000	774	2039.994	Mountain-100 Silver, 48
8	2001-07-01 00:00:00.000	714	28.8404	Long-Sleeve Logo Jersey, M
9	2001-07-01 00:00:00.000	716	28.8404	Long-Sleeve Logo Jersey, XL
10	2001-07-01 00:00:00.000	709	5.70	Mountain Bike Socks, M
11	2001-07-01 00:00:00.000	712	5.1865	AWC Logo Cap
12	2001-07-01 00:00:00.000	711	20.1865	Sport-100 Helmet, Blue
13	2001-07-01 00:00:00.000	762	419.4589	Road-650 Red, 44
14	2001-07-01 00:00:00.000	758	874.794	Road-450 Red, 52

Figure 9-6

Outer Join Subqueries

You'll recall from Chapter 8 that in SQL Server 2008 legacy outer joins are now a thing of the past and are no longer supported. This simply means that if you need to match records between two tables and return non-matching rows from either of the tables, you'll need to use a standard LEFT or RIGHT OUTER JOIN query rather than the old legacy *= or =* column matching technique in a subquery, which is still common in some other database products. In the previous edition of this book, we provided examples in this section of old-school subqueries and discussed why they shouldn't be used. Now that the technique is no longer supported, the point is moot. If you run into queries using the old syntax, please refer to Chapter 8 to learn how to convert these to proper ANSI standard outer joins.

Table Aliasing 101

The mechanics of subqueries are sometimes considerably different from standard join operations. The need to refer to columns from one table within an expression using a different table often requires that tables be aliased. In Chapter 5 you learned how to alias columns. This is the same concept but now you're just giving a table an alternate name. Here's a simple example to introduce the technique:

```
SELECT ProductID, Name FROM Production.Product AS P
```

The word AS may also be omitted, as follows:

```
SELECT ProductID, Name FROM Production.Product P
```

The alias in this query doesn't really accomplish anything in its basic form, but it would be useful if this query were used as a nested subquery within another SELECT statement, or in a join. As queries become larger and more complex, the value of aliasing becomes more apparent. Rather than referring to long table names multiple times, it's convenient to simply use a letter or short, abbreviated name. Personally, I'm a fan of using intuitive abbreviations in larger quantities rather than single letters, but this is purely a matter of preference. If you use the graphical query builder to design multi-table joins, you will not see this; however, as you become less dependent on automated tools to write your queries, aliasing becomes a powerful and important tool.

Some queries may reference the same table more than once in a different context. In this case, aliasing may become an absolute requirement. Here's a hypothetical example where the ConsultingActivity is used in an inner subquery as well as the outer main query, referred to as CA1 and CA2, respectively:

```
SELECT CustProject, Hours
FROM ConsultingActivity as CA1
WHERE CustProject IN (SELECT CustProject
        FROM ConsultingActivity as CA2
        WHERE ActivityType = 'Development'
        AND CA1.CustProject = CA2.CustProject)
ORDER BY CustProject
```

Try It Out

This is a simple concept but a very important technique to master as we prepare to raise the bar. To make sure you have the basics down, try out the following simple exercise. In a query window, connect to the AdventureWorks2008 database and then type the following:

```
SELECT ProductID, Name, ListPrice
FROM Production.Product
WHERE ListPrice > 0
```

Execute this script and note the results.

Now make the following modifications, execute the modified query, and note the results. Even though you used SELECT * to include all available columns, only three columns and a limited number of rows were returned.

```
SELECT P.* FROM
(
    SELECT ProductID, Name, ListPrice
    FROM Production.Product
    WHERE ListPrice > 0
) AS P
```

Throughout the rest of this book, you will see several multi-table queries used with aliases to shorten table name references and help make these queries easier to read and to follow their business logic.

Using Aggregate Functions in Subqueries

In Chapter 7, you saw how aggregate functions are used to return summary values over a group of rows rolled up using the GROUP BY clause. In subqueries, a similar result can be achieved by using aggregate functions in a filtered SELECT expression. In a scalar expression, you use the AVG() function to return a single column value and then use that value to perform calculations with other column values.

In row set queries, aggregate functions can be used along with various filtering and matching techniques to achieve more flexible results. For example, we can simulate a top values query by using the COUNT() function. We'll introduce some other techniques first. Aggregate functions allow you to do some very powerful things in correlated subqueries, which are discussed later in the chapter.

The HAVING Clause

Chapter 7 also showed you how to use the HAVING clause to filter aggregated rows when using the GROUP BY statement. Similar results can be achieved using subquery techniques. Until we discuss the mechanics of correlated subqueries, it may not seem to make sense to use the HAVING clause without a GROUP BY. For example, the following expression serves only to include or exclude all rows from this query:

```
SELECT SUM(UnitPrice) FROM Sales.SalesOrderDetail
HAVING SUM(UnitPrice) > 100000
```

In this example, one value is returned if the UnitPrice sum for the entire range meets this criterion; otherwise, the query returns nothing. In effect, the HAVING statement does the same thing as a WHERE clause, but only after the aggregate value has been calculated. The WHERE clause is used to qualify records before they are fed to the aggregate SUM() function within the subquery. This query returns the name of products that have generated sales exceeding two million dollars:

```
SELECT Name FROM Production.Product
WHERE EXISTS
    (
        SELECT SUM(UnitPrice) FROM Sales.SalesOrderDetail
        WHERE SalesOrderDetail.ProductID = Product.ProductID
        HAVING SUM(UnitPrice) > 2000000
    )
```

When you need to use an aggregated value within a subquery, this technique can be quite useful.

Creating a Derived Table

Sometimes you may need to build values into a query that are not obtained from a table. You've seen that the SELECT statement allows you to return literal values that are just part of an expression. For example, the following statement returns a single row result as if it were read from a table:

```
SELECT 'Fred' AS FirstName, 'Flintstone' AS LastName
```

Because tables can be aliased, an expression-type result set can also be aliased and then treated as if it were a table:

```
SELECT * FROM (SELECT 'Fred' AS FirstName, 'Flintstone' AS LastName)
AS CartoonCharacter
```

Derived tables can be used in joins and subqueries. As far as the query processor is concerned, the CartoonCharacter alias is a table, like any other table, and can be joined or used in expressions like a physical table. If we extend the previous example, a UNION statement is used to create two records, returned as an aliased table. This table is then joined to the physical Department table:

```
SELECT FirstName, LastName, Department.Name AS DeptName FROM
  (SELECT 'Fred' AS FirstName, 'Flintstone' AS LastName, 1 AS DepartmentID
  UNION ALL
  SELECT 'Barney' AS FirstName, 'Rubble' AS LastName, 4 AS DepartmentID)
AS CartoonCharacter
INNER JOIN HumanResources.Department
  ON CartoonCharacter.DepartmentID = Department.DepartmentID
```

The result, shown in Figure 9-7, returns the department name based on the join to the Department table and the DepartmentID provided for each of these records.

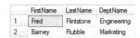

	First Name	Last Name	Dept Name
1	Fred	Flintstone	Engineering
2	Barney	Rubble	Marketing

Figure 9-7

Using the IN( ) Function

In Chapter 5 you saw how the IN() function can be used to match a column to any value in a comma-delimited list of values. This function has a dual purpose in that it also knows how to match a column to the results of a SELECT statement when this statement returns a single column of values. Here's a simple example that returns all products that have been used in orders:

```
SELECT ProductID, Name
FROM Production.Product
WHERE ProductID IN
     (  SELECT ProductID
        FROM Sales.SalesOrderDetail )
```

Subqueries can be nested. Extending the previous example, we can return products that were ordered in March 2003. The OrderDate is stored in the SalesOrderHeader table, and the ProductID for the order is in the SalesOrderDetail table. This requires three expressions — a query within a query within a query, like this:

```
SELECT ProductID, Name
FROM Production.Product
WHERE ProductID IN
     (  SELECT ProductID
        FROM Sales.SalesOrderDetail
        WHERE SalesOrderID IN
             (  SELECT SalesOrderID
                FROM Sales.SalesOrderHeader
                WHERE OrderDate BETWEEN '3-1-03' AND '3-31-03')
     )
```

Note that due to dependencies on records in other tables in the latest versions of the Adventure Works sample databases, the following sample may require other records to be deleted first. Doing so may prevent other examples from working correctly. Therefore, this query is provided only as a hypothetical example and should be executed.

The first product/order example returns a large number of rows. Reversing the logic using the NOT operator will return a list of all the products that haven't sold:

```
SELECT ProductID, Name
FROM Production.Product
WHERE ProductID NOT IN
        (SELECT ProductID FROM Sales.SalesOrderDetail)
```

Perhaps our purpose is to clean up the product inventory and remove those product records that haven't generated revenue. To this end, we can delete products that haven't sold by applying the DELETE command:

```
DELETE FROM Production.Product
WHERE ProductID NOT IN
        (SELECT ProductID FROM Sales.SalesOrderDetail)
```

Using the EXISTS() Function

The EXISTS() function is used to return a row in the outer query when any records are returned by a subquery. The subquery can be any SELECT statement, directly related or not, to the main SELECT statement. The EXISTS() function is often used in correlated subqueries to either mimic the behavior of a join or to implement business rules that wouldn't be possible with a standard join.

It doesn't really matter what column or columns are returned in the subquery because you don't actually use these values. For this reason, it's common to use the asterisk rather than column names. The asterisk is typically used to return all column values from a query but, in this case, it simply allows the query engine to test for the presence of any rows without unnecessarily wasting system resources.

Here's a simple example of this type of subquery:

```
SELECT SalesOrderID, LineTotal
FROM Sales.SalesOrderDetail
WHERE EXISTS
    (SELECT * FROM Production.Product
    WHERE ProductID = Sales.SalesOrderDetail.ProductID
  AND Color = 'Blue')
```

Note the correlation between the inner and outer query using a reference to the SalesOrderDetail table from the subquery based on the Product table. The results, shown in Figure 9-8, return only SalesOrderDetail records that have blue colored products.

	SalesOrderID	Line Total
1	43659	80.746000
2	43661	40.373000
3	43665	40.373000
4	43668	40.373000
5	43671	20.186500
6	43673	20.186500
7	43675	100.932500
8	43678	60.559500
9	43680	20.186500
10	43681	40.373000
11	43683	40.373000
12	43692	60.559500
13	43694	100.932500
14	43849	20.186500

Figure 9-8

NOT EXISTS()

To reverse the logic for this query (to return all the unassigned employees), simply add the NOT operator before the EXISTS statement:

```
SELECT SalesOrderID, LineTotal
FROM Sales.SalesOrderDetail
WHERE NOT EXISTS
    (SELECT * FROM Production.Product
     WHERE ProductID = Sales.SalesOrderDetail.ProductID
  AND Color = 'Blue')
```

The result set, shown in Figure 9-9, returns all the SalesOrderDetail that were excluded in the previous example, with products that are not blue in color.

	SalesOrderID	Line Total
1	43659	2024.994000
2	43659	6074.982000
3	43659	2024.994000
4	43659	2039.994000
5	43659	2039.994000
6	43659	4079.988000
7	43659	2039.994000
8	43659	86.521200
9	43659	28.840400
10	43659	34.200000
11	43659	10.373000
12	43660	419.458900
13	43660	874.794000
14	43661	809.760000

Figure 9-9

Correlated Subqueries

You've just seen some examples of subqueries where the outer query refers to, and conditionally filters rows based on, the inner query. A *correlated subquery* is a subquery where the selection criterion of the inner query refers to values in the outer query. Correlated subqueries can be a bit tricky. One of the restrictions is that the inner query cannot return more than one row matching the outer row. In the following example, we are looking for mountain bike products (where the SubCategoryID is 1) that have been purchased (where there is an existing SalesOrderDetail record). This query contains the proper logic but returns an error because the inner query returns multiple results for some of the products:

```
SELECT ProductID
   , Name
FROM Production.Product AS P
WHERE 1 =
     (SELECT ProductSubCategoryID
      FROM Sales.SalesOrderDetail AS SD
      WHERE P.ProductID = SD.ProductID)
```

The problem is easily corrected by adding a TOP 1 statement:

```
-- Correlated subquery using TOP 1:
SELECT ProductID
   , Name
FROM Production.Product AS P
WHERE 1 =
     (SELECT TOP 1 ProductSubCategoryID
      FROM Sales.SalesOrderDetail AS SD
      WHERE P.ProductID = SD.ProductID)
```

The first few rows of the result set are shown in Figure 9-10.

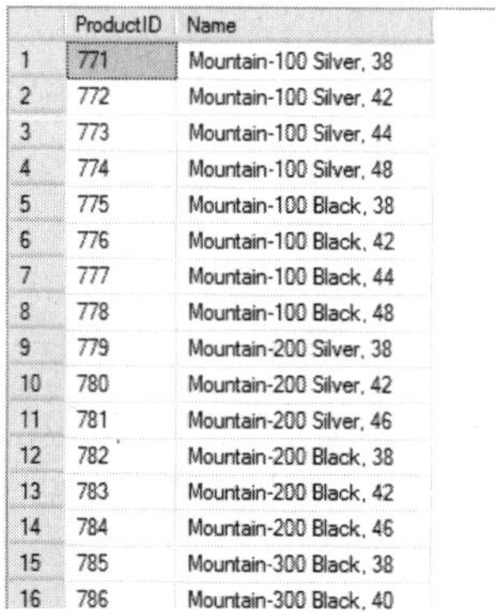

	ProductID	Name
1	771	Mountain-100 Silver, 38
2	772	Mountain-100 Silver, 42
3	773	Mountain-100 Silver, 44
4	774	Mountain-100 Silver, 48
5	775	Mountain-100 Black, 38
6	776	Mountain-100 Black, 42
7	777	Mountain-100 Black, 44
8	778	Mountain-100 Black, 48
9	779	Mountain-200 Silver, 38
10	780	Mountain-200 Silver, 42
11	781	Mountain-200 Silver, 46
12	782	Mountain-200 Black, 38
13	783	Mountain-200 Black, 42
14	784	Mountain-200 Black, 46
15	785	Mountain-300 Black, 38
16	786	Mountain-300 Black, 40

Figure 9-10

The same result could also be achieved using a SELECT DISTINCT statement in the inner query, as shown in the following example:

```
-- Correlated subquery using Distinct:
SELECT ProductID
   , Name
FROM Production.Product AS P
WHERE 1 =
     (SELECT DISTINCT ProductSubCategoryID
      FROM Sales.SalesOrderDetail AS SD
      WHERE P.ProductID = SD.ProductID)
```

One of the significant differences between the outer query value matching (using IN or EXISTS) and the correlated techniques is in how the query processor builds the execution plan. In the case of a correlated subquery, a row is selected from the outer query and then a row is selected from the inner query. Value comparisons are made to determine if an outer row should be output and, if so, the row is typically sent to an output buffer. This process is repeated, processing each of the inner rows for every one of the outer rows until all combinations have been considered. This process is more rigorous than subqueries that use the IN or EXISTS functions and don't match outer query column values within the inner query.

Benchmarking and Best Practices

Several subquery techniques can be used to return the same kind of results you would get from an INNER JOIN or OUTER JOIN query. I don't want to beat the proverbial dead horse, but I'll say it one more time: Using ANSI standard join expressions gives the query processor the opportunity to make intelligent decisions about your stated intentions and then to build an optimal execution plan. Using explicit subquery expressions to achieve the same result doesn't.

Don't just take our word for it. Let's test it out. Using SQL Server Management Studio, enable the feature to Include the Actual Execution Plan. You will find this option on the Query menu and the SQL Editor toolbar. Execute the SELECT DISTINCT correlated subquery example using the AdventureWorks2008 database, and then view the execution plan (see Figure 9-11). You can do this by selecting the Execution Plan tab in the query results pane after the query has completely finished running.

Figure 9-11

The first thing to note is that this query was executed in nine steps. From right to left, you see all of the activities performed by the query-processing engine to process this query. The join was processed using an operation called a **nested loop inner join**. This is exactly what you told the query processor to do: perform an inner join by matching records in two nested loops. Now, place the mouse pointer over and pause on each icon. A pop-up window displays statistical performance information about the execution. Take note of the Subtree Cost value, which will give you an idea about the proportional cost of each operation for the entire query. On the last step, this will also give you a baseline for comparing different queries.

Upon careful evaluation you will see that the majority of time was spent processing an Index Seek operation on the SalesOrderDetail table's index. If you hover over this icon, labeled Index Seek (nonclustered), note that 121,317 total rows were scanned. Hover over the left-most icon and note the Estimated Subtree Cost. On my system, this is about 1.125.

Now, type the following ANSI join version of the same query, highlight the query text, and execute the query:

```
-- ANSI Join:
SELECT DISTINCT Product.ProductID
     , Name
FROM Production.Product INNER JOIN Sales.SalesOrderDetail
     ON Product.ProductID = SalesOrderDetail.ProductID
WHERE ProductSubCategoryID = 1
```

Again, view the execution plan shown in Figure 9-12.

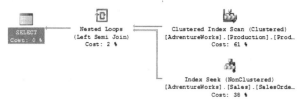

Figure 9-12

This time it took only four steps. Note the Estimated Subtree Cost in the statistics for the left-most icon. In my case, this is only about .022. Now hover over the index seek icon on the right and note that only 32 rows were scanned. Because of this efficiency, it took nearly ¹/₁₀₀ of the time to process this query as it did before. Note that instead of spending nearly all of this time reprocessing the same rows using the index scan, it scanned the index only once. The query optimizer decided that it made more sense to apply filtering at the source than to scan all 121,317 SalesOrderDetail rows.

The real question is: when do you really need to use a subquery instead of a join? So far you've seen that it usually makes sense to use a join wherever you can. However, business doesn't always follow simple rules. The next section looks at some examples of unique business rules that can be solved using various forms of subqueries.

Business Cases for Subqueries

Creating subqueries to solve unique business problems is a fine art, and a source of pride among true database professionals. Often an evolutionary process, queries may progress from crude data selections based on other views or queries, or multi-step inserts and updates to populate temporary tables, finally arriving at a short and elegant solution. This process can take days to years in the life of a database solution. I've learned to think twice before making statements such as "that *can't* be done in a single query," only to later discover otherwise. The following examples, with one exception, use the AdventureWorks2008 database so you can follow along.

Top Sales by Territory

The Director of Sales at Adventure Works Cycles would like to see a report showing the top five sales in each sales territory and the salespeople responsible for those sales. The trick here is that we want to see five sales records in the result for every territory so a top values query won't help unless it is nested in a subquery. We can use a different technique to achieve a similar result. This is done by ordering the SalesOrderHeader rows by the SubTotal column in descending order. This places the largest sales records at the top of the list. The MIN() function is just a trick used to enable the HAVING() function to work. The HAVING expression used in this correlated subquery essentially returns the top five values from matching records within the inner query:

```
SELECT TerritoryID, SubTotal, SalesPersonID, SalesOrderID
FROM Sales.SalesOrderHeader AS SO1
WHERE SubTotal >=
  (
    SELECT Min(SubTotal)
    FROM Sales.SalesOrderHeader AS SO2
```

```
    WHERE SO1.TerritoryID = SO2.TerritoryID
    AND SO1.SubTotal <= SO2.SubTotal
    HAVING Count(*) <= 5
  )
ORDER BY TerritoryID, SubTotal Desc
```

Figure 9-13 shows the first few records in the result set.

	TerritoryID	SubTotal	SalesPersonID	SalesOrderID
1	1	135653.7237	283	46643
2	1	135620.8741	268	51830
3	1	135225.2998	276	57105
4	1	130340.6317	276	51783
5	1	127361.5271	287	69508
6	2	179754.1225	275	47395
7	2	129038.6978	277	53506
8	2	127012.8505	277	50683
9	2	121699.3439	275	48336
10	2	115948.7381	277	49888
11	3	157915.6701	276	51822
12	3	140191.9196	277	43884
13	3	135101.0711	276	57186
14	3	130638.8047	277	44528

Figure 9-13

Unshipped Product Orders

In this scenario, we want a list of sales order records and products where part of the order has been shipped and part has not been shipped. In the outer query, we ask for records from the SalesOrderDetail table (sales order line items) that don't have a tracking number. This indicates that this item has not shipped. For these rows to be output, there must be records with the same SalesOrderID (related to the same SalesOrderHeader record) that do have a tracking number. Before this will work, we need to ship a few products to create partial orders. This script will do the trick:

```
UPDATE Sales.SalesOrderDetail SET CarrierTrackingNumber = 'Z987-1ACD-42'
WHERE SalesOrderDetailID = 94445


UPDATE Sales.SalesOrderDetail SET CarrierTrackingNumber = 'Z987-1ACD-43'
WHERE SalesOrderDetailID = 94441


UPDATE Sales.SalesOrderDetail SET CarrierTrackingNumber = 'Z987-1ACD-44'
WHERE SalesOrderDetailID = 94436
```

Now I have three orders with some products that have shipped and others that have not. The following query may be used to find these orders:

```
SELECT SalesOrderID, ProductID
FROM Sales.SalesOrderDetail AS SD1
WHERE CarrierTrackingNumber IS NULL
AND SalesOrderID IN
  (SELECT SalesOrderID FROM Sales.SalesOrderDetail AS SD2
   WHERE CarrierTrackingNumber IS NOT NULL
   AND SD1.SalesOrderID = SD2.SalesOrderID)
```

Figure 9-14 shows the results.

	SalesOrderID	ProductID
1	66898	933
2	66898	922
3	66900	928
4	66900	921
5	66901	929
6	66901	921
7	66901	871

Figure 9-14

Consulting Billing Time

One of the quandaries in the software development consulting business is just what we should bill our customers for. Inevitably, projects require ramp-up time and, sometimes, projects get cancelled before they really get started. With new clients, the process usually progresses from the sales stage to initiation meetings, specification forming, requirement gathering, and then finally to the development work. We certainly can't bill our customers for the sales calls and all the schmoozing that goes on when building a new business relationship, prior to getting started on a billable project. So, when does the billing clock actually begin to run? Customers want assurance that we can deliver results, and we don't want to waste our time on dead-end projects that we won't get paid for.

For this example, we've created a table called ConsultingActivity with columns containing a description of consulting activities, the number of hours, and the activity type. In a production solution, this data may exist in multiple tables but in this simplified example, we've used only one table. The data looks like that shown in Figure 9-15.

	CustProject	Hours	ActivityType
1	Inventory	2	Investigation
2	Inventory	2	Investigation
3	Inventory	5	Requirement Gathering
4	Invoice	1	Investigation
5	Invoice	3	Requirement Gathering
6	Document Manager	2	Requirement Gathering
7	Inventory	8	Development
8	Inventory	6	Development
9	Inventory	2	Investigation
10	Document Manager	8	Development
11	Inventory	7	Development
12	Inventory	8	Development
13	Document Manager	7	Investigation
14	Document Manager	8	Development
15	Inventory	9	Development
16	Scheduling	3	Investigation
17	Scheduling	4	Investigation
18	Scheduling	6	Requirement Gathering

Figure 9-15

This is the only example in this chapter that doesn't use the AdventureWorks2008 sample database. If you would like to see these results, you will need to create this table and populate it with these values. Otherwise, this example is provided as a hypothetical example. The ActivityType column may contain a number of different values. The business rule is that if your consultants have performed any development work, you will bill the customer for all activities. Otherwise, you don't bill on this project at all.

```
SELECT CustProject, Hours
FROM ConsultingActivity as CA1
WHERE CustProject IN (SELECT CustProject
        FROM ConsultingActivity as CA2
        WHERE ActivityType = 'Development'
        AND CA1.CustProject = CA2.CustProject)
ORDER BY CustProject
```

Of the four projects in various stages of progress, only two have had any development consulting activity performed. The results of this query, shown in Figure 9-16, include all the activities for these two projects.

	CustProject	Hours
1	Document Manager	2
2	Document Manager	8
3	Document Manager	7
4	Document Manager	8
5	Inventory	9
6	Inventory	7
7	Inventory	8
8	Inventory	2
9	Inventory	2
10	Inventory	5
11	Inventory	8
12	Inventory	6
13	Inventory	2

Figure 9-16

Common Table Expressions

Most SQL Server database professionals will agree that the addition of CTEs is one of the most significant improvements introduced in SQL Server 2005. Subqueries can be cumbersome to use at times because all filtering and matching logic must be integrated into the subquery expressions. This is fine when you have a single task to perform and need to use the query expression only once, but subqueries are not reusable and don't support multiple requirements very well. A common work-around to this limitation was to populate a temporary table with the subquery contents. Joins and filter expressions may be applied to the temporary table but at the cost of poor performance and significant physical disk overhead. Using temporary tables also requires permission to create and use another table. The CTE is the best of both worlds: it is a subquery that exists only in memory, so it doesn't require special permissions or unnecessary physical disk operations. Unlike a traditional subquery, the CTE is a named object that can be reused and referenced much like a table, enabling far greater flexibility.

A CTE is defined before it is used in the query script, beginning with the word WITH followed by a list of the output columns in parentheses, then the word AS followed by a complete SELECT statement in parentheses, like this:

```
WITH BlueProducts (ProductID, Name) AS
(
    SELECT ProductID, Name
    FROM Production.Product
    WHERE Color = 'Blue'
)
```

The previous script won't run all by itself because the CTE must be used in a subsequent query. After the CTE is defined, any script using the same connection can simply refer to the CTE as if it were a table.

Any columns that will be used for filtering, sorting. or joining outside of the CTE definition must be included in the column list.

Of course, a CTE is only useful if it's followed by a query. The following query joins the CTE, named BlueProducts, with the SalesOrderDetail table and returns columns from both "tables":

```
SELECT SalesOrderID, Name, UnitPrice
FROM Sales.SalesOrderDetail AS SOD INNER JOIN BlueProducts
    ON SOD.ProductID = BlueProducts.ProductID
```

To test this example, combine the two previous blocks for script and run them as one query. The result is a set of sales order records for only blue products, as shown in Figure 9-17.

	SalesOrderID	Name	UnitPrice
1	43659	Sport-100 Helmet, Blue	20.1865
2	43661	Sport-100 Helmet, Blue	20.1865
3	43665	Sport-100 Helmet, Blue	20.1865
4	43668	Sport-100 Helmet, Blue	20.1865
5	43671	Sport-100 Helmet, Blue	20.1865
6	43673	Sport-100 Helmet, Blue	20.1865
7	43675	Sport-100 Helmet, Blue	20.1865
8	43678	Sport-100 Helmet, Blue	20.1865
9	43680	Sport-100 Helmet, Blue	20.1865
10	43681	Sport-100 Helmet, Blue	20.1865
11	43683	Sport-100 Helmet, Blue	20.1865
12	43683	Sport-100 Helmet, Blue	20.1865

Figure 9-17

Practically any subquery can be replaced with a CTE as long as all the rules are followed. Here's an example based on a query we used earlier to demonstrate the use of the HAVING clause. Note that in the earlier example, it was permissible to omit the GROUP BY clause because the subquery didn't actually return any rows. Here, with the same expression used as a CTE (named PriceyOrderDetails,) we must group by the ProductID because this query returns a complete set of rows prior to being consumed in the latter query.

```
WITH PriceyOrderDetails (UnitPriceSum, ProductID)
AS
(
      SELECT SUM(UnitPrice), ProductID FROM Sales.SalesOrderDetail
      GROUP BY ProductID
      HAVING SUM(UnitPrice) > 2000000
)

SELECT Name FROM Production.Product
WHERE EXISTS
    (
      SELECT * FROM PriceyOrderDetails AS POD
      WHERE POD.ProductID = Product.ProductID
    )
```

The results are displayed in Figure 9-18.

	Name
1	Mountain-200 Black, 38
2	Mountain-200 Black, 42

Figure 9-18

To use a CTE in it simplest form, let's convert the simple query we used to demonstrate a table alias to a CTE. To start, enter the same query as you did earlier:

```
SELECT P.* FROM
(
    SELECT ProductID, Name, ListPrice
    FROM Production.Product
    WHERE ListPrice > 0
) AS P
```

Now convert this query to a CTE using the following expression:

```
WITH NonFreeProducts (ProductID, Name, ListPrice) AS
(
    SELECT ProductID, Name, ListPrice
    FROM Production.Product
    WHERE ListPrice > 0
)

SELECT * FROM NonFreeProducts
```

Execute this query and note that the results are the same as before. This is just to get you started. Your knowledge of this basic technique will prove to be very beneficial as you need to solve more intricate business problems with more complex queries.

Cursors

The definition of the word "cursor" can actually be a little confusing. This is because there are several meanings that have similar context. Before going any further, we'd like to clarify our use of this word. If asked, most computer users would likely tell you that the little blinking bar in a text editor is a cursor. It's a placeholder or position pointer. You could reason that after a SQL query is executed, the cursor would be a pointer to the current record. As much as this makes sense, this isn't the definition of a cursor in the SQL world. In this context, the word "cursor" is an acronym for *CURrent Set Of Rows*. A cursor is a set of records returned from a query.

Unfortunately, it can get a little more confusing than that. It is true that when a SELECT statement is executed, the database engine returns a cursor — or set of records — held in memory or streamed across a network connection. This type of cursor is the basis for programming objects such as recordsets and datasets. In Transact-SQL, when you declare a cursor-type variable, a result set is read into the memory managed by this object for the purpose of iterating through each record. We know — this actually takes us back to the original definition of a cursor as a single record pointer. The fact is that the cursor represents the entire set of records and supports navigation, one record at a time.

Rowset Versus Cursor Operations

Using a cursor to manage or manipulate a set of records is very different from the usual approach. It requires the query processing engine to give up a lot of its built-in optimizations and to hand over a set of data so that you can manage it yourself. Although this may afford you a little more flexibility, it usually comes at a cost of performance and efficiency. There are cases where using a cursor will solve an important business problem. However, it has been my experience that often when I thought I needed to use a cursor to solve a problem, there was a simpler and more efficient method using a standard set-based query. For example, the new MERGE command may eliminate a lot of older cursor code used to loop through records, performing related inserts, updates, and deletes. The MERGE command is introduced in Chapter 10.

Probably one of the greatest challenges for programmers learning to use SQL is the different approach usually taken to handling data. In procedural and object-oriented programming, developers typically work with objects one at a time. Groups of objects are organized into collections, structures, or arrays that support looping and enumeration. So far, you've seen that SQL Server returns sets of rows, all at once, and is optimized to support this paradigm rather than one record at a time. SQL Server performs best when using native set-based operations. There may be times when you will need to loop through a set of individual records, but be forewarned that cursor operations are typically the worst performing operations that occur in T-SQL. If there is a set-based solution that can provide the same functionality as the cursor, you should choose the set-based solution.

T-SQL cursors' default behavior is *forward-only* and *updatable,* unlike their counterparts used in other programming languages, which typically default to *forward-only read-only.* This makes the T-SQL cursor even more expensive as far as performance is concerned. When a cursor is updatable it means that the cursor maintains a link to the underlying data from which it was built. If the underlying data changes, so will the contents of the cursor. To prevent this behavior, the cursor can be declared with an INSENSITIVE option that makes it read-only and decreases the amount of resources needed to maintain it. Another method of mitigating the cost of a cursor is to mark only specific columns in the cursor as updatable rather than the default of all the columns. If you must use a cursor, keep this in mind and use the least expensive cursor possible. The examples used in this chapter follow these performance guidelines.

Creating and Navigating a Cursor

The first order of business is to declare a cursor-type variable. Because this is a special type of non-scalar object, the variable name isn't prefixed with an at symbol (@). The cursor variable can be declared and defined on the same line with the SELECT statement used to populate the cursor:

```
DECLARE curProduct INSENSITIVE CURSOR FOR SELECT ProductID, Name
FROM Production.Product
```

To create a cursor that allows updates only to and from the Name column of the Product table, declare the cursor like this:

```
DECLARE curProduct CURSOR FOR SELECT ProductID, Name
FROM Production.Product
FOR UPDATE OF Name
```

The cursor isn't actually populated until it is opened. Executing the OPEN command loads the cursor structure and data into memory:

```
OPEN curProduct
```

At this point, the record pointer is positioned before the first row. The FETCH NEXT command navigates the pointer to the next record and returns a comma-delimited list of column values. In this case, the pointer is moved to the first row. Individual variables can be used to capture the values of the current row's column values:

```
DECLARE @ProdID Int
DECLARE @ProdName VarChar(100)

FETCH NEXT FROM curProduct INTO @ProdID, @ProdName
```

After FETCH NEXT is executed, one of two things will happen: the record pointer will either be positioned on a valid record or it will navigate beyond the last row. The state of the pointer can be determined using the global variable @@Fetch_Status. On a valid row, it returns 0; otherwise, it returns –1 or –2. It returns –1 if there is no next row to fetch. If a –2 is returned, it means that the next row was deleted in the underlying table when using an updatable cursor. Using this variable, create a simple loop, navigating to the next record as long as @@Fetch_Status is equal to 0:

```
WHILE @@Fetch_Status = 0
   BEGIN
      PRINT @ProdName
      FETCH NEXT FROM curProduct INTO @ProdID, @ProdName
   END
```

In this example, you're simply printing one of the variable values to the query results window. In production, you could use conditional statements to decide whether to perform related operations, such as inserting or deleting records. The real power of using cursors is in using them to conditionally call stored procedures. This way, you can use conditional logic to call different procedures under different conditions, and then a stored procedure can perform practically any combination of operations.

Finally, after navigating past the last record, it's necessary to do some cleanup. Use the CLOSE command to close the cursor, and then use the DEALLOCATE command to recover the memory used by the cursor:

```
CLOSE curProduct
DEALLOCATE curProduct
```

If we put it all together, here's the entire script:

```
DECLARE curProduct INSENSITIVE CURSOR
FOR SELECT TOP 100 ProductID, Name FROM Production.Product
DECLARE @ProdID Int
DECLARE @ProdName VarChar(100)

OPEN curProduct
FETCH NEXT FROM curProduct INTO @ProdID, @ProdName
WHILE @@Fetch_Status = 0
```

(continued)

(continued)

```
    BEGIN
        PRINT @ProdName
        FETCH NEXT FROM curProduct INTO @ProdID, @ProdName
    END
CLOSE curProduct
DEALLOCATE curProduct
```

A list of product names is displayed in the query results pane for the first few products, as shown in Figure 9-19.

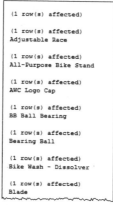

```
(1 row(s) affected)

(1 row(s) affected)
Adjustable Race

(1 row(s) affected)
All-Purpose Bike Stand

(1 row(s) affected)
AWC Logo Cap

(1 row(s) affected)
BB Ball Bearing

(1 row(s) affected)
Bearing Ball

(1 row(s) affected)
Bike Wash - Dissolver

(1 row(s) affected)
Blade
```

Figure 9-19

Just for kicks, display the actual execution plan and run this query again. This should shed some light on any questions of efficiency when using cursors. Each FETCH NEXT command causes a separate look operation, which is slow and resource intensive. Figure 9-20 shows only the first few of these operations. Cursors are powerful and give you procedural control over each row that T-SQL doesn't otherwise allow. Using a cursor is the only way to loop through individual rows and execute explicit code for each. But if there is any other way to do the job, you should consider any alternative to using cursors, especially with large sets of data.

```
Query 1: Query cost (relative to the batch): 5%
OPEN curProduct

 [T-SQL]          [icon]                      [icon]              [icon]            [icon]
OPEN CURSOR      Clustered Index Insert <--- Sequence Project <--- Segment  <---  Index Scan (NonClustered)
Cost: 0 %        [tempdb].[CWT_PrimaryKey]   (Compute Scalar)    Cost: 0 %   [AdventureWorks].[Production].[Prod...
                 Cost: 83 %                  Cost: 0 %                              Cost: 17 %

Query 2: Query cost (relative to the batch): 0%
FETCH NEXT FROM curProduct INTO @ProdID, @ProdName

 [T-SQL]          [icon]
FETCH CURSOR <--- Clustered Index Seek (NonClustered)
Cost: 0 %         [tempdb].[CWT_PrimaryKey]
                  Cost: 100 %

Query 3: Query cost (relative to the batch): 0%
FETCH NEXT FROM curProduct INTO @ProdID, @ProdName

 [T-SQL]          [icon]
FETCH CURSOR <--- Clustered Index Seek (NonClustered)
Cost: 0 %         [tempdb].[CWT_PrimaryKey]
                  Cost: 100 %
```

Figure 9-20

Summary

There may be several ways to write some queries. Although there are some basic rules and guidelines to follow, the best approach will often depend on a number of factors including the volume of data, complexity of the database, and your business rules. Subqueries allow a SELECT statement to feed values or rows to another query. Subqueries can be scalar, single-value expressions, or nested rowset expressions. Joins can be implemented using subqueries rather than ANSI join syntax. Although often more complex and less efficient than standard joins, subquery joins can be used to process specialized business logic. If given the choice between standard join syntax and subqueries, you should typically favor standard joins. In any case, you can test your queries for performance and efficiency using graphical execution plans, SQL Profiler, System Monitor, and other benchmarking and tuning tools. The results are often surprising. Overall, be open to different ways to solve business problems. Try different forms of queries and explore various query expressions and techniques. Taking time to experiment, you will either confirm that you are using the best approach or find a better way to solve the problem.

Exercises

The following exercises will test your knowledge of advanced query techniques. To simplify the relationships and standardize differences between the 2005 and 2008 sample databases, you will create views to use in place of tables.

If you are using SQL Server 2008, run the following script:

```
CREATE VIEW vw_Employee
AS
SELECT E.VacationHours, P.FirstName, P.LastName, E.BusinessEntityID AS
EmployeeID
FROM HumanResources.Employee E INNER JOIN Person.Person P
   ON E.BusinessEntityID = P.BusinessEntityID
```

If you are using SQL Server 2005, run the following script:

```
CREATE VIEW vw_Employee
AS
SELECT E.VacationHours, C.FirstName, C.LastName, E.EmployeeID
FROM HumanResources.Employee AS E INNER JOIN Person.Contact AS C
   ON E.ContactID = C.ContactID
```

Exercise 1

Write a query to return a list of products in order of the product name, the list price, and the highest price for which that product has sold. Use an in-line, scalar query to calculate the highest sales price for the product. Columns in the result set should be labeled ProductName, ProductListPrice, and MaxSalesPrice.

Exercise 2

The following query returns the top 10 employees' accumulated vacation hours and employee names:

```
SELECT TOP 10
    FirstName + ' ' + LastName AS Name
  , VacationHours
FROM vw_Employee AS E
ORDER BY VacationHours DESC
```

This query returns the average vacation hours for all other employees as one summary row labeled "(other)" in-place of the employee's name. A subquery is used to join the all employee rows to the results of the top 10 expression and then to eliminate these from the aggregated group:

```
SELECT '(Other)' AS Name, AVG(E1.VacationHours) AS VacationHours
FROM vw_Employee AS E1
    LEFT OUTER JOIN
    ( SELECT TOP 10 EmployeeID, VacationHours
      FROM vw_Employee ORDER BY VacationHours DESC
    ) AS E2
    ON E1.EmployeeID = E2.EmployeeID
    WHERE E2.EmployeeID IS NULL
```

These two query results need to be combined into a UNION query to return a single result set. However, simply adding the UNION statement between them raises errors because of restrictions of the UNION statement. You can work around these limitations by creating two alias tables similar to the one in the join statement of the second query, and selecting columns from them. Rewrite these statements so the final query has two alias table subqueries based on these two provided queries. Call them EMP1 and EMP2. Union the two subquery results together. Execute the query to verify that it returns 11 rows.

Exercise 3

Rewrite the first of these queries as a CTE named Top10VacHours. Select all records from this CTE.

Transactions

We live in a transactional world. In the not-too-distant future, some of us may be trying to explain the concept of using cash to our grandchildren: "Some people carried paper and small metal disks in their pockets. They had pictures of dead government leaders on them and each one was worth a different value. When you wanted to purchase something, you would hand the paper or metal money to a store clerk in exchange for the stuff you bought." What a strange idea!

In the physical world, things move from one place to another. Like the money the customer hands to the store clerk, this transfer of ownership is a simple concept that even the least sophisticated members of the animal kingdom comprehend. In recent decades, however, mankind has managed to change the mechanics of moving things from one place to another within the information world. For example, on payday, chances are that you don't actually receive real money directly from your employer. I haven't seen a real paycheck for many years. My bank account balance is magically increased as my employer's contracted payroll service provider posts a credit to my bank account. Of course, this happens right before the balance decreases due to a similar transaction performed by my mortgage company.

We perceive that things such as money, files, and data *move* from one place to another. Although the paradigm is the same — modeled after things in the physical world — it's really all made up. We understand that data doesn't *really* move. It gets copied from storage and the new copy is inserted into a new storage location, and then the original copy is deleted from its initial location. If you really want to get technical, the fact is that we're not really moving, inserting, or deleting anything. We're simply telling computers to transmit electronic pulses and then switch memory states and realign iron crystals on spinning hard drive platters. Was that too geeky? Sorry.

Anyone who has worked with computer files or a word processor understands these basic concepts. We think it's important, occasionally, to revisit the facts and to fully understand what happens during this process of supposedly creating, copying, and moving things around within the computer space. Although we may or may not fully understand what happens at a low level within the system, as far as we're concerned, records in databases are inserted, updated, deleted, and "moved" from one location to another.

Introducing Transactions

When we count money for a purchase and hand it to a store clerk, we have confidence that it's all going to make it into the cash drawer. No matter what happens, we're either going to leave that store with our money or the stuff we bought. If the power goes out or the cash register malfunctions, this shouldn't greatly affect our transaction because one of us has the money physically in our hand. As data is processed and moved from one place to another, electronic impulses cause memory registers to "remember" our data. In simple computer processes, this exchange can take place thousands of times before a record reaches its destination. Until it is written to some form of permanent storage, the process can be easily interrupted and the data lost. Most of us have learned that the most effective way to prevent data loss is to make sure you always have at least two copies of your data. For example, if you intend to move an important file from one stand-alone computer's hard disk to another, you copy it from the hard disk to a portable disk or memory device; but you leave the original copy on the source computer's hard disk. Only after you verify that it has been copied to the target computer's storage would you consider deleting it from the source. And, you always make a backup copy of important files from the hard disk in case it fails, right? Sure you do.

In a database, a transaction is simply a mechanism to ensure and verify that data gets to its intended destination. Just like a purchase or bank transaction, both parties must be satisfied with the results based upon some kind of pre-defined rule. They must agree on the anticipated outcome. After the transaction has been completed, they should agree that all of the conditions of the transaction have been met and that everything is in the proper place. After both parties agree that the transaction meets the pre-defined rules, they call it good and move on.

A transaction defines the scope or context of one or more database actions. SQL Server manages transactions in this manner: a T-SQL statement is used to state the intended outcome of a query. The relationships, constraints, and data types in the database define certain rules of behavior and the conditions for modifying data. The database engine must decide whether the query action can be conducted within these parameters before it inserts, deletes, or modifies any data within the transactional scope. Based on these conditions, the database engine decides to allow the operation to succeed or to fail, returning an error.

Transaction Types

All modifications to data take place in the context of a transaction. SQL Server is capable of using three types of optional transaction modes to manage data modification:

- ❑ **Explicit transaction** — The explicit transaction is defined by the presence of an explicit BEGIN TRANSACTION statement followed by one or more dependent data modification statements and completed with an explicit COMMIT TRANSACTION statement. Error checking is added prior to the COMMIT TRANSACTION statement so that if an error occurred in any of the operations, the transaction can be reversed with a ROLLBACK TRANSACTION statement.

- ❑ **Implicit transaction** — The implicit transaction follows the behavior of some other database products in that whenever a data modification is executed it *implicitly* begins a transaction. However, it does not complete the transaction and release the modified data until an explicit COMMIT TRANSACTION or ROLLBACK TRANSACTION statement is issued. Implicit transactions are enabled on a connection basis with the SET IMPLICIT_TRANSACTIONS ON command.

❑   **Auto-commit transaction** — If a data modification statement is executed against the database without an explicit or implicit transaction, it is considered an auto-commit transaction. The modification contained in an auto-commit transaction follows the same pattern as other transactions as described in the next section. In short, it applies to only one operation at a time.

Which option is best? That depends on the application and whom you ask. Personally, we're of the opinion that if you want SQL Server to behave a certain way, you should explicitly state this so there is no room for confusion. We are fans of explicit transactions. If we have five different operations that need to be performed as a unit, we can wrap them in an explicit transaction and we know they will either all succeed or fail as a unit. If we don't want this behavior, we simply don't define an explicit transaction and each statement will be performed separately, with no dependency on another. Anyone reading our code should be able to tell if multiple operations will behave within a transaction or not.

The ACID Test

Most of us have been burned by data loss problems enough times to realize that steps must be taken to ensure that data reliably gets from one place to another. Although there are a number of additional benefits, this is what transactions are all about. A bona fide transaction must meet the following criteria:

❑   **Atomic** — All steps and operations that are part of a transaction are treated as an *atomic* unit. Either *all* succeed or *all* fail together.

❑   **Consistent** — The outcome of any transaction is always predictable; all of the operations either fail or succeed. All operations abide by consistency rules and checks to ensure data integrity within the database.

❑   **Isolated** — Any operations performed before, during, or after the transaction will see related data in a consistent state, rather than in a state of partial completion. Any user or operation that queries data affected by a transaction will perceive that the entire transaction was committed instantaneously.

❑   **Durable** — If a transaction succeeds, data is written to disk and does not revert to its previous state. Data can survive system failure.

The Transaction Log

Meeting all of these criteria may seem like a rather tall order, but the way it works is actually quite elegant. SQL Server pulls this off by using redundancy. When a request is made to modify any data, the following actions take place:

1.   All data is managed in 8 kB storage units called *pages*. The appropriate data pages, containing the records needing to be modified, are located in memory. If these pages are not yet in memory, they are placed in memory from the disk.

2.   The modifications (insert, update, or delete) are made to the applicable pages in memory.

3.   The modifications are written to the transaction log.

4.   The server issues a checkpoint that causes the changed (dirty) pages in memory to be written back to the hard disk. The pages in memory then have their "dirty" flag removed. If the transaction making the changes has been committed, the pages are released and other requests or transactions have access to them. If the checkpoint occurs prior to the transaction being committed, the pages are still locked until the transaction is committed.

The transaction log is a separate file on disk, which is used to collect all successful data modification requests from all users and applications. During the execution of a data modification request, the transaction exists in the buffer cache and log cache. During the changes to the data pages in memory, the pages (and the pages on disk representing the data to be changed) are locked (or isolated) from access by other requests or transactions. The pages remain locked until they are released from the transaction. Figure 10-1 illustrates the transaction process.

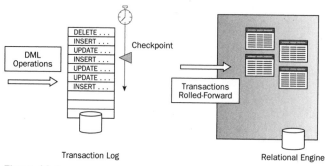

Figure 10-1

Depending on a database setting, the transaction log either continues to fill with archived transaction processes or gets truncated (removing all check-pointed transaction processes by setting the area of the transaction log up for overwrite). In a production database, the transaction log is typically allowed to grow until a scheduled backup cycle. This way, if the main database is damaged or lost, the transaction log becomes a short-term backup solution for new data.

Logged Operations

SQL Server's default behavior is to log all insert, update, and delete operations. For the reasons we explained in the previous section, this generally makes sense. However, the transaction log and its related processes can burden the server with unnecessary work if you don't need this level of protection. For example, if we had exported several thousand records to a text file, intending to load this data into our SQL Server database, this would be an exception to the day-to-day inserts normally performed by applications. Because we have a copy of the data in the export file and have backed up the data in our database, if this operation failed, we would simply correct the problem and try again. In this case, we could speed things up by performing a non-logged insert and bypass the transaction log. This is usually done using the Bulk Copy Task feature of SQL Server Integration Services (SSIS) or the Bulk Copy command-line utility, known as BCP. Non-logged operations are really the exception to the rule. Bulk operations are not a core feature of SQL and are beyond the scope of this book. For more information, use Books Online to read about the BCP utility and DTS.

Let's Do CRUD with Data

As previously mentioned, you can really only do four things with data: Create it, Read it, Update it, and Delete it. These four operations form the basis of what is commonly called CRUD operations. So far, you've been doing a lot of reading using the SELECT statement. Now it's time to work with data in a way that will affect the data in your database.

Adding Records

Adding rows is done using the INSERT statement. Inserts can be performed one row at a time or on multiple rows, depending on the technique, and target only one table. Before attempting to insert data into a table, it is important to know the following:

❑ Which columns require values

❑ Which columns have data-integrity constraints

❑ Which columns are managed by the database through functions

❑ Which columns have default values or allow null values

❑ What the data types of the destination columns are

To get started, take a look at the Production.Product table in design view (see Figure 10-2).

This table has changed a little in the newer AdventureWorks2008 database, but we're just using it as an example. The table shown has five columns, but only one column, the Name, requires a value because every other column either has a default value or accepts NULL. The LocationID column is the primary key. Because it is designated as an identity column, an incremental value will automatically be generated for this column by the database.

	LocationID	Name	CostRate	Availability	ModifiedDate
1	1	Tool Crib	0.0000	0.00	1998-06-01 00:00:00.000
2	2	Sheet Metal Racks	0.0000	0.00	1998-06-01 00:00:00.000
3	3	Paint Shop	0.0000	0.00	1998-06-01 00:00:00.000
4	4	Paint Storage	0.0000	0.00	1998-06-01 00:00:00.000
5	5	Metal Storage	0.0000	0.00	1998-06-01 00:00:00.000
6	6	Miscellaneous Storage	0.0000	0.00	1998-06-01 00:00:00.000
7	7	Finished Goods Storage	0.0000	0.00	1998-06-01 00:00:00.000
8	10	Frame Forming	22.5000	96.00	1998-06-01 00:00:00.000
9	20	Frame Welding	25.0000	108.00	1998-06-01 00:00:00.000
10	30	Debur and Polish	14.5000	120.00	1998-06-01 00:00:00.000
11	40	Paint	15.7500	120.00	1998-06-01 00:00:00.000
12	45	Specialized Paint	18.0000	80.00	1998-06-01 00:00:00.000
13	50	Subassembly	12.2500	120.00	1998-06-01 00:00:00.000
14	60	Final Assembly	12.2500	120.00	1998-06-01 00:00:00.000

Figure 10-2

INSERT Statement

If you only need to provide a value for this column, the statement would be quite simple:

```
INSERT INTO Production.Location ( Name )
SELECT 'Secret Hiding Place'
```

The INTO keyword is optional and is often omitted. We like to include it because we think it reads more like natural language. Two different styles are used with the INSERT statement, and each has its own subtleties. Generally, you could select one technique and pretty much use it for all of your insert operations. We'll show you some examples of each and let you decide when to use them.

INSERT . . . Values

The pattern of the INSERT statement is to provide a list of column names and then a list of values in parentheses. If values are provided for all columns or all columns with the exception of the identity column (only one identity column is allowed per table), the values are inserted in order, so no column name list is required. This technique is used to insert only one row into the table.

The Contact table is a good example going forward, but, like most of the tables in the new version of the AdventureWorks sample database, it includes some complicated features that will only get in the way right now. For the following examples, we will create a new table, similar to the Contact table, named MyContacts, by executing the following script. Note that the extra spaces and carriage returns are unnecessary and are added only to make this query more readable.

```
CREATE TABLE MyContacts
    ( ContactID      int Identity(1, 1) NOT NULL
    , Title          nvarchar(8)   NULL
    , FirstName      nvarchar(50)  NOT NULL
    , MiddleName     nvarchar(50)  NULL
    , LastName       nvarchar(50)  NOT NULL
    , Suffix         nvarchar(10)  NULL
    , EMailAddress   nvarchar(50)  NULL
    , Phone          nvarchar(25)  NULL
    , IsActive       bit           DEFAULT 1
    )
```

The specific commands and options used to create this table will be covered in Chapter 13. For now, just execute this script to help demonstrate how new records are inserted into this table.

For our first example, we are going to include values for only four of the columns. Note that we are skipping the ContactID column. If we were to include a value for the ContactID column, our INSERT statement would fail because this column can only be managed by the IDENTITY() function of the database. In the INSERT statement itself, we include the column names and in the Values list, we provide a corresponding value:

```
INSERT INTO MyContacts (Title, FirstName, LastName, Phone)
VALUES ('Ms.', 'Pebbles', 'Flintstone', '123-4567')
```

Note the use of single quotes to denote literal values to be inserted into the table. If we had a numeric value to insert, we would not use the quotes. The order of the values must match the order of the columns in the table if no column list is provided, with the exception of any identity column that is omitted as the following example shows:

```
INSERT INTO MyContacts
VALUES ( 'Mr.', 'Fred', 'Caveman', 'Flintstone'
       , 'Phd', 'fredf@bedrock.com', '(111) 123-4567'
       , DEFAULT)
```

There are a couple of things to think about in this query that we are not quite ready to cover. First, not all of the table columns are included in the query. Second, one of the columns has a DEFAULT rule defined for it. Because we are just working on the basics right now, don't worry about this. It will be covered in the upcoming section "Inserting NULL, Defaults, and Other Column Considerations."

INSERT ... SELECT

This form of the INSERT statement is similar to the previous values form except it uses a statement to provide values. As discussed in earlier chapters, the SELECT statement can literal values, as well as sets of literal values, without even hitting a table in the databas SELECT can be used to include a variety of different types of values (from tables, joins, ..., groups, aggregates, and literals), this is a much more flexible technique. Practically anything can be inserted as long as the column count and data types match. Because a SELECT statement can return multiple rows, this would result in multiple rows being inserted into the destination table. The following is the equivalent of the previous example using this technique. In this example, columns and values for the MiddleName and NameStyle columns have been omitted. This insert is successful because NULL will automatically be inserted as needed (because these columns allow the NULL value):

```
INSERT INTO MyContacts (Title, FirstName, LastName, Phone)
SELECT 'Mr.', 'Bam Bam', 'Rubble', '234-5678'
```

Because we've executed the previous two INSERT statements, we'll just return all the records from the MyContacts table (SELECT * FROM MyContacts) and scroll down to view the last two rows, shown in Figure 10-3.

	ContactID	Title	FirstName	MiddleName	LastName	Suffix	EMailAddress	Phone	IsActive
1	1	Ms.	Pebbles	NULL	Flintstone	NULL	NULL	123-4567	1
2	2	Mr.	Fred	Caveman	Flintstone	Phd	fredf@bedrock.com	111-123-4567	1
3	3	Mr.	Bam Bam	NULL	Rubble	NULL	NULL	234-5678	1

Figure 10-3

You can see that the ContactID column contains an auto-generated, sequential identity value. The MiddleName column is set to NULL and the IsActive is set to its default value of 0.

Inserting Multiple Records

A convenient new addition to SQL Server 2008 T-SQL is the ability to insert multiple rows in one INSERT statement. This is accomplished with a modified version of the INSERT ... VALUES pattern. Just add each record to be inserted in a separate set of parentheses, each separated by a comma, as in the following example:

```
INSERT INTO MyContacts (Title, FirstName, LastName, Phone)
VALUES
    ( 'Mr.', 'Great', 'Gazoo', '234-9999' )
  ,( 'Mr.', 'George', 'Slate', '123-4567' )
```

There is no limit to the number of new records that may be inserted in a single statement. This is a nice and simple addition to the SQL Server product.

Inserting NULL, Defaults, and Other Column Considerations

A NULL is a special value that essentially means that we didn't want to place any other value in a column. It's the SQL standard way of saying "nothing." Most common data types have a default value. For example, a numeric type by default is zero. The problem with this is that zero means something in the numerical world. If you are storing manufacturing unit records and a record stores the number of ιts produced, any number in that column would have meaning. But if your intention is to state that you don't know what that value is, you don't want to store zero because that means that you actually produced zero units. In the MyContacts example, we don't have Bam Bam's middle name. Frankly, we don't even care what it is. Whether we don't know or we don't care, we use the value NULL to store a placeholder for this missing value.

Different settings at the server, database, and user session level for SQL Server can affect the way NULL is available for a particular column. Although not necessarily complicated, this can be a particularly confusing issue because there are a number of variable elements to be considered. Before you read on, please keep in mind that this only becomes an issue if the default settings are altered and, in any case, the situation can be remedied by explicitly defining columns in tables as NULL or NOT NULL.

You can modify database properties through SQL Server Management Studio or by using T-SQL script. To view or change this option, in the Management Studio Object Browser, right-click the name of the database and then choose Properties from the menu. Figure 10-4 shows the Properties dialog (Options tab) for SQL Server 2008 and as you can see, the ANSI NULL Default property is set to False.

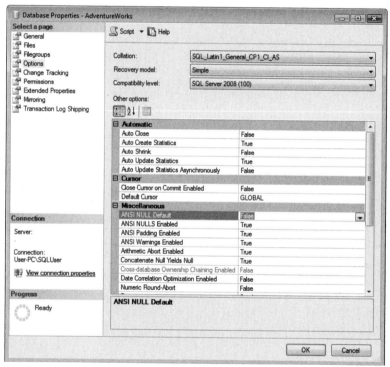

Figure 10-4

The same settings can be applied using script similar to the following:

```
sp_dboption 'AdventureWorks2008', 'ANSI Null Default', 'False'
```

The following script will override the database default setting when executed prior to creating or altering a table:

```
SET ANSI_NULL_DFLT_ON ON
```

When a table is created, the database settings apply unless they are explicitly overridden in the session. When ANSI_NULL_DEFAULT is set to ON (True), all user-defined columns and data types that have not explicitly been defined as NOT NULL during the creation or altering process of the table default to allowing NULL values. This is the opposite of the default setting for SQL Server when installed. It is good practice to explicitly define NULL and NOT NULL regardless of the current or eventual resetting of ANSI_NULL_DEFAULT. If this setting has been altered, the INSERT statements assume that the opposite will fail. Note that Constraints (Check and Default) will apply before NULL.

The Contact table in AdventureWorks for SQL Server 2005 is roughly equivalent to the Person table in AdventureWorks2008. To keep things simple, we are only going to use a subset of the columns from these tables in the following examples. We will provide an example for each of the two product versions.

The AdventureWorks2008 Person table contains these columns that are explicitly NOT NULL:

- BusinessEntityID
- PersonType
- NameStyle
- FirstName
- LastName
- EmailPromotion
- rowguid
- ModifiedDate

The AdventureWorks Contact table contains these columns that are explicitly NOT NULL:

- ContactID
- NameStyle
- FirstName
- LastName
- EmailPromotion
- rowguid
- PasswordHash
- PasswordSalt
- ModifiedDate

Of these, the primary key (BusinessEntityID or ContactID) value is supplied by the IDENTITY() function. The NameStyle, ModifiedDate, and rowguid are supplied by Default Constraints if no values are explicitly provided (the rowguid's Default Constraint employs the NEWID() function, which can be used to generate a globally unique identifier [GUID]). All other columns, as previously stated, are explicitly defined to either prohibit or allow NULL values.

Inserting Rows from Another Table

Using the INSERT ... SELECT pattern, we can bring data from another table or complex query. Conveniently, because we modeled the MyContacts table after the Contact table, we can use it to populate our table. Columns in our select list don't have to have the same names but do have to be compatible data types. First, we'll just use a SELECT statement to view the Person or Contact row we intend to insert:

AdventureWorks2008:

```
SELECT FirstName, LastName, Title
FROM Person.Person
WHERE BusinessEntityID = '273'
```

AdventureWorks:

```
SELECT FirstName, LastName, Title
FROM Person.Contact
WHERE ContactID = '1010'
```

This returns one record, as shown in Figure 10-5.

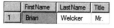

Figure 10-5

It is the best practice to always test the SELECT statements that will be used in transaction statements to prevent failures within the Insert, Update, or Delete statement. The second step is to add the INSERT statement to the front of this query and make sure the columns match up between the two lists:

AdventureWorks2008:

```
INSERT INTO MyContacts (FirstName, LastName, Title)
SELECT FirstName, LastName, Title
FROM Person.Person
WHERE BusinessEntityID = '273'
```

AdventureWorks:

```
INSERT INTO MyContacts (FirstName, LastName, Title)
SELECT FirstName, LastName, Title
FROM Person.Contact
WHERE ContactID = '1010'
```

Finally, execute a SELECT statement against the MyContacts table and scroll to the bottom of the list to check the result, as shown in Figure 10-6.

	ContactID	Title	FirstName	MiddleName	LastName	Suffix	EMailAddress	Phone	IsActive
1	1	Ms.	Pebbles	NULL	Flintstone	NULL	NULL	123-4567	1
2	2	Mr.	Fred	Caveman	Flintstone	Phd	fredf@bedrock.com	111-123-4567	1
3	3	Mr.	Bam Bam	NULL	Rubble	NULL	NULL	234-5678	1
4	4	NULL	Brian	NULL	Welcker	NULL	NULL	716-555-0127	1

Figure 10-6

Great care should be taken to limit the size (rows returned) of the SELECT statement with a WHERE clause when querying another table. Each row requested in the SELECT statement will remain locked from changes during the Insert process. This will momentarily block other requests for operations performed on the same table. In an active, multi-user database, nearly every operation carries a statistical possibility of coinciding with a conflicting operation. Most of the time, these operations are simply queued to execute in turn. The database engine will retry a blocked transaction before it times out in error. However, if two competing operations happen to lock the same tables and are waiting for the availability of locked objects before they can continue, this could result in a deadlock situation in the database. The specific behavior will depend on transaction-level locking options and database settings.

SELECT INTO

At times, you may want to populate a new or a temporary table with the results of a query, a technique that can be a real time-saver. Instead of creating a new table the old-fashioned way (by defining all of the columns and data types), and then using an INSERT statement to populate the new table from existing data, this statement simply creates the table on-the-fly using the output and data types from a SELECT statement. Although we try to avoid storing duplicate data when it's not necessary, sometimes it's just easier to copy results into a table for temporary storage — sort of a snapshot of information that alleviates locking of the transactional table by read requests for reports and so on. This might be especially useful to support a complicated report. The results of a complex query may be written to a table either in the current database, a reporting database or warehouse, or the TempDB database, where the data can be reused in other queries. The INSERT INTO statement requires that you target an existing table. If you want to create a new table from the results of the query (from one or multiple tables), use the SELECT INTO statement. In this example, we select a subset of contact records and create a new table called MyContacts:

AdventureWorks2008:

```
SELECT FirstName, LastName, Title INTO MyOtherContacts
FROM Person.Person WHERE Suffix = 'Jr.'
```

AdventureWorks:

```
SELECT FirstName, LastName, Title INTO MyOtherContacts
FROM Person.Contact WHERE Suffix = 'Jr.'
```

Keep in mind that the new table is a permanent member of the database like any other table, unless you have placed it in the TempDB database as a temporary table. Typically, in a production environment, a database administrator wouldn't grant the privilege to create new tables to all users. If you only need to use the data for a short time, you can create a temporary table by starting the table name with a pound sign (#) or double pound sign (##). A single pound sign denotes a local temporary object that is only visible from the current connection. A double pound sign denotes a global temporary object that is visible to all connections as long as the connection that created it is still active. Here is the same statement that creates a temporary table:

AdventureWorks2008:

```
SELECT FirstName, LastName, Title INTO #MyOtherContacts
FROM Person.Person WHERE Suffix = 'Jr.'
```

AdventureWorks:

```
SELECT FirstName, LastName, Title INTO #MyOtherContacts
FROM Person.Contact WHERE Suffix = 'Jr.'
```

The difference between this and the previous example is that the table will be created in the TempDB database. When the connection used to create this table is closed, SQL Server automatically removes the table and reclaims the storage space. The local temporary table is often used in a stored procedure where cursors are inefficient. The stored procedure first creates the temporary table using a SELECT INTO statement and then returns rows from this table as a result set. When the stored procedure completes and the connection is closed, the local temporary table in TempDB is dropped.

Managing Inserts Using Stored Procedures

In a large-scale production environment, administrators often limit users' ability to insert, update, and delete records directly. Implementing such restrictions while accommodating all user and application needs requires careful planning and can be a lot of work. One popular approach is to deny users all transactional activity against tables and create stored procedures to manage the inserts, updates, and deletes. For each major entity in the database, there will typically be at least three stored procedures: to insert, update, and delete records in that table. Using stored procedures offers the added benefit of enforcing any special business rules, simplifying complex tables and returning custom error messages.

Chapter 13 takes a comprehensive look at stored procedures. For now, we'll keep this simple by creating a stored procedure to insert rows into the MyContacts table. The input parameters are listed first. As you can see in the following code example, each of these parameters corresponds to a column in the table.

```
CREATE PROCEDURE spIns_MyContacts
    @FirstName      nvarchar(50),
    @LastName       nvarchar(50),
    @Phone          nvarchar(25)
AS
    INSERT INTO MyContacts (FirstName, LastName, Phone)
    SELECT @FirstName, @LastName, @Phone
RETURN @@Identity
```

This procedure accepts three input parameters: @FirstName, @LastName, and @Phone. These parameters are used to pass values to the INSERT statement. The global constant @@Identity is used to obtain the last identity value — in this case, the new ContactID value generated by this INSERT statement. To test this procedure, execute the following SQL statement:

```
spIns_MyContacts 'Betty', 'Rubble', '(111) 234-9876'
```

And just to keep things real, here is an example of a more production-like stored procedure that will insert records into the AdventureWorks Product table. Note that the required (non null) parameters are listed first. This is to simplify the execution call so optional parameters may be omitted.

```
CREATE PROCEDURE spIns_Product
   @ProductName              nVarChar(50)
 , @StandardCost             Money
 , @SafetyStockLevel         SmallInt
 , @ReorderPoint             SmallInt
 , @ListPrice                Money
 , @DaysToManufacture        Int
 , @SellStartDate            DateTime
 , @DiscontinuedDate         DateTime = Null
 , @MakeFlag                 Bit = 1
 , @FinishedGoodsFlag        Bit = 1
 , @Color                    nVarChar(15) = Null
 , @Size                     nVarChar(50) = Null
 , @SizeUnitMeasureCode      nChar(3) = Null
 , @WeightUnitMeasureCode    nChar(3) = Null
 , @Weight                   Float = Null
 , @ProductLine              nChar(2) = Null
 , @Class                    nChar(2) = Null
 , @Style                    nChar(2) = Null
 , @ProductSubCategoryID     SmallInt = Null
 , @ProductModelID           Int = Null
 , @SellEndDate              DateTime = Null
AS
INSERT INTO Production.Product
 (
    Name
 , DiscontinuedDate
 , MakeFlag
 , StandardCost
 , FinishedGoodsFlag
 , Color
 , SafetyStockLevel
 , ReorderPoint
 , ListPrice
 , Size
 , SizeUnitMeasureCode
 , WeightUnitMeasureCode
 , Weight
 , DaysToManufacture
 , ProductLine
 , Class
 , Style
 , ProductSubCategoryID
 , ProductModelID
 , rowguid
 , SellStartDate
 , SellEndDate
 )
```

(continued)

(continued)

```
SELECT
      @ProductName
    , @DiscontinuedDate
    , @MakeFlag
    , @StandardCost
    , @FinishedGoodsFlag
    , @Color
    , @SafetyStockLevel
    , @ReorderPoint
    , @ListPrice
    , @Size
    , @SizeUnitMeasureCode
    , @WeightUnitMeasureCode
    , @Weight
    , @DaysToManufacture
    , @ProductLine
    , @Class
    , @Style
    , @ProductSubCategoryID
    , @ProductModelID
    , NEWID()
    , @SellStartDate
    , @SellEndDate
-- Return the new ProductID key identity value --
RETURN @@IDENTITY
```

Modifying Records

When any data in a record or group of records is modified, the user or application making the changes must have exclusive access to the record or records for a short period of time. This locking mechanism is an important part of SQL Server's transaction management model. So, what exactly gets locked? This depends on different factors. SQL Server supports row-level locking and, when feasible, will lock a single row so that neighboring rows don't get locked, affecting other users. This was an issue in earlier versions of SQL Server that supported only page-level locking. In truth, SQL Server will sometimes lock all of the records in an 8KB page, SQL Server's native storage allocation unit. It may do this because it deems this method to be faster or more efficient than locking individual records. Based on inter-table relationships, when a row is modified in one table, locks may be placed on dependent rows in the related table. It may also choose to lock an entire table, groups of tables, or even the entire database, under certain circumstances.

The database engine must make decisions about how it will process each transaction. Based on the scope or number of records involved in a transaction, different locking options may be invoked to manage the transaction as efficiently as possible. With rare exception, this should be completely transparent to all users and operations. Any concurrent or conflicting requests are simply queued and executed in turn. Only after a transaction request has waited several seconds will it time-out and return an error. Fortunately, SQL Server manages record-locking and data modification automatically. Understanding the fundamentals of SQL Server's locking behavior will help you work with the database engine as you modify data. Multi-table updates and other conditions where you should be mindful of these issues are discussed at the end of this chapter.

UPDATE Command

Data is modified one table at a time. A single UPDATE statement can affect one, many, or all records in a table depending on filtering criteria. The syntax is uncomplicated. Column values are modified using the SET keyword.

Filtering Updates

There is no undo feature in T-SQL, short of restoring a backup. Because an update can affect many records, it is important to be absolutely sure of the records you intend to modify. To be cautious, a trial is advisable using only a SELECT query. Inspect the rows returned and then, after you verify that these are the rows you want to change and that the target values are correct, add the UPDATE command to your query. Here's an example. Our objective is to raise the standard cost for all mountain bikes by 10 percent. We are going to break this down into steps to verify the records and our calculation before actually performing the update.

You may recall that we used a similar query in Chapter 4 to raise the StandardCost. If you have worked through either of these exercises, the StandardCost values in your Product table may be different than ours.

The first step is to perform a simple SELECT query. This query returns the product name and current cost:

```
SELECT Name, StandardCost
FROM Production.Product
WHERE ProductSubCategoryID = 1
```

In the results, shown in Figure 10-7, we verify that these are all mountain bikes and that the StandardCost column contains the values we want to modify.

	Name	StandardCost
1	Mountain-100 Silver, 38	2103.3698
2	Mountain-100 Silver, 42	2103.3698
3	Mountain-100 Silver, 44	2103.3698
4	Mountain-100 Silver, 48	2103.3698
5	Mountain-100 Black, 38	2087.9038
6	Mountain-100 Black, 42	2087.9038
7	Mountain-100 Black, 44	2087.9038
8	Mountain-100 Black, 48	2087.9038
9	Mountain-200 Silver, 38	1392.1815
10	Mountain-200 Silver, 42	1392.1815
11	Mountain-200 Silver, 46	1392.1815

Figure 10-7

The next step is to calculate the new value for the StandardCost column. We'll create an additional column with the calculated value:

```
SELECT Name, StandardCost, StandardCost * 1.1
FROM Production.Product
WHERE ProductSubCategoryID = 1
```

Now, we check the calculated value and take a quick look over the entire list to make sure everything is in order (see Figure 10-8).

	Name	StandardCost	(No column name)
1	Mountain-100 Silver, 38	2103.3698	2313.70678
2	Mountain-100 Silver, 42	2103.3698	2313.70678
3	Mountain-100 Silver, 44	2103.3698	2313.70678
4	Mountain-100 Silver, 48	2103.3698	2313.70678
5	Mountain-100 Black, 38	2087.9038	2296.69418
6	Mountain-100 Black, 42	2087.9038	2296.69418
7	Mountain-100 Black, 44	2087.9038	2296.69418
8	Mountain-100 Black, 48	2087.9038	2296.69418
9	Mountain-200 Silver, 38	1392.1815	1531.39965
10	Mountain-200 Silver, 42	1392.1815	1531.39965

Figure 10-8

The calculated value is correct — a 10 percent increase — and the row selection is correct, so we'll move on to the next step and prepare to modify these rows.

The FROM clause gets moved to the top and becomes the UPDATE statement. We are dropping the Name column because it is not affected by this query, and then we are using the remaining two references to the StandardCost column to form the SET statement:

```
UPDATE Production.Product
SET StandardCost = StandardCost * 1.1
WHERE ProductSubCategoryID = 1
```

When this statement is executed in the Query Editor, no results are returned. The following message is displayed on the Messages tab after the name of your server and user name:

```
(32 row(s) affected)
```

To verify the results, we'll execute the first query again:

```
SELECT Name, StandardCost
FROM Production.Product
WHERE ProductSubCategoryID = 1
```

This time, the StandardCost values have increased by 10 percent, as shown in Figure 10-9.

	Name	StandardCost
1	Mountain-100 Silver, 38	2313.7068
2	Mountain-100 Silver, 42	2313.7068
3	Mountain-100 Silver, 44	2313.7068
4	Mountain-100 Silver, 48	2313.7068
5	Mountain-100 Black, 38	2296.6942
6	Mountain-100 Black, 42	2296.6942
7	Mountain-100 Black, 44	2296.6942
8	Mountain-100 Black, 48	2296.6942
9	Mountain-200 Silver, 38	1531.3997
10	Mountain-200 Silver, 42	1531.3997

Figure 10-9

When working with important data, we try to make it a point to test our queries in this way before actually performing the update. Often, we won't if it's a simple query and we are certain that we have it right the first time. However, we have learned that it's better to err on the side of caution. In any case, make sure you have a current backup copy of the data just in case things don't go as planned.

Now, let's look at some variations of the UPDATE statement. In the previous example, we updated one column value. Modifying multiple values is quite easy. You'll perform this exercise with a little less hand-holding. Begin by executing the following query to view all mountain bike products:

```
SELECT ProductID, Name, StandardCost, Color
FROM Production.Product
WHERE ProductSubCategoryID = 1
```

Make note of the first record. Unless you've run the next query before, the name should be *Mountain-100 Silver, 38*. Also make note of the StandardCost and Color column values. We want to change the color, cost, and the name. The name value will reflect the new color and a more descriptive frame size. Figure 10-10 shows these records.

	ProductID	Name	StandardCost	Color
1	771	Mountain-100 Silver, 38	2103.3698	Silver
2	772	Mountain-100 Silver, 42	2103.3698	Silver
3	773	Mountain-100 Silver, 44	2103.3698	Silver
4	774	Mountain-100 Silver, 48	2103.3698	Silver
5	775	Mountain-100 Black, 38	2087.9038	Black
6	776	Mountain-100 Black, 42	2087.9038	Black
7	777	Mountain-100 Black, 44	2087.9038	Black
8	778	Mountain-100 Black, 48	2087.9038	Black
9	779	Mountain-200 Silver, 38	1392.1815	Silver
10	780	Mountain-200 Silver, 42	1392.1815	Silver

Figure 10-10

Now update this record. Each column value assignment is included in a comma-delimited list in the SET statement. This statement shows how to update a product record with multiple column values:

```
UPDATE Production.Product
SET  Name = 'Mountain-100 Gold, 38mm'
   , StandardCost = 2200
   , Color = 'Gold'
WHERE ProductID = 771
```

This, of course, modifies only the silver 100 model, 38mm mountain bike. If you run the first of these two queries, you should see that it is now a gold bike along with the other changes made to the cost and name. The results are shown in Figure 10-11.

	ProductID	Name	StandardCost	Color
1	771	Mountain-100 Gold, 38mm	2200.0000	Gold
2	772	Mountain-100 Silver, 42	2103.3698	Silver
3	773	Mountain-100 Silver, 44	2103.3698	Silver
4	774	Mountain-100 Silver, 48	2103.3698	Silver
5	775	Mountain-100 Black, 38	2087.9038	Black
6	776	Mountain-100 Black, 42	2087.9038	Black
7	777	Mountain-100 Black, 44	2087.9038	Black
8	778	Mountain-100 Black, 48	2087.9038	Black
9	779	Mountain-200 Silver, 38	1392.1815	Silver
10	780	Mountain-200 Silver, 42	1392.1815	Silver

Figure 10-11

Updating Rows Based on Multiple Tables

Sometimes you will need to modify records in one table based on conditions in another table. This can be accomplished using a join or subquery. The rule is that you can only update column values in one table. In the following example, we join the SalesOrderHeader and SalesOrderDetail tables. Based on criteria in the header table, we modify the order quantity value in the related detail row:

```
UPDATE    SOD
SET       OrderQty = 10
FROM      Sales.SalesOrderDetail SOD
INNER JOIN Sales.SalesOrderHeader SOH
          ON SOD.SalesOrderID = SOH.SalesOrderID
WHERE     SOH.PurchaseOrderNumber = 'PO29199294'
```

In this case, there is only one related detail row but there could be multiple detail rows related to the header row.

When setting values, it's common to derive those values from various system functions. One of the simplest and most common of these functions is GETDATE(), which returns the current date and time. Using this function, we'll stamp an order record to indicate that it has been shipped. First, we'll set the stage for this scenario. In the AdventureWorks2008 database, all the order records have already been marked as having been shipped. Suppose that a customer calls your customer service department asking about their order. You look up the order and see that it is marked as having been shipped to the customer. Upon careful investigation, you discover that the package was returned because the customer's address was incorrect. Your first order of business is to update the record to indicate that it was not shipped (or at least not received by the customer). The order in question is SalesOrderID 5005. This statement will remove the ship date, setting it to NULL:

```
UPDATE Sales.SalesOrderHeader
SET ShipDate = NULL
WHERE SalesOrderID = 43659
```

Now you obtain the correct address and schedule the package for shipment. Once confirmed, you update the order record with the current data and time using the GETDATE() function:

```
UPDATE Sales.SalesOrderHeader
SET ShipDate = GETDATE()
WHERE SalesOrderID = 43659
```

Updating Using Views

Most database professionals agree that the traditional purpose for views is to provide a read-only view of data from tables. One of the most compelling capabilities is that sensitive data can be secured and protected — both selected rows and columns hidden from the user's view. Complicated queries and joins can be represented as if they were a single table. We don't normally think of these "virtual tables" as being updatable, but it is possible to update records through views under certain conditions. Updates can only affect the columns of one table at a time. Further, values created by grouping and aggregation cannot be updated. As a rule, if you intend to create a view to support updates, it should either reference only one table or multiple tables through inner joins. All required columns must be included, and update statements must include only references to a single table within the view. If you plan to perform updates through existing views, be prepared for a bumpy ride as there are very specific requirements about indexes and locking options that can make this practice quite restrictive.

Updating Records Using Stored Procedures

Probably the most comprehensive and secure method for managing record updates is to allow updates only through stored procedures. When this approach is taken, a separate stored procedure is typically used to modify the records for each major entity in the database. The following example is a stored procedure to modify a record in the MyContacts table we created earlier.

```
CREATE PROCEDURE spUpd_MyContacts
    @ContactID      int
  , @FirstName      nvarchar(50)
  , @LastName       nvarchar(50)
  , @Phone          nvarchar(25)
AS
    UPDATE MyContacts
    SET FirstName = @FirstName
      , LastName = @LastName
      , Phone = @Phone
```

Executing this procedure is simple. We just pass the ContactID used to identify the record we want to update along with the values for each column as parameters defined in the procedure script:

```
spUpd_MyContacts 5, 'Betrice', 'Rubble', '(222) 234-7654'
```

Here's an example of a slightly more sophisticated stored procedure that updates a record in the Product table. Note that the required parameters are listed first, followed by those with defaults that can be ignored when the procedure is called. We've made a point to include all of the columns in this table just to demonstrate what this would normally look like:

```
CREATE PROCEDURE spUpd_Product
    @ProductID           Int
  , @ProductName         nVarChar(50)
  , @StandardCost        Money
  , @SafetyStockLevel    SmallInt
  , @ReorderPoint        SmallInt
  , @ListPrice           Money
  , @DaysToManufacture   Int
  , @SellStartDate       DateTime
  , @DiscontinuedDate    DateTime = Null
  , @MakeFlag            Bit = 1
  , @FinishedGoodsFlag   Bit = 1
  , @Color               nVarChar(15) = Null
  , @Size                nVarChar(50) = Null
  , @SizeUnitMeasureCode   nChar(3) = Null
  , @WeightUnitMeasureCode nChar(3) = Null
  , @Weight              Float = Null
  , @ProductLine         nChar(2) = Null
  , @Class               nChar(2) = Null
  , @Style               nChar(2) = Null
  , @ProductSubCategoryID  SmallInt = Null
  , @ProductModelID      Int = Null
  , @SellEndDate         DateTime = Null
```

(continued)

315

(continued)

```
AS
UPDATE Production.Product
SET
    Name                     = @ProductName
  , DiscontinuedDate         = @DiscontinuedDate
  , MakeFlag                 = @MakeFlag
  , StandardCost             = @StandardCost
  , FinishedGoodsFlag        = @FinishedGoodsFlag
  , Color                    = @Color
  , SafetyStockLevel         = @SafetyStockLevel
  , ReorderPoint             = @ReorderPoint
  , ListPrice                = @ListPrice
  , Size                     = @Size
  , SizeUnitMeasureCode      = @SizeUnitMeasureCode
  , WeightUnitMeasureCode    = @WeightUnitMeasureCode
  , Weight                   = @Weight
  , DaysToManufacture        = @DaysToManufacture
  , ProductLine              = @ProductLine
  , Class                    = @Class
  , Style                    = @Style
  , ProductSubCategoryID     = @ProductSubCategoryID
  , ProductModelID           = @ProductModelID
  , rowguid                  = NEWID()
  , SellStartDate            = @SellStartDate
  , SellEndDate              = @SellEndDate
WHERE ProductID = @ProductID
```

Note that most of the parameters in the list of input parameters (the variable names preceded with @) are assigned default values. Some accept NULL whereas others, such as @MakeFlag and @FinishedGoodsFlag, are set to the bit value 1, or True. This is so these parameters are optional when executing the procedure. The rowguid column is set using the NEWID() function to generate a unique value. This may or may not be appropriate logic in an update procedure and will depend on specific business requirements. We have included this just to demonstrate a variety of techniques for setting values.

This stored procedure is actually simplified. In production, procedures typically include some conditional business logic and error-handling code. These scripts can be time consuming and cumbersome to write. However, once written and debugged, using stored procedures can significantly simplify data management going forward. Chapter 13 revisits this stored procedure when discussing the finer points of database programming.

Removing Records

Removing records from a table is very easy to do — maybe too easy. Depending on your viewpoint, this convenience could be a blessing or a curse. Take care before you start practicing your deleting skills on production data. Having said that, we are going to ask SQL Server to delete all of the product records in the AdventureWorks database.

DELETE Command

As you can see, this is a simple statement. There is no need to address specific columns because the DELETE statement removes entire rows of data:

```
DELETE FROM Production.Product
```

The FROM clause is actually optional. Personally, we find it a little easier to read this statement with the FROM clause but that's a minor point. This statement does the same thing:

```
DELETE Production.Product
```

Did it work? No. SQL Server returned an error, fortunately:

```
The DELETE statement conflicted with the REFERENCE constraint
"FK_ProductInventory_Product_ProductID". The conflict occurred in database
"AdventureWorks", table "Production.ProductInventory", column 'ProductID'.
The statement has been terminated.
```

Due to the foreign key constraint displayed in the error the statement failed. The database won't allow rows to be deleted if there are related rows in another table. What about the product records that do not have related records in another table? That's not going to happen either, because every Insert, Update, and Delete statement is automatically wrapped into a transaction. You'll recall that transactions are an all-or-nothing proposition; either all the records are affected or none of them are. In this case, no records are affected.

Embrace the WHERE Clause

Just as when updating records, it's important to test the water and make sure you delete the records you intend to. The Product table has foreign key constraints defined with several tables, which make it difficult to delete existing records. For demonstration purposes, we'll add a few products that we can play with:

```
INSERT INTO Production.Product (Name, ProductNumber, StandardCost, ListPrice,
SafetyStockLevel, ReorderPoint, DaysToManufacture, SellStartDate)
VALUES
   ( 'Widget 2002', 'wi002', 50.05, 49.99, 10, 5, 2, GETDATE() )
 ,( 'Widget 2003', 'wi003', 55.97, 49.99, 10, 5, 2, GETDATE() )
 ,( 'Widget 2004', 'wi004', 42.97, 49.99, 10, 5, 2, GETDATE() )
 ,( 'Widget 2005', 'wi005', 45.97, 49.99, 10, 5, 2, GETDATE() )
```

Your objective is to remove all product records for products that would be unprofitable to sell, where the ListPrice is less than the StandardCost. Before actually deleting any records, test your criteria using a SELECT statement:

```
SELECT ProductID, Name, ProductNumber, ListPrice, StandardCost
FROM Production.Product
WHERE StandardCost > ListPrice
```

Two rows meet these criteria, as shown in Figure 10-12.

	ProductID	Name	ProductNumber	ListPrice	StandardCost
1	1012	Widget 2002	wi002	49.9900	50.0500
2	1014	Widget 2003	wi003	49.9900	55.9700

Figure 10-12

After verifying that these are the records you intend to delete, write the DELETE statement, appending this WHERE clause to the end to affect the same records:

```
DELETE FROM Production.Product
WHERE StandardCost > ListPrice
```

These two records are deleted.

Deleting Records Based on Another Table

You may need to remove records from one table based on conditions in another table. Usually there will be a relationship of some kind between these tables. Deletes can be facilitated using any type of join or subquery expression between multiple tables.

In this scenario, suppose that one of your salespeople, Amy Alberts, has left the company and you want to archive all of the related sales orders and detail records. You've already copied these records to their respective archive tables so now all you need to do is delete them. Amy was the salesperson for 39 sales order records with 586 related order detail records.

Before we continue, we would like to work with backup copies of the SalesOrderDetail and SalesOrderHeader tables. This will allow us to delete records without affecting the existing sample data already in the AdventureWorks database. Execute the following script to create a new copy of this table:

```
SELECT * INTO MySalesOrderDetail FROM Sales.SalesOrderDetail
SELECT * INTO MySalesOrderHeader FROM Sales.SalesOrderHeader
```

The following queries will use the new MySalesOrderDetail and MySalesOrderHeader tables without removing any records from the existing tables. For the purpose of this exercise, assume that we are using the SalesOrderDetail and SalesOrderHeader tables instead of the copies we just created.

Try It Out

Figure 10-13 shows the relationship between the tables involved. By specifying an EmployeeID (on the left side of the diagram), you can delete related SalesOrderDetail rows. The SalesOrderHeader, which defines orders, is related to the SalesPerson table through the SalesPersonID foreign key. This is a many-to-many intersect table between Employee and SalesOrderHeader. Order details, in the SalesOrderDetail table, are related to orders through the SalesOrderID foreign key column. Because it is on the outer side of the relationships and nothing else depends on it, begin by deleting rows from this table first.

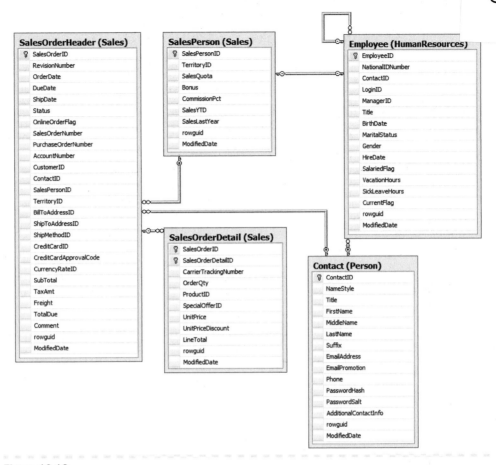

Figure 10-13

There are a few techniques and this is one of the easiest. Earlier you saw how the IN() function is used to compare a value to a comma-delimited list of values. The same function can be used to compare a value with a single-column result set. The mechanics are simple: create any SELECT query that returns a single column, and then pass the results of this query to the IN() function used in the WHERE clause of a DELETE statement.

For the SQL Server 2008 AdventureWorks2008 database:

```
DELETE FROM MySalesOrderDetail
WHERE SalesOrderID IN
        (
         SELECT MSOD.SalesOrderID
         FROM
            MySalesOrderDetail AS MSOD INNER JOIN MySalesOrderHeader AS MSOH
```

```
                   ON MSOD.SalesOrderID = MSOH.SalesOrderID
            INNER JOIN Sales.SalesPerson AS SP
                 ON MSOH.SalesPersonID = SP.BusinessEntityID
            INNER JOIN HumanResources.Employee AS E
                 ON SP.BusinessEntityID = E.BusinessEntityID
            INNER JOIN Person.Person AS C
                 ON E.BusinessEntityID = C.BusinessEntityID
            WHERE C.FirstName = 'Amy' AND C.LastName = 'Alberts'
            )
```

For the SQL Server 2005 AdventureWorks database:

```
DELETE FROM MySalesOrderDetail
WHERE SalesOrderID IN
        (
            SELECT MSOD.SalesOrderID
            FROM
              MySalesOrderDetail AS MSOD INNER JOIN MySalesOrderHeader AS MSOH
                 ON MSOD.SalesOrderID = MSOH.SalesOrderID
            INNER JOIN Sales.SalesPerson AS SP
              ON MSOH.SalesPersonID = SP.SalesPersonID
            INNER JOIN HumanResources.Employee AS E
              ON SP.SalesPersonID = E.EmployeeID
            INNER JOIN Person.Contact AS C
              ON E.ContactID = C.ContactID
            WHERE C.FirstName = 'Amy' AND C.LastName = 'Alberts'
            )
```

This deletes the 586 order detail records. Removing the sales order records is easy and requires only a simple change. Because the SalesOrderID is also the identifying column for records in the MySalesOrderHeader table, all you need to do is change the table name in the DELETE statement and the join.

For the SQL Server 2008 AdventureWorks2008 database:

```
DELETE FROM MySalesOrderHeader
WHERE    SalesOrderID IN
         (
            SELECT MSOH.SalesOrderID
            FROM MySalesOrderHeader AS MSOH
              INNER JOIN Sales.SalesPerson AS SP
                ON MSOH.SalesPersonID = SP.BusinessEntityID
              INNER JOIN HumanResources.Employee AS E
                ON SP.BusinessEntityID = E.BusinessEntityID
              INNER JOIN Person.Person AS C
                ON E.BusinessEntityID = C.BusinessEntityID
            WHERE C.FirstName = 'Amy' AND C.LastName = 'Alberts'
            )
 For the SQL Server 2005 AdventureWorks database:DELETE FROM
MySalesOrderHeader
WHERE    SalesOrderID IN
```

```
        (
            SELECT MSOH.SalesOrderID
            FROM MySalesOrderHeader AS MSOH
                INNER JOIN Sales.SalesPerson AS SP
                    ON MSOH.SalesPersonID = SP.SalesPersonID
                INNER JOIN HumanResources.Employee AS E
                    ON SP.SalesPersonID = E.EmployeeID
                INNER JOIN Person.Contact AS C
                    ON E.ContactID = C.ContactID
            WHERE C.FirstName = 'Amy' AND C.LastName = 'Alberts'
        )
```

This deletes the 39 sales orders. If you were working with the original tables and not the backup copies, it would be necessary to delete the order detail rows first because these records depend on the existence of the sales order records in the SalesOrderHeader table.

TRUNCATE TABLE

The DELETE command is a logged operation. For deletes on a small number of rows or manual operations, there may be a negligible difference in performance. However, for repeated and automated deletes, or on a large volume of records, skipping the transaction logging can improve performance dramatically.

The TRUNCATE TABLE command does only one thing — it removes all of the records in a table without logging a transaction. It performs the deletes in a manner far more efficiently than the DELETE command. You cannot filter specific rows to delete or use any kind of selection criteria. This statement will very efficiently remove all order detail records from the backup copy of the table:

```
TRUNCATE TABLE MySalesOrderDetail
```

We are going to do a performance test, comparing the DELETE and TRUNCATE techniques. We don't intend for you to follow along because it would take a bit of work to set this up. Before running the following script, we have created two additional databases, called AW_1 and AW_2. Using an SSIS package, we copied all of the objects and data from AdventureWorks into each of these two identical databases. The following script gets the current time before and after performing each of these two operations. After each, we compare the two times and display the number of milliseconds that it took to complete the operation.

```
DECLARE @starttime DateTime
DECLARE @endtime DateTime
DECLARE @totaltime Int
USE AW_1 -- Copy 1 of AdventureWorks DB:
SET @starttime = GetDate()
DELETE FROM Sales.SalesOrderDetail
SET @endtime = GetDate()
SET @totaltime = DateDiff(ms, @starttime, @endtime)
PRINT 'Time to Delete:   ' + CONVERT(VarChar(10), @totaltime)
USE AW_2 -- Copy 2 of AdventureWorks DB:
```

(continued)

(continued)

```
SET @starttime = GetDate()
TRUNCATE TABLE Sales.SalesOrderDetail
SET @endtime = GetDate()
SET @totaltime = DateDiff(ms, @starttime, @endtime)
PRINT 'Time to Truncate: ' + CONVERT(VarChar(10), @totaltime)
```

The results are as follows:

```
(121371 row(s) affected)
Time to Delete:   14030ms
Time to Truncate: 130ms
```

The Truncate technique takes less than 1 percent of the time it took to process the DELETE statement. The Delete operation took about 14 seconds and the Truncate operation took about ¹/₇ of a second. That's a big difference! This is because transactional operations are physically written to the transaction log and then rolled forward into the table, one row at a time. The TRUNCATE statement doesn't do all of this. It simply deallocates all the data pages for a table. In reality, data in these pages is not actually changed, but the pointer entries in the index allocation map for these pages are removed. Eventually, data left in the pages gets overwritten but is not really removed.

The only limitation of the TRUNCATE command is that it is a privileged command and only database owners or system administrators can execute it, even if it is encapsulated in a stored procedure.

Automating Inserts, Updates, and Deletes with the MERGE Command

One of the classic challenges when loading a group of records into a table is how to identify and deal with existing records in the target table. A common scenario is to insert a record if it doesn't exist, and update the existing record using the data in the source table if it does exist. In the past, it was necessary to write complex stored procedures to implement all of this logic and explicitly perform the INSERT or UPDATE commands for each record depending on whether certain columns in the source and destination matched up. This technique is commonly referred to as an "UPSERT" (Get it? Update . . . Insert. We guess it wasn't that hard to figure out, huh?)

Thanks to our good friends at Microsoft, SQL Server 2008 now includes a new command called MERGE that automatically implements this "upsert" logic and then performs the appropriate insert or update action based on the criteria provided. The MERGE command can also be used to completely synchronize two different sets of data by also deleting target records based on missing records or other criteria in the source. The language of the MERGE command is not a lot different than you would write yourself in a query using all of the component commands but because the logic is optimized and implemented at a lower level within the query processing engine, it should offer better performance than a custom-written stored procedure. To demonstrate, we will create a new table called MyOtherContacts and populate it with a few Contact records.

For the SQL Server 2008 AdventureWorks2008 database:

```
SELECT TOP 5 CONVERT(nvarchar(10), NULL) AS Title, FirstName, LastName INTO
MyOtherContacts FROM Person.Person
```

For the SQL Server 2005 AdventureWorks database:

```
SELECT TOP 5 CONVERT(nvarchar(10), NULL) AS Title, FirstName, LastName INTO
MyOtherContacts FROM Person.Contact
```

The Title column is set with NULL values so we can update them later. We have made a point to use the nvarchar data type so it is compatible with any incoming Title values. Next, we'll add some records that don't match any existing Contact rows:

```
INSERT INTO MyOtherContacts (FirstName, LastName)
VALUES
    ( 'George', 'Jetson' )
  , ( 'Jane', 'Jetson' )
```

Figure 10-14 shows the target table before we make any changes to the data. Note the five records inserted from the Contact table and the two records we added.

	Title	FirstName	LastName
1	NULL	George	Jetson
2	NULL	Jane	Jetson
3	NULL	Gustavo	Achong
4	NULL	Catherine	Abel
5	NULL	Kim	Abercrombie
6	NULL	Humberto	Acevedo
7	NULL	Pilar	Ackerman

Figure 10-14

Now, let's review the business rules for the merge query:

❑ If the MyOtherContacts table contains any records matching those in the Contact table, we want to update these rows with matching Title values.

❑ If the Contact table contains records that don't match any in the MyOtherContacts, they should be inserted into MyOtherContacts.

❑ If the MyOtherContacts table contains records that don't match any in the Contact, they should be deleted.

The following example performs these operations in one query. We are limiting the records from the Contact table to keep things manageable and because there are some duplicate FirstName and LastName values in the table that could complicate things. The MERGE statement specifies the table to be affected. The USING statement is used to specify a table or query to test for matching records with a special join operator in the ON clause. To make the updated records more obvious, we are converting the Title values to upper case. Note the matching logic in the qualifying statements; MATCHED, NOT

MATCHED, and SOURCE NOT MATCHED. These statements are used to determine whether rows in the first table (the source) match or don't match records in the second table (the target) based on the logic in the ON clause.

```
For the SQL Server 2008 AdventureWorks2008 database:MERGE MyOtherContacts AS
MOC
USING
    (SELECT TOP 10 Title, FirstName, LastName FROM Person.Person) AS C
    ON ( MOC.FirstName = C.FirstName AND MOC.LastName = C.LastName )
WHEN MATCHED THEN
    UPDATE SET MOC.Title = UPPER(C.Title)
WHEN NOT MATCHED THEN
    INSERT ( Title, FirstName, LastName )
    VALUES ( C.Title, C.FirstName, C.LastName )
WHEN NOT MATCHED BY SOURCE THEN
    DELETE
;
```

For the SQL Server 2005 AdventureWorks database:

```
MERGE MyOtherContacts AS MOC
USING
    (SELECT TOP 10 Title, FirstName, LastName FROM Person.Contact) AS C
    ON ( MOC.FirstName = C.FirstName AND MOC.LastName = C.LastName )
WHEN MATCHED THEN
    UPDATE SET MOC.Title = UPPER(C.Title)
WHEN NOT MATCHED THEN
    INSERT ( Title, FirstName, LastName )
    VALUES ( C.Title, C.FirstName, C.LastName )
WHEN NOT MATCHED BY SOURCE THEN
    DELETE
;
```

Finally, take a look at the results in Figure 10-15. Note that the five original contact records have titles in uppercase as a result of the UPDATE statement. The two records that didn't exist in the Contact table have been deleted and an additional five contact records have been inserted.

	Title	First Name	Last Name
2	Ms.	Margaret	Smith
3	Ms.	Carla	Adams
4	Mr.	Jay	Adams
5	Mr.	Ronald	Adina
6	MR.	Gustavo	Achong
7	MS.	Catherine	Abel
8	MS.	Kim	Abercrombie
9	SR.	Humberto	Acevedo
10	SRA.	Pilar	Ackerman

Figure 10-15

A thorough discussion of the MERGE command would require this book to move from the beginning to advanced category. Suffice to say that there is much more you can do with this new product feature by combining the simple application you've seen here with complex joins and conditional logic.

Explicit Transactions

You saw how all insert, update, and delete statements are automatically wrapped into an auto-commit transaction. This means that each of these operations creates a unique entry in the transaction log.

With the exception of the TRUNCATE command, all data modifications are performed in two steps. The two steps are not necessarily sequential and in fact they occur independently of one another. One step is to write all transactions sequentially to the transaction log. This happens quickly because the disk heads don't have to be repositioned and it's not necessary to find free data pages as if writing to a table. The database engine then considers all of the constraints defined for the target table and simply checks to see if the operation would violate those constraints. If not, the transaction succeeds even though the data hasn't been physically written to the table. Any operations that are waiting behind this one are allowed to proceed and users perceive that the database has completed their request.

The second step that occurs is completed by a background process called the *checkpoint*. The checkpoint occurs at dynamic intervals depending on the amount of data modifications occurring in the database. The more modifications and thus transactions that occur, the more checkpoints are issued by the database engine. A checkpoint can occur anywhere in a transaction or at the end of a transaction. Whenever SQL Server detects that a predetermined number of data pages have been modified, it executes a checkpoint. This setting is adjustable but is beyond the scope of this book. It is the database server's job to balance new transaction requests with pending transactions that have been committed but not yet written to disk by the checkpoint process. When the checkpoint runs, it writes all dirty pages (pages modified by transactions) to disk, but does not release them. The pages are freed when released by a completed transaction. Checkpoints are recorded in the transaction log so SQL Server knows where it left off. When SQL Server is restarted, such as in the case of a power failure or during a database restore, SQL Server finds the last checkpoint in the transaction log and rolls all transactions that committed after the checkpoint forward, writing them to disk. All incomplete transactions that were written to disk during the checkpoint are rolled back, or "undone" so that the database is in a consistent state.

Different operations that need to be processed as a unit should be executed within a stated transaction. For example, if you plan to move a group of records from one table to another, you don't want to insert rows into one table if the corresponding delete doesn't take place for the other table. To create an explicit transaction, begin the script with the BEGIN TRANSACTION statement. Any operations that follow will only be completed when the COMMIT TRANSACTION statement is issued.

Explicit transactions should be used whenever multiple modifications are dependent on each other. The chief advantage that explicit transactions bring to data modifications is that you can check for any errors in your operations prior to committing the transaction. If any errors are present you rollback the transaction. If no errors are detected, you commit the transactions. A common misconception is that transactions automatically supply this error detection. Nothing could be further from the truth.

As an example, we will create a Savings account table and a Checking account table and then place a check constraint on the checking account table that enforces a minimum balance of $100.00. We will then populate the tables with data:

```
CREATE TABLE MySavings
(AccountNum Int NOT NULL,
 Amount Money NOT NULL)
CREATE TABLE MyChecking
(AccountNum Int NOT NULL,
 Amount Money NOT NULL)
ALTER TABLE MyChecking ADD CONSTRAINT ckMinBalance
CHECK (Amount > $100.00)
INSERT MySavings
VALUES
   (12345, $1000.00)

INSERT MyChecking
VALUES
   (12345,  $1000.00)
```

Now that we have our two bank accounts set up, we will try to transfer $990.00 from our checking account to our savings account inside an explicit transaction:

```
BEGIN TRANSACTION

  UPDATE MyChecking SET Amount = Amount - $990.00
  WHERE AccountNum = 12345
  UPDATE MySavings SET Amount = Amount + $990.00
  WHERE AccountNum = 12345
COMMIT TRANSACTION
```

The result of this transaction looks like this:

```
The UPDATE statement conflicted with the CHECK constraint "ckMinBalance".
The conflict occurred in database "AdventureWorks2008", table
"dbo.MyChecking",column 'Amount'.
```

The message means that something unintended has happened. A query of the savings account and checking account table reveals an interesting outcome:

```
SELECT Amount AS CheckingAmount FROM MyChecking WHERE AccountNum = 12345
SELECT Amount AS SavingsAmount FROM MySavings WHERE AccountNum = 12345
CheckingAmount
--------------------
1000.00
SavingsAmount
--------------------
1990.00
```

The checking account still has its original balance, but the savings account balance is now increased by $990.00. This is because the update to the checking account was aborted when it violated the minimum balance constraint. However, because we did not do anything about the error, SQL Server continued with the next update and obediently modified the savings account balance, and then committed the transaction, just like we told it to. Good for us, bad for the bank. To prevent this from happening you must add error checking to your transactions.

Chapter 13 covers error handling in greater detail, but for now it is important to see how error handling must be included in transactions to guarantee their consistency. Up to SQL Server 2000, there were very few options for effectively handling errors. This capability was improved considerably in SQL Server 2005 and of course in the current product version. The technique involves the use of TRY . . . CATCH blocks, similar to modern object-oriented programming languages. In T-SQL, TRY and CATCH are separate code blocks. The first code block starts with BEGIN TRY and concludes with END TRY. If this code fails for any reason, execution is set to the first line of code under the BEGIN CATCH statement and then execution continues until the END CATCH statement is reached. In essence, we are saying "Try to run this block of code. If it fails, catch the error and send it to the error-handling code block." Code in the CATCH block runs only if an error is caught within the TRY block.

Executing the following script simply returns an error and does not alter either of the records. This is because an error is thrown in the TRY block and then caught in the CATCH block, causing the entire transaction to be aborted and rolled back:

```
BEGIN TRANSACTION
  BEGIN TRY
    UPDATE MyChecking SET Amount = Amount - $990.00
    WHERE AccountNum = 12345
    UPDATE MySavings SET Amount = Amount + $990.00
    WHERE AccountNum = 12345
    COMMIT TRANSACTION
  END TRY

  BEGIN CATCH
    RAISERROR('Transaction Aborted', 16, 1)
    ROLLBACK TRANSACTION
  END CATCH
```

You can also use the shorthand version of these statements, substituting TRAN for the word TRANSACTION:

```
BEGIN TRAN
COMMIT TRAN
ROLLBACK TRAN
```

Summary

Whether you explicitly declare a transaction or not, all data inserts, updates, and deletes are managed as transactional operations. SQL Server uses the transaction log to queue requested operations and to test validation rules prior to completing the physical operations on rows in the tables. Transactions provide the mechanism to guarantee that all operations either complete successfully or fail altogether. Multiple operations can be explicitly included in a single transaction to ensure that they are managed as an autonomous unit.

Chapter 13 discusses how inserts, updates, and deletes can be managed in secured stored procedures. The INSERT statement supports two different syntax forms, either using the VALUES keyword or SELECT. Using SELECT is more flexible and allows values to be retrieved from other tables and sources.

When updating data, the database engine will lock data at various levels, depending on the scope of the operation and user concurrency. Locking may occur at the row, page, table, or database level. Updates and deletes should always be tested using a SELECT statement before they are performed. These operations may be irreversible without a backup of the database.

The DELETE command allows affected rows to be filtered, based on practically any criteria. For large-scale delete operations, this comes at the cost of transaction management. The TRUNCATE command offers a far more efficient method to effectively remove all rows in a table without the overhead of having to log and manage the deletions as transactions, but can only be executed by a user with elevated privileges.

Exercises

Exercise 1

Create a new product category for Snorkels. Demonstrate two methods to add a record to this table using the SELECT and VALUES statements.

Exercise 2

Populate a new table called RoadBikes with the contents of product records of this subcategory. Your query must filter on the value Road Bike.

Exercise 3

Insert the entire contents of the Product table into a table called MyProducts. Write a query that will delete MyProducts records for products that do not have sales order detail records and where the SubCategoryID is 5. Also write a query that will add a new record to the ProductSubCategory table with the Name column value set to Accessory and ProductCategoryID set to 4. Include both of these statements in a single transaction and execute them in a batch. Check the row count of the MyProducts table before and after to determine whether records were deleted.

Advanced Capabilities

This chapter introduces you to a variety of technologies and features that go beyond standard queries and simple data manipulation. First, you learn to use the new PIVOT and UNPIVOT operators to rotate and rearrange denormalized data structures for reporting and summarization. The next section explores a variety of tools designed to work with text matching and indexing large text fields. These include using the SOUNDEX and DIFFERENCE functions to compare text and to perform approximate phonetic matching. You will learn to use full-text indexes and a collection of functions specifically designed to find patterns and similarities between large text fields, comments, and notes stored in a database.

Pivoting Data

I have to say that this is one of the more interesting newer features in SQL Server. It is interesting for a variety of reasons. Back in 1970, when E. F. Codd first introduced the principles of relational database design in his paper, "A Relational Model of Data for Large Shared Data Banks," for the Association of Computing Machinery, his principles became the foundation on which many of today's fundamental, industry-wide database design patterns are based. The cornerstone of these paramount design rules is the first rule of normal form, which states that an entity shouldn't contain duplicate types of attributes. This means that a table shouldn't have more than one column that represents the same type of non-distinct value; or, in other words, like values shouldn't be repeated across multiple columns in the same row.

Adhering to and practicing this belief is the cornerstone and premise for all our database work. I sincerely believe that rules are meant to be honored and that those who were insightful enough to put these rules into place should be respected and revered. However, I also believe that there is a time and a place where after careful consideration one may cautiously consider breaking certain rules.

So far, all the data we have worked with has been pretty much the same — in columnar structure, adhering to first normal form. Every column in the result set comes from a field in the underlying table and the rows in the results are copied directly from records in the table. Even when we used a GROUP BY clause, each resulting row was derived from a collection of rows having similar values. The structure of the result sets is still the same. Conversely, pivoting data modifies the structure of the underlying data source by repeating like values across rows — essentially breaking first normal form.

Consider the following simple example in this hypothetical table:

OrderYear	Category	SalesAmount
2004	Bikes	45,000
2004	Clothing	22,500
2005	Accessories	28,450
2005	Bikes	57,325
2005	Clothing	31,200
2006	Accessories	32,765
2006	Bikes	61,985
2006	Clothing	34,570
2007	Accessories	39,700
2007	Bikes	75,775
2007	Clothing	42,650

The business user who will use this data primarily for reporting and decision making wants to see product sales by year and then by category. The most effective way to present these values to meet this requirement might be to place the distinct year values on the column headings and the categories in the row labels, with the aggregated sales amounts at the intersect point for each combination of the column and row axes. There are plenty of client tools that can do this within their interface. If you have used an Excel PivotTable, a Microsoft Access Cross Tab query, or the Reporting Services Matrix (or now the SSRS 2008 Tablix in matrix view), you may be familiar with this type of data presentation. Columns are simply derived from groups of distinct values, obtained from one field in the source, just as rows are grouped together in a GROUP BY query.

Let's take a look at a simple example, using Microsoft Office Excel 2007 to build a PivotTable with the values from the previous table. If you have Excel 2007, you are welcome to follow along, but this is not a requirement. Figure 11-1 shows the values from the table typed into a new Excel worksheet.

	A	B	C
1	OrderYear	Category	SalesAmount
2	2004	Bikes	45,000
3	2004	Clothing	22,500
4	2005	Accessories	28,450
5	2005	Bikes	57,325
6	2005	Clothing	31,200
7	2006	Accessories	32,765
8	2006	Bikes	61,985
9	2006	Clothing	34,570
10	2007	Accessories	39,700
11	2007	Bikes	75,775
12	2007	Clothing	42,650

Figure 11-1

I will select the cells in this range and then choose the menu option to insert a PivotTable. After I accept the selected cells as the default source range, a new PivotTable is inserted into a new worksheet. When any part of the PivotTable is selected in the worksheet, a design pane is displayed in a panel to the right. Using the Field List pane, I will drag the OrderYear into the Column Labels, the Category into Row Labels, and the SalesAmount into the Values list box. As shown in Figure 11-2, this builds a PivotTable with summarized sales values at the intersection of each year and category heading.

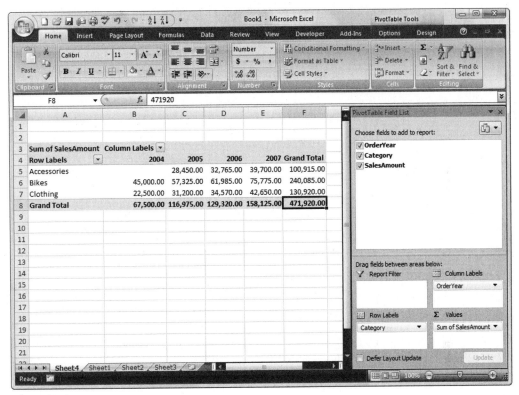

Figure 11-2

The PIVOT Operator

When data is grouped on more than one set of values, it might be convenient to display grouped values as separate columns, rather than as rows. This might not be the optimal way to store this data, but it is how we may want to present it. A similar style of presentation to the PivotTable is now possible in a T-SQL query by using the PIVOT function. Pivoting data allows you to transform data stored in compliance with first normal form but displayed with repeating column attributes.

There is a catch, however. When the Excel PivotTable was applied to the range of SalesYear values, it automatically created a set of distinct column values based on the existing OrderYear values. If you were to modify the source table and add a set of records for 2008, these would simply show up as another column in the PivotTable. The PIVOT command doesn't have this capability. You have to know ahead of time which values you want to include for the column headings, and then you must define static buckets for grouping the data. You do this by providing a list of columns in your query with the values for column grouping.

This is best explained through an example. I'll demonstrate this with a small set of sample records from the SalesOrderHeader table in the AdventureWorks database. The following T-SQL query approximates the PivotTable behavior:

```
SELECT TerritoryID, [7-1-2001], [7-2-2001], [7-3-2001], [7-4-2001], [7-5-2001]
FROM
    (
        SELECT TOP 59
            TotalDue
            , OrderDate
            , TerritoryID
        FROM Sales.SalesOrderHeader
    )   AS Source
PIVOT
    (
        Sum(TotalDue) FOR OrderDate
            IN ([7-1-2001], [7-2-2001], [7-3-2001], [7-4-2001], [7-5-2001])
    )   AS pvt
```

The result is a simple, well-organized matrix of date values along the columns with rows of TerritoryIDs and summed up monetary values at the intersection of each set of column/row headings. Figure 11-3 shows the results — the total amount due for each sales territory and for each day, in the first five days of July, 2001.

	TerritoryID	7-1-2001	7-2-2001	7-3-2001	7-4-2001	7-5-2001
1	1	128233.7408	NULL	NULL	3953.9884	NULL
2	2	28639.5233	NULL	NULL	NULL	NULL
3	3	25480.7357	NULL	NULL	NULL	NULL
4	4	133569.035	3953.9884	7907.9768	NULL	3953.9884
5	5	184509.7436	NULL	NULL	NULL	NULL
6	6	157316.2035	NULL	NULL	NULL	NULL
7	7	3756.989	NULL	NULL	NULL	NULL
8	8	NULL	NULL	NULL	3953.9884	NULL
9	9	3756.989	11440.3414	7907.9768	NULL	8680.4804
10	10	NULL	NULL	772.5036	NULL	3953.9884

Figure 11-3

I'll break this query into pieces so that we can examine its components and the mechanics of how it works. There are three main sections that can be viewed as separate queries: the main SELECT list, an inner query, and the PIVOT operation. I'll show them to you in logical order, beginning with each component.

The inner query

```
SELECT TOP 59 TotalDue, OrderDate, TerritoryID FROM Sales.SalesOrderHeader
```

simply returns 59 rows, including five distinct OrderDate values, ranging from July 1, 2001, through July 5, 2001. These rows also include ten distinct TerritoryID values, ranging from 1 through 10. This result is fed to the main SELECT statement:

```
SELECT TerritoryID, [7-1-2001], [7-2-2001], [7-3-2001], [7-4-2001], [7-5-2001]
FROM
...
```

This is where the pivot columns are set up, providing a "shell" for the PIVOT operation to fill. The last section of the query is the actual PIVOT operation. This performs an aggregation (in this case, using the SUM function) that groups aggregated TotalDue values by distinct OrderDate values within the list provided to the IN function (this is the same list of OrderDate values I included earlier in the column list):

```
PIVOT
  (
      Sum(TotalDue) FOR OrderDate
      IN ([7-1-2001], [7-2-2001], [7-3-2001], [7-4-2001], [7-5-2001])
  ) AS pvt
```

Make sense? It didn't to me when I started working with this. Honestly, I find this pattern a little confusing and, although I understand how it works and what the query engine is doing, it's not particularly intuitive. Once you get over the fact that you must provide a static list of column group values, this may prove to be a very useful part of your T-SQL arsenal.

Can this limitation be worked around? Yes, but it requires a bit of creativity and, well, quite a bit of brute force, frankly. Because the static column list must be present at query time, the only way to build column groups on changing values is to run a different query to get the list of values and then use that to concatenate a string of these comma-delimited values into a variable. Explaining this technique in full goes well beyond the goals for this book and would use techniques we haven't yet discussed. I offer the following example as, well, little more than an example. Using the inner query to populate a cursor allows me to loop through each row. In this loop, I compare the OrderDate with that of the previous row and concatenate together a comma-separated list of unique dates — just like the static list in the previous example. This date list is used to build a big string with the entire contents of the query held in a variable named @Query. The EXECUTE statement is then used to run the whole thing.

```
DECLARE @OrderDate datetime
DECLARE @TotalDue money
DECLARE @TerritoryID int
DECLARE @LastOrderDate datetime
DECLARE @DateList varchar(1000)
DECLARE @InnerQuery nvarchar(1000)
DECLARE @Query nvarchar(4000)
SET @InnerQuery =
'          SELECT TOP 59 ' +
'                  TotalDue ' +
'                , OrderDate ' +
'                , TerritoryID ' +
'          FROM Sales.SalesOrderHeader '
EXEC('DECLARE Cur Cursor for ' + @InnerQuery)
```

(continued)

(continued)

```
OPEN Cur
FETCH NEXT FROM Cur INTO @TotalDue, @OrderDate, @TerritoryID
SET @LastOrderDate = @OrderDate
SET @DateList = '[' + CONVERT(varchar(20), @OrderDate, 110) + ']'
WHILE @@FETCH_STATUS = 0
 BEGIN
            IF @LastOrderDate <> @OrderDate
              SET @DateList = @DateList + ', ['
                    + CONVERT(varchar(20), @OrderDate, 110) + ']'
            SET @LastOrderDate = @OrderDate
            FETCH NEXT FROM Cur INTO @TotalDue, @OrderDate, @TerritoryID
 END
CLOSE Cur
DEALLOCATE Cur
SET @Query =
'SELECT TerritoryID, ' + @DateList +
'FROM ' +
'  ( ' + @InnerQuery + ' )   AS Source ' +
'PIVOT ' +
'  ( ' +
'         Sum(TotalDue) FOR OrderDate IN (' + @DateList + ') ' +
'  )   AS pvt'
EXECUTE (@Query)
```

The results of this query are exactly the same as before. However, you could easily modify the number after the TOP statement or filter this query and get a different set of dates along the columns. I don't expect you to pick this up and run with it. As I said, there are some things in this query we haven't covered yet. The purpose of this example is just to show you that it's possible to work around limitations by using some creative techniques.

The UNPIVOT Operator

As you may have guessed, the UNPIVOT operator does the exact opposite of the PIVOT operator. It enables you to pass it a denormalized set of data with repeating column values and transform it into a standard, columnar format. Because you'll always know the number of columns and their respective header values, UNPIVOT is a little easier to use than the PIVOT operator. This useful tool allows you to take a set of data that breaks first normal form and transform it into a normalized, uniform table of ungrouped rows.

To create a set of unpivotable data, I'll just modify the earlier PIVOT sample query to insert the results into a table named MyPivotData:

```
SELECT TerritoryID, [7-1-2001], [7-2-2001], [7-3-2001], [7-4-2001], [7-5-2001]
INTO MyPivotData
FROM
 (
     SELECT TOP 59
        TotalDue
     , OrderDate
     , TerritoryID
    FROM Sales.SalesOrderHeader
```

```
    )   AS Source
PIVOT
  (
    Sum(TotalDue) FOR OrderDate
        IN ([7-1-2001], [7-2-2001], [7-3-2001], [7-4-2001], [7-5-2001])
  )   AS pvt
```

Executing this query populates a table with the results you saw in Figure 11-3. Transforming this data back into a flat table is somewhat similar to the PIVOT query, in that there are also three different sections. In the first section, you define the structure of the end result set:

```
SELECT
    TerritoryID, OrderDate, DueDateTotal
FROM
...
```

The inner query, or second section, is a simple select from the source table. As a subquery, this SELECT statement is wrapped in parentheses and given a table alias. In this case, the alias name is pvt.

```
  (
    SELECT
      TerritoryID
    , [7-1-2001], [7-2-2001], [7-3-2001], [7-4-2001], [7-5-2001]
    FROM MyPivotData
  )   AS pvt
```

This is followed by the UNPIVOT operator and a statement similar to that used in the PIVOT query. This statement deconstructs the aggregated values from the pivot structure into a column named DueDateTotal that will be grouped on the OrderDate value.

```
UNPIVOT
  (
    DueDateTotal FOR OrderDate
    IN ([7-1-2001], [7-2-2001], [7-3-2001], [7-4-2001], [7-5-2001])
  )
  AS unpvt
```

Finally, here is the entire query:

```
SELECT
  TerritoryID, OrderDate, DueDateTotal
FROM
  (
    SELECT
      TerritoryID
    , [7-1-2001], [7-2-2001], [7-3-2001], [7-4-2001], [7-5-2001]
    FROM MyPivotData
  ) as pvt
UNPIVOT
  (
    DueDateTotal FOR OrderDate
    IN ([7-1-2001], [7-2-2001], [7-3-2001], [7-4-2001], [7-5-2001])
  )
  AS unpvt
```

The results of this query, shown in Figure 11-4, are very similar to what we started with, prior to using the PIVOT operator.

	TerritoryID	OrderDate	DueDate Total
1	1	7-1-2001	128233.7408
2	1	7-4-2001	3953.9884
3	2	7-1-2001	28639.5233
4	3	7-1-2001	25480.7357
5	4	7-1-2001	133569.035
6	4	7-2-2001	3953.9884
7	4	7-3-2001	7907.9768
8	4	7-5-2001	3953.9884
9	5	7-1-2001	184509.7436
10	6	7-1-2001	157316.2035
11	7	7-1-2001	3756.989
12	8	7-4-2001	3953.9884
13	9	7-1-2001	3756.989
14	9	7-2-2001	11440.3414
15	9	7-3-2001	7907.9768
16	9	7-5-2001	8680.4804
17	10	7-3-2001	772.5036
18	10	7-5-2001	3953.9884

Figure 11-4

The cycle of pivoting and then unpivoting a set of data will not always bring you back to exactly where you started. This is because detail rows in the original data source are grouped on the column values. After unpivoting this data, you will have exactly one row per unique column and row combination, with the aggregation of the original source rows.

Full-Text Queries and Approximation Matching

In the late 1980s, I worked as the Tech Support Manager for a growing medical billing software company. We had written most of our own internal support systems, accounting, payroll, and tech support incident management, not to mention our own software products. After a few years and hundreds of thousands of support calls later, we had accumulated what we considered to be a huge repository of support call notes and history. We found ourselves taking calls from customers whose issues seemed vaguely familiar. When a support technician received a call, he or she would page through support incident screens, looking for old records to help find resolutions to repeat problems, often to no avail. Our system didn't store data in a relational database so we couldn't use SQL or any other standard language to query data. All our data lived in flat text files. While attending the Comdex technology exhibition in Las Vegas, I found a company with an interesting product that did indexing over large volumes of text. This software could build searchable indexes for practically anything: encyclopedias, dictionaries, religious books, or hundreds of files in your file system. We quickly built this into our support system, and it changed everything. When a customer called and told one of our support technicians they were getting error 3204 when they entered a new patient diagnosis, the technician could instantly find all incidents related to the same problem by simply typing a few keywords.

Free-form text indexing has been around for many years and has improved and matured since my experience as a Tech Support Manager. Relational databases have largely replaced old flat-file systems, but with that transition, we've actually lost some useful functionality — namely the ability to simply store a large volume of searchable text. Systems evolve to fill gaps and to meet users' needs. Today, most relational database products support the ability to store large volumes of data in a structure called *binary large objects (BLOBs)*. SQL Server offers three different implementations of BLOB types in the data types `text`, `ntext`, and `image`. When the *text* and *image t*ypes were originally added to the SyBase and Microsoft SQL Server products in the early 1990s, they didn't support indexing or ordering. Even today, you cannot use these columns with a standard `WHERE` or `ORDER BY` clause — and for good reason. Can you imagine sorting rows using all of the text in a 15-page document?

T-SQL includes some simple tools for inexact text comparisons. This includes functionality such as Soundex phonetic and approximate word matching. By contrast, full-text indexing includes built-in logical operators, "near" matching, and ranked results. Whether you should choose to use full-text searches or standard SQL techniques depends on your specific needs.

Microsoft Search Service

To compensate for this shortcoming, Microsoft implemented a flexible, free-form text indexing technology very similar to the product I used to index our support call system. The Microsoft Search Service was originally adopted to index newsgroup servers and websites. Because it was capable of indexing practically any volume of text stored in files, it was integrated into SQL Server several versions ago. Today, any SQL data type capable of storing text characters can be indexed for free-form searches using full-text indexing and the Microsoft Search Service. Keep in mind that this is not a capability of SQL Server, but rather a separate service made accessible through extensions in both the SQL Server product and the T-SQL language. Because text in practically any form can be indexed, SQL Server can be used as a storage repository for content such as Office documents that can then be indexed and searched using full-text indexing. Word documents, for example, contain both text and binary markup information. This poses no problem because the non-textual data is simply ignored.

Full-text indexing works much differently than standard indexes in SQL Server. Indexed data is not stored in the database. Full-text catalogs store index data in separate catalog files on the server. When the index is populated, the search service weeds out all the noise words, such as "and" and "of." All the remaining words are added to a table-specific index stored within a catalog. Multiple columns can be added to the same index within a catalog.

Most of us use full-text searching every day. Although the Microsoft Search Service is not implemented on the same scale as the Google and Yahoo web search engines, the fundamental technology is the same. If you have used any of the leading web search services online, then you're already familiar with some of the things you can do with the Microsoft Search Service and full-text indexing.

Soundex Matching

One of the great challenges when mixing the nuance of language with the exactness of computing is to make sense of things that are similar to other things, but not exactly the same. My friend Steve, who writes a humorous newspaper column, says that there are people who like things to be black and white, and there are other people who are okay with things in that gray area in between. For the gray people, driving 70 on a 60-mile-per-hour road is perfectly acceptable for the surgeon on his way to the hospital. This is not to say that the gray people are all about breaking rules and cheating their employers; they just have a different way of looking at things. Likewise, at times you may need to match a word or phrase that is similar to another, in that gray area between equal to and not equal to. One of the great challenges, for those of us who spend our lives in the world of Boolean logic, is to cope with the concept of inexact comparisons.

Soundex, as applied in SQL Server, is a standard used to compare words based on their phonetic equivalents, using a mathematical algorithm. This standard is based on the *Consensus Soundex*, developed by Robert Russell and Margaret Odell in the early 1900s. It was used by the United States Census in the 19th and early 20th centuries and in genealogical research to index and deal with spelling variations in surnames. Although the rules are based on English language phonetic rules, it does work with many words in different languages. Here's something to keep in mind: Just as the rules of spoken language can be a bit arbitrary, so is this. Soundex matching is pretty accurate, most of the time, but on occasion some exceptions may occur. Use it for search and matching features to be validated by a user, but don't bet the farm on every result.

The sound of a word is represented by a letter, representing the first sound, followed by a three-digit integer, each numeral representing adjacent consonant sounds. Before processing a word, the letters *A*, *E*, *I*, *O*, *U*, *H*, *W*, and *Y* are ignored unless they have a phonetic significance when combined with another letter. The first three prominent consonant sounds (after the first letter, if it's a consonant) are translated as shown in the following table.

Letters	English Phonetic Description	Represented By
B, F, P, V	Labials and labio-dentals	1
C, G, J, K, Q, S, X, Z	Gutterals and sibilants	2
D, T	Dental-mutes	3
L	Palatal-fricative	4
M, N	Labio-nasal and lingua-nasal	5
R	Dental fricative	6

The resulting value is padded with zeros, if necessary. Here are some simple examples. The words "Two," "To," and "Too" all have the same pronunciation. I'll pass each to the Soundex function:

```
SELECT SOUNDEX('Two')
SELECT SOUNDEX ('To')
SELECT SOUNDEX ('Too')
```

The result is the same for each word, T000, as shown in Figure 11-5.

Figure 11-5

Because there are no consonants after the "T," zeros are added. This happens to be the same value returned for Tea, Tee, Tow, Toe, and Toy. Using a more complex word, the result is more precise. For example, the Soundex value for the word "Microsoft" is M262: 2 for *C*, 6 for *R*, and 2 for *S*.

Try a few different words. Generally, I've found this to work reasonably well for comparing the closeness of words, but using the Soundex function for this purpose is not an exact science. For example, the word "Seattle" has a Soundex value of S340, which is the same as for the word "Settle." However, the word "Subtle" has a Soundex value of S134 because the algorithm missed the fact that the B is silent. This confirms what I've known all along, that people from Seattle are not very subtle.

The SOUNDEX() function returns a character string. With the exception of an exact match, you would need to parse this string and convert the numeric value to a numeric type. This would allow you to make quantitative comparisons. In this example, I use variables to hold the input and output values. The SOUNDEX() function output is parsed using the SUBSTRING() function to return only the numerical value. The difference is calculated and converted to a positive value using the ABS() function. Using this approach, I'll compare Redmond and Renton, two neighboring Washington State cities that many people (including my wife) often confuse:

```
DECLARE @Word1 VarChar(100)
DECLARE @Word2 VarChar(100)
DECLARE @Value1 Int
DECLARE @Value2 Int
DECLARE @SoundexDiff Int
SET @Word1 = 'Redmond'
SET @Word2 = 'Renton'
SELECT @Value1 = CONVERT(Int, SUBSTRING(SOUNDEX(@Word1), 2, 3))
SELECT @Value2 = CONVERT(Int, SUBSTRING(SOUNDEX(@Word2), 2, 3))
SET @SoundexDiff = ABS(@Value1 - @Value2)
PRINT @SoundexDiff
```

According to the SOUNDEX() function, these two words are quite different phonetically. My query returns a difference of 180. If you don't want to go to this much work and don't need such a granular comparison, all this effort isn't necessary.

The DIFFERENCE() Function

The DIFFERENCE() function is really just a wrapper around two SOUNDEX() function calls and some business logic to compare the values. It simplifies the comparison, reducing the result to a scale from 0 to 4, where the value 4 indicates a very close or exact match.

I'll use the DIFFERENCE() function to compare the words To and Two:

```
SELECT DIFFERENCE('To', 'Two')
```

The result is 4, indicating a very close or exact match.

Using the DIFFERENCE() function to compare Redmond with Renton:

```
SELECT DIFFERENCE ('Redmond', 'Renton')
```

returns 3, meaning a similar but not-so-close match.

Managing and Populating Catalogs

Even though the task of managing full-text indexes belongs to the Microsoft Search Service rather than SQL Server, all the management work can be performed within SQL Server Management Studio. The underlying technology hasn't changed significantly, but some architectural improvements have been made to full-text indexing in SQL Server 2005 and again in SQL Server 2008. Subsequently, the tools and methods used to create and manage the catalogs have changed slightly. For detailed information on managing full-text indexes and catalogs, please refer to *Professional Microsoft SQL Server 2008 Programming* and *Professional SQL Server 2008* from Wrox.

Probably the most significant enhancement to full-text indexing introduced in SQL Server 2005 was that the database engine can update indexes as data changes. This can make full-text indexing behave more like standard indexing and greatly reduce data latency. Just keep in mind that this feature can have a significant impact on overall server performance. This may not be a wise option in a busy transactional database environment unless you have a very capable server. An enhancement to SQL Server 2008 provides catalog storage in SQL Server rather than the file system.

The AdventureWorks2008 database already has full-text catalogs and indexes created, so the following steps are unnecessary. However, you will need to run the following script to generate a full-text index for the Product table. This index is created manually in the AdventureWorks2008 database using the steps that follow.

```
CREATE FULLTEXT INDEX
ON Production.Product(Name, ProductNumber, Color)
KEY Index PK_Product_ProductID
```

The process for creating a catalog and indexes is the same for SQL Server 2008 as it is for SQL Server 2005. So, even though this has already been done for you in the sample database, these steps will give you a reference point for any new databases you should need to configure in the future.

If you are using the AdventureWorks database for SQL Server 2005, use the following steps. Otherwise, skip ahead to the section "Creating an Index Manually."

Catalogs and indexes are implemented in SQL Server Management Studio. The Full-Text Indexing Wizard contains several pages. Begin by defining a new catalog for the AdventureWorks database. Under the database, expand the Storage node and right-click Full Text Catalogs. From the menu, select New Full-Text Catalog, as shown in Figure 11-6.

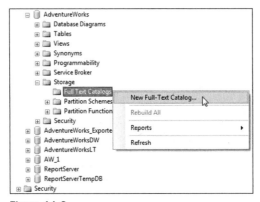

Figure 11-6

The New Full-Text Catalog dialog is used to name, specify a file location (unless you are using SQL Server 2008), and set options for the new catalog file, as shown in Figure 11-7.

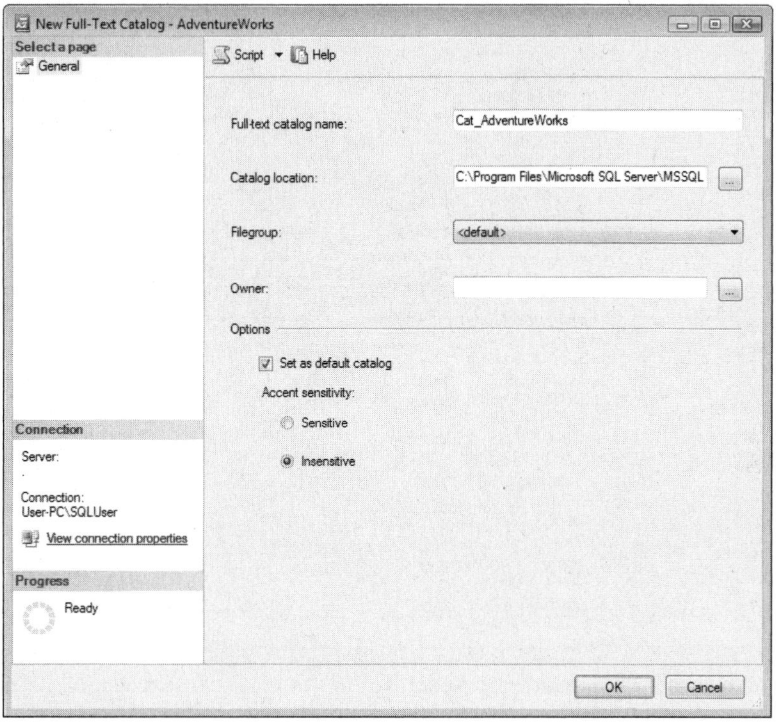

Figure 11-7

After you create a catalog, you can create indexes for tables. To create a new index, right-click a table icon and choose Full-Text Index ⇨ Define Full-Text Index, as shown in Figure 11-8.

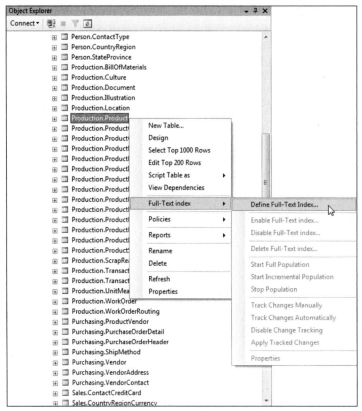

Figure 11-8

When the Full-Text Indexing Wizard opens (see Figure 11-9), navigate past the opening page by clicking Next. Because the wizard was launched from the Product table, it polls the table for a list of indexes. A unique index must exist in order to build a full-text index. Accept the default selection, which is the primary key for this table, as shown in Figure 11-10.

Figure 11-9

Figure 11-10

Next, a list of columns is displayed. These are candidates for full-text indexing. Check any columns that you would like to have included in the full-text index, as demonstrated in Figure 11-11.

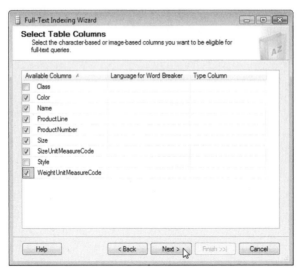

Figure 11-11

If you would like to have SQL Server track and automatically update this full-text index as data is modified, leave the Change Tracking option set to Automatically, as shown in Figure 11-12.

Figure 11-12

The Select a Catalog page gives you the option to select an existing catalog or to create a new catalog. Because I created a catalog to store full-text indexes for this database, select the existing catalog, as shown in Figure 11-13.

Figure 11-13

The next page enables you to manage full-text catalog population schedules. Creating a schedule invokes the SQL Server Agent service, which must be running for this option to function properly. Click Next to skip this page.

The following page displays summary information (see Figure 11-14). Using this dialog, you can review your selections and options. Because no settings have yet been applied, you can use the Back and Next buttons to navigate to any page to make changes. Click the Finish button to apply your selections and build the next full-text index.

Figure 11-14

The next wizard page, shown in Figure 11-15, displays the progress of each step, as it is applied by the wizard.

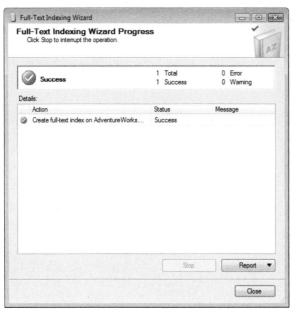

Figure 11-15

Creating an Index Manually

Later in this chapter, I offer some examples of full-text queries on the ProductReview table. Rather than using the wizard, create this index using the following script:

```
CREATE FULLTEXT INDEX
ON Production.ProductReview(Comments, ReviewerName)
KEY Index PK_ProductReview_ProductReviewID
```

An optional statement can be used to explicitly control whether SQL Server tracks changes and whether it automatically populates and updates the index. You may want to disable change tracking to conserve server resources or to give yourself more control over this process.

To explicitly populate the index using change tracking, add this line to the end of the prior script:

```
WITH Change_Tracking Auto
```

To explicitly turn off change tracking, use this option:

```
WITH Change_Tracking OFF
```

If you want to manually populate a full-text index that has not been set up for automatic population, use this option of the `sp_fulltext_table` system stored procedure:

```
sp_fulltext_table 'Production.ProductReview', 'start_full'
```

This stored procedure can be used in place of the Create Full-Text Index expression used previously and includes several related maintenance options.

Full-Text Query Expressions

Full-text indexing in SQL Server extends the T-SQL feature set by adding four language predicates:

- ❏ CONTAINS
- ❏ FREETEXT
- ❏ CONTAINSTABLE
- ❏ FREETEXTTABLE

You'll recall that a predicate is simply a functional statement that yields a Boolean result. Predicates always return a true or false value. Functionally, there are really only two predicate statements with each having an alternate implementation that returns a SQL Server table object — rather than a standard result set — from the query. A predicate is simply an extension to the SQL language, used in a WHERE clause, that provides a conduit from SQL Server to the Microsoft Search Service. As far as you are concerned, you are working with SQL and communicating to the database engine. The reality is that these statements take your request outside of SQL Server and make requests against the search service. The only real evidence of this is in the way you must pass string values.

Quotes in Quotes

This is an interesting idiosyncrasy of the full-text query syntax. As you know, when passing text string values to T-SQL, these values are encapsulated in single quotes. This is still the case when using full-text predicates; however, these string values are then passed from SQL to the search service, which requires that values be passed within double quotes. This means that when you need to pass values to a full-text query expression (if the value contains spaces) you must pass a double-quoted value within single quotes, like this:

```
'"My Value"'
```

T-SQL requires literal string values to be passed in single quotes. Before SQL Server reroutes the statement to the search service, it strips off the single quotes, passing values in the proper format for the search service, which requires literal values that include spaces to be enclosed in double quotes. When using logical operators within a full-text predicate call, you may need to pass multiple quoted values between operators, all of which are enclosed within single quotes for SQL to handle them, and each value in double quotes, as follows:

```
'"My Value" OR "Your Value"'
```

Examples of the entire call syntax follow shortly, but I want to make sure you're comfortable with this requirement to pass double-quoted values (required by the Microsoft Search Service) within single quotes (required by SQL Server).

The CONTAINS Predicate

The CONTAINS predicate lets you find and return rows where one or any combination of indexed column values contains a specified value, or optionally a form of a specified word. The features of this predicate are as follows:

❑ Search criterion can apply to values in one or any number of specified column(s) contained in the full-text index.

❑ Search criterion can apply to values in all columns contained in the full-text index.

❑ The columns' text includes a word or string of characters located anywhere within the text. Matching text can include wildcards indicating that a word starts with, ends with, or contains a string of characters.

❑ Match may be based on a form of a specified word. For example, the text may include a plural, singular, different gender form, or different tense of the word.

The full-text indexing engine includes a vast thesaurus of words in different forms and inflections. This supports multiple languages if different language packs have been installed. To be able to apply language rules to the text, the engine needs to know what language to use. The language parameter for all predicates will accept either the language alias (friendly name) or the LCID, an integer value used internally. Full-text indexing recognizes the languages listed in the following table.

Alias	LCID	Alias	LCID	Alias	LCID
Arabic	1025	French	1036	Portuguese	2070
Brazilian	1046	German	1031	Romanian	1048
British English	2057	Greek	1032	Russian	1049
Bulgarian	1026	Hungarian	1038	Simplified Chinese	2052
Croatian	1050	Italian	1040	Slovak	1051
Czech	1029	Japanese	1041	Slovenian	1060
Danish	1030	Korean	1042	Spanish	3082
Dutch	1043	Latvian	1062	Swedish	1053
English	1033	Lithuanian	1063	Thai	1054
Estonian	1061	Norwegian	2068	Traditional Chinese	1028
Finnish	1035	Polish	1045	Turkish	1055

If the language parameter is omitted, the language will be derived from the column, table, or database.

I'll start with a simple example. I'm interested in returning all Product records where any indexed column contains the value `"Black"`. The first parameter to this function-like statement indicates the indexed columns I want to include in the search. The asterisk (*) represents all available columns. The second parameter is my search criteria:

```
SELECT * FROM Production.Product
WHERE CONTAINS(*, '"Black"')
```

The results are shown in Figure 11-16.

	ProductID	Name	ProductNumber	MakeFlag	FinishedGoodsFlag	Color	SafetyStockLevel
1	317	LL Crankarm	CA-5965	0	0	Black	500
2	318	ML Crankarm	CA-6738	0	0	Black	500
3	319	HL Crankarm	CA-7457	0	0	Black	500
4	322	Chainring	CR-7833	0	0	Black	1000
5	492	Paint - Black	PA-187B	0	0	NULL	60
6	680	HL Road Frame - Black, 58	FR-R92B-58	1	1	Black	500
7	708	Sport-100 Helmet, Black	HL-U509	0	1	Black	4
8	722	LL Road Frame - Black, 58	FR-R38B-58	1	1	Black	500
9	723	LL Road Frame - Black, 60	FR-R38B-60	1	1	Black	500
10	724	LL Road Frame - Black, 62	FR-R38B-62	1	1	Black	500
11	736	LL Road Frame - Black, 44	FR-R38B-44	1	1	Black	500

Figure 11-16

As you can see, rows are returned where the word "Black" is contained in both the Name and Color columns. However, you may be wondering why the word "Black" was found in the middle of a field value when I didn't use any wildcard characters. Something to get used to when using full-text queries is the differences in behavior from this and the SQL LIKE operator. Full-text queries match whole words anywhere within a field without using wildcards. Wildcard matching is performed to match a substring, or part of a word. For example, I'll look for any rows that contain text beginning with the letters "crank":

```
SELECT * FROM Production.Product
WHERE CONTAINS(*, '"crank*"')
```

Note that the wildcard character isn't the percent symbol (%), as it is in T-SQL. It's the asterisk (*). The results are shown in Figure 11-17.

	ProductID	Name	ProductNumber	MakeF
1	317	LL Crankarm	CA-5965	0
2	318	ML Crankarm	CA-6738	0
3	319	HL Crankarm	CA-7457	0
4	949	LL Crankset	CS-4759	1
5	950	ML Crankset	CS-6583	1
6	951	HL Crankset	CS-9183	1

Figure 11-17

You can also specify a list of columns you want to include in the search by specifying a comma-delimited column list within parentheses:

```
SELECT * FROM Production.Product
WHERE CONTAINS((ProductNumber, Name, Color), '"Black"')
```

The full-text indexing engine includes an internal thesaurus of words and their variations. This enables the CONTAINS predicate to match different forms of a word. This might include past-, future-, or present-tense, or different gender inflections. For example, performing a full-text search on the Product table for the word "tour" returns records containing the word "touring," as shown in Figure 11-18.

```
SELECT * FROM Production.Product
WHERE CONTAINS(*, 'FORMSOF(Inflectional, "Tour")')
```

	ProductID	Name	ProductN
1	330	Touring End Caps	EC-T209
2	513	Touring Rim	RM-T801
3	520	LL Touring Seat Assembly	SA-T467
4	521	ML Touring Seat Assembly	SA-T612
5	522	HL Touring Seat Assembly	SA-T872
6	821	Touring Front Wheel	FW-T905
7	829	Touring Rear Wheel	RW-T905
8	842	Touring-Panniers, Large	PA-T100
9	885	HL Touring Frame - Yellow, 60	FR-T98Y-
10	886	LL Touring Frame - Yellow, 62	FR-T67Y-
11	887	HL Touring Frame - Yellow, 46	FR-T98Y-

Figure 11-18

Weighting Values

You can affect the outcome of word matching, and relative ranking of rows, by designating relative weight values for different words. A weight value is a numeric value between 0.0 and 1.0, accurate to one decimal position. Because these values are actually passed as a text string along with the rest of the search criteria, SQL Server doesn't really see this as a numerical type. These values are used only for relative comparison, so it's not necessary to make them add up to anything in particular. A weighted-value word list is passed to the ISABOUT() function, within the CONTAINS predicate expression:

```
ISABOUT (<word> weight (.75), <word> weight (.25))
```

The result of this weighting will affect whether or not some rows are included in the result set but may not otherwise be apparent when using the CONTAINS predicate. This is apparent, however, in the value of the calculated Rank column returned by the CONTAINSTABLE and FREETEXTTABLE predicates.

Ranked Results

Internally, the CONTAINS predicate calculates a qualifying ranking value for each row, based on exact and approximate word matching, logical operators, and explicit weighting value factors. Because the CONTAINS and FREETEXT predicates are only used to qualify selected rows returned in the result set, these techniques can't expose the ranking of each row. The CONTAINSTABLE and FREETEXTTABLE predicates do create a new result set, returned as a SQL table object. A new column, called Rank, is added to the result with the relative ranking value of each row.

The CONTAINSTABLE Predicate

Functionally, this is the CONTAINS predicate, wrapped by functionality that returns a SQL table object. Two additional columns are added to the result. The Key column is just a duplicate of the full-text index key column, which was specified when the full-text index was created. The Rank column appears, as I mentioned previously.

```
SELECT ProductID, Name, ProductNumber, Color, Rank
FROM Production.Product INNER JOIN
CONTAINSTABLE(Production.Product, *
    , 'ISABOUT (Black weight (.2), Blue weight (.8))') AS ConTbl
    ON Product.ProductID = ConTbl.[Key]
ORDER BY Rank DESC
```

Take a look at another example. Full-text queries are ideal for searching large volumes of text. The first thing I'll do is create a full-text index on the ProductReview table. This table contains a Comments column used to hold verbose text. After populating the index, the following query can be executed. Note the weight values for the two words:

```
SELECT Comments, Rank
FROM Production.ProductReview INNER JOIN
CONTAINSTABLE(Production.ProductReview, Comments
    , 'ISABOUT (terrible weight(.9), advertised weight(.1))') AS ConTbl
    ON ProductReview.ProductReviewID = ConTbl.[Key]
ORDER BY Rank DESC
```

When the query is executed, a rank value is calculated based on these words found in the Comments column and the relative weight values. Note the values in the Rank column shown in Figure 11-19.

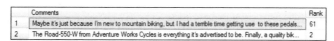

	Comments	Rank
1	Maybe it's just because I'm new to mountain biking, but I had a terrible time getting use to these pedals...	61
2	The Road-550-W from Adventure Works Cycles is everything it's advertised to be. Finally, a quality bik...	2

Figure 11-19

Now I'll change the weight values (reversing .9 and .1) and execute the query again:

```
SELECT Comments, Rank
FROM Production.ProductReview INNER JOIN
CONTAINSTABLE(Production.ProductReview, Comments,
    'ISABOUT (terrible weight(.1), advertised weight(.9))') AS ConTbl
    ON ProductReview.ProductReviewID = ConTbl.[Key]
ORDER BY Rank DESC
```

The FREETEXT Predicate

Can a computer really understand what you want rather than simply give you exactly what you asked it for? The FREETEXT predicate attempts to do just that — to understand the meaning of a phrase or sentence. It does this by breaking a phrase down into individual words and then using the full-text indexing thesaurus to match all forms of these words, applying language rules. It may choose to return text that only contains forms of some of these words. As each row is considered for selection, an algorithm calculates a relative ranking value, used to qualify each record against the matching phrase.

The FREETEXT predicate takes few parameters, and the only optional parameter is the language. As with the CONTAINS predicate, if omitted, the language will be derived from the database. The ranking is not exposed in the result, and the order of records is unaffected by the ranking.

```
SELECT * FROM Production.Product
WHERE FREETEXT (*, 'Yellow road bike')
```

Not only are records returned where indexed columns contain the words "yellow," "road," and "bike," but those records that contain any one of these words or forms of these words are also returned, as shown in Figure 11-20.

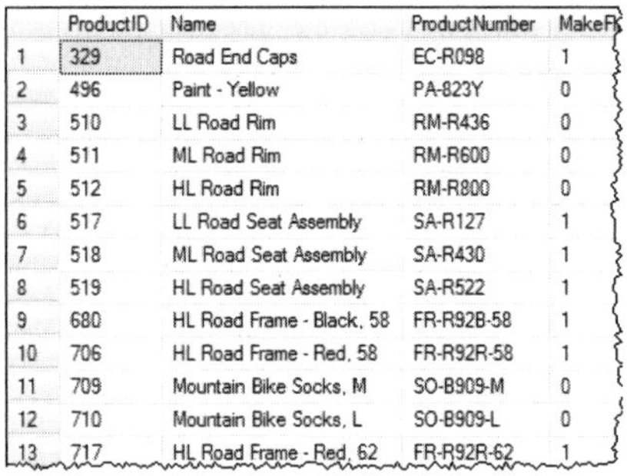

	ProductID	Name	ProductNumber	MakeF
1	329	Road End Caps	EC-R098	1
2	496	Paint - Yellow	PA-823Y	0
3	510	LL Road Rim	RM-R436	0
4	511	ML Road Rim	RM-R600	0
5	512	HL Road Rim	RM-R800	0
6	517	LL Road Seat Assembly	SA-R127	1
7	518	ML Road Seat Assembly	SA-R430	1
8	519	HL Road Seat Assembly	SA-R522	1
9	680	HL Road Frame - Black, 58	FR-R92B-58	1
10	706	HL Road Frame - Red, 58	FR-R92R-58	1
11	709	Mountain Bike Socks, M	SO-B909-M	0
12	710	Mountain Bike Socks, L	SO-B909-L	0
13	717	HL Road Frame - Red, 62	FR-R92R-62	1

Figure 11-20

Logical Operators

Multiple words or text strings can be specified by applying three different forms of logic, as explained in the following table.

Operator	Logic
AND	Criteria on both sides of the operator must match. If two values were provided with the AND operator, a single column value in each qualifying row must match both of the values.
OR	Criteria on either side of the operator must match. If two values were provided with the OR operator, a single column value in each qualifying row must match any provided value.
NEAR	Like the AND operator, both values must match text in a single column value for qualifying rows.

The FREETEXTTABLE Predicate

Like the CONTAINSTABLE predicate, FREETEXTTABLE is functionally the same as the FREETEXT predicate, but it returns a table with ranking values. Using the same technique as before, this table can be joined with the base table to return matching rows and the ranking values.

In this example, I've used a phrase that doesn't match any text exactly but several of the words may be found in the column text:

```
SELECT Comments, Rank
FROM Production.ProductReview INNER JOIN
FREETEXTTABLE(Production.ProductReview, Comments
    , 'mountain biking is new for me') AS FtTbl
    ON ProductReview.ProductReviewID = FtTbl.[Key]
ORDER BY Rank DESC
```

The result returns two rows with one row ranked significantly higher than the other, as shown in Figure 11-21.

	Comments	Rank
1	Maybe it's just because I'm new to mountain biking, but I had a terrible time getting use to the...	419
2	The Road-550-W from Adventure Works Cycles is everything it's advertised to be. Finally, a q...	215

Figure 11-21

The goal of free-text matching is to loosen the matching rules and provide some level of flexibility. Inevitably, this will return some rows that are simply not all that similar to the search text. To make the FREETEXT or FREETEXTTABLE predicate behave in a more predictable manner, you can force it to match the text exactly as it is presented by encapsulating the entire search text in double quotes.

Only one row matches this text exactly, as shown in Figure 11-22.

	Comments
1	Maybe it's just because I'm new to mountain biking, but I had a terrible time getting ...

Figure 11-22

Summary

The PIVOT and UNPIVOT operators transform data, either from a tabular structure into a cross-tabular structure (or "pivot") or from a cross table into a columnar table. Like the GROUP BY clause, multiple rows may be combined and summarized when PIVOT is used along with aggregate functions such as SUM and COUNT. The PIVOT operator is unique in that it combines results into predefined column groups, rather than rows. Although there are reporting tools that will do this in the presentation layer, such as Excel PivotTables, using this technique is a very powerful way to organize data the way users may need to see it presented. The UNPIVOT operator allows you to transform data that is in a cross-tabular, denormalized structure into standard, columnar form. This is a convenient way to take common spreadsheet data and organize it in a structure more appropriate to store in a relational table.

Often in our world of computer-managed precision and rigid logic, it's important to see past exact values and look for information with similar meaning and context. The SOUNDEX() and DIFFERENCE() functions were designed to help you make inexact comparisons, matching words with the same or similar phonetic patterns. Using the SOUNDEX() function is actually an older and fairly unsophisticated technique for matching words based on basic phonetic language rules. It's simple and often useful for matching words that sound similar.

Full-text indexing is a very capable resource for searching and matching content within any text, large or small. The CONTAINS and FREETEXT predicates work very effectively where you may be storing very large volumes of notes, comments, or document content. The CONTAINS predicate gives you fairly precise control over matching logic but will also let you find words, text, and phrases that are grammatically similar to the words you search for. The FREETEXT predicate is generally used for soft-matching a phrase when you don't need text to match exactly, but to find text with similar meaning and content. The CONTAINSTABLE and FREETEXTTABLE predicates expand on their base predicates by returning SQL table types capable of presenting a ranked listing of qualifying values and integrating these features into more sophisticated queries.

Exercises

Exercise 1

Write a T-SQL script to create a new full-text index on the StateProvince table. The index should include all values in the StateProvinceCode, CountryRegionCode, and the Name columns. Execute this script and use SQL Server Management Studio to verify that the index exists.

Exercise 2

Write a query to return all records from the StateProvince table where any indexed columns contain the text "CA." Execute the query and verify the results. You should see the state of California and the country of Canada.

Exercise 3

Use the FREETEXT predicate to find instances of Victoria and BC in the StateProvince table. Is there a record in the table for the city of Victoria, British Columbia?

T-SQL Programming Objects

SQL Server is an enormously capable and powerful relational data store. In general, SQL Server manages transactions and enforces checks and rules to protect the integrity of related records and values. You've seen how the query optimizer makes intelligent decisions and uses indexes to make queries run fast and efficiently. Now we're going to take SQL Server to the next level. Most data is accessed through business applications. SQL Server can be more than just an idle medium for storing this data. A well-designed business solution uses the capabilities of an active database server, programming objects, and other components to distribute the workload and minimize unnecessary network traffic.

I want to take you on a brief tour of history so that you can appreciate the impact of the features we're about to discuss. In the 1980s and early 1990s, PC-based applications ran only on desktops. If data could be shared across networks, it was simply stored in files managed by the file system. Applications supported a small number of users and quickly choked low-bandwidth networks as they moved all of their data to each desktop for processing. Desktop database applications sprang up like weeds in a new garden as inexpensive business applications became available — but the industry quickly hit the technology wall. In the past decade, the PC platform came of age with the advent of client/server database systems. In a nutshell, the enabling technology behind client/ server applications was the cutting-edge concept of running application code on a database server. Products such as SQL Server enabled this capability through the use of database programming objects such as views and stored procedures.

I could stop there and keep things quite simple, but the current state of the industry has moved forward in recent years. Most enterprise database solutions have progressed beyond simple client/ server technology. Now it's easier than ever before to distribute program components across two, three, or more different computers. These may include desktop computers, Web servers, application servers, and database servers.

Sophisticated database applications use complicated queries. For this reason, it is important that queries and other SQL logic are protected and run as efficiently as possible. If SQL statements are managed in server-side database objects rather than in applications, this reduces the overall complexity of a solution. This separation of client-side applications and databases enables programmers and database professionals to each do what they do best, rather than having to write both program code and complex SQL — not to mention the fact that application programmers, unless they have a background in database technologies, have traditionally written very bad SQL.

The very first rule of developing database applications is to avoid the ad-hoc query at all costs. Ad-hoc queries create great efficiency issues, and when it comes to Web applications, great security issues as well. The best practice when creating database-centric applications is to use database programming objects. In SQL Server, these objects include views, stored procedures, functions, and triggers. This chapter covers each of these objects in turn.

Views

A view is one of the simplest database objects. On the surface, a view is nothing more than a SELECT query that is saved with a name in a database. Ask any modern-day programmer what they believe to be the most important and fundamental concept of programming. They will likely tell you that it is code reuse. Writing every line of code, every object, every script, and every query represents a cost or risk. One risk is that there could be a mistake (a bug) in the code. The cost of a bug is that it must be fixed (debugged) and tested. Buggy applications must be redeployed, shipped, installed, and supported. Undiscovered bugs pose a risk to productivity, business viability, and perhaps even legal exposure. One of the few constants in the software universe is change. Business rules will change, program logic will change, and the structure of your databases will also change. For all of these and other reasons, it just makes sense to reduce the number of objects that you create and use in your solutions. If you can create one object and reuse it in several places rather than duplicating the same effort, this limits your exposure to risk. Views promote this concept of code reuse by enabling you to save common queries into a uniform object. Rather than rewriting queries, complex queries can be created and tested and then reused without the added risk of starting over the next time you need to add functionality to an application.

Virtual Tables

One of the great challenges facing users is dealing with the complexity of large business databases. Many tools are available for use by casual database consumers for browsing data and building reports. Applications such as Microsoft Excel and Access are often used by information workers, rather than programmers, to obtain critical business management and operational information. A typical mid-scale database can contain scores of tables that contain supporting or special-purpose data. To reassemble the information stored in a large database, several tables must be joined in queries that take even skilled database professionals time and effort to create effectively. As you've seen in many examples, this is often not a trivial task. From the user's perspective, views are tables. They show up in most applications connecting to a SQL Server, along with the tables. A view is addressed in a SELECT statement and exposed columns, just like a table.

From the developer or database designer's perspective, a view can be a complex query that is exposed as if it were a simple table. This gives you an enormous amount of flexibility and the ability to hide all of the query logic, exposing a simple object. Users simply see a table-like object from which they can select data.

Creating a View

Defining a view is quite simple. First of all, a database user must be granted permission to create a view. This is a task that you may want to have performed only by a database administrator or a select number of trusted users. Because creating a view isn't particularly complicated, you may want certain users to be granted this ability.

Several simplified tools are available that you can use to create views. Microsoft Access, SQL Server Management Studio, and Visual Studio all leverage the T-SQL Query Designer interface to create and manage views. The process is just about the same in all of these tools because they all actually expose the same components. The following section steps through creating a view using Management Studio. I will not demonstrate each tool because the process is nearly identical.

Creating a View in Management Studio

Creating a view with Management Studio is very easy using the graphical query designer. It is basically the same designer used by Visual Studio and Microsoft Access. In Management Studio's Object Explorer, navigate to the AdventureWorks2008 database and then expand the database to expose the Views folder. Right-click the Views folder and choose New View, as shown in Figure 12-1.

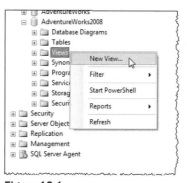

Figure 12-1

After clicking New View, the Add Table dialog appears, as shown in Figure 12-2. Add the Product, ProductCategory, and ProductSubcategory tables. Then click the Close button.

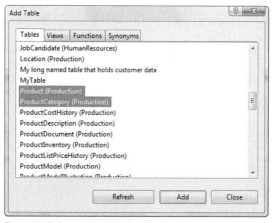

Figure 12-2

After you close the Add Table dialog, the graphical query designer is displayed. It shows the three tables connected by relation links in the top Diagram pane. Because of the relationships that exist between these tables, inner joins are automatically defined in the query. Beneath the Diagram pane is the Criteria pane, SQL pane, and then the Show Results pane, as shown in Figure 12-3.

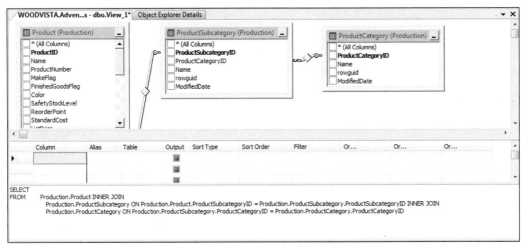

Figure 12-3

Each one of the panes can be displayed or hidden by clicking on the associated button on the View Designer toolbar (see Figure 12-4).

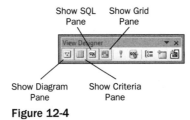

Figure 12-4

Select the Name column from the ProductCategory table and the Name column from the ProductSubcategory table. Then select the ProductID, Name, ProductNumber and ListPrice columns from the Product table (using the checkboxes in the table windows). Using the Alias column in the columns grid, define aliases for the following three columns:

Table.Column	Alias
ProductCategory.Name	Category
ProductSubcategory.Name	Subcategory
Product.Name	Product

Also, designate these three columns for sorting in the order listed by dropping down and selecting the word Ascending in the Sort Type column. Check your results against Figure 12-5 and make any adjustments necessary.

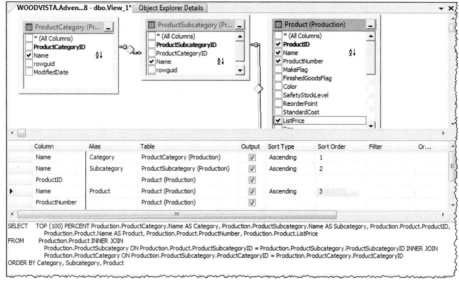

Figure 12-5

Notice that something interesting happens to the SQL that is being written for you when you choose sort criteria: the query designer adds the TOP 100 PERCENT statement to your code.

Back when the original ANSI SQL specification was written, its authors wanted to ensure that database designers wouldn't create SQL queries that would waste server resources. Keep in mind that this was at a time when production servers had 32MB of memory. One common memory-intensive operation is reordering a large result set. So, in their infinite wisdom, the authors imposed a rule that views cannot support the ORDER BY clause unless the results are restricted using a TOP statement.

If you close the window, using the Close button in the top-right corner, Management Studio prompts you to save the view. Click Yes to save the view and enter a name for the new view in the Choose Name dialog, as shown in Figure 12-6. I've always made it a point to prefix view names with v, vw, or vw_ and to use Pascal case (no spaces, with the first letter of each word capitalized). This ensures that when you retrieve objects with older data access methods, the drivers rarely differentiated between tables and views. When creating a data application, it is generally pretty important to know if the object you're referencing is a physical table or a view.

Figure 12-6

After you save the view, it appears in the list of views in Object Explorer and can now be queried as you would query a table, as shown in Figure 12-7.

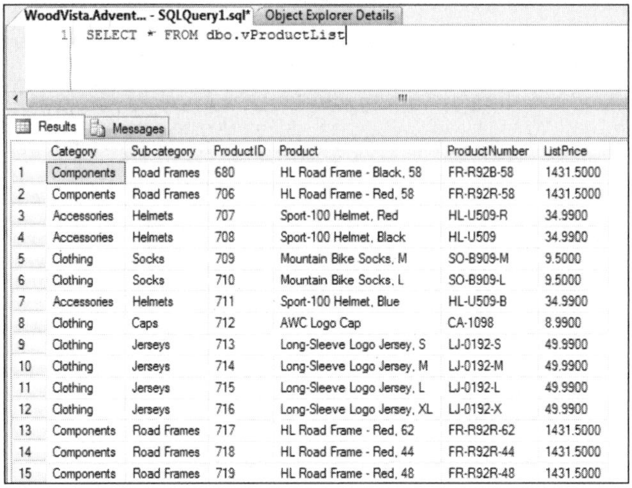

Figure 12-7

Creating a View Using SQL Script

Regardless of the tool or product used to create a view, as you saw in the previous example, SQL script runs in the background and the result will be as varied as handwriting without the use of an automated tool. The syntax for creating a new view is quite simple. The pattern is the same whether the query is very simple or extremely complex. I'll start with a simple view on a single table:

```
CREATE VIEW vProductCosts
AS
SELECT ProductID, Name, StandardCost
FROM Production.Product
```

To continue working with this view and extend its capabilities, I can either use the ALTER command to make modifications to the existing view or drop and create it. Using the ALTER statement rather than dropping and re-creating a view has the advantage of keeping any existing properties and security permissions intact.

Here are examples of these two statements. The ALTER statement is issued with the revised view definition:

```
ALTER VIEW vProductCosts
AS
SELECT ProductID, ProductSubcategoryID, Name, ProductNumber, StandardCost
FROM Production.Product
```

Using the DROP statement will wipe the slate clean, so to speak, reinitializing properties and security permissions. But for the sake of the following example, don't run this code just yet.

```
DROP VIEW vProductCosts
```

What happens if there are dependencies on a view? I'll conduct a simple experiment by creating another view that selects data from the view previously created:

```
CREATE VIEW vProductCosts2
AS
SELECT Name, StandardCost FROM vProductCosts
```

For this view to work the first view has to exist and it must support the columns it references. Now, what happens if I try to drop the first view? I'll execute the previous DROP command. Here's what SQL Server returns:

```
Command(s) completed successfully.
```

The view is gone? What happens if I execute a query using the second view?

```
SELECT * FROM vProductCosts2
```

SQL Server returns this information:

```
Msg 208, Level 16, State 1, Procedure vProductCosts2, Line 3
Invalid object name 'vProductCosts'
Msg 4413, Level 16, State 1, Line 1
Could not use view or function 'vProductCosts2' because of binding errors.
```

Why would SQL Server allow something so silly? I may not be able to answer this question to your satisfaction because I can't answer the question to my own satisfaction. This capability to drop an object and break something else is actually documented as a feature call *delayed resolution*. It's a holdover from the early days of SQL Server, but to a degree it makes sense. The perk of this feature is that if you needed to write script to drop all of the objects in the database and then create them again, this would be difficult to pull off with a lot of complex dependencies. If you're uncomfortable with this explanation, there is good news. An optional directive on the CREATE VIEW statement called SCHEMA BINDING tells SQL Server to check for dependencies and disallow any modifications that would violate them. To demonstrate, the first thing I'll do is drop both of these views and then re-create them:

```
CREATE VIEW vProductCosts WITH SCHEMABINDING
AS
SELECT ProductID, ProductSubcategoryID, Name, ProductNumber, StandardCost
FROM Production.Product
GO
CREATE VIEW vProductCosts2 WITH SCHEMABINDING
AS
SELECT Name, StandardCost
FROM dbo.vProductCosts
```

Some unique requirements are apparent in the example script. First of all, for a view to be schema-bound, any objects it depends on must also be schema-bound. Tables inherently support schema binding, but views must be explicitly schema-bound.

Any dependent objects must exist in the database before they can be referenced. For this reason, it's necessary to use batch delineation statements between dependent CREATE object statements. This example used the GO statement to finalize creating the first view.

When referring to a dependent view, you must use a two-part name. This means that you must use the schema name (which, as you can see in this example, is dbo). A schema-bound view also cannot use the SELECT * syntax. All columns must be explicitly referenced.

Ordering Rows

As mentioned earlier when working with the View designer, ordering rows in a view is not allowed without the TOP statement.

I run into this restriction all of the time. I'll spend some time creating some big, multi-table join or subquery with ordered results. After it's working, I think, "Hey, I ought to make this into a view." So I slap a CREATE VIEW vMyBigGnarlyQuery AS statement on the front of the script and execute the script with this result:

```
The ORDER BY clause is invalid in views, inline functions, derived tables,
subqueries, and common table expressions, unless TOP or FOR XML is also
specified.
```

Then I remember I have to use a TOP statement. This is a no-brainer and is easily rectified using the following workaround:

```
CREATE VIEW vOrderedProductCosts
AS
SELECT TOP 100 PERCENT ProductID, Name, ProductNumber, StandardCost
FROM Production.Product
ORDER BY Name
```

Now that most database servers have 500 times the horsepower and 100 times the memory of those 10 to 15 years ago, ordering a large result set is of much lesser concern.

Partitioned Views

Every system has its limits. Performance-tuning and capacity planning is the science of identifying these gaps and formulating appropriate plans to alleviate them. To partition data is to place tables or other objects in different files and on different disk drives to improve performance and organize data storage on a server. One of the most common methods to increase the performance and fault-tolerance of a database server is to implement RAID storage devices. Although this isn't a book on server configuration, I bring this up for a good reason. In teaching classes on database design and talking about partitioning data across multiple hard disks, I've often heard experienced students ask, "Why don't you just use a RAID device? Doesn't it accomplish the same thing?" Yes, to a point. Disk arrays using RAID 5 or RAID 10 simply spread data across an array of physical disks, improving performance and providing fault-tolerance. However, data partitioning techniques and using RAID are not necessarily mutually exclusive. Categorically, there may be three scenarios for server size and scale:

❑   Small-scale servers

❑   Medium-scale servers

❑   Large-scale servers

Small-scale servers will have system files and data on physical disks. You can implement data partitioning by placing objects in different database files residing on different disks, as depicted in Figure 12-8.

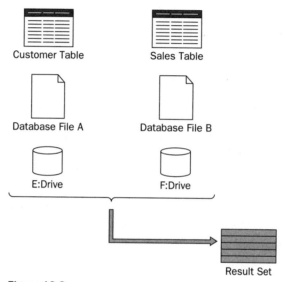

Figure 12-8

Moderate-scale servers may implement a RAID device where an array of identical physical disk drives is treated by the operating system as a single, logical volume. From the database designer's standpoint, the server has one disk, as illustrated in Figure 12-9. The fact that what we perceive to be a single hard disk drive is actually a bank of parallel disks is completely transparent and may have little impact on how we design our database. You could argue that there is no need to be concerned with partitioning because the RAID device does this — as long as we have ample disk space.

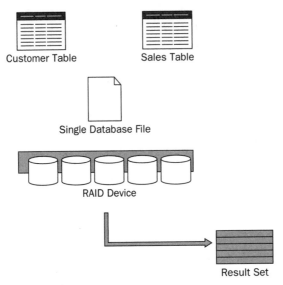

Figure 12-9

In a large-scale server environment, we generally take RAID technology for granted and may have several RAID devices, each acting as if it were an individual disk drive. This brings us back to the same scenario as the first example given where the server has a number of physical disks. In this case, we can partition our data across multiple disks, only each "disk" is actually a RAID device, as shown in Figure 12-10.

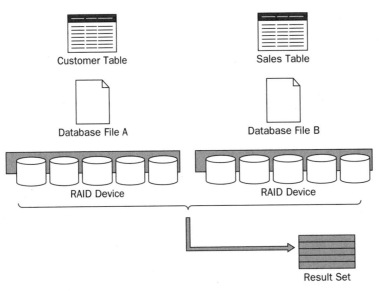

Figure 12-10

For this discussion, I'd like to put the RAID option aside and treat disks as if they are all physical disks, when in fact, each may be a RAID device. Keep in mind that the following SQL examples are given just to describe the methodology behind partitioned views. The code will not actually run on the AdventureWorks2008 database.

What does all this have to do with views? You'll remember that one of the main reasons for views is to treat complex data as if it were a simple table. Partitioning takes this concept to the next level. Here's an example: Suppose that your product marketing business has been gathering sales order data for five years. Business has been good and, on average, you're storing 500,000 sales detail rows each year. At the end of each month your sales managers and executives would like to run comparative sales reports on all of this data but you certainly don't want to keep nearly 3 million rows of data in your active table. When database performance began to slow down a couple of years ago, you decided to archive older records by moving them to a different table. This improved transactional performance because the active sales detail table stored less data. As long as you only accessed the most current records for reporting, performance was fine. However, when you combined the archive tables with the current detail, you were back to where you started. Once again, the server ground to a snail's pace because all of these tables resided on the same physical disk.

Here's a quick computer trivia question: What's the slowest component of almost any computer system? The user? Okay, besides that. The memory? How about the CPU? No, it's the hard disk. Aside from the cooling fans, the hard disk is the only critical component that is still mechanical. The industry hasn't yet found a cost-effective replacement without moving parts. The platter can only spin so fast and the read/write heads can only move back and forth so fast. In earlier chapters you learned that the greatest cost-affecting query performance is disk I/O — the time it takes for the system to position the heads and read data from a physical disk. If the system has one disk, it must find a page of data, reposition the heads, read the next page, and so on until it reads all of the data to return a complete result set. Because one disk has one set of heads, this happens in a linear fashion, one page at a time. If you were able to spread data across multiple disks, SQL Server could retrieve data from each disk simultaneously. The query execution plan makes this possible as it maps out those operations that are dependent and those that can be performed in parallel. This is depicted in Figure 12-11.

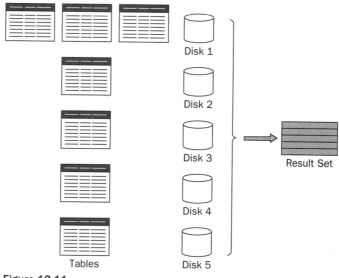

Figure 12-11

The view that makes all this possible is actually quite simple. Using your successful marketing business as an example, the view definition might look like this:

```
SELECT * FROM SalesDetail_1993
UNION ALL
SELECT * FROM SalesDetail_2004
UNION ALL
SELECT * FROM SalesDetail_2005
UNION ALL
SELECT * FROM SalesDetail_2006
UNION ALL
SELECT * FROM SalesDetail_2007
UNION ALL
SELECT * FROM SalesDetail_Current
```

Because these tables are all addressable within the database, they can be referenced in joins, subqueries, or any type of SQL expression. It may not make sense to put every table on its own disk, but if you did, each of these SELECT statements could be processed in parallel. Assuming that each drive had its own independent controller, the data on each of these disks could be read simultaneously.

As you can see, many factors can contribute to the effectiveness of a partitioned view. You would likely choose this route when system performance became an issue. The best indicator that an approach solves a performance or resource problem would be to use performance-tuning tools such as analyzing query execution plans, using the Windows system monitor and SQL Server Profiler.

Federated Views

Federated views are close cousins of partitioned views. The term *federated* means working together, so a federated server solution consists of more than one independent database server working together to solve a business problem. This is not to be confused with a server cluster, where multiple servers appear as a single server on the network. Federated servers may be in close proximity or could be a great distance apart. In fact, one of the significant advantages to a federated server solution is that the database servers are geographically located in close proximity to the users and applications that will use them. With database servers in regional or satellite business locations, the majority of the region's supporting data is typically stored on the local server. Federated views may be used to access data stored on remote servers and in exceptional cases, to connect over the Internet or corporate wide-area network (see Figure 12-12).

Figure 12-12

You could take a few different approaches to make data accessible from one server to another. One of the most common choices is to configure a linked server connection. A linked server maintains a connection to a database on another server as if the remote database were local. Once a linked server connection is established, tables are referenced using a four-part name, as follows:

```
LinkedServer.SalesDatabase.Sales.SalesDetail
```

What does this accomplish? Suppose I have designed the database infrastructure for a banking system. Let's say that credit card transactions may be processed in one of two data centers: one in Atlanta for East Coast accounts, and one in San Francisco for West Coast accounts. All U.S. customers have their account records managed in one of these two data centers. If I live in Seattle and make a purchase anywhere in the western United States, the merchant system sends my transaction to the San Francisco data center where it locates my account record and processes the transaction. However, the system must also be prepared to locate East Coast account records stored in the Atlanta data center. The view used to locate all accounts (from the West Coast server) may be defined like this:

```
CREATE VIEW vAllAccounts
AS
SELECT * FROM Accounts      -- (local West coast)
UNION ALL
SELECT * FROM EastCoastServer.SalesDatabase.dbo.Accounts -- (remote East coast)
```

The query issued from the client would look like this:

```
SELECT TOP 1 * FROM vAllAccounts WHERE CardNumber = @CardNumber
```

The TOP 1 statement tells the query-processing engine to stop looking after it finds one record. If the record is located in the first table (on the local server), no request is made on the remote server. Otherwise, the connection is used to pass the request to the other server, which processes the query until it locates the account record. Figure 12-13 demonstrates this scenario.

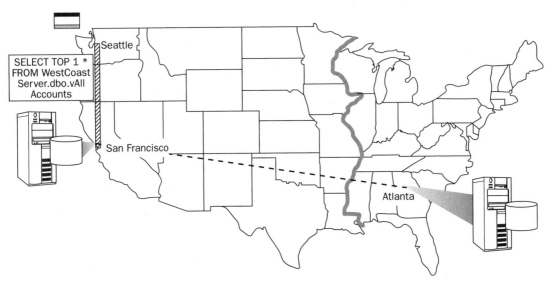

Figure 12-13

Now suppose that I travel to New York and buy a stuffed animal for my daughter's birthday. I find a great deal on a teddy bear wearing a Yankees baseball cap and pay with my credit card, which sends a request to the Atlanta data center to Select Top 1 from a view defined as follows:

```
CREATE VIEW vAllAccounts
AS
SELECT * FROM Accounts       -- (local East coast)
UNION ALL
SELECT * FROM WestCoastServer.SalesDatabase.dbo.Accounts -- (remote West coast)
```

In this example, the East Coast server doesn't find my account record in the local Accounts table so it moves to the remote server, which begins searching in its Accounts table. This part of the query is actually processed on the West Coast server so data isn't unnecessarily transferred across the network connection. After finding one record (my account), it stops looking and terminates the query execution. This scenario is depicted in Figure 12-14.

SELECT TOP 1 *
FROM EastCoast
Server.dbo.vAll
Accounts

Figure 12-14

Securing Data

Another useful offering of views is to provide a layer for user data access without giving users access to sensitive data or other database objects. A common security practice is for the database administrator to lock down all of the tables, denying access to all regular users. Views are then created to explicitly expose selected tables, columns, and/or rows for all or selected users. When the select permission is granted on a view, users gain access to the view's underlying data even if the same user is explicitly denied the select permission on the underlying table(s).

Hiding Complexity

One of the most common, and arguably one of the most important, reasons to use views is to simplify data access. In a normalized database, even the most basic queries can involve many different tables. Views make it possible for programmers, report writers, and users to gain access to data at a reasonably low level without having to contend with the complexities of relationships and database schema. A practical transactional database is broken down into many tables and related information is spread out across these tables to maintain data integrity and to reduce unnecessary redundancy. Reassembling all of these elements can be a headache for someone who doesn't fully understand the data or who may not be versed in relational database design. Even for the experienced developer or DBA, using a view can save time and minimize errors. The following is an example to demonstrate this point. To do something as fundamental as return product inventory information can be a relatively complex proposition.

In this example, I want to return the category, subcategory, product, model, shelf location, inventory quantity, inventory cost, and inventory date for all products. Because this information could be common to more than one product, the category, subcategory, location cost, and inventory data is stored in separate tables. For operational reasons, I have decided to exclude the price information as well as other descriptive data for the products. Using a view, users are not even aware that the columns containing the omitted information exist.

```
CREATE VIEW vProductInventory
AS
SELECT PC.Name AS Category
      ,SC.Name AS Subcategory
      ,P.Name AS Product
      ,P.ProductNumber
      ,PM.Name AS Model
      ,PN.Shelf
      ,PN.Quantity
      ,P.StandardCost
      ,P.StandardCost * PN.Quantity AS InventoryValue
      ,MAX(PN.ModifiedDate) AS InventoryDate
FROM   Production.Product P
INNER JOIN Production.ProductInventory PN
  ON P.ProductID = PN.ProductID
INNER JOIN Production.ProductModel PM
  ON P.ProductModelID = PM.ProductModelID
INNER JOIN Production.ProductSubcategory SC
  ON P.ProductSubcategoryID = SC.ProductSubcategoryID
INNER JOIN Production.ProductCategory PC
  ON SC.ProductCategoryID = PC.ProductCategoryID
GROUP BY PC.Name
        ,SC.Name
        ,P.Name
        ,P.ProductNumber
        ,PM.Name
        ,PN.Shelf
        ,PN.Quantity
        ,P.StandardCost
        ,P.StandardCost * PN.Quantity
```

Here's one more example of a lengthy view. This view will be used a little later in the discussion on processing business logic in stored procedures. I like this view because it contains several columns that can easily be used for reporting purposes, and to sort, group, or filter the resulting data.

```
CREATE VIEW vProductSalesDetail
AS
SELECT DISTINCT
       PC.Name AS Category
      ,PS.Name AS Subcategory
      ,P.Name AS Product
      ,ST.Name AS Territory
      ,SUM(SOD.OrderQty) AS TotalQuantity
      ,SUM(SOD.UnitPrice) AS TotalPrice
      ,SUM(SOD.UnitPriceDiscount) AS TotalDiscount
      ,SUM(SOD.LineTotal) AS LineTotals
      ,SOH.OrderDate
      ,SUM(SOH.SubTotal) AS SubTotal
      ,SUM(SOH.TaxAmt) AS TotalTax
      ,SUM(SOH.TotalDue) AS TotalDue
FROM   Production.ProductCategory PC
```

```
INNER JOIN Production.ProductSubcategory PS
  ON PC.ProductCategoryID = PS.ProductCategoryID
INNER JOIN Production.Product P
  ON PS.ProductSubcategoryID = P.ProductSubcategoryID
INNER JOIN Sales.SalesOrderDetail SOD
  ON P.ProductID = SOD.ProductID
INNER JOIN Sales.SalesOrderHeader SOH
  ON SOD.SalesOrderID = SOH.SalesOrderID
INNER JOIN Sales.SalesTerritory ST
  ON ST.TerritoryID = SOH.TerritoryID
GROUP BY PC.Name
        ,PS.Name
        ,P.Name
        ,ST.Name
        ,SOH.OrderDate
```

Modifying Data Through Views

Can data be modified through a view? Perhaps a better question is *should* data be modified through a view? The definitive answer is maybe. Yes, you can modify some data through views. Because a view can expose the results of a variety of query techniques, some results may be updatable, some may not, and others may allow some columns to be updated. This all depends on various join types, record-locking conditions, and permissions on the underlying tables.

As a rule, I don't think views are for updating records — that's my opinion. After all, doesn't the word view suggest that its purpose is to provide a read-only view of data? I think so, but I've also worked on enough corporate production databases where this was the only option.

The fact of the matter is that over time, databases evolve. Over the years, people come and go, policies are implemented with little evidence of their purpose, and political culture dictates the methods we use. If I ruled the world, no one would have access to data directly through tables; views would provide read-only data access and support all related application features, and stored procedures would be used to perform all transactional operations and filtered data retrieval. These are the guidelines I follow when designing a system from the ground up. However, I acknowledge that this is not always possible in the typical circumstance where one database designer isn't given free license.

In simple terms, these are the most common rules governing the conditions for updating data through views:

❑ In an inner join, columns from one table at a time may be modified. This is due to the record-locking restrictions on related tables. Updates generally cannot be performed on two related tables within the same transaction.

❑ In an outer join, generally columns only for the inner table are updatable.

❑ Updates can't be performed through a view containing a UNION query.

Stored Procedures

If views raise the bar of database functionality, then stored procedures take it to the next level. Unlike views, stored procedures can be used for much more than reading data. They provide a wide range of programming functionality. Categorically, stored procedures can be used to do the following:

- ❏ Implement parameterized views
- ❏ Return scalar values
- ❏ Maintain records
- ❏ Process business logic

Stored Procedures as Parameterized Views

As with views, stored procedures can be used to return a result set based on a SELECT statement. However, I want to clarify an important point about the difference between views and stored procedures. A view is used in a SELECT statement as if it were a table. A stored procedure is executed, rather than selected from. For most programming APIs, this makes little difference. If a programmer needs to return a set of rows to an application or report, any data access layer such as ODBC, OLEDB, ADO.NET, or SQL Client can be used to obtain results from a table, a view, or a stored procedure.

A stored procedure can be used in place of a view to return a set of rows from one or more tables. Earlier in this chapter, I used a simple view to return selected columns from the Product table. Again, the script looks like this:

```
CREATE VIEW vProductCosts
AS
SELECT ProductID, ProductSubcategoryID, Name, ProductNumber, StandardCost
FROM Production.Product
```

Contrast this with the script to create a similar stored procedure:

```
CREATE PROCEDURE spProductCosts
AS
SELECT ProductID, ProductSubcategoryID, Name, ProductNumber, StandardCost
FROM Production.Product
```

To execute the new stored procedure, the name is preceded by the EXECUTE statement:

```
EXECUTE spProductCosts
```

Although this is considered the most proper syntax, the EXECUTE command can be shortened to EXEC:

```
EXEC spProductCosts
```

In addition, when working with Management Studio, a stored procedure can be executed just by referencing its name:

```
spProductCosts
```

However, omitting the EXEC or EXECUTE command will not work when the stored procedure is referenced in other programming objects or programming interfaces. This abbreviated syntax is useful only in ad-hoc executions within Management Studio.

Using Parameters

A parameter is a special type of variable used to pass values into an expression. Named parameters are used for passing values into and out of stored procedures and user-defined functions. Parameters are most typically used to input, or pass values into, a procedure, but they can also be used to return values.

Parameters are declared immediately after the procedure definition and before the term AS. Parameters are declared with a specific data type and are used as variables in the body of a SQL statement. I will modify this procedure with an input parameter to pass the value of the ProductSubcategoryID. This will be used to filter the results of the query. This example shows the script for creating the procedure. If the procedure already exists, the CREATE statement may be replaced with the ALTER statement:

```
ALTER PROCEDURE spProductCosts
@SubCategoryID int
AS
SELECT ProductID, Name, ProductNumber, StandardCost
FROM Production.Product
WHERE ProductSubcategoryID = @SubCategoryID
```

To execute the procedure and pass the parameter value in SQL Query Analyzer or the Query Editor, simply append the parameter value to the end of the statement, like this:

```
EXECUTE spProductCosts 1
```

Alternatively, the stored procedure can be executed with the parameter and assigned value like this:

```
EXECUTE spProductCosts @SubCategoryID = 1
```

Stored procedures can accept multiple parameters and the parameters can be passed in either by position or by value, similar to the previous example. Suppose I want a stored procedure that filters products by subcategory and price. It would look something like this:

```
CREATE PROCEDURE spProductsByCost
@SubCategoryID int, @Cost money
AS
SELECT ProductID, Name, ProductNumber, StandardCost
FROM Production.Product
WHERE ProductSubcategoryID = @SubCategoryID
AND StandardCost > @Cost
```

Using SQL, the multiple parameters can be passed in a comma-delimited list in the order they were declared:

```
EXECUTE spProductsByCost 1, $1000.00
```

Or the parameters can be passed explicitly by value. If the parameters are supplied by value, it doesn't matter in what order they are supplied:

```
EXECUTE spProductsByCost @Cost = $1000.00, @SubCategoryID = 1
```

If a programmer is using a common data access API, such as ADO or ADO.NET, separate parameter objects are often used to encapsulate these values and execute the procedure in the most efficient manner.

Although views and stored procedures do provide some overlap in functionality, they each have a unique purpose. The view used in the previous example can be used in a variety of settings where it may not be feasible to use a stored procedure. However, if I need to filter records using parameterized values, a stored procedure will allow this but a view will not. So, if the programmer building the product browse screen needs an unfiltered result set and the report designer needs a filtered list of products based on a subcategory parameter, do I create a view or a stored procedure? That's easy, both. Use views as the foundation upon which to build stored procedures. Using the previous example, I select from the view rather than the table:

```
ALTER PROCEDURE spProductCosts
@SubcategoryID int
As
SELECT ProductID, Name, ProductNumber, StandardCost
FROM vProductCosts
WHERE ProductSubcategoryID = @SubcategoryID
```

The benefit may not be so obvious in this simple, one-table example. However, if a procedure were based on the nine-table vEmployeeContactDetail view, the procedure call might benefit from optimizations in the view design and the lower maintenance cost of storing this complex statement in only one object.

Returning Values

The parameter examples shown thus far demonstrate how to use parameters for passing values into a stored procedure. One method to return a value from a procedure is to return a single-column, single-row result set. Although there is probably nothing grossly wrong with this technique, it's not the most effective way to handle simple values. A result set is wrapped in a cursor, which defines the rows and columns, and may be prepared to deal with record navigation and locking. This kind of overkill reminds me of a digital camera memory card I recently ordered from a discount electronics supplier. A few days later, a relatively large box arrived and at first appeared to be filled with nothing more than foam packing peanuts. I had to look carefully to find the postage-size memory card inside.

In addition to passing values into a procedure, parameters can also be used to return values for output. Stored procedure parameters with an OUTPUT direction modifier are set to store both input and output values by default. Additionally, the procedure itself is equipped to return a single integer value without needing to define a specific parameter. The return value is also called the return code and defaults to the integer value of 0. Some programming APIs, such as ADO and ADO.NET, actually create a special output parameter object to handle this return value. Suppose I want to know how many product records there are for a specified subcategory. I'll pass the SubCategoryID using an input parameter and return the record count using an output parameter:

```
CREATE PROCEDURE spProductCountBySubCategory
   @SubCategoryID int,
   @ProdCount int OUTPUT
AS
   SELECT @ProdCount = COUNT(*)
   FROM Production.Product
   WHERE ProductSubcategoryID = @SubCategoryID
```

To test a stored procedure with output parameters in Management Studio, it is necessary to explicitly use these parameters by name. Treat them as if they were variables, but you don't need to declare them. When executing a stored procedure using SQL, the behavior of output parameters can be a bit puzzling because they also have to be passed in. In this example, using the same stored procedure, a variable is used to capture the output parameter value. The curious thing about this syntax is that the assignment seems backward. Remember that the OUTPUT modifier affects the direction of the value assignment — in this case, from right to left. The results are shown in Figure 12-15.

```
DECLARE @Out int
EXECUTE spProductCountBySubCategory
@SubCategoryID = 2,
@ProdCount = @Out OUTPUT
SELECT @Out AS ProductCountBySubCategory
```

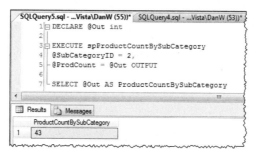

Figure 12-15

It is critical that the OUTPUT modifier also be added to the output parameter when it is passed into the stored procedure. If you don't, the stored procedure will still execute, but it will not return any data, as shown in Figure 12-16.

```
DECLARE @Out int
EXECUTE spProductCountBySubCategory
@SubCategoryID = 2,
@ProdCount = @Out --Missing the OUTPUT directional modifier
SELECT @Out AS ProductCountBySubCategory
```

```
SQLQuery5.sql - ...Vista\DanW (55))*   SQLQuery4.sql - ...Vista\DanW (53))*   SQLQuery3.sql - ...Vista\Dan
    2   EXECUTE spProductCountBySubCategory
    3   @SubCategoryID = 2,
    4   @ProdCount = @Out --Missing the OUTPUT directional modifier
    5
    6   SELECT @Out AS ProductCountBySubCategory
    7
    8
```

```
Results   Messages
    ProductCountBySubCategory
1   NULL
```

Figure 12-16

There is no practical limit to the number of values that may be returned from a stored procedure. The stated limit is 2,100, including input and output parameters.

If you need to return only one value from the procedure, you can do so without the use of an output parameter. You can use the return code of the procedure as long as the value being returned is an integer. Here is the same stored procedure showing this technique:

```
ALTER PROCEDURE spProductCountBySubCategory
   @SubCategoryID int
AS
   DECLARE @Out int
   SELECT @Out = Count(*)
   FROM Production.Product
   WHERE ProductSubcategoryID = @SubCategoryID
RETURN @Out
```

The RETURN statement does two things: it modifies the return value for the procedure from the default value, 0, and it terminates execution so that any statements following this line do not execute. This is significant in cases where there may be conditional branching logic. Typically, the capture of the return value will be done with a programming API. However, you can also execute the return value using Management Studio by setting a variable to the return value of the stored procedure as shown in the following example:

```
DECLARE @Return_Value AS int
EXECUTE @Return_Value =
          spProductCountBySubCategory
                    @SubCategoryID = 2
SELECT @Return_Value
```

Record Maintenance

Using stored procedures to manage the insert, update, and delete operations for each major database entity can drastically reduce the cost of data maintenance tasks down the road. Any program code written to perform record operations should do so using stored procedures and not ad-hoc SQL expressions. As a rule of thumb, when I design a business application, every table that will have records managed through the application interface gets a corresponding stored procedure to perform each of these operations. These procedures are by far the most straightforward in terms of syntax patterns. Although simple, writing this script can be cumbersome due to the level of detail necessary to deal with all of the columns. Fortunately, Management Studio includes scripting tools that will generate the bulk of the script for you. Beyond creating the fundamental INSERT, UPDATE, DELETE, and SELECT statements, you need to define and place parameters into your script.

Insert Procedure

The basic pattern for creating a stored procedure to insert records is to define parameters for all non-default columns. In the case of the Product table, the ProductID primary key column will automatically be incremented because it's defined as an identity column. The rowguid and ModifiedDate columns have default values assigned in the table definition, so they will be set if values are not specified. The MakeFlag and FinishedGoodsFlag columns also have default values assigned in the table definition. It may be appropriate to set these values differently for some records. For this reason, these parameters are set to the same default values in the procedure. Several columns are nullable and the corresponding parameters are set to a default value of null. If a parameter with a default assignment isn't provided when the procedure is executed, the default value is used, which is how you create a procedure with optional parameters. Otherwise, all parameters without default values must be supplied:

```
CREATE  PROCEDURE spProduct_Insert
        @Name                   nvarchar(50)
      , @ProductNumber          nvarchar(25)
      , @MakeFlag               bit             = 1
      , @FinishedGoodsFlag      bit             = 1
      , @Color                  nvarchar(15)    = Null
      , @SafetyStockLevel       smallint
      , @ReorderPoint           smallint
      , @StandardCost           money
      , @ListPrice              money
      , @Size                   nvarchar(5)     = Null
      , @SizeUnitMeasureCode    nchar(3)        = Null
      , @WeightUnitMeasureCode  nchar(3)        = Null
      , @Weight                 decimal         = Null
      , @DaysToManufacture      int
      , @ProductLine            nchar(2)        = Null
      , @Class                  nchar(2)        = Null
      , @Style                  nchar(2)        = Null
      , @ProductSubcategoryID   smallint        = Null
      , @ProductModelID         int             = Null
      , @SellStartDate          datetime
      , @SellEndDate            datetime        = Null
      , @DiscontinuedDate       datetime        = Null
AS
INSERT  INTO Production.Product
    (   Name
      , ProductNumber
      , MakeFlag
      , FinishedGoodsFlag
      , Color
      , SafetyStockLevel
      , ReorderPoint
      , StandardCost
      , ListPrice
      , Size
```

(continued)

(continued)

```
             , SizeUnitMeasureCode
             , WeightUnitMeasureCode
             , Weight
             , DaysToManufacture
             , ProductLine
             , Class
             , Style
             , ProductSubcategoryID
             , ProductModelID
             , SellStartDate
             , SellEndDate
             , DiscontinuedDate   )
     VALUES
             ( @Name
             , @ProductNumber
             , @MakeFlag
             , @FinishedGoodsFlag
             , @Color
             , @SafetyStockLevel
             , @ReorderPoint
             , @StandardCost
             , @ListPrice
             , @Size
             , @SizeUnitMeasureCode
             , @WeightUnitMeasureCode
             , @Weight
             , @DaysToManufacture
             , @ProductLine
             , @Class
             , @Style
             , @ProductSubcategoryID
             , @ProductModelID
             , @SellStartDate
             , @SellEndDate
             , @DiscontinuedDate)
```

It's a lot of script but it's not complicated. Executing this procedure in SQL is quite easy. This can be done in comma-delimited fashion or by using explicit parameter names. Because the majority of the fields and corresponding parameters are optional, they can be omitted. Only the required parameters need to be passed; the optional parameters are simply ignored:

```
EXECUTE spProduct_Insert
      @Name              = 'Widget'
    , @ProductNumber     = '987654321'
    , @SafetyStockLevel  = 10
    , @ReorderPoint      = 15
    , @StandardCost      = 23.50
    , @ListPrice         = 49.95
    , @DaysToManufacture = 30
    , @SellStartDate     = '10/1/04'
```

The procedure can also be executed with parameter values passed in a comma-delimited list. Although the script isn't nearly as easy to read, it is less verbose. Even though this may save you some typing, it often becomes an exercise in counting commas and rechecking the table's field list in the Object Browser until the script runs without error.

```
EXECUTE spProduct_Insert 'Widget', '987654321', 1, 1, Null, 10, 15, 23.50,
49.95, Null, Null, Null, Null, 30, Null, Null, Null, Null, Null, '10/1/04'
```

When using this technique, parameter values must be passed in the order they are declared. Values must be provided for every parameter up to the point of the last required value. After that, the remaining parameters in the list can be ignored.

A useful variation of this procedure may be to return the newly generated primary key value. The last identity value generated in a session is held by the global variable, @@Identity. To add this feature, simply add this line to the end of the procedure. This would cause the Insert procedure to return the ProductID value for the inserted record.

```
RETURN @@Identity
```

Of course, if you have already created this procedure, change the CREATE keyword to ALTER, make changes to the script, and then re-execute it.

Update Procedure

The Update procedure is similar. Usually when I create these data maintenance stored procedures, I write the script for the Insert procedure and then make the modifications necessary to transform the same script into an Update procedure. As you can see, it's very similar:

```
CREATE PROCEDURE spProduct_Update
        @ProductID              int
    ,   @Name                   nvarchar(50)
    ,   @ProductNumber          nvarchar(25)
    ,   @MakeFlag               bit
    ,   @FinishedGoodsFlag      bit
    ,   @Color                  nvarchar(15)
    ,   @SafetyStockLevel       smallint
    ,   @ReorderPoint           smallint
    ,   @StandardCost           money
    ,   @ListPrice              money
    ,   @Size                   nvarchar(5)
    ,   @SizeUnitMeasureCode    nchar(3)
    ,   @WeightUnitMeasureCode  nchar(3)
    ,   @Weight                 decimal
    ,   @DaysToManufacture      int
    ,   @ProductLine            nchar(2)
    ,   @Class                  nchar(2)
    ,   @Style                  nchar(2)
    ,   @ProductSubcategoryID   smallint
    ,   @ProductModelID         int
    ,   @SellStartDate          datetime
    ,   @SellEndDate            datetime
    ,   @DiscontinuedDate       datetime
```

(continued)

(continued)

```
AS
UPDATE Product
SET     Name                    = @Name
      , ProductNumber           = @ProductNumber
      , MakeFlag                = @MakeFlag
      , FinishedGoodsFlag       = @FinishedGoodsFlag
      , Color                   = @Color
      , SafetyStockLevel        = @SafetyStockLevel
      , ReorderPoint            = @ReorderPoint
      , StandardCost            = @StandardCost
      , ListPrice               = @ListPrice
      , Size                    = @Size
      , SizeUnitMeasureCode     = @SizeUnitMeasureCode
      , WeightUnitMeasureCode   = @WeightUnitMeasureCode
      , Weight                  = @Weight
      , DaysToManufacture       = @DaysToManufacture
      , ProductLine             = @ProductLine
      , Class                   = @Class
      , Style                   = @Style
      , ProductSubcategoryID    = @ProductSubcategoryID
      , ProductModelID          = @ProductModelID
      , SellStartDate           = @SellStartDate
      , SellEndDate             = @SellEndDate
      , DiscontinuedDate        = @DiscontinuedDate
  WHERE ProductID = @ProductID
```

The parameter list is the same as the insert procedure with the addition of the primary key, in this case, the ProductID column. However, the defaults have been removed. Defaults are dangerous to use with update procedures because if no value is provided, the procedure will overwrite what is in the table with the default. In our case, most of the defaults are NULL. This would cause any value in the database to be removed and replaced by a NULL if no value were provided.

Delete Procedure

In its basic form, the Delete procedure is very simple. The only necessary parameter for our example is the ProductID column value:

```
CREATE PROCEDURE spProduct_Delete
      @ProductID     int
AS
      DELETE FROM Production.Product
      WHERE ProductID = @ProductID
```

In reality, what needs to be provided is whatever fields uniquely identify the row. This may be a single row, as in the case of the Product table, or a combination of columns in more complex tables.

Remember that deleting rows is not always as easy as it may seem. If the table is referenced with a foreign key constraint, all child records would have to be deleted prior to the deletion of the parent record. For example, the following script will not work:

```
DELETE FROM Production.ProductCategory
WHERE ProductCategoryID = 1
```

This script results in the following error:

```
WoodVista(WoodVista\DanW): Msg 547, Level 16, State 0, Line 2
The DELETE statement conflicted with the REFERENCE constraint
"FK_ProductSubcategory_ProductCategory_ProductCategoryID".
The conflict occurred in database "AdventureWorks2008",
table "Production.ProductSubcategory",
column 'ProductCategoryID'.
WoodVista(WoodVista\DanW):
The statement has been terminated.
```

This leads us smoothly to the next topic, handling errors.

Handling and Raising Errors

In many data maintenance procedures, you may need to decide how to handle errors. Attempting to insert, update, or delete a record that violates constraints or rules will cause the database engine to raise an error. If this is acceptable behavior, you don't need to do anything special in your procedure code. When the procedure is executed, an error is raised and the transaction is aborted. You simply need to handle the error condition in the client program code. Another, often more desirable, approach would be to proactively investigate the potential condition and then raise a custom error. This may have the advantage of offering the user or client application more useful error information or a more graceful method to handle the condition. In the case of the Delete procedure, I could check for existing dependent records and then raise a custom error without attempting to perform the delete operation. This also has the advantage of not locking records while the delete operation is attempted.

Error Messages

There are two general approaches to raising errors. One is to raise the error on-the-fly. This is done using a single statement. The other approach is to add custom error codes and message text to the system catalog. These messages can then be raised from script in any database on the server. Custom errors are added to the system catalog using the sp_addmessage system stored procedure. Here's an example:

```
sp_addmessage @msgnum = 50010
            , @severity = 16
            , @msgtext = 'Cannot delete a category with existing sub-categories. '
            , @with_log = 'True'
            , @replace = 'Replace'
            , @lang = 'us_english'
```

Three parameters are required: the message number, message severity, and message text. There are also three additional optional parameters: one to specify logging the error in the server's application log, one for replacing a current error with the same message number, and one to specify the language of the error if multiple languages are installed on the server. Custom error numbers begin at 50,001. This is user-assigned and has no special meaning. It's just a unique value. The system recognizes severity values within specified numeric ranges and may respond by automatically logging the error or sending alerts. Alerts are configurable within the SQL Server Agent. Messages and errors are distinguished by the Severity Level flag. Those with a severity level from 0 to 10 are considered to be informational messages and will not raise a system exception. Those with a severity level from 11 to 18 are non-fatal errors, and those 19 or above are considered to be the most severe, or fatal errors. This scale was devised for Windows service error logging. The following table shows the system-defined error severity levels.

Severity Level	Description
1	Misc. System Information
2 – 6	Reserved
7	Notification: Status Information
8	Notification: User Intervention Required
9	User Defined
10	Information
11	Specified Database Object Not Found
12	Unused
13	User Transaction Syntax Error
14	Insufficient Permission
15	Syntax Error in SQL Statements
16	Misc. User Error
17	Insufficient Resources
18	Non-Fatal Error in Resource
19 *	Fatal Error in Resource
20 *	Fatal Error in Current Process
21 *	Fatal Error in Database Processes
22 *	Fatal Error: Table Integrity Suspect
23 *	Fatal Error: Database Integrity Suspect
24 *	Fatal Error: Hardware Error
25 *	Fatal Error

This example demonstrates raising the error created in the previous example:

```
RAISERROR (50010, 16, 1)
```

The output from this expression returns the message defined earlier:

```
Msg 50010, Level 16, State 1, Line 1
Cannot delete a product with existing sub-categories.
```

The severity level is actually repeated in the call. This seems like a strange requirement, but that's the way it works. It also does not have to be the same as the defined severity level. If I want to raise the error as a severity level 11 instead of 16, I can. The last parameter is the state. This value is user-defined and has no inherent meaning to the system, but it is a required argument. State can be a signed integer between –255 and +255. State can be used for internal tracking, for example, to track all "State 3" errors.

Here is an example of an ad-hoc message that has not been previously defined:

```
RAISERROR ('The sky is falling', 16, 1)
```

The resulting output is as follows:

```
Msg 50000, Level 16, State 1, Line 1
The sky is falling
```

Note that ad-hoc messages use the reserved message id of 50000. Raising an ad-hoc message with a severity level of 19 or higher requires elevated privileges and must be performed with explicit logging such as the following:

```
RAISERROR ('The sky is falling', 19, 1) WITH LOG
```

If you need to raise an error of this type, it's advisable to define these messages ahead of time because a connection to SQL Server that is not authenticated as a System Administrator will be prevented from using the WITH LOG option.

When an error occurs, the global variable, @@ERROR, changes from its default value of 0 to an integer type standard error number. SQL Server includes more than 6,800 unique errors. All these error numbers and messages are stored in the Master database. The error number can be retrieved by selecting the @@ERROR global variable or by selecting the ERROR_NUMBER() function.

Error Handling in SQL Server

For many years, the ability to handle errors in T-SQL script has been limited to the same type of pattern used in other scripting languages. The query-processing engine was not equipped to respond to error conditions in the same way that an event-driven run-time engine would. Thus, if you suspected that an error might be raised after a specific line of script, you would have to check for an error condition and respond to it. You had to do it for every line where an error could occur. The downside to this approach was that you had to be able to guess where an error might occur and then respond to it.

One of the most significant enhancements to T-SQL with the release of SQL Server 2005 was its new error-handling capability, which works like most true programming languages. Any statements that could possibly cause an error are wrapped within a TRY block. The error-handling script is located in a separate CATCH block. When an error condition occurs in the TRY block, execution is moved to the first line within the CATCH block. The limitation of SQL Server error handling is that it can't always be used to truly "handle" errors. Once an error occurs inside a transaction, very often that transaction enters a "doomed" state. There is no way to commit the transaction; it must be rolled back. However, logic can be added so that the transaction is retried. Other than that, the error can be recorded and maybe some other event code executed. The syntax is fairly straightforward:

```
BEGIN TRY
   ... Transaction
END TRY
BEGIN CATCH
   ... error-handing script
END CATCH
```

If you have experience with other programming languages such as C# or VB.NET, you may be wondering about the "Finally" block that is supported by many programming languages. Sorry to say, it is not supported with T-SQL. To adequately describe the error-handling capabilities, we need to create a table that is used to track and catalog errors. The table is created with the following script:

```
USE AdventureWorks2008
GO
CREATE TABLE ErrorTable
(ErrorID int IDENTITY(1,1) NOT NULL
,ErrorNumber int NOT NULL
,ErrorMessage nvarchar(4000) NOT NULL
,ErrorLine int NOT NULL
,ErrorTime datetime NOT NULL DEFAULT GETDATE())
```

This is an example using this form of error handling:

```
CREATE PROCEDURE spDeleteProduct @Productid int
AS
SET NOCOUNT ON --Inhibits row counts
BEGIN TRY
  BEGIN TRANSACTION
    DELETE Production.Product WHERE ProductID = @ProductID
  COMMIT TRANSACTION
END TRY
BEGIN CATCH
  DECLARE @Err AS int
  DECLARE @Msg AS nvarchar(MAX)
  DECLARE @Line AS int
  SET @Err = ERROR_NUMBER()
  SET @Msg = ERROR_MESSAGE()
  SET @Line = ERROR_LINE()
  ROLLBACK TRANSACTION
  INSERT ErrorTable
  (ErrorNumber,ErrorMessage,ErrorLine)
  VALUES (@err, @msg, @Line)
  RAISERROR(@Msg, 14,1)
END CATCH
```

It is important to remember that the CATCH block does indeed catch and "handle" the error. If the previous procedure did not contain the RAISERROR() function, the calling application would never know that something bad happened.

For example, if you run the following script, it will appear to work just fine:

```
BEGIN TRY
  BEGIN TRANSACTION
    DELETE Production.ProductCategory WHERE ProductCategoryID = 1
  COMMIT TRANSACTION
END TRY
BEGIN CATCH
--Do Nothing
END CATCH
```

However, if you query the ProductCategory table, you will find that the Bikes category is safe and has not been deleted because the ProductSubCategory table has a foreign key that references the ProductCategory table. If the logic is changed to raise an error, the application will be informed and can take appropriate action. Here is the same script with the CATCH block modified so that you can see what happened that aborted the delete:

```
BEGIN TRY
  BEGIN TRANSACTION
    DELETE Production.ProductCategory WHERE ProductCategoryID = 1
  COMMIT TRANSACTION
END TRY
BEGIN CATCH
  DECLARE @Err AS int
  DECLARE @Msg AS nvarchar(MAX)
  DECLARE @Line AS int
  SET @Err = ERROR_NUMBER()
  SET @Msg = ERROR_MESSAGE()
  SET @Line = ERROR_LINE()
  ROLLBACK TRANSACTION
  INSERT ErrorTable
  (ErrorNumber, ErrorMessage, ErrorLine)
  VALUES (@err, @msg, @Line)
  RAISERROR(@Msg, 14,1)
END CATCH
```

The drawback of this method is that the original error number (547) cannot be retrieved by the calling application and instead the number 50000 is returned. SQL Server does not allow the RAISERROR() function to be called with values less than 13000 and messages between 13000 and 50000 are non-configurable. If the application programmer wanted to check for the error number 547, to perform some other logic, he or she would not see it for this procedure, which is where the custom error that was covered earlier can come in.

In some cases T-SQL's error-handling capabilities can be used to handle errors and re-run transactions affected by the error. The following example uses conditional logic to check for an error and to rerun the transaction in the case of that particular error. To set up the example, we must first add a user-defined error to the system catalog with the sp_addmessage stored procedure:

```
sp_addmessage @msgnum = 50100
              ,@severity = 16
              ,@msgtext = 'Testing of error handling capabilities'
              ,@with_log = 'True'
              ,@replace = 'Replace'
              ,@lang = 'us_english'
```

Now that we have our error message, we will build a procedure to test the error-handling capabilities of SQL Server:

```
CREATE PROC dbo.procTestErrorHandling
AS
DECLARE @retry AS int; --Declare retry variable for transaction resubmission
SET @retry = 1;
WHILE @retry BETWEEN 1 AND 3 --Procedure will retry transaction three times
BEGIN
    BEGIN TRY
        BEGIN TRAN
            INSERT Production.ProductCategory
            (Name)
            VALUES
            ('Widgets')
            RAISERROR(50100,16,1)
        COMMIT TRAN
        SET @retry = 0;
    END TRY
    BEGIN CATCH
      -- Output for debug
        PRINT 'In CATCH block.
        Error number: ' + CAST(ERROR_NUMBER() AS nvarchar(10)) + '
        Error message: ' + ERROR_MESSAGE() + '
        Error severity: ' + CAST(ERROR_SEVERITY() AS nvarchar(10)) + '
        Error state: ' + CAST(ERROR_STATE() AS nvarchar(10))

    IF ERROR_NUMBER() = 50100  --If the error is 50100, resubmit the transaction.
        BEGIN
            ROLLBACK TRAN;
            SET @retry = @retry + 1;
            IF @retry <= 3
                BEGIN
                    WAITFOR DELAY '00:00:00:500';
                    --If an error occurs wait a half a second then resubmit
                    PRINT 'Error detected. Attempting try #' + CAST(@retry AS
varchar(10)) + '.';
                END
        END
    ELSE
        BEGIN
            SET @retry = 5
            DECLARE @ErrorMsg nvarchar(MAX)
```

```
            SET @ErrorMsg = ERROR_MESSAGE() + ' Error handling test complete
                                             aborting transaction.'

            ROLLBACK TRAN
            RAISERROR(@ErrorMsg,16, 1)
            RETURN -1
        END
    END CATCH
END
```

Now execute the procedure and check the results.

```
WoodVista(WoodVista\DanW): (1 row(s) affected)
WoodVista(WoodVista\DanW):
In CATCH block.
        Error number: 50100
        Error message: Testing of error handling capabilities
        Error severity: 16
        Error state: 1
WoodVista(WoodVista\DanW):
Error detected. Attempting try #2.
WoodVista(WoodVista\DanW): (1 row(s) affected)
WoodVista(WoodVista\DanW):
In CATCH block.
        Error number: 50100
        Error message: Testing of error handling capabilities
        Error severity: 16
        Error state: 1
WoodVista(WoodVista\DanW):
Error detected. Attempting try #3.
WoodVista(WoodVista\DanW): (1 row(s) affected)
WoodVista(WoodVista\DanW):
In CATCH block.
        Error number: 50100
        Error message: Testing of error handling capabilities
        Error severity: 16
        Error state: 1
```

A query of the ProductCategory table will confirm that the category Widgets was not added.

You are probably wondering what the practical application of this example is. I use this particular logic on production systems to detect modification errors due to a contention error called a *deadlock*. A deadlock occurs when at least two processes are locking resources that each process needs to complete its transaction. This creates a process standoff where neither process can complete while the other process is running. SQL Server automatically detects and terminates deadlocks by selecting one of the processes and killing it. When it does this, it sends the system error 1205 to the associated application to inform the application that the process was selected as the deadlock victim and then terminated. The transaction will need to be resubmitted. Because deadlocks are transient in nature, it is possible that if we detected them, we could wait for a short period of time and resend the modification. That is why I included the WAITFOR DELAY statement in the example. To create a procedure that works for deadlocks or any other predictable error, you simply change the conditional logic of the procedure to look for the error number of interest.

Another useful function that can be used in error handling is XACT_STATE(). XACT_STATE() returns information about what effects an error has had on an associated transaction. The following table describes the possible values returned by XACT_STATE().

XACT_STATE() Return Value	Description
1	There is an active user transaction that is committable.
0	There are no active user transactions.
-1	There is an active user transaction, but it is not committable. It is in a "doomed" state. It must be rolled back.

By using a modified version of the previous example, we can have the CATCH block check the return value of XACT_STATE() and perform the appropriate action:

```
USE AdventureWorks2008
GO
CREATE PROC dbo.InsertCategory @CategoryName nvarchar(50)
AS
BEGIN TRY
    BEGIN TRAN
        INSERT Production.ProductCategory
        (Name)
        VALUES
        (@CategoryName)
        RAISERROR(50100,16,1)
    COMMIT TRAN
END TRY
BEGIN CATCH
  -- Output for debug
    PRINT 'In CATCH block.
    Error number: ' + CAST(ERROR_NUMBER() AS nvarchar(10)) + '
    Error message: ' + ERROR_MESSAGE() + '
    Error severity: ' + CAST(ERROR_SEVERITY() AS nvarchar(10)) + '
    Error state: ' + CAST(ERROR_STATE() AS nvarchar(10)) + '
    Transact state: ' + CAST(XACT_STATE() AS nchar(2))
    IF XACT_STATE() = -1
        BEGIN
            DECLARE @ErrorMsg nvarchar(MAX)
            SET @ErrorMsg = ERROR_MESSAGE()
            PRINT 'Transaction State Doomed, Transaction Rolled Back'
            ROLLBACK TRAN
            RAISERROR(@ErrorMsg,16, 1)
            RETURN -1
        END
    IF XACT_STATE() = 1
        BEGIN
```

```
            COMMIT TRAN
            PRINT 'Transaction State Committable, Transaction Committed'
        END
    IF XACT_STATE() = 0
        BEGIN
            PRINT 'No Transaction Present, Do nothing'
        END
END CATCH
```

Now that we have our new procedure, let's execute it to see what happens:

```
EXECUTE InsertCategory 'Blue Widgets'
```

Here are the results:

```
WoodVista(WoodVista\DanW): (1 row(s) affected)
WoodVista(WoodVista\DanW):
In CATCH block.
   Error number: 50100
   Error message: Testing of error handling capabilities
   Error severity: 16
   Error state: 1
   Transact state: 1
WoodVista(WoodVista\DanW):
        Transaction State Committable, Transaction Committed
```

A query of the ProductCategory table will show that the Blue Widgets category was added. However, when the same procedure is executed again, a different error will occur:

```
WoodVista(WoodVista\DanW): (0 row(s) affected)
WoodVista(WoodVista\DanW):
In CATCH block.
   Error number: 2601
   Error message: Cannot insert duplicate key row in object 'Production
.ProductCategory' with unique index 'AK_ProductCategory_Name'.
   Error severity: 14
   Error state: 1
   Transact state: 1
WoodVista(WoodVista\DanW):
Transaction State Committable, Transaction Committed
```

Even though a unique constraint violation error occurred, the transaction was still committable. This leads us to an important consideration to keep in mind when using this particular functionality. Should we commit a transaction just because it is committable? If the CATCH block was called because of an error, it may not be the wisest of courses to commit the transaction just because you can. Take the following example, for instance. Here we will create a checking account table and a savings account table. Then we will place a check constraint on the amount columns so that they must be greater than zero.

After that we will invoke some code that transfers $100.00 from the savings account to the checking account by updating both tables. Because the savings account currently has a balance of $100.00 this update should cause an error.

```
USE AdventureWorks2008
GO
CREATE TABLE CheckingAccount
(AccountNo int NOT NULL
,Amount money NOT NULL)
ALTER TABLE CheckingAccount
ADD CONSTRAINT CK_CheckingAmount CHECK (Amount > 0)
GO
CREATE TABLE SavingsAccount
(AccountNo int NOT NULL
,Amount money NOT NULL);
ALTER TABLE SavingsAccount
ADD CONSTRAINT CK_SavingsAmount CHECK (Amount > 0)
GO
INSERT CheckingAccount
VALUES
(1111,100.00)
INSERT SavingsAccount
VALUES
(1112,100.00)
BEGIN TRY
    BEGIN TRAN
        UPDATE CheckingAccount
        SET Amount = Amount + 100
        WHERE AccountNo = 1111
        UPDATE SavingsAccount
        SET Amount = Amount - 100
        WHERE AccountNo = 1112
    COMMIT TRAN
END TRY
BEGIN CATCH
  -- Output for debug
    PRINT 'In CATCH block.
    Error number: ' + CAST(ERROR_NUMBER() AS nvarchar(10)) + '
    Error message: ' + ERROR_MESSAGE() + '
    Error severity: ' + CAST(ERROR_SEVERITY() AS nvarchar(10)) + '
    Error state: ' + CAST(ERROR_STATE() AS nvarchar(10)) + '
    Transact state: ' + CAST(XACT_STATE() AS nchar(2))
    IF XACT_STATE() = -1
        BEGIN
            DECLARE @ErrorMsg nvarchar(MAX)
            SET @ErrorMsg = ERROR_MESSAGE()
            PRINT 'Transaction State Doomed, Transaction Rolled Back'
            ROLLBACK TRAN
            RAISERROR(@ErrorMsg,16, 1)
        END
```

```
        IF XACT_STATE() = 1
           BEGIN
                COMMIT TRAN
                PRINT 'Transaction State Committable, Transaction Committed'
           END
        IF XACT_STATE() = 0
           BEGIN
                PRINT 'No Transaction Present, Do nothing'
           END
END CATCH
```

Executing this code gives us the following results:

```
WoodVista(WoodVista\DanW): (1 row(s) affected)
WoodVista(WoodVista\DanW): (1 row(s) affected)
WoodVista(WoodVista\DanW): (1 row(s) affected)
WoodVista(WoodVista\DanW):
In CATCH block.
   Error number: 547
   Error message: The UPDATE statement conflicted with the CHECK constraint
"CK_SavingsAmount". The conflict occurred in database "AdventureWorks2008",
table "dbo.SavingsAccount", column 'Amount'.
   Error severity: 16
   Error state: 0
   Transact state: 1
WoodVista(WoodVista\DanW):
Transaction State Committable, Transaction Committed
```

However, if we query the two account tables, we will find that the checking account now has a balance of $200.00 and the savings account is still at $100.00 — not the best of solutions, especially as far as the bank is concerned.

Processing Business Logic

Handling business rules is all about making decisions. The decision structures in T-SQL are uncomplicated. When writing a decision statement, the first thing I typically do is state the logic using natural language. The roots of T-SQL are in the English language. You'll recall from Chapter 1 that IBM's predecessor to SQL was actually called SEQUEL, which stood for Structured English Query Language. You should be able to break down any process into a decision tree. Even complex logic, once distilled into fundamental components, is just a series of simple logical combinations. This concept is what I call compounded simplicity — each individual piece is simple, there just may be a lot of pieces.

Using logical operators within SQL statements, you should be able to handle quite a lot of relatively complex business logic. I find that my first attempt to address a complex problem is usually a bit convoluted. After taking some time to approach the problem from different angles, I'm usually more successful in using a simpler technique. It takes a little patience and a few iterations to get to the optimal solution.

In the previous section on views, I created a complex view called vProductSalesDetail. This view is an excellent example of the kind of data my sales manager may want to see in a report. Suppose I plan to use SQL Server Reporting Services to design a sales detail report. Users have asked for the ability to provide a variety of parameter values to be used for filtering. As a rule, if a parameter is provided, the report data is filtered accordingly. If the parameter value is not provided, the parameter is ignored and no related filtering takes place. The report parameters are listed in the following table.

Parameters	Logic
Sales Order From Date and Sales Order To Date	The user is prompted to type a date value for each of these parameters. If both parameters contain a value, the sales order data is filtered within the given range of order dates. If either of the parameters is not provided, this criterion is ignored.
Account Number	The user is prompted to type a customer's account number. If this value is not provided, this criterion is ignored.
Product Category	The product category is selected from a drop-down list. The first item of the list displays the word "All." If this value is selected, records are not filtered by the product category.

Combining logical operators may seem to be very complicated but it's actually quite simple when broken down into core components. Each branch of logic must be isolated from others that it shouldn't affect. Using parentheses, group these statements together. For example, if the account number parameter is not provided (the value is Null), you need not consider the value of the corresponding column. In SQL, this logic would look like this:

```
((@ProductCategory IS NULL) OR (CategoryName = @ProductCategory))
```

The inner parentheses, surrounding each individual statement, just make this statement easier to read and could be omitted. The outer parentheses isolate this logic from any other statements. If the value of the parameter @ProductCategory is NULL, then it doesn't matter whether the CategoryName column value matched the parameter value or not. One side of the OR expression has already been satisfied so the expression on other side need not be true as well.

If I want to filter the entire result set based on combinations of multiple parameters, then each group of parameters-related statements must be combined using the AND operator. This is because one of the two statements on the OR statement must be true to return any records for that part of the WHERE clause. Combining the logic for two parameters looks like this:

```
((@ProductCategory IS NULL) OR (CategoryName = @ProductCategory))
AND
((@ProductCategory = 'All') OR (CategoryName = @ProductCategory))
```

I changed the logic for the product category to check for the word "All" just to mix this up a little. It would be convenient if all parameters were compared in the same way, but this is a very realistic scenario. Putting it all together, the stored procedure might look like the following. Notice how the actual selection and column referencing is very simple because I've already handled the complexity of the query in the view. The procedure simply leverages this investment.

```
CREATE PROCEDURE spProductSalesDetail
    @SalesOrderDateFrom  datetime = NULL
    ,@SalesOrderDateTo    datetime = NULL
    ,@Category            nvarchar(50) = 'All'
AS
SELECT * FROM vProductSalesDetail
WHERE
    ((@SalesOrderDateFrom IS NULL) OR (@SalesOrderDateTo IS NULL))
    OR
    (OrderDate BETWEEN @SalesOrderDateFrom AND @SalesOrderDateTo)
    AND
    ((@Category = 'All') OR (Category = @Category))
```

Try It Out

Test this procedure by supplying some parameters and not others. You should be able to use any combination of parameters. You can even leave off the product category because this parameter defaults to the value All. For example, all of the following will work:

```
EXECUTE spProductSalesDetail
    @SalesOrderDateFrom    = '12-1-03'
    ,@SalesOrderDateTo      = '12-31-03'
    ,@Category        = 'Bikes'
EXECUTE spProductSalesDetail
    @SalesOrderDateFrom    = '12-1-03'
    ,@Category        = 'Bikes'
EXECUTE spProductSalesDetail
    @SalesOrderDateFrom    = '12-1-03'
    ,@SalesOrderDateTo      = '12-31-03'
```

Conditional Logic

At the very core of all logic is the simple word "If" in the English language. All other decision structures are variations or extensions of the same basic if concept. Before I show you the specific SQL syntax, take a look at some simple phrases that are examples of conditional logic:

❑   *If* a product record exists, update it.

❑   *If* a product record doesn't exist, create one.

❑   *If* a backorder record exists *and* sufficient inventory exists, delete the backorder and ship the product.

What happens if this condition is not met? That's easy. This is done using an ELSE statement:

- ❏ *If* an account balance is current, calculate the new total.

- ❏ ... or *else if* the account balance is past due, add a late fee and calculate the new total.

- ❏ ... or *else if* the account is seriously past due, add a late fee, close the account, and calculate the new total.

Most programming languages include some other forms of logical branching statements that extend the If statement paradigm. For example, the Visual Basic Select Case command just consolidates what would otherwise be several IF ... ELSE statements. T-SQL contains a Select Case structure that is quite different, which will be introduced shortly.

IF

In SQL, the IF statement is not followed by the word "Then." If a condition is met (if the outcome is True), script beginning on the next line is simply executed. This stored procedure checks for the named table in the database catalog:

```
CREATE PROCEDURE spTableExists
  @TableName varchar(128)
AS
  IF EXISTS(SELECT * FROM sysobjects WHERE name = @TableName)
    PRINT @TableName + ' exists'
```

The ELSE statement, in this case, simply allows me to execute another line of script when the condition is not met:

```
CREATE PROCEDURE spTableExists
  @TableName varchar(128)
AS
  IF EXISTS(SELECT * FROM sysobjects WHERE name = @TableName)
    PRINT @TableName + ' exists'
  ELSE
    PRINT @TableName + ' doesn''t exist'
```

When multiple lines of code follow an IF statement, it is best to wrap the lines in a BEGIN ... END block. Although this is not strictly required, it makes the code much simpler to read and debug.

Try It Out

Using the 2008 database, create a stored procedure to return product information. An optional parameter will be used to determine when records will be filtered. The query uses the Product and ProductSubCategory tables so you can pass the subcategory name for filtering. This is a lot of script to type so you might consider using the Query Builder to create the basic SELECT statement. The input parameter, @Category, is set to Null so it becomes optional.

```
CREATE PROCEDURE spGetProductByCategory
 @Category nvarchar(50) = NULL
AS
IF @Category IS NULL
  BEGIN
     SELECT PC.Name AS ProductCategory
          , P.ProductID
          , P.Name AS ProductName
     FROM   Production.Product AS P
     INNER JOIN Production.ProductSubcategory AS PSC
       ON P.ProductSubcategoryID = PSC.ProductSubcategoryID
     INNER JOIN Production.ProductCategory AS PC
       ON PSC.ProductCategoryID = PC.ProductCategoryID
  END
ELSE
  BEGIN
     SELECT PC.Name AS ProductCategory
          , P.ProductID
          , P.Name AS ProductName
     FROM   Production.Product AS P
     INNER JOIN Production.ProductSubcategory AS PSC
       ON P.ProductSubcategoryID = PSC.ProductSubcategoryID
     INNER JOIN Production.ProductCategory AS PC
       ON PSC.ProductCategoryID = PC.ProductCategoryID
     WHERE PC.Name = @Category
  END
```

If the procedure is executed without a category name value, all product records are returned. Otherwise, the results are filtered. Now, try this out. Execute the procedure with and without a category parameter value:

```
EXECUTE spGetProductByCategory 'Bikes'
```

By passing the category 'Bikes,' only 97 product records are returned because the results are filtered by this category.

Now execute the procedure without a category value:

```
EXECUTE spGetProductByCategory
```

This time, 295 rows (give or take a few depending on other sample queries you may have run) are returned because the products are unfiltered.

CASE

The purpose of the CASE statement is to return a specified value based on a set of business logic. A variety of useful applications for the CASE statement include translating abbreviations into descriptive values and simulating look-up table joins.

The syntax pattern looks like this:

```
SELECT CASE value to evaluate
WHEN literal value 1 THEN return value
WHEN literal value 2 THEN return value
...
END
```

Here's a simple example that could be applied to a status indicator value:

```
DECLARE @Status int
SET @Status = 1
SELECT CASE @Status
   WHEN 1 THEN 'Active'
   WHEN 2 THEN 'Inactive'
   WHEN 3 THEN 'Pending'
END
```

Now, I'll plug the same logic into a query, replacing what would otherwise be an outer join to a related table, with a CASE expression:

```
SELECT ProductID
     , Name
     , ListPrice
     , CASE ProductSubcategoryID
         WHEN 1 THEN 'Mountain Bike'
         WHEN 2 THEN 'Road Bike'
         WHEN 3 THEN 'Touring Bike'
         WHEN NULL THEN 'Something Else'
         ELSE '(No Subcategory)'
       END As SubCategory
FROM Production.Product
```

This script effectively creates an alias column called SubCategory. You can use it with a different aliasing technique, in this case, using the column = . . . syntax. Either way, the results are the same.

```
SELECT ProductID
     , Name
     , ListPrice
     , SubCategory =
         CASE ProductSubcategoryID
            WHEN 1 THEN 'Mountain Bike'
            WHEN 2 THEN 'Road Bike'
            WHEN 3 THEN 'Touring Bike'
            WHEN NULL THEN 'Something Else'
            ELSE '(No Subcategory)'
         END
FROM Production.Product
```

Looping

Statements can be repeated in a conditional looping structure. Looping is performed with the WHILE statement and an expression returning a Boolean result. I used this technique in the previous example when describing error-handling techniques. In the following example, a separate WHERE statement is executed for each iteration of the loop. It filters on the corresponding product subcategory ID.

Try It Out

Switch the query results from grid to text (by selecting Query ⇨ Results to ⇨ Results to Text, or by pressing Ctrl+T) and execute the following:

```
DECLARE @Counter int
SET @Counter = 1
WHILE @Counter < 4
  BEGIN
        PRINT ''
        PRINT 'SubCategory '
            + CONVERT(varchar(10), @Counter) + ':'
        SELECT Name, ProductSubcategoryID, ListPrice
        FROM Production.Product
        WHERE ProductSubcategoryID = @Counter
        SET @Counter = @Counter + 1
  END
```

The results show three separate lists for each of the subcategories:

```
SubCategory 1:
Name                                        ProductSubcategoryID ListPrice
------------------------------------------- -------------------- ----------
Mountain-100 Silver, 38                     1                    3399.99
Mountain-100 Silver, 42                     1                    3399.99
Mountain-100 Silver, 44                     1                    3399.99
...
Mountain-500 Silver, 52                     1                    564.99
Mountain-500 Black, 40                      1                    539.99
Mountain-500 Black, 42                      1                    539.99
Mountain-500 Black, 44                      1                    539.99
Mountain-500 Black, 48                      1                    539.99
Mountain-500 Black, 52                      1                    539.99
(32 row(s) affected)

SubCategory 2:
Name                                        ProductSubcategoryID ListPrice
------------------------------------------- -------------------- ----------
Road-150 Red, 62                            2                    3578.27
Road-150 Red, 44                            2                    3578.27
Road-150 Red, 48                            2                    3578.27
...
Road-350-W Yellow, 44                       2                    1700.99
```

Name		ListPrice
Road-350-W Yellow, 48	2	1700.99
Road-750 Black, 58	2	539.99
Road-750 Black, 44	2	539.99
Road-750 Black, 48	2	539.99
Road-750 Black, 52	2	539.99

(43 row(s) affected)

SubCategory 3:

Name	ProductSubcategoryID	ListPrice
Touring-2000 Blue, 60	3	1214.85
Touring-1000 Yellow, 46	3	2384.07
Touring-1000 Yellow, 50	3	2384.07
...		
Touring-1000 Blue, 60	3	2384.07
Touring-2000 Blue, 46	3	1214.85
Touring-2000 Blue, 50	3	1214.85
Touring-2000 Blue, 54	3	1214.85
Touring-3000 Blue, 44	3	742.35
Touring-3000 Blue, 50	3	742.35

(22 row(s) affected)

During the loop, you may need to modify the logic of some operations. The BREAK statement exits the WHILE structure, resuming execution after the END statement. The CONTINUE statement doesn't exit the loop but sends execution back up to the WHILE statement to repeat the loop:

```
/* If the avg price for all products is below $1200,
   raise all prices by 25% until avg is $1200 or higher
   or highest price is over $4000.
*/
WHILE (SELECT AVG(ListPrice) FROM Production.Product) < $1200
BEGIN
    UPDATE Production.Product SET ListPrice = ListPrice * 1.25
    SELECT MAX(ListPrice) FROM Production.Product
    IF (SELECT MAX(ListPrice) FROM Production.Product) > $4000
        -- Greatest price is too high, quit.
        BREAK
    ELSE
        -- Prices are within range, continue to loop.
        CONTINUE
END
PRINT 'Done.'
```

User-Defined Functions

When user-defined functions were introduced in SQL Server 2000, this opened the door to a whole new level of functionality. Until then, nearly all business logic had to be in compound expressions with little opportunity to reuse code. In traditional programming languages, functions typically accept any number of values and then return a scalar (single) value. Functions are typically used to perform calculations, to compare, parse, and manipulate values. This describes one of the capabilities of user-defined functions (UDFs), but they can also be used to return sets of data.

Set-based functions can be parameterized such as a stored procedure but are used in a SELECT expression such as a view. In some ways this makes UDFs the best of both worlds. Three different categories of user-defined functions exist, two of which return result sets. These categories include the following:

- ❑ Scalar functions
- ❑ Multi-statement table-valued functions
- ❑ Inline table-valued functions

Scalar Functions

A scalar function accepts any number of parameters and returns one value. The term *scalar* differentiates a single, "flat" value from more complex structured values, such as arrays or result sets. This pattern is much like that of traditional functions written in common programming languages.

The script syntax is quite simple. Input parameters are declared within parentheses followed by the return value declaration. All statements must be enclosed in a BEGIN . . . END block. In this simple example, I calculate the age by getting the number of days between the birth date and today's date. Because the function can't call the nondeterministic GETDATE() function, this value must be passed into the function using the @Today parameter. The number of days is divided by the average number of days in a year to determine the result:

```
CREATE FUNCTION fnGetAge (@BirthDate datetime, @Today datetime)
 RETURNS int
AS
 BEGIN
     RETURN DateDiff(day, @BirthDate, @Today) / 365.25
 END
```

When a scalar function is called without specifying the owner or schema, SQL Server assumes it to be a built-in function in the system catalog. For this reason, user-defined scalar functions are always called using multi-part names, prefixed at least with the owner or schema name:

```
SELECT dbo.fnGetAge('1/4/1962', GetDate())
```

Before writing the next sample function, I'd like to create a set of data to use. Assume that you are in charge of preparing invitations to your annual company picnic. The HR department manager has exported a list of employees from the personnel system to a text file. You have used SQL Server Integration Services to import this data into SQL Server. Next, you need to format the data for the invitations. Names are in a single column in the form: LastName, FirstName. You need to separate the first name and last name values into two columns.

The business logic for parsing the last name and first name values is very similar. The logic for extracting the last name is as follows:

1. Find the position of the delimiting comma.

2. Identify the last name value from the first character through the character one position before the comma.

3. Return this value from the function.

Translating this logic into SQL, the function definition looks like this:

```
CREATE FUNCTION fnLastName (@FullName varchar(100))
 RETURNS varchar(100)
AS
 BEGIN
    DECLARE @CommaPosition int
    DECLARE @LastName varchar(100)
    SET @CommaPosition = CHARINDEX(', ', @FullName)
    SET @LastName = SUBSTRING(@FullName, 1, @CommaPosition - 1)
    RETURN @LastName
 END
```

Two built-in functions are used. The CHARINDEX() function returns the position of a character string within another character string, in this case, the position of the comma within the full name. The SUBSTRING() function returns part of a character string from one character position to another. This will be used to carve the last name value from the full name. Because the last name ends one position before the comma, you subtract one from the value returned by the CHARINDEX() function.

If you execute this script, only the last name is returned.

```
SELECT dbo.fnLastName('Washington, George')
```

Try It Out

Create two functions, one to parse the last name and another to parse the first name. Start by executing the script in the previous example. Next, create a new table and populate it with employee records:

```
CREATE TABLE EmployeeList
   (EmployeeName varchar(100))
GO
INSERT INTO EmployeeList (EmployeeName) SELECT 'Flintstone, Fred'
INSERT INTO EmployeeList (EmployeeName) SELECT 'Flintstone, Wilma'
INSERT INTO EmployeeList (EmployeeName) SELECT 'Flintstone, Pebbles'
INSERT INTO EmployeeList (EmployeeName) SELECT 'Rubble, Barney'
INSERT INTO EmployeeList (EmployeeName) SELECT 'Rubble, Betty'
INSERT INTO EmployeeList (EmployeeName) SELECT 'Rubble, BamBam'
```

The easiest way to create the first name function is to copy and paste the script and make a few modifications. The logic is similar to the first function but you want to start two characters after the comma to omit the space character. The SUBSTRING() function returns characters up to the end of the text. This means that if you provide a value greater than the remaining length of text, all characters to the right of the start position will be returned. The LEN() function ensures that this value always exceeds the number of available characters:

```
CREATE FUNCTION fnFirstName (@FullName varchar(100))
 RETURNS varchar(100)
AS
 BEGIN
    DECLARE @CommaPosition int
    DECLARE @FirstName varchar(100)
    SET @CommaPosition = CHARINDEX(', ', @FullName)
    SET @FirstName = SUBSTRING(@FullName, @CommaPosition + 2, LEN(@FullName))
    RETURN @FirstName
 END
```

Test the new function as before:

```
SELECT dbo.fnFirstName('Washington, George')
```

Notice that only "George" is returned.

Finally, use both of these functions in a SQL statement, selecting rows from the table you already created. Remember that the table has only one column. Using each function, you will define two alias columns:

```
SELECT dbo.fnLastName(EmployeeName) As LastName
   , dbo.fnFirstName(EmployeeName) As FirstName
FROM EmployeeList
```

In the result set shown in Figure 12-17, the last and first names are separate and may be used in a form letter.

Figure 12-17

Taking this example just one step further, these two functions can be combined into one by passing in a second parameter to indicate the name to extract:

```
CREATE FUNCTION fnGetName (@FullName varchar(100)
                        , @FirstOrLast varchar(5))
RETURNS varchar(100)
AS
BEGIN
    DECLARE @CommaPosition int
    DECLARE @TheName varchar(100)
    IF @FirstOrLast = 'First'
        BEGIN
            SET @CommaPosition = CHARINDEX(', ', @FullName)
            SET @TheName = SUBSTRING(@FullName, @CommaPosition + 2,
LEN(@FullName))
        END
    ELSE IF @FirstOrLast = 'Last'
        BEGIN
            SET @CommaPosition = CHARINDEX(', ', @FullName)
            SET @TheName = SUBSTRING(@FullName, 1, @CommaPosition - 1)
        END
    RETURN @TheName
END
```

The new function is called just as before but with the addition of a second parameter, like this:

```
SELECT dbo.fnGetName('Washington, George', 'First')
```

Inline Table-Valued Functions

This type of function returns a result set, much like a view. However, unlike a view, functions can accept parameters. The inline function's syntax is quite simple. In the function definition, the return type is set to a table. A RETURN statement is used with a SELECT query in parentheses:

```
CREATE FUNCTION fnProductListBySubCategory (@SubCategoryID int)
RETURNS Table
AS
RETURN
(
    SELECT ProductID, Name, ListPrice FROM Production.Product
    WHERE Production.Product.ProductSubcategoryID = @SubCategoryID
)
```

The function is treated almost like a table using the syntax SELECT . . . FROM (*function name*):

```
SELECT * FROM fnProductListBySubCategory(1)
```

For returning a result set from a function, the inline table-valued function is likely the best choice. It's the most elegant blend of SELECT-compatible syntax with stored procedure style input parameters. Aside from these powerful capabilities, the syntax is simple and easy to manage.

Multi-Statement Table-Valued Functions

Multi-statement functions can be used to do some very unique things outside the context of a standard SELECT statement. As with the preceding inline function, this type of function also returns a table-type result set, but the table is explicitly constructed in script. This can be used to accomplish one of two things: either to process some very unique business logic by assembling a virtual table on the fly, or to duplicate the functionality of an inline function in a more verbose and complicated way. In short, if you need to select records from an existing table to return a result set, use an inline table-valued function.

The following is an example of the same function demonstrated in the previous section, as a multi-statement function. In the declaration, a table-type variable is used to define the return structure. In this case, the variable @ProdList defines a virtual table with three columns. The fact that these columns are the same as the corresponding columns in the Product table is purely a matter of choice. You can see that in the body of the function, I've inserted rows into the variable as if it were a physical table. Finally, the RETURN statement terminates execution and returns the result set:

```
CREATE FUNCTION fnProductListBySubcategory (@SubCategoryID int)
RETURNS @ProdList Table
    (   ProductID int
    , Name nvarchar(50)
    , ListPrice money
    )
AS
 BEGIN
    IF @SubCategoryID IS NULL
      BEGIN
        INSERT INTO @ProdList (ProductID, Name, ListPrice)
        SELECT ProductID, Name, ListPrice
        FROM Production.Product
      END
    ELSE
      BEGIN
        INSERT INTO @ProdList (ProductID, Name, ListPrice)
        SELECT ProductID, Name, ListPrice
        FROM Production.Product
        WHERE ProductSubcategoryID = @SubcategoryID
      END
    RETURN
 END
```

Now, I'll step out of the mainstream and show you a more unique application for this type of function. This function doesn't select data from a table. The records returned by this function are entirely manufactured within the script contained by the function. The filtering logic, implemented by the

@Category parameter, accepts three relevant values: Mainframe, Micro, or All. If the value All is passed, rows for both of the previous categories are returned.

```
CREATE FUNCTION fnComputerTypes(@Category varchar(15))
 Returns @CompType Table
    ( Year int
    , BrandName varchar(50)
    , ModelName varchar(50)
    , Category varchar(25)
    )
AS
 BEGIN
    IF @Category IN ('MainFrame', 'All')
       BEGIN
          INSERT INTO @CompType (Year, BrandName, ModelName, Category)
          SELECT 1945, 'US Ordinance Dept. ', 'ENIAC', 'Mainframe'
          INSERT INTO @CompType (Year, BrandName, ModelName, Category)
          SELECT 1951, 'Remington Rand', 'Univac', 'Mainframe'
          INSERT INTO @CompType (Year, BrandName, ModelName, Category)
          SELECT 1952, 'IBM', '701', 'Mainframe'
          INSERT INTO @CompType (Year, BrandName, ModelName, Category)
          SELECT 1964, 'IBM', 'System/360', 'Mainframe'
          INSERT INTO @CompType (Year, BrandName, ModelName, Category)
          SELECT 1988, 'IBM', 'AS/400', 'Mainframe'
       END
    IF @Category IN ('Micro', 'All')
       BEGIN
          INSERT INTO @CompType (Year, BrandName, ModelName, Category)
          SELECT 1977, 'Tandy Radio Shack', 'TSR-80', 'Micro'
          INSERT INTO @CompType (Year, BrandName, ModelName, Category)
          SELECT 1981, 'Commodore ', 'VIC-20', 'Micro'
          INSERT INTO @CompType (Year, BrandName, ModelName, Category)
          SELECT 1982, 'Commodore', 'Commodore 64', 'Micro'
          INSERT INTO @CompType (Year, BrandName, ModelName, Category)
          SELECT 1981, 'IBM', 'PC', 'Micro'
          INSERT INTO @CompType (Year, BrandName, ModelName, Category)
          SELECT 2004, 'Dell', 'PowerEdge 1855', 'Micro'
       END
 RETURN
 END
```

I'll test the function using the value All:

```
SELECT * FROM dbo.fnComputerTypes('All')
```

The result is shown in Figure 12-18.

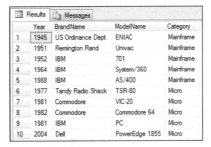

Figure 12-18

As far as the consumer of this data is concerned, it behaves like, and appears to have been selected from, a table in the database.

Transaction Management

You'll recall that in Chapter 10, you learned how to explicitly control transactions. I'll briefly review this topic as it applies to database programming objects. Transaction statements (BEGIN, ROLLBACK, and COMMIT TRANSACTION) are used to queue up a set of statements and control the sequence and dependency of a group of operations. For example, if a stored procedure or user-defined function were to update several sales records and then delete sales records based on some criteria that may have been modified in the UPDATE statement, it would be important to let the update operation finish before deleting any records. In its ever-zealous quest to be efficient, SQL Server may perform operations in parallel, thus working against important business logic. In such cases, it would be important to serialize these dependent operations into separate transactions.

Another important purpose for transactions is to manage the atomicity of a group of operations. If multiple operations are grouped into a single transaction, they are executed as a unit. The outcome of the entire transaction is dependent upon the success of all statements. If they all succeed, the transaction is rolled forward from the transaction log and succeeds. If any operations are unsuccessful, or an error is otherwise raised; the transaction is rolled back, and none of the operations result in committed (inserted, updated, or deleted) records.

Stored procedures are the ideal environment for transactional management. Using the techniques demonstrated in Chapter 10, it's a simple matter to wrap groups of statements into a transactional batch. You can also use error-handling script with transaction management to make your procedures even more bulletproof.

Locking Options

One of the database engine's important jobs is to balance the task of record locking (to protect data as it's modified) and to present consistent result sets of data to queries. This behavior is performed automatically and usually requires no intervention. SQL Server implements locking at various levels based on requested operations and concurrent users sharing the same or adjacent data. On some occasions, it may be necessary to override the default locking behavior within a transaction. This can be done in a couple of different ways. The first is by changing the locking behavior for the entire process by using the `SET TRANSACTION ISOLATION LEVEL` statement. The locking options described in the following table are supported by SQL Server.

Locking Option	Description
READ UNCOMMITTED	Records are read from the transaction log if they have been modified. This includes "dirty" records that have yet to be rolled forward into table data pages.
READ COMMITTED	This is the default behavior. Records are read only from data pages after newly committed rows have been rolled forward into the database. This option prevents inaccurate dirty reads of data within the context of the current transaction. However, concurrent statements could modify records between operations creating an anomaly known as a *phantom read*. This typically only happens in cases where multiple users are frequently modifying multiple records.
REPEATABLE READ	This option locks the transaction unconditionally so that no other operations can modify records. This is an extreme measure that can cause increased locking contention, and is recommended only in rare cases.
SERIALIZABLE	This option serializes transactions so that no concurrent operations can be performed that would affect the state of records within the current transaction. This is done by locking records within a range of key values or other search criteria. This has the advantage of simplifying locking contention problems; however, it can impair functionality and performance.
SNAPSHOT	Snapshot isolation allows users to access the last committed version of data even if that data is undergoing modification. With Snapshot isolation, when data is modified, a copy of the data is written to TempDB. Any other transaction that attempts to read the data being modified will be redirected automatically to the copy stored in TempDB.

The behavior of these options may appear to be easily predictable. However, the actual locking behavior of individual rows, tables, and other objects is a result of the locking options specified by the combined transactions as multiple operations are performed on the same data. The following example serializes these other operations of users on the same data. This way, no modifications would be allowed to these records between the two UPDATE statements:

```
SET TRANSACTION ISOLATION LEVEL SERIALIZABLE
GO
BEGIN TRANSACTION
    UPDATE Production.Product SET StandardCost = StandardCost * 1.15
    WHERE ProductSubcategoryID = 1
    UPDATE Production.Product SET ListPrice = ListPrice * 1.15
    WHERE ProductSubcategoryID = 1
    AND StandardCost < 1000
COMMIT TRANSACTION
```

The second way to alter the default locking behavior is to use table hints. Table hints are applied at the statement level, not at the connection level. For instance, suppose you wanted to retrieve a list of all the data in the SalesOrderHeader table, but you didn't want your query to prevent sales from being inserted into the table while you were running your query. This could happen because a SELECT query is granted a shared lock on the data while an INSERT is granted an exclusive lock. Because exclusive locks are not compatible with shared locks, the INSERT would have to wait until such time as the SELECT query was complete. To avoid this, you can use the (NOLOCK) hint with our query. The (NOLOCK) hint tells SQL Server to read the data but not to issue any shared locks.

```
SELECT *
FROM Sales.SalesOrderHeader WITH (NOLOCK)
```

The (NOLOCK) hint is essentially the same as the READ UNCOMMITTED isolation level, in that it will be possible to read dirty, or uncommitted, data. So in our case, if a sale was inserted and we ran our query, we would see the new sale. However, if the transaction that inserted the sales was rolled back instead of being committed, we might make a bad decision based on inaccurate data.

On the other hand, you may want to apply changes to a table and keep everyone else out of the table while you make the update. To do this, you could use the (TABLOCKX) hint.

```
BEGIN TRANSACTION
    UPDATE Production.Product WITH (TABLOCKX)
    SET StandardCost = StandardCost * 1.15
    WHERE ProductSubcategoryID = 1
COMMIT TRANSACTION
```

There are several more table hints that you can use. For more information, check out the SQL Server Books Online article titled "Table Hints (Transact-SQL)."

Always use caution when using table hints and when changing the default isolation level, and always make sure you fully understand the repercussions of your actions.

Summary

When designing a database solution, it is important to see the bigger picture. Ideally, queries and other database operations should be contained in manageable database objects. In the long run, views, stored procedures, and user-defined functions provide improved security, performance, and simplicity. In most databases, this is a significant investment and may take time and considerable effort.

Views are SELECT statements that can be treated as a table. By organizing complex queries into views, users and programmers don't have to contend with the complexities of a database design and can focus on their pertinent data and business problems. Federated and partitioned views allow data to be stored on different physical media and in different locations, all of which may be transparent to the consumer.

Stored procedures can simplify common operations, providing a standard approach for managing records and high-level data entities. Complex business logic can be processed in a stored procedure, complete with decision branching and error handling. Stored procedures are reusable objects that run efficiently because the SQL script is compiled and optimized.

User-defined functions can provide the same functionality as views and have many of the same capabilities as stored procedures. In some ways, UDFs are the best of both approaches because they support the more common SELECT statement rather than having to be executed like a stored procedure.

Each of these three objects still has its place in SQL programming. Views are far more common than UDFs and under certain conditions may be more efficient. Stored procedures can use nondeterministic functions, which are not allowed in UDFs. The one thing that functions provide that views and procedures do not is the ability to encapsulate the logic to return scalar values. Use UDFs to simplify parsing, calculations, and value manipulation.

Exercises

Exercise 1

Create a new view called vBikePriceSheet. The view should return the product name, subcategory name, model name, color, list price, standard cost, and a calculated column of margin using the price and cost columns. The view should restrict the products to just bikes.

Exercise 2

Create a stored procedure called spAddDepartment. This procedure accepts two parameters: department name and group name. Define logic in the procedure to check for an existing department with the same name. If the department exists and the group name is different, update the group name. If not, insert the new department.

Exercise 3

Add a comment header block and error-handling logic to the procedure you created in Exercise 2. The block should contain a description of the procedure, parameters, your contact information, the date created, and revision information.

Add error-handling logic to catch any errors that may occur. If an error is caught, raise a custom error message.

Creating and Managing Database Objects

No book about T-SQL would be complete without spending some time talking about how to create and manage database objects. As a development DBA, I work predominantly with application developers, who believe that creating and managing databases is boring and strictly for uptight DBA types. However, anyone who works with T-SQL, whether a DBA or a developer, will invariably find themselves having to create and sometimes manage database objects. It may be just a temporary object inside a stored procedure, or a new object to support an application change, but it will happen, so you should probably learn how to do it correctly.

Anything you can do with SQL Server's graphical tools you can do with script. The opposite, however, is not true. Most of the menu options in Management Studio actually create and use T-SQL script to perform changes. Because this is a book about T-SQL, we will not spend any time explaining how to use the graphical tools. Instead, we will concentrate on how to use the T-SQL language to create and manage database objects. For many of the examples in this section I am going to use a table called MyTable. In order to duplicate the examples in this chapter, you will need to drop the MyTable table repeatedly, because the table can exist only once. To drop a table, simply run the command DROP TABLE tablename.

Data Definition Language

You can do only three things with any database object, other than actually use it: you can create it, alter it, or drop it. Every type of database object at least supports the CREATE and DROP statements. Of course, there is actually a lot more to this story. Depending on the object type, a number of options affect certain capabilities and settings. You've already seen a number of these statements because it would have been difficult to cover earlier topics without showing you how to create some objects.

Unless permissions are explicitly assigned, only members of the following roles can execute these statements:

- ❑ sysadmin
- ❑ dbcreator
- ❑ db_ddladmin
- ❑ db_owner

It's a good idea to use role assignments rather than changing permissions for individual users. In the long run, this creates a more manageable environment.

SQL Server has myriad objects that have corresponding CREATE and DROP statements. Many of these objects also have a corresponding ALTER statement. Managing all of these special-purpose objects is beyond the scope of this book. This chapter is limited to the use of T-SQL as related to tables, views, stored procedures, and user-defined functions.

Creating Objects

The basic pattern of the CREATE statement is the same for all objects. However, due to the unique characteristics of different objects, each statement may have a number of different options. To keep things simple, this chapter does not include examples of every incarnation of CREATE statements, but it does includes the most common.

Altering Objects

Generally, any options or changes that can be applied with the CREATE statement can be applied to an existing object using the ALTER statement. If security permissions have been granted or denied for an object, it's a good idea to use the ALTER statement to make changes to an object rather than dropping and re-creating it. This way, the security settings are preserved. A consequence of dropping and re-creating some objects is that this may affect related dependencies. For example, dropping a table with indexes is a cumbersome task and any dependent objects created with schema binding will cause errors to be raised. Altering tables instead wouldn't have the same impact, especially if you didn't make changes to columns that would affect other objects.

Dropping Objects

The syntax for dropping most any object is pretty much the same. You cannot drop objects that would render schema-bound dependencies invalid. For example, you cannot drop a table if it is referenced in a dependent foreign key constraint. In this case, you must either drop the related table or alter the table and remove the constraint.

Naming Objects

The rules for naming objects in SQL Server are extraordinarily flexible. In fact, they are so flexible that it becomes very easy to create objects with names that will cause pain and suffering from the moment you create them. The following sections explain two naming guidelines. The first is more a set of rules than a guideline, and the second is strictly a naming convention. You can disagree with it if you like, but examine the merits of the convention and then come up with your own.

Naming Rules

SQL Server limits the maximum number of characters in any object's name to 128, with the exception of local temporary tables, which are limited to 116 characters. If you choose to create data objects in SQL Server that push this limitation, I can guarantee that you will not be very popular with anyone who must write queries against your objects. For maximum compatibility, all permanent SQL objects should begin with a letter, should not contain any embedded spaces, and should not use any reserved words. After the first letter, the name can contain any combination of numbers and letters. It can also contain some special characters, but these should be avoided like the plague. SQL Server's loose naming rules actually enable you to create an object with the same name as a reserved word. However, you will have to use delimiter characters. If, for some reason, you actually wanted to create a table called Select with columns called From, Insert, and Delete, SQL Server would let you as long as you delimit the names so that SQL Server does not recognize the reserved words as reserved words, as the following example illustrates:

```
CREATE TABLE [Select]
([From] Int,
[Insert] nvarchar(50),
[Delete] nvarchar(50))
```

There are two different delimiter characters: the square bracket and the double quote. The square bracket delimiter is the default in SQL Server, as illustrated in the previous example. The ANSI standard, however, designates the double quote as the standard delimiter. To use double quotes as delimiters, you must set the database or connection-specific QUOTED_IDENTIFIER option to ON. The .NET Native SQL Client, Microsoft OLE DB Provider for SQL Server, and the SQL Server ODBC driver set the QUOTED_IDENTIFIER option to ON by default when they connect:

```
SET QUOTED_IDENTIFIER ON
CREATE TABLE "Select"
(
"From" int,
"Insert" nvarchar(50),
"Delete" nvarchar(50)
)
```

An object's name should be as short as possible but still identify what the object is all about. A table that is used to store data about an employee could simply be called Employee. It's simple and descriptive.

Here is a simple and effective way of checking your names: If you type the name in Management Studio and it shows up blue, you should probably not use it as an object name. As mentioned in Chapter 3, Management Studio automatically changes the color of any reserved word to blue by default. Management Studio is a bit aggressive on what it considers a reserved word because it includes SQL, ODBC, and "Future" keywords, but discretion is not just the better part of valor, it is also the better part of SQL programming. If it turns blue and you don't have a very good reason to keep that name, choose a different one. When it comes to embedded spaces, they are not prohibited; they are just, in the opinion of these authors, stupid. Remember that database object names are limited to 128 characters, so you could conceivably create a table using the following script:

```
CREATE TABLE [This is my table that contains employee data]
(
[My primary key to uniquely track employees] int,
[The employee's last name goes here] nvarchar(50),
[The employee's first name goes here] nvarchar(50)
)
```

However, you would not want to write queries against a database that adhered to this type of naming, and in fact, many database and database application tools do not support embedded spaces.

Sometimes I want to give an object a name that contains more than one word. So, as with many database developers, I avoid the embedded space problem by using either underscores or what is known as "Pascal case," which was introduced in Chapter 4. If you choose underscores, just replace the embedded spaces with an underscore. For example, the table "Order Detail" would end up as Order_Detail. I prefer Pascal case, probably because I am not a very good typist and having to use the Shift key unnecessarily causes me discomfort. My reason for using Pascal case is that underscores disappear in hyperlinks. Even though object names probably won't ever show up in a hyperlink, that's my story and I'm sticking to it. Pascal case comes in handy by avoiding both spaces and underscores by pushing multiple words together and capitalizing each individual word. Order Detail becomes OrderDetail. There is no hard and fast rule concerning underscores and Pascal case, so it really comes down to personal preference or company coding guidelines. The most important aspect of naming objects is to avoid reserved words, embedded spaces, and most importantly, to be consistent.

Naming Guidelines

The basic rules outlined previously will prevent a large amount of pain and frustration. The following naming guideline is just one of many. While I prefer it, many developers do not. Naming guidelines, or conventions, boil down to naming rules, best practices, and personal preference. As a general rule, when I name a table or view, I express it in the singular. A view and table represent a single instance of the entity described by the table. Therefore, the table that describes an employee is called Employee, not Employees. This may seem a bit picky, but when you do a great deal of data modeling with Entity Relationship Diagram (ERD) tools, Object Relational Modeling (ORM) tools, or United Modeling Language (UML), it becomes rather significant. These tools typically enforce singularity for the object and plurality with the relationship.

Most of the organizations I have worked with have had some sort of established naming convention that dictated the use of a prefix on some objects so that they were identifiable in their own right without database context. This is another one of those areas where some developers cringe and others celebrate. The following table is an example of a typical naming convention.

Object Type	Name
Table	Employee
View	vwOpsEmployee
Stored Procedure	spInsertEmployee
Function	fnNewEmployees
Trigger	trVerifyEmployee
Check Constraint	ckPhoneNumber
Foreign Key Constraint	fkSalesEmployeeLink
Primary Key Constraint	pkEmployeeID
Default	dfRegion
Clustered Index	clRegionID
Non-Clustered Index	ncLastName

As the table illustrates, data objects take on the name of a single instance of their data. Programming objects, such as stored procedures, triggers, and functions, take on the name of what they do.

Creating DDL Scripts

A common error when creating scripts that create database objects is trying to combine multiple non-combinable CREATE statements. The following CREATE statements must be the first statement in any batch, which means that they must either be the first statement in the script or be preceded by a GO batch delimiter command:

❑   CREATE PROCEDURE

❑   CREATE VIEW

❑   CREATE TRIGGER

❑   CREATE RULE

❑   CREATE DEFAULT

The following example will fail if it executes, resulting in the error message shown in Figure 13-1.

```
CREATE TABLE MyTable
(MyID Int NOT NULL
,MyDescription nvarchar(50) NULL)
CREATE VIEW MyView
AS
SELECT MyDescription
FROM MyTable
```

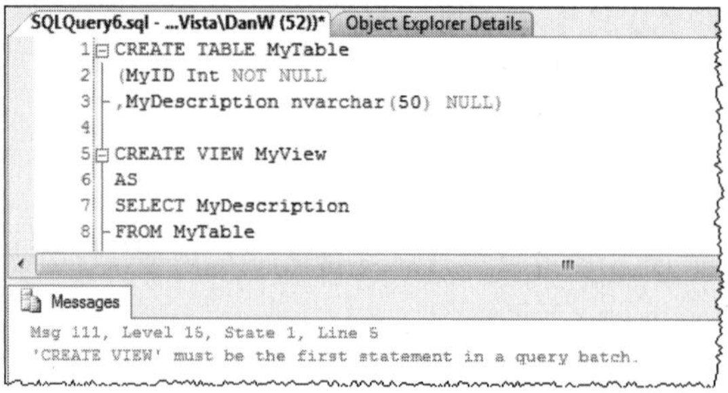

Figure 13-1

In order to get this code to run, a GO command needs to be placed before the CREATE VIEW statement, as the following example depicts:

```
CREATE TABLE MyTable
(MyID Int NOT NULL
,MyDescription nvarchar(50) NULL)
GO
CREATE VIEW MyView
AS
SELECT MyDescription
FROM MyTable
```

CREATE TABLE

In its simplest form, the CREATE TABLE statement contains the name of the new table followed by its column definitions in parentheses. For each column, a name, data type specification, and NULL specification are provided, as in the following example:

```
CREATE TABLE MyTable
(MyID Int NOT NULL
,MyDescription nvarchar(50) NULL)
```

This example script creates a table called MyTable that is made up of two columns. The first column is called MyID, which has a data type of integer and cannot hold a NULL. The second column is called MyDescription. It has a Unicode variable character data type and can be NULL. This may be sufficient to get started, but it certainly isn't comprehensive. Tables are typically a little more sophisticated than this. Several options are available to us as this partial syntax for CREATE TABLE suggests:

```
CREATE TABLE
    [ database_name.[ owner ] . | owner. ] table_name
    ( { < column_definition >
        | column_name AS computed_column_expression
        | < table_constraint > ::= [ CONSTRAINT constraint_name ] }
            | [ { PRIMARY KEY | UNIQUE } [ ,...n ]
    )
```

Most of the time, when a table is created the options that are defined are the table name, the column names, whether or not the columns are nullable, and what column is the primary key. Chapters 1 and 2 reviewed all the possible data types that can be assigned to a column and briefly explained the concept of NULLs and primary keys, so I won't repeat them here except as it applies to the CREATE TABLE statement.

Nullability

You can enable a column to optionally not require a value by designating it as a nullable column. This simply means that if no value is provided it defaults to NULL. NULL is defined as the absence of data, so it does not have any real value. To enable a column to be nullable, the NULL keyword is added immediately after the data type. To prevent nulls, the NOT NULL keywords are added. NOT NULL is actually considered a column constraint, which is covered later in this chapter. If NULL or NOT NULL is not specified, the default setting is to allow nulls, as the next two examples show. This behavior is controlled with the connection option settings ANSI_NULL_DFLT_ON and ANSI_NULL_DFLT_OFF. However, it is a best practice to always designate the nullability of a column when creating or altering a table and not rely on the connection setting.

```
--Relying on the Connection Settings
CREATE TABLE MyTable
    ( Category nvarchar(50) NOT NULL
    , MyDescription nvarchar(50)
)

--Explicitly specifying the nullability
CREATE TABLE MyTable
    ( Category nvarchar(50) NOT NULL
    , MyDescription nvarchar(50) NULL
)
```

With either of the two preceding examples, the MyTable table requires only the value for Category to be provided for an insert operation. Figure 13-2 shows the results of the query after inserting the new row.

```
INSERT MyTable (Category)
VALUES ('Category1')
SELECT * FROM MyTable
```

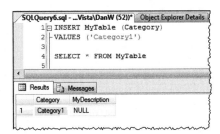

Figure 13-2

Identity

Very often the database developer will want to have a numerical value automatically assigned to a row any time a new row is added. This is the purpose of a column assigned the IDENTITY property. It is very similar to the AutoNumber feature of Microsoft Access, which automatically assigns an integer to every new row. However, the IDENTITY property is much more powerful and flexible. Typically what happens is that a table is created with the default values, which is equivalent to how Access functions:

```
CREATE TABLE MyTable (MyID int IDENTITY(1, 1) NOT NULL
                    , MyDescription nvarchar(50) NOT NULL)

CREATE TABLE MyTable (MyID int IDENTITY NOT NULL
                    , MyDescription nvarchar(50) NOT NULL)
```

Both of the preceding examples cause an incremental value to be assigned starting at 1 and incrementing by 1. The actual syntax for the IDENTITY property is as follows:

```
IDENTITY [ (seed , increment ) ]
```

As the syntax infers, the seed and increment values are not restricted to 1, and they are not strictly limited to integers. Supported data types for the IDENTITY property are tinyint, smallint, int, bigint, decimal, and numeric. However, the decimal and numeric data types are of limited usefulness because they can only be assigned a scale of 0. The scale of these data types defines how many digits are supported to the right of the decimal point. Specifying a decimal or numeric data type with a scale of 0 makes the data type behave like an integer.

The increment value of the IDENTITY property is restricted to whole numbers regardless of the data type used, but it is not limited to a value of 1 or even to positive numbers. A table could be created with an IDENTITY property that is set to start at 1,000,000 and decrement by 100 for every row added. The CREATE statement would look like this:

```
CREATE TABLE MyTable (MyID int IDENTITY(1000000, -100) NOT NULL
                    ,MyDescription nvarchar(50) NOT NULL )
```

If you were designing a database that tracked ticket sales for a venue that could seat 3000 people, you could conceivably seed a tracking table at 3000 with an incremental value of –1 and not allow the number to go negative (through the use of a constraint). This way, every sale could also return the number of tickets remaining without writing an expression to calculate the value.

A table could also be created so that the seed value was negative and the increment was positive:

```
CREATE TABLE MyTable
(MyID int IDENTITY(-1000000, 100) NOT NULL
,MyDescription nvarchar(50) NOT NULL)
```

A column with an IDENTITY property is probably the most common form of primary key value, but be aware that the IDENTITY property by itself does not guarantee uniqueness. If a value is explicitly inserted in the IDENTITY column, SQL Server will not prevent a duplicate unless a constraint has been added to the column to prevent duplicates. Also, keep in mind that a table can have only one IDENTITY column defined.

By default, once a column has been assigned the IDENTITY property, SQL Server does not allow explicit values to be inserted into it. Any attempt to manually enter a value will result in the error shown in Figure 13-3.

```
INSERT MyTable (MyID, MyDescription)
VALUES (5, 'This will not work')
```

```
SQLQuery6.sql - ...Vista\DanW (52))*   Object Explorer Details
   1 □ INSERT MyTable (MyID, MyDescription)
   2 │-VALUES (5, 'This will not work')
   3 │
                                        III
 Messages
 Msg 544, Level 16, State 1, Line 1
 Cannot insert explicit value for identity column in table 'MyTable' when IDENTITY_INSERT is set to OFF.
```

Figure 13-3

Although SQL Server by default doesn't allow explicit values to be inserted into an IDENTITY column, there may well be times when you need to do exactly that. As the error message infers, this is done through the IDENTITY_INSERT property on the table. The IDENTITY_INSERT property defines whether a value is automatically generated for new rows. To change the value of IDENTITY_INSERT, use the SET command, as follows:

```
SET IDENTITY_INSERT MyTable ON
INSERT MyTable (MyID, MyDescription)
VALUES (5, 'This will work')
SET IDENTITY_INSERT MyTable OFF
```

It is very important to turn IDENTITY_INSERT off after the transaction is complete because any normal insertions into the table (by not specifying the INDENTITY value) within the same connection context will fail if the IDENTITY column is not explicitly identified. Only one table at a time can have IDENTITY_INSERT set to ON for a single connection. The SET IDENTITY_INSERT option is also effective only on the connection on which it is used and will be terminated if the connection is closed, even if the option is not reset. Best practices in database design, however, are a lot like the rules our parents tried to teach us: If you use or borrow something, put it back where you found it. So, if you alter a database or connection setting and you do not intend for the change to be permanent, put it back the way you found it. All other connections will continue to work normally by having the IDENTITY value automatically supplied.

It may be a goofy way of remembering how the IDENTITY property works, but for me, I just make a mental note to remember that it is the opposite of what it sounds like. SET IDENTITY_INSERT tablename ON actually turns the IDENTITY property off. SET IDENTITY_INSERT tablename OFF turns the IDENTITY property back on.

Another aspect of explicitly entering a value into an IDENTITY column is the impact on the IDENTITY property's current value. For instance, you create a table with the following script:

```
CREATE TABLE MyTable
(MyID Int IDENTITY(1, 10) NOT NULL
, MyDescription nvarchar(50) NOT NULL)
```

After the table is created, you add two records:

```
INSERT MyTable (MyDescription)
VALUES ('Auto Record 1')
INSERT MyTable (MyDescription)
VALUES ('Auto Record 2')
```

A query of the table reveals the data shown in Figure 13-4.

Figure 13-4

Now you explicitly enter a MyID value with the following script:

```
SET IDENTITY_INSERT MyTable ON
INSERT MyTable (MyID, MyDescription)
VALUES (5, 'Manual Record 1')
SET IDENTITY_INSERT MyTable OFF
```

What is the next value that SQL Server will automatically assign for MyID? Will it be 15 (incrementing 10 from 5) or will it be 21? The answer is that SQL Server will always choose the highest number as its current seed for a positive increment value or the lowest for a negative increment value. So, the results will look like those shown in Figure 13-5.

```
INSERT MyTable (MyDescription)
VALUES ('Auto Record 3')
SELECT * FROM MyTable
```

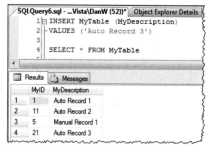

Figure 13-5

Often, when working with IDENTITY values, you will want to know what the last value supplied was. SQL Server provides the @@IDENTITY global variable to hold that value as well as the function SCOPE_IDENTITY(). Retrieving the IDENTITY value is as simple as selecting the variable using one of the available methods, as shown in Figure 13-6.

```
INSERT MyTable (MyDescription)
VALUES ('Auto Record 4')
SELECT * FROM MyTable
SELECT @@IDENTITY AS LastIdentity
INSERT MyTable (MyDescription)
VALUES ('Auto Record 5')
SELECT * FROM MyTable
SELECT SCOPE_IDENTITY() AS LastIdentity
```

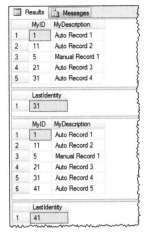

Figure 13-6

Because @@IDENTITY is a global variable, it will work on every connection, but it will only return the last IDENTITY value issued on the connection that the variable is retrieved. The same goes for the SCOPE_IDENTITY() function. If you need to discover what the last IDENTITY value for a table is regardless of your current scope, you can use the IDENT_CURRENT function. So opening a different connection from that used in the previous example would return the results shown in Figure 13-7.

```
SELECT @@IDENTITY AS LastIdentity
      ,SCOPE_IDENTITY() AS LastScopeIdentity
      ,IDENT_CURRENT('MyTable') AS CurrentIdentity
```

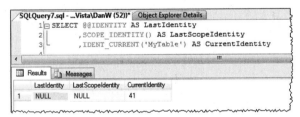

Figure 13-7

Notice that the values for @@IDENTITY and SCOPE_IDENTITY are NULL because no identity value was generated on the new connection.

Defaults

In its simplest form, a default is simply a hard-coded value that is assigned to a column if it isn't specified in an INSERT statement. In Chapter 1, I mentioned a deep-rooted prejudice against NULL. Whenever possible I avoid allowing nulls in my table designs. However, there are many times when I need to allow for a value not to be provided by a calling application in a table insert. In these instances, a default is very handy. For example, let's go back to my MyTable example. This time I will add a new column called Region. This column will contain a three-character region code. Because I live in the Seattle area, I want this value to be PNW, for Pacific Northwest, if no value is provided.

There are three different ways to create a default for a column. The first two use the CREATE TABLE statement. In this first example the default is added without a name, which tells SQL Server to give the default a system-generated name:

```
CREATE TABLE MyTable1 (MyID Int IDENTITY(1, 1) NOT NULL
            ,MyDescription nvarchar(50) NOT NULL
            ,MyRegion nchar(3) NOT NULL DEFAULT 'PNW')
```

I prefer to explicitly name all my objects. Using this technique, a search of the system view sys .default_constraints shows us the name SQL Server picked for our default, as shown in Figure 13-8.

```
SELECT name
FROM sys.default_constraints
WHERE parent_object_id = OBJECT_ID(N'MyTable')
```

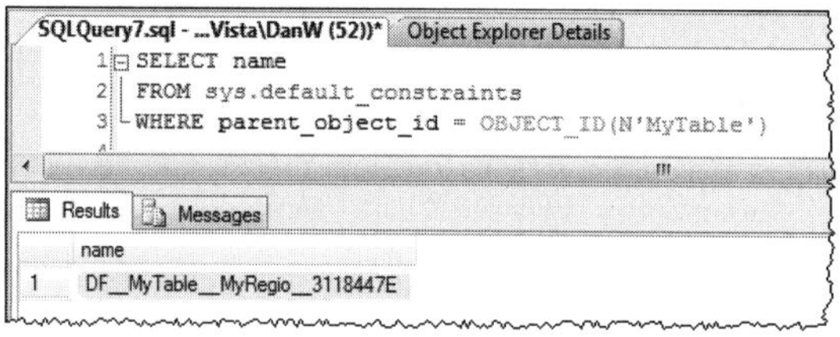

Figure 13-8

A more structured way of adding a default is by explicitly giving the default a name. In this way, the database is more defined and easier to script.

```
CREATE TABLE MyTable (MyID Int IDENTITY(1, 1) NOT NULL
            ,MyDescription nvarchar(50) NOT NULL
            ,MyRegion nchar(3) NOT NULL CONSTRAINT dfMyRegion DEFAULT 'PNW')
```

Now you know the exact name of the default, in case you need to drop it later or script it out for a new database.

The third way of creating a column default is by using the ALTER TABLE command. If you need to add a constraint after it has been created, this is how you would do it:

```
ALTER TABLE MyTable
ADD CONSTRAINT dfMyTableMyRegion
DEFAULT 'PNW' FOR MyRegion
```

Keep in mind that this example will not work if you have already created the table with the default defined. A column can only have one default.

Now if an insert is made to MyTable and a region is not provided, the value PNW will automatically be used.

This is the preferred method for using defaults, but it is not the only way. A default can also be created as a stand-alone object in the database and then bound to any number of columns in any number of tables in the database:

```
CREATE DEFAULT db_df_Region AS 'PNW'
GO
CREATE TABLE MyTable2 (MyID int IDENTITY(1, 1) NOT NULL
              , MyDescription nvarchar(50) NOT NULL
              , MyRegion nchar(3) NOT NULL)
GO
sp_bindefault db_df_Region, MyTable2.MyRegion
```

The use of the database default object has been deprecated by Microsoft and will be removed in a future release. Microsoft recommends that you do not use these anymore, but use the table defaults instead.

Unique Identifiers

A problem with using an auto-incrementing IDENTITY is that this system only works when users or clients are creating records and they are concurrently connected to the same database server and a single table contains the values. This introduces problems for replicated systems or off-line applications that need to synchronize data from other sources. For example, I was recently involved with a project where user data needed to be joined from a SQL Server database and an Active Directory domain. Microsoft's Active Directory uniquely identifies all of its resident objects with a Globally Unique Identifier (GUID, pronounced "goo-id"). As a result, a column needed to be defined in the database that could hold this GUID. To complicate matters even more, part of the application design specified that not all of the system's users would reside in Active Directory. Some would exist only in SQL Server. A method was needed to either use existing GUIDs or to generate new ones. That is where SQL Server's uniqueIdentifier data type and NEWID() function come into play. The uniqueIdentifier type stores a 128-bit integer value that is usually displayed as an alpha-numeric representation of its hexadecimal form. These values are not intended for human consumption because they are quite large and fairly random in composition.

In SQL Server, uniqueidentifier values are either explicitly provided or they are generated by the NEWID() system function. To define a new table with an ID of this type, I'll use the following script:

```
CREATE TABLE MyTable
(MyID uniqueidentifier NOT NULL DEFAULT NEWID()
, MyDescription nvarchar(50) NOT NULL)
```

Once the table is created I can either specify a GUID to be inserted or allow a new GUID to be generated by the NEWID() function, which has been specified as the default value. The NEWID() function only works as a default value for a table's UniqueIdentifier column when no value is provided, as demonstrated in the following:

```
INSERT MyTable (MyID, MyDescription)
VALUES ('2BD9307D-5AAD-417C-AE3A-C1ACDCA0F6C9', 'Explicitly provided GUID')

INSERT MyTable (MyID, MyDescription)
VALUES (DEFAULT, 'SQL Server generated GUID')
SELECT * FROM MyTable
```

The results of the query are shown in Figure 13-9.

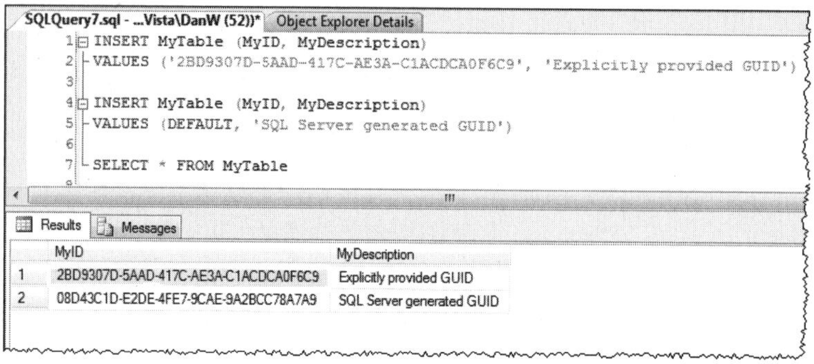

Figure 13-9

Keep in mind that as with the IDENTITY property, the uniqueidentifier type does not in and of itself guarantee uniqueness. A unique constraint, index, or primary key constraint must be used in conjunction with the uniqueidentifier data type. The NEWID() function, however, will never generate the same value twice on any database server in the world (at least that is the theory).

Constraints

SQL Server constraints fall into one of five categories, as described in the following table.

Constraint Type	Description
Not Null	Ensures that the column has a defined non-null value.
Primary Key	Enforces uniqueness for the purpose of identifying a row. Doesn't accept Null values.
Check	Validates a row based on the value of a column. Uses a clause, similar to that following a WHERE statement, to identify acceptable values.
Unique	Requires each value in a column to have a unique value. Column will accept a single Null value unless used in conjunction with Not Null.
Foreign Key	Enforces referential integrity rules by checking the value of a column against that of the primary key value in a related table. Null values are allowable unless explicitly restricted.

Primary Key Constraint

The Primary Key object was introduced in Chapter 1, but I will review it here in more detail. A table's primary key is the primary value that is used to uniquely identify every row in the table. The primary key designation is specified as a constraint on the table. Although we often think of constraints as being applied to a specific column, they are defined at the table level and really apply to each row. Constraints can be created during the initial CREATE TABLE statement or can be added later with an ALTER TABLE statement. A couple of different ways exist to designate a primary key during the table creation process:

```
CREATE TABLE MyTable
(MyID Int IDENTITY(1,1) NOT NULL CONSTRAINT pkMyTable PRIMARY KEY
,Description nvarchar(50) NOT NULL
,MyRegion nchar(3) NOT NULL CONSTRAINT dfMyRegion DEFAULT 'PNW')

CREATE TABLE MyTable
(MyID Int IDENTITY(1,1) NOT NULL
,Description nvarchar(50) NOT NULL
,MyRegion nchar(3) NOT NULL CONSTRAINT dfMyRegion DEFAULT 'PNW'
,CONSTRAINT pkMyTable PRIMARY KEY (MyID))
```

In the preceding examples, pkMyTable is the name of the constraint and PRIMARY KEY is the type of constraint. You can omit the name attribute of the constraint for a primary key constraint if the constraint is defined in the column definition. As with the default constraint explained previously, SQL Server will automatically assign the primary key constraint the name PK_TableName_xxxxxxxx. However, giving constraints a user-friendly name is still a best practice.

To enforce uniqueness, SQL Server builds an index on the key column. This makes perfect sense if you think about it. If you were handed a deck of cards and told to ensure that there were no duplicate cards in the deck, what would you do? Most likely you would sort the cards so that you could easily identify if any duplicates existed. SQL Server does the same thing, except it keeps the column values sorted to prevent a duplicate from occurring in the first place. The index that SQL Server creates to support a primary key will be either a clustered or non-clustered index. If you do not specify one way or the other, SQL Server will create the index as a clustered index if one does not already exist. This is by no means a recommendation that all of your primary key columns also be the clustered index column. The decision on which column to define as the primary key and which column a clustered index is ordered on are very separate design decisions that are beyond the scope of this book. To specify a non-clustered index, add the keyword NONCLUSTERED to the constraint definition immediately following the PRIMARY KEY keywords:

```
CREATE TABLE MyTable
(MyID Int IDENTITY(1,1) NOT NULL CONSTRAINT pkMyTable PRIMARY KEY NONCLUSTERED
,Description nvarchar(50) NOT NULL
,MyRegion nchar(3) NOT NULL CONSTRAINT dfMyRegion DEFAULT 'PNW')


CREATE TABLE MyTable
(MyID Int IDENTITY(1,1) NOT NULL
,Description nvarchar(50) NOT NULL
,Region nvarchar(10) NOT NULL CONSTRAINT dfMyRegion DEFAULT 'PNW'
,CONSTRAINT pkMyTable PRIMARY KEY NONCLUSTERED (MyID))
```

You can also apply the primary key constraint to multiple columns by including the columns in a comma-delimited list. This is often the case for bridge tables used to join two tables and form a many-to-many relationship. A multi-column primary key constraint is defined using similar syntax:

```
CREATE TABLE MyTable
(MyID Int IDENTITY(1,1) NOT NULL
,CategoryID Int NOT NULL
,Description nvarchar(50)
,Region nvarchar(10)NOT NULL CONSTRAINT dfMyRegion DEFAULT 'PNW'
,CONSTRAINT pkMyTable PRIMARY KEY NONCLUSTERED (MyID,CategoryID))
```

If the table has already been created without a primary key, the table will have to be altered to add the constraint, as shown in the following example:

```
ALTER TABLE MyTable
ADD CONSTRAINT pkMyTable PRIMARY KEY NONCLUSTERED (MyID))
```

The syntax is fairly straightforward.

1. After the ALTER statement, you specify what it is you want to add: a constraint.

2. Specify the name of what you want to add: PK_ID.

3. Specify what type of constraint it is: Primary Key.

4. Specify what column the constraint is being applied to: MyID.

The syntax is the same regardless of which type of constraint you add.

Unique Constraint

Primary keys enforce uniqueness and are very often used to manage relationships, as briefly explained in Chapter 1. Sometimes, however, you need to enforce uniqueness on a column that is not the column used to primarily identify each row. Chapter 1 used the Employee table as an example, so let's return to that. In the following example the script creates a table called Employee. The table's primary key is an integer that is automatically generated by the IDENTITY function, but the table also contains the employee's Social Security number:

```
CREATE TABLE Employee (
        EmployeeID Int IDENTITY(1,1) NOT NULL
    , LastName nvarchar(50) NOT NULL
    , FirstName nvarchar(50) NOT NULL
    , SSN Char(9) NOT NULL)
```

It will probably be very important for the company not to have any duplicate Social Security numbers, so you need to find a way to enforce that uniqueness without making the column your primary key. The answer is the unique constraint. Unique constraints are very similar to primary keys with a couple of distinct differences. A unique constraint also requires an index to enforce the uniqueness so SQL Server automatically creates one, but it doesn't create a clustered index by default. Unique constraints will also allow one NULL, whereas primary keys will not. If a NULL is not appropriate, a NOT NULL constraint must be added to the column. Unique constraints, as with all other constraints, can be created when initially creating the table or added after, as the following two examples show:

```
CREATE TABLE Employee (
       EmployeeID Int IDENTITY(1,1) NOT NULL
     , LastName nvarchar(50) NOT NULL
     , FirstName nvarchar(50) NOT NULL
     , SSN Char(9) NOT NULL
     , CONSTRAINT ukEmployeeSSN UNIQUE NONCLUSTERED (SSN))

ALTER TABLE Employee
ADD CONSTRAINT ukEmployeeSSN UNIQUE NONCLUSTERED (SSN)
```

Check Constraint

A *check constraint* uses an expression to qualify records that are acceptable for any inserts or updates performed on the table:

```
CREATE TABLE MyTable
       (MyID Int IDENTITY(1, 1) NOT NULL
     ,MyDescription nvarchar(50) NOT NULL
     ,Region nvarchar(10) NOT NULL CONSTRAINT dfMyRegion DEFAULT 'PNW'
     ,CONSTRAINT pkMyTable PRIMARY KEY CLUSTERED (MyID)
     ,CONSTRAINT ckMyTableRegion CHECK
       (Region IN('PNW', 'SW', 'MT', 'CENTRAL', 'EAST', 'SOUTH')))
```

If a proof were inserted with a Region value other than those in the list, an error would be raised and the insert would be aborted. If an update were performed on the table that attempted to modify the value of Region and make it any value other than those on the list, it would also fail.

Check constraints, as with primary key constraints, can be added to a table after the table is created. Unlike primary key constraints, the data in the table does not have to conform to the check constraint. For example, I create the table MyTable with the following script:

```
CREATE TABLE MyTable
       (MyID Int IDENTITY(1, 1) NOT NULL
     ,MyDescription nvarchar(50) NOT NULL
     ,Region nvarchar(10) NOT NULL CONSTRAINT dfMyRegion DEFAULT 'PNW'
     ,CONSTRAINT pkMyTable PRIMARY KEY CLUSTERED (MyID)
     )
```

Shortly after creating the table, I find that rows are being added with Region values that were not expected or wanted, like those shown in the following INSERT:

```
INSERT MyTable
(MyDescription,Region)
VALUES
('A Bad Region', 'BadRegion')
```

I want to add a check constraint to the table to prevent additional rows being added that don't conform to my business rules, but when I try to add a constraint I get the following error:

```
ALTER TABLE MyTable
ADD CONSTRAINT ckRegion CHECK
(REGION IN ('PNW', 'SW', 'MT', 'CENTRAL', 'EAST', 'SOUTH'))


Server: Msg 547, Level 16, State 1, Line 1
ALTER TABLE statement conflicted with COLUMN CHECK constraint 'ckRegion'.
The conflict occurred in database 'AdventureWorks', table 'MyTable',
column 'Region'.
```

When I tried to add the constraint, there were already records that did not conform to the constraint, so the ALTER TABLE command failed. However, if I modify my ALTER statement to specify that SQL Server should not check existing data, I can add the constraint and prevent any additional bad rows from being added:

```
ALTER TABLE MyTable WITH NOCHECK
ADD CONSTRAINT ckRegion CHECK
(REGION IN ('PNW', 'SW', 'MT', 'CENTRAL', 'EAST', 'SOUTH'))
```

Foreign Key Constraint

Foreign key constraints are used to enforce relationships between tables. Chapters 1 and 2 explained one-to-many, one-to-one, and many-to-many relationships. These relationships between tables can exist without the use of foreign key constraints, and I have seen many databases where this was the case. In my experience, the reason for not using foreign key constraints is for one of two reasons. The first is to optimize performance on a table that is heavily inserted into and that there is a very low probability that an invalid record would be inserted. The second is because the database design was intentionally made complex to prevent organizations from developing internal tools to examine the data. Both cases are fairly common. The database I most often use comprises several tables that contain almost a billion rows. Foreign keys linking tables of this size can have a very negative impact on performance, so we decided to omit them between very large tables. I also must manage a database created by a third party in which the designers intentionally confused the design in order to make it difficult for anyone to create tools that could extract data from it. Columns in this database that linked tables would have different names and sometimes even different data types. This process is euphemistically called *obfuscation,* which is a developer's way of saying "made confusing on purpose." The problem with this approach is that inconsistencies in the data can appear because of an application bug or the data being manipulated outside of the application. As long as performance allows, the preferred method of managing table relationships is through Declarative Relational Integrity (DRI). Foreign keys are an implementation of DRI. The *Declarative* part means that the constraint is a declared part of the table's structure. As a DRI object, foreign keys are a part of the child table's structure.

Let's return to the employee example. I have two tables for this example, as shown in Figure 13-10: Employee and Department.

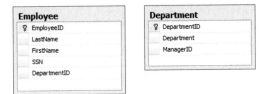

Figure 13-10

I want to ensure that I can identify every employee by the department they work in, so I add the department ID to my employee table. I also want to ensure that when an ID for a department is added to my employee table that the department ID actually exists. I can do this declaratively through the use of a foreign key constraint when creating the employee table or after the creation by altering the employee table:

```
CREATE TABLE Department
        (DepartmentID int NOT NULL
        ,DepartmentName nvarchar(50) NOT NULL
        ,CONSTRAINT pkDepartment PRIMARY KEY CLUSTERED (DepartmentID))
GO

CREATE TABLE Employee
        (EmployeeID Int IDENTITY(1,1) NOT NULL
        ,LastName nvarchar(50) NOT NULL
        ,FirstName nvarchar(50) NOT NULL
        ,SSN Char(9) NOT NULL
        ,DepartmentID Int NOT NULL
        ,CONSTRAINT pkEmployee PRIMARY KEY CLUSTERED (EmployeeID)
        ,CONSTRAINT fkEmployeeDepartment FOREIGN KEY (DepartmentID)
                REFERENCES Department (DepartmentID))

CREATE TABLE Employee
        (EmployeeID Int IDENTITY(1,1) NOT NULL
        ,LastName nvarchar(50) NOT NULL
        ,FirstName nvarchar(50) NOT NULL
        ,SSN Char(9) NOT NULL
        ,DepartmentID Int NOT NULL
        ,CONSTRAINT pkEmployee PRIMARY KEY CLUSTERED (EmployeeID))

ALTER TABLE Employee
ADD CONSTRAINT fkEmployeeDepartment FOREIGN KEY (DepartmentID)
REFERENCES Department (DepartmentID)
```

Foreign key constraints also prevent the parent record from being modified or deleted if it is referenced by a child record. For example, it is decided to change a department's identifier. If the foreign key has been created in the default manner and employees exist that are in the respective department, the update will fail:

```
INSERT Department
VALUES
(1,'Operations')

INSERT Employee
VALUES
('Rubble','Betty','123456789',1)

UPDATE Department
SET DepartmentID = 25
WHERE DepartmentID = 1

Server: Msg 547, Level 16, State 1, Line 1
UPDATE statement conflicted with COLUMN REFERENCE constraint
'fkEmployeeDepartment'.
  The conflict occurred in database ' AdventureWorks2008', table 'Employee',
  column 'DepartmentID'.
The statement has been terminated.
```

SQL Server allows for the creation of the constraint in such a way that any changes to the parent table, instead of causing an error, will make the same changes to the child table. All that is required is to create the foreign key constraint with the CASCADE option. The CASCADE option can be configured so that an update, and/or delete, made to the parent table is reflected in the child table, as shown in the following example:

```
ALTER TABLE Employee
DROP CONSTRAINT fkEmployeeDepartment
GO
ALTER TABLE Employee
ADD CONSTRAINT fkEmployeeDepartment FOREIGN KEY (DepartmentID)
REFERENCES Department (DepartmentID) ON DELETE CASCADE ON UPDATE CASCADE
```

Now if we try to make the change to the Department table, the update will not fail:

```
UPDATE Department
SET DepartmentID = 25
WHERE DepartmentID = 1
```

Overriding Constraints

Foreign key and check constraints are very effective at maintaining data in a consistent state by enforcing all insert and update operations to conform to a set of rules. However, they do not come without cost. Any insert or update must be compared to the rules that were established for the constraint, and that takes time and CPU resources, especially for large inserts. I often load a large number of rows into an existing table with a check or foreign key constraint and I know that the data being loaded already conforms to the constraint. In these instances I will disable the constraint before I add the data and then re-enable the constraint after the load is complete. An example of this is provided here:

```
ALTER TABLE Employee
NOCHECK CONSTRAINT fkEmployeeDepartment
INSERT Employee
SELECT LastName, FirstName, SSN, DepartmentID
FROM NewEmployee
ALTER TABLE Employee
CHECK CONSTRAINT fkEmployeeDepartment
```

CREATE VIEW

Views are the simplest of all the SQL programming objects and were covered in detail in Chapter 12. However, let's review the basics. The syntax for a view is little more than that of a query preceded by an object definition:

```
CREATE VIEW view_name [ ( column [ ,...n ] ) ]
[ WITH [ENCRYPTION | SCHEMABINDING | VIEW_METADATA] ]
AS
select_statement
[ WITH CHECK OPTION ]
```

To create a view, simply write a query that returns the data you want to expose with the view:

```
SELECT P.Name AS ProductName
      ,S.Name AS SubCategoryName
      ,P.ProductNumber
      ,P.ListPrice
FROM Production.Product P
INNER JOIN Production.ProductSubCategory S
   ON P.ProductSubCategoryID = S.ProductSubCategoryID
INNER JOIN Production.ProductCategory C
   ON S.ProductCategoryID = C.ProductCategoryID
WHERE P.FinishedGoodsFlag = 1
```

Then insert the object definition before the SELECT statement:

```
CREATE VIEW vwFinishedProductsAndCategories
AS
SELECT P.Name AS ProductName
      ,S.Name AS SubCategoryName
      ,P.ProductNumber
      ,P.ListPrice
FROM Production.Product P
INNER JOIN Production.ProductSubCategory S
   ON P.ProductSubCategoryID = S.ProductSubCategoryID
INNER JOIN Production.ProductCategory C
   ON S.ProductCategoryID = C.ProductCategoryID
WHERE P.FinishedGoodsFlag = 1
```

If the column names are not defined in the SELECT statement or if different column names are desired and aliases in the SQL statement are not desired, then the column names can be defined in the CREATE statement:

```
CREATE VIEW vwFinishedProductsAndCategories
(ProductName, CategoryName, ProductNumber, ListPrice)
As
SELECT P.Name AS ProductName
      ,S.Name AS SubCategoryName
      ,P.ProductNumber
      ,P.ListPrice
FROM Production.Product P
INNER JOIN Production.ProductSubCategory S
   ON P.ProductSubCategoryID = S.ProductSubCategoryID
INNER JOIN Production.ProductCategory C
   ON S.ProductCategoryID = C.ProductCategoryID
WHERE P.FinishedGoodsFlag = 1
```

Four common options are used to modify the default behavior of views in the CREATE VIEW statement:

- ❑   WITH CHECK OPTION

- ❑   WITH SCHEMABINDING

- ❑   WITH ENCRYPTION

- ❑   WITH VIEW_METADATA

The last option is used by programming components to return information about the view.

WITH CHECK OPTION

In Chapter 12, you learned that data can be modified through a view using an UPDATE statement, just as you would with a table. For views that filter results, the WITH CHECK OPTION keeps the results synchronized with the table(s). This line of script is added to the end of the view definition. To demonstrate with the same view I just created, I can either drop the view and re-create it or use the ALTER statement, like so:

```
ALTER VIEW vwFinishedProductsAndCategories
AS
SELECT P.Name AS ProductName
      ,S.Name AS SubCategoryName
      ,P.ProductNumber
      ,P.ListPrice
FROM Production.Product P
INNER JOIN Production.ProductSubCategory S
   ON P.ProductSubCategoryID = S.ProductSubCategoryID
INNER JOIN Production.ProductCategory C
   ON S.ProductCategoryID = C.ProductCategoryID
WHERE P.FinishedGoodsFlag = 1
WITH CHECK OPTION
```

The rest of the options are specified immediately after the view name, in the CREATE VIEW statement.

WITH SCHEMABINDING

By default, views employ a feature called *delayed name resolution*. This means that any changes to an object that other objects depend on are allowed. Of course, this means that it's possible to create problems that won't be revealed until later. When I first learned about delayed name resolution, I thought it was a bit silly to promote this as a feature rather than a shortcoming of SQL Server; but the reason for it is to enable you to make changes to a database design. As with trying to delete a record in a highly normalized database, it is difficult to make changes or delete objects in a large database when so many objects (typically views, functions, and stored procedures) are dependent on each other.

After the database design has been stabilized, you can consider altering views so that the database engine prevents changes to underlying tables or other dependent objects, which would break the view:

```
CREATE VIEW vwFinishedProductsAndCategories
  (ProductName, CategoryName, ProductNumber, ListPrice)
WITH SCHEMABINDING
AS
SELECT P.Name        ,S.Name
      ,P.ProductNumber
      ,P.ListPrice
FROM Production.Product P
INNER JOIN Production.ProductSubCategory S
    ON P.ProductSubCategoryID = S.ProductSubCategoryID
INNER JOIN Production.ProductCategory C
    ON S.ProductCategoryID = C.ProductCategoryID
WHERE P.FinishedGoodsFlag = 1
```

This view is created using the WITH SCHEMABINDING option. If I were to try to make changes to the dependent table, an error would be raised and the action would be aborted. To schemabind a view, the objects referenced in the SELECT statement must be referenced with their two-part name.

The SCHEMABINDING option is also required to support indexed views.

WITH ENCRYPTION

When a view is created using the WITH ENCRYPTION option, the view is defined and stored in encrypted form. This would make it impossible, even for a system administrator, to see the syntax of the view. Encrypted objects cannot be decrypted by anyone, regardless of their permissions. If you decide to encrypt a view, you should probably save the script in a safe place so you can make changes or regenerate the view later on. Encrypting a view doesn't affect performance to any noticeable degree because the views are generally compiled and stored when referenced.

WITH VIEW_METADATA

The VIEW_METADATA option specifies that client applications will not see the view's underlying table structure. Instead, they will see the view essentially as a table. The reason for this is that some applications try to be smart and expose the underlying table objects so that changes are directed to the tables instead of the view. If that is not a desired configuration, the VIEW_METADATA option can be used to return just the view metadata and not the underlying structure.

Try It Out

The following examples show the effects of definition encryption. The first example shows the result of an `sp_helptext` stored procedure on a view created in the clear. The `sp_helptext` procedure returns the statement used to create the object. The second example shows the result of encryption on the availability of the definition information.

To see the effects of encryption on an object's definition, first create a view without the encryption option:

```
CREATE VIEW vwProductList
AS
SELECT ProductID, Name AS ProductName
FROM Production.Product
```

Next, use the system stored procedure `sp_helptext` to retrieve the views definition:

```
EXEC sp_helptext vwProductList
```

Notice that the results are the same as the original statement used to create the view.

Now alter the view to add the encryption option to the view definition:

```
ALTER VIEW vwProductList
WITH ENCRYPTION
AS
SELECT ProductID, Name AS ProductName
FROM Production.Product
```

Run the system stored procedure `sp_helptext` again to retrieve the view definition. Observe that no results are returned other than a statement letting you know that the object was encrypted.

Indexed Views

At first, the idea of indexing views may seem to be a bit unusual. After all, isn't a view just a SELECT query on one or more tables, and don't indexes really just apply to a table? From a performance and efficiency standpoint, designing a relational database is about finding the right balance between optimizing for transactional performance and data retrieval queries. This feature tips the scales heavily into the data retrieval camp.

I'd like to revisit the topic of indexes briefly. An index is more than just something you tack onto a table to make it find data more efficiently. Indexes contain the actual values for one or more specific columns, stored in presorted order. If an index were to contain all of the column values to support a query, there would be no need for SQL Server to read data from the table pages. All of the necessary data already exists in the data pages allocated to the index. This condition is known as "covering a query" with an index.

If a covering index could be associated with a view, the query optimizer would not only benefit from the caching and stored execution plan for the view, but it wouldn't need to analyze the query to decide which indexes should be used. Such is the case with indexed views. This is by far the most efficient method for returning a subset of sorted data from one or more large tables. The trade-off is that for every insert, update, or delete operation performed on related rows, values in the index must be maintained in real time. In highly transactional systems on a busy server, this performance cost can be quite significant.

A view is indexed using a unique clustered index, which actually creates an index object that is not very different than a clustered index defined for a table. The underlying tables aren't modified, but the index itself contains a separate copy of all the data.

Try It Out

The first order of business in creating an indexed view is to create (or alter) a view using the WITH SCHEMABINDING option:

```
CREATE VIEW vwFinishedProductsAndCategories
  (ProductName, CategoryName, ProductNumber, ListPrice)
WITH SCHEMABINDING

AS
SELECT P.Name
      ,S.Name
      ,P.ProductNumber
      ,P.ListPrice
FROM Production.Product P
INNER JOIN Production.ProductSubCategory S
    ON P.ProductSubCategoryID = S.ProductSubCategoryID
INNER JOIN Production.ProductCategory C
    ON S.ProductCategoryID = C.ProductCategoryID
WHERE P.FinishedGoodsFlag = 1
```

After the view has been schema bound, to index the view, a unique clustered index is created on the view. Remember that a clustered index is the actual data organized in the order of the column the index is created on. A unique clustered index is pretty much the same as a primary key constraint with a clustered index on a table; each row must be uniquely identifiable and stored in the order of that unique column.

```
CREATE UNIQUE CLUSTERED INDEX clFinishedProducts
ON vwFinishedProductsAndCategories (ProductID)
```

Additional non-clustered indexes can then be created on additional columns of the view, if desired.

CREATE PROCEDURE

Procedures were covered in Chapter 12, but in the spirit of thoroughness, a brief description is given here. The basic syntax for creating a stored procedure looks like this:

```
CREATE PROCEDURE procedure_name
    [ { @parameter data_type }[ OUTPUT ]
    ] [ ,...n ]
[ WITH
    { RECOMPILE | ENCRYPTION } ]
AS sql_statement [ ...n ] >
```

Stored procedures are the principle method by which changes are made to the database. Any time you want to insert, update, or delete rows in a table you should use a stored procedure. Stored procedures are also very useful for filtering tables or views by limiting the rows returned through the use of parameters. There are two primary reasons why stored procedures are the preferred method for making changes to a database. The first is security. When a stored procedure is created to make changes, only the changes programmed into the procedure can be executed. Users or even application developers do not need to have any permission granted to the underlying table or tables to make changes to them. The second reason you always want to use stored procedures is efficiency. Stored procedures are compiled and cached on the server upon initial execution. Subsequent executions will be very fast because the compiled version of the stored procedure is being used. The compiled plan stays in cache until SQL Server ages it out or SQL Server is restarted. Typically, SQL Server will leave an active stored procedure in cache indefinitely unless SQL Server runs out of available memory.

Using Parameters

Input and output parameters are declared after the CREATE PROCEDURE statement. Parameter names begin with the @ symbol and are followed by any number of spaces and then the data type. The Input or Output keywords can be used to designate the direction for each parameter. If not specified otherwise, it's assumed that parameters are used for input.

In this SQL script fraction, all four parameters are used for input. The third and fourth parameters are optional because default values are provided:

```
     @WidgetID         int
   , @Description      nvarchar(100)
   , @Category         varchar(20) = Null
   , @StatusCode       char(2) = Null
```

If a procedure is to return one single (scalar) value, whether you should use an output parameter or the return value of the procedure may just be a matter of preference. However, there is one argument for using the return value rather than an output parameter. Because all stored procedures are equipped to return a value by default, using an output parameter can add a slight degree of additional overhead. The following examples demonstrate both of these techniques:

```
/**************************************
     Stored procedure returning value
     using an Output parameter
**************************************/
CREATE PROCEDURE spCalculateOutput
```

```
        @Value1         float
       ,@Value2         float
       ,@Operator       char(10)
       ,@Result         float        Output
   AS
     IF @Operator = 'Add'
           SET @Result = @Value1 + @Value2
     ELSE IF @Operator = 'Subtract'
           SET @Result = @Value1 - @Value2
     ELSE IF @Operator = 'Multiply'
           SET @Result = @Value1 * @Value2
     ELSE IF @Operator = 'Divide'
           SET @Result = @Value1 / @Value2
```

To test this procedure in Management Studio, first declare a variable to hold the output value. This value is assigned in reverse order compared to a typical value assignment statement (remember, you've changed the direction using the Output statement). After executing the procedure, print the result using the variable:

```
-- Declare a variable for the result value
Declare @Out float
-- Execute the procedure & assign the result
Execute spCalculateOutput 123, 456, 'Add', @Result = @Out Output
-- Print the result value
Print @Out
```

The logic for the return-value technique is the same but the syntax varies slightly. Instead of declaring an output parameter, a private variable is declared after the AS keyword. This variable simply holds the calculated value until it is returned at the end of the procedure script. Another valid technique would be to use the Return keyword in each of the branch expressions (that is, Return @Value1 + @Value2), rather than using the variable at all.

```
/*************************************
       Stored procedure returning value
       using Return value
 *************************************/
CREATE PROCEDURE spCalculateReturn
   @Value1         float
  ,@Value2         float
  ,@Operator       char(10)
AS
  Declare @Result float
  IF @Operator = 'Add'
        SET @Result = @Value1 + @Value2
  ELSE IF @Operator = 'Subtract'
        SET @Result = @Value1 - @Value2
  ELSE IF @Operator = 'Multiply'
        SET @Result = @Value1 * @Value2
  ELSE IF @Operator = 'Divide'
        SET @Result = @Value1 / @Value2
RETURN @Result
```

To test the return value procedure the syntax is slightly different:

```
-- Declare a variable for the result value
Declare @Out AS float
-- Execute the procedure by assigning it to the variable
EXECUTE @Out = spCalculateReturn 123, 456, 'Add'
-- Print the result value
Print @Out
```

The ability to capture the value of a stored procedure's return value is built into Visual Studio, but to capture it with T-SQL you must again declare a variable to hold the output, in this case, the return value:

```
DECLARE @Result AS float
exec @Result = spCalculateReturn 10,10, 'Add'
SELECT @Result AS 'spCalculateReturn Return Value'
```

WITH ENCRYPTION

The definition of a stored procedure can be encrypted, just like the view definition, by using the WITH ENCRYPTION option. Remember that an encrypted procedure cannot be decrypted, so it is advisable to keep a copy of the script used to create it for safekeeping.

WITH RECOMPILE

The first time a stored procedure executes, the query optimizer builds an execution plan based on the conditions present in the database. This means that decisions are made based upon the volume, selectivity, density, and distribution of data values in tables accessed by the stored procedure. This execution plan is compiled and then cached with the stored procedure. Rather than repeating the process when the procedure is subsequently called, the same execution plan is used to save time and resources. However, as the data changes in the tables, the efficiency of the execution plan also changes. Over a period of time, the execution plan of a stored procedure could become very inefficient, especially if indexes are added to the tables to optimize data access after the stored procedure is created. A stored procedure execution plan does not become invalid if an index is added because the original plan will still work. However, if an index that is referenced by a query plan is dropped, SQL Server will invalidate the execution plan and cause the stored procedure to be recompiled.

If the database has been optimized with additional indexes after the creation of the stored procedures or a lot of changes have occurred to indexed values, it is generally a good idea to recompile the affected stored procedures or to clear out the procedure cache. Stored procedures can be recompiled in one of three ways. One way is to use the WITH RECOMPILE statement when executing the procedure, like this:

```
EXECUTE spDeleteCreditCard @CreditCardId = 15 WITH RECOMPILE
```

This method really isn't that useful in a production environment because the stored procedures are almost always called from an application. It generally wouldn't make much sense to redesign your applications to force procedure recompilation. The second way is to create or alter the stored procedure so that a compiled plan is never cached:

```
CREATE PROC spDeleteCreditCard
 @CreditCardID Int
WITH RECOMPILE
AS
DELETE Sales.CreditCard
WHERE CreditCardID = @CreditCardID
```

Every time this stored procedure is executed a new plan will be compiled and used and then immediately discarded. This method is also of limited usefulness and would be implemented in an environment where the database structure was expected to change frequently.

The last and most frequently used method is to execute the `sp_recompile` stored procedure against any stored procedure or table. This system stored procedure marks the cached plan of the stored procedure, or all the stored procedures that reference the table if run with the table name invalid, which causes them to be recompiled at their next execution:

```
EXECUTE sp_recompile 'spDeleteCreditCard'
EXECUTE sp_recompile 'Sales.CreditCard'
```

When a table or view is specified as the object in `sp_recompile`, only those compiled plans that reference the table or view are affected.

To globally clear all cached plans, you can either restart SQL Server or execute the DBCC FREEPROCCACHE command.

EXECUTE AS

This feature in SQL Server allows a stored procedure to be executed within an explicit security context. Regardless of the user or login used to execute the procedure, all contained script will execute with the permissions provided in this statement.

Valid options for this statement are described in the following table.

Option	Description
Caller	Executes all code or objects called by the procedure in the context of the user executing the procedure.
Self	Executes all code or objects called by the procedure with default permissions.
Owner	Executes all code or objects called by the procedure in the context of the owner of the procedure.
'user_name'	Executes all code or objects called by the procedure in the context of a specific user or login.

When using the EXECUTE AS option, it is very important to control access to the procedure. This could enable users to execute statements that they would otherwise not be granted the ability to execute.

CREATE FUNCTION

User-defined functions are built using the CREATE FUNCTION statement, much as with any other type of object. In Chapter 12, you looked at the syntax for creating each of the three different types of UDFs. As with views and procedures, the CREATE FUNCTION statement accepts the WITH ENCRYPTION, WITH SCHEMABINDING, and EXECUTE AS options.

Remember that a function cannot call any nondeterministic functions. This means that any function that doesn't consistently return the same value every time can't be used in the body of a user-defined function.

IF EXISTS

In my job I have to write scripts that can be run repeatedly, even if those scripts create objects. As mentioned in the introduction of this chapter, if you try to create an object that already exists, you will receive an error. So, how do you create an object that already exists? Easy, you either drop the object first, or you place conditional logic around the creation of the object so that it will only be created if it doesn't exist already.

In the first scenario, I want to drop any object that exists first because the new object may have the same name, but behave differently. In this scenario we use the IF EXISTS statement to test if an object exists and if so, we drop it before we create the new object as the following example illustrates:

```
IF EXISTS
(SELECT *
 FROM sys.objects
 WHERE name = 'spDeleteCreditCard'
   AND type_desc = 'SQL_STORED_PROCEDURE')
DROP PROCEDURE spDeleteCreditCard
GO
CREATE PROCEDURE spDeleteCreditCard
 @CreditCardID Int
AS
DELETE Sales.CreditCard
WHERE CreditCardID = @CreditCardID
```

The second way of using the EXISTS keyword is by using the IF NOT EXISTS statement. In this way, you can check to see if the object exists and if it does, skip trying to create it, as shown in the following example:

```
IF NOT EXISTS
(SELECT *
 FROM INFORMATION_SCHEMA.TABLES
 WHERE TABLE_NAME = 'CreditCard'
   AND TABLE_SCHEMA = 'Sales'
   AND TABLE_TYPE = 'BASE TABLE')
CREATE TABLE Sales.CreditCard
 (CreditCardID int IDENTITY(1,1) NOT NULL,
```

```
CardType nvarchar(50) NOT NULL,
CardNumber nvarchar(25) NOT NULL,
ExpMonth tinyint NOT NULL,
ExpYear smallint NOT NULL,
ModifiedDate datetime NOT NULL,
CONSTRAINT PK_CreditCard_CreditCardID
PRIMARY KEY CLUSTERED (CreditCardID))
```

The limitation of the IF NOT EXISTS statement is that when working with some objects, such as stored procedures, the CREATE object statement must be the first command in the batch, so the IF NOT EXIST will not work. However, it works great with tables, views, and constraints.

Securing Database Objects

SQL Server's security mechanism is both elegant and flexible. When SQL Server first came to be, it included a role-based security model where all roles and logins were defined within the database server. Users are similar to logins but defined at the database level. Users could be made members of a role and then permissions for various database objects could be assigned at the individual or role level. This approach met all of the necessary requirements except that it duplicated much of the security assignments managed by the network system. As SQL Server was integrated into the Windows platform, it made sense to integrate the existing Windows security model. Today, you have the option to use either Windows Integrated Security or both Windows and SQL Server security mechanisms to secure database objects. Whether or not you choose to utilize the Windows security integration is up to you, but this option is always enabled.

Typically, it makes sense to use Windows Integrated Security if you have the luxury of managing the network security as well. This is convenient considering you don't have to create duplicate login names and groups. In some situations, it may not be feasible to use integrated security. On a departmental database server, where the server is managed separately from the corporate network, this can be a challenge. Another common exception is the Internet service provider that creates accounts for its customers to manage their databases on a common server. In this scenario, there may be no reason to allow access to any other network resources.

The coverage of this topic focuses on the language rather than the administrative tasks and practices. In brief, SQL Server defines eight fixed server roles that can be used to map various server and database object permissions. Logins defined at the server level may have membership in these roles. Logins can be defined using the SQL Server security model or can map to a user or group in Windows. At the database level, custom roles can be defined that may also be used to grant or deny object permissions. Users are defined at the database level that map to a login at the server level. This may seem a little complicated at first, but it really isn't. The short version is that users, in one form or another, are grouped into roles so that you don't have to assign permissions for every individual user. Ideally, all permissions are assigned to a role with the occasional exception for the user who needs to have special permissions or restrictions.

SQL Server also provides the ability to enforce complex passwords and password expiration on SQL Server logins. SQL Server retrieves the password policy from the local security policy on the server and uses it. If complex passwords are required on the server, then, by default, they will also be required for SQL Server logins. The same goes for password expirations.

Managing Security Objects

SQL Server logins, users, and roles have their own corresponding CREATE and DROP statements. The syntax for creating a new login is slightly different depending on whether the new login is a Windows login or a SQL Server login. This first example shows how to create a SQL Server login:

```
/*****************************************************
 * Creates a new SQL Server login and then maps
 * that login to a new database user
 *****************************************************/
USE Master
GO
CREATE LOGIN Paul WITH Password = 'P@ssword1'
USE AdventureWorks2008
GO
CREATE USER Paul FOR Login Paul
```

And the following example shows how to create a login for a Windows account:

```
/*****************************************************
 * Creates a new Windows login and then maps
 * that login to a new database user
 *****************************************************/
USE Master
GO
CREATE LOGIN [AdventureWorks\Paul]
USE AdventureWorks2008
GO
CREATE USER WindowsPaul FOR Login [AdventureWorks\Paul]
```

The syntax for dropping users or logins is simple. Just use the DROP USER or DROP LOGIN statement:

```
/*****************************************************
 * Drops SQL Server login and user
 *****************************************************/
USE AdventureWorks2008
GO
DROP USER Paul
GO
USE Master
GO
DROP LOGIN Paul
```

Data Control Language

Three SQL statements are used to control permission to all database objects and securable user resources (that is, users and roles). Each statement accepts the permission type (select, insert, update, delete, execute, and so on), the object name, and the user or role to which the setting applies.

GRANT

To *grant* permission is to give or allow permission to perform a type of operation on an object. The following are examples:

```
USE AdventureWorks2008
GO
GRANT INSERT ON Production.Product TO Paul
GRANT EXECUTE ON dbo.uspGetBillOfMaterials TO Paul
```

DENY

The DENY statement is used to explicitly prohibit a user or role members from performing a specific action on an object. Even if a user is a member of a role or is otherwise granted permission, they will not be able to perform the action if they are denied permission explicitly or through any role membership:

```
USE AdventureWorks2008
GO
DENY INSERT ON Production.Product TO Paul
DENY EXECUTE ON dbo.uspGetBillOfMaterials TO Paul
```

REVOKE

This statement is often misunderstood, as the term revoke means to take away. Revoking a permission doesn't necessarily mean that a user loses the ability to perform an action. To revoke permission means to remove the current set of permissions for an object and user or role. This could have the effect of removing an explicit GRANT or DENY, if either exists. This would cause the permission set for a user to revert to those applied through a role membership or to the default permissions.

```
USE AdventureWorks2008
GO
REVOKE INSERT ON production.Product TO Paul
REVOKE EXECUTE ON dbo. uspGetBillOfMaterials TO Paul
```

Summary

After you get past the fine points, managing all database objects is a fairly simple matter of using the CREATE, ALTER, and DROP statements for each type of object. These three SQL statements comprise Data Definition Language (DDL), which is the most common method used by administrative tools to design a database and its objects.

Many types of database objects exist, some of which are specialized, and others are more common. In this chapter, you learned to create and manage tables, views, stored procedures, and user-defined functions.

Security permissions are applied for a combination of an object and a user or role. Roles allow groups of users with similar requirements to be managed as a cohesive unit, rather than as individuals. Because SQL Server lets you define logins and users separately or integrated with existing Windows users and groups, security can be managed at a very granular level. This provides a great deal of flexibility for both simple database applications and complex enterprise solutions. Applicable, object-specific actions can be enabled or restricted on each object for individual users or those belonging to a defined role. Permissions to perform an action (such as insert, update, delete, select, or execute) may be explicitly granted or denied, and revoking a permission removes that permission, whether it be a grant or deny.

There is much to consider when planning the security requirements for your system. This is one of a database administrator's most important tasks. This chapter just scratched the surface of this important topic in focusing only on the SQL language related to this topic.

Exercises

Exercise 1

Write the SQL script to define two tables to track customers buying wristbands from an on-line store. Decide on an appropriate name, data type, and nullability option for each column. Due to strict storage requirements, use the most conservative data types possible. Guidelines for the columns in the tables are as follows:

For the customer table, define a column to be used to uniquely identify each customer. Create two columns for the customer's first and last name. The columns should allow between 1 and 50 characters and are required entries. Four columns are needed to store the customer's address: a street address, city, state, and zip code. All addresses and cities will contain only U.S. domestic names, and none of these columns require a value. The address column should allow up to 200 characters, the city should allow up to 100 characters, the state will always be a two-character abbreviation, and the postal code will be between five and ten characters in length.

The sales data should be recorded in a table that identifies the product number, the price of the product, who purchased it, and when it was purchased.

Exercise 2

Wristbands are sold on two separate websites that use two copies of the database. Sales records will be merged together on occasion into one database.

Using the query you created in Exercise 1, add a column to serve as a primary key and to uniquely identify each sales record across multiple databases. Records should not be stored in physical order using this value.

Also, we're currently licensed to sell wristbands in only three countries. Add a constraint to the customer table so that it accepts customers only in the United States (US), United Kingdom (UK), and Canada (CA).

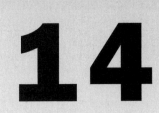

Analyzing and Optimizing Query Performance

I hope you have seen that writing T-SQL is straightforward and fairly easy to learn. However, writing T-SQL is different from writing *efficient* T-SQL. Making sure that the code you write executes quickly and efficiently is very important. Too many times, I have seen developers create a very large and complex script with absolutely no thought to what the impact of the code will be on the database engine. This can lead to complicated, hard-to-diagnose performance problems down the road, especially if the inefficient code is encapsulated in one or more programming objects, such as stored procedures and functions.

This chapter will only scratch the surface of the massive topic of optimizing query performance because the primary focus is to teach you how to write good queries in the first place. Optimizing query performance also includes many other facets of database technologies, such as table indexing and statistics.

The best approach to writing efficient T-SQL is to understand how SQL Server retrieves data, and then writing your code to match the technology. This chapter provides a brief description of how the database engine processes queries and retrieves data, as well as some basic recommendations on which techniques to avoid and which techniques to leverage in your quest to write good queries. I won't go into low-level specifics here; the goal is for you to understand the basics of data retrieval so that you can leverage this knowledge to write good queries.

Data Retrieval

In previous chapters, you learned how to create a query with the SELECT statement and to filter the data returned with the WHERE clause. It is natural to think of the query in those terms, selecting columns from a table or tables where the rows meet a certain criteria. However, the database engine doesn't process the queries in the same way that you write them. Let's take a look at a simple two-table join query and break down how SQL server processes the query.

```
SELECT P.Name AS Product
     ,SUM((S.OrderQty * S.UnitPrice)) AS MountainBikeSales2004
FROM Production.Product P
INNER JOIN Sales.SalesOrderDetail S
  ON P.ProductID = S.ProductID
WHERE YEAR(S.ModifiedDate) = 2004
  AND P.ProductSubCategoryID = 1 --Mountain Bikes
GROUP BY P.Name
HAVING SUM((S.OrderQty * S.UnitPrice)) > $1000.00
ORDER BY MountainBikeSales2004 DESC
```

It would be grossly inefficient for the database engine to retrieve all the product names, their price, and the quantity of products purchased for all products, and then filter out the values that didn't meet the criteria of the WHERE clause. So, the query processor was designed to retrieve the data in the most efficient way possible. The following table breaks the query down in the steps that the query processor takes to execute the query. Notice that the query is not processed in the same order we wrote it in order to retrieve the requested data efficiently.

Order	Statement
4	SELECT P.Name AS Product,SUM((S.OrderQty * S.UnitPrice)) AS MountainBikeSales2004
1	FROM Production.Product PINNER JOIN Sales.SalesOrderDetail S
2	ON P.ProductID = S.ProductID
3	WHERE YEAR(S.ModifiedDate) = 2004AND P.ProductSubCategoryID = 1 --Mountain Bikes
5	GROUP BY P.Name
6	HAVING SUM((S.OrderQty * S.UnitPrice)) > $1000.00
7	ORDER BY MountainBikeSales2004 DESC

As shown in the preceding table, the first operation to occur in this query is the FROM statement. Included in this first phase is the table referenced by the JOIN clause. In our case, that means that the query processor has determined that it must retrieve data from the Production.Product and Sales. SalesOrderDetail tables. However, it does not retrieve any data yet. It simply creates a virtual table that has the potential of holding all the possible combinations of rows from both tables. The next phase of query processing is the ON clause. The ON clause tells the query processor how to combine the rows from the tables. In this example, it is the products that exist in both the Product table and the SalesOrderDetail table. The virtual table that was initially created by the FROM and INNER JOIN statements is now further limited by this additional criteria. Once again, no data has been physically retrieved from disk or memory. The query processor is simply creating a plan to retrieve data based on the query.

The next step is the application of any filter, as specified in the WHERE clause. The filter statement limits the rows from the SalesOrderDetail table to the ones that have a modified date in the year 2004 and products with a SubCategoryID of 1, which equates to the subcategory of Mountain Bikes. Keep in mind that we have already limited the results to those products that exist in both the Product and

SalesOrderDetail tables with the ON clause, so only mountain bikes that have a sales history in 2004 will be returned by the query processor.

Now that the query processor has limited the rows to a specific subset of data, the database engine will identify the location of the rows needed to satisfy the query and retrieve the data from the tables that matches the criteria established by the FROM, INNER JOIN, ON, and WHERE statements. In this way, no extra data is retrieved, which makes the query more efficient.

The first set of data the database engine retrieves in this example is the product name and the product ID for every row in the Product table that has a product subcategory ID of 1. This data is placed in a memory location to be compared to the next set of data retrieved from the SalesOrderDetail table. The query processor retrieves the product ID, unit price, and order quantity of every row from the SalesOrderDetail table where the year of the modified date value is 2004. It also performs the mathematical operation specified in the SELECT statement (Order Quantity * Unit Price) by multiplying the order quantity by the unit price for each sales record returned. At this point, the query processor places all the product ID and expression results in another memory location. It then matches every record from the first operation to every record in the second operation by comparing the product ID values. Rows from the second operation that do not have a matching product ID are discarded, and matching rows are combined with the associated product name in a new memory location that contains only the product name and the associated expression value. This last memory location is sorted by the expression from highest value to lowest. As a last step before the data is returned by the query processor, all the rows that have an expression value less than $1000.00 are discarded.

Analyzing Queries

As you can see, the process of running a query can be a bit more complicated than it appears. The query processor does its best to create the most efficient query plan and then to execute that plan systematically. Understanding the process will help you write queries that run efficiently. In the previous section, I explained the basic process of building and executing a query plan, but how can we look into the query to identify the steps described? The answer is by using various T-SQL commands and tools included with Management Studio. This section explores in more depth how to analyze queries for optimization using the tools provided with SQL Server.

Before I describe the techniques for analyzing queries, it is important to review the process that SQL Server uses to execute a query and return the results. This process is essentially broken down into six steps:

1. **Parsing** — In the parsing phase, the query processor simply ensures that the query meets syntactic requirements.

2. **Resolution** — In the resolution phase, the query processor ensures that all the object names specified in the query actually exist and are accessible.

3. **Optimization** — During the optimization phase, the query processor evaluates a number of possible execution plans to determine which plan would cost the least. It will evaluate whether a single-processor or multiple-processor query would be the most efficient, as well as whether to use any existing indexes or column statistics. The query processor will not always choose the fastest plan. Sometimes it chooses a slower query plan because it costs less as far as CPU expenditures.

4. **Compilation** — The optimized query plan is then compiled into a small executable during the compilation phase.

5. **Caching** — This compiled plan is placed in cache during the caching phase.

6. **Execution** — The compiled plan is executed during the execution phase.

There are two caches that concern us when dealing with query analysis and optimization: the buffer cache and the procedure cache. When the compiled plan is cached, it is placed in the procedure cache. Data from tables and indexes are placed in the buffer cache. During the execution phase, the query processor looks first in the buffer cache to locate the specified data. If it cannot find the data in the cache, it will read the data from disk and place it in cache for future reference. Query plans and data will stay in the respective caches until they are either "aged out" or SQL Server removes the cache entries to make room for new plans or data.

When analyzing queries, it is important to understand the mechanics of query plan caching and data caching. It's important to compare "apples to apples" when analyzing queries. For this reason, it is often desirable to clear out the cached values before executing the queries. Be very careful if you decide to clear the cache. Clearing either the procedure or buffer cache on a production system will severely degrade performance until the cache is refilled.

The following command is used to empty the buffer cache:

```
DBCC DROPCLEANBUFFERS
```

This command clears out of the cache all data pages that have not been modified or have been committed to disk after a write operation.

The following command is used to empty the procedure cache:

```
DBCC FREEPROCCACHE
```

This command clears out all the stored plans, including those associated with programming objects such as stored procedures, functions, views, and so on. Individual query plans cannot be removed from the procedure cache. However, individual object plans can be removed. To remove a plan associated with a programming object, use the system stored procedure sp_recompile. For example, the following query marks the stored procedure uspGetBillOfMaterials for recompilation:

```
USE AdventureWorks2008;
GO
sp_recompile 'dbo.uspGetBillOfMaterials';
```

Running sp_recompile on an object does not actually recompile it at that moment. It marks the object for recompilation, which means it will be recompiled and re-cached the next time it is executed or referenced.

To get consistent results while analyzing queries, it will often be useful to start from a common point by clearing the caches prior to executing the query.

Session Options

SQL Server provides several session options that you can use to return information about the query being executed.

Session Option	Description
STATISTICS IO	Returns the number of read and scan operations required to run the query.
STATISTICS TIME	Returns the number of milliseconds required to parse, compile, and execute a query.
STATISTICS PROFILE	Returns a textual showplan and query statistics.
STATISTICS XML	Returns an XML document that contains a query plan and query statistics.
SHOWPLAN_TEXT	Returns an estimated textual showplan. Does not actually run the query.
SHOWPLAN_ALL	Returns an estimated textual showplan and query statistics. Does not actually run the query.
SHOWPLAN_XML	Returns an XML document that contains an estimated query plan and query statistics. Does not actually run the query.

We haven't yet discussed *showplans,* so a little background is in order. Showplans come in three forms: XML showplans, text showplans, and graphical showplans. Each form will be described later in this chapter. What they all share in common is a human-friendly way to represent and describe the steps that the query processor takes to return or manipulate data.

STATISTICS IO

STATISTICS IO is one of the most useful session options. It returns information about the number of scans and reads the query processor needed to perform to retrieve the query results. The following table describes the information that STATISTICS IO returns.

Output	Description
Scan count	The number of table or index scans performed.
Logical reads	The number of pages read from the buffer cache.
Physical reads	The number of pages read from disk.
Read-ahead reads	The number of pages read into the buffer cache from disk to be available for logical reads.
LOB logical reads	The number of large-object data pages read from the cache.
LOB physical reads	The number of large-object pages read from disk.
LOB read-ahead reads	The number of large-object pages read into the buffer cache from disk to be made available for logical reads.

The scan count details how many table or index scans were required to execute the query. A scan is the reading of every row in the table or index, as opposed to a seek operation, which reads only a subset of an index's rows. Generally speaking, seeks are more efficient than scans because less data is read to retrieve the desired data.

Logical reads occur when the query processor is able to find the data it needs in the buffer cache. Logical reads typically are a 100 times faster than physical reads because the data is being read from memory and not from a physical disk.

Physical reads occur when the data needed to process the query isn't in the cache. The query processor is forced to go to the disk to get the data. When it does, it also caches it for future use.

Read-ahead reads, like physical reads, also occur when the data required to satisfy a query is not available in the buffer cache. What makes them different from physical reads is how the data is retrieved. A physical read is a page read. Remember that a SQL Server data page is an 8KB storage object. So, a physical read retrieves data 8KB at a time. A read-ahead read is an extent read. SQL Server extents comprise eight 8KB data pages for a total of 64KB. A read-ahead read quickly reads an entire data extent and places it in the cache so that the data is available to logical reads.

LOB logical reads, physical reads, and read-ahead reads are conceptually the same as their regular-sized counterparts. The difference is that the data retrieved is specifically for the storage of large-object data types, such as `text` and `image`, or for `varbinary(MAX)`, `varchar(MAX)`, and `nvarchar(MAX)` values exceeding 8KB (or a specified in-row limit).

Before we get started with table structuring, we need to level the playing field between SQL Server 2005 and 2008 so that we can use one set of examples, not two, to explain the coming topics. While your results might be slightly different, that would be true regardless of the database version.

In the following results, I will be omitting the messages returned when running DBCC commands. As long as no errors are encountered, DBCC commands return the following message on the message tab, which is not pertinent to our discussion:

```
DBCC execution completed. If DBCC printed error messages, contact your system
administrator.
```

This message has always amused me. Most DBCC commands can be run only by a user with very elevated permissions, such as the system administrator. But who are the system administrators supposed to contact?

Run the following script on either the SQL Server 2008 or 2005 version of AdventureWorks database:

```
USE AdventureWorks2008 --(or AdventureWorks)
GO
CREATE TABLE MyContact
(ContactID int IDENTITY(1,1) NOT NULL
,Title nvarchar(8) NULL
,FirstName nvarchar(50) NOT NULL
,LastName nvarchar(50) NOT NULL
,EmailAddress nvarchar(50) NULL
,Phone nvarchar(25) NULL)
CREATE CLUSTERED INDEX IX_MyContact
ON MyContact(ContactId)
```

Now that we have our table, let's populate it with contact data. On SQL Server 2008, run the following script:

```
USE AdventureWorks2008
GO
INSERT MyContact
(Title, FirstName, LastName, EmailAddress, Phone)
SELECT PP.Title
      ,PP.FirstName
      ,PP.LastName
      ,PE.EmailAddress
      ,PH.PhoneNumber AS Phone
FROM Person.Person PP
JOIN Person.EmailAddress PE
ON PE.BusinessEntityID = PP.BusinessEntityID
JOIN Person.PersonPhone PH
ON PH.BusinessEntityID = PP.BusinessEntityID
ORDER BY PP.Lastname
```

On the SQL Server 2005 version of AdventureWorks, run the following:

```
USE AdventureWorks
GO
INSERT MyContact
(Title, FirstName, LastName, EmailAddress, Phone)
SELECT Title
      ,FirstName
      ,LastName
      ,EmailAddress
      ,Phone
FROM Person.Contact
ORDER BY Lastname
```

Now let's take a look at a simple query and see what kind of information we can learn from the STATISTICS IO session option.

```
DBCC DROPCLEANBUFFERS;
DBCC FREEPROCCACHE;
SET STATISTICS IO ON;
GO
USE AdventureWorks2008;
GO
SELECT LastName
      ,FirstName
      ,EmailAddress
FROM MyContact
WHERE LastName = 'Ayers';
GO
SET STATISTICS IO OFF;
GO
```

This query returns the following results:

```
LastName               FirstName                EmailAddress
-----------------      ----------------------   ----------------------
Ayers                  Stephen                  stephen1@adventure-works.com
(1 row(s) affected)
Table 'MyContact'. Scan count 1, logical reads 341, physical reads 4,
read-ahead reads 42, lob logical reads 0, lob physical reads 0,
lob read-ahead reads 0.
```

As you can see from the results, the retrieval of a single row required a scan, 341 logical page reads, 4 physical page reads, and 42 read-ahead page reads, which are primarily in the form of 64KB extent reads. There were no large-object reads because none of the data for the MyContact table is stored as large objects.

If you were to change the query to filter on ContactID instead of LastName, as follows, the results would be quite different:

```
DBCC DROPCLEANBUFFERS;
DBCC FREEPROCCACHE;
SET STATISTICS IO ON;
GO
USE AdventureWorks2008;
GO
SELECT LastName
      ,FirstName
      ,EmailAddress
FROM MyContact
WHERE ContactID = 911;
GO
SET STATISTICS IO OFF;
GO
```

And the results would be:

```
LastName               FirstName                EmailAddress
-----------------      ----------------------   ----------------------
Ayers                  Stephen                  stephen1@adventure-works.com
(1 row(s) affected)
Table 'MyContact'. Scan count 1, logical reads 2, physical reads 0, read-ahead
reads 0, lob logical reads 0, lob physical reads 0, lob read-ahead reads 0.
```

We get the same data results, but the work that SQL Server had to perform is dramatically reduced because the MyContact table is built on a clustered index ordered by ContactID. The query processor could just seek out the corresponding key and find all the data it needed. However, there may very well be a legitimate need to search on the Contact table by last name. The amount of work could again be reduced significantly by placing an index on the LastName column, as the following example shows:

```
USE AdventureWorks2008;
GO
CREATE NONCLUSTERED INDEX IX_LastName
ON MyContact (LastName);
GO
DBCC DROPCLEANBUFFERS;
DBCC FREEPROCCACHE;
SET STATISTICS IO ON;
GO
USE AdventureWorks2008;
GO
SELECT LastName
      ,FirstName
      ,EmailAddress
FROM MyContact
WHERE LastName = 'Ayers';
GO
SET STATISTICS IO OFF;
GO
```

Here are the results with an index on the LastName column:

```
LastName             FirstName               EmailAddress
------------------   ---------------------   ----------------------
Ayers                Stephen                 stephen1@adventure-works.com
Table 'MyContact'. Scan count 1, logical reads 4, physical reads 3, read-ahead
reads 0, lob logical reads 0, lob physical reads 0, lob read-ahead reads 0.
```

The performance isn't as good as when using ContactId, but it is much better than the original query without a supporting index. Now you may be thinking "I'm a developer, not a DBA. I will not be building indexes." You may be right. However, it is very important for the SQL developer to understand where a new index would be beneficial to the database performance. Specific recommendations can be given to the DBA to make your queries perform better.

STATISTICS TIME

STATISTICS TIME returns how long the query processor takes to parse and compile a query and then the total execution time for a query. This session option is useful for creating query baselines. The duration of queries can be recorded and compared over time to evaluate ongoing performance.

Let's take a look at our original mountain bike query from earlier in the chapter, but with some session settings added to analyze the query performance.

```
USE AdventureWorks2008;
GO
DBCC DROPCLEANBUFFERS;
DBCC FREEPROCCACHE;
SET STATISTICS TIME ON;
GO
SELECT P.Name AS Product
       ,SUM((S.OrderQty * S.UnitPrice)) AS MountainBikeSales2004
FROM Production.Product P
INNER JOIN Sales.SalesOrderDetail S
   ON P.ProductID = S.ProductID
WHERE YEAR(S.ModifiedDate) = 2004
   AND P.ProductSubCategoryID = 1 --Mountain Bikes
GROUP BY P.Name
HAVING SUM((S.OrderQty * S.UnitPrice)) > $1000.00
ORDER BY MountainBikeSales2004 DESC;
GO
SET STATISTICS TIME OFF;
GO
```

Here are the message results:

```
SQL Server parse and compile time:
   CPU time = 47 ms, elapsed time = 141 ms.
 SQL Server Execution Times:
   CPU time = 94 ms,  elapsed time = 317 ms.
```

In this case the query consumed 47 milliseconds of CPU time and a total server time of 141 milliseconds just on the parse and compile phases of query execution. Total query execution consumed 62 milliseconds of CPU time and a total of 317 milliseconds. Keep in mind that these times are on my server. Your times will vary.

Remember that SQL Server caches a query plan and the data pages associated with a query. So what happens if we run the query again, as follows, without clearing these caches?

```
USE AdventureWorks2008;
GO
SET STATISTICS TIME ON;
GO
SELECT P.Name AS Product
       ,SUM((S.OrderQty * S.UnitPrice)) AS MountainBikeSales2004
FROM Production.Product P
INNER JOIN Sales.SalesOrderDetail S
   ON P.ProductID = S.ProductID
WHERE YEAR(S.ModifiedDate) = 2004
```

```
     AND P.ProductSubCategoryID = 1 --Mountain Bikes
GROUP BY P.Name
HAVING SUM((S.OrderQty * S.UnitPrice)) > $1000.00
ORDER BY MountainBikeSales2004 DESC;
GO
SET STATISTICS TIME OFF;
GO
```

Now look at the results:

```
SQL Server parse and compile time:
   CPU time = 0 ms, elapsed time = 0 ms.
 SQL Server Execution Times:
   CPU time = 72 ms,  elapsed time = 118 ms.
```

Notice that the parse and compile times are now zero, and the total CPU and execution times are less than before. This will not always be the case. Because the CPU time is based on several variables, you may encounter times when the CPU time is the same or even more than when running the query with a clean cache. The total elapsed time, however, will almost always be less.

STATISTICS PROFILE

STATISTICS PROFILE returns a query "profile." The profile consists of a textual showplan along with several statistics about the query. The textual showplan details the steps taken by the query processor to retrieve the data. The statistics detail information about the cost of the query.

Let's re-examine the query from the MyContact table with STATISTICS PROFILE turned on.

```
USE AdventureWorks2008;
GO
DBCC DROPCLEANBUFFERS;
DBCC FREEPROCCACHE;
SET STATISTICS PROFILE ON;
SELECT LastName
      ,FirstName
      ,EmailAddress
FROM MyContact
WHERE LastName = 'Ayers';
GO
SET STATISTICS PROFILE OFF;
GO
```

The first thing that is returned is the results of the query, "Stephen Ayers," which we have seen before. After that is the query profile. The columns of the output are described briefly in the following table.

Column	Description
Rows	The number of rows returned by the query processor.
Executes	How many times the query is executed in the batch.
Stmt Text	The first row is generally the text of the T-SQL statement. The remaining rows contain a description of an operation performed to process the query. The rows in the Stmt Text column are divided into two different types. They are either of the type of the query operation, such as SELECT, UPDATE, INSERT, or DELETE, or they are of the PLAN_ROW type, which described the operation being performed, such as an index seek.
StmtId	An integer representing the number of the statement in the query batch.
NodeId	The number of the node of the query. Each query has a number of nodes, or sub-steps, that were executed to perform the action.
Parent	The steps of a query are hierarchical, with the Parent value identifying the hierarchy of the nodes.
PhysicalOp	The physical operation associated with the step — for instance, an index scan or index seek.
LogicalOp	The logical operation associated with the step — for instance, an index scan or index seek.
Argument	Information about the operation, such as the key being searched for in an index seek.
DefinedValues	A comma-separated list of values being used for the operation — for instance, LastName, Firstname, and EmailAddress for the MyContact table query.
EstimateRows	The estimated number of rows output from the operation.
EstimateIO	The estimated IO cost for the operation.
EstimateCPU	The estimated CPU cost for the operation.
AvgRowSize	The average size of the row (in bytes) being processed by the operation.
TotalSubTreeCost	The estimated cost of the operation and any child operations.
OutputList	A comma-separated list of fields returned by the operation.

Column	Description
Warnings	A comma-separated list of warnings associated the operation, such as Missing Index or No Stats.
Type	Either the type of operation (SELECT, UPDATE, INSERT, DELETE, EXECUTE) or PLAN_ROW.
Parallel	Indicates whether the operation will be run on multiple processors (O for no parallelism; 1 for parallel).
EstimateExecutions	The number of times the operator will be executed for the current batch.

Now that we know what we're looking at, let's take a look at the query profile. In each of the following tables, I will describe the column of interest and also return the Logical Operation column to make it easier to follow. The first column of interest is the statement text.

LogicalOp	StmtText
NULL	SELECT [LastName],[FirstName],[EmailAddress] FROM [MyContact] WHERE [LastName]=@1
Inner Join	|--Nested Loops(Inner Join, OUTER REFERENCES:([Uniq1002], [AdventureWorks2008].[dbo].[MyContact].[ContactID]))
Index Seek(NonClustered)	|--Index Seek(OBJECT:([AdventureWorks2008].[dbo] .[MyContact].[IX_LastName]), SEEK:([AdventureWorks2008] .[dbo].[MyContact].[LastName]=N'Ayers') ORDERED FORWARD)
Clustered Index Seek	|--Clustered Index Seek(OBJECT:([AdventureWorks2008] .[dbo].[MyContact].[IX_MyContact]), SEEK:([AdventureWorks 2008].[dbo].[MyContact].[ContactID]=[AdventureWorks2008] .[dbo].[MyContact].[ContactID] AND [Uniq1002]=[Uniq1002]) LOOKUP ORDERED FORWARD)

The rows of the StmtText column are not listed top to bottom in the order of execution; instead, they are listed from right to left, top to bottom. The pipe (|) symbol separates the operations and indicates their hierarchy. In the above example you will notice that the index seek and clustered index seek operations are indented identically and are the operations most "to the right" in the query, indicating that they are the first operations. The first operation executed is the index seek on the LastName index we created earlier. We know this because it is the topmost operation of the two right operations. Immediately after the index seek is the clustered index seek. After that is a nested loop, where the output of the index seek is joined with the output of the clustered index seek, and then lastly the data is returned by the SELECT statement.

After the StmtText column, the next column that provides detailed information about the query is the Argument column, which is described in the following table:

LogicalOp	Argument
Inner Join	OUTER REFERENCES:([Uniq1002], [AdventureWorks2008].[dbo].[MyContact].[ContactID])
Index Seek (NonClustered)	OBJECT:([AdventureWorks2008].[dbo].[MyContact].[IX_LastName]), SEEK:([AdventureWorks2008].[dbo].[MyContact].[LastName]=N'Ayers') ORDERED FORWARD
Clustered Index Seek	OBJECT:([AdventureWorks2008].[dbo].[MyContact].[IX_MyContact]), SEEK:([AdventureWorks2008].[dbo].[MyContact].[ContactID]=[AdventureWorks2008].[dbo].[MyContact].[ContactID] AND [Uniq1002]=[Uniq1002]) LOOKUP ORDERED FORWARD

Notice that the index seek operation is searching for the LastName of "Ayers" and the clustered index seek is looking for a ContactID because the MyContact table is built on a clustered index on the ContactID column. When the LastName value of "Ayers" is found in the non-clustered index, its corresponding value is that of the ContactID. Therefore, the clustered index seek is looking for the ContactID value returned from the seek of the non-clustered index on the LastName column. We can confirm this by looking at the DefinedValues column.

LogicalOp	DefinedValues
Inner Join	NULL
Index Seek (NonClustered)	[Uniq1002], [AdventureWorks2008].[dbo].[MyContact].[ContactID], [AdventureWorks2008].[dbo].[MyContact].[LastName]
Clustered Index Seek	[AdventureWorks2008].[dbo].[MyContact].[FirstName], [AdventureWorks2008].[dbo].[MyContact].[EmailAddress]

Notice that the ContactID and LastName values are listed for the non-clustered index operation. It is also interesting that the clustered index seek has the defined values of FirstName and EmailAddress. This is because the non-clustered index seek has already identified the other two required values for the query. This is further confirmed by the OutputList column, which lists all the values returned by each operation.

LogicalOp	OutputList
Inner Join	[AdventureWorks2008].[dbo].[MyContact].[FirstName], [AdventureWorks2008].[dbo].[MyContact].[LastName], [AdventureWorks2008].[dbo].[MyContact].[EmailAddress]
Index Seek (NonClustered)	[Uniq1002], [AdventureWorks2008].[dbo].[MyContact] .[ContactID], [AdventureWorks2008].[dbo].[MyContact] .[LastName]
Clustered Index Seek	[AdventureWorks2008].[dbo].[MyContact].[FirstName], [AdventureWorks2008].[dbo].[MyContact].[EmailAddress]

Notice that the inner join operation passes all the columns in our select list out because the bottom two outputs are combined by the join.

STATISTICS XML

STATISTICS XML, like the STATISTICS PROFILE option, returns a query "profile." However, in this case, the data is returned as an XML document. Running the MyContact table query with this session option, as shown in Figure 14-1, causes an XML document to be returned by the query processor.

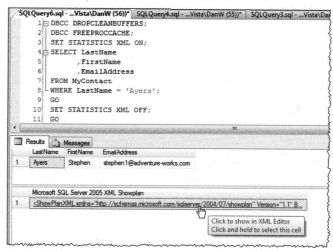

Figure 14-1

What occurs when you click the XML document link in the Results pane depends on whether you are running SQL Server 2005 or SQL Server 2008. SQL Server 2005 will open the XML document in Management Studio. Figure 14-2 shows a partial result set.

```
Microsoft SQL S...ML Showplan1.xml   WoodVista.Advent... - SQLQuery2.sql*   Object Explorer Details
<ShowPlanXML xmlns="http://schemas.microsoft.com/sqlserver/2004/07/showplan" Version="1.0" Build
  <BatchSequence>
    <Batch>
      <Statements>
        <StmtSimple StatementText="SELECT [ContactId],[LastName],[FirstName],[EmailAddress] FROM
          <StatementSetOptions QUOTED_IDENTIFIER="false" ARITHABORT="true" CONCAT_NULL_YIELDS_NU
          <QueryPlan DegreeOfParallelism="1" CachedPlanSize="14" CompileTime="211" CompileCPU="9
            <RelOp NodeId="0" PhysicalOp="Nested Loops" LogicalOp="Inner Join" EstimateRows="1.2
              <OutputList>
                <ColumnReference Database="[AdventureWorks]" Schema="[Person]" Table="[Contact]"
                <ColumnReference Database="[AdventureWorks]" Schema="[Person]" Table="[Contact]"
                <ColumnReference Database="[AdventureWorks]" Schema="[Person]" Table="[Contact]"
                <ColumnReference Database="[AdventureWorks]" Schema="[Person]" Table="[Contact]"
              </OutputList>
              <RunTimeInformation>
                <RunTimeCountersPerThread Thread="0" ActualRows="1" ActualEndOfScans="1" ActualE
              </RunTimeInformation>
              <NestedLoops Optimized="0">
                <OuterReferences>
                  <ColumnReference Database="[AdventureWorks]" Schema="[Person]" Table="[Contact
                </OuterReferences>
                <RelOp NodeId="1" PhysicalOp="Index Seek" LogicalOp="Index Seek" EstimateRows="1
                  <OutputList>
                    <ColumnReference Database="[AdventureWorks]" Schema="[Person]" Table="[Conta
                    <ColumnReference Database="[AdventureWorks]" Schema="[Person]" Table="[Conta
                  </OutputList>
                  <RunTimeInformation>
                    <RunTimeCountersPerThread Thread="0" ActualRows="1" ActualEndOfScans="1" Act
```

Figure 14-2

The XML document contains the same data as the profile data, but in XML format. This ability makes it very handy to programmatically process the results, which several third-party software vendors have done when building tools to help with the analysis of SQL queries.

In SQL Server 2008, Management Studio interprets the XML and displays it as a graphical execution plan, which will be described later. The source XML can be viewed by right-clicking the graphical plan and selecting the Show Execution Plan XML choice in the resulting context menu, as shown in Figure 14-3.

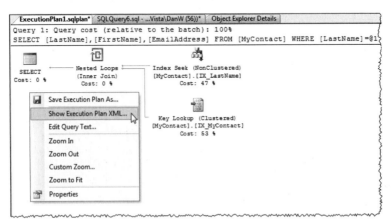

Figure 14-3

SHOWPLAN_TEXT

The SHOWPLAN_TEXT option, as shown in Figure 14-4, returns the same type of textual showplan that the STATISTICS PROFILE option returns. However, it does not return any information other than the showplan. When this option is on, executing a query will not actually run the query. Instead, the query processor calculates a query plan and returns the plan to the results window. No data is actually retrieved.

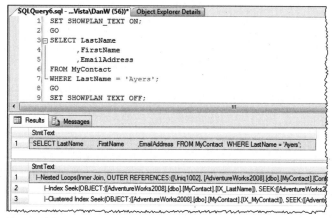

Figure 14-4

SHOWPLAN_ALL

The SHOWPLAN_ALL option, as shown in Figure 14-5, is identical to the STATISTICS PROFILE option except that it, like SHOWPLAN_TEXT, does not actually run the query. SHOWPLAN_TEXT and SHOWPLAN_ALL are good ways of returning query information without the cost of actually running the query. This can be very handy when analyzing a query that takes a very long time to run.

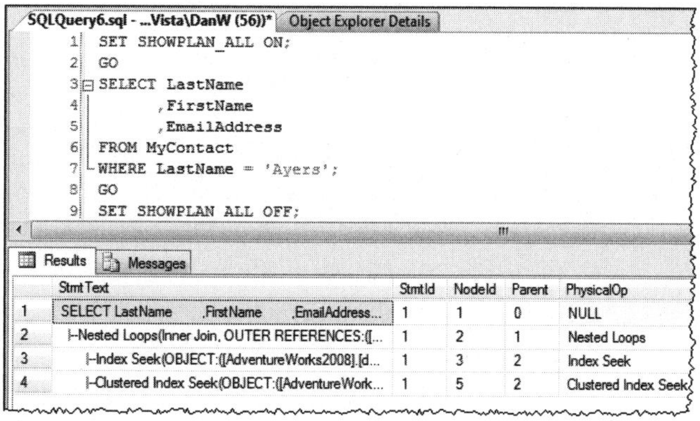

Figure 14-5

SHOWPLAN_XML

The SHOWPLAN_XML option is identical to the STATISTICS XML option except that it, like the other showplan options, does not actually run the query, but instead returns an XML document that contains the operations that would be performed if the query were actually run.

Graphical Execution Plans

The information returned with the session options can also be returned in a graphical format. As with the session options, the graphical execution plans can be created as the corresponding query is run (actual execution plan), or created without running the query (estimated execution plan). The only real difference between the two methods is that the estimated execution plan does not return the actual row count affected by the query or the value of rebinds and rewinds, which I'll explain later in this section.

You can launch or configure graphical execution plans with a button on the SQL Editor toolbar of Management Studio (see Figure 14-6) or with keyboard hotkeys (Ctrl+L for an estimated execution plan and Ctrl+M for an actual execution plan).

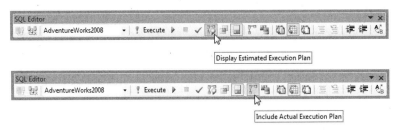

Figure 14-6

The graphical execution plans can get very large and complicated, but they all build on some basic operations. For the purpose of this book, we will keep to fairly basic plans.

For the first example, let's go back to the simple query on the MyContact table. To set up for the example, however, we need to drop the index on the LastName column we created earlier by running the following script:

```
USE AdventureWorks2008;
GO
IF EXISTS(SELECT *
          FROM sys.indexes
          WHERE name = 'IX_LastName'
            AND OBJECT_NAME([object_id]) = 'MyContact')
    DROP INDEX MyContact.IX_LastName;
```

Now that we have put the table back to its original state, we'll analyze the query to see which steps the query processor executes to run the query. Open a new query window and make sure that the database context is set to AdventureWorks2008 on the SQL Editor toolbar, and then type the following query in the new window:

```
SELECT ContactID
       ,LastName
       ,FirstName
       ,EmailAddress
FROM MyContact
WHERE LastName = 'Ayers';
```

Now either press Ctrl+L or click the Display Estimated Execution Plan button on the SQL Editor toolbar.

Figure 14-7 shows a simple execution plan. To retrieve the row for the contact with a last name of "Ayers," the query processor performs a clustered index scan. Remember that a scan of a clustered index is the same as a table scan because a clustered index is essentially all the rows of a table sorted by the index key. You'll also recall that in order to retrieve this one row, SQL Server had to read every row of the table.

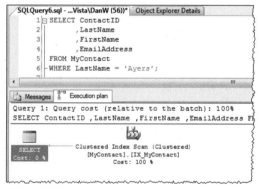

Figure 14-7

Placing the mouse cursor over the clustered index scan icon on the execution plan displays a window that contains information about the operation (see Figure 14-8).

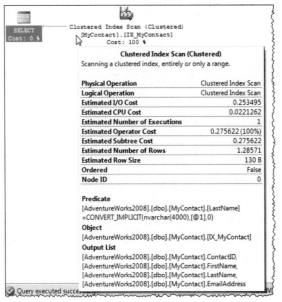

Figure 14-8

As we did earlier in the chapter, replace the LastName search criteria with ContactID, as shown in the following query, and then regenerate the execution plan.

```
SELECT ContactID
      ,LastName
      ,FirstName
      ,EmailAddress
FROM MyContact
WHERE ContactID = 911;
```

Figure 14-9 shows that in order to return the row for the contact with a search criteria of ContactID, a clustered index seek is performed instead of a clustered index scan. Comparing the cost of the two queries shows that the query using LastName is more than 100 times more expensive in CPU and IO cost than the query using ContactID.

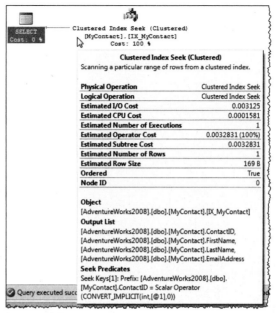

Figure 14-9

Earlier in the chapter when analyzing this query, we added an index to the LastName column and reduced the number of page reads from 341 to 2. To further analyze the impact of adding the index on the query, let's re-add the index on the LastName column and analyze the query again.

First, open a new query window and create the index by running the following script:

```
USE AdventureWorks2008;
GO
CREATE NONCLUSTERED INDEX IX_LastName
ON MyContact(LastName);
```

Now go back to the query window with the Contact table query and change it back so that it is searching on the LastName column again. Once that is done, regenerate the execution plan.

As you can see in Figure 14-10, the plan now contains three different operators: a non-clustered index seek, a key lookup, and a join. These are the same operations we saw when examining the textual showplans; however, the graphical execution plan can make it a little easier to analyze.

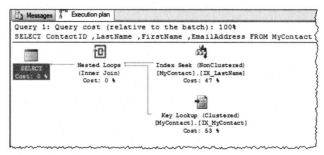

Figure 14-10

In this particular case, we see that the non-clustered index seek searches for the LastName value of "Ayers" and returns both the value of LastName and the value of the corresponding ContactID to the nested loop operator (see Figure 14-11). This occurs because all non-clustered indexes are mapped to the table's clustered index, if one exists. As a result, the row in the index IX_LastName that contains the last name of "Ayers" also has a column with the corresponding clustered index key, which happens to be the ContactID for the MyContact table.

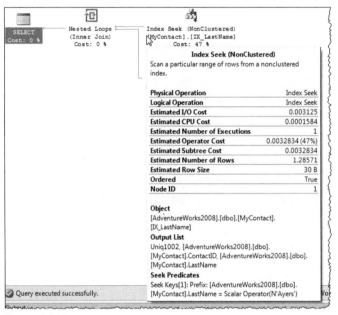

Figure 14-11

The nested loop operator takes the ContactID key value and looks for the associated value from the clustered index in the form of a key lookup, as shown in Figure 14-12. Looking at the associated CPU and IO cost from the original query and comparing it to the same query when an index on the LastName column exists shows again a significant decrease in cost, even though more steps are necessary to perform the operation.

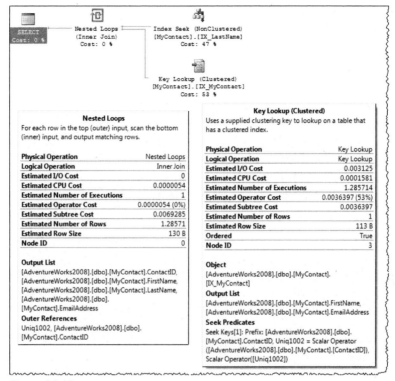

Figure 14-12

As you can see using these very basic examples, the graphical execution plan can be very helpful in analyzing queries in order to provide optimization recommendations, whether those recommendations are for new indexes or a change in search criteria. Let's take a look at our other example query looking for mountain bike sales totals that occurred in the year 2004.

```
USE AdventureWorks2008;
GO
SELECT P.Name AS Product
       ,SUM((S.OrderQty * S.UnitPrice)) AS MountainBikeSales2004
FROM Production.Product P
INNER JOIN Sales.SalesOrderDetail S
  ON P.ProductID = S.ProductID
WHERE P.ProductSubCategoryID = 1 --Mountain Bikes
  AND YEAR(S.ModifiedDate) = 2004
GROUP BY P.Name
HAVING SUM((S.OrderQty * S.UnitPrice)) > $1000.00
ORDER BY MountainBikeSales2004 DESC;
```

This time we'll create the execution plan along with executing the query by either typing the hotkey Ctrl+M and then executing the query or by clicking the Display Actual Execution Plan button on the SQL Editor toolbar and then executing the query. As shown in Figure 14-13, an Execution Plan tab is displayed, along with the usual Results and Messages tabs. You will also notice that I moved things around a little bit so that the execution plan would fit on a single page.

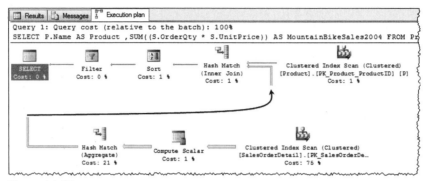

Figure 14-13

Once again, hovering the mouse cursor over an operator icon will display detailed information about that operation. The following table describes the information returned by an actual execution plan. As previously mentioned, the information displayed is identical to that of an estimated execution plan, with the exception of those attributes that specify "Actual." The "Cost" metrics are *not* representative of time or any other concrete metric. Instead, they are an internally generated metric provided by the query processor to enable comparisons when examining different plans.

Attribute	Description
Physical Operation	The physical operation executed by the query processor.
Logical Operation	A conceptual description about the operation performed. For instance, a physical hash-match join is conceptually described as an inner join. (For more information about different types of physical joins, consult SQL Server Books Online.)
Actual Number of Rows	The actual number of rows returned by the operation.
Estimated IO Cost	The estimated IO cost of the operation.
Estimated CPU Cost	The estimated CPU cost of the operation.
Estimated Operator Cost	The total cost associated with the operation.
Estimated Subtree Cost	The cumulative cost of the entire subtree up to the current node. For instance, if you examine the subtree cost value in the mountain bike sales query, you will notice that it continues to increase from the right-most operation to the final SELECT operation. Large, complex queries may have multiple subtrees that are merged as they move from right to left.
Estimated Number of Rows	The number of rows the query optimizer estimated would be affected by the operation. The estimated number is based on column or index statistics and may not match the actual number because statistics are updated dynamically.

Attribute	Description
Estimated Row Size	The estimated size of each row that passes through the operation. Because row size can be affected by variable-length columns in the row, only an estimate is provided.
Actual Rebinds	The number of rebinds executed in a join or spool operator (a spool operator saves an intermediate query result to the tempdb database). A rebind occurs when one or more of the values being joined by the join operator changed during execution and the join required re-initialization.
Actual Rewinds	The number of rewinds executed in a join or spool operator. A rewind occurs when a join or spool is reinitialized but no changes occurred to the join value.
Ordered	Indicates that the index scan or seek was ordered (ascending or descending) by the query processor.
Node ID	The integer identity of the query node (step).

Examining the execution plan shown in Figure 14-13, you can see the exact steps that the query processor took in retrieving our result set. Notice that the lines moving from operator to operator vary in thickness. The thickness of the line indicates the amount of data being passed. The right-most operator, which is the clustered index scan of the SalesOrderDetail table, returns more than 45,000 rows, as you can see in Figure 14-14, which is the number of sale detail records in 2004.

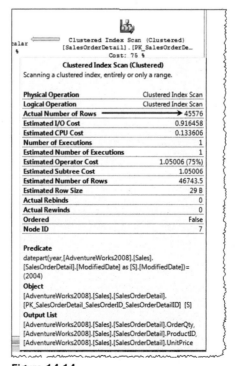

Figure 14-14

But let's not get ahead of ourselves. Remember that the logical order of operation for the execution plans is essentially right to left, top to bottom. With multiple processors and multiple threads processing a query, the logical order will not always match the actual order, but when the query processor puts everything together, the logical sequence is met. With this in mind, we see in Figure 14-13 that the first operation performed by the query processor is a scan of the clustered index on the Product table. The query processor is scanning every row in the Product table to look for those with a ProductSubCategoryID of 1.

At first glance it may seem that a non-clustered index on the ProductSubCategoryID column could reduce the cost of this query. After all, why should the query processor scan all the rows of the Product table if it could just look up the products by ProductSubCategoryID instead? In reality, a non-clustered index on the ProductSubCategoryID column would not change the execution plan at all. The query processor would completely ignore it. It will ignore it for a couple of reasons. The first is that there are not that many rows in the Product table, and spending time correlating an index with a row's location when there are only 505 rows in the table is a waste of time. The second and most significant reason is that the ProductSubCategoryID column is not the only value that is needed from the Product table. The query also needs the Product's name. Looking up the clustered index key value in a non-clustered index built on the ProductSubCategoryID column, only to return to the Product table to retrieve the Name column, would be inefficient.

Looking at the execution plan, we can see that the output of the clustered index scan of the Product table is both the ProductID and the Product Name (see Figure 14-15).

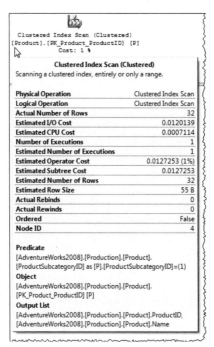

Figure 14-15

The next logical operation that occurs is the clustered index scan of the SalesOrderDetail table, and as mentioned earlier, the output of this operator is wider than the previous operation because this one passes 45,576 rows to the scalar operator. As you can see in Figure 14-16, the scalar operation takes the rows and creates the value of Expr1005 (MountainBikeSales2004) by executing the expression (S.OrderQty * S.UnitPrice). It then passes all 45,576 rows of ProductID and Expr1005 to the hash match operator.

Figure 14-16

The bottom hash match operator is identified as a logical aggregate. The purpose of this hash match operator is to sum the results of the previous expression and group that sum by ProductID. This information isn't readily available with the usual mouse-over window, but it can be seen when launching the Properties window by pressing F4 or selecting the Properties window in the View menu (see Figure 14-17). The hashing algorithm builds a table of all the ProductIDs and then summarizes the expression Expr1005 (S.OrderQty * S.UnitPrice) for each of the distinct ProductIDs that have a sales order detail record in 2004. The aggregate hash match outputs all the identified product records and the expression Expr1004, which equates to SUM(Expr1005) or SUM((S.OrderQty * S.UnitPrice)) to the top hash match operator, which is identified as logical inner join.

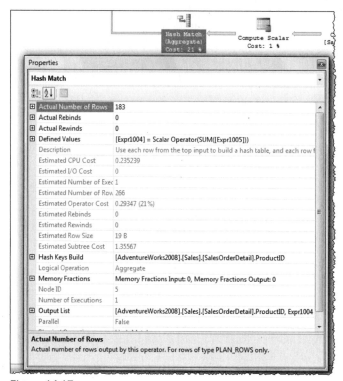

Figure 14-17

The inner join hash match has inputs from the two subtrees. The top input is the ProductID and Name values extracted by the clustered index scan, and the bottom is the ProductID and Expr1004 values from the aggregate hash match, as shown in Figure 14-18. The job of the inner join hash match is to match the ProductID values from the top subtree to the ProductID values of the bottom subtree, and then pass only the ones that match to the sort operator.

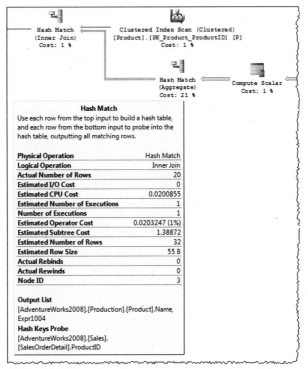

Figure 14-18

The sort operator implements the ORDER BY clause in our query and sorts the expression Expr1004, which is our column alias MountainBikeSales2004. The sort operator passes the final sorted rows to the Select operator, which returns the rows to the query processor.

The two execution plans we have examined are fairly basic, but they have demonstrated the fundamentals of execution plan analysis. There are a few more operators that we have not covered, but a detailed description of them is, unfortunately, beyond the scope of this book. Fortunately, SQL Server Books Online gives adequate coverage of the different operators in the topic titled "Graphical Execution Plan Icons (SQL Server Management Studio)."

Writing Efficient T-SQL (Best Practices)

The true secret to writing good T-SQL is a simple equation and it goes something like this: Understanding of how SQL Server processes T-SQL, combined with good logic, multiplied by good testing, raised to the power of the number of people reviewing the code. Simple, right? The point is this: Almost anybody can learn to write T-SQL. It's fun and it is relatively easy to learn, especially when compared to programming languages such as C or heaven forbid, PERL, which is (in our opinion) more like a mystic art than a language. However, just like everyone who learns how to drive doesn't end up racing in the Daytona 500, everyone who learns T-SQL is not going to write good T-SQL. Writing good, efficient T-SQL takes experience. One of my favorite modern-day proverbs is this: "Good judgment comes from experience. A great deal of experience comes from bad judgment." The same can be said for writing T-SQL. Writing good T-SQL comes from experience. A great deal of experience comes from writing bad T-SQL.

I am not encouraging you to write bad T-SQL in order to write good T-SQL. To be frank, you will probably do that without any help from me, but so did I and so did everyone I know who writes great T-SQL, and many of those write better T-SQL than I do now. So, take every opportunity to learn from other people's mistakes. One of my father's favorite sayings as I grew up was "Smart people learn from their mistakes; smarter people learn from other people's mistakes." In light of that, every time you look at other people's code, ask yourself, "Can I learn something from this code? Is it efficient? Is it logical? Are they implementing their logic in a new way? If it is a new way, is it innovative and cool? Or is it just new?" Many times I have seen a T-SQL developer get enamored with a new capability or function and work very hard to introduce the new capability even when it doesn't make sense. In SQL Server 2000 this was most evident in the new capabilities created with user-defined functions, which are immensely powerful but can introduce significant performance issues if used indiscriminately. With SQL Server 2005, the new Common Language Runtime (CLR) programming objects and XML support saw a massive increase in both capabilities and potential for abuse. SQL Server 2008 also provides some very powerful enhancements that can be used very effectively, but new features should not be introduced to a data application without fully understanding the ramifications of the technology. I work with many databases that are beyond the terabyte size with tables that have billions of rows. Experimenting with and deploying code that runs on a database that is only a few gigabytes in size may be acceptable, but when writing code for a large database that impacts thousands of customers and millions of dollars, you better make sure that your code does not bring the server to its knees. Doing so becomes a singular episode that I, and my colleagues, have come to call an RGE, or "résumé generating event." To avoid RGEs, don't get in a hurry to deploy new code. Test your code, then test it again to make sure it does exactly what you want it to do and nothing else. When you get done, have someone else test it as well. The extra effort will be worth it.

Writing Efficient Filters

The single most important part of any query is the WHERE clause, followed closely by any join criteria when multiple tables are referenced. The primary goal of the WHERE clause is to limit the amount of rows that the query processor must read to return the desired results. In light of this fact, we can establish some basic search criteria.

Positive Searches

The first general guideline for writing efficient filters is to remain positive. Too many times developers go out of their way to use negative search criteria. Although this can be the most efficient way to write equations in a true programming language, doing so in a set-based data manipulation language is not always a good idea. With large result sets, doing a negative search by using the NOT operator can force the query processor to do a table scan, whereas doing a positive search allows the query processor to find just the desired rows. This is not always the case, of course, and there are many variables, such as the existence of indexes and the percentage of rows excluded by the negative criteria. Sometimes logic dictates that a negative criterion be used and there is nothing wrong with that, but to use a negative criterion when a positive one would work just as well can lead to performance issues.

Wildcards

Using the LIKE operator and available wildcard operators is a flexible and powerful method of searching for character data. However, care should be taken to avoid using them excessively or unnecessarily. For example, the two following queries, shown in Figures 14-19 and 14-20, return identical results. However, the query shown in Figure 14-20 is much less efficient.

As you can see in Figure 14-19, this first query takes advantage of the index we created previously on the LastName column. The query processor completes a seek operation on the index to retrieve the row we want.

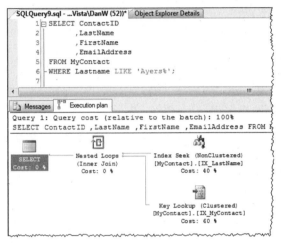

Figure 14-19

The same execution plan would be created even if we changed the search criteria to LIKE 'Ay%'. Trailing wildcards can be optimized by the query processor and take advantage of existing indexes.

Now take a look at Figure 14-20, which shows the query and execution plan with a leading wildcard.

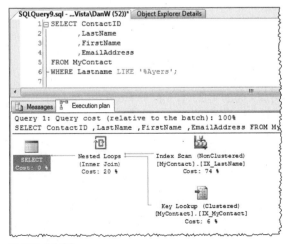

Figure 14-20

Even though both queries return identical results, the query with a leading wildcard is much less efficient. The leading wildcard forces the query processor to complete an index scan instead of an index seek, resulting in increased IO and CPU cost.

Why would a developer write a query like the one shown in Figure 14-20 unless he or she needed to search for a string of characters inside a string of characters? The answer in this case is that the developer was implementing logic whereby the value of last name could be omitted and all contacts returned. Consider the following code:

```
CREATE PROCEDURE uspGetContacts @LastName nvarchar(50) = ''
AS
SELECT ContactID
      ,FirstName
      ,LastName
      ,EmailAddress
FROM MyContact
WHERE LastName LIKE '%' + @LastName + '%';
```

Setting the @LastName variable to an empty string allows the stored procedure to run with a specified last name value or with no last name value specified. As a result, the stored procedure will only return matching rows or all rows. Pretty cool, right? No, actually it's wrong. Every time this query runs, a scan will occur, even when one is not necessary. I discovered code very much like this in a production system that scanned more than 65 million rows. The answer to this problem is to write a bit more code and save the database system a significant amount of processing. Here is a better solution to the previous stored procedure:

```
CREATE PROCEDURE uspGetContacts @LastName nvarchar(50) = ''
AS
IF @LastName = ''
   BEGIN
      SELECT ContactID
            ,FirstName
            ,LastName
            ,EmailAddress
      FROM MyContact
   END
ELSE
   BEGIN
      SELECT ContactID
            ,FirstName
            ,LastName
            ,EmailAddress
      FROM MyContact
      WHERE LastName = @LastName
   END;
```

Using some conditional logic in the stored procedure saves a large amount of overhead any time the procedure is run with a specific last name value.

Logic Operators

I previously mentioned the possible pitfalls in using the NOT operator, but what about the other logic operators, AND and OR? The bottom line when using logic operators is to keep in mind that the OR operator increases the amount of data that must be read, whereas the AND operator limits the amount of data processed. While this sounds obvious, it isn't always. The OR operator is useful, but ask yourself if the logic can be handled without the OR operator. It might be that a few more lines of conditional logic in the stored procedure will eliminate the need for the OR operator and make the overall execution time more efficient.

Join Operators

Be aware that how you join your tables is just as important as how you filter the rows with the WHERE clause. The join criteria of a multi-table query is very much like the WHERE clause. The join criteria specifies which rows from each table are retrieved, just as a WHERE statement does. In fact, you may often encounter developers who use the WHERE clause to join their tables, as the following example illustrates:

```
SELECT P.Name AS Product
    ,SC.Name AS SubCategory
FROM Production.Product P
    ,Production.ProductSubcategory SC
WHERE P.ProductSubcategoryId = SC.ProductSubcategoryId
;
```

There is nothing inherently wrong with using the WHERE clause to join the tables, but it does make the code a bit more complicated when using additional filter criteria. Here is the same query using the more accepted ANSI syntax:

```
SELECT P.Name AS Product
    ,SC.Name AS SubCategory
FROM Production.Product P
INNER JOIN Production.ProductSubcategory SC
ON P.ProductSubcategoryId = SC.ProductSubcategoryId
;
```

Again, there is no real difference between these two queries. If you look at the execution plan for each one, you will see that they are identical. This suggests that the equality operator is not the only operator that can be used in a join. Because the WHERE clause supports a variety of logic and comparison operators, can't we assume that the JOIN operator also supports them? The answer is a conditional yes. While it is possible to use a variety of operators in the joining of tables, chances are that you will not retrieve the results that you initially believed you would. For example, suppose that you wanted to return a list of all subcategories for which there were no products. At first glance, the following query would seem to do the trick:

```
SELECT SC.Name AS SubCategory
FROM Production.ProductSubcategory SC
INNER JOIN Production.Product P
ON SC.ProductSubcategoryID != P.ProductSubcategoryID
;
```

However, if you actually run this query, you will find that it returns more than 10,000 rows when there are only 37 subcategories. What happened? Essentially, this query performs a cross join. That is, it takes the first row from the ProductSubcategory table with a ProductSubcategoryID of 1 and matches it with all the products in the Product table that do not have a ProductSubcategoryID of 1. It then does the same thing with the next subcategory, and the next. The end result is that each subcategory is matched with 503 products — not exactly what we had in mind. The moral to this story is this: Think your logic all the way through and make sure the results are what you expected them to be.

Summary

A great deal more could be written about analyzing and optimizing T-SQL code — enough to fill a couple of books. However, almost all of it would be beyond the scope of this particular *beginning* book on T-SQL. This chapter introduced you to the main concepts regarding T-SQL analysis and optimization, but I will be the first to admit that there is much more to be learned. I hope this chapter encourages you to look critically at your own code and any code you may be called upon to return. While there isn't always room for improvement, very often there is.

Exercises

Exercise 1

Analyze the execution plan of the `uspGetInvoice` stored procedure. Identify inefficiencies in the code and re-write the stored procedure to reduce the amount of CPU and IO cost associated with it.

```
USE AdventureWorks2008
GO
CREATE PROCEDURE uspGetInvoice
    @SalesOrderNumber nvarchar(25) = ''
  , @PurchaseOrderNumber nvarchar(25) = ''
AS
IF @SalesOrderNumber = '' AND @PurchaseOrderNumber = ''
    BEGIN
        RAISERROR('Must provide PurchaseOrder or SalesOrder number', 14,1)
        RETURN
    END
ELSE
    BEGIN
        SELECT SalesOrderNumber
               ,OrderDate
               ,ShipDate
               ,SubTotal
               ,TaxAmt
               ,Freight
               ,TotalDue
        FROM Sales.SalesOrderHeader
        WHERE SalesOrderNumber LIKE '%' + @SalesOrderNumber + '%'
            OR PurchaseOrderNumber LIKE '%' + @PurchaseOrderNumber + '%'
    END;
```

T-SQL in Applications and Reporting

I've always been a firm believer in the principle that any learning experience should lead to a tangible and usable end product. I remember taking a Visual Basic 3.0 programming class at a local college. It was a daytime class so most of the students were typical first-year college kids, just trying to pass the class and get their credits. I, on the other hand, was working in the industry as a database programmer with Hewlett-Packard and was in need of a particular skill. Students would raise their hands and ask questions like, "Will this be on the test?" When I asked questions about user-input validation and concurrent database access, others would grimace because these topics weren't covered in the textbook.

This chapter is all about turning theory into reality. I would like to share some experience (and the experience of others) with you about building applications and database solutions on the concepts you've learned in previous chapters. Throughout this book, I've mentioned that T-SQL isn't really a programming language, although in many ways it acts like one. SQL is best suited for returning and manipulating data and database objects. When it comes to processing complex business logic and interacting with users, the SQL language usually doesn't do the job — that's not what it's for. Fortunately, SQL Server 2008 integrates extremely well with many programming languages and application development environments. It's probably more accurate to say that a number of application development environments work well with SQL Server and other database products that use the SQL query language.

Application Programming Models

An application programming model is a high-level guide, the foundation upon which all of the components of a solution rest. It's also a set of standards and practices that apply to the finer points of application design. This encompasses the concept of *design patterns,* which are repeatable practices and methods for building solutions. There really isn't one application programming model that fits all user and business needs. In fact, it's really hard to say that any one approach is typical. Every software developer, over time, adopts their own toolkit of coding habits, naming conventions, and program code and script snippets to reuse in subsequent projects. This is great for small projects architected and built by one developer. However, larger projects need a more disciplined approach requiring standards applied across the project team or organization.

To appreciate this idea of design patterns, you need only to look around and make some observations. Have you ever noticed how so many cars from different manufacturers are so similar? Why do you think this is? Likely, it's because each company has fed off of the other's success. For example, in the 1980s, the Honda Accord became an icon of style and efficiency. In the 1990s, several competing models suddenly became very similar, including the Toyota Camry, the Nissan Maxima, and others. Someone found a design that worked well, and the industry followed. Innovation is occasionally the result of starting over and applying a pattern radically different than the status quo, but is more often obtained through a series of incremental improvements. In simple terms, the software industry, although relatively young, has matured quickly over the past few decades. Developing software and database solutions is arduous and expensive. The best approach is to build upon the experiences and success of others with a cautious eye toward improvement.

The business of defining usable software programming and design models is not a lightweight topic by any means. Many large businesses have invested millions in defining their own strategies, and a number of industry-wide standards have evolved. The need for reliable and auditable processes has spawned many related, industry, and project type-specific standards. In manufacturing and production, the ISO-9000:9002 standards have prompted businesses of all kinds to maintain specific standards of quality control. Information Technology–related industries have adopted methodologies for better understanding requirements, deliverables, and project lifecycles. Specific methodologies exist for this purpose. These include the Unified Modeling Language (UML) for object-oriented application design and modular solution architecture, and Object Role Modeling (ORM) for high-level data entity modeling and database design. Software project management approaches vary from high-level, principle-centered strategies such as the Microsoft Solutions Framework (MSF) to more rigid, rules-based standards rooted in the top-down waterfall approach. Fully engaged project management deals with core issues and challenges people across different areas of business. For a methodology to work, it requires participants to share a unified belief system. This treads on culture, communication, and trust. It's hard to get two people outside of the same organization to agree on some specifics, but there are a number of principles and practices most of us who have been down this bumpy road can agree upon.

Selecting a Model

The selection of a programming model should be driven by the user and system requirements. When I am enlisted to design and implement a new system, I often go in with preconceived ideas about the size and scope of the final solution. Although it's important to start somewhere, I've learned to keep an open mind. Projects that start small can soon reveal a much larger scope and growth potential, and problems that seemed expansive might be easily solved with small, simple solutions. Likewise, shrink-wrapped commercial applications often need to be customized to such a degree that it is most cost-effective to build the system from scratch; and large, expensive custom applications can sometimes be replaced with off-the-shelf software. In short, an ounce of careful planning and design can be far more beneficial than a pound of brute-force application development.

Database application programming models roughly fall into the following categories:

- ❑ Desktop database applications
- ❑ Client/server database solutions
- ❑ Three-tier component solutions
- ❑ Web server applications
- ❑ Multi-tier Web service solutions
- ❑ Multi-system integrated solutions

Additionally, database systems generally fall into these categories:

- ❑ Online transaction processing databases
- ❑ Online analytical processing databases
- ❑ Hybrid database systems

A database solution is going to involve some combination of application model and database system. Before discussing the finer points of each of these models, I'd like to put some questions in your head. In many database applications, the business requirements aren't always cut-and-dried. You can reason that there may be some opportunity to incorporate pieces of these different models and that a system may need to evolve from one type to another. That's the beautiful thing about modern tools. If you design a system correctly, it can grow and evolve. Ask yourself the following questions about your project or application:

- ❑ **How many users need access to data?** How many users do you have now and how many users will you have in a year, or in five years? Are they employees, customers, or vendors? The volume of concurrent users is a significant factor. After you establish the answer to this question, you also need to know something about the needs of these users. For example, ten users who will consistently enter and modify records can be far more demanding than a thousand users who will occasionally browse data or view reports. It's often difficult to predict the size or profile of your user base years into the future, but this will have a large bearing on your scalability needs — how much the system will need to grow in the future.

- ❑ Modular, multi-tier applications are more scalable but also more complex and expensive to build.

- ❑ **Where are users located?** Are users situated in the same building or on the local-area network (LAN)? Perhaps they are at multiple sites or they need access to the system when they travel. Geographic boundaries have typically been one of the most significant factors in overall solution design.

- ❑ **What is your current infrastructure investment?** Implementing a new software solution involves more than installing a database and writing software. Any solution requires a significant investment in server and network infrastructure. Many companies have already made a sizable investment and are committed to a specific platform, operating system, and maybe even the database product.

❑ Does your company currently manage database servers, Web servers, component hosting services, and a corporate network? Do you have available bandwidth for the increased load? Do you use server clustering or replication? Not only do these services and the related hardware represent a cost, but so do trained and capable personnel. It's important to consider the existing infrastructure and to decide whether you can design a compatible system, or whether it makes sense to take on this additional investment.

❑ **What are your security requirements and restrictions?** How sensitive is the data you are managing? How costly would a security breach be to your business? Consider the legal and regulatory risks and restrictions. If you need a high level of security protection, this represents a greater cost in terms of coding standards, auditing, and testing. Encryption components and certificates are reasonably affordable, but encrypted data slows the system and requires more bandwidth.

❑ **How current does the data need to be?** It's not particularly difficult for a simple database system to let all users see and manipulate current data, but this becomes an issue when the system approaches its capacity limits. If data won't change that often or if data concurrency isn't a big issue, one database may suffice for both data entry and reporting applications. Otherwise, it may be necessary to use two separate databases: one for entry and another for reporting and analysis.

❑ **What data volumes do you anticipate?** Databases grow. That's inevitable. How much storage space will your database require in the next year, or five years? Very large databases have a higher maintenance overhead and need a more capable server. Historical data can be managed by archiving or partitioning portions of the database.

❑ **What are the system availability requirements?** Although allowing a database server to run around the clock isn't very expensive, guaranteeing that it will always be running can be very expensive. When does the data need to be available? During business hours? Week days? 24/7? Unless you invest in redundant, fail-over systems, you must plan for some downtime — both scheduled and unscheduled. A data maintenance and recovery plan will help but cannot guarantee 100 percent uptime unless you have redundancy and measures to mitigate every risk of failure.

❑ **What are your delivery time constraints?** Writing software and building a solution takes time, typically months to years. Usually 20–30 percent of the total time will be spent gathering requirements and designing the system. Another 20–30 percent is required for testing and debugging. After installation, deployment, and training, this leaves only 30–50 percent of the time for the actual system development. Many projects fail because of unexpected schedule overruns because these factors aren't considered or estimated realistically. Pre-built, shrink-wrapped systems can usually be delivered faster, but custom-built solutions often offer greater flexibility.

❑ **What are your budget constraints?** The more complex the project, the more difficult it may be to estimate the final cost. Custom solutions are often budgeted based on the return on investment (ROI) rather than the initial cost because, quite frankly, it's often difficult to justify the cost without considering the long-term benefit.

Desktop Database Applications

This is the most traditional type of database application. Several file-based database products have been around for many years. When I began working with medical billing software in the late 1980s, our application stored data in flat text files and the programmers wrote code that did a lot of the low-level work performed by database engines today. Most desktop database applications, even as early as the 1980s, used integrated database tools such as dBase, Clipper, Clarion, Paradox, FileMaker, and FoxPro. The most popular desktop database for Windows is Microsoft Access. Most modern database products, such as Access, support variations of the SQL language.

Access will support a handful of concurrent network users. Because the database engine doesn't run as a server-hosted service, large data volumes and complex queries can easily create excessive network traffic. Even if the database file is located on a server, data is processed on the user's computer. The advantage of this option is its simplicity and low initial cost. The disadvantage is its lack of scalability and less-efficient query processing.

Microsoft Access includes a forms design environment to create data-centric user interfaces. More sophisticated and lighter-weight applications can also be created using Microsoft Visual Studio or other application development suites.

The Access database engine incorporates an application programming interface (API) called Data Access Objects (DAO). In recent years, Microsoft has all but discouraged the use of the Access JET database engine and DAO for programming. In its place, it has promoted SQL Server 2008 Express Edition. Even though the use of the traditional Access database is being de-emphasized, the fact remains that it can actually be simpler and easier to use for creating small database solutions. Figure 15-1 shows an Access form opened from the Access database window. This form can be used for data entry, viewing, or modifying existing records.

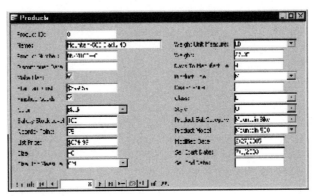

Figure 15-1

Client/Server Database Solutions

The most significant difference between a client/server database and a desktop database is that the client/server database engine runs as a service on a file server. Requests sent to the database are processed on the server, and only results are returned from queries. All query and database processing occurs on the database server. As previously mentioned, the SQL Server 2008 Express Edition is an inexpensive option for getting started and running a small database on a desktop computer.

When client/server databases came onto the scene in the mid 1990s, it was a common practice to pass ad hoc SQL strings from the client application to the server. Although this practice causes a significant performance improvement over the client-side processing of desktop databases, it doesn't take advantage of some of SQL Server's query execution optimizations. By using stored procedures with views and user-defined functions, applications benefit from improved security and compiled execution plan caching.

This model takes advantage of the processing capabilities of two computers: the client and server. That's why it is also known as a *two-tier solution*. This is typically an effective solution for mid-size applications with users connected to a LAN. The client-side application is installed entirely on each user's desktop computer. Data access code routines connect directly to the back-end database server through an API layer, such as ActiveX Data Objects (ADO) or ADO.NET. The first native API for SQL Server was introduced for SQL Server 6.0. Roughly modeled after the existing DAO object model designed for Access/JET databases, Remote Data Objects (RDO) was built on top of Open Database Connectivity (ODBC), Microsoft's first database connectivity and driver standard. In the late 1990s, Microsoft introduced ADO, an upgraded API engineered to work more efficiently with SQL Server 7.0 and above, using the OLEDB connectivity standard. DAO, RDO, and ADO, along with their corresponding connectivity components, implemented Microsoft's original object-oriented programming and execution standard, known as the Component Object Model (COM). Microsoft's latest program execution model is the .NET Common Language Runtime (CLR). This supports updated objects used to connect through ODBC, OLEDB, and the .NET native SQL Server data provider (for SQL Server 7.0 and up).

Client/server applications exist at the entry-level of distributed solution models and have limited scalability. One common practice today is to design the system with three tiers and then deploy the middle-tier components on either the client or server computers, as illustrated in Figure 15-2. This way, if the solution needs to be scaled into a larger environment, it may simply be a matter of reconfiguring existing components to run on three computers. Although this option comes at an elevated initial cost, it may spare the additional cost of rewriting large portions of the application if the solution needs to be scaled up.

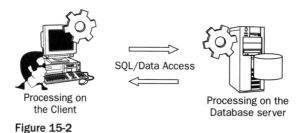

SQL/Data Access

Processing on
the Client

Processing on the
Database server

Figure 15-2

The client application contains the user interface. Figure 15-3 shows a Windows form in design view. Using Visual Studio, a variety of application types can be created to be used on the Windows desktop, in a Web browser, at the command prompt, or on portable mobile devices.

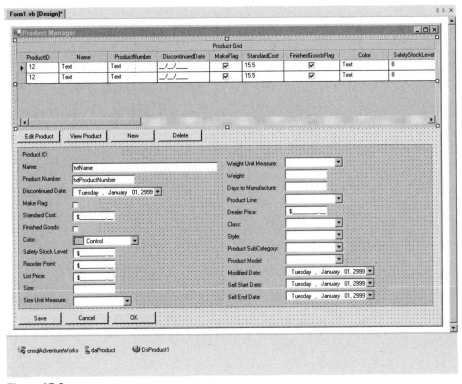

Figure 15-3

Specialized user interface controls give users a rich, interactive experience for entering and modifying record data. In this example, you can see a variety of controls that may be appropriate for different data types and fields. These include the following:

❑ Drop-down list combo boxes

❑ Check boxes

❑ Masked currency text boxes

❑ A color-picker drop-down list box

❑ Date-picker drop-down list boxes

Some of these controls have associated event-handling code, which runs when certain activities are performed by the user. The most common example is the click event of a button. Programmers can write program logic using a programming language of their preference, such as C#, Visual C++, or

Visual Basic.NET. The following simplified Visual Basic code might run when the Save button is clicked after a user enters or modifies a product record:

```
Private Sub btnSave_Click(ByVal sender As System.Object, _
                          ByVal e As System.EventArgs) Handles
btnSave.Click
    '** Determine whether new or existing record
    If bNewRecord Then
        '** New record is being added
        '** Define and open a connection:
        Dim cn As New SqlClient.SqlConnection("Data Source= " _
            & "Corp_DatabaseServer;Initial Catalog=AdventureWorks")
        cn.Open()
        '** define a command object for the Insert SQL:
        Dim cm As New SqlClient.SqlCommand
        cm.Connection = cn
        cm.CommandType = CommandType.Text
        cm.CommandText = "INSERT INTO Product (Name, ProductNumber, " _
                       & "DiscontinuedDate, MakeFlag, StandardCost) " _
            & "SELECT '" _
            & Me.txtName.Text & "', '" _
            & Me.txtProductNumber.Text & "', '" _
            & Me.dtpkDiscontinuedDate.Value & "', " _
            & Me.chkMakeFlag.Checked.ToString & ", " _
            & Me.txtcurStandardCost.Value.ToString
        '** Execute the SQL:
        cm.ExecuteNonQuery()
        '** Close the connection
        cn.Close()
    Else
        '** Existing record is being updated
        '** Define and open a connection:
        Dim cn As New SqlClient.SqlConnection("Data Source= " _
            & "Corp_DatabaseServer;Initial Catalog=AdventureWorks")
        cn.Open()
        '** define a command object for the Insert SQL:
        Dim cm As New SqlClient.SqlCommand
        cm.Connection = cn
        cm.CommandType = CommandType.Text
        cm.CommandText = "UPDATE Product SET " _
            & "Name = '" & Me.txtName.Text & "' ,'" _
            & "ProductNumber = '" & & Me.txtProductNumber.Text _
            & "', '" _
            & "DiscontinuedDate = '" & Me.dtpkDiscontinuedDate.Value _
            & "', " & "MakeFlag = " & Me.chkMakeFlag.Checked.ToString _
            & "', " _
            & "StandardCost = " & Me.txtcurStandardCost.Value.ToString _
            & "WHERE ProductID = " & me.lblProductID.Text
        '** Execute the SQL:
        cm.ExecuteNonQuery()
        '** Close the connection
        cn.Close()
    End If
End Sub
```

In this example, the actual T-SQL statements are assembled in the client code. This may seem to have the advantage of keeping all of the business logic in one place. However, this approach passes uncached, ad hoc SQL statements to the database server that will likely not perform as well as precompiled stored procedures. Allowing queries to be passed to the server on external connections can also be a security risk. This code is simple and relatively easy to maintain, but it may not be a very scalable solution.

n-tier Component Solutions

As two-tier solutions grew and began to run out of steam, many software designers looked for a way to take their applications to the next level. The great challenge was that Windows was designed to primarily run user-interactive applications on the desktop. Developing server-based components has long been difficult and expensive, using capabilities in the hands of large product vendors, not IT application developers. It took a few years for that to change. Visual Basic version 5.0 and 6.0 used COM and ActiveX technology, enabling software developers to create middle-tier components. Although writing components is pretty easy, configuring them to run on a server was quite a hassle in the beginning.

At first, software systems with this added component layer were known as **three-tier solutions** because the entire solution runs on three different physical layers: the database on the database server, middle-tier components on an application server, and the client application running on the desktop. Along with the capability to distribute the workload beyond two layers came the ability to extend the solution to four, five, or more separate computers (thus the term *n-tier*, rather than *three-tier*). One could argue that regardless of the number of servers or desktop computers, there are still conceptually only three tiers. Figure 15-4 depicts an n-tier component solution.

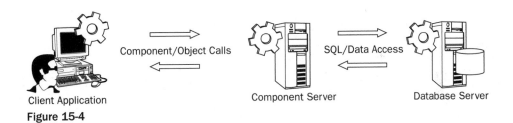

Component/Object Calls   SQL/Data Access

Client Application   Component Server   Database Server

Figure 15-4

Service Oriented Architecture

As application and solution architectures have continued to mature and evolve, standards have been defined to allow component vendors and service providers to formalize the way these middle-tier services are implemented and secured. Proprietary component technologies have given way to platform-agnostic Web services that can allow applications hosted anywhere and developed using practically any toolset to communicate with and use these services. Today the fashionable term for this approach is *SOA,* or Service Oriented Architecture.

The basic tenants of SOA are that different application components, whether developed and maintained within the corporate firewall or hosted by a third party, are segregated by business function. The components participating in an SOA-enabled solution are defined as service providers, services brokers, and service requestors. Industry leaders have defined technical legal standards for the methods used to develop, utilize, and obtain access to SOA components and services.

Database technology plays an important role in a business solution based on any technology or architecture. As information is exchanged between these service components, many of these processes will require data to be read from, modified, or inserted into a database.

Compared with the client/server example we looked at previously, the following demonstrates a more elegant solution. The three following samples are code snippets from a three-tier application. Using Figure 15-4 as a reference, we'll move from right to left. Note that not all fields are used just to keep these examples small and simple. I've made it a point to simplify this code to make it more readable.

Server-Side SQL Objects

In this model, all T-SQL is isolated to the database server as stored procedures, user-defined functions, and views. This provides a layer of security, keeps business logic close to the data, and is a very efficient use of database services and network resources.

```
/*****************************************************************
Adds new product record and returns new ProductID
    3-21-06, Paul Turley
Revisions:
    3-23-06    Added error-handling script
*****************************************************************/
CREATE PROCEDURE spAddProduct
  @Name                   nvarchar(50)
, @ProductNumber          nvarchar(25)
, @DiscontinuedDate       datetime
, @MakeFlag               bit
, @StandardCost           money
, @FinishedGoodsFlag      bit
, @Color                  nvarchar(15)
, @SafetyStockLevel       int
, @ReorderPoint           int
, @ListPrice              money
, @Size                   nvarchar(50)
AS
  INSERT INTO Product
    ( Name
    , ProductNumber
    , DiscontinuedDate
    , MakeFlag
    , StandardCost
    , FinishedGoodsFlag
    , Color
    , SafetyStockLevel
    , ReorderPoint
    , ListPrice
    , Size )
  SELECT
    @Name
  , @ProductNumber
  , @DiscontinuedDate
  , @MakeFlag
  , @StandardCost
```

```
      , @FinishedGoodsFlag
      , @Color
      , @SafetyStockLevel
      , @ReorderPoint
      , @ListPrice
      , @Size
    IF @@ERROR = 0
     RETURN @@IDENTITY
     ELSE
    RETURN -1
```

Middle-Tier Component

The component code, written in Visual Basic .NET in this example, serves as a broker between the presentation layer and the database objects. In this layer, I focus entirely on business logic and don't concern myself with the details of the user interface or the implementation of data storage. Programming objects provide an abstract representation for data access objects such as connections, queries, parameters, and results. This way, application programmers don't concern themselves with different dialects of SQL or other specific requirements of any single data provider.

```
'*****************************************************************
       Product class provides object definition to work with
       product records and product-related maintenance.
       Methods:
               AddProduct()
               UpdateProduct()
               DeleteProduct()
               GetProductList()
               GetProductsByType()
               GetProducts()
       3-23-06, Paul Turley
       Revisions:
'*****************************************************************
Public Class Product
     Public Function AddProduct(ByVal Name As String, _
                          ByVal ProductNumber As String, _
                          ByVal DiscontinuedDate As Date, _
                          ByVal MakeFlag As Boolean, _
                          ByVal StandardCost As Decimal, _
                          ByVal FinishedGoodsFlag As Boolean, _
                          ByVal Color As Color, _
                          ByVal SafetyStockLevel As Integer, _
                          ByVal ReorderPoint As Integer, _
                          ByVal ListPrice As Decimal, _
                          ByVal Size As String) As Boolean
         Dim cn As New SqlClient.SqlConnection(sConnectionString)
         Dim cm As New SqlClient.SqlCommand
         Dim Param As SqlClient.SqlParameter
         Dim iProdID As Integer
         cm.Connection = cn
         cm.CommandType = CommandType.StoredProcedure
         cm.CommandText = "spAddProduct"
```

(continued)

(continued)

```
              ' ** Pass the function arguments/field values to proc. parameters:
              Param = New SqlClient.SqlParameter("Name", Name)
              Param.DbType = DbType.AnsiString
              cm.Parameters.Add(Param)
              Param = New SqlClient.SqlParameter("ProductNumber", ProductNumber)
              Param.DbType = DbType.AnsiString
              cm.Parameters.Add(Param)
              Param = New SqlClient.SqlParameter("DiscontinuedDate",
DiscontinuedDate)
              Param.DbType = DbType.Date
              cm.Parameters.Add(Param)
              ' ** The rest of the parameters are handled here - abbreviated for
demo**
              ' ** Execute the command/stored proc:
              iProdID = cm.ExecuteScalar
              ' ** Return True if successful:
              If iProdID > 0 Then Return True
              cn.Close()
          End Function
          '*** Other Functions to Update, Delete, Get products, etc.:
              Function UpdateProduct() As Boolean
              '***
          End Function
          '*** DeleteProduct()
          '*** GetProductList()
          '*** GetProductsByType()
          '*** GetProducts()
      End Class
```

Presentation Layer

Compare the following code sample with that from the client/server sample. Rather than handling all of the data access and business logic in one chunk, I simply create objects based on the class defined in my middle-tier component. Using this object, I call methods (defined in Visual Basic as "functions") and pass the necessary values. The class method code performs data access and executes stored procedures in the database.

```
      Private Sub btnSave_Click(ByVal sender As System.Object, _
                              ByVal e As System.EventArgs) Handles
btnSave.Click
          '*** Create new instance of an object based on my custom Product class:
          Dim prod As New Product
          If bNewRecord Then
              '** New record is being added
              prod.AddProduct(Me.txtName.Text, Me.txtProductNumber.Text, _
                  Me.dtpkDiscontinuedDate.Value, Me.chkMakeFlag.Checked, ...)
          Else
              '** Existing record is being updated
              prod.UpdateProduct(Me.lblProductID.Text, Me.txtName.Text, _
                  Me.txtProductNumber.Text, Me.dtpkDiscontinuedDate.Value, ...)
          End If
      End Sub
```

Overall, it takes a little more work to design a multi-tier application, but the result is a flexible, scalable solution that is easier to maintain as it grows.

Resource Pooling

Why is a three-tier solution so much more capable than a client/server application? If you have the same number of users running just about the same desktop application connected to the same database, what's the big advantage of having this middle layer? Adding the middle-tier doesn't just raise system capacity by one-third. The middle-tier becomes a broker for pooling and recycling resources. Between the database server and component layer, it enables *connection-pooling*, a feature that was built into ODBC years ago (but largely unused until component technology matured). The database server-side network library keeps a pool of connections active. Each connection will stay open, unused, for a few minutes at a time. When a client or component makes a new connection request, it simply recycles one of the existing idle connections in the pool. Because most operations only take a few seconds at most, this is an effective way to allow lots of clients to utilize a relatively small number of database connections. The catch is that every client has to use the same connection settings and security credentials.

Between the client and component layer, the application server enables *object-pooling*. In a similar way to connection-pooling, after a call is made to run the code (known as a *method call*) in a hosted business object component, a cached copy of the executable code remains in the application server's memory. There it waits for additional requests. Between object-pooling on the application server and connection-pooling on the database server, it's all just a matter of timing. As thousands of users use a few hundred pooled business objects, the business object code uses just a few dozen connections . . . You do the math.

Component Transaction Management

Large-scale applications not only use multiple components but may also use data stored in multiple databases. The ADO and ADO.NET programming objects contain hooks to SQL Server's Distributed Transaction Coordinator (DTC) service. This lets programmers manage and synchronize transactions between different data sources. The benefit is that even with data in separate databases, on separate servers, and even using different database products, application code can have transactional control over multiple operations. Imagine an application that manages the transfer of funds between two different banking systems. After verifying that the interrelated debits and credits are all successfully processed on each separate system, either all operations are explicitly rolled forward or all operations are rolled back.

With the capability to take advantage of this computer horsepower, one significant barrier remained. COM technology (extended in the network-capable implementations, DCOM and COM+) was designed to run only on Microsoft Windows servers and Windows-based networks. These applications would support any number of users, so long as they were all clients on the same network, running Windows applications and components.

Today, both component development and component hosting are much easier than ever before. Microsoft's .NET Framework, integrated server, and development environments have improved upon all the original features of COM and COM+. Though it's true that this style of large-scale application development takes a fair amount of application development expertise, now it's fairly easy to deploy and configure an enterprise-class component server.

LINQ: .NET Standard Query Operators

In the Microsoft .NET Common Language Specification, Microsoft has added a set of language extensions to interface directly with the SQL Server 2008 relational engine through compiled program code, called Language Integrated Query, or LINQ. These extensions can be used in applications developed using Microsoft Visual Studio 2008 for the .NET CLR 3.5. LINQ gives object-oriented programmers a familiar set of programming tools to work with database objects and data without wrapping T-SQL statements into their code.

There are more than 50 operators in the System.Linq namespace that translate roughly to equivalent T-SQL commands. LINQ commands include support for Insert, Update, and Delete operations. Variations of SELECT query operators are applied using several object methods to order, filter, and find records — functionally similar to corresponding SQL clauses. In the Common Language Runtime, LINQ commands are translated to parameterized SQL statements. This occurs at the API level to prevent SQL injection attacks. Although LINQ code essentially executes SQL script against the database engine, this functionality is provided by specific data provider extensions rather than through simple language translation provisions. Using this approach, LINQ code should be able to work on different database platforms without any program code modifications.

LINQ object code generates efficient SQL commands behind the scenes using sophisticated algorithms, reducing the risk of poorly written queries. The same code and LINQ programming techniques used for SQL tables will also work with XML structures, in-memory objects, and other data sources. It fully integrates with any .NET programming language and supports all the coding and debugging tools built into Microsoft Visual Studio.

Web Server Applications

Desktop applications give users tactile control of data. Generally, applications respond quickly, and users can see an immediate response when they perform an action. We've become accustomed to a variety of sophisticated user interface controls that are relatively universal across different systems. For example, most users know what to do when they are presented with a list box, drop-down combo box, a scroll bar, or grill control. However, one of the significant limitations to building custom Windows desktop applications is they must be preinstalled on each user's Windows computer. To share data, they must be connected through a LAN.

Web server applications can make data accessible to users across the Internet. User interface options include Web pages or custom Windows components. Web services make data and application functionality available to custom applications from server to server or desktop to server, across the Internet. Web-based applications have improved significantly over the past few years, and although desktop applications continue to be more responsive and flexible than browser-based solutions, this gap continues to narrow as the Web has become a common medium for business applications. The unique characteristic of a Web server application is that it runs on a Web server, rather than on the user's desktop computer. All, or at least the vast majority, of the processing takes place on a central server running Web server components. The user sees data and changing options as they interact with a user interface that is dynamically regenerated on the Web server and sent back down to the user's Web browser.

The advantage is that users need only a Web browser and a connection to the Internet to use the application. Several challenges continue to be somewhat costly for solution developers. Compared to desktop solutions, performance and response time is slow. Web server applications typically display Web pages using HTML, the mark-up language displayed by Web browsers such as Microsoft Internet Explorer. When a user clicks a button on a Web page to retrieve a record, for example, this request is sent across the Internet to the Web server, where code interacts with the database and server-side components. Code on the server modifies the HTML tags for the copy of the user's Web page in the server's memory and then sends it back across the Internet to the user's browser, displaying a response to the user's request.

Programming Web solutions is still a little more cumbersome than traditional applications, but this has improved in recent years. Microsoft's Web application programming standard matured significantly in 2001 when Active Server Pages (ASP) graduated to ASP.NET. Now using Visual Studio.NET, creating Web server-based applications is a matter of dragging and dropping controls on a design surface and writing event code much like we've been doing to create desktop application interfaces using products such as Access and Visual Basic.

Data-bound Web server components do much of the work of transforming data into an HTML-based user interface. To create a simple data sheet page to display records in a table format, the developer needs only to set properties for a few components and write a minimal amount of code. More sophisticated Web applications may require more advanced-level coding. ASP.NET Web components offer developers the flexibility of working at a lower level when they need to have more control or at a higher level to let the components do more of the work, to develop common applications rapidly. Many of the data access components generate volumes of T-SQL script for common operations. For example, when using drag-and-drop tools to generate a DataAdaptor object, a wizard dialog prompts the developer for a database table. From this, T-SQL script is generated to manage Select, Insert, Update, and Delete operations that are implemented using auto-generated programming code. The DataAdaptor wizard will also generate parameterized stored procedures in the database for managing these operations.

Multi-Tier Web Service Solutions

In a Web server model, the Web server application really becomes the client to the database. As with a desktop application, the client can participate in a number of different application models. Simple Web server applications may use a file-based database or a client/server database. A Web server application can also execute code and use the features exposed by middle-tier components, making it a true three-tier application, with the client code running on the Web server. Additionally, Web applications can run script or separate components in the Web browser, adding yet another layer to the model. To some degree it doesn't make a lot of sense to run custom components in the browser because this really defeats the core objectives of a browser-based solution. However, using common client-side components can enhance the user experience and add more compelling content to Web pages. It's common for Web applications to make use of preinstalled client components such as Macromedia Flash, Windows Media Player, and the Adobe Reader.

Web servers can also act as application servers to host middle-tier components. One of the most exciting recent developments in component technology is the XML Web Service. As with a COM-based component, a Web service can expose functionality for network clients. It can be used as a data source broker to route database requests and return results. The most compelling feature that makes this option so unique is that requests and results are sent as text using the Hypertext Transfer Protocol (HTTP). This means that a Web service can be hosted by a Web server and can communicate with different types of clients using the plumbing of the World Wide Web. Web services are based on industry-wide standards that finally make it a simple matter for applications running on one platform, or type of computer system, to work with those on a different platform.

The magic behind Web services is a programming abstraction layer called *Simple Object Application Protocol* (SOAP). SOAP's job is to provide a standard for translating programming object calls into XML-formatted data on one end of the conversation and then back into objects on the other end. This means that programmers just write program code to work with objects. From a programmer's perspective, working with Web services is much like working with earlier types of components.

Multi-System Integrated Solutions

In a perfect world (at least from a software architect and developer's point of view), all of our business systems should be designed from the ground up to integrate with each other, to exchange information efficiently, and to provide a seamless, unified experience for business users. This just doesn't happen in most businesses. Different systems serve different business users and processes. As business grows and processes evolve, users eventually need to access applications and systems designed for different groups in the organization. This leads to requirements for these systems to interoperate. The almost inevitable outcome is the realization that similar data stored in disparate systems is not stored or used in the same way. This presents a situation common in nearly all large businesses today: To support isolated users and processes, data gets transformed and reshaped in very specific ways, eventually creating scores of special-purpose and incompatible data stores and systems designed to meet some unique business need.

This organic growth of data-related systems can be better managed if database system architects can create flexibly designed databases that can serve multiple business applications. Applications may be designed to share functionality and data through standardized data interfaces and components. Application functionality and data can now be shared by different systems using data-exchange standards such as SOAP, RSS, and XML Web services. Architecting an enterprise-wide application architecture may seem to be a daunting task, especially when integrating commercial application packages, but there are many options today that can make this much easier than before. If applications can't use shared data from a single database, moving and synchronizing copies of similar data can be achieved using resources such as SQL Server 2008 Integration Services.

Database professionals should keep a tight reign on systems that transform multiple copies of the same data for application and reporting use. Remember that information is the context of data — it's what it means and its significance to the business. When people start pushing copies of this data around, it will be easy to lose that context as this data is transformed back into information. This process should be carefully controlled and managed. The control and limitation of access to information is one thing. Every business has to have its own standards regarding information access (that are hopefully not unnecessarily restrictive). However, controlling the ability to change data and information is an entirely different matter. Ensuring that nothing is lost in the translation as data moves around the business will only serve to empower informed information users. This is often best achieved through IT-managed data marts and data warehouse databases that are accessible to all systems and users, who would otherwise be granted access to isolated data sources.

System Integration and Data Exchange

Large organizations manage lots of data. One common reason that large solutions may comprise different databases and applications is that each serves a specific purpose. Dividing data stores between transactional and decision-support systems is a common practice in large business environments. Different systems, each with its own databases, are designed to perform different business functions. Applications may use different database products.

Unfortunately, for system integrators, most specialized business systems aren't intended to integrate or share data with others. In a perfect world, all software would be designed to work together and share common data sources. The reality is that this ideal continues to be a far-off dream in most businesses. As we continue to reengineer disparate systems, we may inch a little closer to this objective in each iteration. For now, the best most of us can hope for are methods to ease the burden of exchanging data between systems.

In recent years, eXtensible Markup Language (XML) has evolved to become a common medium to help connect different databases and applications. XML is not a standard structure for data but a flexible set of standards to define almost any type of data. Unlike rigid data formatting standards of the past (such as EDS) XML allows data to be defined, stored, and documented in the same structure. This makes the data highly portable and easier to transform into that of another system. A number of supporting standards and products are now available to connect systems and synchronize data through the use of XML. Microsoft BizTalk Server allows multiple systems to easily interconnect and exchange data. Databases and specialized business systems can be integrated without cumbersome, manual intervention.

Project Management Challenges

A few years ago, I read that the FBI had commissioned a project to consolidate its many disparate databases and computer systems. After more than a billion dollars in expenses and consulting fees, the project was in shambles. Many business requirements had been revised, and the project scope has been adjusted and expanded to accommodate changing needs and business practices. Budget constraints threaten efforts to complete the work. Fingers were being pointed, and bureaucrats were covering their tracks to avoid blame. Under public scrutiny and executive control, dark clouds of failure were looming.

On a slightly smaller scale, this is all too common. One of the greatest threats to the success of an IT project is time. The larger the scope of the project, the more time it takes to complete. This allows more opportunity for business rules to change. Even if a project is completed to the satisfaction of the original requirements, if it takes too long, requirements will have changed, and the product may not address the current needs of the business.

On a recent consulting assignment, I experienced numerous challenges due to ever-changing scope and requirements. The client was a large technology company with plenty of project experience. In the grand scheme of the product, my component was consistently put on hold as requirements changed in other areas. Although beyond my control, the lack of finite deliverables can be a bit disconcerting.

The ideal solution for managing larger-scale projects is to break them down into manageable pieces with a manageable-sized project team. According to the Microsoft Solutions Framework, Microsoft's internal project management guidelines, teams should consist of no more than eight individuals. If a project requires more people than this, it should be broken down into smaller components. Teams may be divided by features, discipline, or release versions. The larger the project, often the less decision-making control each team member will have over individual components and requirements. This can be demoralizing and frustrating — all the more reason to establish clear requirements and avoid making changes until completing each stage.

SQL Server 2008 Reporting Services

Database reporting solutions are really applications with a user interface, query components, and a data source. Generally speaking, these fit into the client/server application model. Until recently, enterprise-level reporting products were only offered by third-party companies such as Crystal Reports and Business Objects. A number of specialized reporting products, such as Brio and Hyperion, are also available for multi-dimensional, decision-support databases. Microsoft has offered desktop reporting capabilities in Access and Excel, but it wasn't until 2003 that Microsoft released a serious, enterprise-ready reporting extension for SQL Server 2000 called SQL Server Reporting Services. It was originally intended to ship with SQL Server 2005 (which it does) but was completed ahead of the rest of the SQL Server 2005 components. Reporting Services is for serious reporting but it's pretty easy to use. Reporting Services is now a component of both the SQL Server 2005 and 2008 product suites.

A brief tour of SQL Server Reporting Services is provided here. Because the report design experience has changed, two sections follow to demonstrate the report design experience for SQL Server 2008 and then for SQL Server 2005. You'll see how to use some of the query techniques you've learned to support report features. This will be an opportunity to apply some of the techniques and practices you've learned earlier in this book. I'll use Reporting Services to show you how to create and use parameterized queries.

Reporting Services Architecture

Reporting Services is really quite different from other products for a number of significant reasons. The reporting engine runs as a Windows service on a computer configured as a Web server. The core component is an XML Web service sitting on top of ASP.NET and the .NET Common Language Runtime (CLR). This is a highly scalable and extensible architecture, meaning that features and additional capabilities can be added and that it can be expanded to more capable hardware and to multiple servers to handle increased workload. Reports can be integrated into a variety of application types and viewers, but it is most commonly used from a Web browser. Out of the box, Reporting Services can render reports to different formats including variations of the following:

- ❑ HTML
- ❑ Adobe PDF
- ❑ Microsoft Office Excel
- ❑ Microsoft Office Word (SQL Server 2008)
- ❑ Bitmaps (including TIFF, PNG, GIF, JPG, and BMP)
- ❑ XML
- ❑ CSV text

Reports can be viewed on demand or saved to a file. User can subscribe to reports, resulting in the report being sent by email or to a file share at scheduled intervals.

In addition to these standard features, Reporting Services is programmable. Application developers can add additional capabilities for report rendering, data access, security, and delivery. They can also programmatically manage the report server and render reports, embedding report content into custom applications. In a nutshell, Reporting Services has an enormous feature set and with a little custom programming, can be made to do most anything imaginable.

To acquaint you with the Reporting Services design environment, I will walk you through the steps to create a simple report with basic features.

Because our focus is using SQL queries to drive reports, you will create two queries that utilize a parameter to filter report data. Before getting started, here is a quick disclaimer. The book you are reading is not a book on Reporting Services or Visual Studio, so I will not provide an in-depth explanation of all the features you're about to see. Because Visual Studio and Reporting Services are large, complex products, I can't guarantee that I can cover every detail in this short tutorial to get you completely up-to-speed on designing reports with Reporting Services.

SQL Server 2008 Report Design

The report designer comes in two flavors, intended for two different types of users. For the application developer, the integrated report designer is still part of the Business Intelligence Development Studio or Visual Studio. For the information worker, a simplified report design tool is available, called *Report Builder 2.0*. This is the report designer you will use to construct a simple report of product catalog information.

Report Builder 2.0 Updates

The Report Builder 2.0 tool is a new addition to the SQL Server product suite and has undergone several changes since SQL Server 2008 was released. You may notice some minor differences between the screen capture images in this section and the latest edition of the Report Builder 2.0 tool you are using. This is due to the ongoing development of this product. As of this printing, we expect another update to be released shortly. Although the dialog window captions may have changed and there may be other subtle differences in the user interface, the core functionality is unchanged.

Report authoring consists of three general steps. First, you design a data source and then write the query to return a set of data. A query or data command (depending on the specific data provider) is called a *dataset*. Additional dataset queries may be used to feed data to multiple data ranges or report items. Datasets are also used to populate parameter lists for user selection.

Report design is the second step. The report is stored as a single XML file with an RDL file extension. The report definition uses the Report Definition Language XML grammar. This definition is created using graphical design tools that involve dragging-and-dropping items to the report design surface and using menus and toolbar options to set properties.

After testing and validating the design, the last step is to deploy the report to a central report server. This can be performed in the report designer, from SQL Server Management Studio, using automation script, or from the Report Manager Web interface.

In the following exercise, you will create a simple, grouped columnar report using a table data range. It will use one query to populate the table and another query to provide a list of product category values to a parameter drop-down list. After you design the queries, the report layout, and formatting, you will deploy this report to your local report server for users to view in their Web browser.

Open Report Builder 2.0 from the Windows Start menu. Use the shortcut in the SQL Server 2008 Report Builder program group.. This is shown in Figure 15-5.

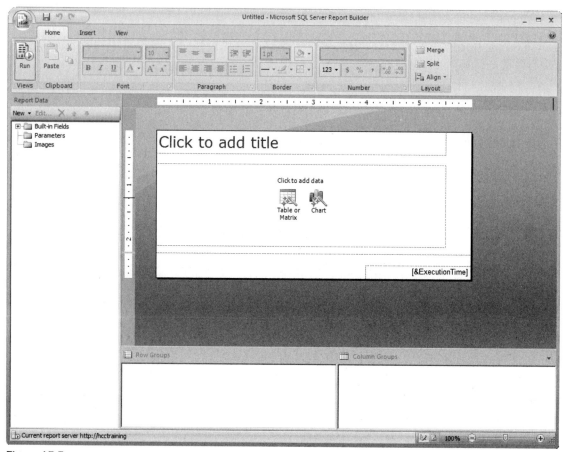

Figure 15-5

The report designer opens to create a new report, as shown in Figure 15-6. The first step is to define a data source and dataset. A dataset is a command string or query used to retrieve records from a data source.

Figure 15-6

Designing the Data Source and Dataset

One of the nice things about the report designer is that there are a few different ways to create these objects. For example, if you place a table data range object on the report, the designer will prompt you to create a data source and then a dataset. If you choose to create a new dataset, you're prompted to create a data source for it. The method we will use is more explicit but a little more logical then either of these. You will define these objects in their natural order.

To get started, in the Report Data pane on the left side of the report designer window, click the New drop-down button and then choose Data Source . . . from the menu. This opens the Data Source Properties dialog.

A data source requires a name containing no spaces. Replace the default data source name with AW2008 in the Name box. This window should look like Figure 15-7.

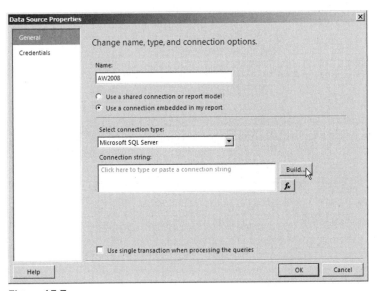

Figure 15-7

This will be an embedded data source, meaning that the connection information will be embedded into a single report and not shared by multiple reports. Shared data sources are generally preferred but require a little more planning. A report can always be directed to a shared data source after it has been designed, tested, and deployed to the report server. Leave the Embedded Connection radio button as it is.

The default connection type is Microsoft SQL Server. This list contains any Reporting Services data processing extensions that are installed and configured for use. Leave this default setting, as you will be connecting to a local SQL Server instance.

To add connection information, click the Edit button on the right side of this page.

The Connection Properties dialog opens, as shown in Figure 15-8. The Data Source type is set automatically based on the Microsoft SQL Server type specified in the previous selection. For reporting on data from different sources, this setting includes access to various .NET native data providers, OLEDB providers, and ODBC drivers that may be available for use on your system. Keep in mind that any data provider you select when you design a report must be available on the report server for use with deployed reports.

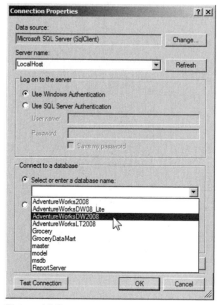

Figure 15-8

For the Server Name setting, you can select or type the name or address of a database server. If your development SQL Server instance is on the same computer as your report design environment, you can use any of the standard local connection aliases, such as *(local)*, *LocalHost* or a single period character. Just enter the word *LocalHost* in this box to continue with this exercise. A word of caution here: if you drop down the Server Name list, a process will explore all available network resources for database server names. If you work in a large, corporate network environment, this may be time-consuming. To avoid this delay, simply type a local alias or the server name rather than selecting it from the list.

After the server name is resolved, all databases on that server are added to the first list in the Connect to a Database section, labeled Select or Enter a Database Name.

Select the AdventureWorks2008 database form this list and then click OK.

Back on the Data Source Properties dialog box, shown in Figure 15-9, you can see the connection string information generated from these selections.

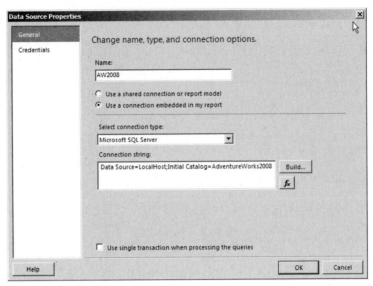

Figure 15-9

Click OK to accept these changes and save the new data source.

A dataset is added by right-clicking the data source in the Report Data pane. On the drop-down menu, select Add Dataset, as shown in Figure 15-10.

Figure 15-10

The Dataset Properties dialog opens. Leave the default properties and click the Query Designer button. Simple queries can just be typed directly into this window. For more complex queries, I prefer to write the query script in the SSMS Query Designer and then paste the text into this window, although this is only a matter of preference. Keep in mind that even though the SSMS query will give you more options with TSQL query scripting, some report-specific features such as query parameters are only supported in the report designer's query design window.

Enter the following query into the Query Designer:

```
SELECT
      Production.ProductCategory.Name AS Category
    , Production.ProductSubcategory.Name AS Subcategory
    , Production.Product.Name AS Product
    , Production.Product.Color
    , Production.Product.ListPrice
FROM
    Production.Product INNER JOIN Production.ProductSubcategory ON
      Production.Product.ProductSubcategoryID =
      Production.ProductSubcategory.ProductSubcategoryID
    INNER JOIN Production.ProductCategory ON
      Production.ProductSubcategory.ProductCategoryID =
      Production.ProductCategory.ProductCategoryID
ORDER BY
    Category, Subcategory, Product
;
```

Remember that tabs and carriage returns are optional; I've added them only for readability.

Click the Run button, as shown in Figure 15-11, to view a sample of the results. Use this to check the column headings and sort order of the first three columns and verify the results of your query output.

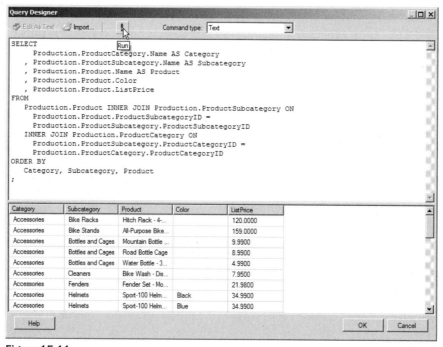

Figure 15-11

Adding a Parameter to the Query

After verifying that the query runs correctly and returns these results, you will make a change to filter records using a parameter. A query parameter named @CategoryID will be used to either filter the query results for a specific category or to indicate that all records should be returned. If a valid ProductCategoryID value is passed in, records are filtered accordingly, but if the parameter value is -1, the filter should be ignored.

In the Report Data pane, right-click the dataset and select Query from the menu.

Add the following WHERE clause in the Query Designer and use the following sample script to validate the syntax.

```
WHERE ProductCategory.ProductCategoryID = @CategoryID
OR CategoryID = -1
```

The query script should now read:

```
SELECT
      Production.ProductCategory.Name AS Category
    , Production.ProductSubcategory.Name AS Subcategory
    , Production.Product.Name AS Product
    , Production.Product.Color
    , Production.Product.ListPrice
FROM
    Production.Product INNER JOIN Production.ProductSubcategory ON
        Production.Product.ProductSubcategoryID =
        Production.ProductSubcategory.ProductSubcategoryID
    INNER JOIN Production.ProductCategory ON
        Production.ProductSubcategory.ProductCategoryID =
        Production.ProductCategory.ProductCategoryID
WHERE
    ProductCategory.ProductCategoryID = @CategoryID OR @CategoryID = -1
ORDER BY
    Category, Subcategory, Product
;
```

Now run the query again, and you should see a dialog displayed, like the one in Figure 15-12, titled Define Query Parameters.

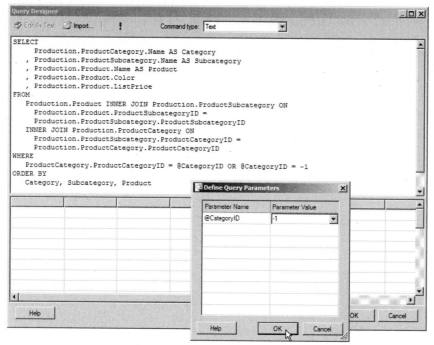

Figure 15-12

Enter **-1** for the @CategoryID parameter value, and then click OK. The results, shown in Figure 15-13, should return all records.

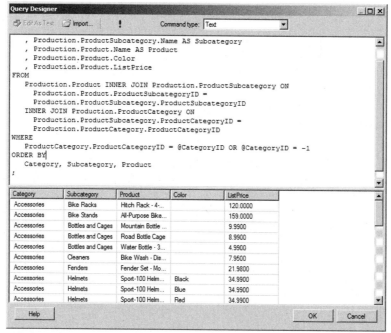

Figure 15-13

Try it again and enter the values 1, 2, 3, or 4 for the parameter value. You should see only records for one product category at a time.

Click OK on the Query Designer to wrap up this part of the process. Our report now has a working dataset with a parameter used for filtering the data at the data source. This is the most efficient method from the data source perspective because the filtered query is processed at the data source rather than on the report server. In a production reporting solution, this would return only the filtered results over the network from the database server to the report server. When this query was parsed, the report designer actually created a separate report definition element, corresponding to the @CategoryID query parameter and added it to a collection of report parameters. The new CategoryID report parameter is visible in the Data utility window on the left side of the designer. When the report runs, users will be prompted to enter a value for this parameter.

Adding a Parameter List Query

I would like to provide a drop-down list of product category values from the ProductCategory table for users to select from. Additionally, I'd also like to add an item to this list prompting users to return the products for all categories. We will add a new dataset to contain this query.

In the Data utility window, right-click the AW2008 data source and select Add Dataset from the menu, as shown in Figure 15-14.

Figure 15-14

The Dataset Properties dialog is displayed. Enter Category_List for the Name, and the data source defaults to the AW2008 data source you defined earlier.

You'll recall that earlier you used the Query Designer to build the last dataset's query. This query is simple enough that you can just type the T-SQL script in the query box. Enter the following script into this box and then check it with Figure 15-15.

```
SELECT  -1 AS ProductCategoryID, '(All Categories)' AS Name
UNION   ProductCategoryID, NAME
FROM    Production.ProductCategory
ORDER BY Name
```

This query returns a static row that will be used to prompt the user to return all categories. The remaining rows will be read from the ProductCategory table and will supply key values used to filter rows based on a selected category.

Click OK to continue.

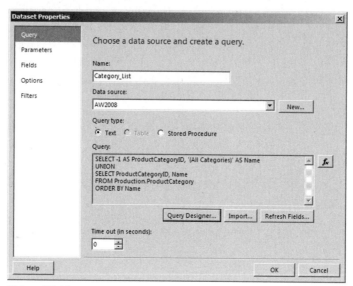

Figure 15-15

Designing the Report Layout

Now that the dataset design is complete, you will design the report body. In the report designer, you can add visual elements to the report by inserting report items from the Insert ribbon to the Data window on the left side of the designer window.

Start by adding the report name to the header of the report. Expand the Built-in Fields branch of the tree in the Report Data pane and drag the ReportName to the top-left corner of the report body, as shown in Figure 15-16.

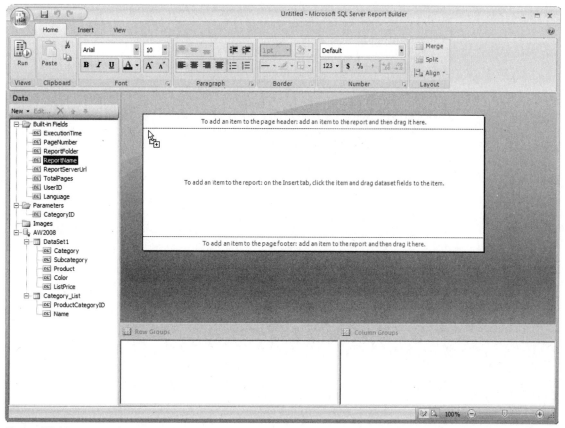

Figure 15-16

A textbox is added with the ReportName expression. With this textbox selected, use the formatting features on the Home ribbon to restyle this text to your liking. You can make it bold, use a larger font, and change the font color. Figure 15-17 shows the textbox with a bold and larger-than-default font.

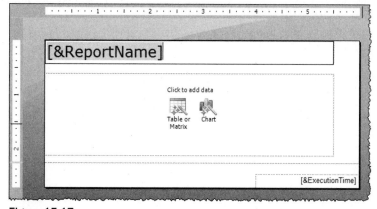

Figure 15-17

Report items and data ranges are added from the Insert ribbon, as shown in Figure 15-18. Choose the Insert tab and then click the Table icon to add a new table to the top-left corner of the report body.

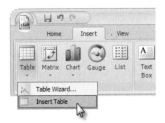

Figure 15-18

To move the table from its inserted position (on top of the report name textbox,) grab it by the selector handle and move it down and just below the textbox. Figure 15-19 shows the automatic snap-to align behavior of the designer, automatically left-aligning the textbox and table items.

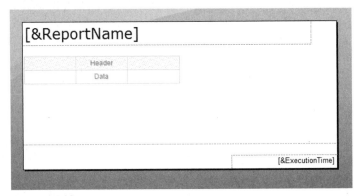

Figure 15-19

The purpose of a table is to repeat rows from a dataset and to group these rows for totaling and navigation. We want to group the product information on a distinct product category and then by subcategory values. The first order of business is to define a row group on the Category field.

Adding Groups and Fields

Groups are managed using the grouping pane below the report designer. First, you can click anywhere within the table to show existing groups.

Drag and drop the Category field from the first dataset to the Row Groups list below the report design pane, shown in Figure 15-20. Because we want this to be the first group, place it above the DetailsGroup item in this list.

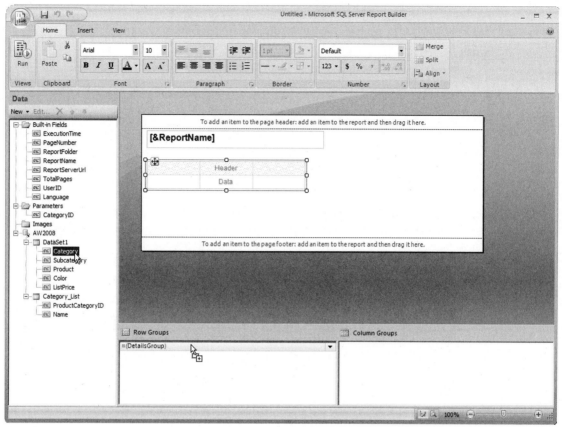

Figure 15-20

Next, drag the Subcategory field from the dataset field list to the Row Groups list and drop it below the Category group, as shown in Figure 15-21.

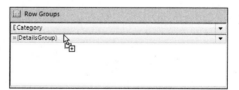

Figure 15-21

Note in Figure 15-22 that row headers and corresponding column headers were added to the table when this new group was defined. This new style of row heading is an improvement from earlier Reporting Services versions that takes advantage of a new data range item called the *tablix*. As the name suggests, the table and matrix are combined into a more capable design element. When adding a table, matrix, or list to a report, you are actually adding a tablix with a template of predefined property settings. Now it's unnecessary to add individual group header rows to a table. As with the matrix in Reporting Services for SQL Server 2000 and 2005, the row headings don't take up extra vertical space.

You don't need to define a row group for products because this is at the detail level of the result set. Simply drag and drop the Product field to the third column detail row.

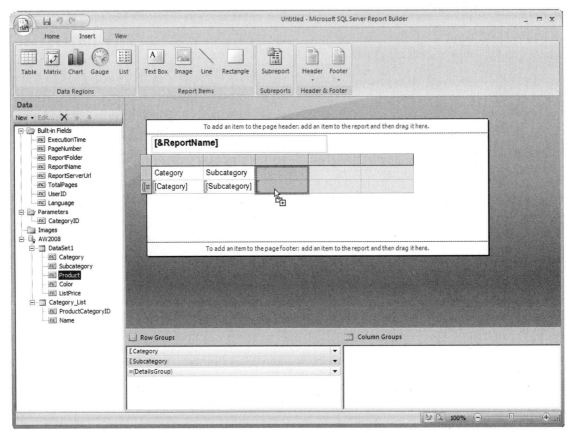

Figure 15-22

Repeat this process for the Color and ListPrice fields, dropping them into the fourth and fifth columns, respectively. This defines an expression in the detail row bound to the field value and adds a textbox value to the header cell with the friendly name of the field.

Formatting a Number Field

Numeric reporting data (called *measures* in the Business Intelligence community) are unformatted by default. Typically, you should display these values using standard formatting such as currency, percentage, thousand separators, and fixed decimals.

To define formatting characteristics for the List Price field cell, right-click the ListPrice detail cell, as shown in Figure 15-23. Select Textbox Properties from the menu.

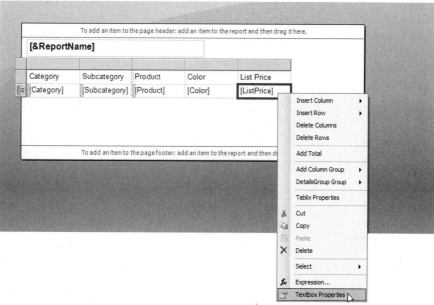

Figure 15-23

Figure 15-24 shows the Text Box Properties dialog box. Use this window to set the format property for the ListPrice numeric field value. On the left side, choose Number to display the numeric formatting page. Select Currency for the Category and check the box labeled Use 1000 Separator (,). Click OK when completed.

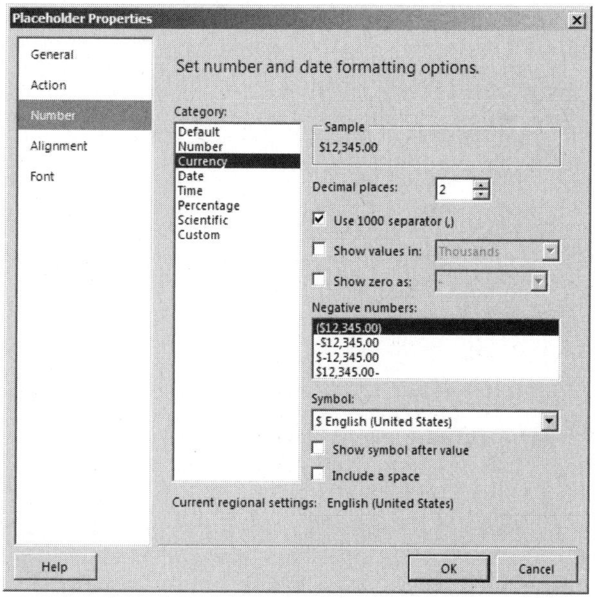

Figure 15-24

Setting Up the Parameter Drop-Down List

Now you'll set-up the CategoryID parameter list. You'll recall that you defined a dataset to return a set of product category keys and names along with an item to select all categories. You need to associate this dataset with the parameter used to filter the first dataset. This is done on the properties for the CategoryID report parameter.

Make sure the Parameters node is expanded, right-click the CategoryID parameter in the Data utility window, and then choose Parameter Properties from the menu (see Figure 15-25).

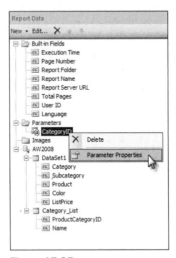

Figure 15-25

The Report Parameter Properties dialog is shown in Figure 15-26. Three pages on this window are used to manage common parameter settings. You will configure the parameter list to display only friendly values, so even though the dataset query will see numeric CategoryID key values, the user will only see descriptive category values.

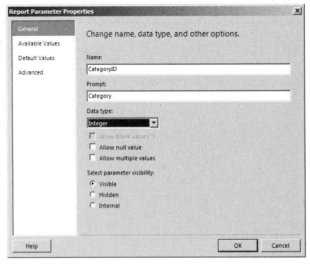

Figure 15-26

510

On the General page, change the Prompt field to read Category.

Click Available Values to switch to the page shown in Figure 15-27. You will specify that you want to display a list of values from a query and then provide field mapping for values and list labels.

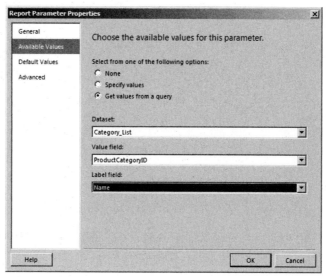

Figure 15-27

Under the heading labeled Select from One of the Following Options, select the radio button labeled Get Values from a Query.

The three drop-down lists are used to bind the dataset supplying parameter values and the corresponding fields.

- ❑ For the Dataset, select the Category_List dataset, which you defined earlier.
- ❑ For the Value Field property, select the ProductCategoryID field.
- ❑ For the Label Field property, select the Name field.

When finished, click OK to close this dialog.

Now to dress up this report and add some chrome to the table, let's start with the table header.

Click the table header row selection handle. This is the small, gray box to the left of the first cell in the table when the table has focus. If this isn't visible, click somewhere in the table and then click the selection handle.

Use the format property icons on the Home ribbon to set the text to bold. Use the background color bucket icon to change the background color to a light color, as shown in Figure 15-28.

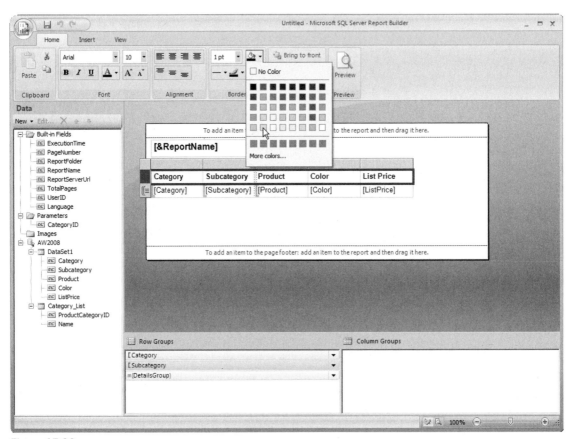

Figure 15-28

Saving the Report

One lesson I learned long ago was to save my work at regular intervals. This is probably a good time to practice this important life skill. Just click the save button (blue floppy disk icon) on the Quick Access toolbar.

When prompted, name the report "Product List Report" and save the RDL file to your Documents folder or another location of your choice. In production, I like to save my reports to project- and client-specific folders on my local hard drive.

Preview the report by clicking the Preview button on the Home ribbon. A smaller version of this button is also accessible on the window frame, just to the left of the zoom slider control.

The CategoryID parameter (labeled Category) drop-down list is displayed above the report toolbar. Drop this list down and select (All Categories), and then click the View Report button.

The animated "spinny" icon will be displayed as the report renders, followed by the report output, as displayed in Figure 15-29. Compare your results with this preview and then review any necessary adjustments to the report design.

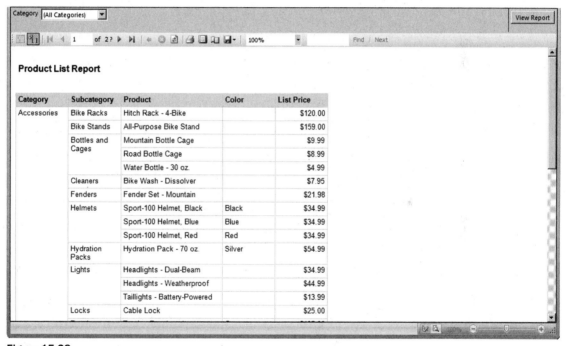

Figure 15-29

Adding Group Totals

So far, the report includes a table header with titles for each column and row headers for each of the two groups. Each row in the table will show the List Price measure value. It might be useful to get this value summarized for each of the groups. Totals can be added to the end of the table, and subtotals can be added to a row at the end of each group. To add a subtotal for the Subcategory group, use the steps illustrated in Figure 15-30.

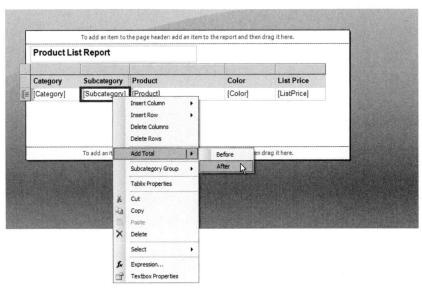

Figure 15-30

Right-click the Subcategory row header. This cell represents the row group and provides access to a menu with several features. From the menu, select Add Total ➪ After.

This menu action inserts a new row below the details, within the Subcategory group. Note that an aggregate expression for the ListPrice field is automatically added to this row.

Use the format settings on the Home ribbon to set the background color and font to bold for this group of cells. If you don't find the color you're looking for on the fill color drop-down pallet, click the More Colors link to reveal a list of named Web colors and the custom color mixer tools.

Figure 15-31 shows the selected range of cells with the font set to bold and the background color set to white smoke, a light shade of gray.

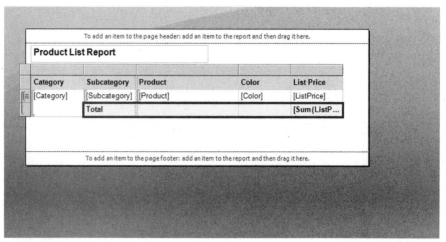

Figure 15-31

Adding a total to the Category group is similar. Right-click this cell and choose Add Total ⇨ After from the menu (see Figure 15-32).

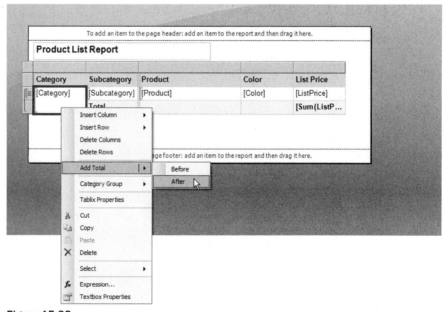

Figure 15-32

Figure 15-33 shows the new group footer row cells set to a slightly darker shade of gray and bold font.

Select all of the cells in this row and use the formatting tools on the Home ribbon to set these properties as you did in the previous step.

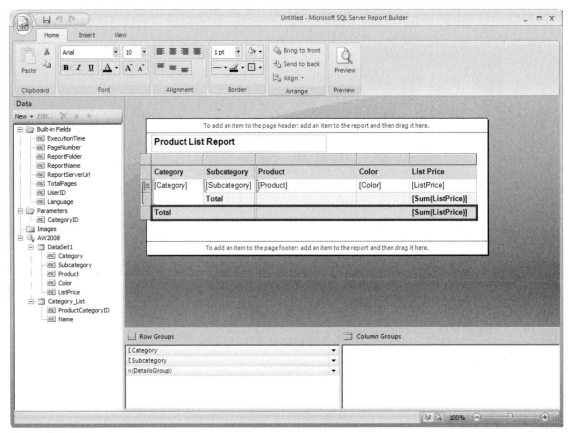

Figure 15-33

The report is done! Before you preview the results, save your changes using the Save icon in the Quick Access toolbar at the top of the designer window.

Click the Preview button on the ribbon and take a look at the results shown in Figure 15-34. If your report looks like the one in this figure, the next step is to take your right hand, place it behind your left shoulder, and pat yourself on the back. Good job!

Product List Report

Category	Subcategory	Product	Color	List Price
Accessories	Bike Racks	Hitch Rack - 4-Bike		$120.00
	Bike Stands	All-Purpose Bike Stand		$159.00
	Bottles and Cages	Mountain Bottle Cage		$9.99
		Road Bottle Cage		$8.99
		Water Bottle - 30 oz.		$4.99
	Cleaners	Bike Wash - Dissolver		$7.95
	Fenders	Fender Set - Mountain		$21.98
	Helmets	Sport-100 Helmet, Black	Black	$34.99
		Sport-100 Helmet, Blue	Blue	$34.99
		Sport-100 Helmet, Red	Red	$34.99
	Hydration Packs	Hydration Pack - 70 oz.	Silver	$54.99
	Lights	Headlights - Dual-Beam		$34.99
		Headlights - Weatherproof		$44.99
		Taillights - Battery-Powered		$13.99
	Locks	Cable Lock		$25.00
	Panniers	Touring-Panniers, Large	Grey	$125.00
	Pumps	Minipump		$19.99
		Mountain Pump		$24.99
	Tires and Tubes	HL Mountain Tire		$35.00
		HL Road Tire		$32.60
		LL Mountain Tire		$24.99
		LL Road Tire		$21.49
		ML Mountain Tire		$29.99
		ML Road Tire		$24.99
		Mountain Tire Tube		$4.99
		Patch Kit/8 Patches		$2.29
		Road Tire Tube		$3.99
		Touring Tire		$28.99
		Touring Tire Tube		$4.99
	Total			**$996.12**
Bikes	Mountain Bikes	Mountain-100 Black, 38	Black	$3,374.99
		Mountain-100 Black, 42	Black	$3,374.99
		Mountain-100 Black, 44	Black	$3,374.99
		Mountain-100 Black, 48	Black	$3,374.99
		Mountain-100 Silver, 38	Silver	$3,399.99
		Mountain-100 Silver, 42	Silver	$3,399.99
		Mountain-100 Silver, 44	Silver	$3,399.99
		Mountain-100 Silver, 48	Silver	$3,399.99
		Mountain-200 Black, 38	Black	$2,294.99
		Mountain-200 Black, 42	Black	$2,294.99

Figure 15-34

As you can see from this short exercise, using Reporting Services you can easily transform practically any T-SQL query into presentable information for the benefit of business information workers and company leaders.

Deploying the Report

Deploying a report is a simple matter of saving the report to the report server. Click the Office Pearl button in the top-left corner of the designer and select Save As from the menu, as shown in Figure 15-35.

Figure 15-35

In Report Builder 2.0, there is really no difference between saving a report to the file system or to the report server. In the Name box, type the address of your report server in the form of http://<server name>/ReportServer into the Name box and press Enter. Enter a name for the report (see Figure 15-36) and then click the Save button to deploy the report to the server.

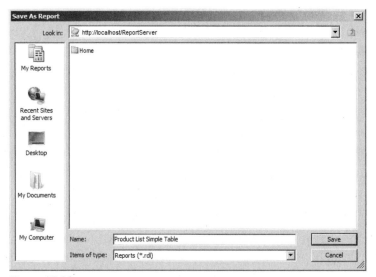

Figure 15-36

Viewing the Report with Report Manager

After Reporting Services is installed, a shortcut is created in the SQL Server group for the Report Manager Web application. This shortcut can be found under Start ⇨ All Programs ⇨ Microsoft SQL Server 2008 ⇨ Reporting Services ⇨ Report Manager. This opens a page located at http://localhost/Reports.

Open Internet Explorer and enter the Web address for the Report Manager application on your report server. The default address on a local server is `http://localhost/reports`.

Figure 15-37 shows the local Report Manager with no previous folders or reports prior to the deployment of this report. The newly deployed report is displayed as a link in the Home folder. Simply click this link to view the report.

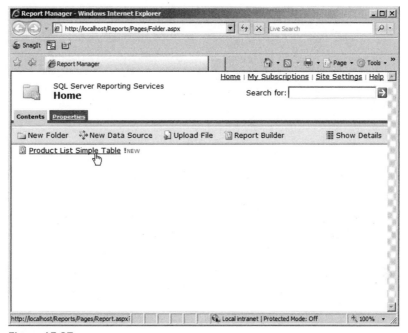

Figure 15-37

The report appears exactly as it did in Figure 15-34, only this time within a frame in the Report Manager Web page.

Report Data Caching

Possibly one of the most compelling features of Reporting Services is its ability to cache report data so that subsequent requests don't require the database to be re-queried. There are a number of ways that reports can be cached and that parameters can be used in combination to refresh cached data and filter cached results.

Report snapshots are a form of cached reports that are completely static. Snapshots are lightweight and simple. This may be an appropriate option for common reports that are produced at regular intervals and usually don't contain parameterized options. Snapshots can be placed into history so that one snapshot doesn't overwrite a previously cached rendering of the same report. Each snapshot is marked with a date and time stamp, and a specific number are typically held in history before they are overwritten. Snapshots typically are generated on a predefined schedule, and users don't need to wait while queries run against live data.

Cached-instance reports are more flexible than snapshots but take a little planning and design effort. When a report is configured for instance caching, each unique combination of query parameters causes a separate cached copy of the report data to be stored in the report server database. Further, non-query report parameters can be used to filter the data stored in the cache. A cached instance can be configured to "live" for a specific period of time or to expire on a regular schedule. Because the cache is populated when a report is requested, the first user who views the report must wait for the query to run. Subsequent users or requests run against the cache until it expires.

Business Intelligence and Business Reporting

One of the inevitable facts about business reporting solutions is that the complexity of reports tends to grow over time — usually just a short period of time. Deriving meaningful information from a large, transactional database often requires the use of several tables that may be joined together in a query, view, or stored procedure.

An unfortunate side effect is that large queries tend to run slowly and demand server resources at the cost of other concurrent processes and applications. When reporting requirements reach this level, it's usually necessary to copy data into a separate database — a data warehouse or data mart with the data stored in simplified tables optimized to support reports rather than online transactions.

You already know how to join tables together, define subqueries, use groups, and aggregate functions. The purpose of the following exercise is to demonstrate how to design a report, so I'm going to keep the T-SQL query very simple. Once you have mastered the report design basics, you can write more complex queries to add additional functionality to your reports. Note, however, that a discussion of data warehouse concepts is beyond the scope of this book.

A sample data warehouse database is available from Microsoft, based on the data in the AdventureWorks2008 and AdventureWorks databases we've used throughout this book. For your reference, the following query uses the AdventureWorksDW2008 data warehouse database. This example is borrowed from the Wrox book *Professional SQL Server 2008 Reporting Services*.

```
SELECT
    D.CalendarYear
  , D.CalendarQuarter
  , ST.SalesTerritoryCountry
  , ST.SalesTerritoryRegion
  , SUM(F.OrderQuantity) AS QtySum
  , SUM(F.SalesAmount) AS AmtSum
FROM
    DimDate D INNER JOIN FactResellerSales F ON D.DateKey = F.OrderDateKey
    INNER JOIN DimSalesTerritory ST ON F.SalesTerritoryKey = ST.SalesTerritoryKey
```

```
        INNER JOIN DimProduct P ON F.ProductKey = P.ProductKey
    WHERE
        D.CalendarYear = @Year AND P.ProductSubcategoryKey = @SubcatKey
    GROUP BY
        D.CalendarYear
      , D.CalendarQuarter
      , ST.SalesTerritoryCountry
      , ST.SalesTerritoryRegion
    ORDER BY
        D.CalendarYear
      , D.CalendarQuarter
      , ST.SalesTerritoryCountry
      , ST.SalesTerritoryRegion
    ;
```

This query contains attribute fields from two different dimensional hierarchies: Sales Territory and Order Date. These values are stored in the dimension table fields. For report users who want to see these measure values, the ideal presentation for this data is a matrix (also called a PivotTable), where the two dimension levels are grouped on both the rows and columns axes. The measure values are expressed as aggregated numeric values at the intersect point of each row and group dimension level. To summarize the same data in summary form, a chart is often the appropriate medium.

Figure 15-38 shows a report containing both a chart and matrix based on the same query results.

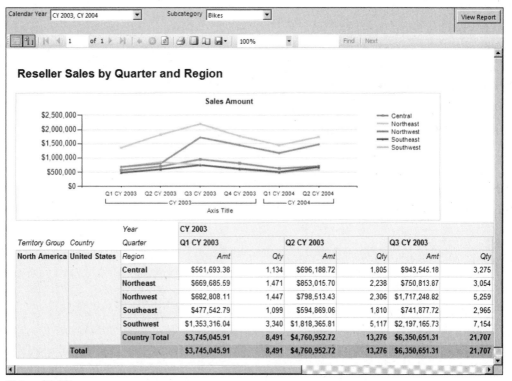

Figure 15-38

Report Application Integration

Reporting Services can be integrated into applications in several ways. These range from a simple hyperlink to fully embedded reports within custom and commercial applications. Using a hyperlink to open a report is uncomplicated. The following URL opens a report in a Web browser window:

```
http://localhost/ReportServer?/FarmAnimal_Reports/Farm Animal Sales_BW&rs:
Command=Render
```

Parameters can either be left to be filled with default values, be provided by users, or may be provided in the URL request:

```
http://localhost/ReportServer?/FarmAnimal_Reports/Farm Animal
Sales_BW&rs:Command=Render&DateFrom='1/1/2005`&DateTo='3/5/2005`&GroupBy=
AnimalName&Animals='Cow','Horse','Chicken','Llama'
```

This URL opens a browser with the report displayed below a parameter bar, pre-filled with the parameter values supplied in the URL string, as shown in Figure 15-39.

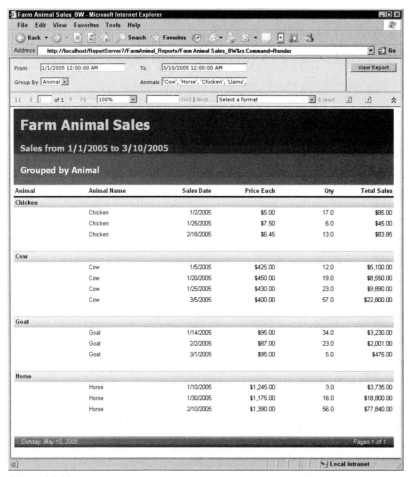

Figure 15-39

This approach is simple and provides a great deal of functionality. However, this may not be an ideal interface for all reporting solutions. A more customized approach uses an ASP.NET Web Form, such as that shown in Figure 15-40. Sophisticated Web controls may be used to prompt users for parameter values.

Figure 15-40

Parameter values are gathered from these controls and then concatenated into a URL like the previous example. A hyperlink control uses this URL to target an HTML frame on the Web Form. After using the custom parameter interface to choose a user's selection criteria, the link renders the report to the in-line frame embedded in the Web page. As far as the user is concerned, this is simply a feature of a Web browser-based custom business application (see Figure 15-41).

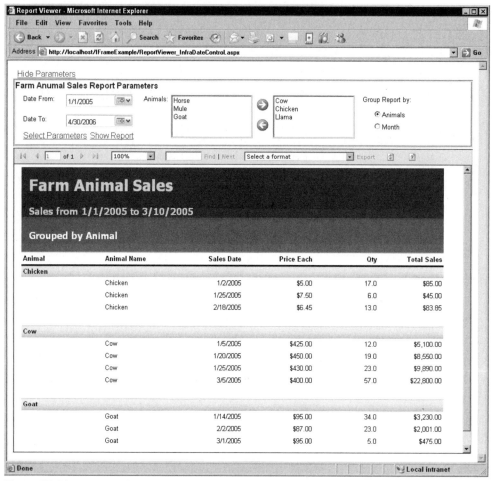

Figure 15-41

Summary

This chapter demonstrated how T-SQL is used in common applications and reporting solutions. A wide range of options are available for architecting and building database application solutions. Programming models vary in purpose and complexity. It's senseless to over-engineer a solution with capabilities that won't ever be used — but it's also important to plan for future requirements. Striking the appropriate balance between these two principles is often the greatest challenge in database solution design.

Scalable solutions can accommodate a larger number of users without redesigning the fundamental application architecture. Scalable solutions make appropriate use of program components to separate the user interface from business logic and data access. How you implement T-SQL in an application plays an important role in its ability to handle whatever requirements may be discovered or imposed after the fact. Isolating database connections to separate reusable application components can simplify ongoing application design. Keeping SQL queries in database server objects, such as views, stored procedures, and user-defined functions, not only offers improved performance, but is also much more secure.

Finding the optimal balance between an application architecture that just gets the job done quickly and being able to adapt to any needs that could potentially arise is often a challenge. Ultimately, it is the long-term business requirements and objectives that should lead to choosing an application model that meets these needs. Fortunately, building scalable solutions is less costly using more capable programming objects and development tools.

You were introduced to the new report design experience in SQL Server 2008 Reporting Services. Reporting is an important part of many business applications. SQL Server Reporting Services makes use of ad hoc TSQL statements, views, and stored procedures. These queries can include parameters to filter results and modify business logic. Reporting Services takes this concept to a level beyond SQL queries by allowing reports to filter cached data results and to provide rich, dynamic reporting capabilities, using report parameters and other advanced Reporting Services features.

Command Syntax Reference

SQL Server 2005 and SQL Server 2008 recognize up to four parts of object names. Depending on the context of an expression, some parts may or may not be necessary when referencing an object. When a script runs on a different server or when you are using a different database, related object names may be required. Note that both SQL Server 2005 and SQL Server 2008 recognize the schema name in the third position, whereas SQL Server 2000 and earlier versions recognized the object owner name in the third position. The following table summarizes valid syntax for referencing database objects.

Object Reference	Use and Context
`object`	Used in the context of the local database, on the same server. Object is part of the dbo schema and there are no duplicate object names.
`schema.object`	Used in the context of the local database, on the same server. Duplicate object names that have schema names (and subsequently, different owners) are permitted. Also uses a standard convention for clarity.
`database..object`	Used in the context of the same or different database on the same server. If you haven't specified the owner or schema, assumes the dbo schema.
`database.schema.object`	A three-part name fully describes an object on the same server, in the same or different database.

(Continued)

Object Reference	Use and Context
`server.database.schema.object`	A four-part name is valid in the context of a remote server or the local server, in the local or a different database, and for any schema.
`server.database..object`	The database owner or schema in the third position can be omitted to use the default dbo schema.
`server..schema.object`	The database name can be omitted to use the default database on that server. This is not a typical practice.
`server...object`	Omitting the database and owner or schema name causes the default database and the default dbo schema to be used. This is valid syntax but not a typical practice.

T-SQL Commands, Clauses, and Predicates

Following are the core components of the T-SQL language. New commands for SQL Server 2008 are explicitly called out in this section.

WITH

Introduced in SQL Server 2005, this method is used to define an alias for the result set returned by a `SELECT` expression.

```
WITH MyCTE
AS
( SELECT * FROM Product WHERE ListPrice < 1000 )
```

Optionally, column aliases can be defined in parentheses following the Common Table Expression (CTE) name:

```
WITH MyCTE ( ID, ProdNumber, ProdName, Price )
AS
( SELECT
    ProductID
  , ProductNumber
  , Name
  , ListPrice
  FROM Product WHERE ListPrice < 1000
)
```

SELECT

To return all columns from a table or view:

```
SELECT * FROM table_name
```

To return specific columns from a table or view:

```
SELECT Column1, Column2, Column3 FROM table_name
```

Column alias techniques:

```
SELECT Column1 AS Col1, Column2 AS Col2 FROM table_name
SELECT Column1 Col1, Column2 Col2 FROM table_name
SELECT Col1 = Column1, Col2 = Column2 FROM table_name
```

To return literal values:

```
SELECT 'Some literal value'
SELECT 'Some value' AS Col1, 123 AS Col2
```

To return an expression value:

```
SELECT (1 + 2) * 3
```

To return the result of a function call:

```
SELECT CONVERT( varchar(20), GETDATE(), 101 )
```

SELECT TOP

To return a fixed number of rows:

```
SELECT TOP 10 * FROM table_name ORDER BY Column1
SELECT TOP 10 Column1, Column2 FROM table_name ORDER BY Column2
```

To return a fixed number of rows with the ties for last position:

```
SELECT TOP 10 WITH TIES Column1, Column2 FROM table_name ORDER BY Column2
```

To return a percentage of all available rows:

```
SELECT TOP 25 PERCENT * FROM table_name ORDER BY Column2
SELECT TOP 25 PERCENT Column1, Column2 FROM table_name ORDER BY Column2
```

To substitute a variable or expression for a top values number:

```
DECLARE @TopNumber Int
SET @TopNumber = 15
SELECT TOP @ TopNumber * FROM table_name ORDER BY Column2
```

To return top values based on an expression:

```
SELECT TOP (SELECT a_column_value FROM some_table) * FROM another_table
```

SELECT INTO

To create and populate a table from a result set:

```
SELECT Column1, Column2 INTO new_table_name FROM existing_table_or_view_name
```

FROM

Single table query:

```
SELECT * FROM table_name
```

Multi-table join query:

```
SELECT *
FROM table1.key_column INNER JOIN table2 ON table1.key_column =
table2.key_column
```

Derived table:

```
SELECT DerTbl.Column1, DerTbl.Column2
FROM
    ( SELECT Column1, Column2 FROM some_table ... ) AS DerTbl
```

WHERE

Exact match:

```
SELECT ... FROM ...
WHERE Column1 = 'A literal value'
```

Not NULL:

```
SELECT ... FROM ...
WHERE Column1 IS NOT NULL
```

Any trailing characters:

```
SELECT ... FROM ...
WHERE Column1 LIKE 'ABC%'
```

Any leading characters:

```
SELECT ... FROM ...
WHERE Column1 LIKE '%XYZ'
```

Any leading or trailing characters:

```
SELECT ... FROM ...
WHERE Column1 LIKE '%MNOP%'
```

Placeholder wildcard:

```
SELECT ... FROM ...
WHERE Column1 LIKE '_BC_EF'
```

Criteria using parentheses to designate order:

```
SELECT ... FROM ...
WHERE
    (Column1 LIKE 'ABC%' AND Column2 LIKE '%XYZ')
    OR
    Column3 = '123'
```

GROUP BY

All non-aggregated columns in the SELECT list must be included in the GROUP BY list:

```
SELECT COUNT(Column1), Column2, Column3
FROM ... WHERE ...
GROUP BY Column2, Column3
```

Designating order:

```
SELECT COUNT(Column1), Column2, Column3
FROM ... WHERE ...
GROUP BY Column2, Column3
ORDER BY Column2 DESC, Column3 ASC
```

WITH ROLLUP

Legacy method to implement a rollup subtotal break:

Note that ROLLUP *and* CUBE *operators cause SQL Server to return a non–two-dimensional result set that is not supported by many APIs and client interfaces.*

```
SELECT Column1, Column2, SUM(Column3)
FROM table_name
GROUP BY Column1, Column2
WITH ROLLUP
```

This syntax is still supported in SQL Server 2008, but the new BY ROLLUP syntax is preferred.

BY ROLLUP

New syntax introduced in SQL Server 2008 for implementing a rollup subtotal break:

```
SELECT Column1, Column2, SUM(Column3)
FROM table_name
GROUP BY ROLLUP(Column1, Column2)
```

WITH CUBE

Legacy method to implement a cube subtotal break:

```
SELECT Column1, Column2, SUM(Column3)
FROM table_name
GROUP BY Column1, Column2
WITH CUBE
```

This syntax is still supported in SQL Server 2008 but the new BY CUBE syntax is preferred.

BY CUBE

New syntax introduced in SQL Server 2008 for implementing a cube subtotal break.

```
SELECT Column1, Column2, SUM(Column3)
FROM table_name
GROUP BY CUBE(Column1, Column2)
```

HAVING

To filter results based on values available after the aggregations and groupings are performed:

```
SELECT COUNT(Column1), Column2, Column3
FROM ... WHERE ...
GROUP BY Column2, Column3
HAVING COUNT(Column1) > 5
```

UNION

To combine multiple results with the same column count:

```
SELECT Column1, Column2 FROM table1_name
UNION
SELECT Column1, Column2 FROM table2_name
```

To combine literal values and query results:

```
SELECT -1 AS Column1, 'A literal value' AS Column2
UNION
SELECT Column1, Column2 FROM table1_name
```

To include non-distinct selection (UNION performs SELECT DISTINCT by default):

```
SELECT Column1, Column2 FROM table1_name
UNION ALL
SELECT Column1, Column2 FROM table2_name
```

EXCEPT and INTERSECT

To select the differences (EXCEPT) or common values (INTERSECT) between two queries:

```
SELECT * FROM TableA EXCEPT SELECT * FROM TableB
SELECT * FROM TableA INTERSECT SELECT * FROM TableB
```

ORDER BY

To order a result set by one or more column values:

```
SELECT * FROM table_name ORDER BY Column1
SELECT * FROM table_name ORDER BY Column1 DESC, Column2 ASC
```

The default order is ascending. If ordering by more than one column, each column can have a different order.

COMPUTE and COMPUTE BY Clauses

To generate totals that are appended to the end of an aggregate query result set:

```
SELECT Column1, Column2, Column3
FROM table_name
ORDER BY Column1, Column2
COMPUTE SUM(Column3)
```

The COMPUTE and COMPUTE BY clauses are not very useful in applications because the aggregated results are not in relational form and cannot be utilized in a dataset.

As of SQL Server 2008, the CUBE and ROLLUP operators are appended to the COMPUTE BY clause (see CUBE and ROLLUP.)

FOR Clause

The FOR clause is used with either the XML or BROWSE option in a SELECT statement. However, the BROWSE and XML options are completely unrelated. FOR XML specifies that the result set is returned in XML format. FOR BROWSE is used when accessing data through the DB-Library so that rows can be browsed and updated one row at a time in an optimistic locking environment. There are several requirements when using the FOR BROWSE option. For more information, consult SQL Server Books Online, under the topic "Browse Mode."

```
SELECT * FROM table_name FOR XML {XML Option}
SELECT * FROM table_name FOR BROWSE
```

OPTION Clause

The OPTION clause is used in a SELECT statement to provide a query hint that will override the query optimizer and specify an index or specific join mechanism to be used along with other hint options.

CASE

To evaluate one or more expression and return one or more specified values based on the evaluated expression:

```
SELECT expression = CASE Column
WHEN value THEN resultant_value
WHEN value2 THEN resultant_value2
...
ELSE alternate_value
END
FROM table
SELECT value =
        CASE
        WHEN column IS NULL THEN value
        WHEN column {expression true} THEN different_value
        WHEN column {expression true} and price {expression true} THEN
other_value
        ELSE different_value
        END,
        column2
FROM table
```

INSERT

To add a new row to a table:

```
INSERT table (column list)
VALUES
(column values)
INSERT table
SELECT columns FROM source expression
INSERT table
EXEC stored_procedure
```

The following is new, multi-table INSERT syntax introduced in SQL Server 2008:

```
INSERT table (column list)
VALUES
(column values),
(column values),
(column values)
```

Note that column values are comma-separated and must appear in the same order as in the column list or in the same order as they are defined in the table.

UPDATE

To update selected columns in a table:

```
UPDATE table SET column1 = expression1, column2 = expression2
WHERE filter_expression
```

To update a table based on the contents of another table:

```
UPDATE table SET column1 = expression
FROM table INNER JOIN table2
ON table.column = table2.column
WHERE table.column = table2.column
```

DELETE

To delete selected rows from a table:

```
DELETE table
WHERE filter_expression
```

To delete rows from a table based on the contents of a different table:

```
DELETE table
FROM table INNER JOIN table2
ON table.column = table2.column
WHERE column = filter_expression
```

DECLARE @local_variable

This creates a named object that temporarily holds a value with the data type defined in the declaration statement. Local variables have scope only within the calling batch or stored procedure. The value of a local variable can be set with either a SET or SELECT operation. SELECT is more efficient than SET and has the advantage of populating multiple variables in a single operation, but the SELECT operation cannot be confined with any data retrieval operation.

```
DECLARE @local_variable AS int
SET @local_variable = integer_expression
DECLARE @local_variable1 AS int, @local_variable2 AS varchar(55)
SELECT @local_variable1 = integer_column_expression, @local_variable2 =
character_column_expression FROM table
```

SET

The SET operator has many functions, from setting the value of a variable to setting a database or connection property. The SET operator is divided into the categories listed in the following table.

Category	Alters the Current Session Settings For
Date and time	Handling date and time data
Locking	Handling SQL Server locking
Miscellaneous	Miscellaneous SQL Server functionality
Query execution	Query execution and processing
SQL-92 settings	Using the SQL-92 default settings
Statistics	Displaying statistics information
Transactions	Handling SQL Server transactions

LIKE

LIKE is a pattern-matching operator for comparing strings or partial strings.

To compare a string value where the compared string is anywhere in the string:

```
SELECT * FROM table WHERE column1 LIKE '%string%'
```

To compare a string value where the compared string is at the beginning of the string:

```
SELECT * FROM table WHERE column1 LIKE 'string%'
```

To compare a string value where the compared string is at the end of the string:

```
SELECT * FROM table WHERE column1 LIKE '%string'
```

To compare a string value where a specific character or character range is in the string:

```
SELECT * FROM table WHERE column1 LIKE '[a-c]'
SELECT * FROM table WHERE column1 LIKE '[B-H]olden'
```

To compare a string value where a specific character or character range is not in the string:

```
SELECT * FROM table WHERE column1 LIKE '[M^c]%' -Begins with M but not Mc
```

ALTER TABLE

To alter the structure of a table by adding or removing table objects such as columns, constraints, and partitions, or by enabling and disabling triggers:

```
ALTER TABLE table_name ADD new_column int NULL;
ALTER TABLE table_name ADD CONSTRAINT new_check CHECK (check expression) ;
ALTER TABLE table_name DROP COLUMN existing_column;
ALTER TABLE table_name ENABLE TRIGGER trigger_name;
ALTER TABLE table_name DISABLE TRIGGER trigger_name;
```

PIVOT Operator

To cause a normalized columnar set to be transformed and restructured with repeating column values according to a predefined column list specification:

```
SELECT Column3, [Col2_List_Val1], [Col2_List_Val2], [Col2_List_Val3]... FROM
(
    SELECT
        Column1  -- Value to aggregate as measure value in pivot cells
      , Column2  -- Value for column headers as column list
      , Column3  -- Value for row headers
    FROM source_table_name
)  AS Source
PIVOT
(
    Sum(Column1) FOR MeasureValue
        IN ([Col2_List_Val1], [Col2_List_Val2], [Col2_List_Val3]...)
)  AS pvt
```

UNPIVOT Operator

To cause a pivoted result set to be transformed into a normalized, columnar table structure:

```
SELECT
 Column3, Column2, Column1  -- columns same as pivot source above
FROM
 (
    SELECT
      Column1
    , [Col2_List_Val1], [Col2_List_Val2], [Col2_List_Val3]... FROM
    FROM pivot_source_table_name
 ) AS pvt
UNPIVOT
 (
     Column1 FOR MeasuresValue
       IN ([Col2_List_Val1], [Col2_List_Val2], [Col2_List_Val3]...)
 )
 AS unpvt
```

CREATE DATABASE

To create a database and all associated files:

```
CREATE DATABASE new_database
ON (
   NAME = 'logical_name',
   FILENAME = 'physical_file_location',
   SIZE = initial_size_in_MB,
   MAXSIZE = max_size_in_MB, --If no MAXSIZE specified unlimited growth
is assumed
   FILEGROWTH = percentage_OR_space_in_MB)
LOG ON
( NAME = 'logical_log_name',
   FILENAME = 'physical_file_location',
   SIZE = initial_size_in_MB,
   MAXSIZE = max_size_in_MB, --If no MAXSIZE specified unlimited growth
is assumed
   FILEGROWTH = percentage_OR_space_in_MB)
COLLATE database_collation
```

CREATE DEFAULT

To create a database-wide default value that can then be bound to columns in any table to provide a default value:

```
CREATE DEFAULT default_name AS default_value
--bind the default to a table column
sp_bindefault default_name, 'table.column'
```

CREATE PROCEDURE

To create a new stored procedure:

```
CREATE PROCEDURE proc_name @variable variable_data_type ...n
AS
...procedure code
```

or

```
CREATE PROC proc_name @variable variable_data_type ...n
AS
...procedure code
```

CREATE RULE

To create a database-wide rule, much like a check constraint, that can then be bound to individual columns in tables throughout the database:

```
CREATE RULE rule_name AS rule_expression
--bind the rule to a table column
sp_bindrule rule_name, 'table.column'
```

CREATE TABLE

To create a new table:

```
CREATE TABLE table_name (
Column1 data_type nullability column_option,
Column2 data_type nullability column_option,
Column3 data_type nullability column_option,
--Column_option = Collation, IDENTITY, KEY...
```

To create a new, partitioned table:

```
CREATE TABLE partitioned_table_name (Column1 int, Column2 char(10))
Column1 data_type nullability column_option,
Column2 data_type nullability column_option,
Column3 data_type nullability column_option
ON partition_scheme_name (column)
```

CREATE TRIGGER

To create a new trigger on a table that fires *after* a DML event:

```
CREATE TRIGGER trigger_name
ON table_name FOR dml_action -INSERT, UPDATE or DELETE
AS
...trigger_code
```

And to create a new trigger on a table that fires *instead of* a DML event:

```
CREATE TRIGGER trigger_name
ON view_or_table_name INSTEAD OF dml_action -INSERT, UPDATE or DELETE
AS
...trigger_code
```

CREATE VIEW

To create a new view:

```
CREATE VIEW view_name
AS
...Select Statement
```

CREATE SCHEMA

To create a new database schema with the option of specifying a non-dbo owner with the AUTHORIZATION clause:

```
CREATE SCHEMA schema_name AUTHORIZATION user_name
```

CREATE PARTITION FUNCTION

To create a partition function to use when physically partitioning tables and indexes:

```
CREATE PARTITION FUNCTION partition_function_name ( input_parameter_type )
AS RANGE LEFT --or RIGHT
FOR VALUES (value1, value2, value3, ...n)
```

CREATE PARTITION SCHEME

To create a partition scheme to use when physically partitioning tables and indexes:

```
CREATE PARTITION SCHEME partition_scheme_name
AS PARTITION partition_function_name
TO (filegroup1, filegroup2, filegroup3, ...n)
```

Script Comment Conventions

In-line comment:

```
SELECT ProductID, Name AS ProductName    -- Comment text
```

Single-line comment:

```
/* Comment text */
```

or

```
-- Comment text
```

Comment block:

```
/*******************************************************
    spProductUpdateByCategory
    Created by Paul Turley, 5-21-08
    nospam@sqlreportservices.com
    Updates product price info for a category
    Revisions:
    5-22-08 - Fixed bug that formatted C:
              drive if wrong type was passed in.
*******************************************************/
```

Reserved Words

Chapter 13 gave some recommendations and guidance about the naming of objects in SQL Server. One of the recommendations was that reserved words should not be used as names of objects. Reserved words typically are easy to see in SQL Server Management Studio, which changes the color of reserved words to blue. If the object names are delimited with double quotes or square brackets, which they often are if you are using a graphical tool to create queries, then they may not show up as being color-coded.

The following keywords have significant meaning within T-SQL and should be avoided in object names and expressions. If any of these words must be used in a SQL expression, they must be contained within square brackets [ ].

ADD	CASCADE	CONVERT
ALL	CASE	CREATE
ALTER	CHECK	CROSS
AND	CHECKPOINT	CURRENT
ANY	CLOSE	CURRENT_DATE
AS	CLUSTERED	CURRENT_TIME
ASC	COALESCE	CURRENT_TIMESTAMP
AUTHORIZATION	COLLATE	CURRENT_USER
BACKUP	COLUMN	CURSOR
BEGIN	COMMIT	DATABASE
BETWEEN	COMPUTE	DBCC
BREAK	CONSTRAINT	DEALLOCATE
BROWSE	CONTAINS	DECLARE
BULK	CONTAINSTABLE	DEFAULT
BY	CONTINUE	DELETE

DENY	GRANT	OFF
DESC	GROUP	OFFSETS
DISK	HAVING	ON
DISTINCT	HOLDLOCK	OPEN
DISTRIBUTED	IDENTITY	OPENDATASOURCE
DOUBLE	IDENTITY_INSERT	OPENQUERY
DROP	IDENTITYCOL	OPENROWSET
DUMMY	IF	OPENXML
DUMP	IN	OPTION
ELSE	INDEX	OR
END	INNER	ORDER
ERRLVL	INSERT	OUTER
ESCAPE	INTERSECT	OVER
EXCEPT	INTO	PERCENT
EXEC	IS	PIVOT
EXECUTE	JOIN	PLAN
EXISTS	KEY	PRECISION
EXIT	KILL	PRIMARY
FETCH	LEFT	PRINT
FILE	LIKE	PROC
FILLFACTOR	LINENO	PROCEDURE
FOR	LOAD	PUBLIC
FOREIGN	NATIONAL	RAISERROR
FREETEXT	NOCHECK	READ
FREETEXTTABLE	NONCLUSTERED	READTEXT
FROM	NOT	RECONFIGURE
FULL	NULL	REFERENCES
FUNCTION	NULLIF	REPLICATION
GOTO	OF	RESTORE

(Continued)

RESTRICT	SOME	UNPIVOT
RETURN	STATISTICS	UPDATE
REVOKE	SYSTEM_USER	UPDATETEXT
RIGHT	TABLE	USE
ROLLBACK	TEXTSIZE	USER
ROWCOUNT	THEN	VALUES
ROWGUIDCOL	TO	VARYING
RULE	TOP	VIEW
SAVE	TRAN	WAITFOR
SCHEMA	TRANSACTION	WHEN
SELECT	TRIGGER	WHERE
SESSION_USER	TRUNCATE	WHILE
SET	TSEQUAL	WITH
SETUSER	UNION	WRITETEXT
SHUTDOWN	UNIQUE	

ODBC Reserved Words

Although the ODBC keywords in the following table are not strictly prohibited, as a best practice to prevent driver inconsistencies, they should be avoided.

ABSOLUTE	AS	BOTH
ACTION	ASC	BY
ADA	ASSERTION	CASCADE
ADD	AT	CASCADED
ALL	AUTHORIZATION	CASE
ALLOCATE	AVG	CAST
ALTER	BEGIN	CATALOG
AND	BETWEEN	CHAR
ANY	BIT	CHAR_LENGTH
ARE	BIT_LENGTH	CHARACTER

CHARACTER_LENGTH	DECLARE	FOR
CHECK	DEFAULT	FOREIGN
CLOSE	DEFERRABLE	FORTRAN
COALESCE	DEFERRED	FOUND
COLLATE	DELETE	FROM
COLLATION	DESC	FULL
COLUMN	DESCRIBE	GET
COMMIT	DESCRIPTOR	GLOBAL
CONNECT	DIAGNOSTICS	GO
CONNECTION	DISCONNECT	GOTO
CONSTRAINT	DISTINCT	GRANT
CONSTRAINTS	DOMAIN	GROUP
CONTINUE	DOUBLE	HAVING
CONVERT	DROP	HOUR
CORRESPONDING	ELSE	IDENTITY
COUNT	END	IMMEDIATE
CREATE	END-EXEC	IN
CROSS	ESCAPE	INCLUDE
CURRENT	EXCEPT	INDEX
CURRENT_DATE	EXCEPTION	INDICATOR
CURRENT_TIME	EXEC	INITIALLY
CURRENT_TIMESTAMP	EXECUTE	INNER
CURRENT_USER	EXISTS	INPUT
CURSOR	EXTERNAL	INSENSITIVE
DATE	EXTRACT	INSERT
DAY	FALSE	INT
DEALLOCATE	FETCH	INTEGER
DEC	FIRST	INTERSECT
DECIMAL	FLOAT	INTERVAL

(Continued)

543

INTO	NUMERIC	REVOKE
IS	OCTET_LENGTH	RIGHT
ISOLATION	OF	ROLLBACK
JOIN	ON	ROWS
KEY	ONLY	SCHEMA
LANGUAGE	OPEN	SCROLL
LAST	OPTION	SECOND
LEADING	OR	SECTION
LEFT	ORDER	SELECT
LEVEL	OUTER	SESSION
LIKE	OUTPUT	SESSION_USER
LOCAL	OVERLAPS	SET
LOWER	PAD	SIZE
MATCH	PARTIAL	SMALLINT
MAX	PASCAL	SOME
MIN	POSITION	SPACE
MINUTE	PRECISION	SQL
MODULE	PREPARE	SQLCA
MONTH	PRESERVE	SQLCODE
NAMES	PRIMARY	SQLERROR
NATIONAL	PRIOR	SQLSTATE
NATURAL	PRIVILEGES	SQLWARNING
NCHAR	PROCEDURE	SUBSTRING
NEXT	PUBLIC	SUM
NO	READ	SYSTEM_USER
NONE	REAL	TABLE
NOT	REFERENCES	TEMPORARY
NULL	RELATIVE	THEN
NULLIF	RESTRICT	TIME

TIMESTAMP	UNIQUE	VIEW
TIMEZONE_HOUR	UNKNOWN	WHEN
TIMEZONE_MINUTE	UPDATE	WHENEVER
TO	UPPER	WHERE
TRAILING	USAGE	WITH
TRANSACTION	USER	WORK
TRANSLATE	USING	WRITE
TRANSLATION	VALUE	YEAR
TRIM	VALUES	ZONE
TRUE	VARCHAR	
UNION	VARYING	

Future Reserved Words

The following table contains keywords that may be reserved in future editions of SQL Server.

ABSOLUTE	BLOB	CONNECT
ACTION	BOOLEAN	CONNECTION
ADMIN	BOTH	CONSTRAINTS
AFTER	BREADTH	CONSTRUCTOR
AGGREGATE	CALL	CORRESPONDING
ALIAS	CASCADED	CUBE
ALLOCATE	CAST	CURRENT_PATH
ARE	CATALOG	CURRENT_ROLE
ARRAY	CHAR	CYCLE
ASSERTION	CHARACTER	DATA
AT	CLASS	DATE
BEFORE	CLOB	DAY
BINARY	COLLATION	DEC
BIT	COMPLETION	DECIMAL

(Continued)

DEFERRABLE	GROUPING	MINUTE
DEFERRED	HOST	MODIFIES
DEPTH	HOUR	MODIFY
DEREF	IGNORE	MODULE
DESCRIBE	IMMEDIATE	MONTH
DESCRIPTOR	INDICATOR	NAMES
DESTROY	INITIALIZE	NATURAL
DESTRUCTOR	INITIALLY	NCHAR
DETERMINISTIC	INOUT	NCLOB
DICTIONARY	INPUT	NEW
DIAGNOSTICS	INT	NEXT
DISCONNECT	INTEGER	NO
DOMAIN	INTERVAL	NONE
DYNAMIC	ISOLATION	NUMERIC
EACH	ITERATE	OBJECT
END-EXEC	LANGUAGE	OLD
EQUALS	LARGE	ONLY
EVERY	LAST	OPERATION
EXCEPTION	LATERAL	ORDINALITY
EXTERNAL	LEADING	OUT
FALSE	LESS	OUTPUT
FIRST	LEVEL	PAD
FLOAT	LIMIT	PARAMETER
FOUND	LOCAL	PARAMETERS
FREE	LOCALTIME	PARTIAL
GENERAL	LOCALTIMESTAMP	PATH
GET	LOCATOR	POSTFIX
GLOBAL	MAP	PREFIX
GO	MATCH	PREORDER

PREPARE	SECTION	TIMESTAMP
PRESERVE	SEQUENCE	TIMEZONE_HOUR
PRIOR	SESSION	TIMEZONE_MINUTE
PRIVILEGES	SETS	TRAILING
READS	SIZE	TRANSLATION
REAL	SMALLINT	TREAT
RECURSIVE	SPACE	TRUE
REF	SPECIFIC	UNDER
REFERENCING	SPECIFICTYPE	UNKNOWN
RELATIVE	SQL	UNNEST
RESULT	SQLEXCEPTION	USAGE
RETURNS	SQLSTATE	USING
ROLE	SQLWARNING	VALUE
ROLLUP	START	VARCHAR
ROUTINE	STATE	VARIABLE
ROW	STATEMENT	WHENEVER
ROWS	STATIC	WITHOUT
SAVEPOINT	STRUCTURE	WORK
SCROLL	TEMPORARY	WRITE
SCOPE	TERMINATE	YEAR
SEARCH	THAN	ZONE
SECOND	TIME	

System Variables and Functions Reference

Variables and functions are often used interchangeably. SQL Server Books Online documents some variables as though they were functions. However, it's important to note that variables are used in expressions to obtain a value, whereas functions process specific business logic and may return a value. Many functions accept input arguments.

This appendix, specific for SQL Server 2008, is not meant to be a comprehensive reference, but to provide a convenient guide to many functions and variables. For complete details and samples of usage, consult Books Online.

System Global Variables

The system-supplied global variables are organized into the following categories:

- ❏ Configuration
- ❏ Cursor
- ❏ System
- ❏ System Statistics

Configuration

Variable	Return Type	Description
@@DATEFIRST	tinyint	The system setting for the first day of the week. 1 = Monday 2 = Tuesday 3 = Wednesday 4 = Thursday 5 = Friday 6 = Saturday 7 = Sunday U.S. default is 7.
@@DBTS	varbinary	The last assigned unique TimeStamp value.
@@LANGID	smallint	The current language ID for the server. 0 = US English 1 = German 2 = French . . . and so on.
@@LANGUAGE	nvarchar	The current language string for the server. Returns the language name in the native language form (us_english, Deutsch, Français, Dansk, Español, Italiano, and so on).
@@LOCK_TIMEOUT	int	Lock time-out setting for the current session in milliseconds.
@@MAX_CONNECTIONS	int	The maximum concurrent connections setting for the server.
@@MAX_PRECISION	tinyint	The maximum precision setting for decimal and numeric types. Default is 38 significant digits (total to the left and right of the decimal point).
@@MICROSOFTVERSION	int	An internal tracking number used by product development and support groups at Microsoft.
@@NESTLEVEL	int	The current number of nested stored procedure or trigger calls. This may be used to limit cascading and/or recursive calls prior to reaching the system limit of 32 recursive calls.

Variable	Return Type	Description

@@OPTIONS	int	The set of query-processing options for the current user session. Multiple options are combined mathematically using bitwise addition (that is, `If SELECT @@OPTIONS & (512 + 8192) > 0...`).
		
		 Any combination of option values can be added to determine whether all these options are enabled.
		
		 Option values:
		
		 `1 = DISABLE_DEF_CNST_CHK`
		`2 = IMPLICIT_TRANSACTIONS`
		`4 = CURSOR_CLOSE_ON_COMMIT`
		`8 = ANSI_WARNINGS`
		`16 = ANSI_PADDING`
		`32 = ANSI_NULLS`
		`64 = ARITHABORT`
		`128 = ARITHIGNORE`
		`256 = QUOTED_IDENTIFIER`
		`512 = NOCOUNT`
		`1024 = ANSI_NULL_DFLT_ON`
		`2048 = ANSI_NULL_DFLT_OFF`
		`4096 = CONCAT_NULL_YIELDS_NULL`
		`8192 = NUMERIC_ROUNDABORT`
		`16384 = XACT_ABORT`

@@REMSERVER	nvarchar	Name of the remote server if executing remote procedures.
@@SERVERNAME	nvarchar	Name of the current server.
@@SERVICENAME	nvarchar	Name of the Windows service for the current SQL Server instance.
@@SPID	int	The process/session ID assigned to the current user's connection.
@@TEXTSIZE	int	The current value of the TEXTSIZE option for a query returning data from a text, ntext, or image type. The default setting is 4096 (4KB).
@@VERSION	nvarchar	A text string with detailed information about the current version of SQL Server. This includes the major version, build number, service pack, and copyright information.

Cursor

Variable	Return Type	Description
@@CURSOR_ROWS	int	The row count for the currently open cursor. Used for explicit cursor processing following an OPEN command. If an asynchronous cursor is opened, the row count will not be known and this variable returns –1.
@@FETCH_STATUS	int	Used as a flag to indicate whether the open cursor has navigated past the last row (EOF). Status values include: 0 = Normal fetch operation –1 = Fetch past last row or unsuccessful –2 = Fetched row has been removed

System

Variable	Return Type	Description
@@ERROR	int	Value of the most recent error within the current user session. Error numbers (from the sysmessages table) are used to determine the status of an error condition.
@@IDENTITY	numeric	Value of the most recently generated identity value. This is typically the result of an identity column insert.
@@ROWCOUNT	int	Number of rows affected by, or returned by, the last operation.
@@TRANCOUNT	int	Number of currently active transactions. Used to determine the number of nested transactions. The maximum number of nested transactions is 11.

System Statistical

Variable	Return Type	Description
@@CONNECTIONS	int	The total connects that have been opened or attempted since the SQL Server service was last started.
@@CPU_BUSY	int	The total time in milliseconds that the server has not been idle since the SQL Server service was last started.
@@IDLE	int	The total time in milliseconds that the server has been idle since the SQL Server service was last started.
@@IO_BUSY	int	The total time in milliseconds that the server has performed physical disk I/O operations since the SQL Server service was last started.
@@PACK_RECEIVED	int	The total number of network packets received by the server since the SQL Server service was last started.
@@PACK_SENT	int	The total number of network packets sent by the server since the SQL Server service was last started.
@@PACKET_ERRORS	int	The total number of network packet errors that have occurred since the SQL Server service was last started.
@@TIMETICKS	int	The number of milliseconds per CPU tick. Each tick takes 1/32 of a second.
@@TOTAL_ERRORS	int	The total number of disk read/write errors that have occurred, while performing physical disk I/O, since the SQL Server service was last started.
@@TOTAL_READ	int	The total number of physical disk reads that have occurred since the SQL Server service was last started.
@@TOTAL_WRITE	int	The total number of physical disk writes that have occurred since the SQL Server service was last started.

System Functions

The system functions are organized into the following categories:

❑ Aggregation

❑ Checksum

❑ Conversion

❑ Cursor

- ❏ Date and Time
- ❏ Image/text
- ❏ Mathematical
- ❏ Metadata
- ❏ Ranking
- ❏ Security
- ❏ System
- ❏ System statistics

Aggregation

Function	Return Type	Description
AVG()	(numeric — depends on input)	Calculates the arithmetic average for a range of column values. Internally, this function counts rows and calculates the sum for all non-null values in the column and then divides the sum by the count. Returns the same numeric data type as the column.
COUNT()	int	Counts all non-null values for a column. The row count is returned using COUNT(*) regardless of null values.
COUNT_BIG()	bigint	Same as COUNT() but returns a bigint type rather than an int type.
GROUPING()	int	Used in conjunction with ROLLUP and CUBE operations in a GROUP BY query, this function returns 0 to indicate that it is on a detail row and 1 to indicate a summary row.
MAX()	(numeric or date — depends on input)	Returns the largest value in a range of column values.
MIN()	(numeric or date — depends on input)	Returns the smallest value in a range of column values.
STDEV()	float	Calculates the standard deviation for a range of non-null column values.
STDEVP()	float	Calculates the standard deviation over a population for a range of non-null column values.

Function	Return Type	Description
SUM()	(numeric — depends on input)	Calculates the arithmetic sum for a range of non-null column values. If all values are NULL, returns NULL.
VAR()	float	Calculates the statistical variance for a range of non-null column values. If all values are NULL, returns NULL.
VARP()	float	Calculates the statistical variance over a population for a range of non-null column values. If all values are NULL, returns NULL.

Checksum

Function	Return Type	Description
CHECKSUM()	int	Calculates a checksum value for a row or range of column values. This function accepts a single column name, a comma-delimited list of columns, or an asterisk (*) to use the entire row. Accepts columns of all types except text, ntext, image, cursor, and sql_variant. The returned value itself is meaningless but will consistently yield the same result for a column or row unless a value changes. String comparisons are case-insensitive.
BINARY_CHECKSUM()	int	Calculates a checksum value for a row or range of column values. This function accepts a single column name, a comma-delimited list of columns, or an asterisk (*) to use the entire row. Accepts columns of all types except text, ntext, image, cursor, and sql_variant. The returned value itself is meaningless but will consistently yield the same result for a column or row unless a value changes. String comparisons are case-sensitive.
CHECKSUM_AGG()	int	Calculates a single checksum value for a range of int type column values. When applied to the result of the CHECKSUM() or BINARY_CHECKSUM() functions, returns a scalar (single value) checksum value for the entire range of values. Can be used to detect value changes over a table or range of column values.

Conversion

Function	Return Type	Description
CAST()	(Returns a specified type)	Converts a value to a specified data type. CAST(the_value AS the_type)
CONVERT()	(Returns a specified type)	Converts (and optionally formats) a value to a specified data type. Formatting can be applied to numeric and date types. CONVERT(the_type, the_value) or CONVERT(the_type, the_value, format_number)

Cryptographic

Function	Return Type	Description
AsymKey_ID()	int	Returns the ID of an asymmetric key.
Cert_ID	int	Returns the ID of a certificate.
CertProperty()	sql_variant	Returns the value of a specified certificate property.
DecryptByAsmKey()	varbinary	Decrypts data with an asymmetric key.
DecryptByCert()	varbinary	Decrypts data with the private key of a certificate.
DecryptByKey()	varbinary	Decrypts data by using a symmetric key.
DecryptByKeyAutoCert()	varbinary	Decrypts by using a symmetric key that is automatically decrypted with a certificate.
DecryptByPassPrase()	varbinary	Decrypts data that was encrypted with a passphrase.
EncryptByAsmKey()	varbinary	Encrypts data with an asymmetric key.

Function	Return Type	Description
EncryptByCert()	varbinary	Encrypts data with the public key of a certificate.
EncryptByKey()	varbinary	Encrypts a string of text using a uniqueidentifier key.
EncryptByPassPhrase()	varbinary	Encrypts a string of text using a passphrase.
Key_GUID()	uniqueidentifier	Returns the global unique identifier of a named encryption key.
Key_ID()	int	Returns the integer ID of a named symmetric key.
SignByAsymKey()	varbinary	Applies a digital signature generated by an asymmetrical key to a block of plain text.
SignByCert()	varbinary	Applies a digital signature generated by a certificate key to a block of plain text.
VerifySignedByAsmKey()	int	Verifies that text signed by an asymmetrical key has not been altered.
VerifySignedByCert()	int	Verifies that text signed by a certificate has not been altered.

Cursor

Function	Return Type	Description
CURSOR_STATUS()	smallint	Returns the status of a previously opened cursor. 1 = Open and populated 0 = Contains no records −1 = Closed −2 = No cursor or deallocated −3 = Doesn't exist

Date and Time

Function	Return Type	Description
CURRENT_TIMESTAMP()	datetime	Returns the current date and time and is synonymous with the GETDATE() function. It exists for ANSI-SQL compliance.
DATEADD()	datetime or smalldatetime (depending on input type)	Returns a date value (datetime or smalldatetime) from a date value added by X number of date interval units. Units may be Year, Quarter, Month, DayOfYear, Day, Hour, Minute, Second, or Millisecond.
DATEDIFF()	int	Returns an integer representing the difference between two date values (datetime or smalldatetime) in specified date interval units. Units may be Year, Quarter, Month, DayOfYear, Day, Hour, Minute, Second, or Millisecond.
DATENAME()	nvarchar	Similar to DATEPART(). Returns a character string representing the specified datepart for a date value. The datepart parameter is the same as the DATEDIFF() interval and includes Year, Quarter, Month, DayOfYear, Day, Hour, Minute, Second, or Millisecond.
DATEPART()	int	Similar to DATENAME(). However, it returns the integer value representing the specified datepart for a date value. The datepart parameter is the same as the DATEDIFF() interval and includes Year, Quarter, Month, DayOfYear, Day, Hour, Minute, Second, or Millisecond.
DAY()	int	Returns the day date part for a date as an integer.
GETDATE()	datetime	Returns the current date and time value.
GETUTCDATE()	datetime	Returns the current date and time value for the Universal Time Zone (UTC), based on the server's time zone settings. UTC is the same as Greenwich Mean Time (GMT).

Function	Return Type	Description
ISDATE()	int	Returns a flag to indicate whether a specified value is, or is capable of being converted to, a date value.
MONTH()	int	Returns the month part for a date as an integer.
SWITCHOFFSET	datetimeoffset (Date)	Returns and/or modifies the UTC offset for a time zone.
SYSDATETIME	datetime	Returns the current database system timestamp.
SYSDATETIMEOFFSET	datetimeoffset (Date)	Returns the current database time offset.
SYSUTCDATETIME	datetime2	Returns the current database system UTC timestamp.
TODATETIMEOFFSET	datetimeoffset	Modifies the time zone offset for a date and time.
YEAR()	int	Returns the year part for a date as an integer.

Image/Text

Function	Return Type	Description
PATINDEX()	bigint or int (depending on input type)	Returns the character index (first position) for a character string pattern occurring within another character string. Similar to CHARINDEX() but supports wildcards. Returns bigint for varchar(max) and nvarchar(max) type strings; otherwise, returns int.
TEXTPTR()	varbinary	Returns a varbinary text pointer handle to be used with the READTEXT(), WRITETEXT(), and UPDATETEXT() functions. Used for performing special operations on text, ntext, and image type column data.
TEXTVALID()	int	Verifies a varbinary text pointer value, obtained from the TEXTPTR() function.

Error Handling

Function	Return Type	Description
ERROR_LINE	int	Returns the line number of the last error when called in a CATCH block.
ERROR_MESSAGE	nvarchar	Returns the full error text for the last error when called in a CATCH block.
ERROR_NUMBER	int	Returns the system- or user-defined error number for the last error when called in a CATCH block.
ERROR_PROCEDURE	nvarchar	Returns the name of the stored procedure or function that raised the last error when called in a CATCH block.
ERROR_SEVERITY	int	Returns the system- or user-defined severity value for the last error when called in a CATCH block.
ERROR_STATE	int	Returns the state number for the last error when called in a CATCH block.
XACT_STATE()	smallint	Tests the commitability of the current transaction within a CATCH block. Returns –1 if the transaction is uncommittable.

Mathematical

Function	Return Type	Description
ABS()	(numeric — same type as input)	Returns the absolute value for a numeric value.
ACOS()	float	Computes the arccosine (an angle) in radians.
ASIN()	float	Computes the arcsine (an angle) in radians.
ATAN()	float	Computes the arctangent (an angle) in radians.
ATN2()	float	Computes the arctangent of two values in radians.
CEILING()	(numeric — same type as input)	Returns the smallest integer value that is greater than or equal to a number.
COS()	float	Computes the cosine of an angle in radians.

Function	Return Type	Description
COT()	float	Computes the cotangent of an angle in radians.
DEGREES()	(numeric — same type as input)	Converts an angle from radians to degrees.
EXP()	float	Returns the natural logarithm raised to a specified exponent. Result is in exponential form.
FLOOR()	(numeric — same type as input)	Returns the largest integer value that is less than or equal to a number.
LOG()	float	Calculates the natural logarithm of a number using base-2 (binary) numbering.
LOG10()	float	Calculates the natural logarithm of a number using base-10 numbering.
PI()	float	Returns the value for PI.
POWER()	float	Raises a value to a specified exponent as FLOAT(the_value, the_exponent).
RADIANS()	(numeric — same type as input)	Converts an angle from degrees to radians.
RAND()	float	Returns a fractional number based on a randomizing algorithm. Accepts an optional seed value.
ROUND()	(numeric — same type as input)	Rounds a fractional value to a specified precision.
SIGN()	float	Returns –1 or 1 depending on whether a single argument value is negative or positive.
SIN()	float	Computes the sine of an angle in radians.
SQRT()	float	Returns the square root of a value.
SQUARE()	float	Returns the square (n^2) of a value.
TAN()	float	Computes the tangent of an angle in radians.

Metadata

Function	Return Type	Description
ASSEMBLYPROPERTY()	sql_variant	Returns descriptive information about a specified assembly property.
COL_LENGTH()	int	Returns the length of a column from the column name.
COL_NAME()	sysname (nvarchar)	Returns the name of a column from the object ID.
COLUMNPROPERTY()	int	Returns a flag to indicate the state of a column property.
DATABASEPROPERTY()	int	This function is maintained for backward compatibility with older SWL Server versions. Returns a flag to indicate the state of a database property.
DATABASEPROPERTYEX()	sqlvariant	Returns a numeric flag or string to indicate the state of a database property.
DB_ID()	smallint	Returns the database ID from the database name.
DB_NAME()	nvarchar	Returns the database name from the database ID.
FILE_ID()	smallint	Returns the file ID from the file name.
FILEGROUP_ID()	int	Returns the ID for a file group name.
FILEGROUP_NAME()	nvarchar(128)	Returns the file group name for a file group ID.
FILEGROUPPROPERTY()	int	Returns a specified file group property value for a file group name and property name.
FILEPROPERTY()	int	Returns a specified file property value for a filename and property name.
FILE_NAME()	nvarchar	Returns the filename from the file ID.
fn_listextendedproperty()	table	Returns a table object populated with extended property names and their settings.

Function	Return Type	Description
FULLTEXTCATALOGPROPERTY()	int	Returns a flag to indicate the state of a full-text catalog property.
FULLTEXTSERVICEPROPERTY()	int	Returns a flag to indicate the state of a full-text service property.
INDEX_COL()	nvarchar	Returns the name of a column contained in a specified index, by table, index, and column ID.
INDEXKEY_PROPERTY()	int	Returns a flag to indicate the state of an index key property.
INDEXPROPERTY()	int	Returns a flag indicating the state of an index property.
OBJECT_ID()	int	Returns an object ID from the object name.
OBJECT_NAME()	nchar	Returns an object name from the object ID.
OBJECTPROPERTY()	int	Returns property information from several different types of objects. It is advisable to use a function designed to query specific object types, if possible. Returns a flag indicating the state of an object property.
OBJECTPROPERTYEX()	sql_variant	Similar to OBJECTPROPERTY() but returns descriptive property values.
SCHEMA_ID()	int	Returns the schema ID for a schema name.
SCHEMA_NAME()	sysname (nvarchar)	Returns the schema name for a schema ID.
SQL_VARIANT_PROPERTY()	sql_variant	Returns the base data type and other information about a sql_variant value.
TYPE_ID()	int	Returns the ID for a specified data type name.
TYPE_NAME()	sysname	Returns the data type name of a specified type ID.
TYPEPROPERTY()	int	Returns information about data type properties.

563

Ranking

Function	Return Type	Description
DENSE_RANK()	bigint	Returns a running incremental value based on an ORDER BY clause passed into the function. Doesn't preserve the ordinal position of the row in the list if there are ties.
NTILE(n)	bigint	Returns an evenly distributed ranking value, dividing the result into a finite number of ranked groups.
RANK()	bigint	Returns a running incremental value based on an ORDER BY clause passed into the function. Preserves the ordinal position of the row in the list with duplicate values for ties followed by subsequent skips.
ROW_NUMBER()	bigint	Returns a running incremental value based on an ORDER BY clause passed into the function.

Rowset

Function	Return Type	Description
CONTAINSTABLE()	table	Returns a table object that can be used in a join operation. Each row in this table contains a Key column value, which is the primary key value for qualifying rows of the queried table. This key value is useful for joining the resulting table object back to the physical table to obtain column values. Two arguments are passed: the name of the indexed table and a search string containing words to be matched.
FREETEXTTABLE()	table	Similar to CONTAINSTABLE() but the search condition can match inexact phrasing rather than exact words.
OPENDATASOURCE()	table	Used to open an ad-hoc connection to a remote OLE DB data source and return a table reference to a database object. Arguments include the name of a registered OLE DB provider, a connection string and the four-part name of a database object.
OPENQUERY()	table	Used to reference an existing linked server and return the results of a query. Arguments include the name of the linked server and a query string.

Function	Return Type	Description
OPENROWSET()	table	Used to connect to a remote OLE DB data source and return the results of a query. Arguments include the name of a registered OLE DB provider, a connection string, and a query string.
OPENXML()	table	Transforms an XML document string into a rowset table. The table structure conforms to the standard "edge" table format. The sp_xml_preparedocument system stored procedure must be called first to obtain a document handle ID, which is then passed to this function, along with the document text.

Security

Function	Return Type	Description
fn_trace_geteventinfo()	table	Returns a table type populated with event information for a specified trace ID.
fn_trace_getfilterinfo()	table	Returns a table type populated with information about filters applied to a trace, for a specified trace ID.
fn_trace_getinfo()	table	Returns a table type populated with trace information for a specified trace ID.
fn_trace_gettable()	table	Returns a table type populated with file information for a specified trace ID.
HAS_DBACCESS()	int	Returns a flag indicating whether the current user has access to a specified database.
IS_MEMBER()	int	Returns a flag indicating whether the current user is a member of a Windows group or SQL Server role.
IS_SRVROLEMEMBER()	int	Returns a flag indicating whether the current user is a member of a database server role.
ORIGINAL_LOGIN()	sysname (varchar)	Returns the first user or login name for the first system login in the current session context.
SUSER_SID()	varbinary	Returns the security ID for a specified username.
SUSER_SNAME()	nvarchar	Returns the username for a specified security ID.
USER_ID()	int	Returns a username for a specified user ID.
fn_trace_geteventinfo()	table	Returns a table type populated with event information for a specified trace ID.

String Manipulation

Function	Return Type	Description
ASCII()	int	Returns the numeric ASCII character value for a standard character.
CHAR()	char	Returns the ASCII character for a numeric ASCII character value.
CHARINDEX()	int	Similar to PATINDEX(), returns the index (character position) of the first occurrence of a character string within another character string.
DIFFERENCE()	int	Returns the numeric difference between two character strings based on the consensus Soundex values.
LEFT()	varchar or nvarchar	Returns the left-most X characters from a character string.
LEN()	int	Returns the length of a character string.
LOWER()	varchar or nvarchar	Converts a character string to all lowercase characters.
LTRIM()	varchar or nvarchar	Removes leading spaces from the left side of a character string.
NCHAR()	nchar	As with the CHAR() function, returns the Unicode character for a numeric character value.
PATINDEX()	int or bigint	Returns the index (first character position) for the first occurrence of characters matching a specified pattern within another character string. Wildcard characters may be used.
QUOTENAME()	nvarchar	Returns a character string with square brackets around the input value. Used with SQL Server object names so they can be passed into an expression.
REPLACE()	varchar or nvarchar	Returns a character string with all occurrences of one character or substring replaced with another character or substring.

Function	Return Type	Description
REPLICATE()	varchar or nvarchar	Returns a character string consisting of a specified number of repeated characters.
REVERSE()	varchar or nvarchar	Returns a character string with all characters in reverse order.
RIGHT()	varchar or nvarchar	Returns a specific number of characters from the right-most side of a character string.
RTRIM()	varchar or nvarchar	Removes trailing spaces from the right side of a character string.
SOUNDEX()	varchar	Returns a four-character alphanumeric string representing the approximate phonetic value of a word, based on the U.S. Census Soundex algorithm.
SPACE()	char	Returns a character string consisting of a specified number of spaces.
STR()	char	Returns a character string value that represents a converted numeric data type. Three arguments include the value, the overall length, and the number of decimal positions.
STUFF()	(character or binary types — depending on input)	Returns a character string with one string placed into another string at a given position and for a specified length.
SUBSTRING()	(character or binary types — depending on input)	Returns a portion of a character string from a specified position and for a specified length.
UNICODE()	int	Returns the numeric Unicode character value for a specified character.
UPPER()	varchar or nvarchar	Converts a character string to all uppercase characters.

System

Function	Return Type	Description
APP_NAME()	nvarchar	Each session is associated with an application name, passed to the database server by explicit program code or by the driver or data provider.
COALESCE()	(same type as input)	Returns the first non-null value from a comma-delimited list of expressions.
COLLATIONPROPERTY()	sql_variant	Returns the value of a specific property for a specified collation. Properties include CodePage, LCID, and ComparisonStyle.
COLUMNS_UPDATED	varbinary	Used only within an Insert or Update trigger. Returns a bitmap of modified column flags for the current table. Bytes are left-to-right with the bits in each byte ordered right-to-left, representing the state (0=unmodified, 1=modified) of each column.
CURRENT_USER()	sysname (varchar)	Returns the name of the current user and is synonymous with the USER_NAME() function.
DATALENGTH()	int	Returns the number of bytes used to store or handle a value. For ANSI string types, this will return the same value as the LEN() function, but for other data types, the value may be different.
fn_Get_SQL()	table	Returns a table type populated with the full text of a query based on a process handle. This value is stored in the sysprocesses table referencing a SPID. This function was introduced with SQL Server 2000 SP3.
fn_HelpCollations()	table	Returns a table type populated with a list of collations supported by the current version of SQL Server.
fn_ServerSharedDrives()	table	Returns a table type populated with a list of drives shared by the server.
fn_VirtualFileStats()	table	Returns a table type populated with I/O statistics for database files, including log files.

Function	Return Type	Description
FORMATMESSAGE()	nvarchar	Returns an error message from the sysmessages table for a specified message number and comma-delimited list of parameters.
GETANSINULL()	int	Returns the nullability setting for the database, according to the ANSI_NULL_DFLT_ON and ANSI_NULL_DFLT_OFF database settings.
HOST_ID()	char	Returns the workstation ID for the current session.
HOST_NAME()	nchar	Returns the workstation name for the current session.
IDENT_CURRENT()	sql_variant	Returns the last identity value generated for a specified table regardless of the session and scope.
IDENT_INCR()	numeric	Returns the increment value specified in the creation of the last identity column.
IDENT_SEED()	numeric	Returns the seed value specified in the creation of the last identity column.
IDENTITY()	(same as input)	Used in a SELECT . . . INTO statement to insert an explicitly generated identity value into a column.
ISNULL()	(same as input)	Determines whether a specified value is null and then returns a provided replacement value.
ISNUMERIC()	int	Returns a flag to indicate whether a specified value is, or is capable of being converted to, a numeric value.
NEWID()	uniqueidentifier	Returns a newly generated uniqueidentifier type value. This is a 128-bit integer, globally unique value, usually expressed as an alphanumeric hexadecimal representation (such as 89DE6247-C2E2-42DB-8CE8-A787E505D7EA). This type is often used for primary key values in replicated and semi-connected systems.

(continued)

Function	Return Type	Description
NULLIF()	(same as input)	Returns a NULL value when two specified arguments have equivalent values.
PARSENAME()	nchar	Returns a specific part of a four-part object name.
ROWCOUNT_BIG()	bigint	Like the @@ROWCOUNT variable, returns the number of rows either returned by or modified by the last statement. Returns a bigint type.
SCOPE_IDENTITY()	sql_variant	Like the @@IDENTITY variable, returns the last Identity value generated but is limited to the current session and scope (stored procedure, batch, or module).
SERVERPROPERTY()	sql_variant	Returns a flag indicating the state of a server property. Properties include Collation, Edition, Engine Edition, InstanceName, IsClustered, IsFullTextInstalled, IsIntegratedSecurityOnly, IsSingleUser, IsSyncWithBackup, LicenseType, MachineName, NumLicenses, ProcessID, ProductLevel, ProductVersion, and ServerName.
SESSION_USER	nchar	Returns the current username. Function is called without parentheses.
SESSIONPROPERTY()	sql_variant	Returns a flag indicating the state of a session property. Properties include ANSI_NULLS, ANSI_PADDING, ANSI_WARNINGS, ARITHABORT, CONCAT_NULL_YIELDS_NULL, NUMERIC_ROUNDABORT, and QUOTED_IDENTIFIER.
STATS_DATE()	datetime	Returns the date that statistics for a specified index were last updated.
SYSTEM_USER	nvarchar	Returns the current username. Function is called without parentheses.
USER_NAME()	nvarchar	Returns the username for a specified User ID.

System Statistical

Function	Return Type	Description
sys.dm_io_virtual_file_stats()	table	Returns a table type populated with I/O statistics for database files, including log files.
sys.dm_db_index_operational_stats()	table	Returns current I/O, locking, latching, and access method activity for each table or index in the database.
sys.dm_db_index_physical_stats()	table	Returns size and fragmentation information for the data and indexes of a specified table or view.
sys.dm_db_index_usage_stats()	rowset	Returns counts of different types of index operations and the time each type of operation was last performed.
sys.dm_db_missing_index_columns()	table	Returns information about database table columns that are missing an index.

System Stored Procedure Reference

This appendix is not meant to be all-inclusive. There are a few types of system stored procedures that are very rarely used in an ad hoc fashion and then only by senior database administrators or programmers. As a result, this appendix intentionally omits inclusion of stored procedures affecting replication data warehouse data collection, notification services (2005 only), and spatial indexes.

SQL Server 2005 and SQL Server 2008 support the following system and extended stored procedures except where indicated.

Active Directory

Procedure	Description
sp_ActiveDirectory_Obj	Adds, updates, or removes the registration record of a SQL Server database in the Active Directory.
sp_ActiveDirectory_SCP	Adds, updates, or removes the registration record of a SQL Server instance in the Active Directory.

Catalog

Procedure	Description
sp_column_privileges	Returns column privileges for a table in the current session.
sp_column_privileges_ex	Returns column privileges for a table on a linked or remote server.
sp_columns	Returns column information for a table or view.
sp_columns_ex	Returns column information for a table or view on a linked or remote server.
sp_databases	Returns information about databases on the local server.
sp_fkeys	Returns foreign key information for a table.
sp_pkeys	Returns primary key information for a table.
sp_server_info	Returns server attributes for the server on a specified connection.
sp_special_columns	Returns columns used to uniquely identify a row (that is, primary key and unique constraints) and columns with programmatically updated values and defaults.
sp_sproc_columns	Returns column information for a stored procedure or user-defined function.
sp_statistics	Returns information about indexes and statistics for a table.
sp_stored_procedures	Returns information about all stored procedures matching a name or wildcard pattern.
sp_table_privileges	Returns information about permissions for a table or tables matching a wildcard pattern in the current session.
sp_table_privileges_ex	Returns information about permissions for a table or tables matching a wildcard pattern on a linked or remote server.
sp_tables	Returns information about all tables matching a name or wildcard pattern.

Change Data Capture (2008)

Procedure	Description
sp_cdc_add_job	Creates a change data capture cleanup or capture job in the current database.
sp_cdc_generate_wrapper_function	Generates scripts to create wrapper functions for the change data capture query functions that are available in SQL Server.
sp_cdc_change_job	Modifies the configuration of a change data capture cleanup or capture job in the current database.
sp_cdc_get_captured_columns	Returns change data capture metadata information for the captured source columns tracked by the specified capture instance.
sp_cdc_cleanup_change_table	Removes rows from the change table in the current database based on the specified low_water_mark value.
sp_cdc_get_ddl_history	Returns the data definition language (DDL) change history associated with the specified capture instance since change data capture was enabled for that capture instance.
sp_cdc_disable_db	Disables change data capture for the current database.
sp_cdc_help_change_data_capture	Returns the change data capture configuration for each table enabled for change data capture in the current database.
sp_cdc_disable_table	Disables change data capture for the specified source table and capture instance in the current database.
sp_cdc_help_jobs	Reports information about all change data capture cleanup or capture jobs in the current database.
sp_cdc_drop_job	Removes a change data capture cleanup or capture job from the current database.
sp_cdc_scan	Executes the change data capture log scan operation.
sp_cdc_enable_db	Enables change data capture for the current database.
sp_cdc_start_job	Starts a change data capture cleanup or capture job in the current database.
sp_cdc_enable_table	Enables change data capture for the specified source table in the current database.
sp_cdc_stop_job	Stops a change data capture cleanup or capture job in the current database.

Cursor Management

Procedure	Description
sp_cursor_list	Returns attributes and information about currently open cursor(s).
sp_describe_cursor	Returns attributes and information about a specific cursor.
sp_describe_cursor_columns	Returns information about columns used to populate a cursor.
sp_describe_cursor_tables	Returns information about tables used to populate a cursor.

Database Engine

Procedure	Description
sp_add_data_file_recover_suspect_db	Adds a database file to a file group after a disk full error. Similar to ALTER DATABASE ADD FILE.
sp_add_log_file_recover_suspect_db	Adds a transaction log file to a file group after a disk full error. Similar to ALTER DATABASE ADD LOG FILE.
sp_addextendedproc	Adds and registers an extended stored procedure to the server metadata.
sp_addextendedproperty	Adds an extended property to the server metadata.
sp_addmessage	Adds a custom error message to the server messages metadata.
sp_addtype	Adds a user-defined data type to a database.
sp_addumpdevice	Adds a backup device (file, tape drive, or other device) to the server.
sp_altermessage	Modifies an existing error message (number, severity, category, or message text).
sp_attach_db	Attaches a database file to a SQL Server instance and makes it available as an active database.
sp_attach_single_file_db	Similar to sp_attach_db but only for single-file databases. Builds a new transaction log file.
sp_autostats	Returns or modifies the UPDATE STATISTICS setting for a table's index or statistics in the current database.

Procedure	Description
sp_bindefault	Associates a defined default with a table's column as a shared default.
sp_bindrule	Associates a defined rule with a table's column as a default check constraint.
sp_bindsession	Allows multiple connections to participate in a single transaction by associating them to an established session.
sp_certify_removable	Verifies (certifies) that a database may be actively used on removable media.
sp_configure	Returns or modifies server configuration settings.
sp_create_removable	Creates a set of files and a new database to be used on removable media.
sp_createstats	Generates statistics for all tables and candidate columns in the current database.
sp_cycle_errorlog	Closes the current error log and initiates a new error log with a default name and settings (as if for a server restart).
sp_datatype_info	Returns detailed information about all current data types or information for a specific data type (system and user-defined data types).
sp_dbcmptlevel	Sets the SQL Server version database compatibility level. Setting the level to an older version number disables certain product features to emulate the capabilities of an older SQL Server version.
sp_dboption	Sets user database options similar to those set using ALTER DATABASE.
sp_dbremove	Removes a database and associated files.
sp_delete_backuphistory	Removes backup history information for a database.
sp_depends	Lists the dependent objects for a database object.
sp_detach_db	Detaches a database's file(s) from the server.
sp_dropdevice	Removes a database or backup device record from the server.
sp_dropextendedproc	Drops an extended stored procedure from the server.
sp_dropextendedproperty	Drops an extended property from the server.
sp_dropmessage	Removes an error message record from the server.
sp_droptype	Removes a user-defined data type from the server.

(continued)

Procedure	Description
sp_executesql	Executes a parameterized Transact-SQL statement.
sp_getapplock	Places a lock on an application or system resource outside of SQL Server for the duration of a transaction or session.
sp_getbindtoken	Uses a varchar type output parameter to return a unique ID for a transaction.
sp_help	Returns descriptive help information specific to a database object.
sp_helpconstraint	Returns help information for a specified constraint.
sp_helpdb	Returns help information for a specified database.
sp_helpdevice	Returns help information for a specified device.
sp_helpextendedproc	Returns help information for a specified extended stored procedure.
sp_helpfile	Returns help information for a specified database file.
sp_helpfilegroup	Returns help information for a specified database file group.
sp_helpindex	Returns help information for a specified index.
sp_helplanguage	Returns help information for a specified server language.
sp_helpserver	Returns help information for a specified server (local or remote).
sp_helpsort	Returns a description of the server's collation and sort order.
sp_helpstats	Returns help information regarding the statistics associated with the indexes for a specified table.
sp_helptext	Returns the definition of a rule, default, stored procedure, user-defined function, trigger, or view.
sp_helptrigger	Returns information about the triggers associated with a specified table.
sp_indexoption	Allows default level-locking options (that is, row, page, table) to be overridden for a specified index.
sp_invalidate_textptr	Invalidates a specified in-row text pointer, or all in-row text pointers in a transaction.

Procedure	Description
sp_lock	Returns information about all active locks.
sp_monitor	Returns the results from several system functions to show the status of server and system resources.
sp_procoption	Enables one of several procedure options to be set.
sp_recompile	Recompiles a stored procedure or trigger.
sp_refreshview	Updates the metadata for a specified view.
sp_releaseapplock	Removes a lock set on an application or external system resource that may have been set using sp_getapplock.
sp_rename	Renames a database object.
sp_renamedb	Renames a database.
sp_resetstatus	Resets the suspect status of a database back to normal status.
sp_serveroption	Sets specified server options for a remote and linked server.
sp_setnetname	Sets the network name for a linked or remote server.
sp_settriggerorder	Sets a specified trigger for a table to execute first or last.
sp_spaceused	Returns information about the disk space used by rows, table, and a database.
sp_tableoption	Sets one of several table options.
sp_unbindefault	Removes a specified default from a column or user-defined data type.
sp_unbindrule	Removes a specified rule from a column or user-defined data type.
sp_updateextendedproperty	Updates the value of a specified extended property.
sp_updatestats	Updates all index statistics in the database.
sp_validname	Checks a specified character string for validity as an object name. If invalid, raises an option error.
sp_who	Returns information about current connections and user sessions on a server.

Database Maintenance Plan

Procedure	Description
sp_add_maintenance_plan	Adds a maintenance plan to the server and returns the plan ID.
sp_add_maintenance_plan_db	Associates a database with a maintenance plan. (A maintenance plan is added using sp_add_maintenance_plan.)
sp_add_maintenance_plan_job	Associates a maintenance plan with an existing job.
sp_delete_maintenance_plan	Deletes a maintenance plan based in the specified plan ID.
sp_delete_maintenance_plan_db	Removes an associated maintenance plan from the specified database.
sp_delete_maintenance_plan_job	Removes an associated maintenance plan from the specified job.
sp_help_maintenance_plan	Returns information about maintenance plans on the server.

Distributed Queries

Procedure	Description
sp_addlinkedserver	Adds a linked server to the current server, allowing persistent access to a remote SQL Server from the current server.
sp_addlinkedsrvlogin	Adds the association of a local login to a linked server login for user connectivity to a linked server.
sp_catalogs	Returns the list of databases on a linked server.
sp_column_privileges_ex	Returns column-level security access privilege information for a specified table on a linked server.
sp_columns_ex	Returns column information for a table or view on a linked server.
sp_droplinkedsrvlogin	Removes the association of a local login to the login on a linked server.
sp_foreignkeys	Returns information about foreign key columns related to a specified primary key for tables on a linked server.

Procedure	Description
sp_indexes	Returns index information for a remote or linked server table.
sp_linkedservers	Returns information about all linked servers.
sp_primarykeys	Returns information about primary key columns for a specified remote or linked server table.
sp_serveroption	Sets server options for remote servers and linked servers.
sp_table_privileges_ex	Returns information about column and table-level security privileges for a specified remote or linked table.
sp_tables_ex	Returns information about tables on a remote or linked server.

External Systems and Extended Procedures

Procedure	Description
xp_cmdshell	Executes an operating system shell command, as if entered at the command prompt on the server.
xp_enumgroups	Returns information about Windows domain groups.
xp_findnextmsg	Uses an output parameter to return a MAPI message ID from the SQL Server Inbox.
xp_grantlogin	Calls sp_grantlogin for backward compatibility. Creates a SQL Server login for an associated Windows user or group.
xp_logevent	Logs a message to the SQL Server log file without raising a SQL Server error.
xp_loginconfig	Returns SQL Server security configuration information.
xp_logininfo	Returns detailed information about a SQL Server login and related privileges.
xp_msver	Returns detailed information about the instance of SQL Server and the operating system environment.
xp_revokelogin	Calls sp_revokelogin for backward compatibility. Revokes permissions of a SQL Server login.
xp_sprintf	Uses an output parameter to return a character string. Used to assemble a character string from parameterized values.
xp_sqlmaint	Calls the SQLMAIN command-line tool to set SQL Server maintenance options.
xp_sscanf	Uses an output parameter to return a character string. Used to disassemble a character string into corresponding parameterized values. This is the converse of the xp_sprintf procedure.

Full-Text Index/Search

Procedure	Description
sp_fulltext_catalog	Creates or maintains a full-text catalog to be used to store and maintain full-text indexes.
sp_fulltext_column	Indicates whether a specified column should be included in a full-text index.
sp_fulltext_database	Enables or disables full-text indexing for a database.
sp_fulltext_service	Used to manage full-text indexing services on a server.
sp_fulltext_table	Manages and enables actions for full-text indexing on a specific table.
sp_help_fulltext_catalogs	Returns information about the tables and attributes for a full-text catalog.
sp_help_fulltext_catalogs_cursor	Returns information about the tables and attributes for a full-text catalog.
sp_help_fulltext_columns	Returns information about the columns contained in a full-text index for a table.
sp_help_fulltext_columns_cursor	Returns information about the columns contained in a full-text index for a table.
sp_help_fulltext_tables	Returns information about the tables contained in a full-text catalog.
sp_help_fulltext_tables_cursor	Returns information about the tables contained in a full-text catalog.

Log Shipping

Log shipping is most easily configured through Management Studio, which in turn calls the various stored procedures listed. However, configuration can be completed directly with the procedures. For more information on these stored procedures, consult Books Online.

Procedure	Description
sp_add_log_shipping_alert_job	Checks to see if an alert job has been created on this server. If an alert job does not exist, this stored procedure creates the alert job and adds its job ID to the log_shipping_monitor_alert table.
sp_delete_log_shipping_secondary_database	Removes a secondary database and removes the local history and remote history.

Procedure	Description
sp_add_log_shipping_primary_database	Sets up the primary database for a log shipping configuration, including the backup job, local monitor record, and remote monitor record.
sp_delete_log_shipping_secondary_primary	Removes the information about the specified primary server from the secondary server, and removes the copy job and restore job from the secondary.
sp_add_log_shipping_primary_secondary	Adds an entry for a secondary database on the primary server.
sp_help_log_shipping_alert_job	Returns the job ID of the alert job from the log shipping monitor.
sp_add_log_shipping_secondary_database	Sets up a secondary databases for log shipping.
sp_help_log_shipping_monitor	Returns a result set containing status and other information for registered primary and secondary databases on a primary, secondary, or monitor server.
sp_add_log_shipping_secondary_primary	Sets up the primary information, adds local and remote monitor links, and creates copy and restore jobs on the secondary server for the specified primary database.
sp_help_log_shipping_monitor_primary	Returns information regarding a primary database from the monitor tables.
sp_change_log_shipping_primary_database	Changes the primary database settings.
sp_help_log_shipping_monitor_secondary	Returns information regarding a primary database from the monitor tables.
sp_change_log_shipping_secondary_database	Sets up a secondary databases for log shipping.
sp_help_log_shipping_primary_database	Retrieves primary database settings.
sp_change_log_shipping_secondary_primary	Changes secondary database settings.
sp_help_log_shipping_primary_secondary	Returns information regarding all the secondary databases for a given primary database.
sp_cleanup_log_shipping_history	Cleans up history locally and on the monitor server based on retention period.

(continued)

Procedure	Description
sp_help_log_shipping_secondary_database	Retrieves the settings for one or more secondary databases.
sp_delete_log_shipping_alert_job	Removes an alert job from the log shipping monitor server if the job exists and there are no more primary or secondary databases to be monitored.
sp_help_log_shipping_secondary_primary	Retrieves the settings for a given primary database on the secondary server.
sp_delete_log_shipping_primary_database	Removes log shipping of primary database including backup job as well as local and remote history.
sp_refresh_log_shipping_monitor	Refreshes the remote monitor tables with the latest information from a given primary or secondary server for the specified log shipping agent.
sp_delete_log_shipping_primary_secondary	Removes the entry for a secondary database on the primary server.

Database Mail

Database Mail is most easily configured through Management Studio, which in turn calls the various stored procedures listed. However, configuration can be completed directly with the procedures. For more information on these stored procedures, consult Books Online.

Procedure	Description
sp_send_dbmail	Sends an e-mail message to the specified recipients. The message may include a query result set, file attachments, or both.
sysmail_help_configure_sp	Displays configuration settings for Database Mail.
sysmail_add_account_sp	Creates a new Database Mail account holding information about an SMTP account.
sysmail_help_principalprofile_sp	Lists information about associations between Database Mail profiles and database principals.
sysmail_add_principalprofile_sp	Grants permission for a database user or role to use a Database Mail profile.
sysmail_help_profile_sp	Lists information about one or more mail profiles.
sysmail_add_profile_sp	Creates a new database mail profile.

Procedure	Description
sysmail_help_profileaccount_sp	Lists the accounts associated with one or more Database Mail profiles.
sysmail_add_profileaccount_sp	Adds a Database Mail account to a Database Mail profile.
sysmail_help_queue_sp	There are two queues in Database Mail: the mail queue and status queue. The mail queue stores mail items that are waiting to be sent. The status queue stores the status of items that have already been sent. This stored procedure allows viewing the state of the mail or status queues.
sysmail_configure_sp	Changes configuration settings for Database Mail.
sysmail_help_status_sp	Displays the status of Database Mail queues.
sysmail_delete_account_sp	Deletes a Database Mail SMTP account.
sysmail_start_sp	Starts Database Mail by starting the Service Broker objects that the external program uses.
sysmail_delete_log_sp	Deletes events from the Database Mail log. Deletes all events in the log or those events meeting a date or type criteria.
sysmail_stop_sp	Stops Database Mail by stopping the Service Broker objects that the external program uses.
sysmail_delete_mailitems_sp	Permanently deletes e-mail messages from the Database Mail internal tables.
sysmail_update_account_sp	Changes the information in an existing Database Mail account.
sysmail_delete_principalprofile_sp	Removes permission for a database user or role to use a public or private Database Mail profile.
sysmail_update_principalprofile_sp	Updates the information for an association between a principal and a profile.
sysmail_delete_profile_sp	Deletes a mail profile used by Database Mail.
sysmail_update_profile_sp	Changes the description or name of a Database Mail profile.
sysmail_delete_profileaccount_sp	Removes an account from a Database Mail profile.
sysmail_update_profileaccount_sp	Updates the sequence number of an account within a Database Mail profile.
sysmail_help_account_sp	Lists information (except passwords) about Database Mail accounts.

OLE Automation

If you use these OLE automation stored procedures, it's possible to execute certain application code from SQL queries to perform actions and automate applications outside of SQL Server. With custom-created COM components, practically any programmatic interaction is possible.

Procedure	Description
sp_OACreate	Instantiates an OLE object from a specified class using either the ProgID or CLSID. If stopped, starts the OLE automation execution process on the server.
sp_OADestroy	Destroys a previously instantiated OLE object.
sp_OAGetErrorInfo	Returns the error information associated with an OLE object instance and actions.
sp_OAGetProperty	Uses either an output parameter or a result set to return the value(s) or structured information for a specified object property.
sp_OAMethod	Calls a method of an OLE object. Uses either an output parameter or a result set to return the value(s) or structured information returned by the method call.
sp_OASetProperty	Sets an object property to a specified value.
sp_OAStop	Stops the OLE automation execution process environment on the server. Immediately terminates all OLE automation activity for all sessions.

SQL Server Profiler

Procedure	Description
sp_trace_create	Creates a new Profiler trace.
sp_trace_generateevent	Creates a new Profiler event.
sp_trace_setevent	Adds an existing event to a trace. These items may be created using the sp_trace_create and sp_trace_generateevent procedures.
sp_trace_setfilter	Adds a filter to an existing trace.
sp_trace_setstatus	Modifies an existing trace.

Security

Stored Procedures marked as "Obsolete" are deprecated and will be removed in a future release.

Procedure	Description
sp_addalias	Matches a server login to a database user. This is an older alternative to using role-based security.
sp_addapprole	Adds an application role to a database to be used for programmatic access from an application component.
sp_addgroup	Adds a user group to a database. This is an older alternative to using role-based security.
sp_addlinkedsrvlogin	Matches a local server login to a linked server login for access to a remote database server.
sp_addlogin	Adds a new server login.
sp_addremotelogin	Adds a login to the local server for use by remote users.
sp_addrole	Adds a new database role.
sp_addrolemember	Adds a SQL Server user, role, Windows user, or group to a SQL Server role.
sp_addserver	Obsolete. Similar to sp_addlinkedserver, adds the metadata representing a registered linked server with persistent access from the local server.
sp_addsrvrolemember	Adds a server login to a server role.
sp_adduser	Obsolete. Similar to sp_grantdbaccess, adds a SQL Server user, role, Windows user, or group to a database.
sp_approlepassword	Modifies the password for an application role.
sp_change_users_login	Modifies the association between a server login and a database user.
sp_changedbowner	Modifies the owner of a database.
sp_changegroup	Obsolete. Similar to sp_addrolemember, modifies the role membership for a user.
sp_changeobjectowner	Modifies the owner of any database object.
sp_dbfixedrolepermission	Returns permission information for all fixed database roles.
sp_defaultdb	Modifies the default database setting for a login.

(continued)

Procedure	Description
sp_defaultlanguage	Modifies the default language setting for a login.
sp_denylogin	Denies access to the server for a Windows user or group.
sp_dropalias	Obsolete. Drops an alias associated with a database user. This is an older technique used before SQL Server role-based security. sp_droprolemember provides similar functionality as a recommended practice.
sp_dropapprole	Drops an application role.
sp_dropgroup	Removes a database role. This is an older procedure provided for compatibility.
sp_droplinkedsrvlogin	Removes the association between a local server login and a linked server login.
sp_droplogin	Drops a local server login.
sp_dropremotelogin	Drops a remote login from the local server.
sp_droprolemember	Removes a user, login, Windows user, or group from a database role.
sp_dropserver	Removes the record of a linked or remote server from a local server.
sp_dropsrvrolemember	Removes a server login, Windows user, or group from a server role.
sp_dropuser	Obsolete. Similar to sp_revokedbaccess, removes access to a database for a SQL Server user, Windows user, or group.
sp_grantdbaccess	Adds access to a database for a server login, Windows user, or group.
sp_grantlogin	Adds access for a Windows user of group to the database server using Windows integrated Security.
sp_helpdbfixedrole	Returns information about fixed database roles.
sp_helpgroup	Obsolete. Returns information about database groups.
sp_helplinkedsrvlogin	Returns information about linked server logins.
sp_helplogins	Returns information about local server logins.
sp_helpntgroup	Returns information about Windows groups.

Procedure	Description
sp_helpremotelogin	Returns information about remote logins registered with the local server.
sp_helprole	Returns information about fixed database roles.
sp_helprolemember	Returns information about the roles for a database.
sp_helprotect	Returns permissions information related to a specified database object.
sp_helpsrvrole	Returns information about server roles.
sp_helpsrvrolemember	Returns information about the logins, Windows user, and groups that are members of a specified server role.
sp_helpuser	Returns information about database users, Windows users, groups, and database roles in a database.
sp_MShasdbaccess	Returns database information accessible to a user.
sp_password	Adds or modifies the password for a login.
sp_remoteoption	Returns or modifies option settings for a remote login.
sp_revokedbaccess	Removes a database user, Windows user, or group from a database.
sp_revokelogin	Removes a login associated with a Windows user or group.
sp_setapprole	Enables an application role for a database. Used to allow programmatic access from an application component.
sp_srvrolepermission	Returns permission information for a server role.
sp_validatelogins	Returns Windows user and group entries in the database server that no longer exist in the operating system or Windows domain.

SQL Server Agent

Procedure	Description
sp_add_alert	Creates a new alert.
sp_add_category	Creates a new category that may be associated with jobs, operators, and so on.
sp_add_job	Creates a new job to contain steps.
sp_add_jobschedule	Creates a new schedule for an existing job.
sp_add_jobserver	Changes the server that will run a job.
sp_add_jobstep	Adds a step to an existing job.
sp_add_notification	Creates and adds a notification for an alert.
sp_add_operator	Creates an operator associated with a job and an alert.
sp_add_proxy	Creates a proxy account for users and roles to execute jobs with elevated permissions, without administrative role membership.
sp_add_schedule	Creates a schedule for use with a job.
sp_add_targetservergroup	Creates a server group to associate a job with a group of servers.
sp_add_targetsvrgrp_member	Adds a server to a target server group.
sp_apply_job_to_targets	Associates a job with one or more target servers.
sp_attach_schedule	Associates a schedule with a job.
sp_cycle_agent_errorlog	Closes the agent error log and initializes a new log file.
sp_cycle_errorlog	Closes the current error log and starts a new log file.
sp_delete_alert	Deletes an alert.
sp_delete_category	Deletes a category.
sp_delete_job	Deletes a job.
sp_delete_jobschedule	Deletes the schedule for a job.
sp_delete_jobserver	Deletes the association between a job and a server.
sp_delete_jobstep	Deletes a specified job step.
sp_delete_jobsteplog	Deletes a specified job step, all job steps for a specified job, or those that meet other criteria.

Procedure	Description
sp_delete_notification	Deletes notifications for an operator and an alert.
sp_delete_operator	Deletes a specified operator.
sp_delete_proxy	Removes a user proxy.
sp_delete_schedule	Deletes a job schedule.
sp_delete_targetserver	Removes a target server designation for a job.
sp_delete_targetservergroup	Deletes a target server group.
sp_delete_targetsvrgrp_member	Removes a target server from a group.
sp_detach_schedule	Associates a schedule to a job.
sp_enum_login_for_proxy	Returns logins associated with a proxy.
sp_enum_proxy_for_subsystem	Returns proxy users that have access to a specified subsystem.
sp_enum_sqlagent_subsystems	Returns the subsystems (process threads) for SQL Agent.
sp_grant_login_to_proxy	Grants a login, user, Windows user, or group access to a proxy.
sp_grant_proxy_to_subsystem	Assigns a DTS/integration Services subsystem to a proxy user.
sp_help_alert	Returns information about an alert or alerts.
sp_help_category	Returns information about a category or categories.
sp_help_downloadlist	Returns information about queued target server download instructions.
sp_help_job	Returns information about a job or jobs.
sp_help_jobactivity	Returns information about job activities.
sp_help_jobcount	Returns the count of jobs for an associated schedule.
sp_help_jobhistory	Returns information about jobs for associated servers.
sp_help_jobs_in_schedule	Returns the information about jobs for an associated schedule.
sp_help_jobschedule	Returns information about automated job scheduling.
sp_help_jobserver	Returns information about a server associated with a job.
sp_help_jobstep	Returns information about the steps for a job.

(continued)

Procedure	Description
sp_help_notification	Returns information about notifications.
sp_help_operator	Returns information about an operator or operators.
sp_help_proxy	Returns information about a proxy user or proxies.
sp_help_schedule	Returns information about a schedule or schedules.
sp_help_targetserver	Returns information about a job target server or servers.
sp_help_targetservergroup	Returns information about a job target server group or groups.
sp_manage_jobs_by_login	Removes or modifies jobs for a specified login.
sp_msx_defect	Modifies the system registry to remove the server from target multiserver operations.
sp_msx_enlist	Modifies the system registry to add the server to the available multiserver target list.
sp_msx_get_account	Returns credentials information for a target server, used to log into a master server.
sp_msx_set_account	Sets credentials for a target server to log into a master server.
sp_notify_operator	Sends an e-mail message to an operator by using SQLiMail.
sp_post_msx_operation	Inserts job information into the sysdownloadlist table for target servers to execute.
sp_purge_jobhistory	Removes history metadata associated with a job.
sp_remove_job_from_targets	Removes the association between a job and a target server.
sp_resync_targetserver	Synchronizes all job metadata from remote servers to the target server.
sp_revoke_login_from_proxy	Removes access to a proxy for a security principal.
sp_revoke_proxy_from_ subsystem	Removes access to a subsystem for a proxy.
sp_start_job	Starts executing a job regardless of its schedule.
sp_stop_job	Stops executing a job.
sp_update_alert	Modifies the settings for an alert.
sp_update_category	Modifies the name of a category.

Procedure	Description
sp_update_job	Modifies the settings for a job.
sp_update_jobschedule	Modifies the settings for a job's schedule.
sp_update_jobstep	Modifies the settings for a step.
sp_update_notification	Modifies the settings for a notification.
sp_update_operator	Modifies the information for an operator.
sp_update_proxy	Modifies the information for a proxy user.
sp_update_schedule	Modifies an agent schedule.
sp_update_targetservergroup	Modifies the name of a target server group.

XML

Procedure	Description
sp_xml_preparedocument	Uses an output parameter to return a numeric handle to a cached copy of a well-formed and prepared XML document structure. The initial XML document is passed into this procedure as a varchar type.
sp_xml_removedocument	Removes data from the server's XML cache.

Information Schema Views Reference

The following views can be used in any database to obtain metadata about database objects. Select from each view as if it were a table in the database, prefixing the view with INFORMATION_SCHEMA., as in the following example:

```
SELECT * FROM INFORMATION_SCHEMA.CHECK_CONSTRAINTS
```

Information schema views are stored in the Master database. Note that the sysname user-defined data type that is preconfigured and used in instances of SQL Server is functionally equivalent to nvarchar(128).

CHECK_CONSTRAINTS

Returns one row for each CHECK constraint in the current database. This information schema view returns information about the objects to which the current user has permissions.

Column Name	Data Type
CONSTRAINT_CATALOG	nvarchar(128)
CONSTRAINT_SCHEMA	nvarchar(128)
CONSTRAINT_NAME	sysname
CHECK_CLAUSE	nvarchar(4000)

COLUMN_DOMAIN_USAGE

Returns one row for each column in the current database that has an `alias` data type. This information schema view returns information about the objects to which the current user has permissions.

Column Name	Data Type
DOMAIN_CATALOG	nvarchar(128)
DOMAIN_SCHEMA	nvarchar(128)
DOMAIN_NAME	sysname
TABLE_CATALOG	nvarchar(128)
TABLE_SCHEMA	nvarchar(128)
TABLE_NAME	sysname
COLUMN_NAME	sysname

COLUMN_PRIVILEGES

Returns one row for each column that has a privilege that is either granted to or granted by the current user in the current database.

Column Name	Data Type
GRANTOR	nvarchar(128)
GRANTEE	nvarchar(128)
TABLE_CATALOG	nvarchar(128)
TABLE_SCHEMA	nvarchar(128)
TABLE_NAME	sysname
COLUMN_NAME	sysname
PRIVILEGE_TYPE	varchar(10)
IS_GRANTABLE	varchar(3)

COLUMNS

Returns one row for each column that can be accessed by the current user in the current database.

Column Name	Data Type
TABLE_CATALOG	nvarchar(128)
TABLE_SCHEMA	nvarchar(128)
TABLE_NAME	nvarchar (128)
COLUMN_NAME	nvarchar (128)
ORDINAL_POSITION	int
COLUMN_DEFAULT	nvarchar(4000)
IS_NULLABLE	varchar(3)
DATA_TYPE	nvarchar (128)
CHARACTER_MAXIMUM_LENGTH	int
CHARACTER_OCTET_LENGTH	int
NUMERIC_PRECISION	tinyint
NUMERIC_PRECISION_RADIX	smallint
NUMERIC_SCALE	int
DATETIME_PRECISION	smallint
CHARACTER_SET_CATALOG	nvarchar(128)
CHARACTER_SET_SCHEMA	nvarchar(128)
CHARACTER_SET_NAME	nvarchar(128)
COLLATION_CATALOG	nvarchar(128)
COLLATION_SCHEMA	nvarchar(128)
COLLATION_NAME	nvarchar(128)
DOMAIN_CATALOG	nvarchar(128)
DOMAIN_SCHEMA	nvarchar(128)
DOMAIN_NAME	nvarchar(128)

CONSTRAINT_COLUMN_USAGE

Returns one row for each column in the current database that has a constraint defined on the column. This information schema view returns information about the objects to which the current user has permissions.

Column Name	Data Type
TABLE_CATALOG	nvarchar(128)
TABLE_SCHEMA	nvarchar(128)
TABLE_NAME	nvarchar(128)
COLUMN_NAME	nvarchar(128)
CONSTRAINT_CATALOG	nvarchar(128)
CONSTRAINT_SCHEMA	nvarchar(128)
CONSTRAINT_NAME	nvarchar(128)

CONSTRAINT_TABLE_USAGE

Returns one row for each table in the current database that has a constraint defined on the table. This information schema view returns information about the objects to which the current user has permissions.

Column Name	Data Type
TABLE_CATALOG	nvarchar(128)
TABLE_SCHEMA	nvarchar(128)
TABLE_NAME	sysname
CONSTRAINT_CATALOG	nvarchar(128)
CONSTRAINT_SCHEMA	nvarchar(128)
CONSTRAINT_NAME	sysname

DOMAIN_CONSTRAINTS

Returns one row for each `alias` data type in the current database that has a rule bound to it and that can be accessed by the current user.

Column Name	Data Type
CONSTRAINT_CATALOG	nvarchar(128)
CONSTRAINT_SCHEMA	nvarchar(128)
CONSTRAINT_NAME	sysname
DOMAIN_CATALOG	nvarchar(128)
DOMAIN_SCHEMA	nvarchar(128)
DOMAIN_NAME	sysname
IS_DEFERRABLE	varchar(2)
INITIALLY_DEFERRED	varchar(2)

DOMAINS

Returns one row for each `alias` data type that can be accessed by the current user in the current database.

Column Name	Data Type
DOMAIN_CATALOG	nvarchar(128)
DOMAIN_SCHEMA	nvarchar(128)
DOMAIN_NAME	sysname
DATA_TYPE	sysname
CHARACTER_MAXIMUM_LENGTH	int
CHARACTER_OCTET_LENGTH	int
COLLATION_CATALOG	varchar (6)
COLLATION_SCHEMA	varchar (3)
COLLATION_NAME	nvarchar (128)
CHARACTER_SET_CATALOG	varchar (6)

(continued)

Column Name	Data Type
CHARACTER_SET_SCHEMA	varchar (3)
CHARACTER_SET_NAME	nvarchar(128)
NUMERIC_PRECISION	tinyint
NUMERIC_PRECISION_RADIX	smallint
NUMERIC_SCALE	tinyint
DATETIME_PRECISION	smallint
DOMAIN_DEFAULT	nvarchar(4000)

KEY_COLUMN_USAGE

Returns one row for each column that is constrained as a key in the current database. This information schema view returns information about the objects to which the current user has permissions.

Column Name	Data Type
CONSTRAINT_CATALOG	nvarchar(128)
CONSTRAINT_SCHEMA	nvarchar(128)
CONSTRAINT_NAME	nvarchar(128)
TABLE_CATALOG	nvarchar(128)
TABLE_SCHEMA	nvarchar(128)
TABLE_NAME	nvarchar(128)
COLUMN_NAME	nvarchar(128)
ORDINAL_POSITION	int

PARAMETERS

Returns one row for each parameter of a user-defined function or stored procedure that can be accessed by the current user in the current database. For functions, this view also returns one row with return value information.

Column Name	Data Type
SPECIFIC_CATALOG	nvarchar(128)
SPECIFIC_SCHEMA	nvarchar(128)
SPECIFIC_NAME	nvarchar(128)
ORDINAL_POSITION	int
PARAMETER MODE	nvarchar(10)
IS_RESULT	nvarchar(10)
AS_LOCATOR	nvarchar(10)
PARAMETER_NAME	nvarchar (128)
DATA_TYPE	nvarchar (128)
CHARACTER_MAXIMUM_LENGTH	int
CHARACTER_OCTET_LENGTH	int
COLLATION_CATALOG	nvarchar (128)
COLLATION_SCHEMA	nvarchar (128)
COLLATION_NAME	nvarchar (128)
CHARACTER_SET_CATALOG	nvarchar (128)
CHARACTER_SET_SCHEMA	nvarchar (128)
CHARACTER_SET_NAME	nvarchar (128)
NUMERIC_PRECISION	tinyint
NUMERIC_PRECISION_RADIX	smallint
NUMERIC_SCALE	tinyint
DATETIME_PRECISION	smallint
INTERVAL_TYPE	nvarchar (30)
INTERVAL_PRECISION	smallint
USER_DEFINED_TYPE_CATALOG	nvarchar (128)
USER_DEFINED_TYPE_SCHEMA	nvarchar (128)
USER_DEFINED_TYPE_NAME	nvarchar (128)
SCOPE_CATALOG	nvarchar (128)
SCOPE_SCHEMA	nvarchar (128)
SCOPE_NAME	nvarchar (128)

REFERENTIAL_CONSTRAINTS

Returns one row for each FOREIGN KEY constraint in the current database. This information schema view returns information about the objects to which the current user has permissions.

CONSTRAINT_CATALOG	nvarchar(128)
CONSTRAINT_SCHEMA	nvarchar(128)
CONSTRAINT_NAME	sysname
UNIQUE_CONSTRAINT_CATALOG	nvarchar(128)
UNIQUE_CONSTRAINT_SCHEMA	nvarchar(128)
UNIQUE_CONSTRAINT_NAME	sysname
MATCH_OPTION	varchar(7)
UPDATE_RULE	varchar(11)
DELETE_RULE	varchar(11)

ROUTINE_COLUMNS

Returns one row for each column returned by the table-valued functions that can be accessed by the current user in the current database.

Column Name	Data Type
TABLE_CATALOG	nvarchar(128)
TABLE_SCHEMA	nvarchar(128)
TABLE_NAME	nvarchar (128)
COLUMN_NAME	nvarchar (128)
ORDINAL_POSITION	int
COLUMN_DEFAULT	nvarchar(4000)
IS_NULLABLE	varchar(3)
DATA_TYPE	nvarchar (128)
CHARACTER_MAXIMUM_LENGTH	int
CHARACTER_OCTET_LENGTH	int
NUMERIC_PRECISION	tinyint
NUMERIC_PRECISION_RADIX	smallint

Column Name	Data Type
NUMERIC_SCALE	tinyint
DATETIME_PRECISION	smallint
CHARACTER_SET_CATALOG	varchar (6)
CHARACTER_SET_SCHEMA	varchar (3)
CHARACTER_SET_NAME	nvarchar(128)
COLLATION_CATALOG	varchar (6)
COLLATION_SCHEMA	varchar (3)
COLLATION_NAME	nvarchar (128)
DOMAIN_CATALOG	nvarchar(128)
DOMAIN_SCHEMA	nvarchar(128)
DOMAIN_NAME	nvarchar(128)

ROUTINES

Returns one row for each stored procedure and function that can be accessed by the current user in the current database. The columns that describe the return value apply only to functions. For stored procedures, these columns will be NULL.

Column Name	Data Type
SPECIFIC_CATALOG	nvarchar(128)
SPECIFIC_SCHEMA	nvarchar(128)
SPECIFIC_NAME	nvarchar(128)
ROUTINE_CATALOG	nvarchar(128)
ROUTINE_SCHEMA	nvarchar(128)
ROUTINE_NAME	nvarchar(128)
ROUTINE_TYPE	nvarchar(20)
MODULE_CATALOG	nvarchar(128)
MODULE_SCHEMA	nvarchar(128)
MODULE_NAME	nvarchar(128)

(continued)

Column Name	Data Type
UDT_CATALOG	nvarchar(128)
UDT_SCHEMA	nvarchar(128)
UDT_NAME	nvarchar(128)
DATA_TYPE	nvarchar(128)
CHARACTER_MAXIMUM_LENGTH	int
CHARACTER_OCTET_LENGTH	int
COLLATION_CATALOG	nvarchar(128)
COLLATION_SCHEMA	nvarchar(128)
COLLATION_NAME	nvarchar(128)
CHARACTER_SET_CATALOG	nvarchar(128)
CHARACTER_SET_SCHEMA	nvarchar(128)
CHARACTER_SET_NAME	nvarchar(128)
NUMERIC_PRECISION	smallint
NUMERIC_PRECISION_RADIX	smallint
NUMERIC_SCALE	smallint
DATETIME_PRECISION	smallint
INTERVAL_TYPE	nvarchar(30)
INTERVAL_PRECISION	smallint
TYPE_UDT_CATALOG	nvarchar(128)
TYPE_UDT_SCHEMA	nvarchar(128)
TYPE_UDT_NAME	nvarchar(128)
SCOPE_CATALOG	nvarchar(128)
SCOPE_SCHEMA	nvarchar(128)
SCOPE_NAME	nvarchar(128)
MAXIMUM_CARDINALITY	bigint(8)
DTD_IDENTIFIER	nvarchar(128)
ROUTINE_BODY	nvarchar(30)

Column Name	Data Type
ROUTINE_DEFINITION	nvarchar(4000)
EXTERNAL_NAME	nvarchar(128)
EXTERNAL_LANGUAGE	nvarchar(30)
PARAMETER_STYLE	nvarchar(30)
IS_DETERMINISTIC	nvarchar(10)
SQL_DATA_ACCESS	nvarchar(30)
IS_NULL_CALL	nvarchar(10)
SQL_PATH	nvarchar(128)
SCHEMA_LEVEL_ROUTINE	nvarchar(10)
MAX_DYNAMIC_RESULT_SETS	smallint
IS_USER_DEFINED_CAST	nvarchar(10)
IS_IMPLICITLY_INVOCABLE	nvarchar(10)
CREATED	datetime
LAST_ALTERED	datetime

SCHEMATA

Returns one row for each schema in the current database.

Column Name	Data Type
CATALOG_NAME	sysname
SCHEMA_NAME	nvarchar(128)
SCHEMA_OWNER	nvarchar(128)
DEFAULT_CHARACTER_SET_CATALOG	varchar (6)
DEFAULT_CHARACTER_SET_SCHEMA	varchar (3)
DEFAULT_CHARACTER_SET_NAME	sysname

TABLE_CONSTRAINTS

Returns one row for each table constraint in the current database. This information schema view returns information about the objects to which the current user has permissions.

Column Name	Data Type
CONSTRAINT_CATALOG	nvarchar(128)
CONSTRAINT_SCHEMA	nvarchar(128)
CONSTRAINT_NAME	sysname
TABLE_CATALOG	nvarchar(128)
TABLE_SCHEMA	nvarchar(128)
TABLE_NAME	sysname
CONSTRAINT_TYPE	varchar(11)
IS_DEFERRABLE	varchar(2)
INITIALLY_DEFERRED	varchar(2)

TABLE_PRIVILEGES

Returns one row for each table privilege that is granted to or granted by the current user in the current database.

Column Name	Data Type
GRANTOR	nvarchar(128)
GRANTEE	nvarchar(128)
TABLE_CATALOG	nvarchar(128)
TABLE_SCHEMA	nvarchar(128)
TABLE_NAME	sysname
PRIVILEGE_TYPE	varchar(10)
IS_GRANTABLE	varchar(3)

TABLES

Returns one row for each table in the current database for which the current user has permissions.

Column Name	Data Type
TABLE_CATALOG	nvarchar(128)
TABLE_SCHEMA	nvarchar(128)
TABLE_NAME	sysname
TABLE_TYPE	varchar(10)

VIEW_COLUMN_USAGE

Returns one row for each column in the current database that is used in a view definition. This information schema view returns information about the objects to which the current user has permissions.

Column Name	Data Type
VIEW_CATALOG	nvarchar(128)
VIEW_SCHEMA	nvarchar(128)
VIEW_NAME	sysname
TABLE_CATALOG	nvarchar(128)
TABLE_SCHEMA	nvarchar(128)
TABLE_NAME	sysname
COLUMN_NAME	sysname

VIEW_TABLE_USAGE

Returns one row for each table in the current database that is used in a view. This information schema view returns information about the objects to which the current user has permissions.

Column Name	Data Type
VIEW_CATALOG	nvarchar(128)
VIEW_SCHEMA	nvarchar(128)
VIEW_NAME	sysname
TABLE_CATALOG	nvarchar(128)
TABLE_SCHEMA	nvarchar(128)
TABLE_NAME	sysname

VIEWS

Returns one row for views that can be accessed by the current user in the current database.

Column Name	Data Type
TABLE_CATALOG	nvarchar(128)
TABLE_SCHEMA	nvarchar(128)
TABLE_NAME	nvarchar(128)
VIEW_DEFINITION	nvarchar(4000)
CHECK_OPTION	varchar(7)
IS_UPDATABLE	varchar(2)

FileStream Objects and Syntax

The `filestream` data type, introduced in SQL Server 2008, provides a mechanism for storing and synchronizing content in the server file system. This is ideal for managing large volumes of unstructured data, typically stored in documents and other application-specific file types. Data for `filestream` type columns is inserted into a database table but actually stored in separate files outside the database — in the NTFS file system, instead of the SQL Server database files. All T-SQL query actions (i.e., INSERT, UPDATE, DELETE, and SELECT) interact with the externally stored data that is managed by the SQL Server database engine.

This feature is disabled by default and must be enabled using the `sp_filestream_configure` system stored procedure.

A database is filestream-enabled by defining a filegroup based on a file system folder, called a *file container*. The database file for this filegroup stores metadata, settings, and header information used to manage the external data.

A table is filestream-enabled by defining a column with the FILESTREAM keyword when the table is created. Data may be written to the filestream type column and subsequently stored in the NTFS file system, using a standard T-SQL INSERT statement for the filestream-enabled table, or by using managed or unmanaged program code.

Because the original content for filestream data will often be contained in source document files, inserting or modifying this data will need to be performed with external program code instead of T-SQL. This typically requires advanced file management and streaming code that cannot be performed with T-SQL queries alone. Programming support is provided by the OpenSQLFileStream API contained in the SQL Server Native Client 10.0 (sqlncli10.dll) library. This is an extension to the Win32 API, and functions may be called from managed .NET code (such as C# or Visual Basic.NET) or unmanaged code (such as C++ or Visual Basic 6).

FileStream Objects

The following table shows system programming objects used to manage filestream types.

Object Name	Return Type	Description
sp_filestream_configure	N/A	Values for the @enable_level return parameter: 0 - Disabled (default) 1 - T-SQL access only 2 - T-SQL and local file system access 3 - T-SQL, local, and remote file system access
PATHNAME()	nvarchar(max)	Returns the file system path for a FileStream type column.
GET_FILESTREAM_TRANSACTION_CONTEXT()	varbinary(max)	Returns a token to coordinate the transactional context of database objects or queries and external program code.

Sample T-SQL Scripts

The following are simple examples of T-SQL scripts to create a database with filestream storage, define a table with a filestream-enabled column, and use an INSERT statement to store column text in an external file.

To Create a Database with FileStream Storage

```
CREATE DATABASE SalesDB ON PRIMARY
  ( NAME = SalesDB_data,
    FILENAME = N'C:\Databases\MyFSDB_data.mdf',
    SIZE = 10MB,
    MAXSIZE = 200MB,
    FILEGROWTH = 10%),
  ---------------------------------------------------
  -- Define a file group for standard data storage --
  ---------------------------------------------------
```

```
FILEGROUP SalesDBData
  ( NAME = SalesData_Group,
    FILENAME = 'C:\Databases\SalesDB_FileStream.ndf',
    SIZE = 10MB,
    MAXSIZE = 200MB,
    FILEGROWTH = 5MB),
------------------------------------------------
-- Define a file group for filestream storage --
------------------------------------------------
FILEGROUP SalesDB_FileStream_Group CONTAINS FILESTREAM
  ( NAME = SalesDB_FileStream,
    FILENAME = 'C:\Databases\SalesDB_FileStreamData')
-----------------------------------
-- Define standard database log --
-----------------------------------
LOG ON
  ( NAME = 'SalesDB_log',
    FILENAME = 'C:\Databases\SalesDB_log.ldf',
    SIZE = 5MB,
    MAXSIZE = 30MB,
    FILEGROWTH = 5MB);
```

To Create a Table with a FileStream-Enabled Column

```
USE SalesDB
CREATE TABLE DocumentData
  (
    DocID UNIQUEIDENTIFIER ROWGUIDCOL
      NOT NULL UNIQUE,                    -- Standard key column
    DocData varbinary(MAX) FILESTREAM    -- filestream type column
  );
```

To Store Column Text in an External File

```
USE SalesDB
INSERT INTO DocumentData
VALUES(NEWID(), CONVERT(varbinary(MAX), 'Sample document content'))
```

Answers to Exercises

Chapter 3
Exercise 1 Solution

```
SELECT ProductID, Name, ListPrice
FROM    Production.Product
ORDER BY Name
```

Exercise 2 Solution

```
SELECT Production.ProductSubcategory.Name AS SubCategory
       ,Production.Product.Name AS ProductName
       ,Production.Product.ListPrice
FROM    Production.Product
INNER JOIN Production.ProductSubcategory
ON Production.Product.ProductSubcategoryID =
Production.ProductSubcategory.ProductSubcategoryID
ORDER BY SubCategory, ProductName
```

Exercise 3 Solution

```
SELECT * FROM Production.Product WHERE ListPrice > 4000
```

Rowcount = 13

Exercise 4 Solution

```
SQLCMD /S localhost /E
>1 USE AdventureWorks2008
>2 GO
>1 SELECT ProductCategoryID, Name FROM Production.ProductCategory
>2 GO
```

Chapter 4
Exercise 1 Solution

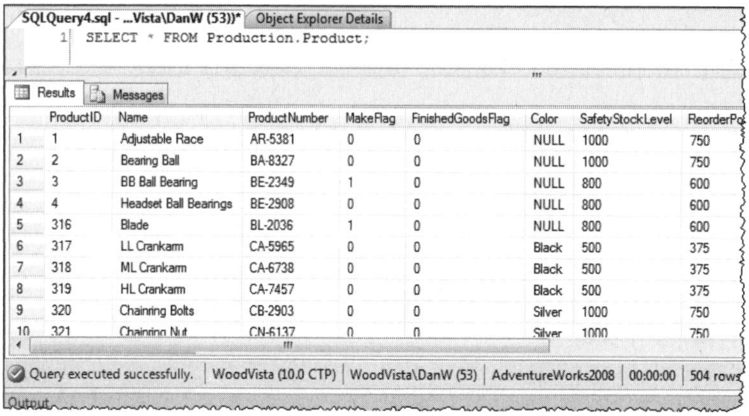

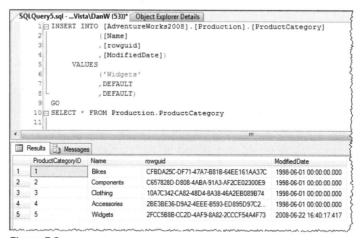

Figure F-1

Exercise 2 Solution

Figure F-2

Chapter 5
Exercise 1 Solution

```
SELECT NationalIDNumber
      ,LoginID
      ,JobTitle
```

```
      ,BirthDate
      ,MaritalStatus
      ,HireDate
FROM HumanResources.Employee
```

Exercise 2 Solution

```
SELECT NationalIDNumber
      ,LoginID
      ,JobTitle
      ,BirthDate
      ,MaritalStatus
      ,HireDate
      ,DATEDIFF(YY,BirthDate,HireDate) AS AgeAtHire
FROM HumanResources.Employee
```

Exercise 3 Solution

```
SELECT Name, ListPrice
FROM Production.Product
WHERE DaysToManufacture >= 3
```

or

```
SELECT Name, ListPrice
FROM Production.Product
WHERE DaysToManufacture > 2
```

Exercise 4 Solution

```
SELECT TOP 10
       ProductId
      ,Name
      ,ProductNumber
      ,Color
      ,ListPrice
FROM Production.Product
WHERE ProductNumber LIKE 'BK%'
ORDER BY ListPrice DESC
SELECT TOP 10 WITH TIES
       ProductId
      ,Name
      ,ProductNumber
      ,Color
      ,ListPrice
FROM Production.Product
WHERE ProductNumber LIKE 'BK%'
ORDER BY ListPrice DESC
```

Chapter 6
Exercise 1 Solution

```
SELECT AVG(Weight)
FROM Production.Product
WHERE ProductSubcategoryID = 3
```

Exercise 2 Solution

```
DECLARE @ProdCount AS char(3)
SELECT @ProdCount = CAST(COUNT(ProductID) AS char(3))
FROM Production.Product
SELECT 'There are ' + @ProdCount + ' products on record'
```

Exercise 3 Solution

```
SELECT SQRT(ABS(COS(PI())))
```

Exercise 4 Solution

```
SELECT DATEDIFF(dd,'06-28-1919',GETDATE())
```

Exercise 5 Solution

```
SELECT FirstName
    ,LastName
    ,LEFT(FirstName,1) + LEFT(Lastname,1) AS Initials
FROM SlateGravelEmployee
```

Chapter 7
Exercise 1 Solution

For SQL Server 2008, using the AdventureWorks2008 database:

```
SELECT JobTitle, MIN(LoginID)
FROM HumanResources.Employee
WHERE OrganizationLevel IN(0, 1, 2)
GROUP BY JobTitle
```

For SQL Server 2005, using the AdventureWorks database:

```
SELECT Title, MIN(LoginID)
FROM HumanResources.Employee
WHERE Title IN('Buyer', 'Recruiter', 'Stocker')
GROUP BY Title
```

Exercise 2 Solution

```
SELECT ProductSubCategoryID, MIN(Name) AS Name, MAX(ListPrice)
FROM Production.Product
GROUP BY ProductSubCategoryID
HAVING COUNT(ProductSubCategoryID) > 20
ORDER BY Name
```

Exercise 3 Solution

For SQL Server 2008, using the AdventureWorks2008 database:

```
SELECT OrganizationLevel, Gender, AVG(VacationHours)
FROM HumanResources.Employee
GROUP by OrganizationLevel, Gender
WITH ROLLUP
```

For SQL Server 2005, using the AdventureWorks database:

```
SELECT Title, Gender, AVG(VacationHours)
FROM HumanResources.Employee
GROUP by Title, Gender
WITH ROLLUP
```

Chapter 8
Exercise 1 Solution

SQL Server 2008 using the AdventureWorks2008 database:

```
SELECT Name, SubTotal
FROM Purchasing.Vendor INNER JOIN Purchasing.PurchaseOrderHeader
ON Vendor.BusinessEntityID = PurchaseOrderHeader.VendorID
ORDER BY Name
```

SQL Server 2005 using the AdventureWorks database:

```
SELECT Name, SubTotal
FROM Purchasing.Vendor INNER JOIN Purchasing.PurchaseOrderHeader
ON Vendor.VendorID = PurchaseOrderHeader.VendorID
ORDER BY Name
```

Exercise 2 Solution

```
SELECT
      Manager.Title AS ManagerTitle
    , Manager.FirstName + ' ' + Manager.LastName AS ManagerName
    , Employee.Title AS EmployeeTitle
    , Employee.FirstName + ' ' + Employee.LastName AS EmployeeName
FROM DimEmployee AS Manager INNER JOIN DimEmployee AS Employee
      ON Manager.EmployeeKey = Employee.ParentEmployeeKey
```

Exercise 3 Solution

```
SELECT
    ProductSubCategory.Name AS SubCategoryName
    , Product.Name AS ProductName
FROM Production.ProductSubCategory
    INNER JOIN Production.Product
        ON ProductSubCategory.ProductSubCategoryID = Product
.ProductSubCategoryID
    LEFT OUTER JOIN Sales.SalesOrderDetail
        ON Product.ProductID = SalesOrderDetail.ProductID
WHERE SalesOrderDetail.ProductID IS NULL
```

Chapter 9
Exercise 1 Solution

```
SELECT
    Name AS ProductName
    , ListPrice AS ProductListPrice
    , (SELECT MAX(UnitPrice) AS MaxSalesPrice
       FROM Sales.SalesOrderDetail
       WHERE ProductID = Product.ProductID
       GROUP BY ProductID) AS MaxSalesPrice
FROM Production.Product
ORDER BY Name
```

Exercise 2 Solution

```
SELECT Emp1.* FROM
(
  SELECT TOP 10
     FirstName + ' ' + LastName AS Name
   , VacationHours
  FROM vw_Employee AS E
  ORDER BY VacationHours DESC
) AS Emp1
UNION
SELECT Emp2.* FROM
(
  SELECT '(Other)' AS Name, AVG(E1.VacationHours) AS VacationHours
  FROM vw_Employee AS E1
        LEFT OUTER JOIN
        ( SELECT TOP 10 EmployeeID, VacationHours
          FROM vw_Employee ORDER BY VacationHours DESC
        ) AS E2
    ON E1.EmployeeID = E2.EmployeeID
    WHERE E2.EmployeeID IS NULL
) AS Emp2
```

Exercise 3 Solution

```
WITH Top10VacHours (VacationHours, Name, EmployeeID)
AS
(
  SELECT TOP 10
    FirstName + ' ' + LastName AS Name
  , VacationHours
  , EmployeeID
  FROM vw_Employee AS E
  ORDER BY VacationHours DESC
)
SELECT * FROM Top10VacHours
```

Chapter 10
Exercise 1 Solution

```
INSERT INTO Production.ProductCategory (Name) SELECT 'Snorkels'
INSERT INTO Production.ProductCategory (Name) VALUES ('Snorkels')
```

Exercise 2 Solution

```
SELECT Product.* INTO RoadBikes
FROM Production.Product
    INNER JOIN Production.ProductSubCategory
      ON Product.ProductSubCategoryID = ProductSubCategory
.ProductSubCategoryID
WHERE ProductSubCategory.Name = 'Road Bikes'
```

Exercise 3 Solution

```
BEGIN TRANSACTION
DELETE FROM Production.Product
WHERE ProductID IN
  (
    SELECT Product.ProductID
    FROM Production.Product LEFT OUTER JOIN Sales.SalesOrderDetail
      ON Product.ProductID = SalesOrderDetail.ProductID
    WHERE SalesOrderDetail.ProductID IS NULL
    AND Product.ProductSubCategoryID = 5
  )
INSERT INTO Production.ProductCategory (Name) SELECT 'Accessory'
COMMIT TRANSACTION
```

No product records were deleted because the second query raised an error, causing the transaction to roll back.

Chapter 11
Exercise 1 Solution

```
CREATE FULLTEXT INDEX
ON Person.StateProvince(StateProvinceCode, CountryRegionCode, Name)
KEY INDEX PK_StateProvince_StateProvinceID
```

Exercise 2 Solution

```
SELECT *
FROM Person.StateProvince
WHERE CONTAINS(*, '"CA"')
```

Exercise 3 Solution

```
SELECT *
FROM Person.StateProvince
WHERE FREETEXT('"Victoria BC"')
```

There is not a record for Victoria, BC. The only city on record for British Columbia is Vancouver, and the only record for Victoria is the province in Australia.

Chapter 12
Exercise 1 Solution

```
CREATE VIEW vBikePriceSheet
AS
SELECT P.Name AS Product
      ,PM.Name AS Model
      ,PS.Name AS Subcategory
      ,P.Color
      ,P.ListPrice
      ,P.StandardCost
      ,P.ListPrice - P.StandardCost AS Margin
FROM   Production.Product P
INNER JOIN Production.ProductSubcategory PS
  ON P.ProductSubcategoryID = PS.ProductSubcategoryID
INNER JOIN Production.ProductModel PM
  ON P.ProductModelID = PM.ProductModelID
WHERE PS.ProductCategoryID = 1
```

Exercise 2 Solution

```sql
CREATE PROCEDURE spAddDepartment
 @Name nvarchar(50)
,@GroupName nvarchar(50)
AS
IF EXISTS (SELECT *
            FROM HumanResources.Department
            WHERE Name = @Name
              AND GroupName != @GroupName)
   BEGIN
      UPDATE HumanResources.Department
      SET GroupName = @GroupName
      WHERE Name = @Name
   END
ELSE
   IF EXISTS(SELECT *
            FROM HumanResources.Department
            WHERE Name = @Name
              AND GroupName = @GroupName)
   BEGIN
      RAISERROR('Duplicate Department Name!', 14,1)
      RETURN
   END
ELSE
   BEGIN
      INSERT HumanResources.Department
      (Name, GroupName)
      VALUES
      (@Name, @Groupname)
   END
```

Exercise 3 Solution

```sql
/*****************************************************************************
* spAddDepartment.sql
* 2008/07/01 Created (D.Wood) dan.wood@adventureworkscycles.com
* Adds or updates department information in the HumanResources.Department
table
* If a department name exists, it will update the groupname if different
* If the name and group name are new it will be added
* Accepts two parameters: @Name = Department Name
*                         @GroupName = Department Group
* 2008/07/10 Modified (P.Turley) paul.turley@adventureworks.com
* Added error checking
*****************************************************************************/
CREATE PROCEDURE spAddDepartment
 @Name nvarchar(50)
,@GroupName nvarchar(50)
AS
BEGIN TRY
   IF EXISTS (SELECT *
```

(continued)

(continued)

```
                    FROM HumanResources.Department
                    WHERE Name = @Name
                        AND GroupName != @GroupName)
        BEGIN
            BEGIN TRAN
                UPDATE HumanResources.Department
                SET GroupName = @GroupName
                WHERE Name = @Name
            COMMIT TRAN
        END
    ELSE
        IF EXISTS(SELECT *
                    FROM HumanResources.Department
                    WHERE Name = @Name
                        AND GroupName = @GroupName)
            BEGIN
                RAISERROR('Duplicate Department Name!', 14,1)
                RETURN
            END
        ELSE
            BEGIN
                BEGIN TRAN
                    INSERT HumanResources.Department
                    (Name, GroupName)
                    VALUES
                    (@Name, @Groupname)
                COMMIT TRAN
            END
END TRY
BEGIN CATCH
    DECLARE @ErrorMsg nvarchar(MAX)
    SET @ErrorMsg = ERROR_MESSAGE()
    IF XACT_STATE() != 0
        BEGIN
            ROLLBACK TRAN
            RAISERROR(@ErrorMsg,16, 1)
            RETURN -1
        END
    ELSE
        BEGIN
            RAISERROR(@ErrorMsg,16, 1)
            RETURN -1
        END
END CATCH
```

Chapter 13
Exercise 1 Solution

```
CREATE TABLE Customer
(CustomerId int IDENTITY(1,1) NOT NULL
,Lastname varchar(50) NOT NULL
,FirstName varchar(50) NOT NULL
,StreetAddress1 varchar(200)
,StreetAddress2 varchar(200)
,City varchar(100)
,StateProvince varchar(100)
,PostalCode varchar(20)
,Country char(2))

CREATE TABLE WristbandSales
(SaleId int IDENTITY(1,1) NOT NULL
,ProductId int NOT NULL
,SalesPrice money NOT NULL
,Quantity int NOT NULL
,CustomerId int NOT NULL
,Salesdate datetime NOT NULL)
```

Exercise 2 Solution

```
ALTER TABLE Wristbandsales
DROP COLUMN SaleId
ALTER TABLE Wristbandsales
ADD SalesId UNIQUEIDENTIFIER NOT NULL DEFAULT NEWID()
ALTER TABLE Customer ADD CONSTRAINT
CK_Country CHECK (Country IN ('US','UK','CA'))
```

Chapter 14
Exercise 1 Solution

```
USE AdventureWorks2008
GO
CREATE PROCEDURE uspGetInvoice
    @SalesOrderNumber nvarchar(25) = ''
   ,@PurchaseOrderNumber nvarchar(25) = ''
AS
IF @SalesOrderNumber = '' AND @PurchaseOrderNumber = ''
   BEGIN
       RAISERROR('Must provide PurchaseOrder or SalesOrder number', 14,1)
       RETURN
   END
IF @SalesOrderNumber = ''
   BEGIN
       SELECT SalesOrderNumber
```

(continued)

(continued)

```
            ,OrderDate
            ,ShipDate
            ,SubTotal
            ,TaxAmt
            ,Freight
            ,TotalDue
        FROM Sales.SalesOrderHeader
        WHERE PurchaseOrderNumber = @PurchaseOrderNumber
    END
IF @PurchaseOrderNumber = ''
    BEGIN
        SELECT SalesOrderNumber
            ,OrderDate
            ,ShipDate
            ,SubTotal
            ,TaxAmt
            ,Freight
            ,TotalDue
        FROM Sales.SalesOrderHeader
        WHERE SalesOrderNumber = @SalesOrderNumber
    END;
```

Index